Handbook of
Legal AI

Handbook of Legal AI

Edited by

Giovanni Casini

Livio Robaldo

Leendert van der Torre

Serena Villata

ISBN 978-1-84890-385-2

College Publications
Scientific Director: Dov Gabbay
Managing Director: Jane Spurr

http://www.collegepublications.co.uk

Cover produced by Laraine Welch

College Publications and the authors have no responsibility for the persistence or accuracy of URLs for external or third-party internet websites referred to in this publication.

CONTENTS

CHAPTERS

0

Introduction to the Handbook of Legal AI

GIOVANNI CASINI
LIVIO ROBALDO
LEENDERT VAN DER TORRE
SERENA VILLATA

1 Introduction

Legal scholars and practitioners are feeling increasingly overwhelmed with the expanding set of legislation and case law available these days, which is assuming more and more of an international character. Consider, for example, European legislation, which is estimated to be 170,000 pages long, of which over 100,000 pages have been produced in the last ten years, with most of them translated into the different languages of the member states of the European Union (EU). The EU is aware of these difficulties and chose as one of its primary objectives to establish an integrated and standardised system of laws that applies in all member states. Furthermore, legislation is available in unstructured formats (i.e., text), which makes it difficult for users to cut through the information overload. As the law gets more complex, conflicting, and ever-changing, more advanced methods, most of them coming from the artificial intelligence (AI) field, are required to analyse, represent and reason with legal knowledge. The discipline that tackles these challenges is now known as "Legal Artificial Intelligence". Legal AI has been experiencing growth in activity, particularly in the last few years and also at the industrial level, covering a variety of issues including analysis of the textual content of the law, reasoning with legal interpretation, and ethical issues pertaining to AI applications in the legal domain (e.g., artificial judges).

This Handbook presents a collection of chapters about three main topics: norm mining (i.e., how to automatically identify, extract, classify and interlink norms from text), reasoning about norms and regulations (i.e., how to derive new legal knowledge from existing legal knowledge bases to address the requirements of automatic legal decision-making), and norm enforcement and compliance (i.e., how to check and ensure that the requirements of the system complies with legal regulations).

Giovanni Casini   Livio Robaldo   Leendert van der Torre   Serena Villata

Concerning norm mining, the idea is to develop new AI methods to classify, index, and interlink legal documents by exploiting natural language processing (NLP) methods and tools [Jurafsky and Martin, 2009] such as parsers, named entity recognizers (NERs), neural classifiers, legal embeddings, and language models (LMs). These methods often rely on structured legal knowledge representation like ontologies [Hitzler *et al.*, 2009] and legal knowledge graphs [Ji *et al.*, 2022] to guide the extraction of this kind of information from unstructured data (i.e., textual documents). The extracted information is then used to populate the ontologies. These methods also bring ethical challenges and raise topical issues in the AI community such as the explainability and transparency of the results obtained through neural computations. Three chapters address these issues in the Handbook.

Chapter 1 reviews and discusses existing approaches and problems relating to automating normative mining from legal documents with an NLP perspective. Ferraro and Lam discuss the issue of automatically extracting normative information from legal documents and present possible approaches to normative mining via a literature review of state-of-the-art approaches. Also discussed are the main problems in this research area like evaluation methodologies and benchmarking for normative mining. The chapter ends by highlighting some preliminary results in extracting normative rules using relation extraction and semantic parsing models.

Chapter 2 introduces a recent research area in NLP called argument mining (AM), which is aimed at extracting natural language arguments and their relations from text, with the final goal of providing machine-processable structured data for computational models of arguments. This research area also includes other forms of processing natural language arguments beyond mining, i.e., searching for arguments on the Web, argument generation and synthesis, and assessing the quality of arguments with respect to specific criteria like persuasiveness. Cabrio and Villata describe classic argument mining tasks, and then present new tasks recently proposed in the literature. They also discuss results obtained in the area from a data-driven perspective, with a focus on legal text.

Chapter 3 focuses on another relevant task in NLP called recognising textual entailment (RTE), which is the task of recognising the relationship between two sentences to measure whether and to what extent one of the two is inferred from the other. In legal documents, from a set of obligations that are known to be complied with, RTE may be used to infer which other norms are complied with as well. In this chapter, Siragusa *et al.* propose a dataset about cybersecurity controls for RTE research in the legal domain. The dataset was constructed using information available online provided by domain experts from the (US) National Institute of Standards and Technology (NIST)[1].

As regards reasoning about norms and regulations, the goal is to aid decisions and derive new knowledge from already encoded legal knowledge (this knowledge may either exist directly via manual encoding, as with legal ontologies, or may be derived via norm mining). One key idea of the most logical accounts of normative reasoning (e.g., moral and, in particular, legal reasoning) is that it is defeasible, that is, that we may have reasons to abandon certain normative conclusions even though there was no apparent mistake in previously supporting them [Billi *et al.*, 2021]. Another key idea of legal reasoning is that legislation is not only a repository of rules but also contains text that state the purpose of the laws and the values and principles that underlie those laws [Jones and Sergot, 1992]. Laws are by design sometimes inconsistent, vague, inherently dynamic, can be violated if not useful, and may repair violations of other norms [Tosatto *et al.*, 2020; Boella *et al.*, 2010]. As such, formal argumentation techniques have been proposed to identify and explain inconsistencies in legal knowledge [Bench-Capon and Sartor, 2003]. In this Handbook, nine chapters address these issues.

Chapter 4 presents an overview of existing ontologies for the legal domain. Ontologies represent the standard way of modelling knowledge about specific domains. This holds also for the legal domain where several ontologies have been put forward to model specific kinds of legal knowledge. In this chapter, Leone *et al.* analyse and classify state-of-the-art legal ontologies and describe their distinctive features. The aim is to guide generic users and legal experts in selecting the legal ontology that best fits their needs and to help them understand its specificity so that they can investigate proper extensions to the selected model.

Chapter 5 investigates a variety of ways to reason with normative systems. In this chapter, Parent and van der Torre discuss the use of examples, inference patterns and more abstract properties. First, they give an overview of several benchmark examples of normative reasoning and deontic logic: van Fraassen's paradox, Forrester's paradox, Prakken and Sergot's cottage regulations, Jeffrey's disarmament example, Chisholm's paradox, Makinson's Mobius strip, and Horty's priority examples. Second, inference patterns can be used to compare different ways of reasoning with normative systems. Parent and van der Torre use inference patterns to analyse them at a higher level of abstraction. They discuss inference patterns reflecting typical logical properties such as strengthening the antecedent or weakening the consequent. Third, more abstract properties can be defined to compare different ways of reasoning with normative systems like factual detachment,

---

[1] https://www.nist.gov

violation detection, substitution, replacement of equivalents, implication, para-consistency, conjunction, factual monotony, norm monotony, and norm induction.

Chapter 6 introduces defeasible deontic logic, which uses techniques from non-monotonic logic to address various challenges in normative reasoning such as *prima facie* permissions and obligations, moral dilemmas, deontic detachment, contrary-to-duty reasoning, and legal interpretation. In this chapter, Dong *et al.* employ formal argumentation to design defeasible deontic logics based on classical deontic logic. They use the ASPIC+ structured argumentation theory to define non-monotonic variants of well-understood monotonic modal logics. They illustrate the ASPIC+-based approach and the resulting defeasible deontic logics using argumentation about strong permission.

Chapter 7 investigates normative change, since changing legal rules poses interpretation problems for determining the content of legal rules. The question of interpretation is tightly linked to questions about determining the validity of rules and their ability to produce effects. Different formal models of normative change appear to be better suited to capturing these different dimensions: the dimension of validity appears to be better captured by the AGM approach, while syntactic methods are better suited to modelling how the effects of rules are blocked or enabled. In this chapter, Maranhão *et al.* first provide a survey of the AGM approach to belief revision along with the main criticisms of it, and then they turn to formal analysis of normative change that combines AGM theory and input/output logic, thereby allowing a clear distinction between norms and obligations.

Chapter 8 discusses the issue of legal dynamics with a focus on temporal aspects. There are several time-based features of law that should be studied, and Tamargo *et al.* discuss two approaches: one based on defeasible logic and the other based on belief revision. Each makes use of one of the two classic forms of reasoning about time: point-based and interval-based. Both formalisms provide the necessary logical infrastructure to characterise the complex behaviour of legal dynamics.

Chapter 9 provides an overview of multi-agent abstract argumentation and dialogue and their application to the formalisation of legal reasoning. The basis of multi-agent abstract argumentation is input/output argumentation, distinguishing between individual acceptance by agents and collective acceptance by the system. The former may also be seen as a type of conditional reasoning, and the latter may be seen as the reasoning of an external observer. In this chapter, Arisaka *et al.* introduce dialogue semantics for abstract argumentation by refining agent communication into dialogue steps.

Chapter 10 discusses, via examples, the potential for integrating the theory of legal reasoning with some recently developed instruments of formal logic. Three zones of contact are highlighted: *(i)* the law of evidence, in the light of labelled deductive systems (LDSs), discussed through the example of the admissibility of hearsay evidence; *(ii)* the give and take of legal debate in general, and regarding the acceptability of evidence in particular, represented using the abstract systems of argumentation developed in logic; and *(iii)* the use of Bayesian networks as tools to analyse the effects of uncertainty on the legal status of actions.

Chapter 11 discusses new challenges of legal reasoning in the big data era. Traditionally, computational knowledge representation and reasoning focused its attention on rich domains such as the law. The main underlying assumption of traditional legal knowledge representation and reasoning is that knowledge and data are both available in main memory. However, in the era of big data, where large amounts of data are generated daily, an increasing range of scientific disciplines as well as business and human activities are becoming data-driven. In this chapter, Antoniou *et al.* summarise existing research on legal representation and reasoning with the aim of revealing technical challenges associated both with the integration of rules and databases and with the main concepts of the big data landscape.

Finally, norm enforcement and compliance have the goal of checking and ensuring that systems' requirements comply with norms through norm enforcement. Compliance requirements may stem from legislation and the guidelines of regulatory bodies (e.g., Sarbanes-Oxley, Basel II, the Health Insurance Portability and Accountability Act (HIPAA)), standards and codes of practice (e.g., the International Organization for Standardization (ISO) 9000 standards), and business partner contracts. Regulatory compliance in computer systems is aimed at ensuring that the specification requirements of such systems are in accordance with a prescribed and/or agreed sets of norms. Two fundamental strategies are identified in the literature for characterising norm enforcement and the concept of compliance in computer systems. First, norms may be hard constraints and system compliance is achieved by design. Second, norms may be soft constraints and therefore do not limit the system's behaviour in advance. Compliance is then ensured by system mechanisms stating that violations should result in sanctions or other normative effects to recover from violations. In this Handbook, two chapters address these issues.

Chapter 12 focuses on the computational complexity of proving the regulatory compliance of business process models. While the topic has never received the attention it deserves, Colombo Tosatto and Governatori argue that existing and future theoretical results may be far reaching for many areas related to the problem of proving the compliance of process models. In this chapter, they discuss existing results concerning the theoretical computational complexity of the problem as well as some further areas that could potentially advance knowledge about this issue.

Chapter 13 discusses legal understanding in a business development context. Given the dynamic environment and the ever-changing international context, it is crucial that companies are able to quickly and effectively identify potential threats and opportunities. This can be done with environmental scanning, which allows for the development and analysis of potential scenarios to help proactively plan responses to potential risks. Yet, the process of scanning, and the design and analysis of scenarios, are extremely expensive as they have to be done manually. In this chapter, Grassi and Vallati propose the use of AI techniques to support political, economic, social, technological, legal, and environmental (PESTLE) analysis — a managerial tool used to identify external factors that might affect a company — with a focus on the legal environment.

Chapter 14 discusses some legal and ethical challenges linked to the use of sophisticated AI services exploiting very large volumes of information from space. These legal and ethical challenges call for solutions that the international treaties currently in force are not able to determine and implement sufficiently. In this chapter, Long *et al.* propose a new methodology to link intelligent systems and services to a system of applicable rules. This methodology refers to existing legal AI-based tools amenable to making space law actionable, interoperable and machine readable for future compliance tools.

The chapters included in this volume are aimed at providing enough introductory material so that the newcomer can get acquainted with the essentials of the field while also covering advanced issues so that the interested reader can have a comprehensive reference on the state of the art for future developments. This Handbook brings together in one volume research carried out in the context of the MIning and REasoning with Legal texts (MIREL) project (funded by Marie Skłodowska-Curie Action — Research and Innovation Staff Exchange (RISE)).

We are pleased to conclude with some dutiful expressions of gratitude. We thankfully acknowledge the contribution of all the authors and the reviewers who made this volume possible and the help of all the colleagues who provided comments, suggestions, critiques and encouragement during the development of the initiative. Last but not least, special thanks go to College Publications and, in particular, Jane Spurr for her invaluable continued support.

BIBLIOGRAPHY

[Bench-Capon and Sartor, 2003] Trevor J. M. Bench-Capon and Giovanni Sartor. A model of legal reasoning with cases incorporating theories and values. *Artif. Intell.*, 150(1-2):97–143, 2003.

[Billi *et al.*, 2021] Marco Billi, Roberta Calegari, Giuseppe Contissa, Francesca Lagioia, Giuseppe Pisano, Galileo Sartor, and Giovanni Sartor. Argumentation and defeasible reasoning in the law. *J*, 4:897–914, 12 2021.

[Boella *et al.*, 2010] Guido Boella, Guido Governatori, Antonino Rotolo, and Leendert W. N. van der Torre. A logical understanding of legal interpretation. In Fangzhen Lin, Ulrike Sattler, and Miroslaw Truszczynski, editors, *Principles of Knowledge Representation and Reasoning: Proceedings of the Twelfth International Conference, KR 2010, Toronto, Ontario, Canada, May 9-13, 2010*. AAAI Press, 2010.

[Hitzler *et al.*, 2009] Pascal Hitzler, Markus Krötzsch, and Sebastian Rudolph. *Foundations of Semantic Web Technologies*. Chapman & Hall/CRC, 2009.

[Ji *et al.*, 2022] Shaoxiong Ji, Shirui Pan, Erik Cambria, Pekka Marttinen, and Philip S. Yu. A survey on knowledge graphs: Representation, acquisition, and applications. *IEEE Trans. Neural Networks Learn. Syst.*, 33(2):494–514, 2022.

[Jones and Sergot, 1992] Andrew J. I. Jones and Marek J. Sergot. Deontic logic in the representation of law: Towards a methodology. *Artif. Intell. Law*, 1(1):45–64, 1992.

[Jurafsky and Martin, 2009] Dan Jurafsky and James H. Martin. *Speech and language processing : an introduction to natural language processing, computational linguistics, and speech recognition*. Pearson Prentice Hall, Upper Saddle River, N.J., 2009.

[Tosatto *et al.*, 2020] Silvano Colombo Tosatto, Guido Governatori, and Antonino Rotolo. Principles and semantics: Modelling violations for normative reasoning. In Víctor Rodríguez-Doncel, Monica Palmirani, Michal Araszkiewicz, Pompeu Casanovas, Ugo Pagallo, and Giovanni Sartor, editors, *AI Approaches to the Complexity of Legal Systems XI-XII - AICOL International Workshops 2018 and 2020: AICOL-XI@JURIX 2018, AICOL-XII@JURIX 2020, XAILA@JURIX 2020, Revised Selected Papers*, volume 13048 of *Lecture Notes in Computer Science*, pages 75–89. Springer, 2020.

1
NLP Techniques for Normative Mining

GABRIELA FERRARO
HO-PUN LAM

ABSTRACT. Natural Language Processing (NLP) is a branch of artificial intelligence that studies the interactions between computers and
human (natural) language. In the field of legal informatics, the focus
has been centered on mining and formalising normative information
such that the legal norms extracted can be interpreted and reasoned
by machines in an automated fashion. In the present chapter, we focus our attention on discussing the challenges of normative mining
from an NLP perspective, and present a detailed overview of existing
techniques on semantic parsing, and their strengths and limitations
on mining legal norms.

1 Introduction

Natural Language Processing (NLP) is a branch of artificial intelligence that
study the interaction between computers and human (natural) language.
NLP deals with the design, development and analysis of computational algorithms for processing natural language, and its theoretical foundations encompasses computer science, mathematics, and linguistics. One of goals of
NLP is to provide language technology capabilities, for example, translating
between languages, extracting information from texts, answering questions,
holding a conversation, taking instructions, and so on.

Modern methods rely mostly on data-driven machine learning algorithms
that learn from examples. Other important methods for language processing
are deterministic models (e.g., state machines), declarative models (e.g., rule
systems), logic (e.g., predicate calculus), and probabilistic methods (e.g.,
weighted state machines).

Some of the characteristics of human language makes NLP particularly
challenging, for instance, human language data is discrete, thus it is not
possible to gradually approach a solution; language follows a power law
distribution [Zipf, 1949], which means that algorithms have to deal with
observations never seeing before; language is compositional, for example,
words combine to create larger units as phrases, hence algorithms have to
model implicit recursivity; and language is ambiguous, thus a construction

may have multiple interpretations [Jurafsky and Martin, 2008]. Despite the difficulties of modelling language, recent NLP methods has demonstrated impressive improvements in complex task as machine translation [Sutskever et al., 2014] and question answering [Sun et al., 2018].

Advances on NLP research are central for modelling the problem of formalising normative information from legal documents. The ultimate goal of normative mining is to automate the extraction and formalisation of laws and regulations in a format that a machine can interpret and reason about. This is a complex and challenging task as it encompasses language understanding at different processing levels: document-collection level, document level, section level, and sentence level. Sentence level processing is especially hard since it require semantic analysis of complex utterances, for example, identification of predicates and their arguments in particularly long sentences. Indeed, the process of extracting normative information from sentences is so complex that, at the moment, it is mostly done manually.

This chapter is intended to provide a review and discussion of the problems and plausible approaches in automating normative mining from legal documents with an NLP perspective. The rest of the chapter is organised as follows. Section 2 discusses the issues and problems of automatically extract the normative information from legal documents. Section 3 discuss the possible approaches to normative mining, and a literature review of the state-of-the-art approaches will be presented herein. Problems related to evaluation methodologies and benchmarking for normative mining will be discussed in Section 4. Section 5 presents preliminary results to normative rules extraction using relation extraction and semantic parsing models. Finally, Section 6 present the conclusions and some of the directions for future research in this area.

2   What are the problems?

Algorithms developed by the NLP community has been used to model the process of extracting normative rules from legal documents with certain success. Extracting normative rules is difficult because it requires sentence semantic analysis, which is one of the most challenging NLP problems. Moreover, some characteristics of legal documents also possess additional problems for NLP methods. Legal documents considerable differ from other documents such as news or Wikipedia articles that are usually used in NLP research. Those differences make off-the-shelf NLP solutions sometimes hard to apply, or insufficient, or inefficient, when analysing legal documents. In particular, legal documents have a peculiar document structure that needs to be captured in order to properly interpret its written content. Within the documents, sentences can be extremely long and complex, which possess important challenges to the semantic analysis methods available. In this section, we review some of the NLP-related challenges towards the formalisation of legal norms. In particular, we elucidate on the following.

- Document level cross-referencing
- Ambiguity and inconsistent terminology
- Sentence semantic analysis
- Identification of normative effects

While dealing with ambiguity, inconsistent terminology and sentence semantic analysis are central problems in NLP, handling sentence complexity and cross-referencing are particular to the legal domain. In what follows, each challenge will be described in detail so that the landscape of the problem and situations that led to the problem can be explored.

2.1 Document Level Cross-referencing

Typically, a legal document is structured into different chapters, articles, sections and subsections, where each of these might contain one or several sentences or even paragraphs. Consider the example as shown in Figure 1 illustrating the structure of the proposed EU regulation on EU administrative law [Evas, 2018]. As can be seen from the figure, the proposed regulation structure is constituted by four main chapters with thirty different articles, which correspond to different stages of the procedure, namely: (i) *initiation* of the procedure, (ii) *management* of the procedure, (iii) *conclusion* of the procedure, (iv) rights related to *rectification* and *withdrawal* of the act. In addition to this, it also consists of a chapter on general provisions related to the *objective*, *scope* and *definitions* (such as terms and concepts being used) of the act; and another chapter on the general scope, such as *evaluation*, and when the act enter into force, etc.

Essentially, each statement in a legal document has their own specific *goals*, *objectives*, and *scopes*, which define the *context* under which a particular set of statements become applicable and the (normative) *effects* that follow from applying it. This modularity nature of legislation allows legal drafters to focus on a particular aspect of legislation when drafting the document. Hence, referencing information from one section to another within the same regulation, or to other regulations, is not uncommon in legal documents.

Technically, *cross-references* are explicit phrases that appear in regulations and can be used to link regulatory requirements within and across regulations [Gordon and Breaux, 2013]. They can help to avoid ambiguity that may occur across different sections of the documents and can help to indicate whether a sentence is an *elaboration*, *subordinate*, or *prevailing* with

11

Chapter I General Provisions
- Article 1 Subject matter and objective
- Article 2 Scope
- Article 3 Relationship between this regulation and other legal acts of the Union
- Article 4 Definitions

Chapter II Initiation of Administrative Procedure
- Article 5 Initiation of the administrative procedure
- Article 6 Initiation by the Union's administration
- Article 7 Initiation by application

Chapter III Management of the Administrative Procedure
- Article 8 Procedural rights
- Article 9 Duty of careful and impartial investigation
- Article 10 Duty to cooperate
- Article 11 Witnesses and experts
- Article 12 Inspections
- Article 13 Conflict of interests
- Article 14 Right to be heard
- Article 15 Right of access to the file
- Article 16 Duty to keep records
- Article 17 Time-limits

Chapter IV Conclusion of the Administrative Procedure
- Article 18 Form of administrative acts
- Article 19 Duty to state reasons
- Article 20 Remedies
- Article 21 Notification of administrative acts

Chapter V Rectification and Withdrawal of Acts
- Article 22 Correction of errors in administrative acts
- Article 23 Rectification or withdrawal of administrative acts which adversely affect a party
- Article 24 Rectification or withdrawal of administrative acts which are beneficial to a party
- Article 25 Management of corrections of errors, rectification and withdrawal

Chapter VI Administrative Acts of General Scope
- Article 26 Respect for procedural rights
- Article 27 Legal basis, statement of reasons and publication
- Article 28 Online information on rules on administrative procedures
- Article 29 Evaluation
- Article 30 Entry into force

Figure 1: Structure of the proposed draft regulation from European Parliamentary Research Service (adopted from [Evas, 2018]).

respect to other sentences or definitions. They can also be used to conferring a priority to reconcile potential conflicts by discarding existing goals or substituting alternative top-level goals [Miall, 2007]. Hence, from NLP point of view, identifying cross-references is an important task in normative mining as they define the context of linguistic utterances and can help to resolve referential and lexical ambiguity, which will be discussed below.

2.2 Ambiguity and Inconsistent Terminology

As in other language related tasks, ambiguity is one of the problems to deal with in normative mining. We often encounter *lexical ambiguity* due to polysemy, *syntactic (or structural) ambiguity* due to different interpretations of a sentence grammatical structure, *referential ambiguity* that happens when it is not clear to what or whom a concept refers, and *logical ambiguity*, which leads to different logic interpretations.

Drafters of legal documents try to avoid ambiguity and ideally, produce a document that results in only one interpretation (e.g., avoid pronouns, avoid synonyms to refer to the same concept, add attributes to identify parties, use punctuation to define the scope of quantifiers, etc.). Furthermore, to avoid lexical ambiguity, legal documents usually include a glossary, sometimes named as Definitions (see Figure 1), which list the most important lexical items from the document and their corresponding definitions. For example, a regulation about *buildings* may contained a glossary with entries such as *commercial building, industrial building, accommodation units*, etc. However, as natural language is used to write the legislation, unintended ambiguities may arise. Lexical and referential ambiguities are usually inferred from the context in which the lexical units appeared. In the case of processing legal documents, in addition to the current (local) context, conditions related to the meaning of linguistic lexical units sometimes need to be inherited from other document sections via cross-referencing (see Section 2.1).

Logical ambiguity, on the other hand, refers to the use of natural language that can be mapped to different logical interpretations [Breaux and Antón, 2007]. Consider the fragment of legislation extracted from [Ministry of Business, Innovation and Employment, 2017a], as shown in Figure 2. Syntactically the terms *commercial building* and *industrial building* in the first sub-condition (a), *household units* and *accommodation units* in the second sub-condition (b), and the two sub-conditions are connected using *and*. However, logically (or semantically), the statement is in fact representing conditions to the four different types of building and should be represented using disjunction, i.e., *or*, in the resulting normative rule(s) generated.

Apart form the ambiguity problems just mentioned, the inconsistent use of terminology across different documents may also affect the normative

1.2 Natural ventilation – General

⋮

1.2.2 Natural ventilation of occupied spaces must be achieved by providing a net openable area of windows or other openings to the outside of no less than 5% of the floor area. The 5% floor area requirement does not apply to:

a) occupied spaces in Commercial **and** Industrial buildings where products listed in NZBC Clause G4.3.3 are generated (mechanical ventilation of these spaces is required), **and**

b) household units **and** accommodation units where there is only one external wall with opening windows (refer to Paragraph 1.3 for additional requirements if natural ventilation is used).

Figure 2: Example of logical ambiguity (Sentence extracted from [Ministry of Business, Innovation and Employment, 2017a]).

mining process as the same entity can be expressed using different terms or the scope of the same term has been defined differently. As mentioned in [Baaij, 2018],

> ... *inconsistencies within a single directive could have significant consequences for the national implementation law, instigating legal uncertainty in commercial and legal practices.*

Consider the case in EU as an example. Due to the divergence of languages being used, discrepancies among language versions are capable of aggravating the adverse consequence and may cause the same regulatory inconsistencies [Baaij, 2018, §2.4]. Hence, the European Commission has declared a requirement to the EU legislature to eliminate differences in terms and concepts that cannot be explained by differences in the problems being addressed [Baaij, 2018, §2.4.2.1]. Recently, [Bajčić, 2018] studied the role of EU legal English as a *lingua franca* in shaping EU legal culture; while [Misra, 2016] studied the terminological inconsistencies problem arising from *term-aliasing* (of the same language), i.e., when the same entity has been referred to by multiple terms across a corpus of documents related to a particular context, so that a better refinement, and possibly unified, glossary of terms can be used across the set of documents.

However, as the problem of dealing with inconsistent terminology does not directly affect the normative rules generation process, it will be skipped for the rest of the chapter.

14

2.3 Sentence Semantic Analysis

The automatic extraction of normative rules from sentences written in natural language required some sort of sentence semantic analysis that produce a meaning representation, for example, a logical statement or a deterministic rule, that is executable by a machine. An expressive meaning representation involves many aspects such as meaning of words, meaning associated with grammatical constructions (syntax), knowledge about the discourse structure (relationship between phrases and sentences), common-sense knowledge about the topic of the sentence, and pragmatic knowledge about the context where the discourse is occurring [Jurafsky and Martin, 2008].

The first problem encountered here is that, currently, there is no NLP computational framework that encompasses all the above aspects of meaning representation. The state-of-the-art semantic analysis methods produce meaning representations by analysing the lexical and grammatical (syntactical) characteristics of language at the sentence level [Montague, 1973; Warren and Pereira, 1982; Zelle and Mooney, 1996; Zettlemoyer and Collins, 2005; Liang et al., 2013; Reddy et al., 2016] and should be considered fairly modest in their scope.

The second problem is that the state-of-the-art semantic analysis struggled to capture predicates in complex sentences. Capturing sentence predicates units such as verbs and their arguments is essential to model meaning. This is particularly challenging in legal domain because sentences from legal documents can be extremely long and contain multiple predicates. As stated by [Burga et al., 2013], sentence length is an indication of sentence complexity. While the average number of lexical units in a sentence written in the English Wikipedia is about nineteen [Woodsend and Lapata, 2011], sentences from legal documents can have more than fifty units, as can be seen in Figure 2. Long sentences tend to have a complex grammatical structure, usually contained several predicates and coordinate and subordinate constructions, and are likely to be poorly analysed even with the use of state-of-the-art syntax analysers. For example, it is well known that automatic methods for syntax analysis straggled to capture the scope of multiple coordinate conjunctions and antecedent of subordinate phrases [Burga et al., 2013]. Similarly, they also straggled to capture long distance dependencies, which sometimes are essential for capturing the scope of predicate arguments.

2.4 Identification of Normative Effects

Capturing the normative effects of legal norms is a crucial task in legal informatics. Typically, a regulation can be seen as a set of *provisions*, carried by speech acts, where a provision can assume different types as *definition*,

Table 1: Example of Deontic Modalities identification and attachment (*obligation* (O))

Sentence	*Accessible showers **shall have** a level threshold.*
Normative rule	$accessibleShowers(X) \Rightarrow_O haveLevelThreshold(X)$

obligation, sanction, competence, amendments, etc. [Biagioli *et al.*, 2005], that are written in a highly structured way and in *legalese*. For instance, consider the fragment of regulation extracted from [Ministry of Business, Innovation and Employment, 2017b], as shown in Table 1. While it can be consider as a part of the physical structure of a legislative text [Francesconi and Passerini, 2007], it can also be qualified as a provision of type *obligation*, whose arguments are:

    Subject: Accessible showers
    Predicate: shall have
    Object: level threshold

As can be seen, such information affect the way that we interpret the legislation from a semantic point of view and the (normative) effects that specify the types of behaviour that it generated or permitted from applying those norms. Hence, it is foreseeable that detrimental impact (such as incorrect rights, duties, or obligations) or damaging effects may be conferred to some stakeholders if information like this is misinterpreted or has not been detected correctly.

3   Literature review

In this section, we examine some promising NLP avenues related to the problem of capturing normative information from legal documents and legal statements, and review existing approaches found in literature. We consider three related work topics. In Section 3.1, we investigate different NLP approaches to capture sentences semantics and discuss their strengths and weaknesses. Techniques on identifying and resolving cross-referencing that appear among different lexical units are discussed in Section 3.2. Section 3.3 discusses the problem of capturing normative information from legal texts using NLP. Finally, Section 3.4 review existing approaches to deal with the problem of extracting legal norms from legal documents.

3.1   Capturing sentence semantics

Traditionally, NLP methods capture semantics through syntax. These approaches are based on the principle of compositionality [Montague, 1973],

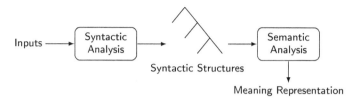

Figure 3: A simple pipeline approach to semantic analysis (adopted from [Jurafsky and Martin, 2008, p. 596]).

which follows the idea that the meaning of a sentence can be constructed by the meaning of its parts, and on the ordering and grouping of words and relations among words [Janssen, 1997]. Recent data-driven methods learn the mapping from sentences to meaning representations without using syntax or other external knowledge. In what follows, we review some of the research streams to address the problem of producing some sort of meaning representation: syntax-driven semantic parsing, and neuronal generative models for semantic parsing

3.1.1   Syntax-Driven Semantic Parsing

The input of syntax-driven semantic parsers is a syntactic tree and the output is a meaning representation, e.g., a first order logic formula or a subject-verb-object triplet [Jurafsky and Martin, 2008]. Figure 3 depicts a simple NLP pipeline approach to semantic analysis, in which an input is first passed through a parser to derive its syntactic structure, i.e., a syntax tree. The structure is then passed as input to a semantic analyser to produce a meaning representation.

In the literature, there are at least, the following NLP research streams that uses syntax as the basics for semantic analysis:

- Relation extraction
- Semantic role labelling
- Grammar-driven semantic parsing
- Data-driven semantic parsing

In what follows, we describe these research areas in more detail.

Relation Extraction refers to the extraction of relation tuples (typically binary relations) from plain text. For instance, from the sentence *"Buildings require ventilation"*, it is possible to extract the tuple as shown below:

$$(require_{pred} = buildings_{arg1}, ventilation_{arg2})$$

where *pred* stands for *predicate* and arg_i denotes the *arguments of the predicate* and i indicates the *argument order* in its syntactic structure. Recent approaches to relation extraction are open to any relation, thus relations do not have to be defined in advance and are able to model long-range dependencies, making it possible to identify multiple relations inside a single sentence. Relation extraction can be also seen as a step towards the formulation of normative rules. After the predicate structure of a sentence is extracted, those building blocks still need to be instantiated in a rule format. However, a drawback of relation extraction is that it does not capture predicate nouns and adjectives, e.g., given the sentence *A large building is any building with a net lettable area greater than 300 m^2*, the relation extraction tool OpenIE [Angeli et al., 2015] extracted the following relation tuples: '*A large building*', '*is building with*', '*net lettable area greater than 300 m^2*', but the arguments of the predicate '*greater than*' are not extracted. A detailed review of the current state-of-the-art on relation extraction can be found in [Pawar *et al.*, 2017]

Semantic Role Labelling refers to the process that assigns labels to the semantic arguments or roles of predicates in a sentence such as *agent, goal, result*, among other semantic roles. This is an important step towards making sense of the meaning of a sentence. A semantic analysis of this sort is at a lower-level of abstraction than a syntax tree, e.g., it has more categories, thus groups fewer clauses in each category. It can be seen as an important step towards the extraction of normative rule since the main predicates and their arguments are the basic building blocks of a rule. For example, the sentence *"For the purposes of subclause 2.4, a person is responsible for an individual if the person is a parent of the individual"* would need four labels such as *verb, purpose, argument(s)*, and *adverbial*, as elicited in Figure 4[1]. The current state-of-the-art on semantic role labeling are deep learning models that uses syntax as [He *et al.*, 2018].

Grammar-driven Semantic Parsing takes a sentence as input and output a meaning representation. The meaning representations can be diverse, e.g., a logical formula, a SQL query, a computer command, among others, as depicted in Table 2. Traditional approaches relied on categorical grammars, which are induced from data [Zettlemoyer and Collins, 2005; Kwiatkowski *et al.*, 2011; Kwiatkowski *et al.*, 2013]. Another research stream has focused on the task of automatically learn-

---

[1]The output of semantic role labeling in Figure 4 is generated using the tool: AllenNLP (`https://demo.allennlp.org/semantic-role-labeling`) (last accessed: 16 July 2019).

Figure 4: Example of Semantic Role Labelling for the sentence: *For the purposes of subclause 2.4, a person is responsible for an individual if the person is a parent of the individual.*

ing the mapping from sentences to meaning representations based on a training set of sentences labelled with their semantics [Ge and Mooney, 2005; Kate and Mooney, 2006; Lu *et al.*, 2008; Dong and Lapata, 2016; Reddy *et al.*, 2016; Duong *et al.*, 2017]. Most of these works rely on manually designed syntactic and lexical features, which are usually domain and meaning representation dependent.

3.1.2   Neuronal Generative Models for Semantic Parsing

Inspired by recent research in machine translation [Kalchbrenner and Blunsom, 2013; Sutskever *et al.*, 2014], neuronal generative models have been successfully applied to semantic parsing [Dong and Lapata, 2016; Jia and Liang, 2016; Ling *et al.*, 2016; Lapata and Dong, 2018]. These models are learn from sentences paired with meaning representations and do not use explicit syntactic knowledge. Indeed, the sequence-to-sequence models are able to generate translations directly from the probability distribution of the network without any external knowledge [Kalchbrenner and Blunsom, 2013]. Thus, they do not rely on domain-dependent features and representation-specific solutions. One of the drawbacks is that these methods are data hungry and creating datasets for semantic parsing is not a trivial task.

The above methods capture semantic aspects from sentences, but are not designed to capture normative rules explicitly. Even though, they can provide certain level of automation to accomplish that task. Recent methods developed by the semantic parsing community are especially promising for facilitating the automation of normative rules extraction. However, they require the creation and release of datasets of sentences pairs with their corresponding normative rules.

3.2   Capturing cross-referencing/scope

Detection of document structure is one of the tools that can be used to determine the context of an argument in which it becomes effective or applicable, and can be used to enhance the quality of cross-referencing information that appear within the same document or among different legislation.

As mentioned before, legislations are presented following a very strict (and formal) structure. Based on this, [de Maat *et al.*, 2006] has categorized the structure of references into four different types, namely: (i) *simple references*, references to other legislations using their name, such as "Building Act", "part 1", or "Paragraph 1.3" (as shown in Figure 2); (ii) *complex references* or *multi-valued references*, a reference label that is constituted by more than one simple references, such as "article 1, section 2, paragraph 2"; (iii) *special cases*, references that contain a list or an exception. For example, a reference is made to the first item of article 1, the first item of article 2 and the first item of article 4 can can shorten to "the first item of articles 1, 2 and 4"; and (iv) *complete and incomplete references*, references that include complete (or respectively, incomplete) information of a particular document. For example, "section 1, article 1" is an incomplete references; while "section 1, article 1, Building Act" is a complete reference.

In addition to this, based on sequence of references appear, [Tran *et al.*, 2013] has characterized references using the notions: *mention* to denote references that contain referring texts, and *antecedent* to denote the text that mentions refer to, and discussed the ways that is used in Japanese legislations.

In the past, regular expressions or context free grammar based approaches have been proposed to address this issue [de Maat *et al.*, 2006; Palmirani *et al.*, 2003; Tran *et al.*, 2013] and promising results have been reported in the literature. However, such approaches have been limited by the list of terms and abbreviations used, and are language dependent.

Recent trends in this area have been emphasised on the use of syntactic structures of the legal texts. For instance, [Sleimi *et al.*, 2018] studied the problem of extracting and analysing semantic legal metadata (such as *actor, artifact, situation, action, constraint,* among others) using NLP-based extraction rules and proposed a conceptual model to capture the extracted information.

Falesse *et al.* [2010], on the other hand, conducted an empirical evaluation on applying different NLP techniques (such as algebraic model (vector space model, latent semantic analysis, etc), term extraction, weighting schema, and similarity metric) and models to identify equivalent requirements (or linkage) across different documents, and concluded that simple measures are more precise than complex ones.

3.3 Capturing normative effects and modalities

The conventions of legalese are not always use consistently and may introduce intended and unintended ambiguities that affect the performance of the automated tools [Kiyavitskaya *et al.*, 2008]. To minimize the effects of such ambiguities, normative sentences are typically classified with the aid of some legal ontologies which explicitly specify a conceptualization, i.e., a formal description of concepts (i.e., the set of normative effects in our case) either as a whole or focus on a particular aspect or activity, and their relations. It can be used to resolve the problem of language heterogeneities (and ambiguities) that appear in legal documents, and allow the information interchange between different diverse information systems [Gómez-Pérez *et al.*, 2004].

Based on [Jiang and Tan, 2005], Winkels and Hoekstra [2012] proposed an approach to extract legal concepts by parsing and extracting noun phrase in every sentence individually. Lee [2006] proposed an ontological approach to categorize and extract normative requirements from regulations, which helped knowledge engineers in rigorously identifying inconsistencies between the model and regulation. Breaux [2009; 2008] proposed an upper ontology, which has *two* tiers, for formalizing *frames* in legal provision. Deontic Concepts such as *permission, obligations, refrainments, exclusions, facts* and *definitions* are defined in the first tier; while the second tier describes concepts related to constituent phrases, such as *subject, acts, objects, purposes, instruments* and *locations*. Sleimi [2018] used syntactic structures and handwritten rules to identify entities (*agent, action, condition, exception*, among others) and linked action to a (normative/deontic) *modality* such as *obligations, permissions*, and *prohibitions*, and further divided constraints into *conditions, violations*, and *exceptions*, which are relevant in legal knowledge representation.

In [Visser and Bench-Capon, 1998], the authors have compared legal ontologies in three different dimensions, namely: (i) *epistemological adequacy* (such as *epistemological clarity, epistemological intuitiveness, epistemological relevance, epistemological completeness*, and *discriminative power*), (ii) *operationality* (such as *encoding bias, coherence*, and *computationality*), and (iii) *reusability* (such as *task-and-method reusability* and *domain reusability*). Their results have found that different ontology authors were using different conceptualisations of the legal domain and despite their purposes were similar, and have not have much agreement to what are the most important block of legal knowledge. However, their results also showed that there are not many differences in knowledge types distinguished but difference in priorities of these knowledge can be found. Recently, several legal ontologies have been proposed [Benjamins *et al.*, 2005; Ajani *et al.*, 2006; Rubino *et al.*, 2006; Hoekstra *et al.*, 2007], providing a more update-to-date conceptual architecture for the development of a legal system.

3.4   Related work

Algorithms developed by the NLP community has been used to model the process of extracting normative information from legal texts with certain success. van Engers *et al.* [2004] proposed an automated concept and norm extraction framework by exploiting the use of a Juridical (Natural) Language Constructs (JLC) as an intermediate format between the legal texts and a formal model. In their approach, the JLC is essentially a set of patterns that can appear in the legal document. Legal knowledge is identified and constructed using noun and verb phrases patterns, that will later be transformed into formal rules. However, the effectiveness or efficiencies of their approach is still an unknown as no evaluation results has been reported in the paper.

Likewise, similar approaches have been used to transform legal text into an intermediate formalism, to improve the efficiencies of the legal norms generation process. For instance, [Selway *et al.*, 2015; Bajwa *et al.*, 2011] used Semantics of Business Vocabulary and Rules (SBVR) [Object Management Group, 2017] — a controlled natural language, as a tool to aid the information extraction process by clarifying ambiguities and inconsistencies that may appear in the regulations. Kimura *et al.* [2009] andNakamura *et al.* [2008] proposed to convert sentences into a logical formalism that conform to Davidsonian Style [Zucchi, 1993], which is suitable for some languages that allow zero-pronouns (such as Japanese). In [van Gog and van Engers, 2001], the authors proposed an approach to translate legal texts into a formal language, such as UML, to support automatic legislation modelling. However, information about how much their system can help in reducing the burden of the normative information extraction process is still an unknown issue.

Instead of using pattern matching methods based on lexico-syntactic patterns, which are manually crafted or deduced automatically [Auger and Barrière, 2008], [Boella *et al.*, 2013] presented a technique to automatically extract semantic knowledge from legal texts based on the syntactic dependencies between terms extracted with a syntactic parser, which is also the technique used in [Dragoni *et al.*, 2016] but with different kinds of information extracted. Wyner and Peters [2011] proposed a linguistic oriented rule-based approach to extract deontic rule from regulations that build on top of General Architecture for Text Engineering (GATE) framework [Cunningham *et al.*, 2013] and found that serious issues may appear when mapping thematic roles to syntactic position. Gaur *et al.* [2014], on the other hand, developed a translation systems called NL2KR to learn the semantics of unknown words from syntactically similar words with known meaning, which can later be translated into a variety of formal language representations. However, their evaluation was based on a few small sentences picked from the literature, and further enhancements is needed when dealing with long and more complicated sentences that frequently appear in legal documents.

The automated processing of extracting a certain types of information (such as the definitions of terms, metadata of a particular version of the regulation, etc.) is another challenging task that needs to be addressed. In the past, researchers in knowledge representation community has proposed different schemas, such as ᴹᴱᵀᴬLex [Boer *et al.*, 2002], to encode legislation documents and content with annotated metadata in a structural and standardised format (mainly XML), which helps to improve the efficiency of managing and processing information in legal knowledge base systems. Maxwell *et al.* [2011], on the other hand, proposed a legal taxonomy to address the problems, such as conflicting requirements, conflicting definition, refining an existing requirement, etc., that can appear when cross-referencing legal documents. Gordon and Breaux [2013] developed a legal requirements specification language (LRSL) as a standard notation of extracted requirements and proposed a frame-based approach called *"requirements water marking"* to systematically align, manually extract and reconcile cross-references from multi-jurisdictions, as illustrated in Figure 5. Recently, LegalDocumentML [Palmirani and Vitali, 2018], an OASIS standard, has been proposed to provide a common legal document standard to exchange legislative and judicial information between different institutions.

Biagioli *et al.* [2005] proposed an automated framework for the semantic annotation of provisions to ease the retrieval process of norms, from the semantic, [de Araujo *et al.*, 2013] presented a tool for extracting requirements from regulations where texts are annotated to identify fragments describing normative concepts, [Kiyavitskaya *et al.*, 2008] present a tool for extracting requirements from regulations where texts are annotated to identify fragments describing normative concepts, and then a semantic model is constructed from these annotations and transformed into a set of requirements. [Sleimi *et al.*, 2018] used the syntactic structures and hand-written rules to identify different types of entities (*agent, action, condition, exception*, among others), which are relevant in legal knowledge representation and can be useful in assisting the legal norms extraction process.

In another line of research, argumentation mining (AM) is intended to extract arguments from generic text corpora automatically, to provide structured data for computational models of argument and reasoning engines [Cabrio and Villata, 2018; Lippi and Torroni, 2016; Mochales-Palau and Moens, 2011]. Most of the AM systems developed so far implement a pipeline architecture, as depicted in Figure 6, where a set of unstructured text are taken input and generate a set of structured/annotation document as output, and arguments and their relations are extracted and annotated so

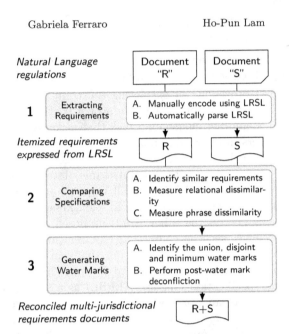

Figure 5: Overview of regulatory water mark construction (adopted from [Gordon and Breaux, 2013])

as to form an *argument graph* showing their linguistic structure, the relationship between different arguments, and recognizing the underlying concepts, evidences and consequences (a.k.a. conclusions or claims in some literature) of the legal texts.

Over the years, different techniques have been proposed to address a variety of tasks in the AM process. Most relevant to us, among others, are approaches that focus on the identification of argumentation structure, such as: *component identification*, *component classification*, and *structure identification* [Stab and Gurevych, 2017]. For instance, [Mochales-Palau and

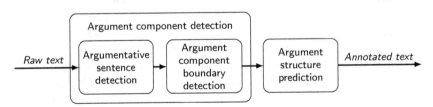

Figure 6: Argumentation Mining Pipeline architecture (adopted from [Lippi and Torroni, 2016])

Moens, 2011], classify arguments as either premises, claims, or proposes using convolution kernel methods with domain-dependent key phrases and text statistics, and have achieved an accuracy of 65%, which is a bit lower than [Mochales-Palau and Moens, 2009] (73%). Cabrio and Villata [2012], on the other hand, adopt the notion of *textual entailment* to recognize features characterizing legal arguments and have applied different abstract argumentation frameworks over the set of generated arguments to determine the set of acceptable arguments with respect to the chosen semantics. More detailed discussions on this topic can be found in the next chapter in this *Handbook: A Data-informed Analysis of Argument Mining* by Elena Cabrio and Serena Villata.

Legal documents considerably differ from other types of documents with respect to structure, language, length, etc. As a result, the desired generation of formalised legal norms may pose some significant challenges to the NLP community. In this section, we have provided an overview of the NLP approaches that have been developed for mining normative information from legal texts. Some research has been devoted to the task of generating legal norms from sentences in legal documents with some success [Dragoni *et al.*, 2015] but are still not yet sufficient to cater the needs in practical use. Hence, more works need to be done to further enhance the efficiency and quality of normative information extracted. In the following section, we are going to address problems that may appear from evaluation and benchmarking perspectives.

4 Evaluation and Benchmarking

Reporting meaningful evaluations is essential for comparing, replicating and benchmarking methods, and is crucial for scientific progress and technical innovation [Peng, 2011]. However, evaluation and benchmarking have always been problematic in normative mining related research due to the lack of evaluation datasets, i.e., there are no available gold-standard with text snippets written in natural language paired with their corresponding normative rules, nor standards/tools to benchmark approaches that have been developed. Thus, making it difficult to compare and reproduce existing results.

In this section, we explore two fundamental questions concerning the evaluation of normative rule extraction: *what* to evaluate, and *how* to evaluate? We will response to each of these questions in turn and will discuss important aspects to be taken into account to prompt method comparisons and replications.

4.1   What to evaluate?

A fundamental question in evaluation methodology is what to evaluate. On one hand, it is possible to *intrinsically* or directly evaluate a system on a set of desire functionalities, for example, the measure to what extent the automatically generated normative rules corresponds to correct outputs. On the other hand, it is possible to *extrinsically* assess the impact of a task external to the system, for example, the disclosure of reasoning of the generated normative rules.

NLP system are intrinsically evaluated in terms of *one input, one output* or *multiple outputs per input*. In the case of normative rules extraction, intrinsic evaluation should be done considering *one input, one output*, therefore avoiding multiple competing rules that can negatively affect the reasoning process, for example, by increasing complexity due to the number of rules.

Besides, it is also important to take into consideration the architecture of the proposed systems. Usually, NLP systems are not monolithic, but rather a set of modules in a processing pipeline. An advantage of implementing a system like this is that one can artificially manipulate a component input and observe its impact to the system's final effectiveness, and evaluation can be done at both an *individual* component level or at group level. For instance, syntax parsing heavily depends on the quality of the POS-Tags associated with each word. Artificially corrupting the POS-Tags can help to study the sensibility of the syntax parser to POS-Tagging errors. This is particularly relevant when evaluating modular architectures for normative rules extraction since the quality of off-the-shelf tools, such as POS-Taggers and syntax parsers, are seriously affected when analysing complicated sentences from legal documents. Interestingly, modern NLP approaches are shifting from pipeline architectures to an end-to-end ones. Some modern NLP solutions are implemented as end-to-end neuronal machine learning systems, such that the entire system is trained as a whole from the processing of input text to the output predication, and evaluation is to be done only on the final outputs.

Overall, system's architectures play a key role in deciding what to evaluate and should be taken into consideration when designing an evaluation methodology.

4.2   How to evaluate?

NLP systems are can be manually or automatically evaluated. Nowadays, manual evaluation in NLP are not uncommon. They usually require a well designed methodology, large investment in resources, and the results can be inconsistent and slow. Automatic evaluation is the most popular way of evaluating NLP systems, and they is usually designed to mimic human assessments. It require the creation of evaluation material (or gold-standard) and its cost depends on the complexity of the task to evaluate. It allows fast development and is cheap, in the sense that it is possible to re-use the evaluation material multiple times and sometimes it is possible to automate its creation process. As already mentioned, one of the main bottlenecks for advancing research in normative rules extraction is the lack of annotated gold-standard material for evaluation. Creating gold-standards can be an immense task, and its creation process needs to be scrutinised and evaluated to ensure certain quality. For example, it is expected that the same statement is to be annotated and agreed by at least two independent annotators, and inter-annotator agreement calculation, upper bounds discovery, etc., has to be done accordingly to measure the acceptability of the proposing standard. In the following, we provide some guidelines on creating a gold-standard for normative rules extraction.

4.2.1 How to create a gold-standard for normative rules extraction

Having a gold-standard for normative rules extraction allows to carry-out intrinsic evaluations. Creating a gold-standard implies the compilation of a data set consisting of sentences written in natural language paired with their corresponding normative rules. With a gold-standard such as that, it is possible to perform evaluations in terms of *one input, one output*, and therefore, assess the quality of the normative rules directly, without having to execute the reasoning process.

Creating a gold-standard is can immense task. In what follows we discussed some important considerations to take into account when building a gold-standard data set for normative rules extraction.

- Agnostic to reasoning: there is no consensus about to what extent normative rules should be formalism independent, and whether normative rules should be agnostic to the reasoning machinery. In an ideal situation, the output of the normative mining algorithms is agnostic to the reasoning machinery that used them, which implies that the normative rules generated should be written in a format that can be transformed into a formalism that can be reasoned with at the later stage of the process.

- Annotator expertise level: the manual annotation of normative rules require humans with experience in the areas of logic, and/or linguistics, and/or law.

- Inter-annotator agreement and upper-bound calculation: Inter-annotator agreement is a measure of how well two (or more) annotators can make the same annotation decision for a certain instance. Calculating inter-annotator agreement gives an idea about the difficulty of the problem, thus how trustworthy is the annotation (the lower the agreement, the less trust-able the annotation) The agreement rate can be thought of as an upper bound (human ceiling), on accuracy of a system evaluated using the annotation.

- Gold-standard size and instance diversity: machine learning based approaches require about 1000 instances to learn a decent performing model. Meanwhile, other approaches might not require big gold-standard material for training, they should use gold-standards for development and evaluation with at least 100 instances. Making a gold-standard representative of a problem is hard, however, diversity in terms of rules complexity, regulation topics (rules from many different, unrelated regulations), and jurisdictions are likely to make a gold-standard more representative.

- Annotation of Deontic Modalities : it is necessary to characterise normative rules legally by attaching Deontic modalities to them.

- Annotation guidelines: annotation guidelines are useful to document conventions in annotation and should contemplate solutions for generic cases, for example, how to annotate negation, coordinate constructions, prepositional verbs (verbs coupled with specific prepositions e.g., *correlate with*), prepositional phrases as modifiers (prepositions are context dependent e.g., *corresponds with, corresponds to*) Annotation guidelines are important to help annotators to produce consistent annotations and help users to interpret the data correctly.

4.3 How to evaluate given the gold-standard?

Having a gold standard means there is a reference for evaluation. As mentioned, a gold standard for normative rules consist of a set of sentences aligned with their normative rules. During evaluation, sentences from the gold standard are input to a computational model for rule extraction, which outputs normative rules.

Since normative rules are statements executable by a machine by a reasoning engine, they quality of the rules directly impact the reasoning process. Therefore, rules are either right or wrong, and there is no middle ground or partially correct rules. Hence, the most appropriate evaluation metric to assess the correctness of the rules is Accuracy.

Formally, accuracy is the fraction of predictions a model got right and it is defined as follows:

(1)
$$Accuracy = \frac{\text{Number of correct predictions}}{\text{Total number of predictions}}$$

The calculation of the predicted rules against the gold standard ones can be done by comparing the tokens of both rules sequentially from left to right. While the sequence of tokens is the same in both rules Accuracy is 1, otherwise is 0.

4.4 Road map for evaluation and benchmarking

Here we summarised key aspects towards the design of meaningful evaluations for normative rules extraction methods, and highlight some good practises to encourage methods comparison and facilitate replication.

Encourage *one input, one output intrinsic* evaluations: intrinsic evaluations focus on directly evaluating a desire functionality, for example, the correctness of the a normative rule given a sentence in natural language. This makes development more focus and faster than extrinsic evaluations, making easier to optimise the number of correct rules, thus minimising the risk of having multiple competing rules that can negatively affect the reasoning process.

Data sets creation: data sets creation is essential for evaluating methods for normative rules extraction. Using crowdsourcing platforms, which offers online workers with several levels of expertise, are probable the fasted way of annotating large amounts of data. For example, it is possible to crowdsource the construction of a data set of sentences paired with they corresponding normative rules. Performing a quality control it is important when eliciting annotations from online workers.

Data sets partitioning: data set partitioning is fundamental for reporting meaningful evaluations. Data sets should be partitioned into, at least, two disjoint subsets: test set and development set, so that the data in the test set a remain completely untouched and unseen until the system is frozen just prior to evaluation.

Data sets sharing: data sharing provides others with access to data. It avoids the generation of equivalent data sets, brings new perspectives from the re-analysis of the data set, and make possible method comparison and experiment replication.

Code sharing: code sharing provides other with access to implementation details and code of an existing method. Code sharing under open source licenses has become an standard good practise in computer science research. It avoids re-implementation of existing methods, improves their understanding, and facilitates method comparison.

5 Neuronal Semantic Parsing for Normative Rule Extraction

In this section, we assess the feasibility of using neuronal semantic parsing for the extraction of normative rules. To do so, we applied and evaluate an state-of-the-art neuronal semantic parsing approach using a small dataset of sentences from regulations and their corresponding representation in lambda calculus.

As discussed in Section 3, current NLP tools cannot be used to directly distil normative rules. Nevertheless, there are some promising avenues in that direction such as applying neuronal semantic parsing.

Semantic parsing is the task of mapping sentences in natural language to a meaning representation such as a logic formula (see Section 3.1). It can be seen as an intermediate step towards the extraction of normative rules due to its predicate-argument structure, which can be used as building blocks for normative rules extraction. Table 3 shows some example sentences written in natural language, their correspondent logic formula in lambda calculus (we follow the notation from [Kwiatkowski *et al.*, 2011]), and their corresponding normative rules represented using PCL [Governatori and Rotolo, 2010].

We chose to evaluate neuronal semantic parsing since it does not require hand-crafted features that usually require knowledge from domain experts in their design. In addition, it does not use syntactic structures to represent sentences, which can have poor quality when dealing with long sentences and domain-specific text, such as the legal one. Finally, neural network architectures are now the dominant machine learning approaches in NLP and produce the state-of-the-art results in semantic parsing.

In our experiments, we evaluate sequence-to-sequence model with LSTM [Hochreiter and Schmidhuber, 1997] with Attention proposed by [Dong and Lapata, 2016], as depicted in Figure 7. It consists of an encoder and decoder with two different L-layer recurrent neural networks with LSTM units, which recursively process tokens one by one. A sentence in natural language x is encoded into a vector representation, and decoded into a sequence $y_1, \ldots, y_{|y|}$ that is learned conditioned on the encoded vector $p(y|x)$. Additionally, to integrate encoder side information (also referred to as context vector), this approach incorporates an Attention Mechanism [Bahdanau *et al.*, 2015; Luong *et al.*, 2015].

5.1 Data Sets for Training Semantic Parsers

The neuronal semantic models are trained using the following data sets, which cover texts from different domains and their corresponding meaning representations is in lambda calculus.

GEO This is a standard semantic parsing benchmark. It consist of a set of queries to a database of U.S. geography. We used the splits provided by [Dong and Lapata, 2016] (see Table 4). The meaning representation of this data set is lambda-calculus. Values for variables city, state, country, river and number are identified beforehand.

RegTech [Ferraro *et al.*, 2019] This data set is developed for evaluating the performance of semantic parsing in the legal domain. At the moment, the data set consists of 140 sentences extracted from regulations from New Zealand and Australia. Following the annotation schema of [Dong and Lapata, 2016], sentences in the data set are paired with logical expressions that are used to indicate the scope of the predicates and their arguments. The annotations were carried out by annotators with a background in logic. Each annotator annotated a set of 10 sentences (without overlap). Next, two annotators reviewed the logical expressions, agreed on the best practises and produce a consistent final version of the data set.

Information and examples of the data sets are shown in Tables 4 and 5, respectively.

5.2 Experimental Settings

Semantic parsing is evaluated on accuracy, which is defined as the proportion of the input sentences that are correctly parsed to their gold standard logical form. All models are trained on GPU with their default hyper-parameters.

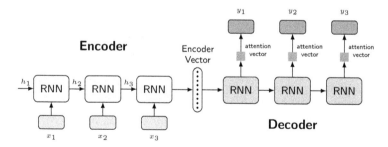

Figure 7: Sequence-to-Sequence Model with LSTM and Attention Architecture

5.3 Experimental results

Table 7 shows the results of the semantic parsing experiments. We first verify the ability of the method in analysing sentences of different complexity, assuming the sentence length is an indicator of sentence complexity (the longer the sentence, the more likely it is to contain complicated semantic structures). As already shown in Table 5, sentences in the legal domain (for example, in RegTech) have an average input length that is significantly higher than sentences in standard semantic parsing data sets such as GEO. Since the size RegTech is small and potentially not sufficient to properly train a semantic parser, we evaluate the parsers performance on long sentences by splitting the GEO test set in two subsets, respectively: a set containing sentences with less than 10 tokens; and a set containing sentences with more than 10 tokens. For comparison, we also report the evaluation results with the full test sets: GEO (all). As expected, results shows considerable drops when parsing long sentences, The model performance dropped about 14 points when parsing long sentences with GEO (from 83.57 to 68.99).

As mentioned, the size of RegTech is potentially too small to train a semantic parser. Results shows an accuracy of 18.28 for sequence-to-sequence. For comparison, we report results on GEO trained only with 140 sentences that were randomly chosen. Results indicate that models trained with limited amount of data are not able to generalise well. A qualitative error analysis performed on the output of the semantic parsers trained with RegTech indicates that the models are able to correctly output the structure of the logic formulas, but failed to instantiate the appropriate vocabulary. Cf. Table 6. We attribute this limitation to the vocabulary mismatch between the training and testing sets. The main take away from these experiments is that current technologies for semantic parsing are data hungry, and creating data sets for semantic parsing is not a trivial task. As mentioned before, in the GEO data set values for in-domain variables e.g., city, airport, etc. are anonymised before training, thus the vocabulary size is reduced, making encoding and decoding easier. Note that variables in RegTech are not anonymised, consequently, the vocabulary size is bigger, which impacts the generalisation power of the model. Nevertheless, we argue that is less costly to increase the size of RegTech and train a semantic parser, than investing in a syntax-based approach, which require to manually annotate in-domain syntactic structures to re-train a syntax analyser and to write grammars to distil the rules from the trees.

6 Conclusion

In this chapter, we have identified some of the problems of extracting normative rules from legal texts from an NLP perspective. One of the main challenges is the semantic analysis of sentences such as the identification of predicates and their arguments in complex sentences. Other important aspects to take into account in the design and development of methods for normative rule extraction are: cross-referencing between document sections and document collections; the identification of normative effects or normative modalities; and the intrinsic ambiguities that might arise as natural language is use to write legislation and regulations.

Despite the difficulties of extracting normative rules from text, several approaches have been developed with certain success. While syntax driven approaches are the most popular strategy for normative rule extraction, the current limitations of syntax parsing in the legal domain make these approaches insufficient. The most obvious limitation of syntactic analysis is related to structural ambiguity, which occurs when a parser produces a competitive analysis, hence producing more than one possible parsed outcome to a sentence. Another limitation of the current state-of-the-art approaches is the lack of an standard evaluation methodology. The lack of publicly available data sets for evaluation makes model comparison and replication not possible. We argue that to overcome the evaluation issues just mentioned and to advance research in this area it is necessary to encourage researchers to share their data and models.

This chapter also includes experiments on neuronal semantic parsing as an intermediate step towards the extraction of normative rules. In our experiments, we have used a publicly available data set of sentences from legal documents aligned with lambda calculus formulas, which is the only resource available for semantic parsing in the legal domain. We believed this is an promising research avenue as neuronal models for semantic parsing are receiving a lot of attention from the NLP and machine learning community.

The field of NLP is moving fast, and it is a challenge for the legal informatics community to keep up with the advances. Therefore, encouraging multi-disciplinary teams with NLP researchers and legal informatics experts is the key to advance research in this area.

BIBLIOGRAPHY

[Ajani et al., 2006] Gianmaria Ajani, Guido Boella, L. Lesmo, Macro Martin, Alessandro Mazzei, and Piercarlo Rossi. A Development Tool For Multilingual Ontology-based Conceptual Dictionaries. In *Proceedings of the 5th International Conference on Language Resources and Evaluation*, LREC06, pages 479–484, Genoa, Italy, May 2006.

[Angeli et al., 2015] Gabor Angeli, Melvin Jose Johnson Premkumar, and Christopher D. Manning. Leveraging Linguistic Structure For Open Domain Information Extraction. In *Proceedings of the 53rd Annual Meeting of the Association for Computational Linguistics and the 7th International Joint Conference on Natural Language Processing (Volume 1: Long Papers)*, pages 344–354, Beijing, China, July 2015. Association for Computational Linguistics.

[Auger and Barrière, 2008] Alain Auger and Caroline Barrière. Pattern-based approaches to semantic relation extraction: A state-of-the-art. *Terminology*, 14(1):1–19, January 2008.

[Baaij, 2018] C. J. W. Baaij. *Legal Integration and Language Diversity: Rethinking Translation in EU Lawmaking*. Oxford University Press, Inc., 2018.

[Bahdanau et al., 2015] Dzmitry Bahdanau, Kyunghyun Cho, and Yoshua Bengio. Neural machine translation by jointly learning to align and translate. In *3rd International Conference on Learning Representations, ICLR 2015, San Diego, CA, USA, May 7-9, 2015, Conference Track Proceedings*, 2015.

[Bajčić, 2018] Martina Bajčić. The Role of EU Legal English in Shaping EU Legal Culture. *International Journal of Language & Law*, 7:8–24, 2018.

[Bajwa et al., 2011] Imran Sarwar Bajwa, Mark G. Lee, and Behzad Bordbar. SBVR Business Rules Generation from Natural Language Specification. In Knut Hinkelmann and Barbara Thönssen, editors, *2011 AAAI Spring Symposium: AI for Business Agility*, pages 2–8, 2011.

[Benjamins et al., 2005] V. Richard Benjamins, Pompeu Casanovas, Joost Breuker, and Aldo Gangemi, editors. *Law and the Semantic Web: Legal Ontologies, Methodologies, Legal Information Retrieval, and Applications*. Springer Berlin Heidelberg, Berlin, Heidelberg, 2005.

[Biagioli et al., 2005] C. Biagioli, E. Francesconi, A. Passerini, S. Montemagni, and C. Soria. Automatic Semantics Extraction in Law Documents. In *Proceedings of the 10th International Conference on Artificial Intelligence and Law*, ICAIL '05, pages 133–140, Bologna, Italy, June 2005. ACM.

[Boella et al., 2013] Guido Boella, Luigi Di Caro, and Livio Robaldo. Semantic Relation Extraction from Legislative Text Using Generalized Syntactic Dependencies and Support Vector Machines. In Leora Morgenstern, Petros Stefaneas, François Lévy, Adam Wyner, and Adrian Paschke, editors, *Proceedings of the 7th International Web Rule Symposium: Theory, Practice, and Applications of Rules on the Web*, RuleML 2013, pages 218–225, Seattle, WA, USA, 2013. Springer Berlin Heidelberg.

[Boer et al., 2002] Alexander Boer, Rinke Hoekstra, and Radboud Winkels. METALex: Legislation in XML. In T. Bench-Capon, A. Daskalopulu, and R. Winkels, editors, *Proceedings of the 15th Annual Conference on Legal Knowledge and Information Sytems*, JURIX 2002, pages 1–10. IOS Press, 2002.

[Breaux and Antón, 2007] Travis D. Breaux and Annie I. Antón. A Systematic Method for Acquiring Regulatory Requirements: A Frame-Based Approach. In *Proceedings of the 6th International Workshop on Requirements for High Assurance Systems*, RHAS-6, Pittsburg, PA, USA, September 2007. Software Engineering Institute (SEI).

[Breaux and Anton, 2008] T.D. Breaux and A.I. Anton. Analyzing Regulatory Rules for Privacy and Security Requirements. *IEEE Transactions on Software Engineering*, 34(1):5–20, January 2008.

[Breaux, 2009] Travis Durand Breaux. *Legal Requirements Acquisition for the Specification of Legally Compliant Information Systems*. Ph.D. Thesis, North Carolina State University, Raleigh, NC, USA, 2009.

[Burga et al., 2013] Alicia Burga, Joan Codina, Gabriela Ferraro, Horacio Saggion, and Leo Wanner. The Challenge of Syntactic Dependency Parsing Adaptation for the Patent Domain. In *Proceedings of ESSLLI-13 Workshop on Extrinsic Parse Improvement*, EPI, Düsseldorf, Germany, August 2013.

[Cabrio and Villata, 2012] Elena Cabrio and Serena Villata. Natural Language Arguments: A Combined Approach. In *Proceedings of the 20th European Conference on Artificial Intelligence*, ECAI'12, pages 205–210, Montpellier, France, August 2012. IOS Press.

[Cabrio and Villata, 2018] Elena Cabrio and Serena Villata. Five Years of Argument Mining: a Data-driven Analysis. In *Proceedings of the 27th International Joint Con-

ference on Artificial Intelligence, IJCAI 2018, pages 5427–5433. International Joint Conferences on Artificial Intelligence Organization, July 2018.

[Cunningham *et al.*, 2013] Hamish Cunningham, Valentin Tablan, Angus Roberts, and Kalina Bontcheva. Getting More Out of Biomedical Documents with GATE's Full Lifecycle Open Source Text Analytics. *PLOS Computational Biology*, 9(2):1–16, 02 2013.

[de Araujo *et al.*, 2013] Denis A. de Araujo, Sandro J. Rigo, Carolina Muller, and Rove Chishman. Automatic Information Extraction from Texts with Inference and Linguistic Knowledge Acquisition Rules. In *2013 IEEE/WIC/ACM International Joint Conferences on Web Intelligence (WI) and Intelligent Agent Technologies (IAT)*, volume 3, pages 151–154, Atlanta, GA, USA, November 2013. IEEE.

[de Maat *et al.*, 2006] Emile de Maat, Radboud Winkels, and Tom van Engers. Automated Detection of Reference Structures in Law. In Tom M. van Engers, editor, *Proceedings of the 19th International Conference on Legal Knowledge and Information Systems*, JURIX 2006, pages 41–50, Amsterdam, The Netherlands, December 2006. IOS Press.

[Dong and Lapata, 2016] Li Dong and Mirella Lapata. Language to Logical Form with Neural Attention. In Katrin Erk and Noah A. Smith, editors, *Proceedings of the 54th Annual Meeting of the Association for Computational Linguistics (Volume 1: Long Papers)*, ACL 2016, pages 33–43, Berlin, Germany, August 2016. Association for Computational Linguistics.

[Dragoni *et al.*, 2015] Mauro Dragoni, Serena Villata, Williams Rizzi, and Guido Governatori. Combining Natural Language Processing Approaches for Rule Extraction from Legal Documents. In Ugo Pagallo, Monica Palmirani, Pompeu Casanovas, Giovanni Sartor, and Serena Villata, editors, *AI Approaches to the Complexity of Legal Systems International Workshops*, AICOL 2015, pages 287–300. Springer International Publishing, 2015.

[Dragoni *et al.*, 2016] Mauro Dragoni, Serena Villata, Williams Rizzi, and Guido Governatori. Combining NLP Approaches for Rule Extraction from Legal Documents. In Ugo Pagallo, Monica Palmirani, Pompeu Casanovas, Giovanni Sartor, and Serena Villata, editors, *1st Workshop on MIning and REasoning with Legal texts*, MIREL 2016, Sophia Antipolis, France, December 2016.

[Duong *et al.*, 2017] Long Duong, Hadi Afshar, Dominique Estival, Glen Pink, Philip Cohen, and Mark Johnson. Multilingual Semantic Parsing And Code-Switching. In Roger Levy and Lucia Specia, editors, *Proceedings of the 21st Conference on Computational Natural Language Learning*, CoNLL 2017, pages 379–389, Vancouver, Canada, August 2017. Association for Computational Linguistics.

[Evas, 2018] Tatjana Evas. EU law for an open independent and efficient European administration: Summary report of the public consultation. Study PE 621.830, European Added Value Unit, European Parliament Research Service, July 2018.

[Falessi *et al.*, 2010] Davide Falessi, Giovanni Cantone, and Gerardo Canfora. A Comprehensive Characterization of NLP Techniques for Identifying Equivalent Requirements. In *Proceedings of the 2010 ACM-IEEE International Symposium on Empirical Software Engineering and Measurement*, ESEM '10, pages 18:1–18:10, Bolzano-Bozen, Italy, September 2010. ACM.

[Ferraro *et al.*, 2019] Gabriela Ferraro, Ho-Pun Lam, Silvano Colombo Tosatto, Francesco Oliveri, Nick van Beest, and Guido Governatori. Automatic Extraction of Legal Norms: Evaluation of Natural Language Processing Tools. In *Proceedings of the 13th International Workshop on Juris-Informatics*, JURISIN 2019, Kanagawa, Japan, November 2019. Springer. [to appear].

[Francesconi and Passerini, 2007] E. Francesconi and A. Passerini. Automatic Classification of Provisions in Legislative Texts. *Artificial Intelligence and Law*, 15(1):1–17, March 2007.

[Gaur et al., 2014] Shruti Gaur, Nguyen H. Vo, Kazuaki Kashihara, and Chitta Baral. Translating Simple Legal Text to Formal Representations. In Tsuyoshi Murata, Koji Mineshima, and Daisuke Bekki, editors, 8th International Workshop on Juris-Informatics, JURISIN 2014, pages 259–273, Kanagawa, Japan, October 2014. Springer Berlin Heidelberg.

[Ge and Mooney, 2005] Ruifang Ge and Raymond Mooney. A Statistical Semantic Parser that Integrates Syntax and Semantics. In Ido Dagan and Daniel Gildea, editors, Proceedings of the Ninth Conference on Computational Natural Language Learning, CoNLL-2005, pages 9–16, Ann Arbor, MI, USA, June 2005. Association for Computational Linguistics.

[Gómez-Pérez et al., 2004] Asunción Gómez-Pérez, Mariano Fernándex-López, and Oscar Corcho. Ontological Engineering: with Examples from the areas of Knowledge Management, e-Commerce and the Semantic Web. Springer London, London, UK, 2004.

[Gordon and Breaux, 2013] David G. Gordon and Travis D. Breaux. A cross-domain empirical study and legal evaluation of the requirements water marking method. Requirements Engineering, 18(2):147–173, June 2013.

[Governatori and Rotolo, 2010] Guido Governatori and Antonino Rotolo. A Conceptually Rich Model of Business Process Compliance. In Proceedings of the 7th Asia-Pacific Conference on Conceptual Modelling, APCCM 2010, pages 3–12, Brisbane, QLD, Australia, January 2010. ACS.

[He et al., 2018] Shexia He, Zuchao Li, Hai Zhao, and Hongxiao Bai. Syntax for Semantic Role Labeling, To Be, Or Not To Be. In Proceedings of the 56th Annual Meeting of the Association for Computational Linguistics (Volume 1: Long Papers), pages 2061–2071, Melbourne, Australia, July 2018. Association for Computational Linguistics.

[Hochreiter and Schmidhuber, 1997] Sepp Hochreiter and Jürgen Schmidhuber. Long short-term memory. Neural Comput., 9(8):1735–1780, November 1997.

[Hoekstra et al., 2007] Rinke Hoekstra, Joost Breuker, Marcello Di Bello, and Alexander Boer. The LKIF Core Ontology of Basic Legal Concepts. In Pompeu Casanovas, Maria Angela Biasiotti, Enrico Francesconi, and Maria Teresa Sagri, editors, Proceedings of the Workshop on Legal Ontologies and Artificial Intelligence Techniques, LOAIT 2007, Stanford, CA, USA, June 2007. CEUR Workshop Proceedings.

[Janssen, 1997] Theo M. V. Janssen. Compositionality – with an appendix by b. partee, 1997.

[Jia and Liang, 2016] Robin Jia and Percy Liang. Data Recombination for Neural Semantic Parsing. In Katrin Erka and Noah A. Smith, editors, Proceedings of the 54th Annual Meeting of the Association for Computational Linguistics (Volume 1: Long Papers), ACL 2016, pages 12–22, Berlin, Germany, August 2016. Association for Computational Linguistics.

[Jiang and Tan, 2005] Xing Jiang and Ah-Hwee Tan. Mining ontological knowledge from domain-specific text documents. In Proceedings of the 5th IEEE International Conference on Data Mining, ICDM'05, Houston, TX, USA, November 2005. IEEE.

[Jurafsky and Martin, 2008] Daniel Jurafsky and James H. Martin. Speech and Language Processing. Prentice-Hall, Inc., Upper Saddle River, NJ, USA, 2nd edition, 2008.

[Kalchbrenner and Blunsom, 2013] Nal Kalchbrenner and Phil Blunsom. Recurrent Continuous Translation Models. In David Yarowsky, Timothy Baldwin, Anna Korhonen, Karen Livescu, and Steven Bethard, editors, Proceedings of the 2013 Conference on Empirical Methods in Natural Language Processing, EMNLP 2013, pages 1700–1709, Seattle, Washington, USA, October 2013. Association for Computational Linguistics.

[Kate and Mooney, 2006] Rohit J. Kate and Raymond J. Mooney. Using String-Kernels for Learning Semantic Parsers. In Rohit J. Kate and Raymond J. Mooney, editors, Proceedings of the 21st International Conference on Computational Linguistics and 44th Annual Meeting of the Association for Computational Linguistics, pages 913–920, Sydney, NSW, Australia, July 2006. Association for Computational Linguistics.

[Kimura *et al.*, 2009] Yusuke Kimura, Makoto Nakamura, and Akira Shimazu. Treatment of Legal Sentences Including Itemized and Referential Expressions – Towards Translation into Logical Forms. In Hiromitsu Hattori, Takahiro Kawamura, Tsuyoshi Idé, Makoto Yokoo, and Yohei Murakami, editors, *Proceedings of the 22nd Annual Conference of the JSAI: New Frontiers in Artificial Intelligence*, JSAI 2008, pages 242–253, Asahikawa, Japan, June 2009. Springer Berlin Heidelberg.

[Kiyavitskaya *et al.*, 2008] Nadzeya Kiyavitskaya, Nicola Zeni, Travis D. Breaux, Annie I. Antón, James R. Cordy, Luisa Mich, and John Mylopoulos. Automating the Extraction of Rights and Obligations for Regulatory Compliance. In Qing Li, Stefano Spaccapietra, Eric Yu, and Antoni Olivé, editors, *Proceedings of the 27th International Conference on Conceptual Modeling*, ER 2008, pages 154–168, Barcelona, Spain, October 2008. Springer Berlin Heidelberg.

[Kwiatkowski *et al.*, 2011] Tom Kwiatkowski, Luke Zettlemoyer, Sharon Goldwater, and Mark Steedman. Lexical Generalization in CCG Grammar Induction for Semantic Parsing. In Regina Barzilay and Mark Johnsn, editors, *Proceedings of the 2011 Conference on Empirical Methods in Natural Language Processing*, EMNLP 2011, pages 1512–1523, Edinburgh, Scotland, UK, July 2011. Association for Computational Linguistics.

[Kwiatkowski *et al.*, 2013] Tom Kwiatkowski, Eunsol Choi, Yoav Artzi, and Luke Zettlemoyer. Scaling Semantic Parsers with On-the-Fly Ontology Matching. In David Yarowsky, Timothy Baldwin, Anna Korhonen, Karen Livescu, and Steven Bethard, editors, *Proceedings of the 2013 Conference on Empirical Methods in Natural Language Processing*, EMNLP 2013, pages 1545–1556, Seattle, WA, USA, October 2013. Association for Computational Linguistics.

[Lapata and Dong, 2018] Mirella Lapata and Li Dong. Coarse-to-Fine Decoding for Neural Semantic Parsing. In Iryna Gurevych and Yusuke Miyao, editors, *Proceedings of the 56th Annual Meeting of the Association for Computational Linguistics (Volume 1: Long Papers)*, ACL 2018, pages 731–742, Melbourne, Australia, July 2018. Association for Computational Linguistics.

[Lee *et al.*, 2006] Seok-Won Lee, Robin Gandhi, Divya Muthurajan, Deepak Yavagal, and Gail-Joon Ahn. Building Problem Domain Ontology from Security Requirements in Regulatory Documents. In *Proceedings of the 2006 International Workshop on Software Engineering for Secure Systems*, SESS '06, pages 43–50, Shanghai, China, May 2006. ACM.

[Liang *et al.*, 2013] Percy Liang, Michael I. Jordan, and Dan Klein. Learning dependency-based compositional semantics. *Comput. Linguist.*, 39(2):389–446, June 2013.

[Ling *et al.*, 2016] Wang Ling, Phil Blunsom, Edward Grefenstette, Karl Moritz Hermann, Tomáš Kočiský, Fumin Wang, and Andrew Senior. Latent Predictor Networks for Code Generation. In Katrin Erk and Noah A. Smith, editors, *Proceedings of the 54th Annual Meeting of the Association for Computational Linguistics (Volume 1: Long Papers)*, ACL 2016, pages 599–609, Berlin, Germany, August 2016. Association for Computational Linguistics.

[Lippi and Torroni, 2016] Marco Lippi and Paolo Torroni. Argumentation Mining: State of the Art and Emerging Trends. *ACM Transactions on Internet Technology*, 16(2):10:1–10:25, March 2016.

[Lu *et al.*, 2008] Wei Lu, Hwee Tou Ng, Wee Sun Lee, and Luke S. Zettlemoyer. A Generative Model for Parsing Natural Language to Meaning Representations. In Mirella Lapata and Hwee Tou Ng, editors, *Proceedings of the 2008 Conference on Empirical Methods in Natural Language Processing*, EMNLP 2008, pages 783–792, Honolulu, HI, USA, October 2008. Association for Computational Linguistics.

[Luong *et al.*, 2015] Thang Luong, Hieu Pham, and Christopher D. Manning. Effective approaches to attention-based neural machine translation. In *Proceedings of the 2015*

Conference on Empirical Methods in Natural Language Processing, pages 1412–1421, Lisbon, Portugal, September 2015. Association for Computational Linguistics.

[Maxwell *et al.*, 2011] Jeremy C. Maxwell, Annie I. Antón, and Peter Swire. A Legal Cross-References Taxonomy for Identifying Conflicting Software Requirements. In *2011 IEEE 19th International Requirements Engineering Conference*, RE 2011, pages 197–206, Trento, Italy, August 2011. IEEE.

[Miall, 2007] Hugh Miall. *Emergent Conflict and Peaceful Change*. Palgrave MacMillan, 2007.

[Ministry of Business, Innovation and Employment, 2017a] Ministry of Business, Innovation and Employment. *New Zealand Building Code Clause G4 Ventilation: Acceptable Solutions and Verification Methods*. New Zealand Government, New Zealand, 4th edition, 2017.

[Ministry of Business, Innovation and Employment, 2017b] Ministry of Business, Innovation and Employment. *New Zealand Building Code Clause H1 Energy Efficiency: Acceptable Solutions and Verification Methods*. New Zealand Government, New Zealand, 4th edition, 2017.

[Misra, 2016] Janardan Misra. Terminological inconsistency analysis of natural language requirements. *Information and Software Technology*, 74:183 – 193, 2016.

[Mochales-Palau and Moens, 2009] Raquel Mochales-Palau and Marie-Francine Moens. Argumentation Mining: The Detection, Classification and Structure of Arguments in Text. In *Proceedings of the 12th International Conference on Artificial Intelligence and Law*, ICAIL '09, pages 98–107, Barcelona, Spain, June 2009. ACM.

[Mochales-Palau and Moens, 2011] Raquel Mochales-Palau and Marie-Francine Moens. Argumentation mining. *Artificial Intelligence and Law*, 19(1):1–22, March 2011.

[Montague, 1973] Richard Montague. The proper treatment of quantification in ordinary English. In K. J. J. Hintikka, J. Moravcsic, and P. Suppes, editors, *Approaches to Natural Language*, pages 221–242. Reidel, Dordrecht, 1973.

[Nakamura *et al.*, 2008] Makoto Nakamura, Shunsuke Nobuoka, and Akira Shimazu. Towards Translation of Legal Sentences into Logical Forms. In Ken Satoh, Akihiro Inokuchi, Katashi Nagao, and Takahiro Kawamura, editors, *Proceedings of the 21st Annual Conference (and Workshops) of the Japanese Society for Artificial Intelligence*, JSAI 2007, pages 349–362, Miyazaki, Japan, June 2008. Springer Berlin Heidelberg.

[Object Management Group, 2017] Object Management Group. *Semantics of Business Vocabulary and Rules (SBVR)*, 1.4 edition, May 2017. [accessed: 1 August 2019].

[Palmirani and Vitali, 2018] Monica Palmirani and Fabio Vitali. *OASIS LegalDocumentLegal (LegalDocML)*, 2018.

[Palmirani *et al.*, 2003] Monica Palmirani, Raffaella Brighi, and Matteo Massini. Automated Extraction of Normative References in Legal Texts. In *Proceedings of the 9th International Conference on Artificial Intelligence and Law*, ICAIL '03, pages 105–106, Scotland, UK, June 2003. ACM.

[Pawar *et al.*, 2017] Sachin Pawar, Girish K. Palshikar, and Pushpak Bhattacharyya. Relation Extraction : A Survey. *CoRR*, abs/1712.05191, 2017.

[Peng, 2011] Roger D. Peng. Reproducible research in computational science. *Science*, 334, 12 2011.

[Reddy *et al.*, 2016] Siva Reddy, Oscar Täckström, Michael Collins, Tom Kwiatkowski, Dipanjan Das, Mark Steedman, and Mirella Lapata. Transforming dependency structures to logical forms for semantic parsing. *Transactions of the Association for Computational Linguistics*, 4:127–141, 2016.

[Rubino *et al.*, 2006] Rossella Rubino, Antonino Rotolo, and Giovanni Sartor. An OWL Ontology of Fundamental Legal Concepts. In *Proceedings of the 9th Annual Conference on Legal Knowledge and Information Systems*, JURIX 2006, pages 101–110, Amsterdam, The Netherlands, 2006. IOS Press.

[Selway *et al.*, 2015] Matt Selway, Georg Grossmann, Wolfgang Mayer, and Markus Stumptner. Formalising natural language specifications using a cognitive linguistic/-configuration based approach. *Information Systems*, 54:191 – 208, 2015.

[Sleimi *et al.*, 2018] Amin Sleimi, Nicolas Sannier, Mehrdad Sabetzadeh, Lionel Briand, and John Dann. Automated Extraction of Semantic Legal Metadata Using Natural Language Processing. In *The 26th IEEE International Requirements Engineering Conference*, pages 124–135, Banff, AB, Canada, August 2018. IEEE.

[Stab and Gurevych, 2017] Christian Stab and Iryna Gurevych. Parsing Argumentation Structures in Persuasive Essays. *Computational Linguistics*, 43(3):619–659, 2017.

[Sun *et al.*, 2018] Kai Sun, Dian Yu, Dong Yu, and Claire Cardie. Improving Machine Reading Comprehension with General Reading Strategies. In Jull Burstein, Christy Doran, and Thamar Solorio, editors, *Proceedings of the 2019 Conference of the North American Chapter of the Association for Computational Linguistics: Human Language Technologies*, NAACL 2019, pages 2633–2643, Minneapolis, MN, USA, June 2018. Association for Computational Linguistics.

[Sutskever *et al.*, 2014] Ilya Sutskever, Oriol Vinyals, and Quoc V. Le. Sequence to sequence learning with neural networks. *CoRR*, abs/1409.3215, 2014.

[Tran *et al.*, 2013] Oanh Thi Tran, Minh Le Nguyen, and Akira Shimazu. Reference Resolution in Legal Texts. In *Proceedings of the Fourteenth International Conference on Artificial Intelligence and Law*, ICAIL '13, pages 101–110, Rome, Italy, June 2013. ACM.

[van Engers *et al.*, 2004] Tom M. van Engers, Ron van Gog, and Kamal Sayah. A Case Study on Automated Norm Extraction. In Thomas Gordon, editor, *The 17th International Conference on Legal Knowledge and Information Systems*, JURIX 2004, pages 49–58, Amsterdam, The Netherlands, 2004. IOS Press.

[van Gog and van Engers, 2001] Ron van Gog and Tom M. van Engers. Modeling legislation using natural language processing. In *2001 IEEE International Conference on Systems, Man and Cybernetics. e-Systems and e-Man for Cybernetics in Cyberspace (Cat.No.01CH37236)*, volume 1, pages 561–566, Tucson, AZ, USA, October 2001. IEEE.

[Visser and Bench-Capon, 1998] Pepijn R. S. Visser and Trevor J. M. Bench-Capon. A Comparison of Four Ontologies for the Design of Legal Knowledge Systems. *Artificial Intelligence and Law*, 6(1):27–57, March 1998.

[Warren and Pereira, 1982] David H. D. Warren and Fernando C. N. Pereira. An Efficient Easily Adaptable System for Interpreting Natural Language Queries. *Computational Linguistics*, 8(3-4):110–122, July 1982.

[Winkels and Hoekstra, 2012] Radboud Winkels and Rinke Hoekstra. Automatic Extraction of Legal Concepts and Definitions. In Burkhard Schäfer, editor, *The 25th International Conference on Legal Knowledge and Information Systems*, JURIX 2012, pages 157–166, Amsterdam, The Netherlands, December 2012. IOS Press.

[Woodsend and Lapata, 2011] Kristian Woodsend and Mirella Lapata. WikiSimple: Automatic Simplification of Wikipedia Articles. In *Proceedings of the 25th AAAI Conference on Artificial Intelligence*, AAAI 2011, pages 927–932, San Francisco, CA, USA, August 2011. AAAI Press.

[Wyner and Peters, 2011] Adam Z. Wyner and Wim Peters. On rule extraction from regulations. In *International Conference on Legal Knowledge and Information Systems*, JURIX, 2011.

[Zelle and Mooney, 1996] John M. Zelle and Raymond J. Mooney. Learning to Parse Database Queries Using Inductive Logic Programming. In William J. Clancey and Daniel S. Weld, editors, *Proceedings of the 13th National Conference on Artificial Intelligence*, volume 2, pages 1050–1055, Portland, Oregon, USA, August 1996. AAAI Press / The MIT Press.

[Zettlemoyer and Collins, 2005] Luke S. Zettlemoyer and Michael Collins. Learning to map sentences to logical form: Structured classification with probabilistic categorial grammars. In *Proceedings of the Twenty-First Conference on Uncertainty in Artificial Intelligence*, UAI'05, pages 658–666, Arlington, Virginia, United States, 2005. AUAI Press.

[Zipf, 1949] George K. Zipf. *Human Behavior and the Principle of Least Effort*. Addison-Wesley, 1949.

[Zucchi, 1993] Alessandro Zucchi. *The Language of Propositions and Events: Issues in the Syntax and the Semantics of Nominalization*. Springer Netherlands, Dordrecht, Germany, 1993.

Gabriela Ferraro
Data61, CSIRO
Acton ACT 2601
Australia
Email: gabriela.ferraro@csiro.au

Ho-Pun Lam
Data61, CSIRO
Eveleigh NSW 2015
Australia
Email: brian.lam@csiro.au

Table 2: Examples of instances from three semantic parsing data set. The Input column refers to sentences written in natural language and the Output column refers to their corresponding mapping into different meaning representations: computer command, SQL, and Lambda calculus.

Input	Output
	Computer command
if I post something on blogger it will post it to wordpress	Blogger: Any new post $\Longrightarrow$ WordPress: Create a pos
	SQL
How many engine types did Val Musetti use?	SELECT COUNT Engine WHERE Driver = Val Musetti
	Lambda calculus
flight from Los Angeles to Phoenix	(lambda $0 e (and (flight $0) (from $0 Los Angeles) (to $0 Phoenix)))

Table 3: Examples of semantic parsing as an intermediate steps towards the generation of normative rules

	Example
Sentence	*A large building is any building with a net lettable area greater than* $300 \, \text{m}^2$.
Logic formula	`lambda. $0 (if (A large building: $0) then (is any building with a lettable area greater than ($0 300m2)))`
Normative rule	$largeBuilding \rightarrow greaterThan(netLettableArea, 300)$
Sentence	*For the purposes of subclause 2.4, a person is responsible for an individual if the person is a parent of the individual.*
Logic formula	`lambda. $0 $1 (if (and (person:$0) (individual: $1) (parent of ($0 $1))) then (responsible for (for purpose of subclause 2.4 ($0 $1))))`
Normative rule	$subclause(2.4), parentOf(A, B) \Rightarrow_O responsible(A, B)$

Table 4: Data sets splits and average length of input and output sequences

	GEO	RegTech
Training set	600	144
Test set	280	-
Total	880	144
Avg. input length	7.3	26.75

Table 5: Examples of sentences written in natural language and their corresponding meaning representation from three data sets

Data set	Example
GEO	*what is the capital of the state with the largest population density?* `( capital:c ( argmax $1 ( state:t $1 ) ( density:i $1 ) ) )`

RegTech	*a large building is any building with a net lettable area greater than 300 m2.*
	 `lambda. $0 (if (A large building:$0) then (is any building with a`
	 `lettable area greater than ( $0 300m2)))`

Table 6: Examples of gold-standard formulas from RegTech and their corresponding predicted formulas generated by the semantic parsing model

Gold-standard formulas

```
1. lambda $0 $1 $2 (and ((endorsing body or) (supplier of:$1)))
             then (must (be replaced by ($0 $1)))
2. lambda $0 (and ((claim:$0)) (must (not (refer to
   ($0 prevention of (or ((disease) (disorder) (condition)))))))))
```

Predicated formulas

```
1. lambda $0 $1 $2 (and (( endorsing body:$0 )
        (supplier of:$1 ( food:$2)) (must ( <U> ( $0 $1 )))))
2. lambda $0 (and((claim:$0)) (must (not (refer to
   ($0 diagnosis of (or (( disease) (disorder) (condition)))))))))
```

Table 7: Semantic parsing evaluation on test sets (short sentences contained less than 0 tokens (< 10 tokens) and long sentences contained more than 10 tokens (> 10 tokens))

	seq2seq+LSTM+Attention
GEO (all)	83.57
GEO (< 10 tokens)	92.09
GEO (> 10 tokens)	68.93
GEO (140)	29.28
RegTech (140)	18.28

2

A Data-Informed Analysis of Argument Mining

ELENA CABRIO
SERENA VILLATA

ABSTRACT. Argument Mining (AM) is the research area aiming at extracting natural language arguments and their relations from text, with the final goal of providing machine-processable structured data for computational models of argument. This research topic has started to attract the attention of a small community of researchers around 2014, and it is nowadays counted as one of the most promising research areas in Artificial Intelligence and Natural Language Processing in terms of growing of the community, funded projects, and involvement of companies. Recently, this research area includes also further forms of processing natural language arguments than mining, i.e., searching for arguments on the Web, argument generation and synthesis, and assessing the quality of arguments with respect to specific criteria like persuasiveness. In this chapter, we start by describing the classic argument mining tasks, and then we present the new tasks proposed lately in the literature. We discuss the obtained results in the area from a data-driven perspective. An open discussion highlights the main weaknesses suffered by the existing work in the literature, and proposes open challenges to be faced in the future.

1 Introduction

Argument(ation) mining [Peldszus and Stede, 2013; Lippi and Torroni, 2016b; Cabrio and Villata, 2018; Lawrence and Reed, 2019] is a recent research area in Artificial Intelligence (AI), mainly across the areas of Knowledge Representation and Reasoning (KRR) on the one side, and Natural Language Processing (NLP), on the other side. Few approaches to what is now called argument mining started to appear around 2010, when the first methods to mine (different connotations of) *arguments* from natural language documents were proposed: [Teufel *et al.*, 2009] introduced the definition of argumentative zoning for scientific articles, and [Mochales and Moens, 2011] proposed a way to detect arguments from legal texts. Since these seminal approaches, the need for automated methods to mine arguments and the relations among them from natural language text was brought to light, but it was only briefly touched upon. The parallel advances, from the formal point of view in the research field of computational models of argument, and from the point of view of the computational techniques for learning and understanding human language content in the NLP and the Machine Learning fields, boosted the almost contemporary organization of two events in 2014 targeting open discussions about the challenge of mining arguments from text. Both the workshop on Argument Mining[1] co-located with ACL, and the workshop on Frontiers and Connections between Argumentation Theory and Natural Language Processing [2] we organized, shared the same goal: bringing together the communities of NLP and of formal argumentation to jointly work towards the definition of the new research area of *argument mining*. Since then, two Dagstuhl Seminars have been organized on such topic[3], the Argument Mining workshop holds every year, three tutorials on AM have been given at IJCAI-2016[4], ACL-2016[5] and ACL-2019[6], three ESSLLI courses[7] in 2017, and AM has became a topic in major AI and NLP conferences.

Argument mining involves several research areas from the AI panorama: NLP provides the methods to process natural language text, to identify the arguments and their components (i.e., premises and claims) in texts and to predict the relations among such arguments, KRR contributes with the reasoning capabilities upon the retrieved arguments and relations so that, for instance, fallacies and inconsistencies can be automatically identified in such texts, and Human-Computer Interaction guides the design of good human-computer digital argument-based supportive tools.

The classic argument mining pipeline is composed of three main steps: first, the argument components are identified in the text; second, the boundaries of such components are defined; third, the intra-argument relations (relations among the evidences and the claims composing the same argument) and the inter-argument relations (relations among different arguments, e.g., support and attack) are predicted. Usually supervised learning methods are used to face these tasks, leading to the need of defining beforehand annotated datasets for the specific task and application scenario.

Recently, the area of argument mining has evolved to go beyond this pipeline, and new challenges lead to the definition of novel computational

---

[1]https://goo.gl/kF4Eep

[2]https://goo.gl/ttVUZk

[3]I.e., Debating Technologies (https://goo.gl/osqEY3) and Natural Language Argumentation: Mining, Processing, and Reasoning over Textual Arguments (https://goo.gl/jS1Co6)

[4]https://goo.gl/kd4456

[5]http://acl2016tutorial.arg.tech/

[6]http://arg.tech/~chris/acl2019tut/index.html

[7]https://goo.gl/Cw1FLC

tasks in processing natural language arguments. Among them, we can highlight the task of assessing the quality of an argument (e.g., its strength, its persuasiveness degree), the task of synthesising argumentative text, and the task of generating natural language arguments.

The goal of this chapter is to provide an overview of the existing approaches in the AM literature, mainly focusing on recent developments in NLP. With respect to the state-of-the-art contributions [Peldszus and Stede, 2013; Lippi and Torroni, 2016b; Lawrence and Reed, 2019], we adopt a different perspective, and we propose a data-driven analysis of the existing work in AM, structuring it around precise axes, i.e., application scenarios, algorithms, features, and produced resources for systems evaluation[8].

In the remainder of the chapter, Section 2 provides the definition of argument mining, and describes the AM pipeline, together with some examples to clarify the tasks to the reader. Section 3 discusses the recent tasks addressed in the AM community to process natural language arguments. Section 4 investigates the weaknesses of current approaches and open challenges.

2   Argument Mining

In the last 10 years, the growing of the Web and the daily increasing number of textual data published there with different purposes have highlighted the need to process such data in order to identify, structure and summarize this huge amount of information. Online newspapers, blogs, online debate platforms and social networks, but also normative and technical documents provide a heterogeneous flow of information where natural language arguments can be identified, and analyzed. The availability of such data, together with the advances in Natural Language Processing and Machine Learning, supported the rise of a new research area called *Argument Mining*. The main goal of argument mining is the automated extraction of natural language arguments and their relations from generic textual corpora, with the final goal to provide machine-readable structured data for computational models of argument and reasoning engines.

Argument(ation) Mining is defined as "the general task of analyzing discourse on the pragmatics level and applying a certain argumentation theory to model and automatically analyze the data at hand" [Habernal and Gurevych, 2017]. Two main stages are crucial in the argument mining framework:

Arguments' extraction : The first stage is the identification of arguments within the input natural language text. This step may be further split in two different stages such as the detection of argument

---

[8]This chapter updates and extends our previous review [Cabrio and Villata, 2018].

components (e.g., claim, premise) and the further identification of their textual boundaries. Many approaches have recently been proposed to address such task, that adopt different methods like Neural Networks [Mayer *et al.*, 2020; Eger *et al.*, 2017; Potash *et al.*, 2017], SVM [Mochales and Moens, 2011; Lippi and Torroni, 2016c; Niculae *et al.*, 2017], Naïve Bayes classifiers [Duthie *et al.*, 2016], Latent Dirichlet Allocation (LDA) based approaches, and Logistic Regression [Levy *et al.*, 2014].

Relations' prediction : The second stage consists in predicting the relations between the arguments identified in the first stage. This is an extremely complex task, as it involves high-level knowledge representation and reasoning issues. The relations between the arguments may be of heterogeneous nature, like *attacks* and *supports*. They are used to build the argument graphs, in which the relations connecting the retrieved arguments (i.e., the nodes in the graph) correspond to the edges. Different methods have been employed to address this task, from Neural Networks, to standard SVMs to Textual Entailment [Cabrio and Villata, 2013]. This stage is also in charge of predicting, in structured argumentation, the internal relations of the argument's components, such as the connection between the premises and the claim [Stab and Gurevych, 2017].

Some of the models proposed in the literature operate on the argument component and on the relation component levels separately, while more recent approaches propose end-to-end computational argumentation mining solutions, applied to different scenarios [Eger *et al.*, 2017; Morio and Fujita, 2018; Mayer *et al.*, 2020].

Referring to standard *argument graphs*, the retrieved arguments will thus represent the nodes in the final argument graph returned by the system. To clarify such tasks, let us consider the following example from the political debate of the Campaign "Trump – Clinton" on September 2016.[9] The first task of the argument mining framework consists in detecting the arguments from the text. In the example below, we highlight the arguments that can be identified (premises underlined and claims in bold):

A_1: *She talks about solar panels. We invested in a solar company, our country.* **That was a disaster.** *They lost plenty of money on that one. Now, look, I'm a great believer in all forms of energy, but we're putting a lot of people out of work.*

---

[9]Debate extracted from the Commission on Presidential Debates (http://debates.org).

A_2: *Well, **I'm really calling for major jobs*** *because* the wealthy are going create tremendous jobs. They're going to expand their companies. They're going to do a tremendous job.

It appears evident that the argumentative sentences "in the wild", i.e., in natural language text as the ones reported in the examples, are pretty far from the prototypical argumentation patterns usually investigated in KRR, increasing the complexity of the task.

Let us consider now another example from an online debate about *Random sobriety tests for drivers*[10], where we identify again premises and claims.

A_3: Little evidence random alcohol tests deter drunk driving. *There is a dearth of research regarding the deterrent effect of checkpoints. The only formally documented research regarding deterrence is a survey of Maryland's "Checkpoint Strikeforce" program. The survey found no deterrent effect:* **"To date, there is no evidence to indicate that this campaign, which involves a number of sobriety checkpoints and media activities to promote these efforts, has had any impact on public perceptions, driver behaviors, or alcohol-related motor vehicle crashes and injuries.** This conclusion is drawn after examining statistics for alcohol-related crashes, police citations for impaired driving, and public perceptions of alcohol-impaired driving risk.*"*

A_4: **Random breath testing doesn't necessarily lower drunk driving.** Many countries have had random testing for some time and have seen no real fall in drink driving figures.

A_5: **Random sobriety tests for drivers are effective at deterring drunk driving.**

Given these three arguments, the relations among them have to be predicted. Let us consider that the two relations we aim at identifying are *attack* (a negative relation between two arguments, e.g., a contradiction) and *support* (a positive relation between two arguments) only. In this case, we have that argument A_3 supports argument A_4, and argument A_4 attacks argument A_5.

It is important to underline at this point that argument mining differs from well-known *opinion mining* (or *sentiment analysis*): while opinion mining focuses on understanding *what* users think about a certain topic or product, argument mining revolves around *why* users have a certain opinion about a

---

[10]http://www.debatepedia.com/en/index.php/Debate:_Random_sobriety_tests_for_drivers

topic or product. It is also important to discuss the difference with another well-known task in NLP, i.e., *stance detection* [Walker *et al.*, 2012a; Hasan and Ng, 2013; Ferreira and Vlachos, 2016; Du *et al.*, 2017]. Stance detection is a sub-task in argument mining and it aims to detect an author's stance towards a certain topic. Stance detection represents a main component in argument mining applications like claim validation or argument search, where there is the need to check both what is the stance of the author towards a certain topic (e.g., why the author is against Covid-19 vaccination) and how this stance is supported through arguments (e.g., the arguments justifying the fact that the author is against Covid-19 vaccination).

Both the main argument mining tasks require high-quality annotated corpora to train and to evaluate the performances of automated approaches. The reliability of an annotated corpus is guaranteed by the calculation of the inter-annotator agreement that measures the degree of agreement in performing the annotation task among the involved annotators. It must be underlined that the creation of the annotations is quite a critical point for the quality of a dataset. Often there is a tradeoff between the number and size of documents that are included in a dataset, and the quality of its annotations. They can be assigned by experts of the domain, crowdsourced, or even generated automatically.

This section provides an overview of the main recent contributions in the argument mining research area. Given the multitude of research papers addressing this topics from multiple perspectives, we made the choice of selecting and focusing on the most recent research papers published in main AI and NLP conferences, minimizing the redundancy in the same authors' citations. For older (till 2015) contributions, we refer the reader to [Lippi and Torroni, 2016b].[11] We propose a data-driven approach to the analysis of the existing work in the area, structuring it around precise axes, i.e., coarse-grained application scenarios (Sections 2.1, 2.3, 2.4, and 2.5), most performing algorithms (Table 1) and released datasets (Table 2).

---

[11]An updated list of external resources in Argument Mining is maintained at http://argumentationmining.disi.unibo.it/resources.html.

Approaches	Component Detection		Relations prediction
	Sentence classification	Boundaries Detection	
SVM	[Mochales and Moens, 2011], [Duthie et al., 2016] [Lippi and Torroni, 2016a; Lippi and Torroni, 2016c] [Habernal and Gurevych, 2017] [Bar-Haim et al., 2017], [Haddadan et al., 2019b]	[Mochales and Moens, 2011] [Lippi and Torroni, 2016c]	[Naderi and Hirst, 2015] [Niculae et al., 2017] [Stab and Gurevych, 2017] [Menini et al., 2018]
P	[Villalba and Saint-Dizier, 2012] [Peldszus and Stede, 2015] [Eger et al., 2017]	[Eger et al., 2017]	[Villalba and Saint-Dizier, 2012] [Peldszus and Stede, 2015] [Eger et al., 2017]
LR and LDA	[Levy et al., 2014], [Rinott et al., 2015] [Nguyen and Litman, 2018]	[Dusmanu et al., 2017] [Ibeke et al., 2017] [Nguyen and Litman, 2018]	[Nguyen and Litman, 2018]
RNN	[Eger et al., 2017], [Mayer et al., 2020] [Potash et al., 2017], [Morio and Fujita, 2018]	[Eger et al., 2017], [Mayer et al., 2020] [Potash et al., 2017], [Morio and Fujita, 2018]	[Niculae et al., 2017], [Mayer et al., 2020] [Eger et al., 2017], [Potash et al., 2017] [Morio and Fujita, 2018]
ME	[Mochales and Moens, 2011], [Duthie et al., 2016]	[Mochales and Moens, 2011]	
CRF	[Stab and Gurevych, 2017]		
NB	[Duthie et al., 2016]		
RF		[Dusmanu et al., 2017]	
TES			[Cabrio and Villata, 2013]
ML		[Levy et al., 2014]	

Table 1. A comparison of the approaches applied to AM tasks. They are ordered starting from the most frequently applied methods. As for other tasks in NLP, SVMs have proved to be the most performing algorithms in different settings, and for different AM sub-tasks. The acronyms stand for: Support Vector Machine (SVM), Parsing algorithms (P), Logistic Regression (LR), Recurrent Neural Networks for language models (RNN), Maximum Entropy models (ME), Conditional Random Fields (CRF), Naïve Bayes (NB), Random Forests (RF), Textual Entailment Suites (TES) and Maximum Likelihood (ML).

2.1 Education

In the education field, argument mining has been applied to two genres of text, namely, student essays written in response to controversial topics, and scientific articles.

Persuasive essays. A persuasive essay explains a specific topic and attempts to persuade the audience that the speaker's point of view is the most informed, logical and valid perspective on the topic. This makes such kind of texts an excellent playground to test AM tasks. For instance, [Stab and Gurevych, 2017] propose an approach to identify argument components using sequence labeling at the token level, and apply a joint model for detecting argumentation structures (optimized using Integer Linear Programming). They also build an annotated corpus of persuasive essays.[12]

Eger *et al.* [2017] use the same corpus of persuasive essays to propose a neural end-to-end AM system. Neural computational AM is at least as good as the competing feature-based Integer Linear Programming formulation, with the advantage of eliminating the need for manual feature engineering and constraint designing. They firstly highlight that, even if coupling argument component detection and relation prediction is not optimal, both tasks should be treated separately, but modeled jointly, and secondly that the relation prediction task is more challenging than the argument component detection one.

With the goal of improving the automated scoring of persuasive essays, [Nguyen and Litman, 2018] implement another end-to-end argument mining system that parses argumentative structures of free-text essays and creates argumentative features from these structures.

Peldszus and Stede [2015] jointly predict different aspects of the argumentation structure by combining the different subtasks prediction in the edge's weights of an evidence graph; they then apply a standard Minimum Spanning Tree decoding algorithm on a small corpus of English-German microtexts.[13] They rely on Freeman's dialectical theory using the moves of proponent and challenger in a dialectical situation as a model of the structure of the argumentation in texts.This corpus has been extended doubling the size of the original corpus by means of crowdsourcing [Skeppstedt *et al.*, 2018].

Lugini and Litman [2020] introduce a new dataset consisting of 3,135 Argumentative Discourse Units (ADUs) in a corpus of 29 text-based multiparty classroom discussions between high school students (average 15 students per discussion), where the discussion is centered around a book, play,

---

[12]https://goo.gl/3tXibr
[13]https://github.com/peldszus/arg-microtexts

or other literature piece. The discussions were audio-recorded, manually transcribed, and ADUs were manually annotated according to a simplified version of Toulmin's model consisting of three labels: claims, evidence, and warrant. They also analyze the impact of context for predicting argument components in these multi-party discussions.Two types of context are defined, namely local context and speaker context, to analyze how different models perform when varying the context size.

Potash *et al.* [2017] propose an architecture that applies Pointer Network sequence-to-sequence attention modeling to both tasks of extracting links between argument components and classifying their type on the persuasive essays dataset.

2.2 Scientific literature

In the following, we describe the argument mining approaches tested on scientific articles and on medical data (mainly Randomized Clinical Trials).

Scientific articles. Among the earliest work that can be considered as forerunner of AM, in [Teufel *et al.*, 2009] a rhetorical-level analysis of scientific articles is introduced (*argumentative zoning*). Data annotation is based on the typical argumentation to be found in scientific articles. It reflects the attribution of intellectual ownership in scientific articles, expressions of authors' stance towards the related work, and typical statements about problem-solving processes. [Lauscher *et al.*, 2018] analyze the information shared by the rhetorical and argumentative structure of scientific documents. In order to do this, they add an argumentation layer to the Dr Inventor Scientific Corpus [Fisas *et al.*, 2016], which includes 40 computer graphics papers. The enriched corpus is used to trained new models for the automatic identification of claims and evidence. More recently, [Accuosto and Saggion, 2019] propose to tackle the limitations posed by the lack of annotated data for AM in the scientific domain by conducting a pilot annotation experiment in which they enrich a subset of the SciDTB corpus [Yang and Li, 2018] with an additional layer of argumentative structures; then, they explore the potential of a transfer learning approach to improve the performance of an AM model trained with a small volume of data. Their goal is to predict the acceptance or rejection of scientific papers in computer science conferences based on the automatic identification of argumentative components and relations in the abstracts.

Medical data. We created a dataset of 659 abstracts from the Randomized Controlled Trials (RCTs) (extracted from PubMed) annotated with the different argument components (evidence, claims and major claims). In total, it contains 4198 argument components and 2601 argument relations on different diseases (i.e., *neoplasm, glaucoma, hepatitis, diabetes, hypertension*)

[Mayer *et al.*, 2018; Mayer *et al.*, 2020]. We then propose a complete AM pipeline for RCTs, classifying argument components as *evidence* and *claims*, and predicting the relation, i.e., *attack* or *support*, holding between those argument components. We experiment with deep bidirectional transformers in combination with different neural architectures (i.e., LSTM, GRU and CRF). As a result, we implemented ACTA, a tool to support doctors and clinicians in identifying the RCTs of interest about a certain disease, and in analyzing the main argumentative content and PICO elements [Mayer *et al.*, 2019].

2.3   Web-based Content

In the following, we present relevant contributions experimented on heterogeneous data extracted from the Web.

Wikipedia articles. IBM is putting a lot of effort in the development of debating technologies[14]. Among their contributions, [Levy *et al.*, 2014] address the task of automatically detecting *context dependent claims* in Wikipedia articles, i.e., a general, concise statement that directly supports or contests the given topic, discussed in the debate motions database[15]. As a follow up, [Rinott *et al.*, 2015] address the task of automatically detecting evidences in Wikipedia articles supporting a given claim (*context dependent evidence detection*). More recently, [Bar-Haim *et al.*, 2017] introduce the task of *claim stance classification*, decomposed into the detection of: *i)* the targets of the given topic and the claim, *ii)* the polarity (sentiment) towards each of the targets, and *iii)* whether the targets are consistent or contrastive. To evaluate this task, the Wikipedia-based IBM dataset for claim classification is extended by adding Pro/Con annotations.

Lippi and Torroni [2016c] present MARGOT (Mining ARGuments frOm Text),[16] a tool for argument component classification (both premises and claims) and boundaries detection, tested on the IBM datasets [Bar-Haim *et al.*, 2017; Rinott *et al.*, 2015].

Recently, the argument classification task on the IBM dataset was addressed with contextualized word embeddings [Reimers *et al.*, 2019] (they assume components are given, and boundary detection is not considered).

Microblogs and web debating platforms. Habernal and Gurevych [2017] propose a sequence labeling approach to identify argument components (following a modified Toulmin's model) in user-generated Web discourses, i.e., on a sample of controversial topics about education.

---

[14]IBM Debater Datasets (https://goo.gl/MxfB7N), the EPSRC Argument Mining project (https://goo.gl/444uu8).

[15]https://idebate.org/

[16]Demo available at http://margot.disi.unibo.it/.

Niculae *et al.* [2017] propose a structured prediction model for AM (comparing SVMs and RNNs algorithms), jointly learning to classify elementary units and to identify the argumentative relations between them. Two datasets are used for evaluation: the Cornell eRulemaking Corpus - CDCP,[17] and the persuasive essays dataset [Stab and Gurevych, 2017].

Cabrio and Villata [2013] tackle the relation prediction task on a corpus of online debates from Debatepedia (now called `idebate.com`).[18] Starting from the opinions put forward from the users and the main issue of the debate, we investigate how Textual Entailment suites can be exploited to predict the support (i.e., entailment) and the attack (i.e., contradiction) relations among these text snippets.

In [Khatib *et al.*, 2016], a large corpus annotated with argumentative text segments is acquired through distant supervision from the same online debate portal, and used to test a binary classifier of text argumentativeness.

Moro and Fujita [2018] annotated a large-scale online civic discussion dataset for AM with micro-level inner- and inter- post scheme, and they apply a neural end-to-end AM method for relations identification.

Online product reviews. Argument mining techniques enable to capture the underlying motivations expressed by the consumers in their reviews, which provide more detailed information compared to a basic attitude like "I do/do not like product A". Villalba and Saint-Dizier [2012] discuss how the automatic recognition of arguments can be implemented on the TextCoop platform. In [Ibeke *et al.*, 2017], the authors address the task of mining contrastive opinions using a unified latent variable model on the El Capitan dataset,[19] where reviews are manually annotated with topic and sentiment labels. Analyzing arguments in user reviews suffers from the vague relation between argument mining and sentiment analysis. This is because sentiments about individual aspects of the implied claim (for/against the product) sometimes express also the reasons why the product is considered good or bad.

Newspaper articles. As a second scenario, [Lippi and Torroni, 2016c] evaluate MARGOT on ten newspaper articles from the New York Times, that cover various topics.[20]

Social media. In [Dusmanu *et al.*, 2017], we collected a dataset of tweets, DART, where we addressed the tasks of distinguishing argumentative tweets from non-argumentative ones. The topics of the tweets range from politics like Brexit and Grexit to the release of the new Apple Watch.

---

[17]http://joonsuk.org
[18]http://www-sop.inria.fr/NoDE/
[19]https://github.com/eibeke/El-Capitan-Dataset
[20]https://goo.gl/mmxv9i

Moreover, MARGOT [Lippi and Torroni, 2016c] is applied to the comments in two Reddit threads (a sub Reddit focused on the New Hampshire primaries held on February 9th, 2016, and a sub Reddit focused on climate shift).

2.4 Legal Documents

In the legal domain, argument mining approaches have been proposed to detect premises, claims and argumentation schemes in judgments to ease the work of judges and law scholars in identifying similarities and differences among a number of judgments, the arguments proposed therein, and the ultimate outcome of the cases. More precisely, [Mochales and Moens, 2011] propose a system for argument component detection and inter-argument relation prediction for the legal domain. They identify premises and claims using statistical classifiers, and they define a context-free grammar to predict the relations among the different argument components. They created a corpus from the European Court of Human Rights (ECHR) judgments. Following this line of work, [Teruel et al., 2018] recently present a new corpus of ECHR judgments[21] annotated with premises and claims as well as with support and attack relations among the argument components. Grabmair et al. [2015] work with a set of U.S. Court of Federal Claims cases deciding whether compensation claims comply with a federal statute establishing the National Vaccine Injury Compensation Program. The Legal UIMA system they propose extracts argument-related semantic information from such legal documents: the principal argumentation roles of clauses, e.g., evidence-based finding of fact, evidence-based intermediate reasoning, and case-specific process or procedural facts.

2.5 Political Debates and Speeches

The political domain allows for intuitive applications of the argument mining framework with the final aim of detecting fallacies, persuasiveness degree and coherence in the candidate's argumentation. [Lippi and Torroni, 2016a] address the problem of argument extraction, and more precisely claim detection, over a corpus based on the 2015 UK political election debates. They aim to study the impact of the vocal features of speech on the claim detection task. This approach also relies on an audio dataset with the recording of the political speeches, showing that such a kind of multi-modal approach achieves promising results. The Internet Argument Corpus[22] (IAC) [Walker et al., 2012b] collects the posts from 4forums.com, a website for political debate. The debates have been annotated for argumentative markers like

---

[21] https://github.com/PLN-FaMAF/ArgumentMiningECHR
[22] http://nlds.soe.ucsc.edu/software

54

degrees of agreement with a previous post, cordiality, audience direction, combativeness, assertiveness, emotionality of argumentation, and sarcasm. [Duthie *et al.*, 2016] apply AM methods to detect the presence and polarity of ethotic arguments from UK parliamentary debates.[23] The authors also investigate how their results can be visualized to support user understanding.[24] Naderi and Hirst [2015] show how features based on embedding representations can improve discovering various frames in argumentative political speeches. They propose a corpus of speeches from the Canadian Parliament, and they examine the statements with respect to the position of the speaker towards the discussed topic (pro, con, or no stance). In [Menini *et al.*, 2018], we address the relation prediction task on political speeches in monological form, where there is no direct interaction between the opponents. We created a corpus, based on the transcription of speeches and official declarations issued by Nixon and Kennedy during 1960 Presidential campaign, of argument pairs annotated with the support and attack relations.[25] In the same direction, in [Haddadan *et al.*, 2019b] we created a corpus of 39 political debates from the last 50 years of US presidential campaigns, and we annotated 29k argument components, labeled as *premises* and *claims*. We then carried out the tasks of argumentative components identification, and classification as *premises* and *claims*, applying both feature-rich SVM learners and Neural Network architectures [Haddadan *et al.*, 2019a] describes the DISPUTool, to explore and automatically identify argumentative components over the 39 political debates.

Only few contributions tackle the issue of generalizing across different text types. Among them, Araucaria[26] collects arguments from heterogeneous sources, e.g., newspapers, parliamentary records, judgments and discussion fora. The annotation is based on Walton's argumentation schemes. Daxenberger *et al.* [2020] introduce a heterogeneous web-based resource. The model they propose is capable of analyzing the controversial topics discussed in online forums and political debates. Other work in this direction has been proposed by [Hua and Wang, 2017] and [Stab *et al.*, 2018b].

Stab *et al.* [2018c] introduce a corpus of heterogeneous text types (including news reports, editorials, blogs, debate forums, and encyclopedia articles) annotated with topic-based arguments. The corpus (UKP Sentential Argument Mining Corpus) includes over 25,000 instances covering eight controversial topics. Such resource can be used to evaluate the performance of

---

[23]http://arg.tech/Ethan3Train, http://arg.tech/Ethan3Test
[24]https://goo.gl/P9fyzi
[25]https://dh.fbk.eu/resources/political-argumentation
[26]https://goo.gl/tU7dCr

argument mining methods across topics in heterogeneous sources.

Visser *et al.* [2020] present the US2016 dataset containing annotated dialogical argumentation. The corpora comprise the transcriptions of television debates leading up to the 2016 US presidential election, and the subsequent reactions to the debates posted on the Reddit social network. The annotation covers argumentative relations, dialogue acts and pragmatic features.

	Datasets	Document source	Size	Comp. Det. Sent. Clas.	Comp. Det. BD	RP
Educ	[Stab and Gurevych, 2017]	persuasive essays	402 essays	✓		✓
	[Peldszus and Stede, 2015]	microtexts	112 short texts	✓	✓	✓
	[Skeppstedt et al., 2018]	microtexts	205 short texts	✓		✓
	[Lugini and Litman, 2020]	multi-party classroom discussions (high school)	29 text-based discussions	✓		
Scient	[Mayer et al., 2020]	Randomized Controlled Trials	659 abstracts	✓	✓	✓
	[Accuosto and Saggion, 2019]	scientific articles (EMNLP conf.)	60 abstracts	✓	✓	✓
	[Lauscher et al., 2018]	scientific articles	40 computer graphics publications	✓	✓	✓
Web-based content	[Bar-Haim et al., 2017]	debate motions DB	55 topics	✓		
	[Rinott et al., 2015]	Wikipedia, debate motions DB	58 topics, 547 articles	✓		
	[Bar-Haim et al., 2017]	Wikipedia, debate motions DB	33 topics, 586 articles	✓		
	IAC	4forums.com	11,800 discussions	✓		
	[Habernal and Gurevych, 2017]	i-debate	524 documents			
	[Khatib et al., 2016]	comments, forum, blog posts	445 documents		✓	
	NoDE	online debates	260 pairs	✓		✓
	DART	Twitter	4,713 tweets	✓	✓	✓
	Araucaria	newspapers, legal, debates	660 arguments			
	[Stab et al., 2018c]	news, blogs, debate forums, and encyclopedia	400 doc., 25,492 sentences	✓		✓
Legal	[Teruel et al., 2018]	ECHR judgments	7 judgments	✓	✓	✓
	[Mochales and Moens, 2011]	ECHR judgments	47 judgments	✓	✓	✓
	[Niculae et al., 2017]	eRule-making discussion forum	731 comments	✓		✓
Politics	[Menini et al., 2018]	Nixon-Kennedy Presid. campaign	5 topics (1,907 pairs)	✓		✓
	[Lippi and Torroni, 2016a]	Sky News debate for UK elections	9,666 words	✓		
	[Duthie et al., 2016]	UK parliamentary record	60 sessions	✓		
	[Naderi and Hirst, 2015]	speeches Canadian Parliament	34 sent., 123 paragr.			
	[Haddadan et al., 2019b]	US political debates (1960-2016)	34,013 sent., 676,227 tokens	(✓)	✓	✓
	[Visser et al., 2020]	US political debates (2016)	97,999 words (tokens)		✓	(✓)[27]

Table 2. Available datasets for AM (sub-)tasks, grouped by their application scenario (BD=boundaries detection; RP=relation prediction).

3 Recent Findings in Processing Natural Language Arguments

Section 2 has focused on the standard definition of the AM framework to highlight its main tasks. However, in the last years, a number of new challenges on processing natural language arguments have been proposed in the literature. In this section, we focus on three main challenges, namely the characterization of the arguments and the assessment of their quality (Section 3.1), the synthesis of argumentative text (Section 3.2), and the generation of natural language arguments (Section 3.3).

3.1 Argument characterization and quality

In this section, we present the recent approaches proposed in the literature to characterize the nature of natural language arguments. Arguments may be characterized along with different features like reporting a factual information vs a personal opinion, their persuasiveness as arguments or counter-arguments, or their strength.

Dusmanu *et al.* [2017], for instance, propose to select argumentative tweets on specific hashtags (namely Grexit and Brexit), and distinguish those arguments conveying an opinion from those containing *factual* information, to detect their source of information (e.g., the BBC). The task consists in classifying argumentative tweets as containing factual information or being opinion-based. This would allow then to rank factual argumentative tweets depending on the reliability or expertise of their source for fact checking. An argument is annotated as factual if it contains a piece of information which can be proved to be true, or if it contains 'reported speech'. All the other arguments are considered as 'opinion' This approach relies on a Logistic Regression classifier based on lexical features, Twitter-specific ones like punctuation and emoticons, syntactic/semantic features, and sentiment.

Many approaches aim to assess the quality of the arguments in a certain context, e.g., the more persuasive argument, the best counter-argument, the strongest argument in a debate.

Toledo *et al.* [2019] investigate how to assess the quality of arguments. In particular, they introduce a dataset of actively collected arguments, annotated for quality, with a quality score in the range [0, 1]. Two approaches are proposed to label argument quality, namely labeling individual arguments (each individual argument is directly labeled for its quality) and labeling argument pairs (each argument pair is labeled with a comparative label determining the higher quality argument). They also define a method for argument-pair classification and for individual argument ranking.

Wachsmuth *et al.* [2017a] investigate the importance of theory and practice in assessing argumentation quality. They empirically analyze the correlations holding in two argument corpora, one annotated for 15 well-defined quality dimensions taken from theory [Wachsmuth *et al.*, 2017c] and one with 17 reasons for quality differences phrased spontaneously in practice [Habernal and Gurevych, 2016a].

Several approaches focus on argument persuasion with the aim to study the persuasive degree of the proposed arguments. The persuasiveness of an argument depends not only on the language employed, but also on the attributes of the source, the audience, and the appropriateness and strength of the argument's claims given the pragmatic and discourse context of the argument [Durmus *et al.*, 2019]. As an example, [Tan *et al.*, 2016] investigates the effect of user interaction dynamics and language features looking at the ChangeMyView forum on Reddit and found that user interaction patterns as well as linguistic features are connected to the success of persuasion.

Habernal and Gurevych [2016b; 2016a] created a crowd-sourced corpus consisting of argument pairs and, given a pair of arguments, asked annotators which is more convincing, i.e., "argument A is more convincing than argument B"? They experiment with different features and machine learning techniques for persuasion prediction.

Starting from Aristotle's definition for modes of persuasion, [Hidey *et al.*, 2017] annotated claims and premises extracted again from the ChangeMyView forum to study whether occurrence of certain semantic types or sequence of semantic types could identify persuasive arguments from non-persuasive arguments.

Durmus and Cardi [2018] analyse persuasion in debates. They identify which features appear to be most important for persuasion, considering the selected user-level factors as well as the traditional linguistic features associated with the language of the debate itself. This approach underlines that prior beliefs associated with the selected user-level factors play a larger role than linguistic features when predicting the successful debater. Durmus *et al.* [2019] study the role of kairos on argument quality prediction by examining the individual claims of an argument for their timeliness and appropriateness in the context of a particular line of argument. They define kairos as the sequence of argumentative text (e.g. claims) along a particular line of argumentative reasoning. The dataset includes different topic categories including Politics, Religion, Health, Science and Music.

Glieze *et al.* [2019] target the task of assessing argument convincingness, and more specifically, they focus on evidence convincingness' given texts representing evidence for a given debatable topic, identify the more convincing ones. They release the IBM-EviConv dataset of evidence pairs which offers a focused view of the argument convincingness task. They propose a model based on a Siamese Network architecture for the argument convincingness task.

Wachsmuth *et al.* [2018b] investigate the task of automatically finding the best counterargument to any argument. Relying on the observation that we cannot expect prior knowledge of an argument's topic, they assume the best counterargument invokes the same aspects as the argument while having the opposite stance. They simultaneously model the topic similarity and stance dissimilarity of a candidate counterargument to the argument in order to find the most dissimilar among the most similar arguments. The corpus is available at `http://www.arguana.com`.

Reisert *et al.* [2019] propose an annotation protocol for collecting user-generated counter-arguments via crowdsourcing. More precisely, they conduct two experiments, where workers are instructed to produce a counter-argument of a certain argument, and a counter-argument after identifying a fallacy in a target argument.

Finally, [Habernal *et al.*, 2018] study how to empirically distinguish wrong argumentative moves like fallacies. Among the set of prototypical fallacies, they consider ad hominem argument, where arguing against the person is considered faulty and it is prevalent in online and offline discourse. The paper investigates three levels of increasing discourse complexity: ad hominem in isolation, direct ad hominem without dialogical exchange, and ad hominem in large inter-personal discourse context. They experiment with various neural architectures, and they propose a list of linguistic and rhetorical triggers of ad hominem based on interpreting the parameters of trained neural models.

3.2 Argumentation synthesis

Several applications necessitate the development of argumentation synthesis technologies. For this reason, a number of recent studies have been proposed to addresses the argumentation synthesis task. These studies propose different approaches to generate claims or reasons for a given topic, with a particular stance towards a topic.

For instance, [Bilu and Slonim, 2016] generate new claims by reusing topics and predicates found in a database of claims. [Egan *et al.*, 2016] produce summaries of the main points in a debate, and [Reisert *et al.*, 2015] synthesize complete arguments from a set of manually curated topic-stance relations based on the fine-grained argument model of Toulmin. [Wang and Ling, 2016] propose an attention-based neural network model for generating abstractive summaries of opinionated text. The proposed system takes as input a set of text units containing opinions about the same topic (e.g., the reviews for a movie), and then outputs a one-sentence abstractive summary describing the opinion consensus of the input. Given the risk to generate text which suffers from incoherence and repetitiveness, [Holtzman *et al.*,

2018] propose to alleviate these issues by training a set of discriminators, which aim to ensure that a text respects the Gricean maxims of quantity, quality, relation, and manner.

More recently, [El Baff *et al.*, 2019] tackles the task to generate complete texts including both argumentative and rhetorical considerations, in order to achieve persuasion with argumentative texts. Based on their previous work [Wachsmuth *et al.*, 2018a], they propose a computational approach that synthesizes argumentative texts following a rhetorical strategy. The proposed approach considers a 'controlled' synthesis setting, with the aim to successively create the models that are able to deal with more complex settings. Given a pool of argumentative discourse units, this approach generates arguments for any unseen pair of topic and stance (e.g., 'pro vegetarianism') together with a basic rhetorical strategy (i.e., logos, pathos or ethos).

3.3 Argument Generation

Recently, a number of empirical approaches have been proposed to tackle the task of generating arguments in different application scenarios. These approaches start from the assumption that employing a retrieval based systems (e.g., [Wachsmuth *et al.*, 2017d; Stab *et al.*, 2018a]) suffers from inflexibility in addressing a potentially controversial issue: firstly with regard to the missing keywords in the input, secondly the unseen topics in the dataset they have been trained upon. Furthermore, it is hard to model a one-to-many relationship which is more suitable for argument generation as a real-world argument may have multiple perspectives.

Park *et al.* [2019] propose a model called ArgDiver (Argument generation model from Diverse perspectives) to face the above mentioned challenges. For a given claim, ArgDiver generates multiple sentential arguments that cover diverse perspectives on the given claim. They adopt a Seq2Seq framework and they evaluate the proposed model with two measures, namely the quality of each of the generated sentential arguments, and their diversities. Hua and Wang [2018] leverage passages retrieved from Wikipedia to improve the quality of generated arguments. Due to the fact that Wikipedia has the limitation of containing mostly facts, [Hua *et al.*, 2019] define a counter-argument generation system to produce paragraph-level arguments with coherent content. More precisely, they introduce the CANDELA framework to generate Counter-Arguments with two-step Neural Decoders and ExternaL knowledge Augmentation. The key feature of this approach is to rely on two decoders, i.e., one fo text planning, selecting talking points to cover for each sentence to be generated, and a second decoder for content realization, producing a fluent argument to reflect the decisions made by the text planner. The output consists in longer arguments containing richer information.

Gretz *et al.* [2020] investigate a pipeline based on GPT-2 for generating coherent claims. They explore the types of claims that the model produces, and their veracity, using an array of manual and automatic assessments. They compare the generated claims to an existing large-scale collection of claims for the same topics, leading to the conclusion that the generated claims tend to be novel, and they might be employed to augment traditional AM techniques in automatically providing claims for a given topic.

Schiller *et al.* [2021] present a new language model, called Arg-CTRL, for argument generation to generate sentence-level arguments for a given topic, stance, and aspect. The argument generation task is defined through an argument aspect detection phase as a necessary method to allow this fine-granular control and crowdsource a dataset of 5,032 arguments annotated with aspects. Results show that the Arg-CTRL language model is able to generate high quality aspect specific arguments.

4   Conclusion

In this chapter, we have provided an overview of AM models and methods, applied to a variety of textual documents, e.g., legal cases, persuasive essays, online debates and tweets, to detect premises and claims, and predict the relations among them. The results obtained so far in AM have attracted the interest (and investment) of companies (e.g., IBM), and have raised high expectations for the future findings in the area.

In addition, AM is strongly connected with hot topics in AI, as deep learning (heavily used in AM), fact checking and misinformation detection (the prediction of the attacks between arguments is a building block for fake news detection), and explanations of machine decisions (AM can disclose how the information on which the machine relies to make its own decisions is retrieved). Other application scenarios where AM can contribute are medicine (where AM can detect information needed to reason upon randomised clinical trials), politics (where AM can provide the means to automatically identify fallacies and unfair propaganda), and for cyberbullism prevention (where AM can support the detection of repeated attacks against a person [Chung *et al.*, 2021b; Chung *et al.*, 2021a]).

Alas, all that glitters is not gold, and some open issues in AM should be tackled to actually attain the expectations. First of all, system performances should improve. Despite the good results obtained in some application scenarios, i.e., persuasive essays [Stab and Gurevych, 2017] (where the structure of the essays themselves eases the argument component detection task), for other kinds of documents, e.g., legal cases [Teruel *et al.*, 2018] and micro-texts [Peldszus and Stede, 2015], more work is still required. It is important to underline here that also human agreement (generally viewed as the upper bound on automatic performance in annotation tasks) is affected by the complexity of the AM tasks. As a result, there still exists a gap between NLP and KRR: *(i)* NLP is error-prone, and *(ii)* there is a lot of uncertainty involved in argumentation, as realized in the natural language. How to close this gap is an open research challenge: hopefully, it is getting smaller by virtue of the efforts of the AM community.

Moreover, various heterogeneous datasets have been produced since the beginning of research in AM. Because of the immaturity of a rising field, and the lack of clear definitions, each dataset has been annotated relying on slightly different definitions of argument components and of the relations holding between them, thus preventing the possibility of a straightforward alignment among datasets. While on the one side, it would be worth trying to unify existing resources, on the other side, this fact shows that AM is flexible enough to adapt to different use case scenarios, e.g., premises and claims are not the same in legal cases, persuasive essays and Twitter. In [Daxenberger *et al.*, 2017], a qualitative analysis of six different datasets used in AM is presented, to underline the different conceptualization of claims. Recently, [Schulz *et al.*, 2018] show that multi-task learning is one possible way to go. More precisely, they study whether conceptually diverse AM datasets from different domains can help deal with new AM datasets when data is limited. The question about the worthiness of unifying the existing datasets is still open and under debate. Wachsmuth *et al.* [2017b] highlight and empirically study a related issue, i.e., the question of how different the theoretical (computational models of argument) and practical views of argumentation quality actually are. Their results show that, on the one hand, most reasons for quality differences in practice seem well-represented in the theory, but on the other hand, some quality dimensions remain hard to assess in practice, resulting in a limited agreement.

Finally, another open challenge in AM deals with multilinguality. Only very few approaches tackled the issue of applying AM methods to texts in other natural languages than English, i.e., [Peldszus and Stede, 2016] address argument component detection for German, [Basile *et al.*, 2016] tackle the relation prediction task for Italian, and [Yamada *et al.*, 2019] present an approach to the automatic extraction of argument structure over a corpus of 89 documents of Japanese judgement documents.

Acknowledgments

The authors have received funding from EU Horizon 2020 research and innovation programme under the Marie Sklodowska-Curie grant agreement No. 690974 (MIREL).

BIBLIOGRAPHY

[Accuosto and Saggion, 2019] Pablo Accuosto and Horacio Saggion. Transferring knowledge from discourse to arguments: A case study with scientific abstracts. In *Proceedings
of the 6th Workshop on Argument Mining*, pages 41–51, Florence, Italy, August 2019.
Association for Computational Linguistics.

[Bar-Haim et al., 2017] Roy Bar-Haim, Indrajit Bhattacharya, Francesco Dinuzzo, Am-
rita Saha, and Noam Slonim. Stance classification of context-dependent claims. In
EACL, pages 251–261, 2017.

[Basile et al., 2016] Pierpaolo Basile, Valerio Basile, Elena Cabrio, and Serena Villata.
Argument mining on italian news blogs. In *CLiC-it*, volume 1749 of *CEUR Workshop
Proceedings*, 2016.

[Bilu and Slonim, 2016] Yonatan Bilu and Noam Slonim. Claim synthesis via predicate
recycling. In *Proceedings of the 54th Annual Meeting of the Association for Computational Linguistics (Volume 2: Short Papers)*, pages 525–530, Berlin, Germany, August
2016. Association for Computational Linguistics.

[Cabrio and Villata, 2013] Elena Cabrio and Serena Villata. A natural language bipolar
argumentation approach to support users in online debate interactions. *Argument &
Computation*, 4(3):209–230, 2013.

[Cabrio and Villata, 2018] Elena Cabrio and Serena Villata. Five years of argument mining: a data-driven analysis. In *Proceedings of the Twenty-Seventh International Joint
Conference on Artificial Intelligence, IJCAI 2018, July 13-19, 2018, Stockholm, Sweden*, pages 5427–5433, 2018.

[Chung et al., 2021a] Yi-Ling Chung, Marco Guerini, and Rodrigo Agerri. Multilingual
counter narrative type classification. In Khalid Al Khatib, Yufang Hou, and Manfred Stede, editors, *Proceedings of the 8th Workshop on Argument Mining, ArgMin-
ing@EMNLP 2021, Punta Cana, Dominican Republic, November 10-11, 2021*, pages
125–132. Association for Computational Linguistics, 2021.

[Chung et al., 2021b] Yi-Ling Chung, Serra Sinem Tekiroglu, and Marco Guerini. Towards knowledge-grounded counter narrative generation for hate speech. In Chengqing
Zong, Fei Xia, Wenjie Li, and Roberto Navigli, editors, *Findings of the Association
for Computational Linguistics: ACL/IJCNLP 2021, Online Event, August 1-6, 2021*,
volume ACL/IJCNLP 2021 of *Findings of ACL*, pages 899–914. Association for Computational Linguistics, 2021.

[Daxenberger et al., 2017] Johannes Daxenberger, Steffen Eger, Ivan Habernal, Christian Stab, and Iryna Gurevych. What is the essence of a claim? cross-domain claim
identification. In *EMNLP*, pages 2055–2066, 2017.

[Daxenberger et al., 2020] Johannes Daxenberger, Benjamin Schiller, Chris Stahlhut,
Erik Kaiser, and Iryna Gurevych. Argumentext: Argument classification and clustering in a generalized search scenario. *Datenbank-Spektrum*, 20(2):115–121, 2020.

[Du et al., 2017] Jiachen Du, Ruifeng Xu, Yulan He, and Lin Gui. Stance classifica-
tion with target-specific neural attention. In Carles Sierra, editor, *Proceedings of the
Twenty-Sixth International Joint Conference on Artificial Intelligence, IJCAI 2017,
Melbourne, Australia, August 19-25, 2017*, pages 3988–3994. ijcai.org, 2017.

[Durmus and Cardie, 2018] Esin Durmus and Claire Cardie. Exploting the role of prior
beliefs for argument persuasion. In *NAACL*, page 1035–1045, 2018.

[Durmus et al., 2019] Esin Durmus, Faisal Ladhak, and Claire Cardie. The role of pragmatic and discourse context in determining argument impact. In *Proceedings of the
2019 Conference on Empirical Methods in Natural Language Processing and the 9th
International Joint Conference on Natural Language Processing (EMNLP-IJCNLP)*,
pages 5668–5678, Hong Kong, China, November 2019. Association for Computational
Linguistics.

[Dusmanu et al., 2017] Mihai Dusmanu, Elena Cabrio, and Serena Villata. Argument
mining on twitter: Arguments, facts and sources. In *EMNLP*, pages 2317–2322, 2017.

[Duthie *et al.*, 2016] Rory Duthie, Katarzyna Budzynska, and Chris Reed. Mining ethos in political debate. In *COMMA*, pages 299–310, 2016.

[Egan *et al.*, 2016] Charlie Egan, Advaith Siddharthan, and Adam Wyner. Summarising the points made in online political debates. In *Proceedings of the Third Workshop on Argument Mining (ArgMining2016)*, pages 134–143, Berlin, Germany, August 2016. Association for Computational Linguistics.

[Eger *et al.*, 2017] Steffen Eger, Johannes Daxenberger, and Iryna Gurevych. Neural end-to-end learning for computational argumentation mining. In *ACL*, pages 11–22, 2017.

[El Baff *et al.*, 2019] Roxanne El Baff, Henning Wachsmuth, Khalid Al Khatib, Manfred Stede, and Benno Stein. Computational argumentation synthesis as a language modeling task. In *Proceedings of the 12th International Conference on Natural Language Generation*, pages 54–64, Tokyo, Japan, October–November 2019. Association for Computational Linguistics.

[Ferreira and Vlachos, 2016] William Ferreira and Andreas Vlachos. Emergent: a novel data-set for stance classification. In Kevin Knight, Ani Nenkova, and Owen Rambow, editors, *NAACL HLT 2016, The 2016 Conference of the North American Chapter of the Association for Computational Linguistics: Human Language Technologies, San Diego California, USA, June 12-17, 2016*, pages 1163–1168. The Association for Computational Linguistics, 2016.

[Fisas *et al.*, 2016] Beatríz Fisas, Francesco Ronzano, and Horacio Saggion. A multi-layered annotated corpus of scientific papers. In *LREC*, 2016.

[Gleize *et al.*, 2019] Martin Gleize, Eyal Shnarch, Leshem Choshen, Lena Dankin, Guy Moshkowich, Ranit Aharonov, and Noam Slonim. Are you convinced? choosing the more convincing evidence with a Siamese network. In *Proceedings of the 57th Annual Meeting of the Association for Computational Linguistics*, pages 967–976, Florence, Italy, July 2019. Association for Computational Linguistics.

[Grabmair *et al.*, 2015] Matthias Grabmair, Kevin D. Ashley, Ran Chen, Preethi Sureshkumar, Chen Wang, Eric Nyberg, and Vern R. Walker. Introducing LUIMA: an experiment in legal conceptual retrieval of vaccine injury decisions using a UIMA type system and tools. In *ICAIL*, pages 69–78, 2015.

[Gretz *et al.*, 2020] Shai Gretz, Yonatan Bilu, Edo Cohen-Karlik, and Noam Slonim. The workweek is the best time to start a family - A study of GPT-2 based claim generation. In Trevor Cohn, Yulan He, and Yang Liu, editors, *Findings of the Association for Computational Linguistics: EMNLP 2020, Online Event, 16-20 November 2020*, volume EMNLP 2020 of *Findings of ACL*, pages 528–544. Association for Computational Linguistics, 2020.

[Habernal and Gurevych, 2016a] Ivan Habernal and Iryna Gurevych. What makes a convincing argument? empirical analysis and detecting attributes of convincingness in web argumentation. In Jian Su, Xavier Carreras, and Kevin Duh, editors, *Proceedings of the 2016 Conference on Empirical Methods in Natural Language Processing, EMNLP 2016, Austin, Texas, USA, November 1-4, 2016*, pages 1214–1223. The Association for Computational Linguistics, 2016.

[Habernal and Gurevych, 2016b] Ivan Habernal and Iryna Gurevych. Which argument is more convincing? analyzing and predicting convincingness of web arguments using bidirectional LSTM. In *ACL*, page 1589–1599, 2016.

[Habernal and Gurevych, 2017] I. Habernal and I. Gurevych. Argumentation mining in user-generated web discourse. *Comput. Linguist.*, 43(1):125–179, 2017.

[Habernal *et al.*, 2018] Ivan Habernal, Henning Wachsmuth, Iryna Gurevych, and Benno Stein. Before name-calling: Dynamics and triggers of ad hominem fallacies in web argumentation. In *Proceedings of the 2018 Conference of the North American Chapter of the Association for Computational Linguistics: Human Language Technologies, Volume 1 (Long Papers)*, pages 386–396, New Orleans, Louisiana, June 2018. Association for Computational Linguistics.

[Haddadan et al., 2019a] Shohreh Haddadan, Elena Cabrio, and Serena Villata. Disputool - A tool for the argumentative analysis of political debates. In *Proceedings of the Twenty-Eighth International Joint Conference on Artificial Intelligence, IJCAI 2019, Macao, China, August 10-16, 2019*, pages 6524–6526, 2019.

[Haddadan et al., 2019b] Shohreh Haddadan, Elena Cabrio, and Serena Villata. Yes, we can! mining arguments in 50 years of US presidential campaign debates. In *Proceedings of the 57th Conference of the Association for Computational Linguistics, ACL 2019, Florence, Italy, July 28- August 2, 2019, Volume 1: Long Papers*, pages 4684–4690, 2019.

[Hasan and Ng, 2013] Kazi Saidul Hasan and Vincent Ng. Extra-linguistic constraints on stance recognition in ideological debates. In *Proceedings of the 51st Annual Meeting of the Association for Computational Linguistics, ACL 2013, 4-9 August 2013, Sofia, Bulgaria, Volume 2: Short Papers*, pages 816–821. The Association for Computer Linguistics, 2013.

[Hidey et al., 2017] Christopher Hidey, Elena Musi, Alyssa Hwang, Smaranda Muresan, and Kathy McKeown. Analyzing the semantic types of claims and premises in an online persuasive forum. In Ivan Habernal, Iryna Gurevych, Kevin D. Ashley, Claire Cardie, Nancy Green, Diane J. Litman, Georgios Petasis, Chris Reed, Noam Slonim, and Vern R. Walker, editors, *Proceedings of the 4th Workshop on Argument Mining, ArgMining@EMNLP 2017, Copenhagen, Denmark, September 8, 2017*, pages 11–21. Association for Computational Linguistics, 2017.

[Holtzman et al., 2018] Ari Holtzman, Jan Buys, Maxwell Forbes, Antoine Bosselut, David Golub, and Yejin Choi. Learning to write with cooperative discriminators. In *Proceedings of the 56th Annual Meeting of the Association for Computational Linguistics (Volume 1: Long Papers)*, pages 1638–1649, Melbourne, Australia, July 2018. Association for Computational Linguistics.

[Hua and Wang, 2017] Xinyu Hua and Lu Wang. Understanding and detecting diverse supporting arguments on controversial issues. In *ACL*, pages 203–208, 2017.

[Hua and Wang, 2018] Xinyu Hua and Lu Wang. Neural argument generation augmented with externally retrieved evidence. In *Proceedings of the 56th Annual Meeting of the Association for Computational Linguistics (Volume 1: Long Papers)*, pages 219–230, Melbourne, Australia, July 2018. Association for Computational Linguistics.

[Hua et al., 2019] Xinyu Hua, Zhe Hu, and Lu Wang. Argument generation with retrieval, planning, and realization. In *Proceedings of the 57th Annual Meeting of the Association for Computational Linguistics*, pages 2661–2672, Florence, Italy, July 2019. Association for Computational Linguistics.

[Ibeke et al., 2017] Ebuka Ibeke, Chenghua Lin, Adam Z. Wyner, and Mohamad Hardyman Barawi. Extracting and understanding contrastive opinion through topic relevant sentences. In *IJCNLP*, pages 395–400, 2017.

[Khatib et al., 2016] Khalid Al Khatib, Henning Wachsmuth, Matthias Hagen, Jonas Köhler, and Benno Stein. Cross-domain mining of argumentative text through distant supervision. In *NAACL*, pages 1395–1404, 2016.

[Lauscher et al., 2018] Anne Lauscher, Goran Glavaš, and Simone Paolo Ponzetto. An argument-annotated corpus of scientific publications. In *Proceedings of the 5th Workshop on Argument Mining*, pages 40–46, Brussels, Belgium, November 2018. Association for Computational Linguistics.

[Lawrence and Reed, 2019] John Lawrence and Chris Reed. Argument mining: A survey. *Computational Linguistics*, 45(4):765–818, 2019.

[Levy et al., 2014] Ran Levy, Yonatan Bilu, Daniel Hershcovich, Ehud Aharoni, and Noam Slonim. Context dependent claim detection. In *COLING*, pages 1489–1500, 2014.

[Lippi and Torroni, 2016a] Marco Lippi and Paolo Torroni. Argument mining from speech: Detecting claims in political debates. In *AAAI*, pages 2979–2985, 2016.

[Lippi and Torroni, 2016b] Marco Lippi and Paolo Torroni. Argumentation mining: State of the art and emerging trends. *ACM Trans. Internet Techn.*, 16(2):10, 2016.

[Lippi and Torroni, 2016c] Marco Lippi and Paolo Torroni. Margot: A web server for argumentation mining. *Expert Systems with Applications*, 65:292–303, 12 2016.

[Lugini and Litman, 2020] Luca Lugini and Diane J. Litman. Contextual argument component classification for class discussions. In Donia Scott, Núria Bel, and Chengqing Zong, editors, *Proceedings of the 28th International Conference on Computational Linguistics, COLING 2020, Barcelona, Spain (Online), December 8-13, 2020*, pages 1475–1480. International Committee on Computational Linguistics, 2020.

[Mayer et al., 2018] Tobias Mayer, Elena Cabrio, Marco Lippi, Paolo Torroni, and Serena Villata. Argument mining on clinical trials. In *Computational Models of Argument - Proceedings of COMMA 2018, Warsaw, Poland, 12-14 September 2018*, pages 137–148, 2018.

[Mayer et al., 2019] Tobias Mayer, Elena Cabrio, and Serena Villata. ACTA A tool for argumentative clinical trial analysis. In *Proceedings of the Twenty-Eighth International Joint Conference on Artificial Intelligence, IJCAI 2019, Macao, China, August 10-16, 2019*, pages 6551–6553, 2019.

[Mayer et al., 2020] Tobias Mayer, Elena Cabrio, and Serena Villata. Transformer-based argument miningfor healthcare applications. In *Proceedings of the 24th European Conference on Artificial Intelligence (ECAI 2020)*, 2020.

[Menini et al., 2018] Stefano Menini, Elena Cabrio, Sara Tonelli, and Serena Villata. Never retreat, never retract: Argumentation analysis for political speeches. In *AAAI*, pages 4889–4896, 2018.

[Mochales and Moens, 2011] Rachele Mochales and Marie-Francine Moens. Argumentation mining. *Artificial Intelligence and Law*, 19(1):1–22, 2011.

[Morio and Fujita, 2018] Gaku Morio and Katsuhide Fujita. End-to-end argument mining for discussion threads based on parallel constrained pointer architecture. In *Proceedings of the 5th Workshop on Argument Mining*, pages 11–21, Brussels, Belgium, November 2018. Association for Computational Linguistics.

[Naderi and Hirst, 2015] Nona Naderi and Graeme Hirst. Argumentation mining in parliamentary discourse. In *CMNA*, pages 16–25, 2015.

[Nguyen and Litman, 2018] Huy V. Nguyen and Diane J. Litman. Argument mining for improving the automated scoring of persuasive essays. In *AAAI*, pages 5892–5899, 2018.

[Niculae et al., 2017] Vlad Niculae, Joonsuk Park, and Claire Cardie. Argument mining with structured svms and rnns. In *ACL*, pages 985–995, 2017.

[Park et al., 2019] ChaeHun Park, Wonsuk Yang, and Jong Park. Generating sentential arguments from diverse perspectives on controversial topic. In *Proceedings of the Second Workshop on Natural Language Processing for Internet Freedom: Censorship, Disinformation, and Propaganda*, pages 56–65, Hong Kong, China, November 2019. Association for Computational Linguistics.

[Peldszus and Stede, 2013] Andreas Peldszus and Manfred Stede. From argument diagrams to argumentation mining in texts: A survey. *IJCINI*, 7(1):1–31, 2013.

[Peldszus and Stede, 2015] Andreas Peldszus and Mandred Stede. Joint prediction in mst-style discourse parsing for argumentation mining. In *EMNLP*, page 938–948, 2015.

[Peldszus and Stede, 2016] Andreas Peldszus and Manfred Stede. An annotated corpus of argumentative microtexts. In *ECA*, pages 801–815, 2016.

[Potash et al., 2017] Peter Potash, Alexey Romanov, and Anna Rumshisky. Here's my point: Joint pointer architecture for argument mining. In *Proceedings of the 2017 Conference on Empirical Methods in Natural Language Processing*, pages 1364–1373, Copenhagen, Denmark, September 2017. Association for Computational Linguistics.

[Reimers et al., 2019] Nils Reimers, Benjamin Schiller, Tilman Beck, Johannes Daxenberger, Christian Stab, and Iryna Gurevych. Classification and clustering of arguments with contextualized word embeddings. In *Proceedings of the 57th Annual Meeting of the Association for Computational Linguistics*, pages 567–578, Florence, Italy, July 2019. Association for Computational Linguistics.

[Reisert *et al.*, 2015] Paul Reisert, Naoya Inoue, Naoaki Okazaki, and Kentaro Inui. A computational approach for generating toulmin model argumentation. In *Proceedings of the 2nd Workshop on Argumentation Mining*, pages 45–55, Denver, CO, June 2015. Association for Computational Linguistics.

[Reisert *et al.*, 2019] Paul Reisert, Gisela Vallejo, Naoya Inoue, Iryna Gurevych, and Kentaro Inui. An annotation protocol for collecting user-generated counter-arguments using crowdsourcing. In Seiji Isotani, Eva Millán, Amy Ogan, Peter M. Hastings, Bruce M. McLaren, and Rose Luckin, editors, *Artificial Intelligence in Education - 20th International Conference, AIED 2019, Chicago, IL, USA, June 25-29, 2019, Proceedings, Part II*, volume 11626 of *Lecture Notes in Computer Science*, pages 232–236. Springer, 2019.

[Rinott *et al.*, 2015] Ruty Rinott, Lena Dankin, Carlos Alzate, Mitesh M. Khapra, Ehud Aharoni, and Noam Slonim. Show me your evidence - an automatic method for context dependent evidence detection. In *EMNLP*, pages 440–450, 2015.

[Schiller *et al.*, 2021] Benjamin Schiller, Johannes Daxenberger, and Iryna Gurevych. Aspect-controlled neural argument generation. In Kristina Toutanova, Anna Rumshisky, Luke Zettlemoyer, Dilek Hakkani-Tür, Iz Beltagy, Steven Bethard, Ryan Cotterell, Tanmoy Chakraborty, and Yichao Zhou, editors, *Proceedings of the 2021 Conference of the North American Chapter of the Association for Computational Linguistics: Human Language Technologies, NAACL-HLT 2021, Online, June 6-11, 2021*, pages 380–396. Association for Computational Linguistics, 2021.

[Schulz *et al.*, 2018] Claudia Schulz, Steffen Eger, Johannes Daxenberger, Tobias Kahse, and Iryna Gurevych. Multi-task learning for argumentation mining in low-resource settings. In *NAACL*, page 35–41, 2018.

[Skeppstedt *et al.*, 2018] Maria Skeppstedt, Andreas Peldszus, and Manfred Stede. More or less controlled elicitation of argumentative text: Enlarging a microtext corpus via crowdsourcing. In *Proceedings of the 5th Workshop on Argument Mining*, pages 155–163, Brussels, Belgium, November 2018. Association for Computational Linguistics.

[Stab and Gurevych, 2017] Christian Stab and Iryna Gurevych. Parsing argumentation structures in persuasive essays. *Comput. Linguist.*, 43(3):619–659, 2017.

[Stab *et al.*, 2018a] Christian Stab, Johannes Daxenberger, Chris Stahlhut, Tristan Miller, Benjamin Schiller, Christopher Tauchmann, Steffen Eger, and Iryna Gurevych. ArgumenText: Searching for arguments in heterogeneous sources. In *Proceedings of the 2018 Conference of the North American Chapter of the Association for Computational Linguistics: Demonstrations*, pages 21–25, New Orleans, Louisiana, June 2018. Association for Computational Linguistics.

[Stab *et al.*, 2018b] Christian Stab, Tristan Miller, and Iryna Gurevych. Cross-topic argument mining from heterogeneous sources using attention-based neural networks. *CoRR*, abs/1802.05758, 2018.

[Stab *et al.*, 2018c] Christian Stab, Tristan Miller, Benjamin Schiller, Pranav Rai, and Iryna Gurevych. Cross-topic argument mining from heterogeneous sources. In *Proceedings of the 2018 Conference on Empirical Methods in Natural Language Processing*, pages 3664–3674, Brussels, Belgium, October-November 2018. Association for Computational Linguistics.

[Tan *et al.*, 2016] Chenhao Tan, Vlad Niculae, Cristian Danescu-Niculescu-Mizil, and Lillian Lee. Winning arguments: Interaction dynamics and persuasion strategies in good-faith online discussions. In Jacqueline Bourdeau, Jim Hendler, Roger Nkambou, Ian Horrocks, and Ben Y. Zhao, editors, *Proceedings of the 25th International Conference on World Wide Web, WWW 2016, Montreal, Canada, April 11 - 15, 2016*, pages 613–624. ACM, 2016.

[Teruel *et al.*, 2018] Milagro Teruel, Cristian Cardellino, Fernando Cardellino, Laura Alonso Alemany, and Serena Villata. Increasing argument annotation reproducibility by using inter-annotator agreement to improve guidelines. In *LREC*, pages 4061–4064, 2018.

[Teufel *et al.*, 2009] Simone Teufel, Advaith Siddharthan, and Colin Batchelor. Towards domain-independent argumentative zoning: Evidence from chemistry and computational linguistics. In *EMNLP*, pages 1493–1502, 2009.

[Toledo *et al.*, 2019] Assaf Toledo, Shai Gretz, Edo Cohen-Karlik, Roni Friedman, Elad Venezian, Dan Lahav, Michal Jacovi, Ranit Aharonov, and Noam Slonim. Automatic argument quality assessment - new datasets and methods. In *Proceedings of the 2019 Conference on Empirical Methods in Natural Language Processing and the 9th International Joint Conference on Natural Language Processing (EMNLP-IJCNLP)*, pages 5625–5635, Hong Kong, China, November 2019. Association for Computational Linguistics.

[Villalba and Saint-Dizier, 2012] María Paz García Villalba and Patrick Saint-Dizier. A framework to extract arguments in opinion texts. *IJCINI*, 6(3):62–87, 2012.

[Visser *et al.*, 2020] Jacky Visser, Barbara Konat, Rory Duthie, Marcin Koszowy, Katarzyna Budzynska, and Chris Reed. Argumentation in the 2016 US presidential elections: annotated corpora of television debates and social media reaction. *Lang. Resour. Evaluation*, 54(1):123–154, 2020.

[Wachsmuth *et al.*, 2017a] Henning Wachsmuth, Nona Naderi, Ivan Habernal, Yufang Hou, Graeme Hirst, Iryna Gurevych, and Benno Stein. Argumentation quality assessment: Theory vs. practice. In *Proceedings of the 55th Annual Meeting of the Association for Computational Linguistics (Volume 2: Short Papers)*, pages 250–255, Vancouver, Canada, July 2017. Association for Computational Linguistics.

[Wachsmuth *et al.*, 2017b] Henning Wachsmuth, Nona Naderi, Ivan Habernal, Yufang Hou, Graeme Hirst, Iryna Gurevych, and Benno Stein. Argumentation quality assessment: Theory vs. practice. In *ACL*, pages 250–255, 2017.

[Wachsmuth *et al.*, 2017c] Henning Wachsmuth, Nona Naderi, Yufang Hou, Yonatan Bilu, Vinodkumar Prabhakaran, Tim Alberdingk Thijm, Graeme Hirst, and Benno Stein. Computational argumentation quality assessment in natural language. In *Proceedings of the 15th Conference of the European Chapter of the Association for Computational Linguistics: Volume 1, Long Papers*, pages 176–187, Valencia, Spain, April 2017. Association for Computational Linguistics.

[Wachsmuth *et al.*, 2017d] Henning Wachsmuth, Martin Potthast, Khalid Al-Khatib, Yamen Ajjour, Jana Puschmann, Jiani Qu, Jonas Dorsch, Viorel Morari, Janek Bevendorff, and Benno Stein. Building an argument search engine for the web. In *Proceedings of the 4th Workshop on Argument Mining*, pages 49–59, Copenhagen, Denmark, September 2017. Association for Computational Linguistics.

[Wachsmuth *et al.*, 2018a] Henning Wachsmuth, Manfred Stede, Roxanne El Baff, Khalid Al-Khatib, Maria Skeppstedt, and Benno Stein. Argumentation synthesis following rhetorical strategies. In *Proceedings of the 27th International Conference on Computational Linguistics*, pages 3753–3765, Santa Fe, New Mexico, USA, August 2018. Association for Computational Linguistics.

[Wachsmuth *et al.*, 2018b] Henning Wachsmuth, Shahbaz Syed, and Benno Stein. Retrieval of the best counterargument without prior topic knowledge. In *Proceedings of the 56th Annual Meeting of the Association for Computational Linguistics (Volume 1: Long Papers)*, pages 241–251, Melbourne, Australia, July 2018. Association for Computational Linguistics.

[Walker *et al.*, 2012a] Marilyn A. Walker, Pranav Anand, Rob Abbott, and Ricky Grant. Stance classification using dialogic properties of persuasion. In *Human Language Technologies: Conference of the North American Chapter of the Association of Computational Linguistics, Proceedings, June 3-8, 2012, Montréal, Canada*, pages 592–596. The Association for Computational Linguistics, 2012.

[Walker *et al.*, 2012b] Marylin Walker, Jean Fox Tree, Pranav Anand, R. Abbott, and Joseph King. A corpus for research on deliberation and debate. In *LREC*, pages 812–817, 2012.

[Wang and Ling, 2016] Lu Wang and Wang Ling. Neural network-based abstract generation for opinions and arguments. In *Proceedings of the 2016 Conference of the North American Chapter of the Association for Computational Linguistics: Human Language Technologies*, pages 47–57, San Diego, California, June 2016. Association for Computational Linguistics.

[Yamada *et al.*, 2019] Hiroaki Yamada, Simone Teufel, and Takenobu Tokunaga. Building a corpus of legal argumentation in japanese judgement documents: towards structure-based summarisation. *Artif. Intell. Law*, 27(2):141–170, 2019.

[Yang and Li, 2018] An Yang and Sujian Li. SciDTB: Discourse dependency TreeBank for scientific abstracts. In *Proceedings of the 56th Annual Meeting of the Association for Computational Linguistics (Volume 2: Short Papers)*, pages 444–449, Melbourne, Australia, July 2018. Association for Computational Linguistics.

Elena Cabrio
Université Côte d'Azur
CNRS Inria, I3S
France
Email: elena.cabrio@univ-cotedazur.fr

Serena Villata
Université Côte d'Azur
CNRS
Inria, I3S
France
Email: serena.villata@inria.fr

and

Laboratoire I3S, Campus Sophia Tech
Polytech'Nice-Sophia, 930 route des Colles
BP 145, 06903 Sophia Antipolis CEDEX, France
Email: villata@i3s.unice.fr

3

Textual Entailment for Cybersecurity: an Applicative Case

Giovanni Siragusa
Livio Robaldo
Luigi Di Caro
Andrea Violato

ABSTRACT. Recognizing Textual Entailment (RTE) is the task of recognize the relation between two sentences, in order to measure whether and to what extent one of the two is inferred from the other. It is used in many Natural Language Processing (NLP) tasks. In the last decades, with the digitization of many legal documents, NLP applied to the legal domain has became prominent, due to the need of knowing which norms are complied with in case other norms are. In this context, from a set of obligations that are known to be complied with, RTE may be used to infer which other norms are complied with as well. We propose a dataset, regarding cybersecurity controls, for RTE on the legal domain. The dataset has been constructed using information available online, provided by domain experts from NIST (https://www.nist.gov).

1 Introduction

It is well-known that laws can be pragmatically interpreted in multiple, and often incompatible, ways, even in the same context. Handling multiple interpretations of legal norms is perhaps the best known problem in Legal Informatics.

On the one hand, since it is impossible to predict a priori every possible context where the norms will be deployed, legislators tend to use vague terms that are flexible enough to be adapted to a multitude of contexts and, within certain limits, to the technological advancements of the society.

On the other hand, what makes legal texts so much dependent on subjective human interpretation is that they are used in disputes that represent different interests, so that the interpretation of the norms tends to be stretched depending on the interest involved.

It is eventually up to judges and other appointed authorities to decide the interpretation of norms in context. According to the seminal work in [Hart,

1994], legal authorities expand or restrict the core of determinate meaning of norms by filling legal gaps to connect *legal requirements* (formal compliance) and *operational requirements* (substantive compliance), i.e., how and to what extent the legal requirements from legislation are met in real-world scenarios.

More generally, the connection from legal to operational requirements recalls the notion of "concept holism" (see [Boella *et al.*, 2010; Grossi. *et al.*, 2008; Rotolo and Roversi, 2012; Ajani *et al.*, 2016], among others): one cannot say to have the complete meaning of a legal requirement without knowing the whole system of constitutive rules and the web of concepts with which the meaning of that requirement is intertwined.

In order to take decisions about the interpretation of norms, judges often consult the relevant literature in the area. For this reason, other legal authorities, standardization bodies, or associations representing categories of involved entities produce additional documents that contain recommendations, guidelines, standards, etc. specifying how to be compliant with the legislation in specific situations. In many cases, this is even explicitly required by the legislation itself, as in the case of the General Data Protection Regulation (GDPR), which requires controllers to define their own data protection policies (cf. GDPR, Artt. 13, 14, and 24(2)), invites associations and other bodies representing categories of controllers or processors to prepare codes of conducts (see, e.g., GDPR, Art. 40), the European Data Protection Board has the duty to release guidelines and recommendations (see, e.g., GDPR, Art. 70(1)(d)), etc. The interested reader is addressed to [Robaldo *et al.*, 2019], who proposes a recent formal account to handle correlations between GDPR legal and operational requirements.

Recommendations, guidelines, standards, etc. are not typically part of legislation; therefore, their adoption do not automatically provide compliance with the regulations. However, by certifying the adoption of a standard, an organisation can argue in favour of its proactive attitude and best efforts to be compliant with the regulations. In other words, such certifications provide strong arguments of compliance to be possibly used in auditing procedures or even in court.

On the other hand, since operational requirements are usually scattered around several documents in different format released, at different times, by different associations and other bodies, with different authoritative power and reputation in a certain domain, finding correlations between legal and operational requirements requires to build, maintain, and analyze an up-to-date archive of all these documents, which may be rather time-consuming, burdensome, and, therefore, unmanageable.

In light of this, Natural Language Processing (NLP) applications, in particular Textual Entailment (TE) applications [Korman *et al.*, 2018], can provide valid help in creating and maintaining such an holistic network of legal/operational requirements, specifically in identifying when a requirement semantically entails another one.

The main problem of TE regarding legal documents is the availability of dataset used to train machine learning algorithms to recognize the relation expressed. The few existing ones are generally based on case laws, as the one proposed in Competition on Legal Information Extraction/Entailment (COLIEE) Workshop[1]. There is no dataset regarding standard procedures that a company has to implement to protect their data, where the adoption of TE techniques are crucial to verify if they have been defined.

Such procedures are generally defined by ISO[2] (the International Organization for Standardization). The standard includes 114 *controls*, that a company needs to check in order to be consider itself as "secure" enough from cybersecurity attacks. In order to assess compliance with the standard, a company hires specialized auditors, who, after an inspection, decides whether the company is compliant with the standard or has to revise some of its internal business processes.

However, the ISO/IEC 27001:2013 controls, expressed in Natural Language, are quite vague and leave plenty of room for subjective interpretations.

For this reason, several public institutions, e.g., NIST[3] (National Institute of Standards and Technology), release more context-specific standards that refine the ISO/IEC 27001:2013. In this Chapter, we focus in particular on the NIST 800-53 rev.4[4], which implements 256 controls while specifying how they relate to the 114 controls of ISO/IEC 27001:2013 and viceversa. Specifically, it contains annexes that explain which controls of one of the two standards are satisfied by the controls of the other (and viceversa), in the sense that if a company implements one of the two, then it is assumed that the company also implements the associated controls in the other standard.

The present chapter starts from the assumption that the ISO/IEC 27001: 2013 and NIST 800-53 rev.4, and, in particular, the annexes included in the latter, which specify correspondences between the two standards, are precious raw sources for building a dataset for RTE. The latter has been recently identified in [Bentivogli *et al.*, 2017] as a challenging research topic.

Note that ISO/IEC 27001:2013 and NIST 800-53 rev.4 are just the two running examples that we will use in this Chapter. Many other cybersecurity standards are available on the Web, as well as corresponding tables inter-

---

[1]https://sites.ualberta.ca/~rabelo/COLIEE2019/
[2]https://www.iso.org/home.html
[3]https://www.nist.gov
[4]https://nvd.nist.gov/800-53

linking their controls. In other words, this Chapter has to be considered as the first step of a bigger research project to create a dataset made of a *network* of inter-connected technical documents in the cybersecurity domain. The advocated dataset, and the RTE classifiers trained, tuned, and evaluated on it, would be a precious resource for cybersecurity auditors and companies collaborating with them, e.g., Nomotika SRL.

In this Chapter, we propose:

- A dataset for RTE regarding cybersecurity. We constructed the dataset using the correspondences between controls that we found in the ISO/IEC 27001:2013 and NIST 800-53 rev.4.

- An evaluation of several RTE classifiers on the dataset, where we conducted a three-step evaluation. In the first step, we evaluated the dataset using cross-fold validation to see if it could be used to train the RTE classifiers. In the second step, we trained the classifiers using the COLIEE dataset[5] for Legal Textual Entailment; the idea is to check whether it is possible to transfer the knowledge acquired from a domain-oriented dataset to our one. Finally, in the third step, we checked if it is possible to transfer the knowledge acquired on our dataset to other legal ones.

The remain of the Chapter is structured as follows: Section 2 describes the construction of the dataset, reporting the number of pairs it contains, the average length of sentences and the vocabulary size; Section 3 describes the used models and their performance on the two datasets. Section 4 describes some related work on legal domain and RTE. Section 5 concludes the Chapter.

2   A dataset for Recognizing Textual Entailment (RTE)

We defined a dataset for RTE in the cybersecurity domain, called *cybersecurity entailment*. We constructed the dataset using ISO controls covered by the NIST ones[6], and the controls of the same NIST document[7] covered by the ISO/IEC 27001. For NIST and ISO documents, each <NIST control, ISO control> pair is constructed using the table[8] reported in the NIST

---

[5]https://sites.ualberta.ca/~rabelo/COLIEE2019/

[6]https://nvlpubs.nist.gov/nistpubs/SpecialPublications/NIST.SP.800-53r4.pdf, appendix H

[7]https://nvlpubs.nist.gov/nistpubs/SpecialPublications/NIST.SP.800-53r4.pdf, appendix F

[8]The table is created by a domain expert when the document is redacted.

document, and it could be seen as an entailment pair. We then extended the entailment pairs with neutral ones, applying a cartesian product between NIST and ISO controls and removing duplicated ones. An example of positive <NIST control, ISO control> pair follows:

NIST: *"The organization employs the principle of least privilege, allowing only authorized accesses for users (or processes acting on behalf of users) which are necessary to accomplish assigned tasks in accordance with organizational missions and business functions."*

ISO: *"The allocation and use of privileged access rights shall be restricted and controlled."*

The following one is an example of neutral <NIST control, ISO control> pair:

NIST: *"The information system enforces approved authorizations for logical access to information and system resources in accordance with applicable access control policies."*

ISO: *"Users shall ensure that unattended equipment has appropriate protection."*

We repeated the process of constructing the pairs for the controls between the NIST document and the ISO/IEC 27001. In this case, each ISO/IEC control has a *related_to* tag that express connections with other NIST ones, reporting their IDs. The IDs in each tag are assigned by a domain expert. We used the tag to construct the entailment pairs. We then extended the set with neutral pairs as for the previous set. A <NIST control, ISO/IEC control> pair that expresses an entailment relation follows:

sent.: *The organization implements a tamper protection program for the information system, system component, or information system service.*

related_to: *The organization protects against supply chain threats to the information system, system component, or information system service by employing as part of a comprehensive, defense-in-breadth information security strategy.*

The following pair is an example of neutral <NIST control, ISO/IEC control> pair:

sent.: *The information system maintains a separate execution domain for each executing process.*

related_to: *The information system separates user functionality (including user interface services) from information system management functionality.*

Finally, we merged the two sets of pairs to create the *cybersecurity entailment* dataset. We balanced the resulting dataset in order to have the same number of entailment and neutral pairs. An interesting fact is that the constructed datasets do not contain contradiction pairs because a control cannot be in contraposition with an another one.

Table 1 reports the number of pairs, the average sentence length, and the size of unique terms. The table highlights that the vocabulary of neutral pairs is contained in the entailment one. We also report the frequency of the Part-Of-Speech (POS) tags in Figure 1. We used OpenNLP[9] to assign the POS tags. From the image, it is possible to see that the majority of words are nouns, followed by adjectives.

The proposed dataset is availabled at https://drive.google.com/drive/folders/1swYciO8yOtaM1pCTS9ySEpNZ-Ac8A569?usp=sharing

	# pairs	avg. sentence length	vocabulary size
all dataset	2898	110.0	1912
entailment	1449	115.37	1912
neutral	1449	104.59	1905

Table 1. The table reports the number of pairs, the average sentence length, and the size of unique terms of the *cybersecurity entailment* dataset.

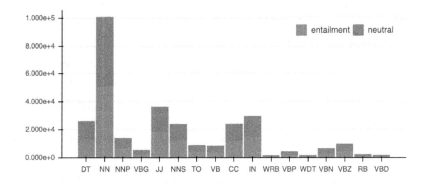

Figure 1. The POS frequency of the *cybersecurity entailment* dataset.

---

[9]https://opennlp.apache.org

2.1 XML representation of the dataset

We stored the dataset into an XML file to simplify sharing and interoperability. We encapsulated each <premise, hypothesis> pair inside the *pair* tag. In each tag, the first element of the pair is contained in the *t* tag (the premise) and the second element in the *h* tag (the hypothesis). Furthermore, each *pair* tag has the attribute *entailment* which expresses the relation: entailment or neutral. It also has two other attributes: *id* which is an identifier of the pair, and *task* which is required by Excitement Open Platform (EOP) framework [Magnini *et al.*, 2014; Padó *et al.*, 2015]. All those entries are contained under the tag *entailment-corpus*. Figure 2 depicts an excerpt of the xml.

Figure 2. The image shows a small section of the xml.

The main advantage of such XML structure is that it can be passed in input to EOP framework (or another one for TE) in order to train a classifier.

3 Evaluation Study of the Cybersecurity Dataset

In this section, we will perform three different analysis on our dataset:

- we will evaluate whether it is possible to train a classifier for RTE in order to recognize the entailment relation expressed in the <NIST, ISO> pair. For this evaluation, we will perform a cross-fold validation on our dataset;

- we will evaluate whether it is possible to transfer the knowledge acquired from another dataset to our one. In this evaluation, we would like to check the complexity of our dataset, i.e. if the relation expressed in the pairs can be easily recognized;

- we will evaluate whether it is possible to use our dataset to recognize the TE relations present in another dataset for legal domain, i.e. if a classifier trained on our dataset can generalize on unseen data. For this evaluation, we will train the classifiers on the *cybersecurity entailment* dataset and we will test them on the COLIEE testset.

We will follow RTE evaluation using *accuracy* measure: the ratio between the number of test instances correctly predicted and the number of test instances.

3.1 Preprocessing of the Sentences

In order to train the classifiers, we have to process the dataset sentences to extract the relevant features. The preprocessing consists of the following steps: tokenization, stopwords removal, stemming and feature extraction.

We started computing the Part-Of-Speech (POS) tags of the words. Those are necessary to extract the features in the last step. We used OpenNLP[10] to obtain the POS tags of each word. Then, we tokenized the sentences using the NLTK[11] module. We filtered the stopwords out using the list provided by this latter framework. We also used a regular expression to remove all non-alphanumerical tokens because they are not relevant to recognize the TE relation. Finally, we stemmed and lowercased the remaining tokens to obtain a less diversified vocabulary.

Once the list of salient tokens is obtained through the above mentioned steps, we proceeded to extract the features for the classifiers. We first selected the POS tags corresponding to the remaining words; then, we computed words n-grams and POS n-grams with n comprises in the range $[1, 5]$. We used a Term Frequency - Inverse Document Frequency schema to weight the extracted n-grams and to obtain the features.

3.2 Ablation Study

In the previous section, we said that the classifiers will use both word n-grams and POS n-grams. In this section, we will analyze the impact of these features on the performances. For this evaluation, we will compare the *Support Vector Machine* (SVM) classifier with the *Maximum Entropy* (ME) of EOP framework one since both generally perform well in RTE tasks. We

---

[10]https://opennlp.apache.org
[11]https://www.nltk.org

will use a *Random* classifier, which assigns the entailment relation with a probability of 0.5, as a baseline one.

We will train and test the classifiers on the *cybersecurity entailment* dataset to check the impact of the features. Since we do not have a testset, we will perform a cross-fold evaluation, with the fold number sets to 10. Each fold contains about 175 TE pairs. In detail, we will train the classifier on 9 folds and test on the remaining one. We will repeat this process leaving out a different fold for the test. Each classifier will be trained using the following features:

unigram: The classifier uses only unigrams as features. We decided to use such features as a baseline;

n-grams: The classifier uses n-grams as features, with n comprises in the range $[1, 5]$;

n-grams + POS: The classifier uses both word n-grams and POS tag n-grams, with n comprises in the range $[1, 5]$.

Table 2 reports the result of this evaluation. We can see that the n-grams slightly increased the accuracy of both classifiers. The accuracy is further increased with the adoption of the POS n-grams. It is interesting to notice that the n-grams had a major impact on the ME classifier than on the SVM one.

Model	Accuracy
SMV + unigrams	82.12%
+ unigram + n-grams	82.58%
+ n-grams + POS	83.06%
ME + unigrams	82.04%
+ unigram + n-grams	82.75%
+ n-grams + POS	83.10%

Table 2. The table reports the accuracy of ME and SVM classifiers with the different features.

3.3 Evaluation

In this section, we will evaluate several classifiers to check which one performs better in recognizing the expressed TE relation. The proposed classifiers are:

Random: it assigns a label randomly to each pair in the *cybersecurity entailment* dataset, which has a fixed accuracy of 50%. We used this classifier as baseline;

SVM: a Support Vector Machine that uses the extracted features (word and POS n-grams) to classify the pairs;

NB: a Naive Bayes classifier that uses the same features of SVM;

RF: since each pair of premise and hypothesis could contain specific words or POS tags that bring the entailment or neutral relation out, we decided to use a Random Forest classifier to capture them. The Random Forest creates a decision tree in which each branch contains word and POS n-grams features useful to distinguish the relation;

ME: a Maximum Entropy classifier with word and POS n-grams features. We used the implementation provided by the EOP framework since it contains state-of-the-art methods and classifiers for the TE task;

ME+WN+VO: it extends the features of the previous Maximum Entropy classifier with Wordnet [Miller, 1995] synsets (WN) and Verb Ocean [Chklovski and Pantel, 2004] (VO) classes, i.e. a semantic network for verbs. VO reports for each verb: (1) the semantic relation with other verbs (e.g., to make and to create have a similarity relation), (2) if the verb is transitive and (3) if it is symmetric. Those features are used to handle possible periphrases and synonyms in the pairs. As for *ME*, we used the implementation provided by the EOP framework.

For the first evaluation, we decided to check if it is possible to train a classifier on the *cybersecurity entailment* dataset and generalize on similar data. Since we do not have a testset, we used the cross-fold validation. We divided the dataset in 10-fold, training the classifiers on nine folds and testing on the remaining one. Table 3 reports the results of this evaluation.

Classifier	Avg. Accuracy
Random	50%
SVM	83.06%
NB	82.90%
RF	79.42%
ME	83.10%
ME+WN+VO	83.10%

Table 3. The table reports the average accuracy for the cross-fold evaluation.

From the table, we can see that the SVM, the ME and the ME+WN+VO classifiers are able to recognize the relations expressed in those pairs, obtaining outstanding results. We can also notice that both the ME classifiers obtained an accuracy higher than the SVM, about 0.04 percentage points; since such difference is not significative, it is possible to use either the SVM or the ME. Both ME and ME+WN+VO classifiers have the same accuracy, meaning that the addition of WordNet synsets and Verb Ocean classes to the features is not relevant to recognize the TE relation.

We analyzed the errors made by SVM and ME classifiers. We found that they tend to mistake a neutral relation for an entailment one when both the premise and the hypothesis regard different topics of the same argument (e.g., auditing records storage vs. auditing events). An example of missclassified pair follows:

NIST: *"The organization: Schedules, performs, documents, and reviews records of maintenance and repairs on information system components in accordance with manufacturer or vendor specifications and/or organizational requirements; Approves and monitors all maintenance activities, whether performed on site or remotely and whether the equipment is serviced on site or removed to another location; Requires that [Assignment: organization-defined personnel or roles] explicitly approve the removal of the information system or system components from organizational facilities for off-site maintenance or repairs; Sanitizes equipment to remove all information from associated media prior to removal from organizational facilities for off-site maintenance or repairs; Checks all potentially impacted security controls to verify that the controls are still functioning properly following maintenance or repair actions; and Includes [Assignment: organization-defined maintenance-related information] in organizational maintenance records."*

ISO: *"The organization: Documents and monitors individual information system security training activities including basic security awareness training and specific information system security training; and Retains individual training records for [Assignment: organization-defined time period]."*

In the proposed example, both the controls regard the *information system*, but they are not related to the same topic. The NIST one describes that the organization should maintain documents regarding maintenance activities and changes to the information systems, while the ISO one regards the training activities on the information systems.

We conducted a second evaluation to see whether it is possible to train the classifiers on a dataset different from our one, and use such acquired knowledge to recognize the relation expressed in the controls. In other words, we would like to verify if it is possible to generalize on our TE pairs. For this evaluation, we trained the classifiers using the legal textual entailment dataset proposed in COLIEE 2019[12] task 2. The dataset is composed of 362 pairs, divided into 182 pairs that express an entailment relation and 182 that express a contradiction one. Since this dataset does not present any neutral relation, we treated the neutral pairs of our dataset as negative ones to perform a proper evaluation. We applied the same preprocessing phase to the COLIEE trainset. Table 4 reports the results of this second evaluation. From the table, we can notice that only the SVM classifier slightly surpassed the Random one. Those results highlight the fact that our cybersecurity dataset contains complex pairs, making hard to generalize from a legal TE dataset to our one.

Classifier	Accuracy
Random	50%
SVM	50.48%
NB	49.44%
RF	48.86%
ME	50%
ME+WN+VO	50%

Table 4. The table reports the results obtained training the classifier on COLIEE dataset and testing on our one.

Finally, we conducted a third evaluation to see whether it is possible to transfer the knowledge that the classifier acquired from our dataset to other legal-based ones. For this experiment, we decided to evaluate the classifiers on the COLIEE testset. For a completed evaluation, we also reported the accuracy of the classifiers when they are trained and tested on only the COLIEE one. We expect that the accuracy will be high in this latter case, surpassing certainly the random classifier, while being lower for the generalization from the *cybersecurity entailment* dataset to the COLIEE one. Table 5 reports the results of this last evaluation.

As we expected, the accuracy of the classifiers trained and tested on COLIEE surpassed the Random one. However, if we train them on our dataset, we obtain very poor performances; in this latter case, the classifiers have a lower accuracy, meaning that they found difficult to generalize on unseen data. Those results confirm again that our dataset contains more complex and semantic distant pairs than one presented in COLIEE. This could be verified computing the cosine distance between premise (or hypothesis) of our dataset with the one of COLIEE. More in detail, we calculated the cosine

---

[12]https://sites.ualberta.ca/~rabelo/COLIEE2019/

Trainset	Classifier	Accuracy
-	Random	50%
COLIEE	SVM	71.11%
	NB	64.44%
	RF	67.80%
	ME	71.20%
	ME+WN+VO	71.06%
Cybersecurity	SVM	45.55%
	NB	46.70%
	RF	47.00%
	ME	47.00%
	ME+WN+VO	47.00%

Table 5. The table reports the results obtained training the classifier on Excitement dataset and testing on our one.

distance between each premise (or hypothesis) sentence of the *cybersecurity entailment* dataset and the COLIEE ones; we then averaged the obtained scores. Table 6 reports the cosine distance for premise and hypothesis sentences, where it is possible to see that the two datasets, despite their are related to legal documents, do not have neither a jargon nor a syntactic structure in common.

Pairs	Cosine Distance
Premise	0.97
Hypothesis	0.95

Table 6. This table shows the cosine distance between the Cybersecurity dataset and the Coliee one.

4 Related Works

Nowadays, Recognizing Textual Entailment (RTE) is an interesting task since it predicts the relation of two sentences. For instance, in legal domain could be used to see whether a law has a relation (i.e., entails) another one, or in case of European Union, we can see whether a law of a member state implements a directive of the EU (cf. [Nanda *et al.*, 2017]).

In general, research on generic RTE is conducted with the use of Neural Networks, where one important research works is [Bowman *et al.*, 2015]. In the article, the authors proposed both a dataset constructed through crowd-sourcing, and a Multi-Layer Perceptron (MLP) to classify the relation of a <premise, hypothesis> pair. After this article, researcher started to experiment with deep-learning models, also re-adapting idea coming from different NLP fields, such as Machine Translation. [Rocktäschel et al., 2015] proposed an encoder with attention for textual entailment. First, the authors sequentially read the premise and the hypothesis tokens with an LSTM, producing a list of encoded representation for the words. Then, they applied an attention mechanism to understand the correlation between the premise and the hypothesis words. They found that the attention mechanism is able to capture small semantic difference (e.g., the colour) in similar sentences. Finally, [Tsuchiya, 2018; Gururangan et al., 2018; Poliak et al., 2018b] found that, for some datasets, the hypothesis is all you need. According to them, the hypothesis contains very salient information that can be used by a Neural Network to unravel the relation. Poliak et al. [2018a] used such models to evaluate Natural Language Inference Problems, defining several evaluation frameworks.

Other researchers, instead, tried to apply the Recognizing Textual Entailment task on different domains, also starting competitions to see which models could perform well. In the field of Legal Informatics, we can find COLIEE (Competition on Legal Information Extraction/Entailment)[13]. COLIEE started in 2014, and defined a competition every year up to now. Each competition is composed of four tasks: two regarding information retrieval on legal text, one regarding question answering and one regarding RTE on legal text. The task datasets are free to access upon request. In this Chapter, we decided to use their dataset for RTE in order to train our classifiers, since our dataset, to the best of our knowledge, is the first one regarding the cybersecurity domain. In this competition, [Son et al., 2017] proposed a Multi-Layer Perceptron (MLP), composed of two hidden layers, with a decomposable attention model to find relations between words pairs. In detail, they started collecting articles from a civil code. Then, they ranked those articles according to a given query. Finally, they paired the best article (after the ranking) with the query to construct the training dataset for the MLP. Carvalho et al. [2015] proposed a method similar to the one in [Son et al., 2017], where they used n-grams, extracted using lexical and morphological characteristics, to retrieve articles from the civil code. Another one close to the work of Son et al. is [Kim et al., 2015]. In this work, the authors tried a convolutional neural network to see whether two legal articles are related to each other or not. Finally, [Kim et al., 2016] proposed a complex model to solve both legal information retrieval and textual entailment for COLIEE 2016. For the former one, they proposed an ensemble similarity method us-

---

[13]https://sites.ualberta.ca/~rabelo/COLIEE2019/

ing least mean square and linear discriminant analysis. For the latter, they applied a majority vote schema of three classifiers: a decision tree, an SVM, and a convolutional neural network. As features for the classifiers, they used word overlap, cosine similarity, WordNet [Miller, 1995] similarity score, and substring similarity.

5 Conclusion

We presented a dataset for Recognizing Textual Entailment on the legal domain. All pairs of the dataset regard cybersecurity controls extracted from NIST, ISO and ISO/IEC 27001 documents. To the best of our knowledge, this is the first dataset for cybersecurity RTE.

We conducted three evaluations on our dataset using several classifiers. We first checked whether it is possible to train a classifier to recognize the relations expressed in our dataset. Since there is no testset, we used a cross-fold evaluation. We obtained an average accuracy of about 83% for the Support Vector Machine and the Maximum Entropy classifiers. We also reported that only word and POS tag n-grams are relevant as features to predict the relation. This is also confirmed by the ablation study. However, the classifiers tend to predict the wrong label when both the premise and hypothesis regard different aspects of the same topic (e.g., information system training vs information system maintenance). To solve this problem, we think that the classifiers require features that are able to capture the the topics of the NIST and ISO controls. For such reason, we will adopt the Topic Model proposed by [Blei et al., 2003].

We then performed a second evaluation, checking whether it is possible to transfer the knowledge acquired from a legal dataset for RTE to our one. Thus, we trained the classifiers using Task 2 dataset of COLIEE competition. We obtained an accuracy of about 50.48%, slightly surpassing the Random classifier. Such analysis showed that our dataset contains complex pairs, for both language and content, that do not allow classifiers trained on other datasets to generalize well. This has been also confirmed by the third evaluation, where we evaluated if it is possible to transfer the knowledge acquired on our dataset to other legal ones for RTE. We decided to test the classifiers on the COLIEE testset, obtaining an accuracy of about 47%.

In our future works, we aim at integrating and inter-linking more cybersecurity standards. Specifically, we want to create a *unified* inter-connected corpus of technical documents in Natural Language for the cybersecurity domain, on which training and evaluating RTE classifiers to be later used by auditors as well as by companies collaborating with them, such as Nomotika SRL.

Giovanni Siragusa   Livio Robaldo   Luigi Di Caro   Andrea Violato

Acknowledgments

This research was supported by the EU's Horizon 2020 research and innovation programme under the Marie Skodowska-Curie grant agreement No 690974 for the project "MIREL: MIning and REasoning with Legal texts" (http://www.mirelproject.eu). We would like to thank prof. Cleo Condoravdi for fruitful discussions and feedback during the secondment of Giovanni Siragusa and Livio Robaldo at Stanford University in the context of the MIREL project.

BIBLIOGRAPHY

[Ajani et al., 2016] G. Ajani, G. Boella, L. DI Caro, L. Robaldo, L. Humphreys, S. Praduroux, P. Rossi, and A. Violato. The european taxonomy syllabus: A multilingual, multi-level ontology framework to untangle the web of european legal terminology. *Applied Ontology*, 11(4), 2016.

[Bentivogli et al., 2017] Luisa Bentivogli, Ido Dagan, and Bernardo Magnini. *The Recognizing Textual Entailment Challenges: Datasets and Methodologies*, pages 1119–1147. Springer Netherlands, Dordrecht, 2017.

[Blei et al., 2003] David M Blei, Andrew Y Ng, and Michael I Jordan. Latent dirichlet allocation. *Journal of machine Learning research*, 3(Jan):993–1022, 2003.

[Boella et al., 2010] G. Boella, G. Governatori, A. Rotolo, and L. van der Torre. A logical understanding of legal interpretation. In *Int. Conference on the Principles of Knowledge Representation and Reasoning*, 2010.

[Bowman et al., 2015] Samuel R Bowman, Gabor Angeli, Christopher Potts, and Christopher D Manning. A large annotated corpus for learning natural language inference. In *Proceedings of the 2015 Conference on Empirical Methods in Natural Language Processing*, 2015.

[Carvalho et al., 2015] Danilo S Carvalho, Minh-Tien Nguyen, Chien-Xuan Tran, and Minh-Le Nguyen. Lexical-morphological modeling for legal text analysis. In *JSAI International Symposium on Artificial Intelligence*, pages 295–311. Springer, 2015.

[Chklovski and Pantel, 2004] Timothy Chklovski and Patrick Pantel. Verbocean: Mining the web for fine-grained semantic verb relations. In *Proceedings of the 2004 Conference on Empirical Methods in Natural Language Processing*, 2004.

[Grossi. et al., 2008] D. Grossi., C. Meyer, and F. Dignum. The many faces of counts-as: A formal analysis of constitutive-rules. *Journal of Applied Logic*, 6(2), 2008.

[Gururangan et al., 2018] Suchin Gururangan, Swabha Swayamdipta, Omer Levy, Roy Schwartz, Samuel R Bowman, and Noah A Smith. Annotation artifacts in natural language inference data. In *Proceedings of the 2018 Conference of the North American Chapter of the Association for Computational Linguistics: Human Language Technologies*, volume 2, pages 107–112, 2018.

[Hart, 1994] H. Hart. *The Concept of Law*. Oxford: Clarendon Press, 1994.

[Kim et al., 2015] Mi-Young Kim, Randy Goebel, and S Ken. Coliee-2015: evaluation of legal question answering. In *Ninth International Workshop on Juris-informatics (JURISIN 2015)*, 2015.

[Kim et al., 2016] Kiyoun Kim, Seongwan Heo, Sungchul Jung, Kihyun Hong, and Young-Yik Rhim. An ensemble based legal information retrieval and entailment system. In *Tenth International Workshop on Juris-informatics (JURISIN)*, 2016.

[Korman et al., 2018] Daniel Z. Korman, Eric Mack, Jacob Jett, and Allen H. Renear. Defining textual entailment. *Journal of the Association for Information Science and Technology*, 69(6), 2018.

[Magnini *et al.*, 2014] Bernardo Magnini, Roberto Zanoli, Ido Dagan, Kathrin Eichler, Günter Neumann, Tae-Gil Noh, Sebastian Pado, Asher Stern, and Omer Levy. The excitement open platform for textual inferences. In *Proceedings of 52nd Annual Meeting of the Association for Computational Linguistics: System Demonstrations*, pages 43–48, 2014.

[Miller, 1995] George A Miller. Wordnet: a lexical database for english. *Communications of the ACM*, 38(11):39–41, 1995.

[Nanda *et al.*, 2017] Rohan Nanda, Luigi Di Caro, Guido Boella, Hristo Konstantinov, Tenyo Tyankov, Daniel Traykov, Hristo Hristov, Francesco Costamagna, Llio Humphreys, Livio Robaldo, and Michele Romano. A unifying similarity measure for automated identification of national implementations of european union directives. In *Proceedings of the 16th Edition of the International Conference on Articial Intelligence and Law*, ICAIL '17, pages 149–158, New York, NY, USA, 2017. ACM.

[Padó *et al.*, 2015] Sebastian Padó, Tae-Gil Noh, Asher Stern, Rui Wang, and Roberto Zanoli. Design and realization of a modular architecture for textual entailment. *Natural Language Engineering*, 21(2):167–200, 2015.

[Poliak *et al.*, 2018a] Adam Poliak, Aparajita Haldar, Rachel Rudinger, J Edward Hu, Ellie Pavlick, Aaron Steven White, and Benjamin Van Durme. Collecting diverse natural language inference problems for sentence representation evaluation. In *Proceedings of the 2018 Conference on Empirical Methods in Natural Language Processing*, pages 67–81, 2018.

[Poliak *et al.*, 2018b] Adam Poliak, Jason Naradowsky, Aparajita Haldar, Rachel Rudinger, and Benjamin Van Durme. Hypothesis only baselines in natural language inference. In *Proceedings of the Seventh Joint Conference on Lexical and Computational Semantics*, pages 180–191, 2018.

[Robaldo *et al.*, 2019] L. Robaldo, C. Bartolini, M. Palmirani, A. Rossi, M. Martoni, and G. Lenzini. Formalizing gdpr provisions in reified i/o logic: The dapreco knowledge base. *Journal of Logic, Language and Information*, to appear, 2019.

[Rocktäschel *et al.*, 2015] Tim Rocktäschel, Edward Grefenstette, Karl Moritz Hermann, Tomáš Kočiskỳ, and Phil Blunsom. Reasoning about entailment with neural attention. In *Proceedings of the 2015 International Conference on Learning Representations*, 2015.

[Rotolo and Roversi, 2012] A. Rotolo and C. Roversi. Constitutive rules and coherence in legal argumentation: The case of extensive and restrictive interpretation. *Legal Argumentation Theory*, 2012.

[Son *et al.*, 2017] Nguyen Truong Son, Viet-Anh Phan, and Nguyen Le Minh. Recognizing entailments in legal texts using sentence encoding-based and decomposable attention models. In *COLIEE@ ICAIL*, pages 31–42, 2017.

[Tsuchiya, 2018] Masatoshi Tsuchiya. Performance impact caused by hidden bias of training data for recognizing textual entailment. In *Proceedings of the Eleventh International Conference on Language Resources and Evaluation*, 2018.

Giovanni Siragusa
University of Turin
Italy
Email: siragusa@di.unito.it

Livio Robaldo
University of Luxembourg, Nomotika SRL
Luxembourg
Email: livio.robaldo@uni.lu

Luigi Di Caro
University of Turin, Nomotika SRL
Italy
Email: dicaro@di.unito.it

Andrea Violato
Nomotika SRL
Italy
Email: andrea.violato@nomotika.it

4

Legal Ontologies: An Overview

VALENTINA LEONE
LUIGI DI CARO
SERENA VILLATA

ABSTRACT.   Ontologies represent the standard way to model the
knowledge about specific domains. This holds also for the legal domain where several ontologies have been put forward to model specific
kinds of legal knowledge. Both for standard users and for law scholars,
it is often difficult to have an overall view on the existing alternatives,
their main features and their interlinking with the other ontologies.
To answer this need, this chapter addresses an analysis of the state-
of-the-art in legal ontologies and characterises them along with some
distinctive features. The aim is to guide generic users and law experts in selecting the legal ontology that better fits their needs and in
understanding its specificity so that proper extensions to the selected
model could be investigated.

1   Introduction

The modelling and the formalisation of legal knowledge are crucial aspects to
implement in order to increase the automatic approach to the law field thus
supporting the work of legal experts, enhancing legal information extraction
and question answering systems and enabling automatic reasoning over legal
cases.

Overlooking the first theoretical approaches to the formalisation of legal
ontologies, such as the Functional Ontology of Law by [Valente *et al.*, 1994]
or the frame-based ontology proposed by [van Kralingen, 1997], in the early
2000s most of the efforts focused on the modelling of core ontologies and
knowledge interchange formats, such as LRI-Core by [Breuker and Hoekstra,
2004], CLO-Core Legal Ontology by [Gangemi *et al.*, 2005] and LKIF by
[Hoekstra *et al.*, 2007].

Starting from the second decade of this century, the attempts to formally
represent the legal knowledge moved towards the modelling of specific legal
sub-fields due to a greater awareness of the specificity which characterises
each of them. This change of focus was accompanied by the consolidation
of the Semantic Web [Berners-Lee *et al.*, 2001] as a reality for knowledge

Handbook of Legal AI

Valentina Leone   Luigi Di Caro   Serena Villata

management and sharing. The Linked Data principles [Bizer *et al.*, 2011] and the adoption of standardised knowledge representation formalisms, as RDF[1] and OWL[2], are now common choices for publishing resources automatically accessible and processable through the Web.

However, despite the general acceptance of these good practices to release resources, the overall objective of a shared representation of legal knowledge has not been reached yet. In order to evaluate the possible reuse of a resource, all the actors involved in the ontology building process, i.e., legal experts as well as developers, need to be constantly up-to-date about the existing alternatives modelling the domain of interest. Moreover, the ontological commitment and the methodological choices adopted by each resource need to be carefully analysed. If not, the risk is to create and release on the Web redundant representations of knowledge, which obstruct the economy of information promoted by the Semantic Web.

Considering that the last decade has seen a proliferation of ontologies and vocabularies for different legal fields, it can be a good opportunity to take stock of the state-of-the-art concerning legal knowledge representation. Therefore, this chapter proposes a structured comparative analysis of the most recent legal ontologies and vocabularies. The aim is to provide developers and legal experts involved in the ontology building process with a practical source of information to consult in order to make an informed choice about the already modelled and reusable pieces of knowledge provided by other ontologies.

The chapter is organised as follows: Section 2 introduces the ontologies the comparative analysis is based on, Section 3 provides a description of the main features used to study and classify them, Section 4 discusses some insights resulting from the proposed classification and Section 5 ends the chapter with final remarks.

2   Selected legal ontologies

In the past years, some studies aiming at analysing and classifying legal ontologies have already been published. Casellas [2011] proposed a comprehensive survey about legal ontologies spanning a fifteen-years' time range approximately, from early 90's to 2011. The features she considered in her analysis mainly concern the intended use of the ontology, the level of generality (core or domain), the degree of formalisation, the methodology used to build and evaluate the ontology, and its availability for reuse.

Recently, de Oliveira Rodrigues *et al.* [2019] enlarged the time-frame of their literature review and they analysed the legal ontologies proposed from

---

[1]https://www.w3.org/TR/rdf11-primer
[2]https://www.w3.org/TR/owl2-overview/

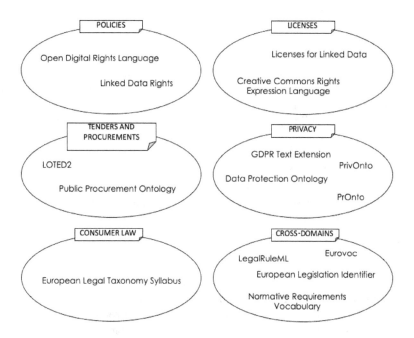

Figure 1. The six domains according to which the ontologies are grouped.

Valentina Leone   Luigi Di Caro   Serena Villata

late 90's to 2017. Their work presents different classification studies aimed at grouping ontologies among different dimensions, some of them similar to those already proposed by Casellas [2011]. The new categorisation dimensions introduced by the authors concern the country and the venue where the literature about an ontology was published, its underlying legal theory, the syntactic and semantic peculiarities of legal texts that were addressed while producing the ontology (e.g., the dynamism of normative texts or the overlap of jurisdictions) and the legal subdomain it models.

If, on the one hand, the work of Casellas [2011] seems now out of date due to the lack of many recently developed ontologies, in de Oliveira Rodrigues [2019] literature review it is difficult to identify the current emerging trends in the field due to the wide temporal interval their study focuses on. Moreover, their analysis was mainly developed on a theoretical level, relying on the scientific papers published to describe the ontologies. Features emerging from the documentation and the actual implementation of the resources, when available, seem not to have been included. However, experts involved in the ontology building task who are planning to reuse an existing resource need to consider a wide set of details. Usually, those details are not limited to the theoretical features of an ontology, but also include more practical information, e.g., the on-line availability of the ontology source file or the presence of a specific class inside the ontology.

Starting from these considerations, the classification of legal ontologies can be pushed one step further by analysing the details of their implementation and including practical information concerning their actual availability for reuse. As an ideal continuation and extension of Casellas [2011] work, this chapter proposes a comparative analysis of the ontologies released from 2012, by the addition of two older ontologies which are still well known and used, i.e., Eurovoc[3] and ELI[4]. The ontologies whose source files are not available for the download are excluded in order to enable readers to analyse just those actually available to reuse. Only three ontologies do not accomplish this requirement, i.e., ELTS [Ajani et al., 2016], PrivOnto [Oltramari et al., 2018] and PrOnto [Palmirani et al., 2018]. This is because they are very recent (less three years old) and the eventuality that they will be released can be still considered as possible. Moreover, the chapter analyses the resources that model a legal domain referring to some European or globally applicable legal framework. The ontologies that focus on a national jurisdiction are not included in the analysis.

---

[3]https://publications.europa.eu/en/web/eu-vocabularies/th-dataset/-/resource/dataset/eurovoc

[4]https://publications.europa.eu/en/web/eu-vocabularies/model/-/resource/dataset/eli

According to these selection criteria, a set of eleven ontologies belonging to five domains related to different legal fields are analyzed:

1. *Policies*: it refers to the ontologies which model the permitted, mandatory and prohibited actions that can be made on a digital or material asset;

2. *Licences*: it includes the ontologies modelling the actions allowed on a resource protected by the intellectual property rights;

3. *Tenders and procurements*: this domain includes the ontologies modelling the processes used by public administrations and authorities to find contractors to entrust with services or supplies;

4. *Privacy*: the ontologies model the concepts concerning the protection of personal data;

5. *Consumer Law*: it refers to the ontologies modelling the protection of consumers.

Each domain is characterised by the different sources of law it refers to and by a distinctive jargon usually reflected in the classes and properties' names of each related ontology.

In addition to the aforementioned domains, another set of four "cross-domains" ontologies is analysed. These ontologies are difficult to associate to a specific legal field because they were proposed as a more generic model for expressing deontic operators (Normative Requirement Vocabulary [Gandon *et al.*, 2017]), representing the content of legal texts in a machine-readable format (LegalRuleML [Palmirani *et al.*, 2011]) and indexing documents for search (Eurovoc and European Legislation Identifier).

Figure1 shows the distribution of the ontologies across the aforementioned domains. The following part of this Section provides a short description of each ontology.

2.1 Policies

Open Digital Rights Language. Open Digital Rights Language[5] (ODRL) is a language promoted by the ODRL Community Group [6] in order to model policies for digital content and media [Steyskal and Polleres, 2014]. ODRL offers a Core Vocabulary to specify the minimum set of terms suitable to model the policies and a Common Vocabulary of general terms to model, for example, actions regulated by the obligations, permission and prohibitions expressed in the policies.

---

[5] https://www.w3.org/TR/odrl-vocab/
[6] https://www.w3.org/community/odrl/

It models different types of policies, making a distinction between *(i)* a policy which is an agreement between an assigner and an assignee, *(ii)* a policy which is an offer from an assigner to an undefined wide audience and *(iii)* a policy which is a generic set of rules with no specified assigner and assignee.

Concerning the deontic logic, ODRL allows the expression of the effects associated to the non-compliance of an obligation, the effects of the non-compliance of some preliminary duties to obtain a permission and the duties to be accomplished for remedying to a violated prohibition. Finally, it is possible to associate a policy with some meta-information concerning, for example, its creator, its coverage (i.e., the jurisdiction applied upon the policy) and the reference to older versions of the policy.

Linked Data Rights ontology. The Linked Data Rights (LDR) ontology[7] was developed by the Ontology Engineering Group[8] and it is specifically designed to model the rights which can be exercised on a Linked Data resource. LDR ontology is based on ODRL from which it extends the classes *Action, Asset, Policy* and *Rule* in order to model the conditions of use of the Linked Data resources.

In detail, LDR defines three subsets of the ODRL *Action* class in order to represent the actions permitted on a resource protected by the intellectual property rights, to use a database of Linked Data and to access a resource via the REST and SPARQL services. Moreover it defines which are the types of Linked Data resources (data-sets, link-sets, ontologies, resources and statements) and which are the types of policy that can be concluded (contract or licence).

It is important to note that this ontology contains also a reference to the intellectual property rights. Even if they are not the main focus, it can be useful to take into account this ontology for the intellectual property field when the other models do not fit the needs of the users.

2.2 Licences

Creative Commons Rights Expression Language. The Creative Commons Rights Expression Language (ccREL)[9] is the standard promoted by Creative Commons[10] (CC) to express the copyright licensing terms in a machine readable way. This ontology is more than six years old, but its analysis is worthwhile because of the wide dissemination of the Creative

---

[7]http://oeg-dev.dia.fi.upm.es/licensius/static/ldr/

[8]http://www.oeg-upm.net/

[9]https://www.w3.org/Submission/ccREL/

[10]https://creativecommons.org/

Commons licensing terms to regulate the use of resources protected by copyright.

The ccREL ontology models all the relevant actions provided by the Creative Commons standard, distinguishing among permissions, requirements and prohibitions. All of them are further specialised by the actions which allow the sharing of a work with third parties while maintaining the copyright. Moreover, the ontology allows the specification of the legal jurisdiction which applies on the modelled licence to be represented.

Licence for Linked Open Data. The Licence for Linked Open Data (L4LOD)[11] vocabulary uses a light ontological structure to organise the terms concerning licensing in the Web of Data. The deontic operators (permission, prohibition, obligation) are further specified in order to detail which actions can be necessarily or possibly made and avoided on Linked Open Data sources.

2.3 Tenders and procurements

LOTED2. LOTED2[12], by [Distinto *et al.*, 2016], is a legal ontology which aims to represent the knowledge concerning the public procurements domain in the European Union. This ontology exploits the terminology contained in TED[13], the reference online platform where all the public institutions of European and EEA countries publish their procurement notices. Starting from this website, LOTED2 enriches the TED lexicon with an ontological structure legally rooted on two European Union directives about the public contracts field: the Directive 2004/18/EC[14] and the Directive 2004/17/EC[15]. LOTED2 uses these two directives in order to model the legal concepts involved in the process of awarding a public contract, among which there are: the roles that an agent can play in the process, the different types of competition, the different types of documents used for the publication of a notice, the legal resources that regulate the field and the offers submitted for awarding a public contract.

The aforementioned aspects are all contained in the core version of LOTED2. An extended version of the ontology in which the concepts modelled in LOTED2 are integrated with some concepts and properties of the Good Relations ontology[16] is also available.

---

[11] http://ns.inria.fr/l4lod/v2/l4lod_v2.html
[12] https://code.google.com/archive/p/loted2/source
[13] https://ted.europa.eu/TED/main/HomePage.do
[14] https://eur-lex.europa.eu/legal-content/en/ALL/?uri=CELEX%3A32004L0018
[15] https://eur-lex.europa.eu/legal-content/EN/ALL/?uri=CELEX%3A32004L0017
[16] http://www.heppnetz.de/projects/goodrelations/

Public Procurement ontology. The Public Procurement ontology[17] (PPROC), by [Muñoz-Soro *et al.*, 2016] aims to semantically represent the information published in official procurement documents, focusing on the Spanish law and in the EU law in general. Besides representing the usual information about tenders, PPROC objective is to represent the whole process of execution of tenders, starting from the publication of the contract until its termination.

Among its distinctive features, PPROC provides a classification of contracts according to different criteria, e.g., their administrative type or their subdivision in lots. Moreover it allows the specification of the criteria used for the evaluation of a tender, distinguishing them between subjective and objective criteria. The agents involved in a contract are expressed in the form of roles played during its execution and some hierarchies of roles are modelled. PPROC also represents the aspects which do not belong strictly to the set of properties of a tender or a contract, but which could be of interest for the suppliers (e.g., the kind of procedure followed during the execution of the procurement or its urgency).

In its attempt to model the public procurements and tenders domain, PPROC makes a big effort to try to reuse information already modelled in other existing ontologies, limiting the introduction of new classes and properties to very specific modelling requirements.

2.4 Privacy

Data Protection Ontology. The Data Protection Ontology[18] by [Bartolini *et al.*, 2015] concerns the data protection field, as it is modelled in the General Data Protection Regulation 2016/679[19] (GDPR). The Regulation came into force in May 2018, three years after the ontology published by [Bartolini *et al.*, 2015] . However, even if the ontology is not based on the final version of the GDPR text, we decided to include this ontology to enable the interested reader to compare it with other two ontologies modelling the same field, that is GDPRtEXT (see Subsection 2.4) and PrOnto (see Subsection 2.4). This ontology is part of a more complex system where it plays the role of a knowledge base used to express data protection requirements as annotations inside a workflow model (e.g., a business process). The Data Protection Ontology was developed manually, extracting the terms of the domain of competence from a corpus of official normative sources. The main concepts modelled by the ontology concern the data protection principles, the rules of data processing and the rights of the data subject. In particu-

---

[17]http://contsem.unizar.es/def/sector-publico/pproc.html
[18]https://bit.ly/2uhumDv
[19]https://eur-lex.europa.eu/eli/reg/2016/679/oj

lar, the data protection principles are the glue that relates and justifies the duties of the data controller as well as the rights of the data subjects, making explicit the relation between a data subject right and the corresponding obligation for a data controller to guarantee this right.

GDPRtEXT. The GDPRtEXT[20] (GDPR text extensions), by [Pandit *et al.*, 2018], is one of the most recent ontologies analysed in this chapter and it deals with a currently central topic in the privacy domain: the aforementioned General Data Protection Regulation.

The aim of GDPRtEXT is to represent the GDPR as a Linked Data resource, assigning an URI to each relevant part of the text. To do this, it extends some classes and properties of the ELI ontology (presented in Subsection 2.6) in order to specify the different parts in which the GDPR's text is structured (such as articles, recitals, citations and so on) and the properties that hold among them.

The ontology also provides more than 200 classes suitable to represent the relevant concepts introduced by the regulation and concerning the data protection field. The concepts' macro-areas modelled by the ontology are related to the categories of personal data, the concept of consent, the agents involved in the processing of the data, the actions that can be made on data, the rights of the data subject and the obligations of each agent which deals with the data.

GDPRtEXT also introduces a special property *isDefinedBy* which exploits the URI scheme created according to the Linked Data principles in order to link its classes to the relevant part of the text of the GDPR explaining the concepts they represent.

PrivOnto. PrivOnto is an ontology developed by [Oltramari *et al.*, 2018] in the context of the Usable Privacy Policy project[21] and its aim is to model annotated privacy policies explaining the data practices implemented by a website.

PrivOnto was built from a corpus of 115 privacy policies of websites belonging to US-based companies. This corpus was annotated by some domain experts who were asked to identify the main categories representing data practices, together with their attributes. The result was a set of ten categories of data practices represented as frames. Each frame has its set of attributes together with the corresponding values, that refer to the fragment of the privacy policy they are taken from. Indeed, PrivOnto allows the mod-

---

[20]https://bit.ly/2xwjTZJ
[21]https://www.usableprivacy.org/

elling, with specific classes, of different parts of the text and the annotations associated to each of them.

As an application of this resource, a set of 57 different SPARQL queries was engineered in order to browse the annotated corpus over its different dimensions (categories, attributes and values).

PrOnto. Similarly to the Data Protection Ontology and GDPRtEXT (see Subsection 2.4 and Subsection 2.4), PrOnto (Privacy Ontology), proposed by [Palmirani *et al.*, 2018], focuses on the modelling of the knowledge concerning the GDPR. The purpose of PrOnto is not only to support information retrieval, but also to provide a model on which techniques of legal reasoning and compliance checking could be applied.

Among its distinctive features, PrOnto focuses on the distinction between agents and roles, with the former able to cover particular roles inside different contexts and for a limited interval of time. Moreover, PrOnto models the sequence of actions aimed at processing personal data. Specifically, it makes a distinction between a planned sequence of actions named *workflow* and the real execution of this plan, named *workflow execution*. A temporal reference can be associated to each action and some boolean attributes are associated to the workflow in order to represent and automatically infer its lawfulness, fairness and transparency.

Besides the traditional deontic operators, (i.e., permissions, prohibitions, obligations and duties) PrOnto explicitly models compliance with and violation of an obligation by relating the *obligation* class with the *compliance* and *violation* classes as well as a *right* with the corresponding *permission*.

Within the DAPRECO project by [Bartolini *et al.*, 2016], the PrOnto ontology has been associated to fine-grained if-then rules in reified Input/Output logic [Robaldo and Sun, 2017]. Rules represent GDPR norms and are encoded in LegalRuleML (see Section 2.6). To date, this the biggest knowledge base in LegalRuleML freely available online[22].

2.5 Consumer law

European Legal Taxonomy Syllabus. The European Legal Taxonomy Syllabus (ELTS) [Ajani *et al.*, 2016] was modelled to provide a conceptual structure to the vocabulary created in the context of the Uniform Terminology project [Ajani and Ebers, 2005] and based on the EU consumer protection law. By organizing the terminology provided by the vocabulary, ELTS makes a clear distinction between the terminological and the conceptual layers it is made of.

---

[22]https://github.com/dapreco/daprecokb/blob/master/gdpr/rioKB_GDPR.xml

The authors describe ELTS as a *lightweight* ontology, lacking of an axiomatic formalization. This choice was made to handle the specificity of the consumer protection law at the European level as well as in each national jurisdiction in the European Union. In particular, ELTS models an ontology to represent the domain concepts of the European level and a separate ontology for each Member State to represent the concepts of their national jurisdiction.

Moreover, to manage the multi-lingual landscape of the European Union, ELTS associates to each concept at the European level the corresponding lexicalizations in all the Member States languages. By contrast, the concepts belonging to an ontology at the national level are associates only with terms in the corresponding national language.

The concepts belonging to the same ontology are interlinked through ontological relations, some of them more generic (e.g.*is a* and *part of*), some of them more specific (e.g., *purpose* and *concerns*). Similarly, other relations allows the connection between concepts of different levels (e.g., *implementation* and *translation*).

2.6   Cross-domains ontologies

Eurovoc. Eurovoc[23] is a multilingual and multidisciplinary thesaurus managed by the Publications Office of the European Union. Its function is to index the documents issued by the European Union Institutions in order to ease their retrieval.

The concepts are organised in 21 sectors which in turn are composed by micro-thesauri. Each sector concerns a field of competence of the European Union and each concept can be associated with only one sector to avoid ambiguities (except for the sector *Geography* which allows a polihierarchy).

Each concept is lexicalised by a set of terms in which only one is the *preferred term* (i.e., the term used for the indexing of the concept), while the others are the *non preferred terms* (i.e., synonyms of the preferred term not used for the indexing of the concept they represent). All the terms associated to a concept are provided with their translations in all the 23 languages spoken inside the European Union and Macedonian, Serbian and Albanian. Nevertheless, while there is a unique correspondence between the different translations of a preferred term, the set of the non preferred terms associated to a concept can vary considering their representation in different languages in order to maintain the linguistic nuances of each national legal lexicon.

The terms in Eurovoc are also linked to each other through some semantic

---

[23]https://publications.europa.eu/en/web/eu-vocabularies/th-dataset/-/resource/dataset/eurovoc

relations: beside the classical hierarchical one, also associative relations can be found among terms that are semantically related but are not on the same hierarchical structure.

Although the project which led to the creation of Eurovoc is more than twenty years old, its updating is constant and frequent: the thesaurus is continuously enriched with new terms concerning the topics dealt by the EU and cleaned up by removing obsolete terms.

LegalRuleML. LegalRuleML[24], by [Palmirani *et al.*, 2011] and [Athan *et al.*, 2015], is a project promoted by the OASIS LegalRuleML Technical Committee[25] which aims to develop a standard for the legal knowledge representation and exchange. To reach this goal, LegalRuleML offers a markup language which permits the harmonisation of different types of legal texts, such as norms, guidelines and policies.

Even though LegalRuleML is not properly an ontology but a markup language, we decided to include this resource inside our survey because it provides a rich set of concepts and properties which enable the management of the complexities of a formal representation of legal texts in a machine-readable way. Among its distinctive features, LegalRuleML provides some parameters to model the different interpretations that could be associated to a rule, to keep track of the author of a document or its fragments, to manage the temporal evolution of the norms and to take into account the defeasibility of the law.

Thus, the advantage and the final goal of LegalRuleML is the possibility to maintain the same expressive power independently from the way the norm is expressed, using the natural language or a formal machine-readable representation.

European Legislation Identifier ontology. The European Legislation Identifier (ELI) ontology[26] [Francart *et al.*, 2019] is a model which allows the publication of legal documents of different European Union countries using a shared and uniform set of metadata in order to enhance interoperability among the national administrations. Nowadays, this resource is used by 11 of the 28 EU countries and by the EU Publication Office.

The ELI ontology reflects many of the basic principles of FRBR (Func-

---

[24]http://docs.oasis-open.org/legalruleml/legalruleml-core-spec/v1.0/legalruleml-core-spec-v1.0.html

[25]https://www.oasis-open.org/committees/tc_home.php?wg_abbrev=legalruleml

[26]https://publications.europa.eu/en/web/eu-vocabularies/model/-/resource/dataset/eli

tional Requirements for Bibliographic Records) vocabulary[27], contextualising them into the legal field. While the FRBR provides the description of a bibliographic record in terms of *work, expression, manifestation* and *item,* the ELI ontology describes a legal document through the concepts of *legal resource, legal expression* and *format.* In detail, *legal resource* refers to the intellectual creation, independently from its translation in more than one language and from the format used for its publishing; it corresponds to the *work* property in FRBR. The *legal expression* concept is the realisation of a *legal resource* using a sequence of signs (e.g., the alphanumeric characters) and it corresponds to the *expression* property in FRBR. The *format* refers to the physical means used to store the *legal expression* (could be paper or an electronic format) and it corresponds to the *manifestation* property on FRBR. However, the *item* property of FRBR does not have a correspondence in the ELI ontology.

Since the documents issued by different EU countries could be described with different metadata according to the national jurisdiction they refer to, the ELI ontology overlooks these differences in order to represent only the common metadata of the national legal documents, providing the user the possibility to personalise and extend the set of metadata according to its needs. Therefore, the set of properties that can be established among the aforementioned three classes is not so large and they mainly concern the type of the represented document, the topics it deals with, the entry into force and the legal value of the document according to the format it is represented with.

Normative Requirements Vocabulary. The Normative Requirements Vocabulary[28] (NRV), by [Gandon *et al.,* 2017], is an ontology which extends LegalRuleML and whose aim is to exploit the standard frameworks offered by the Semantic Web in order to represent normative requirements and rules. Differently from other existing legal ontologies, NRV is not limited to the representation of the three main deontic operators (i.e., permission, obligation and prohibition), but it specifies and organises them in a hierarchical structure according to different criteria which concern: the need for compensation, the possibility to breach or fulfil a requirement and the temporal aspects involved in their validity and compliance.

NRV also uses the named graphs of RDF 1.1 in order to represent the states of affairs, that is the contexts on which the deontic operators can be applied. Then, given that OWL does not support the named graph structure, a SPARQL approach is tested for making complex inferences in which the

---

[27] https://sparontologies.github.io/frbr/current/frbr.html
[28] http://ns.inria.fr/nrv/v1/nrv_v1.html

formalised normative requirements are applied upon a state of affairs.

3   Features Description

This Section contains a description of each feature used to classify the legal ontologies. The overall set of features is organised in three macro-classes according to the type of property modelled by the features they include. More specifically, the three macro-classes are:

- *general information* class: it contains several features about the ontology disclosure and the purpose of its creation;

- *modelling information* class: it refers to the methodological and technological choices followed in order to build the ontology;

- *semantic information* class: it groups all the features concerning the way in which the ontology models the knowledge it refers to.

As mentioned before, each of these macro-classes is a set of more specific features as detailed in Table 1. The following part of the Section provides a description of each feature used to classify the analysed legal ontologies.

3.1   *General information* class

The features contained in this class refer to the generic purpose for which the ontology was built together with some practical information useful for those who are actually interested in using the resource. Eight features belong to this class.

The first information concerns the *extended name* of the ontologies. As they are often referenced by their acronyms in literature, their full name could provide to the reader a first insight of the scope of the ontology, also helping her to memorise the acronym itself.

The *legal domain* feature refers to one of the six domains listed in Section 2 and it corresponds to the visual information represented in Figure 1. This feature is further specified by *purpose* which contains a brief description of the main scope and function of the ontology inside the specified domain. Finally, the *year* feature indicates the year of the ontology first release.

Together with this general information, some more specific features provides the reader with useful information concerning the retrieval of an ontology on the Web and its reuse. To this purpose, the *current version* feature refers to the most recent released version of the ontology, while *licence* provides the information concerning the licence under which a resource is made available for reuse. Such feature could help interested users to fairly use the ontology, respecting any limitation and constraint in its adoption. The *updates frequency* feature represents an assessment of the frequency of updates

Table 1. The macro-classes and the corresponding features used to classify the legal ontologies

Macro-classes	Features
general information	extended name
	legal domain
	purpose
	year
	current version
	licence
	updates frequency
	references
	link
modelling information	development
	construction
	language
	knowledge sources for terms extraction
	external vocabularies references
	ground ontology
	level of structure
	knowledge representation formalism
	axioms
	design patterns
	evaluation
semantic information	modelling of temporal aspects
	adopted normative model
	deontic logic model

made to an ontology. Its possible values are: *low*, *medium* and *high*. and they are followed by the date of the last update. This feature is important to understand if the resource already reached a stable point and to evaluate if it is kept up-to-date according to the changes of the domain that it models.

The *references* feature provides an estimate on how much an ontology is known. In particular, it corresponds to the number of references to the paper describing the ontology (and included in the bibliography of this chapter) from its publication date until May 2019, as returned by Google Scholar[29]. For the resources which do not have a reference paper, it corresponds to the number of citations starting from 2012, i.e., the year the analysis proposed in the chapter starts from (see Section 2). Two research keywords were used: the first one contained the extended name of the ontology followed by the term "ontology" (except for Eurovoc, where term "thesaurus" was used as

---

[29]https://scholar.google.it/

it is usually associated to this resource), while the second one contained the corresponding acronym (if available) followed again by the term "ontology". The two keywords were then linked by a disjunction operator (i.e., the OR operator). For instance,for the ELI ontology the following string was built: *"European Legislation Identifier ontology" OR "ELI ontology"*, where the quote marks were used to obtain only exact matches.

Finally, the *link* feature specifies the at-present active link to the Web page containing the ontology documentation. Usually, if available, this Web page also contains the link to download the ontology source file.

Table 2, Table 3 and Table 4 classify the ontologies presented in Section 2 according to these features.

3.2 *Modelling information* class

The eleven features contained in this class concern all the modelling choices which are immediately reflected in methodologies and standards used to build the ontologies.

The *language* feature refers to the main natural language used to specify the concepts, the relations and the lexicon inside the ontology. The *development* feature indicates the approach adopted in the ontology building process, i.e., a bottom-up approach (from lexicon to concepts), a top-down approach (from legal foundations to lexicon) or a middle-out approach, which merges the techniques of the previous two methods.

The *construction* feature specifies if the modelling of the concepts and the relations of an ontology was performed manually or using some Natural Language Processing (NLP) technique to partially automatise the process of building the ontology. Linked to this aspect, two features concern the sources from which the concepts inserted in the ontology were chosen. The first one is *knowledge source (KS) for terms extraction*, that is legal documents or websites used to extract the relevant concepts and the corresponding ontology lexicon. In contrast, the *external vocabulary (EV) reference* feature refers to the existing ontologies and vocabularies which the ontology reuses specifying the URIs of some of its concepts and properties. Therefore, the difference between these two last features is that the legal documents listed in correspondence of the first feature only provide the raw concepts which are relevant for the domain but which needed to be formally modelled before being inserted in the ontology. By contrast, the second feature looks at the reuse of some parts of existing ontologies in order to adopt some concepts and relations already modelled by them. Similarly, the *ground ontology* feature refers to the main ontology which is extended by the analysed resource. This feature can be seen as a specialisation of *external vocabulary reference*. The difference is that an ontology which uses another one as ground ontology inherits from it the great part of its concepts and structure, while an ontology that makes some references to external vocabularies adopts its own structure and reuses only some concepts of other existing resources.

The *level of structure* feature is a quantitative evaluation of the number of concepts and relations modelled by the ontology. This property can be expressed by three values that denote a growing number of classes and relations: *lightly structured, moderately structured* and *highly structured*. The *knowledge representation (KR) formalism* refers to the formal language used to represent the ontology in a machine readable way. At present, the two *de facto* standards used to represent ontologies are RDF and OWL. Connected to this feature, the *axioms* feature is also considered. The feature refers to the three possible level of axioms allowed by the OWL 2 specification: class expression axioms, object property axioms and data property axioms.

Taking into account the principle of reuse promoted by the Semantic Web, the *ontology design patterns* feature is used to represent some parts of knowledge whose modelling was already codified in a standard representation. Finally, the *evaluation* feature analyses which methods were adopted to evaluate the created knowledge model provided by the ontology.

Tables 5 to 7 classify the analysed ontologies according to the features of this class.

3.3 *Semantic information* class

The two sets of features presented so far are independent from the legal domain and they could be applied potentially to analyse and compare the ontologies belonging to every domain of interest. By contrast, the three features belonging to this class specifically refer to the way in which the legal knowledge is modelled.

The *modelling of temporal aspects* feature allows to specify if an ontology models some temporal aspects concerning the legal field of interest and provides a brief description of the way in which this is done. There are a lot of different possibilities to model a temporal feature inside an ontology: it could be a simple time mark associated to the issue of a policy, or an interval of time which specifies the validity of an obligation or, again, it could be an implicit representation of time which focuses on the parameters that could vary over it, e.g., the status of a norm or the jurisdiction under which it is valid.

When an ontology permits the modelling of norms and rules, the *adopted normative model* feature specifies the type of rules that the ontology can represent (e.g., constitutive rules, prescriptive norms, etc.). Finally, the *deontic logic model* feature provides a short description of the deontic operators modelled inside the ontology (i.e., obligation, duties, permissions and rights).

As for the previous feature, this one holds only if the ontology deals with norms and rules. However, since norms are one of the main focus of the legal domain, a lot of the analysed ontologies model the deontic operators. For example, some of them only represent permissions, obligations and prohibitions, others model also the violations of obligations and prohibitions, while others provide a hierarchy of deontic operators organising them according to different criteria (e.g., temporal criteria or need for compensation of a violated norm).

Tables 8 to 10 classify the ontologies according to these three features.

4   Concluding remarks

From the analysis of the ontologies contained in this chapter and for each macro-class of feature used to classify them, it is possible to identify some issues and future challenges to be addressed in the field of legal knowledge representation.

Considering the general information about an ontology (summarised in the *general information* class), some lacks of standardisation still exists in the graphical user interfaces (GUIs) used to make the ontology content available to the final user. Currently, the LODE[30] tool is one of the most common Web services used to automatically create these GUIs. LODE processes the *owl* file of an ontology to create an HTML page which lists classes, properties and axioms of the ontology together with some metadata indicating the author(s), the release date, the current version and the licence of the ontology, as shown in Figure 2.

A unified look for the GUIs exposing the content of an ontology could be helpful for users concerned with ontology building and reuse, as it could reduce the time spent to look for the information within websites.

Linked to this problem, the second issue is related to the need of making explicit all the details concerning the download and the licence of an ontology. Browsing the Web pages of the different resources, it is sometimes difficult to find this information. However, it seems clear that without them, a fair reuse of the ontologies would not be promoted.

A special case concerns the resources made available by the European Union whose orientation towards the Semantic Web and the Linked Open Data is remarkable. They are all collected in the EU vocabularies portal[31] where a tab-like GUI organises all the information about a resource as it shown in Figure 3. However, even if the download links are well visible, the type of licence which regulates the use of each resource is not specified. Moreover, in the current interface of the EU vocabularies portal, the title of

---

[30]github.com/essepuntato/LODE
[31]publications.europa.eu/en/web/eu-vocabularies

Figure 2. An excerpt of the NRV GUI, automatically generated using the LODE tool.

each tab sometimes does not clarify the information associated with it, and the documentation of the different resources is not standardized. For example, the documentation of ELI is an *xlsx* file which must be downloaded and opened with a commercial software in order to be visualized. In contrast, the description of Eurovoc is better organized into expandable windows inside the tab.

Therefore, according to these remarks, some improvement would be desirable to harmonize the way in which the metadata on legal ontologies issued by the EU are organised inside the portal.

Concerning the methodological and technological choices made during the development of an ontology, this information is never displayed on the aforementioned GUIs and it could be difficult to find it also reading the literature published together with the ontology. However, this information is important for several reasons: first of all, it provides a scientific foundation to the work allowing other researchers to analyse and verify it, secondly, it enables an easy and understandable interpretation of the corresponding literature in which this information is sometimes implicit, even if it is at the basis of the development of the ontology.

The analysed resources show a positive trend towards the reuse and the extension of concepts and the properties, while a lack of sensitivity to the adoption of the ontology design patterns (ODPs) in the ontology building process still exists. As outlined by Gangemi and Presutti [2009], ODPs are

Valentina Leone   Luigi Di Caro   Serena Villata

Figure 3. Some information about ELI as displayed on the EU vocabularies portal.

modelling solutions to solve recurrent ontology design problems. The ODPs differ from the reuse of single concepts as they are micro-ontologies which model a piece of knowledge which occurs frequently in different domains. The low use of ontology patterns could be associated to the difficulty to identify, inside a complex modelling problem, the parts which could be covered by an ODP because it requires the knowledge of the full landscape of available ODPs. However, some portals ease their retrieval collecting the existing design patterns (the most famous being www.gong.manchester.ac.uk/odp/html and www.ontologydesignpatterns.org).

Finally, from the classification of the ontologies according to the *modelling information* class, a lack of standard methodologies to evaluate the resources is evident. In the literature related to the resources, the criteria used to evaluate the proposed models are sometimes omitted. However, as shown in Table 7, the current trend is to provide SPARQL queries to test the validity of some competencies questions and the fulfilment of some objectives which the ontology should reach. This is done especially by the most recent ontologies as for example NRV and PrOnto. In contrast, older ontologies mention in they literature the fact that they are adopted by real users, as in the case of PPROC or the resources released by the European Union.

The weaknesses concerning the *semantic information* class call back the aforementioned problem of the ontologies design patterns. Indeed, each ontology models a specific legal domain and adopts its own ontological commitment, with a consequent proliferation of different knowledge models referring to similar use cases. For example, the deontic operators, being one of the main focus of different legal domains, are modelled in many ontologies but the aspects that each of them considers are different. For example, some ontologies associate a temporal reference to the validity of an operator (as LegalRuleML or ODRL do) while others do not (e.g., L4LOD). Or, again, some ontologies make a distinction between an obligation which is respected and an obligation which is violated (as NRV), while others not (e.g., LDR). Thus, even if the legal domain has plenty of recurrent use cases, few efforts are dedicated to find a standardized solution to design problems which recur often within the legal domain.

5 Future perspectives

According to the remarks proposed in the previous Section, some improvements could be done to enhance an ontology building process oriented towards the reuse of existing resources.

First of all, the creation of a new set of metadata to include inside the ontology source file should be evaluated in order to complete the information that is already showed in the graphical interfaces displaying the content of an ontology. The most needed information are both of a general and of a legal nature. In the first instance, some metadata for indicating the methodology of development followed to create the ontology and the embedded design patterns would be useful to ensure the reuse of the ontology itself. In the second instance, a set of metadata able to summarise some of the purely legal aspects modelled into an ontology could be useful. Some of these metadata could recall some of the features used inside this chapter to classify the ontologies, as for example the modelled deontic operators and the type of modelled norms (if this feature is applicable).

In addition to a new set of metadata for the description of the ontology features, it could be important to address the problem pointed out at the end of Section 4 concerning the need of legal design patterns to reuse inside the ontologies. Some witnesses in this direction are provided by [Haapio and Hagan, 2016] and [Haapio *et al.*, 2018]. An effort to discover recurrent legal knowledge and to model it in the form of a standardises legal use case with the corresponding ontology design pattern could improve the quality of the released ontologies reducing the efforts required to model legal knowledge.

Valentina Leone   Luigi Di Caro   Serena Villata

This is especially true considering that usually the design of ontology-based systems is assigned to computer scientists who need, in addition to the technical background, a further knowledge about the legal domain which usually they do not hold.

	Eurovoc	ccREL	LegalRuleML	ODRL	LALOD
Extended name	European Vocabulary	Creative Commons Rights Expression Language licences	Legal Rule Modelling Language	Open Digital Rights Language	Licenses for Open Linked Data
Legal domain	cross-domains	licences	cross-domains	policies	licences
Purpose	indexing of the documentary information of the EU institutions	machine-readable standard to express licensing terms	modelling of legal norms allowing legal reasoning	representation of the conditions of usage of digital assets	representation of existing licensing terms in the Web of Data
Year	1984	2008	2011	2012	2013
Current version	4.9	unique version	1.0	2.2	0.2
Licence	commercial or non-commercial use allowed providing appropriate acknowledgement	CC BY 3.0	OASIS Intellectual Property Rights Policy	W3C Community Contributor License Agreement (CLA)	CC-BY-SA
Updates frequency	high (29 Mar 2019)	low (1 May 2008)	high (8 May 2018)	high (15 Feb 2018)	low (10 May 2013)
References	280	190	56	21	31
Link	bit.ly/2MY0TpM	bit.ly/2Lua4gp	bit.ly/2sxpskV	bit.ly/2J75JPj	bit.ly/2m40FSn

Table 2. Classification of ontologies published from 1984 to 2013 according to the *general information* class of features. Last revision of the information contained in the table: May 2019.

	ELI	LOTED2	PPROC	LDR	Data Protection Ontology
Extended name	European Legislation Identifier	not found	Public Procurement Ontology	Linked Data Rights ontology	not applicable
Legal domain	cross-domains	tenders and procurements	tenders and procurements	policies	privacy
Purpose	metadata for the description of legal documents issued by the EU and its Member States	indexing, search and retrieval of European public procurement notices	management of public procurements and the execution of contracts	representation of policies of Linked Data resources	Model the GDPR concepts, focusing on the obligation of the data controller in relation with the rights of the data subject
Year	2014	2014	2014	2014	2015
Current version	1.2	unique version	1.0.0	unique version	unique version
Licence	reuse allowed providing appropriate acknowledgement	GNU GPL v3	CC BY-SA 4.0	CC BY 4.0	not found
Updates frequency	low (21 Nov 2018)	low (16 Jan 2014)	low (29 Oct 2014)	low (1 Sep 2014)	low (16 Feb 2016)
References	27	23	10	4	10
Link	bit.ly/2NyUimC	bit.ly/2m5os4q	bit.ly/2MWxGPq	bit.ly/2KU59cx	bit.ly/2uhumDv

Table 3. Classification of ontologies published from 2014 to 2015 according to the *general information* class of features. Last revision of the information contained in the table: May 2019.

	ELTS	GDPRtEXT	NRV	PrivOnto	PrOnto
Extended name	European Legal Taxonomy Syllabus	GDPR text extensions	Normative Requirements Vocabulary	not found	Privacy Ontology
Legal domain	consumer law	privacy	cross-domains	privacy	privacy
Purpose	provide a conceptual structure to a domain terminology vocabulary	representation of the GDPR concepts with a direct link to the Regulation text	representation of annotated privacy policies of websites	representation of normative requirements and rules as LOD	representation of the GDPR concepts for legal reasoning and compliance checking
Year	2016	2017	2017	2017	2018
Current version	not released	0.6	unique version	unique version	not released
Licence	not applicable	CC by 4.0	not found	not found	not applicable
Updates frequency	not applicable	high (31 July 2018)	law (last update not found)	not found	not applicable
References	14	10	6	20	5
Link	not applicable	bit.ly/2xwjTZJ	bit.ly/2KFwkIC	not found	not applicable

Table 4. Classification of ontologies published from 2016 to 2018 according to the *general information* class of features. Last revision of the information contained in the table: May 2019.

Valentina Leone   Luigi Di Caro   Serena Villata

	Eurovoc	ccREL	LegalRuleML	ODRL	L4LOD
Development	not found	not found	not found	not found	not found
Construction	manual	manual	manual	manual	manual
Language	EU's languages, Macedonian, Albanian, Serbian	English	English	English	English
KS for terms extraction	ECLAS thesaurus, SCAD, EC-01, Official Gazette indices	not found	not applicable	not applicable	not found
EV references	FRBR, Dublin Core, SKOS	not found	not found	Dublin Core, SKOS, FOAF	not found
Ground ontology	none	none	RuleML	none	none
Level of structure	lightly structured	lightly structured	highly structured	highly structured	lightly structured
KR formalism	RDF	RDF	RelaxNG and XML Schema, RDFS, XSLT	RDF	RDF
Axioms	not found	class level, property level	class level, property level	class level, property level	class level
Design patterns	not found	not found	container, collection, recursive element, marker, composite	not found	not found
Evaluation	EU institutions, Publication Office, national and regional parliaments	not found	not found	not found	not found

Table 5. Classification of ontologies published from 1984 to 2013 according to the *modelling information* class of features. Last revision of the information contained in the table: May 2019.

	ELI	LOTED2	PPROC	LDR	Data Protection Ontology
Development	not found	middle-out	bottom-up	not found	bottom-up
Construction	manual	manual	manual	manual	manual
Language	English	English	English	English	English
KS for terms extraction	not applicable	TED website, EI Directive 2004/17/EC and EU Directive 2004/17/EC	buyer profiles, EU directives, public procurements' announcement models of Spanish legislation	not found	GDPR, Data Protection Directive (DPD), Handbook on European data protection law
EV references	FRBR, Dublin Core, SKOS	LKIF-core, GoodRelations	CPV, PCO, FOAF, SKOS, DC, Organization Ontology, schema.org, Good Relations	ODRL, SKOS	LKIF-Core, SKOS
Ground ontology	FRBR/RDA	none	none	ODRL	none
Level of structure	lightly structured	moderately structured	highly structured	lightly structured	lightly structured
KR formalism	OWL	OWL	OWL	OWL	OWL
Axioms	class level	class level	class level	class level, property level	class level
Design patterns	not found	Social Reality	not found	not found	not found
Evaluation	provided by users	not found	provided by two Spanish public authorities	not found	not found

Table 6. Classification of ontologies published from 2014 to 2015 according to the *modelling information* class of features. Last revision of the information contained in the table: May 2019.

Valentina Leone   Luigi Di Caro   Serena Villata

	ELTS	GDPR&EXT	NRV	PrivOnto	PrOnto
Development	bottom-up	bottom-up	not found	middle-out	top-down following the MeLOn methodology
Construction	manual	manual	manual	manual	manual
Language	EU's languages	English	English	English	English
KS for terms extraction	vocabulary for the Uniform Terminology Project	GDPR, document issued by official sources, industry-based sources	not applicable	115 privacy policies of US-based companies	GDPR, terms of use, information, privacy policies, consent forms
EV references	not found	ELI ontology	LegalRulemML, RuleML	not found	ALLOT, FRBR, LKIF Core, PWO, LegalRuleML metamodel
Ground ontology	none	ELI ontology	LegalRuleML	none	none
Level of structure	lightly structured	lightly structured	moderately structured	lightly structured	highly structured
KR formalism	not used	OWL	RDF	OWL	OWL
Axioms	not applicable	class level	class property	class level	class level
Design patterns	not applicable	not found	not found	not found	Time-indexed Value in Context, Time interval
Evaluation	legal experts in the loop	not found	SPARQL queries	not found	SPARQL queries

Table 7. Classification of ontologies published from 2016 to 2018 according to the *modelling information* class of features. Last revision of the information contained in the table: May 2019.

116

	Eurovoc	ccREL	LegalRuleML	ODRL	L4LOD
Modelling of temporal aspects	not applicable	not found	modelling of the aspects of a rule that vary over time (e.g., status, validity, jurisdiction)	modelling of the date and time a policy is issued or modified. Date and time constraint on the validity of a deontic operator.	not found
Adopted normative model	not applicable	prescriptive rules	constitutive, technical and prescriptive rules	prescriptive rules	prescriptive rules
Deontic logic model	not applicable	requirements and prohibitions set by the Creative Commons standard	permission, rights, obligation, prohibition, compliance with a prohibition or an obligation, violation of a prohibition or an obligation, reparation of a violation	permissions, prohibitions and obligations over a digital or material asset	permissions, obligations and prohibitions over the licensed data

Table 8. Classification of ontologies published from 1984 to 2013 according to the *semantic information* class of features. Last revision of the information contained in the table: May 2019.

117

	ELI	LOTED2	PPROC	LDR	Data Protection Ontology
Modelling of temporal aspects	not applicable	date and time associated to tenders	only to indicate the deadline for submissions of tenders and requests of participation	not found	not found
Adopted normative model	not applicable	not applicable	not applicable	prescriptive rules	prescriptive rules
Deontic logic model	not applicable	not applicable	additional obligations that a contract needs, requirements that a tender needs in order to be submitted	right over a Linked Data resource	obligation (of the data controller) and rights (of the data subject)

Table 9. Classification of ontologies published from 2014 to 2015 according to the *semantic information* class of features. Last revision of the information contained in the table: May 2019.

	ELTS	GDPRtEXT	NRV	PrivOnto	PrOnto
Modelling of temporal aspects	use of the ontological relation "replaced by" to model the evolution of concepts definitions	information about personal data retention and storage period are modelled as ontology classes	temporal aspects are modelled through the concepts of perdurance, persistence, co-occurrence and preemptiveness of a deontic operator	not applicable	temporal intervals associated to actions in workflows, to agents' roles and to deontic operators
Adopted norms model	constitutive and prescriptive rules	prescriptive rules	prescriptive rules	prescriptive rules	constitutive and prescriptive rules
Deontic logic model	permissions, prohibitions, obligations and rights are complex concepts that are linked to the basic concepts they involve (e.g., "right of withdrawal" is linked to the concept of "withdrawal" intended as an act)	obligations of different agents mentioned in the GDPR (Controller, Processor, Data Protection Officer) and right of the data subject	permissions, obligations and prohibition are organised according to the principles of compensation, compliance, violation, temporal validity and realisation	not applicable	permissions, prohibitions, obligations, rights, compliance with an obligation and violation of an obligation. Some references are modelled between obligations and compliance/violation and between rights and permissions

Table 10. Classification of ontologies published from 2016 to 2018 according to the *semantic information* class of features. Last revision of the information contained in the table: May 2019.

BIBLIOGRAPHY

[Ajani and Ebers, 2005] Gianmaria Ajani and Martin Ebers. Uniform terminology for european contract law: introduction. *Uniform terminology for European contract law. Nomos, Baden-Baden*, pages 11–20, 2005.

[Ajani et al., 2016] Gianmaria Ajani, Guido Boella, Luigi Di Caro, Livio Robaldo, Llio Humphreys, Sabrina Praduroux, Piercarlo Rossi, and Andrea Violato. The european legal taxonomy syllabus: a multi-lingual, multi-level ontology framework to untangle the web of european legal terminology. *Applied Ontology*, 11(4):325–375, 2016.

[Athan et al., 2015] Tara Athan, Guido Governatori, Monica Palmirani, Adrian Paschke, and Adam Wyner. Legalruleml: Design principles and foundations. In *Reasoning Web International Summer School*, pages 151–188. Springer, 2015.

[Bartolini et al., 2015] Cesare Bartolini, Robert Muthuri, and Cristiana Santos. Using ontologies to model data protection requirements in workflows. In *JSAI International Symposium on Artificial Intelligence*, pages 233–248. Springer, 2015.

[Bartolini et al., 2016] Cesare Bartolini, Andra Giurgiu, Gabriele Lenzini, and Livio Robaldo. Towards legal compliance by correlating standards and laws with a semi-automated methodology. In *Benelux Conference on Artificial Intelligence*, pages 47–62. Springer, 2016.

[Berners-Lee et al., 2001] Tim Berners-Lee, James Hendler, Ora Lassila, et al. The semantic web. *Scientific American*, 284(5):28–37, 2001.

[Bizer et al., 2011] Christian Bizer, Tom Heath, and Tim Berners-Lee. Linked data: The story so far. In *Semantic services, interoperability and web applications: emerging concepts*, pages 205–227. IGI Global, 2011.

[Breuker and Hoekstra, 2004] Joost Breuker and Rinke Hoekstra. Epistemology and ontology in core ontologies: Folaw and lri-core, two core ontologies for law. In *In Proceedings of the EKAW04 Workshop on Core Ontologies in Ontology Engineering*, pages 15–27. Northamptonshire, UK, 2004.

[Casellas, 2011] Núria Casellas. *Legal ontology engineering: Methodologies, modelling trends, and the ontology of professional judicial knowledge*, volume 3. Springer Science & Business Media, 2011.

[de Oliveira Rodrigues et al., 2019] Cleyton Mário de Oliveira Rodrigues, Frederico Luiz Gonçalves de Freitas, Emanoel Francisco Spósito Barreiros, Ryan Ribeiro de Azevedo, and Adauto Trigueiro de Almeida Filho. Legal ontologies over time: A systematic mapping study. *Expert Systems with Applications*, 130:12–30, 2019.

[Distinto et al., 2016] Isabella Distinto, Mathieu d'Aquin, and Enrico Motta. Loted2: An ontology of european public procurement notices. *Semantic Web*, 7(3):267–293, 2016.

[Francart et al., 2019] Thomas Francart, John DANN, Roberto Pappalardo, Carmen Malagon, and Marco Pellegrino. The european legislation identifier. *Knowledge of the Law in the Big Data Age*, 317:137, 2019.

[Gandon et al., 2017] Fabien Gandon, Guido Governatori, and Serena Villata. Normative requirements as linked data. In *The 30th international conference on Legal Knowledge and Information Systems (JURIX 2017)*, 2017.

[Gangemi and Presutti, 2009] Aldo Gangemi and Valentina Presutti. Ontology design patterns. In *Handbook on ontologies*, pages 221–243. Springer, 2009.

[Gangemi et al., 2005] Aldo Gangemi, Maria-Teresa Sagri, and Daniela Tiscornia. A constructive framework for legal ontologies. In *Law and the semantic web*, pages 97–124. Springer, 2005.

[Haapio and Hagan, 2016] Helena Haapio and Margaret Hagan. Design patterns for contracts. In *Networks. Proceedings of the 19th International Legal Informatics Symposium IRIS*, pages 381–388, 2016.

[Haapio et al., 2018] Helena Haapio, Margaret Hagan, Monica Palmirani, and Arianna Rossi. Legal design patterns for privacy. In *Data Protection/LegalTech. Proceedings of the 21th International Legal Informatics Symposium IRIS*, pages 445–450, 2018.

[Hoekstra *et al.*, 2007] Rinke Hoekstra, Joost Breuker, Marcello Di Bello, Alexander Boer, et al. The LKIF core ontology of basic legal concepts. *LOAIT*, 321:43–63, 2007.

[Muñoz-Soro *et al.*, 2016] José Félix Muñoz-Soro, Guillermo Esteban, Oscar Corcho, and Francisco Serón. Pproc, an ontology for transparency in public procurement. *Semantic Web*, 7(3):295–309, 2016.

[Oltramari *et al.*, 2018] Alessandro Oltramari, Dhivya Piraviperumal, Florian Schaub, Shomir Wilson, Sushain Cherivirala, Thomas B Norton, N Cameron Russell, Peter Story, Joel Reidenberg, and Norman Sadeh. Privonto: A semantic framework for the analysis of privacy policies. *Semantic Web*, (Preprint):1–19, 2018.

[Palmirani *et al.*, 2011] Monica Palmirani, Guido Governatori, Antonino Rotolo, Said Tabet, Harold Boley, and Adrian Paschke. Legalruleml: Xml-based rules and norms. In *Rule-Based Modeling and Computing on the Semantic Web*, pages 298–312. Springer, 2011.

[Palmirani *et al.*, 2018] Monica Palmirani, Michele Martoni, Arianna Rossi, Cesare Bartolini, and Livio Robaldo. Pronto: Privacy ontology for legal reasoning. In *International Conference on Electronic Government and the Information Systems Perspective*, pages 139–152. Springer, 2018.

[Pandit *et al.*, 2018] Harshvardhan J Pandit, Kaniz Fatema, Declan O'Sullivan, and Dave Lewis. Gdprtext-gdpr as a linked data resource. In *European Semantic Web Conference*, pages 481–495. Springer, 2018.

[Robaldo and Sun, 2017] Livio Robaldo and Xin Sun. Reified input/output logic: Combining input/output logic and reification to represent norms coming from existing legislation. *Journal of Logic and Computation*, 27(8):2471–2503, 2017.

[Steyskal and Polleres, 2014] Simon Steyskal and Axel Polleres. Defining expressive access policies for linked data using the odrl ontology 2.0. In *Proceedings of the 10th International Conference on Semantic Systems*, pages 20–23. ACM, 2014.

[Valente *et al.*, 1994] Andre Valente, Jost Breuker, et al. A functional ontology of law. *Towards a global expert system in law*, pages 112–136, 1994.

[van Kralingen, 1997] Robert van Kralingen. A conceptual frame-based ontology for the law. In *Proceedings of the First International Workshop on Legal Ontologies*, pages 6–17, 1997.

Valentina Leone
University of Turin
Computer Science Department
via Pessinetto 12, 10149, Turin, Italy
Email: leone@di.unito.it

Luigi Di Caro
University of Turin
Computer Science Department
via Pessinetto 12, 10149, Turin, Italy
Email: dicaro@di.unito.it

Serena Villata
Laboratoire I3S, Campus Sophia Tech
Polytech'Nice-Sophia, 930 route des Colles
BP 145, 06903 Sophia Antipolis CEDEX, France
Email: villata@i3s.unice.fr

5

Detachment in Normative Systems: Examples, Inference Patterns, Properties

XAVIER PARENT

LEENDERT VAN DER TORRE

ABSTRACT.   There is a variety of ways to reason with normative systems. This partly reflects a variety of semantics developed for deontic logic, such as traditional semantics based on possible worlds, or alternative semantics based on algebraic methods, explicit norms or techniques from non-monotonic logic. This diversity raises the question how these reasoning methods are related, and which reasoning method should be chosen for a particular application. In this chapter we discuss the use of examples, inference patterns, and more abstract properties. First, benchmark examples can be used to compare ways to reason with normative systems. We give an overview of several benchmark examples of normative reasoning and deontic logic: Van Fraassen's paradox, Forrester's paradox, Prakken and Sergot's cottage regulations, Jeffrey's disarmament example, Chisholm's paradox, Makinson's Möbius strip, and Horty's priority examples. Moreover, we distinguish various interpretations that can be given to these benchmark examples, such as consistent interpretations, dilemma interpretations, and violability interpretations. Second, inference patterns can be used to compare different ways to reason with normative systems. Instead of analysing the benchmark examples semantically, as it is usually done, in this chapter we use inference patterns to analyse them at a higher level of abstraction. We discuss inference patterns reflecting typical logical properties such as strengthening of the antecedent or weakening of the consequent. Third, more abstract properties can be defined to compare different ways to reason with normative systems. To define these more abstract properties, we first present a formal framework around the notion of detachment. Some of the ten properties we introduce are derived from the inference patterns, but others are more abstract: factual detachment, violation detection, substitution, replacements of equivalents, implication, para-consistency, conjunction, factual monotony, norm monotony, and norm induction. We consider these ten properties as desirable for a reasoning method for

Handbook of Legal AI
© *2022, Xavier Parent and Leendert van der Torre*

normative systems, and thus they can be used also as requirements for the further development of formal methods for normative systems and deontic logic.

1   Introduction

The *Handbook of Deontic Logic and Normative Systems* [Gabbay *et al.*, 2013] describes a debate between the traditional or standard semantics for deontic logic and alternative approaches. The traditional semantics is based on possible world models, whereas many alternative approaches refer to foundations in normative systems, algebraic methods, or non-monotonic logic. In particular, whereas Anderson [1956] argued to refer explicitly to normative systems and also Åqvist [2002] builds on it, various alternative approaches such as input/output logic [Makinson, 1999; Makinson and van der Torre, 2000] represent norms explicitly in the semantics.

Proponents of alternative approaches typically refer to limitations in the traditional approach, although the traditional approach has been generalised or extended to handle many of these limitations [Horty, 2014]. The development of formal and conceptual bridges between traditional and alternative approaches is one of the main current challenges in the area of normative systems and deontic logic. The following three limitations are frequently discussed.

Dilemmas. Examples discussed in the literature are those of Van Fraassen [1973], Makinson [1999]'s Möbius strip, Prakken and Sergot [1996]'s cottage regulations, and Horty [2007]'s priority examples.

Defeasibility. The traditional approach does not distinguish various kinds of defeasibility. Legal norms are often assumed to be defeasible, and there is an increasing interest in philosophy in defeasibility, such as the defeasibility of moral reasons [Horty, 2007; Parent, 2011].

Identity. Many traditional deontic logics validate the formula $\bigcirc(\alpha \mid \alpha)$, read as "$\alpha$ is obligatory given α," "whose intuitive standing is open to question" [Makinson, 1999]. This has been dismissed as a harmless borderline case by proponents of the traditional semantics, but it hinders the representation of fulfilled obligations and violations, playing a central role in normative reasoning. Consider a logic validating identity: the formula $\bigcirc(\alpha \mid \neg\alpha)$, which represents explicitly that there is a violation, is not satisfiable; the obligation of α disappears, in context $\neg\alpha$. (See Section 2 in this chapter.)

Different disciplines and applications have put forward different requirements for the development of formal methods for normative systems and deontic logic. For example, in linguistics compositionality is an important requirement, as deontic statements must be integrated into a larger theory of language. In legal informatics, constitutive and permissive norms play a central role, and legal norms may conflict. It is an open problem whether there can be a unique formal method which can be widely applied across disciplines, or even whether there is a single framework of formal methods which can be used. In this sense, there may be an important distinction between classical and normative reasoning, since there is a unique first order logic for classical logic reasoning about the real world using sets, relations and functions. The situation for normative reasoning may be closer to the situation for non-monotonic reasoning, where also a family of reasoning methods have been proposed, rather than a unique method.

In this chapter we do not want to take a stance on these discussions, but we want to provide techniques and ideas to compare traditional and alternative approaches. We focus on inference patterns and proof-theory instead of semantical considerations. In particular, in this chapter we are interested in the question:

> Which obligations can be detached from a set of rules or conditional norms in a context?

Our angle is different from the more traditional one in terms of inference rules.

There are many frameworks for reasoning about rules and norms, and there are many examples about detachment from normative systems, many of them problematic in some sense. However, there are few properties to compare and analyse ways to detach obligations from rules and norms, and they are scattered over the literature. We are not aware of a systematic overview of these properties. We address our research question by surveying examples, inference patterns and properties from the deontic logic literature.

Examples: Van Fraassen's paradox, Forrester's paradox, Prakken and Sergot's cottage regulations, Jeffrey's disarmament example, Chisholm's paradox, Makinson's Möbius strip, and Horty's priority example. They illustrate challenges for normative reasoning with deontic dilemmas, contrary-to-duty reasoning, defeasible obligations, reasoning by cases, deontic detachment, prioritised obligations, and combinations of these.

Inference Patterns: Conjunction, weakening of the consequent, forbidden conflict, factual detachment, strengthening of the antecedent, violation detection, compliance detection, reinstatement, deontic detachment, transitivity, and various variants of these patterns.

Framework: We develop a *framework* for deontic logics representing and resolving conflicts. By framework we mean that we do not develop a single logic, but many of them. This reflects that there is not a single logic of obligation and permission, but many of them, and which one is to be used depends on the application.

Properties: Factual detachment, violation detection, substitution, replacements of equivalents, implication, paraconsistency, conjunction, factual monotony, norm monotony, and norm induction.

The term "property" is more general than the term "inference pattern". An inference pattern describes a property of a certain form. The inference patterns listed above appear also in the list properties. For instance, factual monotony echoes strengthening of the antecedent. In some cases, we use the same name for both the inference pattern and the corresponding property.

A formal framework to compare formal methods should make as little assumptions as possible, so it is widely applicable. We only assume that the context is a set of facts $\{a, b, \ldots\}$ and that the conditional norms are of the type "if a is the case, then it ought to be the case that b" where a and b are sentences of a propositional language. This is more general than some rule-based languages based on logic programming, where a is restricted to a conjunction of literals and b is a single literal. However, it is less expressive than many other languages, that contain, for example, modal or first order sentences, constitutive and permissive norms, mixed norms such as "if a is permitted, then b is obligatory," nested operators, time, actions, knowledge, and so on. There are few benchmark examples discussed in the literature for such an extended language (see [Governatori and Hashmi, 2015] for a noteworthy exception) and we are not aware of any properties specific for such extended languages. Extending our formal framework and properties to such extended languages is therefore left to further research.

Our framework is built upon the notion of detachment. In traditional approaches "if a, then it ought that b" is typically written as either $a \rightarrow \bigcirc b$ or as $\bigcirc(b|a)$, and in alternative approaches it is sometimes written as (a, b). To be able to compare the different reasoning methods, we will not distinguish between these ways to represent normative systems. The challenge for comparing the formal approaches is that traditional methods typically derive conditional obligations, whereas alternative methods typically do not, maybe because they assume norms do not have truth values and thus they cannot be derived from other norms. Instead, they derive only unconditional obligations. To compare these approaches, one may assume that the derivation of a conditional obligation "if a, then it ought that b" is short for "if the context is exactly $\{a\}$, then the obligation $\bigcirc b$ is detached." Alternatively, the detachment of an obligation for b in context a in alternative systems may be written as the derivation of a pair (a, b), as it is done in the proof theory of input/output logics [Makinson, 1999; Makinson and van der Torre, 2000]. These issues are discussed in more detail in Section 3 of this chapter.

A remark on notation and terminology. We use Greek letters α, β, γ, ... for propositional formulas, and roman letters $a, b, c, \ldots, p, q, \ldots$ for (distinct) propositional atoms. Throughout this chapter the terms "rule" and "conditional norm" will be used interchangeably. The term "rule" is most often used in computer science (with reference to so-called rule-systems and expert systems), and the term "conditional norm" in philosophy and linguistics. Readers should feel free to use the term they prefer. The unconditional obligation for α will be written as $\bigcirc \alpha$, while the conditional obligation for α given β will be written as $O(\alpha|\beta)$, or as (β, α). We do not assume a specific semantics for these constructs.

We give two examples below.

Example 1.1 (Deontic explosion) *The deontic explosion requirement says that we should not derive all obligations from a dilemma. Now consider a dilemma with obligations for $\alpha \wedge \beta$ and $\neg\alpha \wedge \gamma$. It may be tempting to think that an obligation for $\beta \wedge \gamma$ should follow:*

$$\frac{\dfrac{\bigcirc(\alpha \wedge \beta)}{\bigcirc\beta} \quad \dfrac{\bigcirc(\neg\alpha \wedge \gamma)}{\bigcirc\gamma}}{\bigcirc(\beta \wedge \gamma)}$$

Assuming that we have replacements by logical equivalents, if we substitute a for α, $a \vee b$ for β, and $\neg a \vee b$ for γ, then we would derive from the obligations for a and $\neg a$ the obligation for c: deontic explosion. We should not derive the obligation for $\beta \wedge \gamma$, because $\alpha \wedge \beta$ and $\neg\alpha \wedge \gamma$ are classically inconsistent. As we show in Section 2.1, the obligation for $\beta \wedge \gamma$ should be derived only under suitable assumptions.

Example 1.2 (Aggregation) *Consider an iterative approach deriving from the two norms "obligatory c given $a \wedge b$" and "obligatory b given a" that in some sense we have in context a that c is obligatory. This derivation of the obligation for c is made by so-called deontic detachment, because it is derived from the fact a together with the obligation for b. However, if the input is a together with the negation of b, then (intuitively) c should not be derived. However, we can (still intuitively) make the following two derivations. First, we can derive "obligatory a and b given c," a norm which is accepted by the* *two norms (Parent and Van der Torre [2014a; 2014b]).*

$$\frac{\bigcirc(\alpha|\beta \wedge \gamma), \bigcirc(\beta|\gamma)}{\bigcirc(\alpha \wedge \beta|\gamma)} \qquad \frac{(\gamma, \beta), (\gamma \wedge \beta, \alpha)}{(\gamma, \beta \wedge \alpha)}$$

Second, we can also derive the ternary norm "given α, and assuming β, γ is obligatory." However, we would need to extend the language with such expressions as done by Van der Torre [2003] and Xin & Van der Torre [2014]. Different motivations for using a ternary operator can be given. For instance, one may want to reason about exceptions to norms. This is the approach taken by Van der Torre [2003], who works with expressions of the form "given α, γ is obligatory unless β."

This chapter is organised as follows. In Section 2 we introduce benchmark examples of deontic logic, and discuss them using inference patterns. In Section 3, we introduce the formal framework and its properties. Our approach is general and conceptual, and we abstract away from any specific system from literature. The reader will find in the *Handbook of Deontic Logic and Normative Systems* sample systems which can serve to exemplify the general considerations offered in this chapter.

The present chapter does not cover the notion of permission nor does it cover the notion of counts-as conditional. These topics will be a subject for future research. The reader is referred to the chapter by S. O. Hansson and to the chapter by A. Jones and D. Grossi in the aforementioned handbook for an overview of the state-of-the-art and perspectives for future research regarding these notions.

2   Benchmark Examples and Inference Patterns

In this section we discuss benchmark examples of deontic logic. The analysis in this section is based on a number of inference patterns. We do not consider ways in which deontic statements can be given a semantics. These principles must be understood as expressing strict rules. For future reference, we list the inference patterns in Table 1, in the order they are discussed in this section.

pattern	name
$\bigcirc\alpha_1, \bigcirc\alpha_2 \,/\, \bigcirc(\alpha_1 \wedge \alpha_2)$	AND
$\bigcirc\alpha_1, \bigcirc\alpha_2, \Diamond(\alpha_1 \wedge \alpha_2) \,/\, \bigcirc(\alpha_1 \wedge \alpha_2)$	RAND
$\bigcirc\alpha_1 \,/\, \bigcirc(\alpha_1 \vee \alpha_2)$	W
$\bigcirc(\alpha_1\|\beta), \bigcirc(\alpha_2\|\beta), \Diamond(\alpha_1 \wedge \alpha_2) \,/\, \bigcirc(\alpha_1 \wedge \alpha_2\|\beta)$	RANDC
$\bigcirc(\alpha_1\|\beta) \,/\, \bigcirc(\alpha_1 \vee \alpha_2\|\beta)$	WC
$\bigcirc(\alpha_1\|\beta), \bigcirc(\alpha_2\|\beta), \Diamond(\alpha_1 \wedge \alpha_2 \wedge \beta) \,/\, \bigcirc(\alpha_1 \wedge \alpha_2\|\beta)$	RANDC2
$\bigcirc(\alpha_1 \wedge \alpha_2\|\beta_1), \bigcirc(\neg\alpha_1 \wedge \alpha_3\|\beta_1 \wedge \beta_2) \,/\, \bigcirc(\neg\beta_2\|\beta_1)$	FC
$\bigcirc(\alpha\|\beta), \beta \,/\, \bigcirc\alpha$	FD
$\bigcirc(\alpha\|\beta_1) \,/\, \bigcirc(\alpha\|\beta_1 \wedge \beta_2)$	SA
$\bigcirc(\alpha\|\beta_1), \Diamond(\alpha \wedge \beta_1 \wedge \beta_2) \,/\, \bigcirc(\alpha\|\beta_1 \wedge \beta_2)$	RSA
$\bigcirc(\alpha\|\beta) \,/\, \bigcirc(\alpha\|\beta \wedge \neg\alpha)$	VD
$\bigcirc(\alpha\|\beta \wedge \neg\alpha) \,/\, \bigcirc(\alpha\|\beta)$	VD$^-$
$\bigcirc(\alpha\|\beta_1), C \,/\, \bigcirc(\alpha\|\beta_1 \wedge \beta_2)$	RSA$_C$
$\bigcirc(\alpha\|\beta) \,/\, \bigcirc(\alpha\|\beta \wedge \alpha)$	CD
$\bigcirc(\alpha\|\beta \wedge \alpha) \,/\, \bigcirc(\alpha\|\beta)$	CD$^-$
$\bigcirc(\alpha_1\|\beta_1), \bigcirc(\neg\alpha_1 \wedge \alpha_2\|\beta_1 \wedge \beta_2) \,/\, \bigcirc(\alpha_1\|\beta_1 \wedge \beta_2 \wedge \neg\alpha_2)$	RI
$\bigcirc(\alpha_1\|\beta_1), \bigcirc(\neg\alpha_1 \wedge \alpha_2\|\beta_1 \wedge \beta_2),$	
$\bigcirc(\neg\alpha_2\|\beta_1 \wedge \beta_2 \wedge \beta_3) \,/\, \bigcirc(\alpha_1\|\beta_1 \wedge \beta_2 \wedge \beta_3)$	RIO
$\bigcirc(\alpha\|\beta_1), \bigcirc(\alpha\|\beta_2) \,/\, \bigcirc(\alpha\|\beta_1 \vee \beta_2)$	ORA
$\bigcirc(\alpha\|\beta), \bigcirc\beta \,/\, \bigcirc\alpha$	DD
$\bigcirc(\alpha\|\beta), \bigcirc(\beta\|\gamma) \,/\, \bigcirc(\alpha\|\gamma)$	T
$\bigcirc(\alpha\|\beta \wedge \gamma), \bigcirc(\beta\|\gamma) \,/\, \bigcirc(\alpha\|\gamma)$	CT
$\bigcirc(\alpha\|\beta \wedge \gamma), \bigcirc(\beta\|\gamma) \,/\, \bigcirc(\alpha \wedge \beta\|\gamma)$	ACT

Table 1. Inference patterns

The letter C in RSA$_C$ stands for the condition: there is no premise $\bigcirc(\alpha'|\beta')$ such that $\beta_1 \wedge \beta_2$ logically implies β', β' logically implies β_1 and not vice versa, α and α' are contradictory and $\alpha \wedge \beta'$ is consistent. RSA$_C$ is not a rule in the usual proof-theoretic sense. For it has a statement that quantifies over all other premises as an auxiliary condition. Thus the rule is not on a par with the other rules, like for instance weakening of the output.

2.1 Van Fraassen's Paradox

We first discuss deontic explosion in Van Fraassen's paradox, then the trade-off between on the one hand "ought implies can" and on the other hand the representation of violations in the violation detection problem, whether it is forbidden to put oneself into a dilemma, and finally the use of priorities to resolve conflicts.

2.1.1 Deontic Explosion: Conjunction versus Weakening

It is a well-known problem from paraconsistent logic that the removal of all inconsistent formulas from the language is insufficient to reason in the presence of a contradiction, because there may still be explosion in the sense that all formulas of the language are derived from a contradiction. The following derivation illustrates how we can derive q from p and $\neg p$ in propositional logic, where all formulas in the derivation are classically consistent.

$$\frac{\dfrac{p}{q \vee p} \quad \neg p}{\dfrac{q \wedge \neg p}{q}}$$

The rules of replacements of logical equivalents, $\vee$-introduction, $\wedge$-introduction, and $\wedge$-elimination are used in this derivation.

A similar phenomenon occurs in deontic logic, if we reason about deontic dilemmas or conflicts, that is situations where $\bigcirc p$ and $\bigcirc \neg p$ both hold. Van der Torre and Tan [2000] call this deontic explosion problem "Van Fraassen's paradox," because Van Fraassen [1973] gave the following (informal) analysis of dilemmas in deontic logic. He rejects the conjunction pattern AND:

$$\text{AND:} \frac{\bigcirc \alpha_1, \bigcirc \alpha_2}{\bigcirc (\alpha_1 \wedge \alpha_2)}$$

This is because AND warrants the move from $\bigcirc p \wedge \bigcirc \neg p$ to $\bigcirc (p \wedge \neg p)$, and such a conclusion is not consistent with the principle 'ought implies can', formalised as $\neg \bigcirc (p \wedge \neg p)$. However, he does not want to reject the conjunction pattern in all cases. In particular, he wants to be able to derive $\bigcirc (p \wedge q)$ from $\bigcirc p \wedge \bigcirc q$ when p and q are distinct propositional atoms. His suggestion is that a restriction should be placed on the conjunction pattern: one derives $\bigcirc (\alpha_1 \wedge \alpha_2)$ from $\bigcirc \alpha_1$ and $\bigcirc \alpha_2$ only if $\alpha_1 \wedge \alpha_2$ is consistent. He calls the latter inference pattern *Consistent Aggregation*, renamed to restricted conjunction (RAND) by Van der Torre and Tan in their following variant of Van Fraassen's suggestion.

Example 2.1 (Van Fraassen's paradox [Van der Torre & Tan, 2000])
Consider a deontic logic without nested modal operators in which dilemmas like $\bigcirc p \wedge \bigcirc \neg p$ are consistent, but which validates $\neg \bigcirc \bot$, where $\bot$ stands for any contradiction like $p \wedge \neg p$. Moreover, assume that it satisfies replacement of logical equivalents and at least the following two inference patterns Restricted Conjunction (RAND), also called consistent aggregation, and Weakening (W), where $\Diamond \phi$ can be read as "ϕ is possible" (possibility is not

necessarily the same as consistency).

$$\text{RAND:} \frac{\bigcirc\alpha_1, \bigcirc\alpha_2, \Diamond(\alpha_1 \wedge \alpha_2)}{\bigcirc(\alpha_1 \wedge \alpha_2)} \qquad \text{W:} \frac{\bigcirc\alpha_1}{\bigcirc(\alpha_1 \vee \alpha_2)}$$

Moreover, assume the two premises 'Honor thy father or thy mother!' $\bigcirc(f \vee m)$ *and* 'Honor not thy mother!' $\bigcirc\neg m$. *The left derivation of Figure 1 illustrates how the desired conclusion* 'thou shalt honor thy father' $\bigcirc f$ *can be derived from the premises. Unfortunately, the right derivation of Figure 1 illustrates that we cannot accept restricted conjunction and weakening in a monadic deontic logic, because we can derive* every $\bigcirc\beta$ *from* $\bigcirc\alpha$ *and* $\bigcirc\neg\alpha$.

$$\frac{\dfrac{\bigcirc(f \vee m) \quad \bigcirc\neg m}{\bigcirc(f \wedge \neg m)} \text{ RAND}}{\bigcirc f} \text{ W} \qquad \frac{\dfrac{\dfrac{\bigcirc\alpha}{\bigcirc(\alpha \vee \beta)} \text{ W} \quad \bigcirc\neg\alpha}{\bigcirc(\neg\alpha \wedge \beta)} \text{ RAND}}{\bigcirc\beta} \text{ W}$$

Figure 1. Van Fraassen's paradox

Van Fraassen's paradox has a counterpart in dyadic deontic logic. The paradox consists in deriving $\bigcirc(\gamma|\beta)$ from $\bigcirc(\alpha|\beta)$ and $\bigcirc(\neg\alpha|\beta)$ using the following rules of *Restricted Conjunction for the Consequent* (RANDC) and *Weakening of the Consequent* (WC).

$$\text{RANDC:} \frac{\bigcirc(\alpha_1|\beta), \bigcirc(\alpha_2|\beta), \Diamond(\alpha_1 \wedge \alpha_2)}{\bigcirc(\alpha_1 \wedge \alpha_2|\beta)} \qquad \text{WC:} \frac{\bigcirc(\alpha_1|\beta)}{\bigcirc(\alpha_1 \vee \alpha_2|\beta)}$$

2.1.2 Violation Detection Problem: Unrestricted versus Restricted Conjunction

Whereas $p \wedge \neg p$ can not be derived in a paraconsistent logic, we can consistently represent the formula $\bigcirc(p \wedge \neg p)$ in a modal logic, and we can block deontic explosion using a minimal modal logic [Chellas, 1980]. This raises the question whether we should accept the conjunction pattern unrestrictedly or in its restricted form.

The choice between the two can be illustrated as follows. Suppose we can derive the obligation $\bigcirc(p \wedge \neg p)$ from $\bigcirc(p)$ and $\bigcirc(\neg p)$ without deriving $\bigcirc f$, or any other counterintuitive consequence. In that case, is $\bigcirc(p \wedge \neg p)$ by itself a consequence we want to block? This presents us with a choice. On the one hand we would like to block $\bigcirc(p \wedge \neg p)$, because it contradicts the "ought implies can" principle. On the other hand, we would like to allow the derivation of $\bigcirc(p \wedge \neg p)$, because such a formula represents explicitly the fact that there is a dilemma.

This choice is even more subtle in dyadic deontic logic. There is the extra question as to whether the "ought implies can" reading implies that the obligation in the consequent must only be consistent in itself, or consistent with the antecedent too. The latter requirement is represented by the following variant of the *Restricted Conjunction for the Consequent* pattern, which we call RANDC2.

$$\text{RANDC2} : \frac{\bigcirc(\alpha_1|\beta), \bigcirc(\alpha_2|\beta), \Diamond(\alpha_1 \wedge \alpha_2 \wedge \beta)}{\bigcirc(\alpha_1 \wedge \alpha_2|\beta)}$$

On the one hand, given $\bigcirc(p|\neg p \vee \neg q)$ and $\bigcirc(q|\neg p \vee \neg q)$, we would like to block the derivation of $\bigcirc(p \wedge q|\neg p \vee \neg q)$ because "ought implies can". On the other hand, we would like to be able to derive it in order to make explicit that $\neg p \vee \neg q$ gives rise to a dilemma, and is not consistent with the fulfillment of the two obligations appearing as premises.

The alternative restricted conjunction pattern RANDC2 highlights the distinction between what we call the violability and the temporal interpretation of dyadic deontic logic. The former interprets the obligation $O(\alpha|\beta)$ as "given that β has been settled beyond repair, we should do α to make the best out of the sad circumstances" [Hansson, 1969] and the latter as "if α is the case now, what should be the case next?" The violability interpretation says that $O(\neg \alpha|\alpha)$ represents that α is a violation. For example, if you are going to kill, then do it gently. The temporal interpretation says that the present situation must be changed—which may or may not indicate a violation. For example, the temporal interpretation may be used to express a conditional obligation like "if the light is on, turn it off!"

We would like to point out that the violability interpretation is more expressive, in the sense that the temporal interpretation can be represented by introducing distinct propositional letters for what is the case now, and what is the case in the next moment. For example, "if the light is on, turn it off" can be represented by $\bigcirc(\neg on_2|on_1)$, where on_1 represents that the light is on now, and on_2 that it is on at the next moment in time. In the temporal interpretation, however, it seems impossible to represent all violations in a natural way. Thus, a temporal interpretation with future directed obligations only seems to be a strong limitation.

We use the name "violation detection problem" to refer to the phenomenon that with the restricted conjunction pattern the representation (and hence the detection) of violations is made impossible. We continue the discussion on the violation detection problem in Section 2.2, where we discuss restricted inference patterns formalising contrary-to-duty reasoning.

2.1.3 Forbidden Conflicts

Here is another question raised by dilemmas: is it forbidden to create a dilemma? The following inference pattern is called *Forbidden Conflict* (FC). If the inference pattern is accepted, then it is not allowed to bring about a conflict, because a conflict is sub-ideal.

$$\text{FC} : \frac{\bigcirc(\alpha_1 \wedge \alpha_2 | \beta_1), \bigcirc(\neg \alpha_1 \wedge \alpha_3 | \beta_1 \wedge \beta_2)}{\bigcirc(\neg \beta_2 | \beta_1)}$$

Here is an example, taken from Van der Torre and Tan [1997]. Assume the premises $\bigcirc k$ and $\bigcirc(p \wedge \neg k | d)$, where k can be read as 'keeping a promise', p as 'preventing a disaster' and d as 'a disaster will occur if nothing is done to prevent it'. (FC) yields $\bigcirc \neg d$. There are situations where this is the right outcome. Consider a person having the obligation to keep a promise to show up at a birthday party. We have $\bigcirc k$, but also $\bigcirc(p \wedge \neg k | d)$. She does not want to go, and so before leaving she does something that might result in a disaster later on, like leaving the coffee machine on. During the party, she leaves and goes home, using her second obligation as an excuse. Nobody will contest that leaving the machine on (on purpose) was a violation already, viz. $\bigcirc \neg d$.

An instance of this inference pattern has been discussed in defeasible deontic logic, and we return to it in Section 2.3.

2.1.4 Resolving Dilemmas

To resolve a conflict between an obligation for p and an obligation for $\neg p$, we need additional information. For example, a total preference order on sets of propositions can resolve all dilemmas by picking the preferred set of obligations among the alternatives of the dilemma, and weaker relations on sets of propositions such as a total pre-order or a partial order leaves some dilemmas unresolved.

The most studied source for a preference order over sets of propositions is a preference order over propositions, which is then lifted to an order on sets of propositions. For example, an ordering on obligations can be derived from an ordering on the authorities who created the obligations, or the moment in time they were created. The level of preference of an obligation may reflect its priority.

Consider three obligations with priority 3, 2 and 1, and a dilemma between the first and the latter two. To represent the priority of an obligation, we write it in the $\bigcirc$ notation. A higher number reflects a higher priority.

$$\{③(p \wedge q), ②\neg p, ①\neg q\}$$

In other words, we can either satisfy the most important obligation $③(p \wedge q)$, or two less important obligations $②\neg p$ and $①\neg q$. Can this dilemma be resolved? There are various well known possibilities in the area of non-monotonic logic. Whether they can be used depends on the origin of the priorities and the application.

The issue of lifting priorities from obligations to sets of them gets more challenging when we consider conditional obligations and deontic detachment, as discussed later on in Section 2.7.

2.2 Forrester's Paradox

We first discuss factual detachment in Forrester's paradox, then the problematic derivation of secondary obligations from primary ones, and finally what we call the violation detection problem for Forrester's paradox.

2.2.1 Factual Detachment versus Conjunction

Forrester's paradox consists of the four sentences 'Smith should not kill Jones,' 'if Smith kills Jones, then he should do it gently,' 'Smith kills Jones', and 'killing someone gently logically implies killing him.' The preference based models of dyadic deontic logic give a natural representation of the two obligations: not killing is preferred to gentle killing, and both are preferred to other forms of killing. However, the following example illustrates that it is less clear how to combine dyadic obligation with factual detachment, deriving unconditional obligations from conditional ones.

Example 2.2 (Forrester's paradox) *Assume a dyadic deontic logic without nested modal operators that has at least replacement of logical equivalents, the Conjunction pattern* AND *and the following inference pattern called factual detachment* FD.

$$\text{FD}: \frac{\bigcirc(\alpha|\beta), \beta}{\bigcirc\alpha}$$

Furthermore, assume the following premise set with background knowledge that gentle murder implies murder $\vdash g \to k$.

$$S = \{\bigcirc(\neg k|\top), \bigcirc(g|k), k\}$$

The set S represents the Forrester paradox when k is read as 'Smith kills Jones' and g as 'Smith kills Jones gently.' We say that the last obligation is a contrary-to-duty obligation with respect to the first obligation, because its antecedent is contradictory with the consequent of the first obligation. Figure 2 visualizes how we can represent the concept of contrary-to-duty as a binary relation among dyadic obligations: the obligation $\bigcirc(\alpha_2 \mid \beta_2)$ is a contrary-to-duty with respect to $\bigcirc(\alpha_1 \mid \beta_1)$ if and only if $\beta_2 \wedge \alpha_1$ is inconsistent.

The derivation in Figure 3 illustrates how the obligation $\bigcirc(\neg k \wedge g)$, i.e. $\bigcirc(\bot)$, can be derived from S by FD *and* AND.

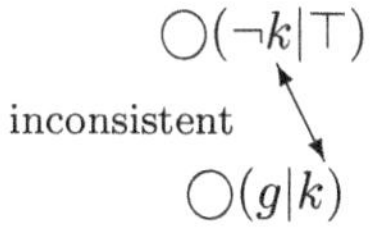

$$\bigcirc(\neg k | \top)$$

inconsistent

$$\bigcirc(g|k)$$

Figure 2. $\bigcirc(g|k)$ is a contrary-to-duty obligation with respect to $\bigcirc(\neg k|\top)$

$$\dfrac{\bigcirc(\neg k|\top) \quad \top}{\bigcirc(\neg k)} \text{ FD} \qquad \dfrac{\bigcirc(g|k) \quad k}{\bigcirc(g)} \text{ FD}$$
$$\dfrac{}{\bigcirc(\neg k \wedge g)} \text{ AND}$$

Figure 3. Forrester's paradox

Forrester's paradox can be given two interpretations. First, the dilemma interpretation says that the two obligations give rise to a dilemma, just like the obligations $\bigcirc p$ and $\bigcirc \neg p$ in Van Fraassen's paradox. Consequently, according to the dilemma interpretation, there is no problem, the derivation of $\bigcirc(\bot)$ just reflects the fact that there is a dilemma.

The coherent interpretation appeals to the independent and seemingly plausible principle 'ought implies can', $\neg \bigcirc (\bot|\alpha)$. According to this interpretation, the Forrester set is intuitively consistent with the 'ought implies can' principle, and so there is no dilemma, just an obligation to act as good as possible in the sub-ideal situation where the primary obligation has been violated.

There is a consensus in the literature that the example should be given a coherent interpretation, and that the dilemma interpretation is wrong.

2.2.2 Deriving Secondary Obligations from Primary Ones: Strengthening of the Antecedent versus Weakening of the Consequent

The following example shows that Forrester's paradox can be used also to illustrate that combining the desirable inference patterns strengthening of the antecedent and weakening of the consequent is problematic in dyadic deontic logic. For example, strengthening of the antecedent is used to derive 'Smith should not kill Jones in the morning' $\bigcirc(\neg k|m)$ from the obligation 'Smith should not kill Jones' $\bigcirc(\neg k|\top)$ and weakening of the consequent is used to derive 'Smith should not kill Jones' $\bigcirc(\neg k|\top)$ from the obligation 'Smith should drive on the right side of the street and not kill Jones' $\bigcirc(r \wedge \neg k|\top)$.

Example 2.3 (Forrester's paradox, cont'd [Van der Torre and Tan, 2000]) *Assume a dyadic deontic logic without nested modal operators that has at least replacement of logical equivalents and the following inference patterns* Strengthening of the Antecedent *(SA), the* Conjunction pattern for the Consequent *(ANDC) and* Weakening of the Consequent *(WC) .*

$$\text{SA} : \frac{\bigcirc(\alpha|\beta_1)}{\bigcirc(\alpha|\beta_1 \wedge \beta_2)} \qquad \text{ANDC} : \frac{\bigcirc(\alpha_1|\beta), \bigcirc(\alpha_2|\beta)}{\bigcirc(\alpha_1 \wedge \alpha_2|\beta)} \qquad \text{WC} : \frac{\bigcirc(\alpha_1|\beta)}{\bigcirc(\alpha_1 \vee \alpha_2|\beta)}$$

The derivation in Figure 4 illustrates how the obligation $\bigcirc(\neg k \wedge g|k)$, *i.e.* $\bigcirc(\bot|k)$, *can be derived from S by* SA *and* ANDC. *Note that the dyadic obligation* $\bigcirc(\neg k \mid k)$ *can be given only a violability interpretation in this example, not a temporal interpretation, because it is impossible to undo a killing. That is, this dyadic obligation can be read only as "if Smith kills Jones, then this is a violation."*

$$\frac{\dfrac{\bigcirc(\neg k|\top)}{\bigcirc(\neg k|k)} \text{ SA} \qquad \bigcirc(g|k)}{\bigcirc(\neg k \wedge g|k)} \text{ ANDC} \qquad\qquad \frac{\dfrac{\dfrac{\bigcirc(\neg k|\top)}{\bigcirc(\neg g|\top)} \text{ WC}}{\bigcirc(\neg g|k)} \text{ RSA} \qquad \bigcirc(g|k)}{\bigcirc(\neg g \wedge g|k)} \text{ ANDC}$$

Figure 4. Forrester's paradox

The derivation is blocked when SA *is replaced by the following inference pattern* Restricted Strengthening of the Antecedent *(RSA).*

$$\text{RSA} : \frac{\bigcirc(\alpha|\beta_1), \Diamond(\alpha \wedge \beta_1 \wedge \beta_2)}{\bigcirc(\alpha|\beta_1 \wedge \beta_2)}$$

However, the obligation $\bigcirc(\bot|k)$ *can still be derived from S by* WC, RSA *and* ANDC. *This derivation from the set of obligations is represented on the right hand side of Figure 4. Like in Example 2.2, we can give the set a dilemma or a coherent interpretation.*

The underlying problem of the counterintuitive derivation in Figure 4 is the derivation of $\bigcirc(\neg g \mid k)$ *from the first premise* $\bigcirc(\neg k \mid \top)$ *by* WC *and* RSA, *because it derives a contrary-to-duty obligation from its own primary obligation.*

Since there is consensus that Forrester's paradox should be given a coherent interpretation, Forrester's paradox in Example 2.3 shows that combining strengthening of the antecedent and weakening of the consequent is problematic for *all* deontic logics.

2.2.3 Violation Detection Problem: Restricted versus Unrestricted Strengthening of the Antecedent

The choice between the unrestricted version and the restricted version of the law of strengthening of the antecedent has some similarity with the choice between the unrestricted version and the restricted version of the law of conjunction. This can be illustrated as follows. Suppose we have the obligation $\bigcirc(\neg k \mid \top)$. In that case, is $\bigcirc(\neg k \mid k)$ a consequence we want to block? This presents us with a choice. On the one hand, we would like to block $\bigcirc(\neg k \mid k)$, because it contradicts the "ought implies can" principle. On the other hand, we would like to allow the derivation of $\bigcirc(\neg k \mid k)$, because this formula represents explicitly that there is a violation. (Cf. our explanatory comments on the violability interpretation, on p. 10.)

The following inference pattern *Violation Detection* (VD) formalizes the intuition that an obligation cannot be defeated by only violating it, and represents a solution to the violation detection problem. The VD pattern models the intuition that after violation the obligation to do α is still in force. Even if you drive too fast, you are still obliged to obey the speed limit.

$$\text{VD} : \frac{\bigcirc(\alpha \mid \beta)}{\bigcirc(\alpha \mid \beta \wedge \neg \alpha)} \qquad \text{VD}^- : \frac{\bigcirc(\alpha \mid \beta \wedge \neg \alpha)}{\bigcirc(\alpha \mid \beta)}$$

The inverse pattern VD$^-$ says that violations do not come out of the blue. Although this inference pattern may seem intuitive at first sight, it appears too strong on further inspection.

Example 2.4 (Metro) *Consider the following derivation.*

$$\frac{\dfrac{\bigcirc(\alpha \mid \beta)}{\bigcirc(\alpha \mid \beta \wedge \neg \alpha)} \text{ VD}}{\bigcirc(\alpha \mid \alpha \vee \beta)} \text{ VD}^-$$

For example, assume that if you travel by metro, you must have a ticket. We can derive that traveling by metro without a ticket is a violation. The two inference patterns together would derive that if you travel by metro or you buy a ticket, then you must buy a ticket. This is counterintuitive, because buying a ticket without traveling by metro does not involve any obligations. The example illustrates how reasoning about violations only can lead to the wrong conclusions.

Normative systems typically associate sanctions with violations, as an incentive for agents to obey the norms. Such sanctions can sometimes be expressed as contrary-to-duty obligations: the sanction to pay a fine if you do not return the book to the library in time, can be modelled as a contrary-to-duty obligation to pay the fine. By symmetry, though this is less often implemented in normative systems, rewards can be associated with compliance of obligations. In modal logic, an obligation for α is fulfilled if we have $\alpha \wedge \bigcirc \alpha$.

The following inference pattern *Compliance Detection* (CD) formalizes the intuition that an obligation cannot be defeated by only complying with it, analogous to the *Violation Detection* (VD) pattern.

$$\text{CD} : \frac{\bigcirc(\alpha|\beta)}{\bigcirc(\alpha|\beta \wedge \alpha)} \qquad \text{CD}^- : \frac{\bigcirc(\alpha|\beta \wedge \alpha)}{\bigcirc(\alpha|\beta)}$$

The following example illustrates that the inference pattern CD should not be confused with the inverse of CD$^-$, which seems to say that fulfilled obligations do not come out of the blue. Although this inference pattern may seem intuitive at first sight, it is highly counterintuitive on further inspection.

Example 2.5 (Forrester, continued) *Consider the following derivation.*

$$\frac{\dfrac{\bigcirc(\alpha \wedge \beta|\alpha)}{\bigcirc(\alpha \wedge \beta|\alpha \wedge \beta)} \text{ CD}}{\bigcirc(\alpha \wedge \beta|\top)} \text{ CD}^-$$

You should kill gently, if you kill $\bigcirc(k \wedge g|k)$. Hence, by CD, you should kill gently, if you kill gently $\bigcirc(k \wedge g\,|\,k \wedge g)$ (a fulfilled obligation). However, this does not mean that there is an unconditional obligation to kill gently $\bigcirc(k \wedge g|\top)$. Hence, the inference pattern CD$^-$ should not be valid.

Without the CD pattern, we say that the fulfilled obligation "disappears," analogous to violations. A fulfilled obligation also disappears when we have as an axiom of the logic that $\bigcirc(\alpha|\beta) \leftrightarrow \bigcirc(\alpha \wedge \beta|\beta)$, because in that case $\bigcirc(\alpha \wedge \beta|\beta)$ does not hold because β is compliant with a norm.

2.3 Prakken and Sergot's Cottage Regulations

We first discuss the extension of Forrester's paradox with defeasible obligations, then we return to the violation detection problem, and finally we discuss reinstatement.

2.3.1 Violations and Exceptions

The so-called cottage regulations are introduced by Prakken and Sergot [1996] to illustrate the distinction between contrary-to-duty reasoning and defeasible reasoning based on exceptional circumstances. It is an extended version of the Forrester or gentle murderer paradox discussed in Section 2.2. The following example is an alphabetic variant of the original example, because we replaced s, to be read as 'the cottage is by the sea,' by d, to be read as 'there is a dog.' Moreover, as is common, instead of representing background knowledge that w implies f, Prakken and Sergot represent a white fence by $w \wedge f$.

Example 2.6 (Cottage regulations [van der Torre and Tan, 1997])
Assume a deontic logic that validates at least replacement of logical equivalents and the inference pattern RSA_C.

$$\text{RSA}_C : \frac{\bigcirc(\alpha|\beta_1), C}{\bigcirc(\alpha|\beta_1 \wedge \beta_2)}$$

C: there is no premise $\bigcirc(\alpha'|\beta')$ *such that* $\beta_1 \wedge \beta_2$ *logically implies* β', β' *logically implies* β_1 *and not vice versa,* α *and* α' *are contradictory and* $\alpha \wedge \beta'$ *is consistent. [van der Torre, 1994]*

RSA_C *formalises a principle of specificity to deal with exceptional circumstances. It is illustrated with Figure 5 (a). Suppose we are given these rules: you ought not to eat with your fingers; if you are served asparagus, you ought to eat with your fingers. One does not want to be able to strengthen the first obligation into: if you are served asparagus, you ought not to eat with your fingers. Such a strengthening is blocked by* RSA_C.
Now, assume the obligations

$$S = \{\bigcirc(\neg f|\top), \bigcirc(w \wedge f|f), \bigcirc(w \wedge f|d)\},$$

where f can be read as 'there is a fence around your house,' $w \wedge f$ as 'there is a white fence around your house' and d as 'you have a dog.' Notice that $\bigcirc(w \wedge f|f)$ *is a contrary-to-duty obligation with respect to* $\bigcirc(\neg f|\top)$ *and* $\bigcirc(w \wedge f|d)$ *is not. If all we know is that there is a fence and a dog $(f \wedge d)$, then the first obligation in S is intuitively overridden, and therefore it cannot be violated. Hence, the obligation* $\bigcirc(\neg f | f \wedge d)$ *should not be derivable. However, if all we know is that there is a fence without a dog (f), then the first obligation in S is intuitively not overridden, and therefore it is violated. Hence, the obligation* $\bigcirc(\neg f|f)$ *should be derivable.*
One should be careful not to treat both $\bigcirc(w \wedge f|f)$ *and* $\bigcirc(w \wedge f|d)$ *as more specific obligations that override the obligation* $\bigcirc(\neg f|\top)$: *this does not hold for* $\bigcirc(w \wedge f|f)$. *The latter obligation should be treated as a contrary-to-duty obligation, i.e. as a case of violation. This interference of specificity and contrary-to-duty is represented in Figure 5. This figure should be read as follows. Each arrow is a condition: a two-headed arrow is a consistency*

check, and a single-headed arrow is a logical implication. For example, the condition C formalizes that an obligation $\bigcirc(\alpha|\beta)$ is overridden by $\bigcirc(\alpha'|\beta')$ if the conclusions are contradictory (a consistency check, the double-headed arrow) and the condition of the overriding obligation is more specific (β' logically implies β). Case (a) represents criteria for overridden defeasibility, and case (b) represents criteria for contrary-to-duty. Case (c) shows that the pair $\bigcirc(\neg f|\top)$ and $\bigcirc(w \wedge f|f)$ can be viewed as overridden defeasibility as well as contrary-to-duty.

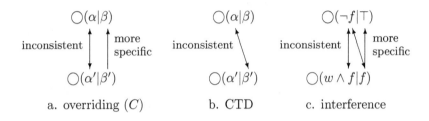

Figure 5. Specificity and CTD

2.3.2 Violation Detection Problem for Defeasible Obligations

What is most striking about the cottage regulations is the observation that when the premise $\bigcirc(\neg f\,|\,\top)$ is violated by f, then the obligation for $\neg f$ should be derivable, but not when $\bigcirc(\neg f|\top)$ is overridden by $f \wedge d$. In other words, we have to distinguish violations from exceptions.

In approaches where $\bigcirc(\alpha|\beta)$ implies that $\alpha \wedge \beta$ is consistent, we cannot represent this difference by deriving $\bigcirc(\neg f|f)$ and not deriving $\bigcirc(\neg f|d \wedge f)$. In this sense, this is again an example of the violation detection problem.

We can use priorities to represent the specificity example, by giving the more specific obligation a higher priority. Many conditional logics have specificity built in, but this must be combined with other conflict resolution methods, for example based on time or authority. This is an issue of reasoning about uncertainty, default reasoning, and nonmonotonic logic.

2.3.3 Reinstatement

The question raised by the inference pattern *Reinstatement* (RI) is whether an obligation can be overridden by an overriding obligation that itself is violated. The obligation $\bigcirc(\alpha_1|\beta_1)$ is overridden by $\bigcirc(\neg\alpha_1 \wedge \alpha_2|\beta_1 \wedge \beta_2)$ for $\beta_1 \wedge \beta_2$, but is it also overridden for $\beta_1 \wedge \beta_2 \wedge \neg\alpha_2$? If the last conclusion is not accepted, then the first obligation α_1 should be in force again. Hence, the original obligation is reinstated.

$$\text{RI} : \frac{\bigcirc(\alpha_1|\beta_1), \bigcirc(\neg\alpha_1 \wedge \alpha_2|\beta_1 \wedge \beta_2)}{\bigcirc(\alpha_1|\beta_1 \wedge \beta_2 \wedge \neg\alpha_2)}$$

Suppose you are in the street, and see a child's bike unattended. As a general rule, you should not take the bike, viz. $\bigcirc\neg t$ where t is for taking the bike. Now, suppose you also observe an elderly neighbor collapse with what might be a heart attack. You are a block away from the nearest phone from which you could call for help. In that more specific situation, you should take the bike and go call for help, $\bigcirc(t \wedge h \,|\, e)$, where e and h are for an elderly neighbor collapses and go call for help, respectively. The obligation $\bigcirc\neg t$ is overriden by $\bigcirc(t \wedge h|e)$ for e. But it is not overriden for $e \wedge \neg g$. Of course, if you do not go for help, then the prohibition of t remains.

The following inference pattern RIO is a variant of the previous inference pattern RI, in which the overriding obligation is not factually defeated but overridden. The obligation $\bigcirc(\alpha_1|\beta_1)$ is overridden by $\bigcirc(\neg\alpha_1 \wedge \alpha_2|\beta_1 \wedge \beta_2)$ for $\beta_1 \wedge \beta_2$, and the latter is overridden by $\bigcirc(\neg\alpha_2|\beta_1 \wedge \beta_2 \wedge \beta_3)$ for $\beta_1 \wedge \beta_2 \wedge \beta_3$. The inference pattern RIO says that an obligation cannot be overridden by an obligation that is itself overridden. Hence, an overridden obligation becomes reinstated when its overriding obligation is itself overridden.

$$\text{RIO} : \frac{\bigcirc(\alpha_1|\beta_1), \bigcirc(\neg\alpha_1 \wedge \alpha_2|\beta_1 \wedge \beta_2), \bigcirc(\neg\alpha_2|\beta_1 \wedge \beta_2 \wedge \beta_3)}{\bigcirc(\alpha_1|\beta_1 \wedge \beta_2 \wedge \beta_3)}$$

Example: you should not kill; if you find yourselves in a situation of self-defence, you should kill; if you find yourselves in a situation of self-defence, but your opponent is weak, you should not kill.

Van der Torre and Tan [1997] argue that Reinstatement does not hold in general, for example it does not hold for obligations under uncertainty. However, they argue also that these patterns hold for so-called prima facie obligations. The notion of prima facie obligation was introduced by Ross [1930]. He writes: 'I suggest '*prima facie* duty' or 'conditional duty' as a brief way of referring to the characteristic (quite distinct from that of being a duty proper) which an act has, in virtue of being of a certain kind (e.g. the keeping of a promise), of being an act which would be a duty proper if it were not at the same time of another kind which is morally significant' [Ross, 1930, p.19]. A prima facie duty is a duty proper when it is not overridden by another prima facie duty. When a prima facie obligation is overridden, it is not a proper duty but it is still in force: 'When we think ourselves justified in breaking, and indeed morally obliged to break, a promise [...] we do not for the moment cease to recognize a prima facie duty to keep our promise' [Ross, 1930, p.28].

Van der Torre and Tan argue also that the inference pattern Forbidden Conflict, discussed in Section 2.1.3, does not hold in general, but it holds for prima facie obligations. If the inference pattern is accepted, then it is not allowed to bring about a conflict, because a conflict is sub-ideal, even when it can be resolved.

2.4   Jeffrey's Disarmament Paradox

In general, reasoning by cases is a desirable property of reasoning with conditionals. In this reasoning scheme, a certain fact is proven by proving it for a set of mutually exclusive and exhaustive circumstances. For example, assume that you want to know whether you want to go to the beach. If you desire to go to the beach when it rains, and you desire to go to the beach when it does not rain, then you may conclude by this scheme 'reasoning by cases' that you desire to go to the beach under all circumstances. The two cases considered here are rain and no rain. This kind of reasoning schemes can be formalized by the following derivation: *If 'α if β' and 'α if not β,' then 'α* **regardless of** *β.'* Formally, if we write the conditional 'α if β' by $\beta > \alpha$, then it is represented by the following disjunction pattern for the antecedent.

$$\text{ORA:} \frac{\beta > \alpha, \neg\beta > \alpha}{\top > \alpha}$$

The following example illustrates that the disjunction pattern for the antecedent combined with strengthening of the antecedent derives counterintuitive consequences in dyadic deontic logic. Example 2.7 is based on the following classic illustration of Jeffrey [1983], see also the discussion by Thomason and Horty [1996].

Example 2.7 (Disarmament paradox [Van der Torre and Tan, 2000])
Assume a deontic logic that validates at least replacement of logical equivalents and the two inference patterns RSA *and the* Disjunction pattern for the Antecedent *(*ORA*),*

$$\text{ORA} : \frac{\bigcirc(\alpha|\beta_1), \bigcirc(\alpha|\beta_2)}{\bigcirc(\alpha|\beta_1 \vee \beta_2)}$$

and assume as premises the obligations 'we ought to be disarmed if there will be a nuclear war', 'we ought to be disarmed if there will be no war' *and* 'we ought to be armed if we have peace if and only if we are armed'. *They may be formalized as* $\bigcirc(d|w)$, $\bigcirc(d|\neg w)$ *and* $\bigcirc(\neg d|d \leftrightarrow w)$, *respectively. The derivation in Figure 6 shows how we can derive the counterintuitive* $\bigcirc(d \wedge \neg d|d \leftrightarrow w)$. *The derived obligation is inconsistent in most deontic logics, whereas intuitively the set of premises is consistent. The derivation of* $\bigcirc(d|d \leftrightarrow w)$ *is counterintuitive, because it is not possible to fulfill this* *obligation together with the obligation $\bigcirc(d \mid \neg w)$ it is derived from. The contradictory fulfillments are respectively $d \wedge w$ and $d \wedge \neg w$.*

$$\frac{\dfrac{\dfrac{\bigcirc(d|w) \quad \bigcirc(d|\neg w)}{\bigcirc(d|\top)} \text{ ORA}}{\bigcirc(d|d \leftrightarrow w)} \text{ RSA} \qquad \bigcirc(\neg d|d \leftrightarrow w)}{\bigcirc(d \wedge \neg d|d \leftrightarrow w)} \text{ AND}$$

Figure 6. The disarmament paradox

In other words, in this derivation the obligation $\bigcirc(d|d \leftrightarrow w)$ is considered to be counterintuitive, because it is not grounded in the premises. If $d \leftrightarrow w$ and w (the antecedent of the first premise) are true then d is trivially true, and if $d \leftrightarrow w$ and $\neg w$ (the antecedent of the second premise) are true then d is trivially false. In other words, if $d \leftrightarrow w$ then the first premise cannot be violated and the second premise cannot be fulfilled. Hence, the two premises do not ground the conclusion that for arbitrary $d \leftrightarrow w$ we have that $\neg d$ is a violation.

The example is difficult to interpret, because it makes use of a bi-implication. An alternative set of premises, also based on bi-implications, with analogous counterintuitive conclusions is $\{\bigcirc(d|d \leftrightarrow w), \bigcirc(d|\neg d \leftrightarrow w), \bigcirc(\neg d|w)\}$.

ORA also plays a role in the so-called miners' scenario introduced recently by Kolodny and MacFarlane [2010].

2.5 Chisholm's Paradox

The second contrary-to-duty paradox we consider is Chisholm [1963]'s paradox. We first discuss the choice between deontic versus factual detachment, and then the representation of deontic detachment. We discuss the violation detection problem for deontic detachment only in Section 2.6 after we have introduced Makinson's Möbius strip example.

2.5.1 Deontic versus Factual Detachment

Chisholm's paradox consists of the three obligations of a certain man 'to go to his neighbours assistance,' 'to tell them that he comes if he goes,' and 'not to tell them that he comes if he does not go,' together with the fact 'he does not go.' The preference-based models of dyadic deontic logic again give a natural representation of the three sentences, just like for Forrester's paradox. For example, going to the assistance and telling is preferred to all the other possibilities, and not going to the assistance and not telling is preferred to not going and telling. It seems that the going and not telling and not going and telling may be ordered in various ways. However, the following example illustrates that it is difficult to combine factual with deontic detachment, and to derive unconditional obligations from conditional and unconditional ones.

Example 2.8 (Chisholm's paradox) *Assume a dyadic deontic logic without nested modal operators that has at least replacement of logical equivalents, the Conjunction pattern* AND *factual detachment* FD *and the following inference pattern deontic detachment* DD.

$$\text{DD}: \frac{\bigcirc(\alpha|\beta), \bigcirc\beta}{\bigcirc\alpha}$$

Furthermore, consider the following premise set S.

$$S = \{\bigcirc(a|\top), \bigcirc(t|a), \bigcirc(\neg t|\neg a), \neg a\}$$

The set S formalizes Chisholm's paradox when a is read as 'a certain man goes to the assistance of his neighbors' *and t as* 'the man tells his neighbors that he will come.' *Chisholm's paradox is more complicated than Forrester's paradox, because it also contains an* According-To-Duty *(ATD) obligation. We can represent the notion of according-to-duty as a binary relation among conditional obligations, just like the notion of contrary-to-duty. A conditional obligation* $\bigcirc(\alpha|\beta)$ *is an ATD obligation of* $\bigcirc(\alpha_1|\beta_1)$ *if and only if* β *logically implies* α_1. *The condition of an ATD obligation is satisfied only if the primary obligation is fulfilled. The definition of ATD is analogous to the definition of CTD in the sense that an ATD obligation is an obligation conditional upon the fulfilment of an obligation and a CTD obligation is an obligation conditional upon a violation. The second obligation is an ATD obligation and the third obligation is a CTD obligation with respect to the first obligation, see Figure 7.*

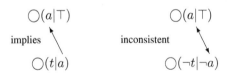

Figure 7. $\bigcirc(t|a)$ is an ATD of $\bigcirc(a|\top)$ and $\bigcirc(\neg t|\neg a)$ is a CTD of $\bigcirc(a|\top)$

The derivation in Figure 8 shows how the counterintuitive obligation $\bigcirc(t \wedge \neg t)$, *or* $\bigcirc\bot$, *can be derived from S by* FD, DD *and* AND. *Just like in Forrester's paradox, we can give a dilemma and a coherent interpretation to the scenario, and there is consensus that the latter one is preferred. This is not surprising, as Forrester's paradox shows that factual detachment and conjunction are problematic in themselves.*

$$\cfrac{\bigcirc(t|a) \quad \cfrac{\bigcirc(a|\top) \quad \top}{\bigcirc(a)}\text{ FD}}{\bigcirc t}\text{ DD} \qquad \cfrac{\bigcirc(\neg t|\neg a) \quad \neg a}{\bigcirc(\neg t)}\text{ FD}$$
$$\cfrac{}{\bigcirc(t \wedge \neg t)}\text{ AND}$$

Figure 8. Chisholm's paradox

2.5.2 Deriving Secondary Obligations from Primary Ones: Three Kinds of Transitivity

Deontic detachment is related to the following three variants of transitivity: plain transitivity T, cumulative transitivity CT, and what Parent and Van der Torre [2014a; 2014b] call aggregative cumulative transitivity ACT.

$$\text{T}: \frac{\bigcirc(\alpha|\beta), \bigcirc(\beta|\gamma)}{\bigcirc(\alpha|\gamma)} \qquad \text{CT}: \frac{\bigcirc(\alpha|\beta \wedge \gamma), \bigcirc(\beta|\gamma)}{\bigcirc(\alpha|\gamma)} \qquad \text{ACT}: \frac{\bigcirc(\alpha|\beta \wedge \gamma), \bigcirc(\beta|\gamma)}{\bigcirc(\alpha \wedge \beta|\gamma)}$$

The left derivation illustrates that T can be derived from ACT together with SA and WC, and likewise CT can be derived from T and SA, and T can be derived from CT and SA. The right derivation illustrates how ANDC can be derived from SA and ACT. RANDC can be derived analogously from RSA and ACT.

$$\cfrac{\cfrac{\bigcirc(\alpha|\beta)}{\bigcirc(\alpha|\beta \wedge \gamma)}\text{ SA} \quad \bigcirc(\beta|\gamma)}{\cfrac{\bigcirc(\alpha \wedge \beta|\gamma)}{\bigcirc(\alpha|\gamma)}\text{ WC}}\text{ ACT} \qquad \cfrac{\cfrac{\bigcirc(\alpha_1|\beta)}{\bigcirc(\alpha_1|\beta \wedge \alpha_2)}\text{ SA} \quad \bigcirc(\alpha_2|\beta)}{\bigcirc(\alpha_1 \wedge \alpha_2|\beta)}\text{ ACT}$$

The following variant of Chisholm's paradox illustrates that only ACT can be combined with restricted strengthening of the antecedent.

Example 2.9 (Chisholm's paradox, continued) *Assume a dyadic deontic logic that validates at least replacement of logical equivalents and the (intuitively valid) inference patterns RSA (or SA), T (or CT), and ANDC.*

The left derivation in Figure 9 illustrates how the counterintuitive $\bigcirc(\bot| \neg a)$ can be derived from S. Again we can give a dilemma and a coherent interpretation, and there is consensus in the literature that it should get a coherent interpretation. The underlying problem is the derivation of $\bigcirc(t|\neg a)$,

$$\dfrac{\dfrac{\bigcirc(t|a) \quad \bigcirc(a|\top)}{\bigcirc(t|\top)}\ \text{T/CT}}{\bigcirc(t|\neg a)}\ \text{RSA} \qquad \bigcirc(\neg t|\neg a)$$

$$\dfrac{}{\bigcirc(t \wedge \neg t|\neg a)}\ \text{AND}$$

$$\dfrac{\dfrac{\dfrac{\bigcirc(t|a) \quad \bigcirc(a|\top)}{\bigcirc(a \wedge t|\top)}\ \text{ACT}}{\bigcirc(t|\top)}\ \text{WC}}{\bigcirc(t|\neg a)}\ \text{RSA} \qquad \bigcirc(\neg t|\neg a)$$

$$\dfrac{}{\bigcirc(t \wedge \neg t|\neg a)}\ \text{AND}$$

Figure 9. Chisholm's paradox

which seems counterintuitive since it derives a contrary-to-duty obligation from the primary $\bigcirc(a|\top)$. If we accept RSA, *then we cannot accept* T *or* CT.

Assume a dyadic deontic logic that validates at least replacement of logical equivalents and the (intuitively valid) inference patterns RSA, ANDC, WC *and* ACT. *The right derivation of Figure 9 illustrates how the counterintuitive* $\bigcirc(\bot|\neg a)$ *can be derived from S. However, without* WC *the counterintuitive obligation cannot be derived.*

When we compare the two derivations of the contrary-to-duty paradoxes in dyadic deontic logic, we find the following similarity. The underlying problem of the counterintuitive derivations is the derivation of the obligation $\bigcirc(\alpha_1|\neg\alpha_2)$ from $\bigcirc(\alpha_1 \wedge \alpha_2|\top)$ by WC and RSA. It is respectively the derivation of $\bigcirc(\neg g|k)$ from $\bigcirc(\neg k|\top)$ in Figure 3 and $\bigcirc(t|\neg a)$ from $\bigcirc(a \wedge t|\top)$ in Figure 9. The underlying problem of the contrary-to-duty paradoxes is that a contrary-to-duty obligation can be derived from its primary obligation. It is no surprise that this derivation causes paradoxes. The derivation of a secondary obligation from a primary obligation confuses the different contexts found in contrary-to-duty reasoning. The context of primary obligation is the ideal state, whereas the context of a contrary-to-duty obligation is a violation state. Preference-based deontic logics were developed to semantically distinguish the different violation contexts in a preference ordering, but it appears more challenging to represent these contexts in derivations.

2.6　Makinson's Möbius Strip

Makinson [1999]'s Möbius strip illustrates that dilemmas and deontic detachment can also be combined, leading to new challenges and distinctions. We discuss also the violation detection problem for deontic detachment.

2.6.1　Iterated deontic detachment

The so-called Möbius strip (whose name comes from the shape of the example in Figure 10) arises when we allow for deontic detachment to be iterated. We give the version of the example presented by Makinson and Van der Torre in their input/output logic, though we use the dyadic representation.

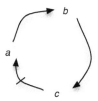

Figure 10. Möbius strip

Example 2.10 (Möbius strip) *Consider three conditional obligations stating $\neg a$ is obligatory given c, that c is obligatory given b, and that b is obligatory given a, together with the fact that a is true.*

$$\bigcirc(\neg a|c), \bigcirc(c|b), \bigcirc(b|a), a$$

For instance, a, b, c could represent "Alice (respectively Bob,Carol) is invited to dinner." The obligation $\bigcirc(b|a)$ says that if Alice is invited then Bob should be, and so on.

Makinson [1999] gives what we call here the coherent interpretation. He mentions that "intuitively, we would like to have" that under condition a, each of b and c is obligatory, even though we may not want to conclude for $\neg a$ under the same condition. He also indicates that "an approach inspired by maxi choice in AGM theory change" (like the one described in the paper in question) leads to three possible outcomes: both b and c are obligatory; only b is obligatory; neither of b and c is obligatory. The three sets of obligations corresponding to these outcomes are linearly ordered under set-theoretical inclusion.

In their input/output logic framework, Makinson and Van der Torre [2001] present what we call here the dilemma interpretation of the example. They change the definitions such that precisely the dilemma among these three alternatives is the desired outcome of the example.

There does not seem to be consensus in the literature on which interpretation is the intuitive answer for this example. Deontic detachment has been severely criticised in the literature, so it may be questioned whether full transitivity is natural. However, the choice between coherent and dilemma interpretation is general and can be found in other examples, such as the following variant of Chisholm's paradox.

Example 2.11 (Chisholm's paradox, continued) *Consider this variant of the Möbius strip:*

$$\{\bigcirc(d|c), \bigcirc(c|b), \bigcirc(b|a), a, \neg d\}$$

By symmetry with the dilemma interpretation of Möbius strip, the dilemma interpretation gives three alternatives, $\{\bigcirc b, \bigcirc c\}$, $\{\bigcirc b\}$ *and* $\emptyset$. *Now consider deontic detachment in Chisholm's paradox, together with the fact that we do not tell.*

$$\bigcirc(t|a), \bigcirc(a|\top), \neg t$$

Again by symmetry, the dilemma interpretation gives two alternatives, $\{\bigcirc a\}$ *and* $\emptyset$.

The following example has been introduced by Horty [2007] in a prioritised setting, and we will consider it again in the section that comes next. Again the question is raised whether one solution can be a subset of another solution.

Example 2.12 (Order) *Consider the following set of obligations. a is for putting the heating on, and b is for opening the window.*

$$\bigcirc(a|\top), \bigcirc(b|\top), \bigcirc(\neg b|a)$$

The example is a dilemma, but the question is whether there are two or three alternatives. According to the first interpretation, the only two alternatives are the obligations for a and b, and the obligations for a and ¬b. According to the second interpretation, there is also the alternative of an obligation for b, without an obligation for a. The latter alternative is a subset of another alternative, analogous to the dilemma interpretation of the Möbius strip example.

2.6.2 Violation detection problem and transitivity

In the previous subsections, like most authors we have assumed that in the Möbius strip the derivation of the obligation for $\neg a$ is intuitively not desirable. However, one can also view it as being intuitively desirable, for the following reason.

Example 2.13 (Möbius strip, continued) *Consider first the coherent interpretation of the Möbius strip, deriving obligations for b and c, but not for ¬a. With the transitivity T pattern, one may consider the derivation of the* *obligation for ¬a. This represents that a was actually a violation. With* ACT, *the violation can be represented by an obligation for b ∧ c ∧ ¬a.*

Consider now the dilemma interpretation, presenting three possible outcomes, either {○b, ○c}, or {○b}, or ∅. In that case, a leads to a choice, and we may thus have an instance of the forbidden conflict pattern FC *that derives that a is forbidden.*

2.7 Priority

We are given a set S of conditional obligations along with a priority relation defined on them.

Example 2.14 (Order [Horty, 2007], continued from Example 2.12])
Numbers represent the priority of the obligation, as in Section 2.1.4. Consider

$$\{③(¬b|a), ②(b|⊤), ①(a|⊤)\}$$

①, ②, *and* ③ *can be thought of as expressing commands uttered by a priest, a bishop, and a cardinal, respectively. There are three interpretations. The greedy interpretation derives obligations for a and b. It looks strange, because complying with* ①(a|⊤) *triggers the most important norm* ③(¬b|a), *which in turn cancels* ②(b|⊤). *To put it another way, complying with* ①(a|⊤) *and* ②(b|⊤) *results in violating* ③(¬b|a).

The last link interpretation derives ○a *and* ○¬b. *This looks strange too, because* ②(b|⊤) *takes precedence over* ①(a|⊤), *and* ③(¬b|a) *will not be triggered (and* ②(b|⊤) *cancelled) unless* ①(a|⊤) *is fulfilled.*

The weakest link interpretation derives ○b *only. In order not to trigger* ③(¬b|a), *and avoid being in a violation state with respect to it, the agent goes for* ②(b|⊤) *only.*

The idea underpinning Parent [2011]'s next example is similar. Parent argues that different outcomes are expected depending on whether the example is instantiated in the deontic or epistemic domain.

Example 2.15 (Cancer [Parent, 2011]) *Assume we have*

$$\{ ③(c|b), ②(b|a), ①(¬b|a)\}$$

a is for the set of data used to set up a treatment against cancer, b is for receiving chemo as per the protocol, and c is for keeping WBCs (White Blood Cells) count to a safe level using a drug. In a diagram:

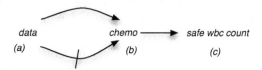

data   chemo ⟶ safe wbc count
(a)   (b)   (c)

Figure 11. Cancer

Assume the input is a. In that case, we get ②$(b|a)$ and ③$(c|b)$, which derives $\bigcirc b$ and $\bigcirc c$. Given a, both ①$(\neg b|a)$ and ②$(b|a)$ are triggered. These two conflict. The stronger obligation takes precedence over the weaker one.

Assume the input is $\{a, \neg c\}$. In that case, we get ①$(\neg b|a)$ which derives $\bigcirc\neg b$. The reason why may be explained as follows. Following one of Hansson [1969]'s suggestions, one might think of the input as someting settled as true. The question is: shall the agent do b or not? The ordering ② > ① says that b has priority over $\neg b$. So it would seem to follow that he should do b. But, in reply, it can be said that the ordering ③ > ② tells us that compliance with the stronger of the two conflicting norms triggers an obligation of even higher rank, namely the obligation to do c. Furthermore, c is already (settled as) false. Hence if the agent goes for b he will put himself in a violation state with respect to a norm with an even higher rank. The only way to avoid the violation of the most important norm is to go for $\neg b$. This is fully in line with what practitioners do: if the WBCs count cannot be maintained at a safe level, chemo is postponed.

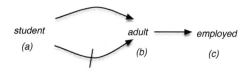

student   adult ⟶ employed
(a)   (b)   (c)

Figure 12. Student example

In the epistemic domain, a different outcome is expected. This can be seen using the reliability interpretation discussed by Horty [2007, p. 391] among others. Under the latter interpretation, an epistemic conditional indicates something like a high conditional probability that its conclusion is satisfied, and the priority ordering measures relative strength of these conditional probabilities. For illustration purposes, assume that these conditional probabilities encode statistical assertions about some population groups, and instantiate a, b and c into (this is the example often used to illustrate the non-transitivity of default patterns) *being a student, being an adult*, and *being employed*. This is shown in Figure 12. Given input $\{a, \neg c\}$, the expected output remains b.

3 Formal Framework

We extract ten basic properties from the examples, falling in three groups. We believe that the properties of factual detachment and violation detection, the logical properties of substitution, replacement by logical equivalents, implication and paraconsistency are desirable for methods to reason with normative systems, and that the properties of aggregation, factual and norm monotony, and norm induction are optional.

In this section we use the detachment terminology instead of the inference rules terminology.

3.1 Norms, Obligations and Factual Detachment

The distinction between norms and obligations is fundamental in the modern approach to deontic logic. They are related via factual detachment, the detachment of an obligation from a norm.

3.1.1 Representing Norms and Imperatives Explicitly

There are two traditions in normative reasoning, as witnessed by the two historical chapters in the *Handbook on Deontic Logic and Normative Systems* [Gabbay *et al.*, 2013]. The first tradition of deontic logic is concerned with logical relations between obligations and permissions, or between the actual and the ideal. The second tradition of normative systems is concerned with normative reasoning, including reasoning about imperatives. Many people suggested a more comprehensive approach, by bringing the two traditions closer to each other, or proposing a uniform approach. For example, when Van Fraassen [1973] is asking himself whether restricted conjunction can be formalized to reason about dilemmas, he suggests to represent imperatives explicitly.

> "But can this [...] be reflected in the logic of the ought-statements alone? Or can it be expressed only in a language in which we can talk directly about the imperatives as well? This is an important question, because it is the question whether the inferential structure of the 'ought' language game can be stated in so simple a manner that it can be grasped in and by itself. Intuitively, we want to say: there are simple cases, and in the simple cases

the axiologist's logic is substantially correct even if it is not in general—but can we state precisely when we find ourselves in such a simple case? These are essentially technical questions for deontic logic, and I shall not pursue them here." [van Fraassen, 1973]

The distinction between norms and obligations was most clearly put forward by Makinson [1999], and we follow his notational conventions. To detach an obligation from a norm, there must be a context, and the norms must be conditional. Consequently, norms are a particular kind of rules.

3.1.2 Formal Representation

In this section, a set of norms is represented by a set of pairs of formulae from a base logic, (a_1, x_1), ..., (a_n, x_n). A norm (a, x) can be read as "if a is the case, then x ought to be the case." A normative system contains at least one set of norms, the regulative norms from which obligations and prohibitions can be detached. It often contains also permissive norms, from which explicit permissions can be detached, and constitutive norms, from which institutional facts can be detached.

The context is represented by a set of formulae of the same logic. A deontic operator $\bigcirc$ factually detaches obligations, represented by a set of formulae of the base logic, from a set of norms N in a context A, written as $\bigcirc(N, A)$. Unless there is a need for it, we adopt the convention that we do not prefix the detached formula with a modal operator. For example, from a norm that if you travel by metro, you must have a valid ticket $(metro, ticket)$ in the context where you travel by metro, we derive $ticket \in \bigcirc(\{(metro, ticket)\}, \{metro\})$, but $ticket$ itself is not prefixed with a deontic modality. Note that there is no risk of confusing facts and obligations. We know that $ticket$ represents an obligation for $ticket$, because it is factually detached by the $\bigcirc$ operator.

To facilitate presentation and proofs, in this Chapter we assume propositional logic as the base logic. We write $\beta \in \bigcirc(N, \alpha)$ for $\beta \in \bigcirc(N, \{\alpha\})$, and $\gamma \in \bigcirc((\alpha, \beta), A)$ for $\gamma \in \bigcirc(\{(\alpha, \beta)\}, A)$.

3.1.3 Arguments

Maybe the most important technical innovation of the modern approach is the following convention of writing an argument for α supported by A, traditionally written as $A \therefore \alpha$, as a pair (A, α):

$$(A, \alpha) \in \bigcirc(N) = \alpha \in \bigcirc(N, A)$$

We can move between $\bigcirc(N)$ and $\bigcirc(N, A)$ as we move between $\vdash$ and Cn in classical logic.

It is crucial to understand that the representation of arguments by a pair (A, α) is just a technical method to develop logical machinery: we use it to give more compact representations, to provide proof systems, and to make relations with other branches of logic. However, if you want to know what the argument $(A, \alpha) \in \bigcirc(N)$ *means*, then you always have to translate it back to $\alpha \in \bigcirc(N, A)$.

We reserve the term "norms" to explicit norms, in N. Obviously, one does not derive norms from norms.

In this section we give both the long and the short version of the properties we discuss, to prevent misreading.

3.1.4 Factual Detachment

Factual detachment says that if there is a norm with precisely the context as antecedent, then the output contains the consequent. On the one hand this is relatively weak, as we require the context to be *precisely* the antecedent. A much stronger detachment principle imposes detachment when the antecedent is *implied* by the context. Between these two extremes, we can have that most obligations are detached, or in the most normal cases the obligation is detached. On the other hand the factual detachment principle is also quite strong, as in context a from the norm $(a, \perp)$ the contradiction $\perp$ is detached, and in case of a dilemma of (a, x) and $(a, \neg x)$, in context a both x and $\neg x$ are detached.

Definition 3.1 (Factual detachment) *A deontic operator* $\bigcirc$ *satisfies the factual detachment property if and only if for all sets of norms N and all sentences α and β we have:*

$$\frac{(\alpha, \beta) \in N}{\beta \in \bigcirc(N, \alpha)}\text{FD} \qquad \frac{(\alpha, \beta) \in N}{(\alpha, \beta) \in \bigcirc(N)}\text{FD} \qquad \frac{(\alpha, \beta) \in N}{(\alpha, \beta)}\text{FD}$$

3.2 Violation Detection

The distinctive feature of norms and obligations with respect to other types of rules and modalities is that they can be violated. Obligations which cannot be violated are not real obligations, but obligations of a degenerated kind. It is not only that ought implies can, but more importantly, ought implies can-be-violated. Issues concerning violations can be found in most deontic examples. For example, dilemma examples arise because some obligation has to be violated, and contrary-to-duty examples arise because some obligation has been violated.

Modal logic offers a simple representation for violations. An obligation for α has been violated if and only we have $\neg \alpha \wedge \bigcirc \alpha$. In our notation with explicit norms, this is $\alpha \in \bigcirc(N, A)$ with $\neg \alpha \in Cn(A)$.

To make sure that violated obligations do not drown, we use the violation detection inference pattern, which we already discussed in Section 2.2.3.

Definition 3.2 (Violation Detection) *A deontic operator $\bigcirc$ satisfies the violation detection property if and only for all sets of norms N, all sets of sentences A and all sentences α we have:*

$$\frac{\alpha \in \bigcirc(N, A)}{\alpha \in \bigcirc(N, A \cup \{\neg\alpha\})}\text{VD} \qquad \frac{(A, \alpha)}{(A \cup \{\neg\alpha\}, \alpha)}\text{VD}$$

Consequently, the restricted strengthening of the antecedent pattern is too weak.

3.3 Substitution

Whereas the first two properties define what is special about *deontic* logic, namely factual detachment and violation detection, the next four properties of substitution, replacements of logical equivalence, implication and paraconsistency say something about *logic*.

The first logical requirement is substitution, well known from classical propositional logic. It says that we can uniformly replace propositional letters by propositional formulae.

Definition 3.3 (Substitution) *Let a uniform substitution map each proposition letter to a propositional formula. A deontic operator $\bigcirc$ satisfies substitution if and only for all sets of norms N, all sets of formulae A, all sentences α and all uniform substitutions σ we have:*

$$\frac{\alpha \in \bigcirc(N, A)}{\alpha[\sigma] \in \bigcirc(N[\sigma], A[\sigma])}\text{SUB}$$

For example, it allows to replace propositional letters by distinct new letters, thus renaming them. This is an example of irrelevance of syntax, a core property of logic.

3.4 Replacement of Logical Equivalents

The following definition introduces two stronger types of irrelevance of syntax.

Definition 3.4 (Irrelevance of Syntax) *Let Cn be closure under logical consequence, and Eq closure under logical equivalence: $\alpha \in Eq(S)$ if and only if there is a β in S such that $Cn(\alpha) = Cn(\beta)$. We write $Eq(a_1, \ldots, a_n)$ for $Eq(\{a_1, \ldots, a_n\})$, and $Cn(a_1, \ldots, a_n)$ for $Cn(\{a_1, \ldots, a_n\})$. Here Cn*

is the consequence operation of the base logic on top of which the deontic operator $\bigcirc$ operates.

A deontic operator $\bigcirc$ satisfies *formula input (output) irrelevance of syntax* if and only for all sets of norms N and all sets of formulae A we have:

$$\bigcirc(N, A) = \bigcirc(N, Eq(A)) \qquad (\bigcirc(N, A) = Eq(\bigcirc(N, A)))$$

and it satisfies *set input (output) irrelevance of syntax* if and only if for all sets of norms N and all sets of formulae A we have:

$$\bigcirc(N, A) = \bigcirc(N, Cn(A)) \qquad (\bigcirc(N, A) = Cn(\bigcirc(N, A)))$$

The following example illustrates the various types of irrelevance of syntax.

Example 3.5 (Irrelevance of syntax) *Let* $N = \{(a, x), (a, y)\}$ *and* $A = \{a\}$. *The following table lists some possibilities for* $\bigcirc(N, A)$:

$\emptyset$	$\{x, y\}$	$\{x, y, x \wedge y\}$
$\{x \wedge y, y \wedge x\}$	$\{x \wedge y, y \wedge x, x, y\}$	$\{x \wedge y, y \wedge x, x, y, x \vee y, y \vee x\}$
$Eq(x \wedge y)$	$Eq(x \wedge y, x, y)$	$Eq(x \wedge y, x, y, x \vee y)$
$Cn(x) \cup Cn(y)$	$Cn(x \wedge y)$	

The first row gives some deontic operators which do not satisfy basic properties. For example, $\emptyset$ does not satisfy factual detachment, $\{x, y\}$ does not satisfy conjunction, and $\{x, y, x \wedge y\}$ does not satisfy variable renaming. That is, if we replace x and y in N, then we end up with the same set, but if we replace x and y in the output, we obtain $y \wedge x$. This violates the most basic property of irrelevance of syntax.

The second row gives some examples satisfying variable renaming for x and y. The set of obligations $\{x \wedge y, y \wedge x\}$ does not satisfy factual detachment again, and the set $\{x \wedge y, y \wedge x, x, y, x \vee y, y \vee x\}$ satisfies besides closure under conjunction also closure under disjunction. Whether this is desired depends on the application. However, all three examples do not satisfy formula output irrelevance of syntax. For example, they all three derive $x \wedge y$, but they do not derive the logically equivalent $x \wedge x \wedge y$.

The third and fourth row close the output under logical equivalence and logical consequence, respectively. $Cn(x \wedge y)$ in the last row satisfies set output irrelevance of syntax.

Input irrelevance is analogous to output irrelevance. For example, when the input is $a \wedge a$ rather than a, it may or may not derive again the same output. If it does not, then the operator violates formula input irrelevance of syntax. Moreover, if it does not treat $\{a, b\}$ and $\{a \wedge b\}$ the same, then it violates input set irrelevance of syntax.

155

The following example illustrates that output set irrelevance of syntax is too strong in the context of dilemmas, because it may lead to deontic explosion.

Example 3.6 (Irrelevance of syntax, continued) *Let*

$$N = \{(a, x \wedge y), (a, \neg x \wedge y)\}$$

and $A = \{a\}$. The following table lists some possibilities for $\bigcirc(N, A)$. We only list options closed under logical equivalence, i.e. which satisfy output formula irrelevance of syntax.

$Eq(x \wedge y, \neg x \wedge y)$	$Eq(x \wedge y, \neg x \wedge y, x \wedge \neg x \wedge y)$
$Eq(x \wedge y, \neg x \wedge y, y)$	$Eq(x \wedge y, \neg x \wedge y, y, x \wedge \neg x \wedge y)$
$Cn(x \wedge y) \cup Cn(\neg x \wedge y)$	$Cn(x \wedge y) \cup Cn(\neg x \wedge y) \cup Eq(x \wedge \neg x \wedge y)$
$Cn(x \wedge y, \neg x \wedge y)$	

The last set $Cn(x \wedge y, \neg x \wedge y)$ derives the whole language, and thus gives rise to explosion. Hence we cannot accept it. The example illustrates that we cannot accept set output irrelevance of syntax.

The difference between the left and right column is that the right column is closed under conjunction, and represents with inconsistent formulae that there is a dilemma.

The difference between the first and the second row is that the second row is closed under disjunction. The difference between the second and the third row is that consistent formulae are closed under logical consequence.

$Cn(x \wedge y) \cup Cn(\neg x \wedge y) \cup Eq(x \wedge \neg x \wedge y))$ has the feature that violations and other obligations are treated in a distinct way.

In this Chapter we require set input irrelevance of syntax, and formula output irrelevance of syntax. In addition, along the same lines we require that we can replace formulae within the norms by logically equivalent ones. All together, it corresponds to the following property of replacement of logical equivalents.

Definition 3.7 (Replacement of logically equivalent expressions) *We say that two norms ar similar, written as $(\alpha_1, \beta_1) \approx (\alpha_2, \beta_2)$, if and only if $Cn(\alpha_1) = Cn(\alpha_2)$, and $N \approx M$ if and only if for all $(\alpha_1, \beta_1) \in N$ there is a $(\alpha_2, \beta_2) \in M$ such that $(\alpha_1, \beta_1) \approx (\alpha_2, \beta_2)$, and vice versa. A deontic operator $\bigcirc$ satisfies the replacement of Logical Equivalents property if and only if for all sets of norms N and M, all sets of formulae A and B, and all sentences α and β we have:*

$$\frac{N \approx M, Cn(A) = Cn(B), Cn(\alpha) = Cn(\beta), \alpha \in \bigcirc(N, A)}{\beta \in \bigcirc(M, B)} \text{RLE}$$

The examples illustrate that there are other options in between formula and set output irrelevance of syntax, such as requiring that the output is closed under conjunction, or under disjunction, or both. We consider them in Section 3.7.

The principle of irrelevance of syntax has been criticized in belief revision theory. It is discussed by [Stolpe, 2010] in the context of a study of the notion of revision of a normative system. This notion falls outside the scope of the present Chapter, and must be left as a topic for future research.

3.5 Implication

The four properties FD, VD, SUB and RLE defined thus far may be called positive properties, in the sense that they require something to be obligatory. That is why we could represent them as Horn rules: given a set of conditions, we require some obligation to be derivable. This contrasts with the examples in Section 2, where typically too much is derived.

The implication requirement in this section and the paraconsistency requirement in the following section may be called negative properties, in the sense that they forbid something to be obligatory. The first requirement makes use of the so-called materialisation of a normative system, which means that each norm (a, x) is interpreted as a material conditional $a \to x$, i.e. as the propositional sentence $\neg a \lor x$. The implication requirement says that if the materializations of N, written as $m(N)$, do not imply $a \to x$, then $(a, x) \notin \bigcirc(N)$. This represents the idea that we cannot derive more than we can derive in propositional logic. In general, implication in the base logic is the upper bound.

Definition 3.8 (Implication) *Let $m(N) = \{a \to x \mid (a, x) \in N\}$ be the set of materializations of N. A deontic operator $\bigcirc$ satisfies the implication property if and only if for all sets of norms N and all sets of sentences A we have $\bigcirc(N, A) \subseteq Cn(m(N) \cup A)$.*

The elements $(\{\alpha\}, \beta)$ of $\bigcirc(N)$ are a subset of $\{(\alpha, \beta) \mid \alpha \to \beta \in Cn(m(N))\}$. In most systems, the base logic is classical propositional logic, but it need not be so. For instance, Cn may be the consequence relation of intuitionistic propositional logic, as in [Parent *et al.*, 2014]. Cn may also be what Makinson calls a pivotal consequence relation Cn_K, defined by $Cn_K(A) = C(A \cup K)$, where K is a set of formulas, and C is the consequence relation of classical propositional logic. Stolpe [2008] defines and studies two such input/output operations. They are aimed to model the interplay between norms and so-called material dependencies. We have $\bigcirc(N, A) \subseteq Cn_K(m(N) \cup A)$.

157

3.6 Paraconsistency

To prevent explosion we do not want to derive the whole language, unless maybe in pathological cases in which the normative system contains a norm for each propositional formula. A consequence relation may be said to be paraconsistent if it is not explosive, though there are various ways to make this formal.

To define our paraconsistency requirement, we distinguish obligations representing violations from other obligations. That is, we decompose an operator $\bigcirc(N, A)$ into two operators $V(N, A)$ and $\overline{V}(N, A)$, such that we have $V(N, A) = \{x \in \bigcirc(N, A) \mid \neg x \in Cn(A)\}$ and $\overline{V}(N, A) = \bigcirc(N, A) \setminus V(N, A)$. Trivially, we have

$$\bigcirc(N, A) = V(N, A) \cup \overline{V}(N, A)$$

The basic idea of our paraconsistency requirement is that obligations in $\overline{V}$ can be derived from a set of norms M in N, such that this set of norms M does not explode.

Definition 3.9 (Paraconsistency) *A deontic operator $\bigcirc$ satisfies the paraconsistency property if and only if for all sets of norms N, all sets of formulae A and all sentences α, if $\alpha \in \overline{V}(N, A)$, then there is a $M \subseteq N$ such that $\alpha \in \bigcirc(M, A)$ and $\bigcirc(M, A) \cup A$ is classically consistent.*

Implication and paraconsistency together imply that if $\alpha \in \overline{V}(N, A)$, then there is a $M \subseteq N$ such that $\alpha \in Cn(m(N) \cup A)$ and $\bigcirc(M, A) \cup A$ is classically consistent. This suggest an additional condition: if $\alpha \in \overline{V}(N, A)$, then there is a $M \subseteq N$ such that $\alpha \in Cn(m(N) \cup A)$ and $m(N) \cup A$ is classically consistent.

The underlying intuition to restrict to a set of norms was already raised in Example 1.1 in the introduction. There we observe that if we can derive $\bigcirc(\beta \wedge \gamma)$ from $\bigcirc(\alpha \wedge \beta)$ and $\bigcirc(\neg\alpha \wedge \gamma)$, and we have substitution and replacements of logical equivalents, then we also derive $\bigcirc(\beta)$ from $\bigcirc(\alpha)$ and $\bigcirc(\neg\alpha)$, in other words, we have deontic explosion. This can be verified by replacing β by $\alpha \vee \beta$ and γ by $\neg\alpha \vee \beta$. Therefore, we restrict the set of norms we use to a set of norms which is in some sense "consistent" with the input A.

3.7 Aggregation

The last four properties of aggregation, factual and norm monotony, and norm induction determine the kind of deontic logics we are going to study in our framework. We believe that other choices at this point may be of interest too, but we do not pursue them in this Chapter.

Aggregation is a core issue in van Fraassen's paradox.

Definition 3.10 (Aggregation) *A deontic operator* $\bigcirc$ *satisfies the aggregation property if and only if for all sets of norms N, sets of sentences A and sentences α and β we have*

$$\frac{\alpha, \beta \in \bigcirc(N, A)}{\alpha \wedge \beta \in \bigcirc(N, A)} \text{AND} \qquad \frac{(A, \alpha), (A, \beta)}{(A, \alpha \wedge \beta)} \text{AND}$$

Van Fraassen's paradox shows that therefore we cannot accept weakening of the consequent. In the context of our present framework, we prefer to call it weakening of the output.

Definition 3.11 *A deontic operator* $\bigcirc$ *satisfies the weakening of the output property if and only if for all sets of norms N, sets of sentences A and sentences α and β we have*

$$\frac{\alpha \wedge \beta \in \bigcirc(N, A)}{\alpha, \beta \in \bigcirc(N, A)} \text{WO} \qquad \frac{(A, \alpha \wedge \beta)}{(A, \alpha), (A, \beta)} \text{WO}$$

Proposition 3.12 *There is no operator* $\bigcirc$ *satisfying simultaneously paraconsistency, aggregation, and weakening of the output.*

Proof. *Assume the statement does not hold, so there is a deontic $\bigcirc$ satisfying paraconsistency, aggregation and weakening of the output. Consider van Fraassen's paradox $N = \{(\top, p), (\top, \neg p)\}$. According to aggregation and weakening of the output, we have $(\top, q) \in \bigcirc(N)$. According to paraconsistency, $(\top, q) \notin \bigcirc(N)$. Contradiction.* ∎

3.8 Factual Monotony

In this Chapter we are interested in monotonic logics. Though non-monotonic logics may have their applications too, we believe they should be build on top of the monotonic ones.

Definition 3.13 (Factual monotony) *The factual monotony property holds for* $\bigcirc$ *if and only if for all sets of norms N, and all sets of sentences A and B, we have $\bigcirc(N, A) \subseteq \bigcirc(N, A \cup B)$.*

As this implies strengthening of the antecedent, Forrester's paradox illustrates that we cannot accept weakening of the consequent.

Proposition 3.14 *There is no operator* $\bigcirc$ *satisfying simultaneously paraconsistency, factual monotony, and weakening of the output.*

Proof. *Assume the statement does not hold, so there is a deontic $\bigcirc$ satisfying paraconsistency, factual monotony and weakening of the output. Consider the first norm of Forrester's paradox $N = \{(\top, \neg k)\}$. According to factual monotony and weakening of the output, we have $(k, \neg k \vee g) \in \bigcirc(N)$. According to paraconsistency, $(k, \neg k \vee g) \notin \bigcirc(N)$. Contradiction.* ■

3.9 Norm Monotony

Definition 3.15 (Norm monotony) *A deontic operator $\bigcirc$ satisfies the property of norm monotony if and only if for all sets of norms N and M we have $\bigcirc(N) \subseteq \bigcirc(N \cup M)$.*

A deontic operator $\bigcirc$ satisfies the property of monotony if and only if it satisfies those of factual and norm monotony, i.e. for all N, M, A, B we have $\bigcirc(N, A) \subseteq \bigcirc(N \cup M, A \cup B)$.

3.10 Norm Induction

Norm induction says that if there is an output β for an input α, and we add the norm (α, β) to the normative system, then for all inputs, the output of the normative system stays the same. We call it norm induction, because the norm is induced from the relation between facts and obligations. The norm induction requirement considers a set M of such pairs (α, β).

Definition 3.16 (Norm induction) *A deontic operator $\bigcirc$ verifies the property of norm induction if and only if for all sets of norms N and M and all sets of sentences A we have $M \subseteq \bigcirc(N) \Rightarrow \bigcirc(N) = \bigcirc(N \cup M)$*

The strong norm induction principle strengthens the norm induction principle to expansion of the normative system with new norms.

Definition 3.17 (Strong norm induction) *A deontic operator $\bigcirc$ satisfies the property of strong norm induction if and only if for all sets of norms N, N', M, and all sets of sentences A we have $M \subseteq \bigcirc(N) \Rightarrow \bigcirc(N \cup N') = \bigcirc(N \cup N' \cup M)$*

Clearly we have that the strong norm induction property implies the norm induction property.

Together, factual detachment, monotony and norm induction are equivalent to requiring that $\bigcirc$ is a closure operator.

Definition 3.18 (Closure operator) *$\bigcirc$ is a closure operator if and only if it satisfies the following three properties:*

INCLUSION $N \subseteq \bigcirc(N)$

MONOTONY $N \subseteq M$ *implies* $\bigcirc(N) \subseteq \bigcirc(M)$

IDEMPOTENCE $\bigcirc(N) = \bigcirc(\bigcirc(N))$

Their counterparts in terms of Cn are knowns as the "Tarskian" conditions, after A. Tarski. They can each be rephrased in terms of $\vdash$ ('proves') as follows.

REFLEXIVITY $A \vdash x$ for all $x \in A$

MONOTONY $A \vdash x$ implies $A \cup B \vdash x$

TRANSITIVITY $A \vdash x$ for all $x \in B$ and $B \vdash y$ imply $A \vdash y$

Inclusion for Cn translates into reflexivity of $\vdash$. Monotony for Cn translates into monotony of $\vdash$. Idempotence of Cn corresponds to the transitivity of $\vdash$.

4 Summary

Table 2 lists the examples we discussed in this Chapter. Given that the world is full of conflicts, we have that normative systems are developed by humans and full of inconsistencies. We need to represent dilemmas consistently, if only to consider their resolution. Van Fraassen's paradox illustrates that doing so presents a basic dilemma: do we accept aggregation or closure under consequence? Forrester's paradox seems to indicate a dilemma too, as it presents two alternatives. In the cottage regulations, such a dilemma interpretation makes sense: either remove the fence, or paint it white. However, in Forrester's gentle murderer example, you cannot undo killing someone. So only the coherent interpretation makes sense. Dilemmas can be resolved by explicit priorities, for example reflecting the authority creating the obligation, or it can be derived from the specificity of the obligations. In the latter case, as illustrated by the cottage regulations, we have to be careful to distinguish violations from exceptions. Jeffrey's disarmament illustrates the problem of reasoning by cases in deontic reasoning. When conditions have an epistemic reading, reasoning by cases may not be valid. Deontic detachment and transitivity originate from Chisholm's paradox, though it is known in the literature as a contrary-to-duty paradox rather than a deontic detachment paradox. Chisholm's paradox illustrates that an alternative representation of the transitivity pattern makes it analogous to Forrester's paradox. Makinson's Möbius strip illustrates many of the problems of reasoning with transitivity. In particular, the dilemma interpretation highlights that we can have solutions being a strict subset of other solutions. More priority

Xavier Parent   Leendert van der Torre

Ex.	obligations	patterns	
2.1	Fraassen	$\bigcirc p, \bigcirc \neg p$	AND, WC
2.2	Forrester	$\bigcirc(\neg k|\top), \bigcirc(g|k), \vdash g \to k$	FD, (R)AND
2.3	Forrester	$\bigcirc(\neg k|\top), \bigcirc(g|k), \vdash g \to k$	(R)SA, ANDC, WC
2.6	Cottage	$\bigcirc(\neg f|\top), \bigcirc(w \wedge f|f), \bigcirc(f|d)$	RSA$_o$
2.7	Jeffrey	$\bigcirc(d|w), \bigcirc(d|\neg w), \bigcirc(\neg d|d \leftrightarrow w)$	RSA, ORA
2.8	Chisholm	$\bigcirc(a|\top), \bigcirc(t|a), \bigcirc(\neg t|\neg a), \neg a$	AND, FD, DD
2.9	Chisholm	$\bigcirc(a|\top), \bigcirc(t|a), \bigcirc(\neg t|\neg a), \neg a$	T/ CT / ACT, ANDC
2.10	Möbius	$\bigcirc(\neg a|c), \bigcirc(c|b), \bigcirc(b|a), a$	T/ CT
2.14	Priority	$③(\neg b|a), ②(b|\top), ①(a|\top)$	T/ CT

Table 2. Summary of the examples

examples are introduced in the area of epistemic reasoning, and reasoning with defaults.

Maybe the most important technical innovation of our formal framework is the convention of writing an argument for α supported by A as a pair (A, α) with $(A, \alpha) \in \bigcirc(N)$, which means the same as $\alpha \in \bigcirc(N, A)$. We can move between $\bigcirc(N)$ and $\bigcirc(N, A)$ as we move between $\vdash$ and Cn in classical logic.

The ten properties of our formal framework listed in Table 3. We believe that all deontic logics have to satisfy the deontic properties of factual detachment and violation detection, and the logical properties of substitution, replacement by logical equivalents, implication and paraconsistency. Moreover, we discussed the optional properties of aggregation, factual and norm monotony, and norm induction.

FD	$(\alpha, \beta) \in N \Rightarrow \beta \in \bigcirc(N, \alpha)$	Factual detachment
VD	$(A, \beta) \Rightarrow (A \cup \{\neg \beta\}, \beta)$	Violation detection
SUB	$\alpha \in \bigcirc(N, A) \Rightarrow \alpha[\sigma] \in \bigcirc(N[\sigma], A[\sigma])$	Substitution
RLE	$N \approx M, Cn(A) = Cn(B), Cn(\alpha) = Cn(\beta),$ $(A, \alpha) \in \bigcirc(N) \Rightarrow (B, \beta) \in \bigcirc(M)$	Replacement of equivalents
IMP	$\bigcirc(N, A) \subseteq Cn(m(N) \cup A)$	Implication
PC	$\alpha \in \overline{V}(N, A) \Rightarrow \exists M \subseteq N : \alpha \in \bigcirc(M, A)$ and $\bigcirc(M, A) \cup A$ consistent	Paraconsistency
AND	$(A, \alpha)(A, \beta) \Rightarrow (A, \alpha \wedge \beta)$	Conjunction
FM	$(A, \alpha) \Rightarrow (A \cup B, \alpha)$	Factual monotony
NM	$\bigcirc(N) \subseteq \bigcirc(N \cup M)$	Norm monotony
NI	$M \subseteq O(N) \Rightarrow O(N) = O(N \cup M)$	Norm induction

Table 3. Properties

There are two ways to look at the operator $\bigcirc$. First, given a set of norms, it derives sentences from sentences: $\alpha \in \bigcirc_N(A)$. This is the classical way deontic logics considered normative systems: facts go in, obligations go out. Secondly, it derives arguments from norms: $(A, \alpha) \in \bigcirc(N)$. These two views can be used to summarise our properties as follows.

First, the operator in $(A, \alpha) \in \bigcirc(N)$ must be a closure operator, which means that it satisfies factual detachment, norm monotony and norm induction. In addition, it must satisfy substitution and replacement of logical equivalents. Secondly, the operator in $\alpha \in \bigcirc_N(A)$ must satisfy violation detection, implication, paraconsistency, factual monotony, and aggregation.

The properties of norm monotony and norm induction have the effect that our logics will behave classically as Tarskian consequence operators. However, it is important to realise that the closure properties on $\bigcirc(N)$ are not as innocent as they are in other branches of philosophical logic. In particular norm induction is very strong, because it says that every argument (A, α) can itself be used as a norm. This may be true of some branches of case law, but it is probably too strong to be accepted as a universal law for norms. We therefore expect that future studies will first relax this requirement, before relaxing the others.

Finally, we may consider our ten properties as requirements for the further development of reasoning methods for normative systems and deontic logic. We have recently presented two logics satisfying all ten properties [Parent and van der Torre, 2014b], which shows that the ten properties are consistent in the sense that they can be satisfied simultaneously.

Acknowledgements

X. Parent's research was funded in whole or in part by the Austrian Science Fund (FWF) [M-3240-N]. For the purpose of open access, the author has applied a CC BY public copyright licence to any Author Accepted Manuscript version arising from this submission.

This is a reprint of an article that appeared under the same title in IfColog Journal of Logics and their Applications, Special Issue "Logic for Normative Multi-Agent Systems" (Guest editors: G. Pigozzi and L. van der Torre), 2017, Volume 4, Number 9, pp. 2996-3039, and in the Handbook of Normative Multiagent Systems (Amit Chopra, Leendert van der Torre, Harko Verhagen and Serena Villata, eds), 2018, College Publications.

BIBLIOGRAPHY

[Anderson, 1956] A. R. Anderson. The formal analysis of normative systems. In N. Rescher, editor, *The Logic of Decision and Action*, pages 147–213. Univ. Pittsburgh, 1967, 1956.

[Åqvist, 2002] L. Åqvist. Deontic logic. In D. Gabbay and F. Guenthner, editors, *Handbook of philosophical logic*, volume 8, pages 147–264. Kluwer Academic publisher, 2002.

[Chellas, 1980] B.F. Chellas. *Modal Logic: An Introduction*. Cambridge University Press, 1980.

[Chisholm, 1963] R.M. Chisholm. Contrary-to-duty imperatives and deontic logic. *Analysis*, 24:33–36, 1963.

[Gabbay et al., 2013] D. Gabbay, J. Horty, R. van der Meyden, X. Parent, and L. van der Torre, editors. *Handbook of Deontic Logic and Normative Systems*, volume 1. College Publications, London, UK, 2013.

[Governatori and Hashmi, 2015] G. Governatori and M. Hashmi. Permissions in deontic event-calculus. In *Legal Knowledge and Information Systems - JURIX 2015: The Twenty-Eighth Annual Conference, Braga, Portual, December 10-11, 2015*, volume 279, pages 181–182. IOS Press, 2015.

[Hansson, 1969] B. Hansson. An analysis of some deontic logics. *Noûs*, 3:373–398, 1969. Reprinted in [Hilpinen, 1971, pp 121-147].

[Hilpinen, 1971] R. Hilpinen, editor. *Deontic Logic: Introductory and Systematic Readings*. Reidel, Dordrecht, 1971.

[Horty, 2007] J. Horty. Defaults with priorities. *Journal of Philosophical Logic*, 36:367–413, 2007.

[Horty, 2014] J. Horty. Deontic modals: why abandon the classical semantics? *Pacific Philosophical Quarterly*, 95:424–460, 2014.

[Jeffrey, 1983] R. Jeffrey. *The Logic of Decision*. University of Chicago Press, 2nd edition, 1983.

[Kolodny and MacFarlane, 2010] N. Kolodny and J. MacFarlane. Iffs and oughts. *Journal of Philosophy*, 107(3):115–143, 2010.

[Makinson and van der Torre, 2000] D. Makinson and L. van der Torre. Input/output logics. *Journal of Philosophical Logic*, 29(4):383–408, 2000.

[Makinson and van der Torre, 2001] D. Makinson and L. van der Torre. Constraints for input-output logics. *Journal of Philosophical Logic*, 30(2):155–185, 2001.

[Makinson, 1999] D. Makinson. On a fundamental problem in deontic logic. In P. Mc Namara and H. Prakken, editors, *Norms, Logics and Information Systems*, Frontiers in Artificial Intelligence and Applications, pages 29–54. IOS Press, Amsterdam, 1999.

[Parent and van der Torre, 2014a] X. Parent and L. van der Torre. Aggregative deontic detachment for normative reasoning (short paper). In T. Eiter, C. Baral, and G. De Giacomo, editors, *Principles of Knowledge Representation and Reasoning. Proceedings of the 14th International Conference - KR 14*. AAAI Press, 2014.

[Parent and van der Torre, 2014b] X. Parent and L. van der Torre. "Sing and dance!": Input/output logics without weakening. In F. Cariani, D. Grossi, J. Meheus, and X. Parent, editors, *Deontic Logic and Normative Systems - 12th International Conference, DEON 2014, Ghent, Belgium, July 12-15, 2014. Proceedings*, volume 8554 of *Lecture Notes in Computer Science*, pages 149–165. Springer, 2014.

[Parent et al., 2014] X. Parent, D. Gabbay, and L. van der Torre. Intuitionistic basis for input/output logic. In S. O. Hansson, editor, *David Makinson on Classical Methods for Non-Classical Problems*, pages 263–286. Springer Netherlands, Dordrecht, 2014.

[Parent, 2011] X. Parent. Moral particularism in the light of deontic logic. *Artificial Intelligence and Law*, 19(2-3):75–98, 2011.

[Prakken and Sergot, 1996] H. Prakken and M.J. Sergot. Contrary-to-duty obligations. *Studia Logica*, 57:91–115, 1996.

[Ross, 1930] D. Ross. *The Right and the Good*. Oxford University Press, 1930.

[Stolpe, 2008] A. Stolpe. Normative consequence: The problem of keeping it whilst giving it up. In G. Governatori and G. Sartor, editors, *Deontic Logic in Computer Science, 10th International Conference, DEON 2010. Proceedings*, volume 6181 of *Lecture Notes in Computer Science*, pages 174–188. Springer, 2008.

[Stolpe, 2010] A. Stolpe. Norm-system revision: Theory and application. *Artif. Intell. Law*, 18(3):247–283, 2010.

[Sun and van der Torre, 2014] X. Sun and L. van der Torre. Combining constitutive and regulative norms in input/output logic. In F. Cariani, D. Grossi, J. Meheus, and X. Parent, editors, *Deontic Logic and Normative Systems - 12th International Conference, DEON 2014. Proceedings*, volume 8554 of *Lecture Notes in Computer Science*, pages 241–257. Springer, 2014.

[Thomason and Horty, 1996] R. Thomason and R. Horty. Nondeterministic action and dominance: foundations for planning and qualitative decision. In *Proceedings of the Sixth Conference on Theoretical Aspects of Rationality and Knowledge (TARK'96)*, pages 229–250. Morgan Kaufmann, 1996.

[van der Torre and Tan, 1997] L. van der Torre and Y.-H. Tan. The many faces of defeasibility in defeasible deontic logic. In D. Nute, editor, *Defeasible Deontic Logic*, pages 79–121. Kluwer, 1997.

[van der Torre and Tan, 2000] L. van der Torre and Y.-H. Tan. Two-phase deontic logic. *Logique et analyse*, 43(171-172):411–456, 2000.

[van der Torre, 1994] L. van der Torre. Violated obligations in a defeasible deontic logic. In *Proceedings of the Eleventh European Conference on Artificial Intelligence (ECAI'94)*, pages 371–375. John Wiley & Sons, 1994.

[van der Torre, 2003] L. van der Torre. Contextual deontic logic: Normative agents, violations and independence. *Ann. Math. Artif. Intell.*, 37(1-2):33–63, 2003.

[van Fraassen, 1973] B.C. van Fraassen. Values and the heart command. *Journal of Philosophy*, 70:5–19, 1973.

Xavier Parent
Vienna University of Technology
Faculty of Informatics
Austria
Email: x.parent.xavier@gmail.com

Leendert van der Torre
University of Luxembourg
Email: leon.vandertorre@uni.lu

6

Defeasible Deontic Logic: Arguing about Permission and Obligation

HUIMIN DONG
BEISHUI LIAO
RÉKA MARKOVICH
LEENDERT VAN DER TORRE

ABSTRACT. Defeasible deontic logic uses techniques from non-monotonic logic to address various challenges in normative reasoning, such as prima facie permissions and obligations, moral dilemmas, deontic detachment, contrary-to-duty reasoning and legal interpretation. In this chapter, we use formal argumentation to design defeasible deontic logics, based on two classical deontic logics. In particular, we use the ASPIC$^+$ structured argumentation theory to define non-monotonic variants of well-understood monotonic modal logics. We illustrate the ASPIC$^+$-based approach and the resulting defeasible deontic logics using argumentation about strong permission.

1 Introduction to defeasible deontic logic

Deontic logic is the logic of permission, obligation, and prohibition [von Wright, 1951], and has been used to formalise reasoning in law, ethics, linguistics, computer science, and elsewhere. See: the deontic logic handbook series [Gabbay *et al.*, 2013; Gabbay *et al.*, 2021] for an in depth discussion of this area, the deontic logic textbook [Parent and van der Torre, 2018] for an introduction into the main formal systems, and the handbook of normative multiagent systems [Chopra *et al.*, 2018] for a recent overview of the challenges in deontic logic and normative reasoning [Pigozzi and van der Torre, 2017], and for an overview of the benchmark examples, inference patterns, and properties [Parent and van der Torre, 2017].

Defeasible deontic logic emerged in the nineteen-nineties when techniques from non-monotonic logic addressed various challenges in normative reasoning. Classical deontic logic is monotonic, meaning that a conclusion derivable from a set of premises remains derivable when new premises are added. However, new premises can block such derivations when normative reasoning involves prima facie permissions, conditional permissions, or where one normative principle is preferred to another. Moreover, many axioms of deontic logic have been criticised, and non-monotonic techniques have been applied widely to address them [Horty, 1993; Prakken, 1996; van der Torre, 1997]. For instance, Horty [1993] formalises normative reasoning in term of conditional obligations. His deontic framework is based on default logic with preference logic. In general, an acceptable derivation may be defeated by a new line of reasoning when new information activates competing normative principles. The Springer volume on defeasible deontic logic [Nute, 1997] appeared over two decades ago, and still provides an excellent overview of challenges in the area of defeasible deontic logic.

Combining *formal argumentation* and deontic logic is an increasingly active research topic in recent years [da Costa Pereira *et al.*, 2017; Beirlaen *et al.*, 2018; Pigozzi and van der Torre, 2018]. For example, Prakken [1996] proposed combining standard deontic logic with an early-generation formal argumentation system to formalise defeasible deontic reasoning, and Prakken and Sartor [2013] formulated arguments about norms as the application of argument schemes to knowledge bases of facts and norms. Young *et al.* [2016] proposed an approach to representing prioritised default logic by using the tool ASPIC$^+$, and Liao *et al.* [2019] represented three logics of prioritised norms using argumentation.

In this chapter, we use a variant of standard deontic logic [van Benthem, 1979; Parent and van der Torre, 2018] as the base logic in an argumentation approach to normative reasoning [Dong *et al.*, 2019b; Straßer and Arieli, 2019]. The technique proposed here provides a *resolution of conflicts* as a treatment of *prima facie permissions* and *obligations*. For example, conflicts among prima facie norms can be resolved using priorities or preferences. The obligation is standard, but we study strong permission instead of weak permission. We argue for choosing strong permission comparing the *moral conflict* pertaining to obligations with that pertaining to permission.

EXAMPLE 1 (Moral Conflict: Obligation) *This phenomenon occurs in deontic logic if we reason about deontic dilemmas or conflicts, that is situations where Op and $O\neg p$ both hold. Van der Torre and Tan [2000] call this deontic explosion problem "van Fraassen's paradox", because van Fraassen [1973] gave the following (informal) analysis of dilemmas in deontic logic. He rejects the* AND *conjunction pattern,*

$$\text{AND:} \frac{O\varphi, O\psi}{O(\varphi \wedge \psi)}.$$

This is because AND *warrants a move from the two assumptions Op and $O\neg p$ to the conclusion $O(p \wedge \neg p)$, while such a conclusion is not consistent with* the principle 'ought implies can' formalised as $\neg O(p \wedge \neg p)$. However, he does not want to reject the conjunction pattern in all cases. In particular, he wants to be able to derive $O(p \wedge q)$ from Op and Oq when p and q are distinct propositional atoms. His suggestion is that a restriction should be placed on the conjunction pattern: one derives $O(\varphi \wedge \psi)$ from $O\varphi$ and $O\psi$ only if $\varphi \wedge \psi$ is consistent.

EXAMPLE 2 (Moral Conflict: Permission) *The sense of moral conflict pertaining to strong permission was first observed by von Wright [1951] and later discussed by Lewis [1979] and many others [Kamp, 1973; Hilpinen, 1982; Alchourrón and Bulygin, 1984; Makinson, 1984; Asher and Bonevac, 2005]. The central property of strong permission can be represented by the following monotonic pattern of free choice permission,* FCP, *as reviewed recently by Hansson [2013]:*

$$\text{FCP:} \frac{P\varphi, \Box(\psi \to \varphi)}{P\psi}$$

The FCP *pattern ensures a move from the assumptions $P\phi$ and $\Box(\psi \to \phi)$ to the conclusion $P\psi$. It then leads from a permission Pp to another permission $P(p \wedge q)$, where q is arbitrary. The moral conflict can arise when q is a proposition bringing moral wrong. An example involving the* FCP *pattern in natural language [Hansson, 2013] is the so–called "vegetarian free lunch" example. In that example, if you are allowed to order a vegetarian lunch, then, by applying the rule* fcp, *you are allowed to order a vegetarian lunch while doing something harmful. In Example 1, the moral conflict is brought by obligation aggregation with inconsistency. In contrast, the "paradox" of strong permission here brings up morally wrong statements.*

Similar to van Fraassen's suggestion, we need to restrict the FCP *pattern. We accept conclusion $P\psi$ derived from $P\varphi$ and $\Box(\psi \to \varphi)$ when there is no prohibition on ψ having priority. Compare the following prima facie permissions:*

(A) *"It is permitted to use private cars." (Pc)*

(B) *"It is permitted to use private cars which exceed the air pollution level." $(P(c \wedge a))$*

(C) *"It is permitted to use private cars in an emergency, even those that exceed the air pollution level." $(P(c \wedge a \wedge e))$*

The FCP *pattern guarantees moves from* **(A)** *to* **(B)** *and to* **(C)**, *but the conclusion* **(B)** *seems to be less acceptable. It is possible to have a prohibition $\neg P(c \wedge a)$ opposing* **(B)** *and another $\neg P(c \wedge a \wedge e)$ opposing* **(C)**. *$\neg P(c \wedge a)$ has a higher priority than* **(B)** *and so* **(B)** *is defeated. The prohibition $\neg P(c \wedge a \wedge e)$ cannot defeat* **(C)**, *because this prohibition has a lower priority.*

The comparison between Example 1 and Example 2 suggests that a compromise is required to accept FCP as is required for AND. The counterintuitive results can be handled with techniques from non-monotonic logic. ASPIC$^+$ is one such recent technique that captures the reasoning of normative statements defeasibly. We develop a variety of defeasible deontic logics using ASPIC$^+$ in order to model possible reasoning patterns regarding prima facie obligations and permissions.

The layout of this chapter is as follows. Section 2 provides an overview of various aspects of permission in natural language in legal contexts. Section 3 introduces the running example of this chapter. Section 4 introduces the basic idea of using formal argumentation as a way to design defeasible deontic logics. Section 5 introduces monotonic deontic logics, and in Section 6 we use these logics to define ASPIC$^+$ argumentation systems. Section 7 defines the defeasible deontic logics in terms of the argumentation systems, and Section 8 presents an alternative based on various premises as a further development. In Section 9, we summarise the logical properties of the defeasible deontic logics. Section 10 proposes some further work regarding, for example, related concepts like conditional permissions, rights and duties, permission to know, and permissive norms. We present basic notions regarding permission in various modal languages. By observing the *defeasible* phenomenon in these permissions, we point to possible applications of our ASPIC$^+$-based defeasible logics in order to capture their reasoning. Section 11 focuses on related work. Section 12 concludes the chapter.

2   Many facets of permission

Permission and permissive norms have many facets, proven by the linguistic richness of legal conceptualisation and reasoning in natural language [Hansson, 2013; Governatori *et al.*, 2020]. This section explores various reasoning patterns underlying permission.

One central distinction between different kinds of permissions regards the notions of *declarative* and *descriptive* norms [Hansson, 2013], which are two sides of the same coin. A declarative permission is defined by the *presence* of a certain normative, legal, or moral source explicitly granting that permission. By contrast, a descriptive permission can be seen as the *absence* of a *mandatory* source or code containing a prohibition. A declarative permission can generate an obligation, a prohibition, or a permission. For instance, a declarative permission to the customer, "You are allowed to order your lunch", generates an obligation on the part of the waiter towards the customer, "I ought to serve the menu". This kind of permission can sometimes be understood as an explicit, strong, or positive permission [von Wright, 1963; Makinson and van der Torre, 2003], because there is a normative source or code that this permission refer to. This is not possible with descriptive permissions. The declarative permission "Every citizen over 18 is allowed to vote" is one instance in the legal context. The civil duty on the state to guarantee the right to vote arises from this permission. Besides, a declarative permission is "action guiding"—the agent would anticipate the deontic status of his or her actions with reference to the permission declared [Makinson and van der Torre, 2003]. A phenomenon framed by this effect is the so-called free-choice permission [Hansson, 2013]: given that "You are permitted to order a croissant or order a baguette" is declarative, the customer would expect to be allowed to have two choices: the permission to order a croissant and a permission to order a baguette. Otherwise the customer might expect a descriptive permission to order a croissant or might expect a permission to order a baguette, but does not know which one is a permissible option.

Another aspect we need to consider is possible relations between prohibition and permission. We have already stated that a declarative permission is defined by the *presence* of a certain normative, legal, or moral source, and that, by contrast, a descriptive permission can be seen as the *absence* of a *mandatory* source or code. Usually the former is called a strong permission while the latter is called a weak permission [von Wright, 1963]. Some may argue that it is not easy to differentiate between strong and weak permissions. In fact, a strong and explicit permission of ϕ can be considered as a free-choice permission—it is action-guiding because of the existence of a norm. Although a strong permission denies a prohibition, we do not consider it to be a weak permission as well. This line follows an idea discussed in several works [von Wright, 1963; Alchourrón and Bulygin, 1984; Hansson, 2013]: it is better not to mix strong and weak permissions. Otherwise, when a permission to ϕ is given, a permission to arbitrary ψ can follow. A strong permission to ϕ can lead to a weak permission to ϕ or ψ, concluding with a strong permission to ψ. Therefore, a clear distinction is required. It is not enough to say that a permission exists because its prohibition is denied. One proper way out is to emphasise which reason supports the existence of such a norm [Ross, 1930; Raz, 1975], as the next point shows.

We therefore address the third view of permission, which is the main theme of this chapter, prima facie permission. Ross [1930] first introduced the notion of prima facie with regard to obligations. There may be a moral reason that requires one to do something, which conflicts with another stronger reason for not doing it, and, therefore, the prima facie obligation could be defeated. Similarly, a prima facie permission could be overtaken by a competing norm when the latter has higher priority. This competing norm can either be a permission granted to a different person or a prima facie obli-

171

gation [Hansson, 2013]. Here, a prima facie permission is considered to be a declarative and strong permission. It is declarative, because it can further generate an implied permission [Hansson, 2013]. A prima facie permission is considered to be a strong permission because it does not necessarily imply that an obligation is denied. A prima facie permission may defeat another permission [Hansson, 2013].

Permission is able to represent different types of right in legal theory. The Hohfeldian theory of legal rights [Hohfeld, 1923] usually equates privilege with weak permission [Kanger and Kanger, 1966; Kanger, 1972], while power is created via constitutive rules [Searle, 1996; Sergot, 2013; Markovich, 2020; Dong and Roy, 2021]. We leave further discussion on rights and permissions to Section 10.2.

There are many other linguistic phenomena pertaining to permissions [Hansson, 2013; Governatori *et al.*, 2020], including: unilateral and bilateral permissions; explicit, implied, and tacit permissions; dynamic permissions; permission as activation and revocation; permission as exception of prohibition; and permission as derogation of prohibition. For a more detailed overview, please refer to the handbook chapter on the varieties of permissions [Hansson, 2013].

Before turning to our benchmark example of permission, we review the intuition behind, and inferential pattern pertaining to, strong permission in the literature [von Wright, 1963; Von Wright, 1968; Hansson, 2013]. Von Wright first stated that an action is strongly permitted if "the authority has considered its normative status and decided to permit it" [von Wright, 1963, p.68]. Later, he put forward the following pattern that a strong permission should follow: "(Strong) [p]ermission (...) means freedom to choose between all the alternatives, if any, covered by the permitted thing" [Von Wright, 1968, p.32]. This flavour of "freedom to choose" is similar to the notion of *at liberty* proposed by Raz [1975]. It is commonly applied in ordinary language in the following way [Hilpinen, 1982; Asher and Bonevac, 2005; Barker, 2010]:

(A) If it is permitted to take a break or continue working, then it is permitted to take a break and it is permitted to continue working.

There are some sentences in the legal context that have a similar sense. We do not take a stand but just present them here: "Exactly how much to tip a server is at the discretion of the customer", "Bail is granted at the discretion of the court". It is usually possible to derive some strong permissions to a certain extent from this kind of sentence. To capture sentences like these, as Example 2 argues, the FCP inferential pattern of strong permission should be restricted.

3 Running example

In this section, we follow the intuition behind Example 2 and present a possible resolution of conflict between prima facie permission and obligation. The principle of this resolution requires that a prima facie permission must stay consistent with any existing obligation. This intuition can be formalised based on the notion of "Obligation as weak permission", represented by the OWP rule, which is an axiom in van Benthem's minimal deontic logic [van Benthem, 1979]:

$$\text{OWP:} \frac{O\varphi, P\psi}{\Box(\psi \to \varphi)}$$

It is necessary that what is permitted is not in conflict with what ought to be.

The following example in legal reasoning illustrates the feature of defeasibility displayed by prima facie permission.

1. It is permitted for the owner to use any of his or her property, for example, a private car.

2. It is prohibited to cause air pollution.

The question now is whether it is permitted to use one's private car which exceeds certain air pollution levels. The solution we adopt is that it is permitted to use private cars in normal situations i.e where the permission is not defeated. So we can derive that:

3. Cars are not used beyond the air pollution level.

If we add information that "this car is used beyond the air pollution level", or "this car can be used beyond the air pollution level", and in addition we *prefer* these *specific* statements, we would expect that the derivation of statement (3) will be blocked. Furthermore, when applying the (OWP) rule to assumption (1), the permission to use cars and cause air pollution may be blocked when assumption (2) is preferable. However, by applying the same rule, we would still expect, for example, a permission to use cars while commuting, because there is *no preferable* argument to the contrary.

From a formal point of view, the problem of strong or prima facie permissions that we focus on in this chapter is the derivation of $P(\varphi \wedge \psi)$ from $P\varphi$. It has been observed by Glavaničová [2018] that this is a rule that should not hold in case it leads to inconsistency.

EXAMPLE 3 (Air Pollution) *Our aim is to define a defeasible logic such that the prima facie permission to use cars, Pc, can infer a permission* *to use a car for commuting, $P(c \wedge m)$. Similarly, from Pc we can infer $P(c \wedge a)$, a permission to use cars and cause air pollution. However, in certain exceptional cases, for instance having using cars permitted but having air pollution prohibited, from $\{Pc, O\neg a\}$ we cannot infer $P(c \wedge a)$, and thus the logic is non-monotonic.*

To capture the non-monotonic reasoning in Example 3, we adopt a variant of van Benthem's [1979] minimal deontic logic as the monotonic base. This logic contains two axioms for the FCP and OWP patterns, which are necessary for the derivations in Example 3.

Each level in our approach can be analysed using the methods pertaining to the relevant discipline, i.e. monotonic logic can be studied using, for example, modal logics based on possible world semantics); argumentation theory can be studied using rationality postulates [Caminada, 2018]; and non-monotonic inference can be analysed using, for example, the approach advocated by Kraus et al. [1990].

4 Using ASPIC+ to design defeasible deontic logics

In this chapter, we explain the basic idea of employing ASPIC$^+$ to design deontic argumentation systems and defeasible deontic logics and, in particular, to study strong permission. The ASPIC+ approach has been discussed in a variety of papers [Straßer and Arieli, 2019; Dong et al., 2019b]. In our opinion, this approach is one of the most transparent ones suitable to put forward our idea in argumentation, and we follow the exposition provided by Modgil and Prakken in the handbook of formal argumentation [Modgil and Prakken, 2018]. ASPIC$^+$ is a framework for specifying argumentation systems, and it leaves one full freedom to choose the logical language, the strict and defeasible inference rules, the axioms and ordinary premises in a knowledge base, and the argument preference ordering [Modgil and Prakken, 2018].

Modgil and Prakken [2018] observe that "in ASPIC$^+$ and its predecessors, going back to the seminal work of John Pollock, arguments can be formed by combining strict and defeasible inference rules and conflicts between arguments can be resolved in terms of a preference relation on arguments. This results in abstract argumentation frameworks (a set of arguments with a binary relation of defeat), so that arguments can be evaluated with the theory of abstract argumentation." In this chapter, we use argumentation systems to define defeasible deontic logics. Our ASPIC$^+$-based methodology consists of three steps.

1) **Arguments:** we take literally Modgil and Prakken's [2018] idea that "rule-based approaches in general do not adopt a single base logic but

two base logics, one for the strict and one for the defeasible rules". We use monotonic modal logics as our base logics with Hilbert-style proof theory.

1.1) Strict arguments use only strict rules defined in terms of a "lower bound" logic that defines the minimal inferences that must be made. We use a variant of von Wright's standard deontic logic [Parent and van der Torre, 2018] for strict arguments.

1.2) Defeasible arguments also use defeasible rules defined in terms of an "upper bound" logic that defines all possible inferences that can be made. We use a variant of van Benthem's logic of strong permission [van Benthem, 1979] for defeasible arguments.

2) Preferences among arguments can be generic or can depend on the logical languages used to build the arguments. We focus on **argument types** defined in ASPIC$^+$ that distinguish between defeasible and plausible arguments.

3) Non-monotonic inference relations can be based on a sceptical or credulous relation, and on one of the argumentation semantics. Here, we only choose the sceptical inferential relation based on stable semantics.

In the following sections, we present the above notions in ASPIC$^+$ step by step.

5 Arguments based on two monotonic logics

We use two monotonic logics to define the strict and defeasible rules in ASPIC$^+$, and use the crude approach to define arguments [Modgil and Prakken, 2018]: "A crude way is to simply put all valid propositional (or first-order) inferences over your language of choice in [the strict rules] R_s. So if a propositional language has been chosen, then R_s can be defined as follows (where $\vdash_{PL}$ denotes standard propositional-logic consequence). For any finite $S \subseteq \mathcal{L}$ and any $\phi \in \mathcal{L}$: $S \to \phi \in R_s$ if and only if $S \vdash_{PL} \phi$." This method can be applied to define defeasible rules, and this application, as stated by Modgil and Prakken [2018], should be based on some cognitive or rational criteria. By using the crude method to define strict rules in the lower-bounded logic $\mathbf{S}^-$ and to define defeasible rules in the upper-bounded logic $\mathbf{S}^+$, the arguments can be short even when Hilbert style derivations are quite long.

Besides this way of defining the defeasible rules, all the other definitions in this section—like the arguments and the extensions—are standard and taken from the handbook chapter by Modgil and Prakken [2018]. In particular, we consider three instantiations of ASPIC$^+$ by taking different monotonic logics ($\mathbf{D}_{-1}$ or $\mathbf{D}_{-2}$, defined later) as the basic logic and then treating either as only FCP or FCP together with OWP (in Table 1) as defeasible. In this section, we define the notion of argumentation theory. In the following section, we use argumentation theory to define non-monotonic logic as a combination of two selected monotonic logics: $\mathbf{S}^-, \mathbf{S}^+$.

We first present a version of van Benthem's [1979] deontic logic of obligation and strong permission. This logic is different from standard deontic logic [Parent and van der Torre, 2018]. Standard deontic logic sees obligation and permission as a dual pair representing that what is permitted is not obligatory not to be. Van Benthem's deontic logic does not take this view. While this logic still interprets obligation as what is necessary for staying ideal, it interprets permission as what is sufficient for staying ideal. This new connection can be formalised as OWP. The modal language contains the classic negation $\neg$, conjunction $\wedge$, universal modality $\Box$, and two additional deontic modalities: O for obligation and P for strong permission.

DEFINITION 4 (Deontic Language) *Let p be any element of a given (countable) set Prop of atomic propositions. The deontic language $\mathcal{L}$ of modal formulas is defined as follows:*

$$\phi := p \mid \neg\phi \mid (\phi \wedge \phi) \mid \Box\phi \mid O\phi \mid P\phi$$

The disjunction $\vee$, the material implication $\rightarrow$ and the existential modality $\Diamond$ are defined as usual: $\phi \vee \psi := \neg(\neg\phi \wedge \neg\psi)$, $\phi \rightarrow \psi := \neg(\phi \wedge \neg\psi)$ and $\Diamond\phi := \neg\Box\neg\phi$.

DEFINITION 5 *The deontic logic $\mathbf{D}$ is a system that includes all the axioms and rules in Table 1.*

The axiomatisation presented in Table 1 is a variant of van Benthem's logic [van Benthem, 1979]. We use $\mathbf{D}$ to denote it. The deontic logic $\mathbf{D}$ not only takes obligation and universal modality into account, but also considers free-choice permission and the connection between obligation and permission. In logic $\mathbf{D}$, except for the essential K$_\Box$, E$_\Box$, T$_\Box$, 4$_\Box$, B$_\Box$, and NEC$_\Box$ (NEC stands for necessity), the axioms $\Box_O$ and $\Box_P$ are the core of the universal modality in normal modal logic. Moreover, $\Box_O$ claims that what is always the case is obligatory, but $\Box_P$ leaves the space for what is never to be permitted. The axiom D$_O$ maintains that an obligation is to be ideally consistent as usual. OWP considers "obligation as the weakest permission" [van Benthem, 1979; Anglberger *et al.*, 2015]. RFC (it stands for "Reverse of free choice permission") represents one direction of free-choice permission, and FCP the other. For further information about the logic and its motivations, see the work of van Benthem [1979].

- PL: all propositional tautologies
- $E_\square$: $\square\phi \leftrightarrow \neg\Diamond\neg\phi$
- $4_\square$: $\square\phi \to \square\square\phi$
- $\square_O$: $\square\phi \to O\phi$
- D_O: $\neg(O\phi \wedge O\neg\phi)$
- RFC: $P\phi \wedge P\psi \to P(\phi \vee \psi)$
- MP: $\phi, \phi \to \psi / \psi$

where $\triangle \in \{\square, O\}$

- $K_\triangle$: $\triangle(\phi \to \psi) \to (\triangle\phi \to \triangle\psi)$
- $T_\square$: $\square\phi \to \phi$
- $B_\square$: $\phi \to \square\Diamond\phi$
- $\square_P$: $P\bot$
- OWP: $O\phi \wedge P\psi \to \square(\psi \to \phi)$
- FCP: $P\psi \wedge \square(\phi \to \psi) \to P\phi$
- $NEC_\triangle$: $\phi / \triangle\phi$

Table 1: The logic **D** of obligation and permission

In this chapter, we consider sub-systems of **D** that contain a strict subset of the axioms and inference rules of **D**. In particular, we define $\mathbf{D}_{-1}$ as an axiomatisation that does not contain FCP, and we define $\mathbf{D}_{-2}$ as an axiomatisation that does not contain OWP and other axioms (FCP, RFC and $\square_P$) used purely for permission.

DEFINITION 6 *The deontic logic $\mathbf{D}_{-1}$ is a system that includes all the axioms and rules in* **D** *except FCP. The deontic logic $\mathbf{D}_{-2}$ is a system that includes all the axioms and rules in* **D** *except RFC, $\square_P$, FCP, and OWP.*

We define the notions of derivation based on modal logic $\mathbf{S} \in \{\mathbf{D}, \mathbf{D}_{-1}, \mathbf{D}_{-2}\}$ in the usual way, see [Blackburn *et al.*, 2002] for instance. Note that modal logic provides two related kinds of derivation according to the application of necessitation, i.e. necessitation can only be applied to theorems and not to an arbitrary set of formulas. We use both notions in the formal argumentation theory.

DEFINITION 7 (Derivations without Premises) *Let $\mathbf{S} \in \{\mathbf{D}, \mathbf{D}_{-1}, \mathbf{D}_{-2}\}$ be a deontic logic. A derivation of ϕ in* **S** *is a finite sequence $\phi_1, \ldots, \phi_{n-1}, \phi_n$ such that $\phi = \phi_n$, and for every $\phi_i(1 \leq i \leq n)$ in this sequence, ϕ is*

1. *either an instance of one of the axioms in* **S***, or*

2. *the result of the application of one of the rules in* **S** *to those formulas appearing before ϕ_i.*

177

We write $\vdash_S \phi$ if there is a derivation of ϕ in **S**, *or,* $\vdash \phi$ *when the context of* **S** *is clear. We say ϕ is a theorem of* **S**, *or* **S** *proves ϕ. We write $Cn(S)$ to represent the set of all the theorems of* **S**.

DEFINITION 8 (Derivations from Premises) *Let* $S \in \{D, D_{-1}, D_{-2}\}$ *be a deontic logic. Given a set Γ of formulas, a derivation of ϕ from Γ in* **S** *is a finite sequence $\phi_1, \ldots, \phi_{n-1}, \phi_n$ such that $\phi = \phi_n$, and for every $\phi_i (1 \leq i \leq n)$ in this sequence, ϕ is*

1. *either $\phi_i \in Cn(S) \cup \Gamma$; or*

2. *the result of the application of one of the rules (which is neither $NEC_\square$ nor NEC_O) to those formulas appearing before ϕ_i.*

We write $\Gamma \vdash_S \phi$ if there is a derivation from Γ for ϕ in **S** [1], *or, $\Gamma \vdash \phi$ when the context of* **S** *is clear. We say that ϕ is derivable in* **S** *from Γ. We write $Cn_S(\Gamma)$ to represent the set of formulas derivable in* **S** *from Γ, or $Cn(\Gamma)$ if the context of* **S** *is clear.*

A system **S** is consistent iff $\perp \notin Cn(S)$; otherwise, it is inconsistent. A set Γ is **S**-consistent iff $\perp \notin Cn_S(\Gamma)$; otherwise, it is inconsistent. A set $\Gamma' \subseteq \Gamma$ is a maximally **S**-consistent subset of Γ, denoted as $\Gamma' \in MC_S(\Gamma')$, iff there is no $\Gamma'' \supset \Gamma'$ such that Γ'' is **S**-consistent.

The following example explains in what sense we can say in monotonic logics that Pc and $O\neg a$ are in conflict. These two assumptions will not be consistent when taken together with the statement "It is not the case that using a car does not lead to air pollution", i.e. $\neg\square(c \to \neg a)$, which can be equally formalised as $\Diamond(c \wedge a)$. This will be explained in Example 9.

EXAMPLE 9 (Air Pollution, continued) *The following derivation shows that the set $\{Pc, O\neg a, \Diamond(c \wedge a)\}$ is inconsistent in* D_{-1} *or* **D**.

1.	$O\neg a \wedge \Diamond(c \wedge a)$	assumptions, PL
2.	$O\neg a \wedge Pc \to \square(c \to \neg a)$	OWP
3.	$\Diamond(c \wedge a) \leftrightarrow \neg\square(c \to \neg a)$	$E_\square$
4.	$O\neg a \wedge \Diamond(c \wedge a) \to \neg Pc$	2, 3, MP
5.	$\neg Pc$	1, 4, MP

To investigate when defeasible *derivations are possible, we use* **D** *only to derive conclusions that are defeasible, and we use one of the subsystems of* **D** *to define monotonic and strict conclusions.*

---

[1]Alternatively, it can be seen as a theorem $\vdash_S \bigwedge \Gamma \to \phi$ by the so-called deduction theorem.

We assume the view of ASPIC$^+$ of considering inference rules as uncertain and fallible defeasible rules, and those rules that are infallible as strict rules. This type of uncertainty or fallibility is represented by distinguishing between lower-bounded and upper-bounded logics. However, to simplify the present issue of how to use ASPIC$^+$ to define non-monotonic logics, it is not necessary to fully adopt all the methods in ASPIC$^+$ to define arguments. We only consider a general knowledge base here. The distinction between different types of knowledge is left until Section 8.

DEFINITION 10 (Argumentation Theory) *Let $\mathcal{L}$ be the deontic language and let $(\mathbf{S}^-; \mathbf{S}^+) \in \{(\mathbf{D}_{-2}; \mathbf{D}_{-1}), (\mathbf{D}_{-2}; \mathbf{D}), (\mathbf{D}_{-1}; \mathbf{D})\}$ be a Cartesian product of two monotonic logics. An argumentation system AS based on $(\mathbf{S}^-; \mathbf{S}^+)$ is a pair $(\mathcal{L}, R)$ where $R = R_s \cup R_d$ is a set of rules such that:*

- *$R_s = \{\phi_1, \ldots, \phi_n \mapsto \phi \mid \{\phi_1, \ldots, \phi_n\} \vdash_{\mathbf{S}^-} \phi\}$ is the set of strict rules, and*

- *$R_d = \{\phi_1, \ldots, \phi_n \Mapsto \phi \mid \{\phi_1, \ldots, \phi_n\} \vdash_{\mathbf{S}^+} \phi \,\&\, \{\phi_1, \ldots, \phi_n\} \nvdash_{\mathbf{S}^-} \phi\}$ is the set of defeasible rules.*

If the context of $(\mathbf{S}^-; \mathbf{S}^+)$ is clear, we mention AS without $(\mathbf{S}^-; \mathbf{S}^+)$. An argumentation theory AT is a pair (AS, K) where $K \subseteq \mathcal{L}$ is a knowledge base.

So the requirement that $R_s \cap R_d = \emptyset$ holds. We define the sets of empty-bodied strict/defeasible rules as $R_s^0 = \{\mapsto \phi \mid \mapsto \phi \in R_s\}$ and $R_d^0 = \{\Mapsto \phi \mid \Mapsto \phi \in R_d\}$. Clearly, $R_s^0 \subseteq R_s$ and $R_d^0 \subseteq R_d$.

Next, we define what are arguments. We will see that arguments have different structures to those of derivations. Although each argument corresponds to a derivation defined as a top rule, the former explicitly considers each step of this derivation as a finite sequence.

DEFINITION 11 (Arguments) *Let AT be an argumentation theory with a knowledge base K and an argumentation system $(\mathcal{L}, R)$. Given each $n \in \mathbb{N}$, the set $\mathcal{A}_n$ where $n \in \mathbb{N}$ is defined as follows:*

$$
\begin{aligned}
\mathcal{A}_0 &= K \cup R_s^0 \cup R_d^0 \\
\mathcal{A}_{n+1} &= \mathcal{A}_n \cup \{B_1, \ldots, B_m \rhd \psi \mid B_i \in \mathcal{A}_n \text{ for all } i \in \{1, \ldots, m\}\}
\end{aligned}
$$

where $\rhd \in \{\mapsto, \Mapsto\}$, and for an element $B \in \mathcal{A}_i$ with $i \in \mathbb{N}$:

- *if $B = \psi \in K$, then $Prem(B) = \{\psi\}$, $Conc(B) = \psi$, $Sub(B) = \{\psi\}$, $Rules_d(B) = \emptyset$, and $TopRule(B) = undefined$;*

- *if $B = \mapsto \psi \in R_s^0$, then $Prem(B) = \emptyset$, $Conc(B) = \psi$, $Sub(B) = \{\mapsto \psi\}$, $Rules_d(B) = \emptyset$, and $TopRule(B) = \mapsto \psi$;*

- if $B = \Rightarrow \psi \in R_d^0$, then $Prem(B) = \emptyset$, $Conc(B) = \psi$, $Sub(B) = \{\Rightarrow \psi\}$, $Rules_d(B) = \{\Rightarrow \psi\}$, and $TopRule(B) = \Rightarrow \psi$;

- if $B = B_1, \ldots, B_m \rhd \psi$ where $\rhd$ is $\mapsto$, then
  $\{Conc(B_1), \ldots, Conc(B_m)\} \mapsto \psi \in R_s$ with
  $Prem(B) = Prem(B_1) \cup \ldots \cup Prem(B_m)$, $Conc(B) = \psi$,
  $Sub(B) = Sub(B_1) \cup \ldots \cup Sub(B_m) \cup \{B\}$,
  $Rules_d(B) = Rules_d(B_1) \cup \ldots \cup Rules_d(B_m)$,
  $TopRule(B) = Conc(B_1), \ldots, Conc(B_m) \mapsto \psi$; and

- if $B = B_1, \ldots, B_m \rhd \psi$ where $\rhd$ is $\Rightarrow$, then each condition is similar to the previous item, except that the rule is defeasible and $Rules_d(B) = Rules_d(B_1) \cup \ldots \cup Rules_d(B_m) \cup \{Conc(B_1), \ldots, Conc(B_m) \Rightarrow \psi\}$.

We define $\mathcal{A} = \bigcup_{n \in \mathbb{N}} \mathcal{A}_n$ as the set of arguments on the basis of AT, and define $Conc(E) = \{\varphi \subseteq Conc(A) \mid A \in E\}$ where $E \subseteq \mathcal{A}$. Let $F(B) = Conc(Sub(B))$ when $B \in \mathcal{A}$. We have $F(E) = \bigcup \{F(B) \mid B \in E \subseteq \mathcal{A}\}$.

The following example illustrates the arguments provided in the running example. We consider the defeats (arrows) in Figure 2 in the next section.

EXAMPLE 12 (Air Pollution, continued) *Let* $K = \{\Diamond(c \wedge a), O\neg a, Pc\}$ *be a knowledge base where the atomic proposition* c *stands for someone using cars, and atomic proposition* a *stands for someone causing air pollution. Prohibition or forbidden means "ought not to". There are three arguments in knowledge base* K:

- $A = O\neg a$: *It is prohibited for someone to cause air pollution;*

- $B = Pc$: *It is permitted for someone to use cars;*

- $C = \Diamond(c \wedge a)$: *It is possible for someone who uses cars to cause air pollution.*

Some arguments constructed from K *are shown as follows:*

1. *the arguments that have top rules as strict rules by using* NEC_O *and* K_O *in* $\mathbf{D}_{-2}$:

   - $A''' = A \mapsto O\neg(c \wedge a)$

2. *the arguments that have top rules as defeasible rules by using* OWP *and* $E_\Box$ *in* $\mathbf{D}_{-1}$:

   - $A' = A, C \Rightarrow \neg Pc$

- $A'' = A, C \Rrightarrow \neg P(c \wedge a)$
- $B' = B, C \Rrightarrow \neg O \neg a$
- $B''' = B, C \Rrightarrow \neg O \neg (c \wedge a)$
- $C' = A, B \Rrightarrow \neg \Diamond (c \wedge a)$

3. *the arguments that have top rules as defeasible rules by using FCP in* $\mathbf{D}_{-1}$:

- $B'' = B \Rrightarrow P(c \wedge a)$
- $B''' = B \Rrightarrow P(c \wedge m)$

where m is short for someone commuting.

Because arguments A' and A''' both have premise $O \neg a$, we consider that these two arguments represent this obligation $O \neg a$. On the other hand, arguments B' and B'' both have Pc as a premise, and we consider that they represent permission Pc.

The formulas pertaining to the set $\{A'', A''', B'''\}$ of arguments are $\{O \neg a, O \neg (c \wedge a), \Diamond (c \wedge a), Pc, \neg P(c \wedge a), P(c \wedge m)\}$. In Section 6, we present a mechanism for selecting this desired set of arguments, so that the defeasible deontic logic corresponds to it.

6   Preferences among arguments

In this chapter, we follow the idea proposed by Modgil and Prakken [2018] of partitioning arguments on the basis of strict, defeasible, and sound arguments. These partitions on arguments can be used to define two orders: rule-based and premise-based. The rule-based order prefers strict arguments to defeasible arguments, while premise-based order prefers unsound arguments to sound ones.

DEFINITION 13 (Argument Properties) *Let* A, B *be arguments and* E *a set of arguments. Then* A *is strict if* $Rules_d(A) = \emptyset$, *it is defeasible if* $Rules_d(A) \neq \emptyset$, *and it is sound if* $Prem(A) \cap K \neq \emptyset$. *We define* $Concs(E) = \{Conc(A) \mid A \in E\}$. *The partial order* $\leq$ *over* E *is rule-based iff we have* $A \leq B$ *iff* A *is defeasible, and it is premise-based iff* $A \leq B$ *iff* A *is sound.*

We use $\leq^{\tau}$ to denote a τ-ordering with $\tau \in \{r, p\}$, where r stands for rule-based and p stands for premise-based. The premise-based ordering $\leq$ is an *universal* order, because given any $A, B \in \mathcal{A}$, it is the case that $A \leq B$.

Next, we introduce the notions of defeat. The first notion is rebuttal and the second is undermining [Modgil and Prakken, 2018]. In order to

181

simplify the discussion, we do not make any additional assumptions like distinguishing between different kinds of defeated knowledge on undermining. In the next section, distinguishing between rebuttal and undermining will give different consequences in defeasible deontic reasoning.

DEFINITION 14 (Argumentation Frameworks) *Given $A, B \in \mathcal{A}$ and an order $\leq$ over $\mathcal{A}$, argument A defeats argument B, or simply call it a* defeat, *denoted as $(A, B) \in \mathcal{D}$ if and only if:*

- *A rebuts B: $Conc(A) = +\phi$ for some $B' \in Sub(B)$ and $TopRule(B') \in R_d$, $Conc(B') = -\phi$, and $A \not< B'$, or*

- *A undermines B: $Conc(A) = +\phi$ for knowledge $-\phi \in Prem(B)$ of B and $A \not< -\phi$,*

where $+\phi$ indicates m negations in front of ϕ, and $-\phi$ indicates n negations in front of ϕ, such that $|m-n|$ is an odd number. An abstract argumentation framework AF corresponding to $\langle AT, \leq^\tau \rangle$ is a pair $(\mathcal{A}, \mathcal{D})$ where $\mathcal{D}$ is the set of all defeats defined by $\leq$ over $\mathcal{A}$.

As the following example shows, the notions of defeat can explain the idea of one rule taking precedence over another. Notice that knowledge, defeasible rules, and preferences are the three key elements to deciding what are defeated.

EXAMPLE 15 (Defeats in knifed murder, continued) *As shown in Figure 1, when in the rule-based ordering, A''' rebuts B'''', but not vice versa. This shows a case of obligation defeating permission but not vice versa.*

Now we turn to the premise-based ordering. As shown in Figure 2, we have that B' undermines A''', which indicates a permission defeating an obligation. Here, we can see that all rebuttals in the rule-based ordering are also maintained in the premise-based ordering. So the straight arrows in Figure 2 represent defeat relations under the rule-based ordering, and the dashed arrows represent the additional defeat relations under the premise-based ordering.

DEFINITION 16 (Dung Extensions) *Let $AF = (\mathcal{A}, \mathcal{D})$ and let $E \subseteq \mathcal{A}$ be a set of arguments. Then:*

- *E is conflict-free iff $\forall A, B \in E$, we have $(A, B) \notin \mathcal{D}$;*

- *$A \in \mathcal{A}$ is acceptable w.r.t. E iff when $B \in \mathcal{A}$ such that $(B, A) \in \mathcal{D}$, then $\exists C \in E$ such that $(C, B) \in \mathcal{D}$;*

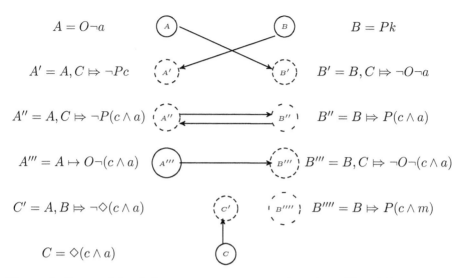

$A = O\neg a$

$A' = A, C \Rrightarrow \neg Pc$

$A'' = A, C \Rrightarrow \neg P(c \wedge a)$

$A''' = A \mapsto O\neg(c \wedge a)$

$C' = A, B \Rrightarrow \neg\Diamond(c \wedge a)$

$C = \Diamond(c \wedge a)$

$B = Pk$

$B' = B, C \Rrightarrow \neg O\neg a$

$B'' = B \Rrightarrow P(c \wedge a)$

$B''' = B, C \Rrightarrow \neg O\neg(c \wedge a)$

$B'''' = B \Rrightarrow P(c \wedge m)$

Figure 1: Some of the defeats among arguments based on $(\mathbf{D}_{-2}; \mathbf{D})$ in the rule-based ordering. Straight arrows are defeats among these arguments.

- E is an admissible set iff E is conflict-free, and if $A \in E$, then A is acceptable w.r.t. E;

- E is a complete extension iff E is admissible, and if $A \in \mathcal{A}$ is acceptable w.r.t. E, then $A \in E$;

- E is a stable extension iff E is conflict-free and $\forall B \notin E \exists A \in E$ such that $(A, B) \in \mathcal{D}$.

The following example illustrates a different sense of consistency in ASPIC$^+$ by using stable extensions in order to explain, given the inconsistent knowledge base K, why $B \Rrightarrow P(c \wedge a)$ is sometimes defeated and why $B \Rrightarrow P(c \wedge m)$ is always undefeated.

EXAMPLE 17 (Air Pollution, continued) *Consider the arrows in Figure 1. The straight arrows represent defeat relations under the rule-based ordering, and the dashed arrows represent additional defeat relations under the premise-based or universal ordering. Under the rule-based ordering, arguments A, B and C will not be defeated in every extension, whereas in premise-based or universal ordering, they will be. For this reason, we prefer the rule-based ordering in this example. Furthermore, under the rule-based ordering, we have at least two stable extensions, one containing $B \Rrightarrow P(c \wedge a)$*

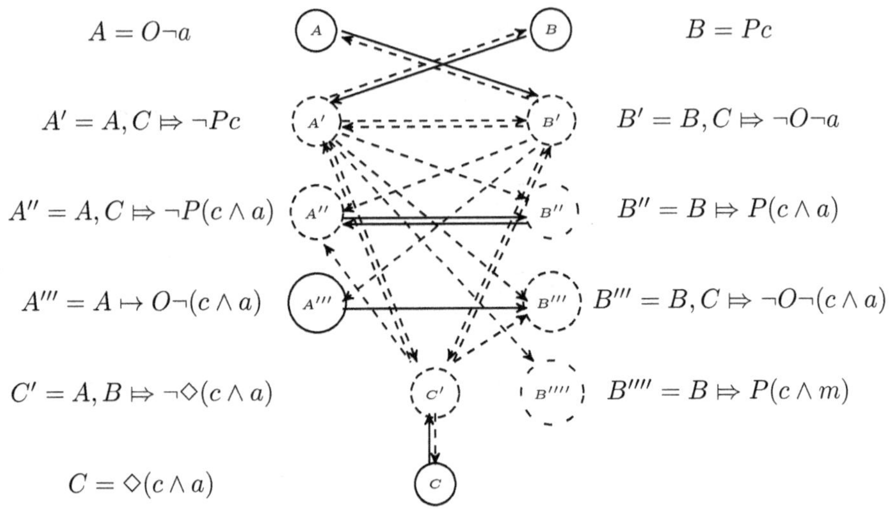

$A = O\neg a$

$B = Pc$

$A' = A, C \Rrightarrow \neg Pc$

$B' = B, C \Rrightarrow \neg O\neg a$

$A'' = A, C \Rrightarrow \neg P(c \wedge a)$

$B'' = B \Rrightarrow P(c \wedge a)$

$A''' = A \mapsto O\neg(c \wedge a)$

$B''' = B, C \Rrightarrow \neg O\neg(c \wedge a)$

$C' = A, B \Rrightarrow \neg\Diamond(c \wedge a)$

$B'''' = B \Rrightarrow P(c \wedge m)$

$C = \Diamond(c \wedge a)$

Figure 2: Some of the defeats among arguments based on $(\mathbf{D}_{-2}; \mathbf{D})$ in the premise-based ordering. Straight arrows are rebuttals while dashed arrows are underminings.

and another containing $A, C \Rrightarrow \neg P(c \wedge a)$. Since $B'''' = B \Rrightarrow P(c \wedge m)$ will not be defeated, we have B'''' in every stable extension. Similarly, arguments in the form of $A_1, \ldots, A_n \mapsto Pk \vee O\neg a \vee \Diamond(c \wedge a)$ are contained in every stable extension.

Not only can plausible and defeasible arguments be compared in the preference ordering, factual statements can be preferred to deontic statements, and prohibitions to permissions or vice versa. We leave such further investigations until Section 8.

7 Designing defeasible deontic logics

Our defeasible deontic logics are designed by using the stable extensions pertaining to different monotonic logics and different orderings. The proposition that follows provides a guideline for searching for these stable extensions. In the case of premise-based ordering, strict rules are equally preferable to defeasible rules. So a stable extension can be considered as a maximally consistent subset of knowledge base K in the upper-bounded logic. We call this an *undermining*-based construction, for details see e.g. [Arieli *et al.*, 2018; Straßer and Arieli, 2019]. But this is not enough to capture the case of rule-based ordering in which the defeasible argument is less preferable compared to the others. So the second item of this proposition provides a rule-based method for constructing the desired extensions, stable extensions. We construct each stable extension in the style of Lindenbaum's Lemma [Blackburn et al., 2002]. That is, we first consider the maximally consistent subset K' of the knowledge base with regard to the lower-bounded logic $\mathbf{S}^-$ for strict rules, and then a consistent subset of K' with regard to the upper-bounded logic $\mathbf{S}^+$ for defeasible rules, such that no argument with regard to $\mathbf{S}^+$ defeats that with regard to $\mathbf{S}^-$, and K' is a maximal set satisfying these two conditions. This is called a *rebuttal*-based construction. It can be considered as a way of fibring—combining two logics [Gabbay, 1996]. See the following proposition for details.

PROPOSITION 18 *Consider the deontic language $\mathcal{L}$ and a pair of two monotonic logics $(\mathbf{S}^-; \mathbf{S}^+) \in \{(\mathbf{D}_{-2}; \mathbf{D}_{-1}), (\mathbf{D}_{-2}; \mathbf{D}), (\mathbf{D}_{-1}; \mathbf{D})\}$. Let AF, corresponding to $\langle AT, \leq^\tau \rangle$, be an abstract argumentation framework $(\mathcal{A}, \mathcal{D})$ such that AT is based on $(\mathbf{S}^-; \mathbf{S}^+)$, K is a knowledge base, and $\tau \in \{p, r\}$. Given a set $\Gamma \subseteq \mathcal{L}$ of formulas, we define:*

- *a stable set generated by Γ as $\{D \in \mathcal{A} \mid F(D) \subseteq Cn_{\mathbf{S}^+}(\Gamma)\}$;*

- *a proper set generated by Γ as $\bigcup_{i \in \omega} E_i$, such that*

$$E_0 = \{D \in \mathcal{A} \mid F(D) \subseteq Cn_{\mathbf{S}^-}(\Gamma)\}$$

$$E_{n+1} = \begin{cases} E_n \cup \{D \in \mathcal{A}\}, & \text{if } F(D) \subseteq Cn_{\mathbf{S}^+}(\Gamma) \text{ and} \\ & \quad F(D) \cup F(E_n) \text{ is } \mathbf{S}^- \text{-consistent;} \\ E_n, & \text{otherwise.} \end{cases}$$

1. *When $\tau = p$, then E is a stable set generated by $\Gamma \in MC_{\mathbf{S}^+}(K)$ iff E is a stable extension regarding K.*

2. *When $\tau = r$, E is a proper set generated by $\Gamma \in MC_{\mathbf{S}^-}(K)$ iff E is a stable extension regarding K.*

Given the knowledge base $K = \{Pc, O\neg a, \Diamond(c \wedge a)\}$ of the running example, ASPIC$^+$ provides a mechanism for deciding whether the two arguments $A''' = A \mapsto O\neg(c \wedge a)$ and $B''' = B, C \Mapsto \neg O\neg(c \wedge a)$ can be accepted. In the case of premise-based order, undermining together with stability is a mechanism for ensuring that even when knowledge base K is not consistent, there is still a way to find maximally consistent subsets to construct stable extensions. In the case of rule-based ordering, we cannot use the undermining-based construction to ensure that we derive the first argument but not the second one. Instead, we need to use the rebuttal-based construction. The rebuttal approach can accept both the above arguments, unless one works contrary to the other. That is why the two arguments need to be distinguished in the lower-bounded and upper-bounded logics.

We now present the central definition of the chapter, namely the definition of defeasible deontic logic in terms of formal argumentation theory. This is well in line with current practice in ASPIC$^+$. We first take the desired conclusions in each stable extension (as shown in Proposition 18) and then the intersection of all the stable extensions.

DEFINITION 19 (Defeasible Inferences) *Let $\Gamma \subseteq \mathcal{L}$ and $\phi \in \mathcal{L}$. We let $(\mathbf{S}^-;\mathbf{S}^+) \in \{(\mathbf{D}_{-2};\mathbf{D}_{-1}),(\mathbf{D}_{-2};\mathbf{D}),(\mathbf{D}_{-1};\mathbf{D})\}$ be a Cartesian product of two monotonic logics, and let $\leq^\tau$ be a τ-ordering such that $\tau \in \{r,p\}$. Let AT be a Γ-argumentation theory based on $(\mathbf{S}^-;\mathbf{S}^+)$ iff the argumentation theory AT obtains with $K = \Gamma$, and iff $AF^\tau = \langle AT, \leq^\tau \rangle$. The non-monotonic inference $\Vdash^\tau_{\mathbf{S}^-;\mathbf{S}^+}$ is defined as follows:*

- *$\Gamma \Vdash^{\tau\forall}_{\mathbf{S}^-;\mathbf{S}^+} \phi$ iff every stable extension of the Γ-AT based on $(\mathbf{S}^-;\mathbf{S}^+)$ corresponding to AF^τ contains an argument A with $Conc(A) = \phi$.*

We define the closure operator corresponding to this inference relation as usual: $\mathcal{C}^{\tau\forall}_{\mathbf{S}^-;\mathbf{S}^+}(\Gamma) = \{\phi \mid \Gamma \Vdash^{\tau\forall}_{\mathbf{S}^-;\mathbf{S}^+} \phi\}$. Moreover, we write $\Vdash^{\tau\forall}_{\mathbf{S}^-;\mathbf{S}^+} \phi$ when $\emptyset \Vdash^{\tau\forall}_{\mathbf{S}^-;\mathbf{S}^+} \phi$.

The resulting non-monotonic inference relations are standard relations among sets of formulas pertaining to the logical language, i.e. they no longer refer to ASPIC$^+$. An alternative way to define non-monotonic logics is to first consider the intersection of all stable extensions, and then the conclusions of the arguments that appear in the intersection. For instance, $Pc \vee O\neg a \vee \Diamond(c \wedge a)$ is an element in $\mathcal{C}^{\tau\forall}_{\mathbf{D}_{-2};\mathbf{D}}(\{Pc, O\neg a, \Diamond(c \wedge a)\}$ where $\tau \in \{p,r\}$. With the alternative approach mentioned above, this cannot be inferred because it is possible to have many different arguments, for instance $Pc \Mapsto Pc \vee O\neg a \vee \Diamond(c \wedge a)$ and $O\neg a \Mapsto Pc \vee O\neg a \vee \Diamond(c \wedge a)$, that contain the same conclusion but from different premises.

The following proposition offers a detailed explanation of the mechanisms we have proposed. First, the undermining mechanism states that the non-monotonic consequences are the intersection of all maximally consistent subsets of the knowledge base under an universal or premise-based ordering. Second, and more generally, the rebuttal mechanism states that the non-monotonic consequences are encased in all unions of a maximally consistent subset of the knowledge base with regard to the lower-bounded logic, and are encased in a consistent subset of those unions with regard to the upper-bounded logic in certain maximal behaviour.

186

PROPOSITION 20 *Let* $\Gamma \subseteq \mathcal{L}$, $(\mathbf{S}^-; \mathbf{S}^+) \in \{(\mathbf{D}_{-2}; \mathbf{D}_{-1}), (\mathbf{D}_{-2}; \mathbf{D}), (\mathbf{D}_{-1}; \mathbf{D})\}$ *be a pair of two monotonic logics and let* K *be a knowledge base of AT. We define*

- *an R-set generated by* K *in* $(\mathbf{S}^-; \mathbf{S}^+)$ *as* $\bigcup_{n \in \mathbb{N}} R_n$, *such that*

$$R_0 = Cn_{\mathbf{S}^-}(\Gamma)$$

$$R_{n+1} = \begin{cases} R_n \cup \{\varphi\}, & \text{if } \varphi \in Cn_{\mathbf{S}^+}(\Gamma) \text{ and} \\ & \{\varphi\} \cup R_n \text{ is } \mathbf{S}^-\text{-consistent;} \\ R_n, & \text{otherwise;} \end{cases}$$

where $\Gamma \in MC_{\mathbf{S}^-}(K)$.

The R-collection $R_{\mathbf{S}^-;\mathbf{S}^+}(K)$ *generated by* K *in* $(\mathbf{S}^-; \mathbf{S}^+)$ *is the set of all R-sets generated by* K *in* $(\mathbf{S}^-; \mathbf{S}^+)$. *Then:*

1. $\mathcal{C}^{p\forall}_{\mathbf{S}^-;\mathbf{S}^+}(K) = \bigcap_{\Gamma \in MC_{\mathbf{S}^+}(K)} Cn_{\mathbf{S}^+}(\Gamma)$;

2. $\mathcal{C}^{r\forall}_{\mathbf{S}^-;\mathbf{S}^+}(K) = \bigcap R_{\mathbf{S}^-;\mathbf{S}^+}(K)$.

To prove Proposition 20, and inspired by Proposition 18, we first consider the maximally consistent subset of the knowledge base with regard to the lower-bounded logic $\mathbf{S}^-$, and then consider the consistent subset of the knowledge base with regard to the upper-bounded logic $\mathbf{S}^+$, such that the second consistent set is maximal in the sense that it is consistent with each element of the first consistent set with regard to the lower-bounded logic. In contrast, Proposition 20.2 illustrates a different understanding of maximality of consistency, which not only has to consider the consistency of the upper-bounded logic but also its consistency with each element in the lower-bounded logic. Our method of defining defeasible deontic logic follows from the "layer" method, which has been used to deal with "paraconsistency" [Benferhat *et al.*, 1995]. These methods share a similar spirit of handling maximal consistency when instantiating formal argumentation based on classical logic [Amgoud and Besnard, 2013] or modal logic [Beirlaen *et al.*, 2018]. What we have done here is to explicitly construct a stable extension according to the variants on the upper-/lower-bounded logics as well as the variants on the orders.

We leave to further research a formal analysis of the non-monotonic inference relation, as well as the development of alternative non-monotonic relations in terms of the formal argumentation theory.

EXAMPLE 21 (Air Pollution, continued) *Given a knowledge base* $K = \{\Diamond(c \land a), O\neg a, Pc\}$ *as the premises, we have different non-monotonic consequences* shown in Table 2, depending on the combinations of monotonic logics and orderings. They are non-monotonic in the sense that, even given Pk as one premise, $P(c \wedge a)$ is excluded in every non-monotonic consequence, while $P(c \wedge m)$ is a non-monotonic consequence with regard to $(\mathbf{D}_{-2}; \mathbf{D})$ under the rule-based ordering. Intuitively speaking, in Figure 1 there is no defeat of arguments ending with $P(c \wedge m)$, while there is an argument A'' that defeats a B'' that ends with $P(c \wedge a)$.

	Order	Closure	Example of Consequences
$(\mathbf{D}_{-2}; \mathbf{D}_{-1})$	p	T_p	$\bigvee K$
$(\mathbf{D}_{-2}; \mathbf{D}_{-1})$	r	T_r^1	$\Diamond(c \wedge a), O\neg a, Pc, O\neg(c \wedge a), \bigvee K$
$(\mathbf{D}_{-2}; \mathbf{D})$	p	T_p	$\bigvee K$
$(\mathbf{D}_{-2}; \mathbf{D})$	r	T_r^2	$\Diamond(c \wedge a), O\neg a, Pc, O\neg(c \wedge a),$ $P(c \wedge m), \bigvee K$
$(\mathbf{D}_{-1}; \mathbf{D})$	p, r	T_p	$\bigvee K$

Table 2: Examples of defeasible inferences in the case of knifed murder, based on knowledge base $\{\Diamond(c \wedge a), O\neg a, Pc\}$. We have $T_p = \bigcap_{\Gamma \in MC_{\mathbf{D}_{-1}}(K)} Cn_{\mathbf{D}_{-1}}(\Gamma)$, $T_r^1 = \bigcap R_{\mathbf{D}_{-2}; \mathbf{D}_{-1}}(K)$, and $T_r^2 = \bigcap R_{\mathbf{D}_{-2}; \mathbf{D}}(K)$.

8   Preferences on premises

This section describes further research on defeasible inferences defined by preferences on premises. Example 21 shows that the premise-based ordering equalises all inconsistent results, and then only provides the disjunction of all inconsistent formulas to receive a consistent conclusion. If we have different priorities on the premises, do we have different defeasible consequences? To answer this question, we define defeasible deontic logics based on different priorities on the premises. All defeasible deontic logics instantiated in this section are handled by a more general *undermining* mechanism.

Preferences over arguments can be distinguished according to different taxonomies of premises. Here we investigate two approaches. One suggests splitting arguments into two parts, such that some deontic formulas are more preferable than others. This provides us with different kinds of preferences over arguments based on the language types of their premises. Another approach follows that discussed by Modgil and Prakken [2018], and it divides arguments by strict and defeasible knowledge.

8.1 Preferences on language types

Now, we distinguish between arguments based on the different kinds of premises they have. We first categorise arguments by the premises in which we are interested—in the form of $\Diamond\varphi$, $O\varphi$ or $P\varphi$—and then we propose six different orderings according to these categories. Here, we categorise the deontic language by modalities. We say that φ is a non-permissible formula denoted as $\varphi \in \mathcal{L}_P^-$ iff there is no P-modality appearing in φ, that formula φ is a non-obligatory formula denoted as $\varphi \in \mathcal{L}_O^-$ iff there is no O-modality appearing in φ, that formula φ is a non-factual formula denoted as $\varphi \in \mathcal{L}_\Diamond^-$ iff there is no $\Diamond$- or $\Box$-modality appearing in φ, that formula φ is a permissible formula denoted as $\varphi \in \mathcal{L}_P$ iff the only modality appearing in φ is P-modality, that formula φ is an obligatory formula denoted as $\varphi \in \mathcal{L}_O$ iff the only modality appearing in φ is O-modality, and that formula φ is a factual formula denoted as $\varphi \in \mathcal{L}_\Diamond$ iff the only modalities appearing in φ are either $\Diamond$- or $\Box$-modality. For example, we have $O\neg(c \wedge a) \wedge Pm \in \mathcal{L}_\Diamond^-$.

DEFINITION 22 (Argument Properties, continued) *Let $A, B \in \mathcal{A}$ be arguments and E a set of arguments. The partial order $\leq$ is: strictly factual iff we have $(A \leq B$ iff $Prem(B) \subseteq \mathcal{L}_\Diamond)$, strictly obligated iff $(A \leq B$ iff $Prem(B) \subseteq \mathcal{L}_O)$, strictly permitted iff $(A \leq B$ iff $Prem(B) \subseteq \mathcal{L}_P)$, obligated iff $(A \leq B$ iff $Prem(B) \subseteq \mathcal{L}_P^-)$, permitted iff $(A \leq B$ iff $Prem(B) \subseteq \mathcal{L}_O^-)$, or deontic iff $(A \leq B$ iff $Prem(B) \subseteq \mathcal{L}_\Diamond^-)$.*

We use $\leq^\tau$ to denote the τ-ordering with $\tau \in \{f, o^s, a^s, o, a, d\}$, where f stands for strictly factual, o^s for strictly obligated, a^s for strictly permitted, o for obligated, a for permitted, and d for deontic. We define the argumentation framework, defeat relation and different extensions as before.

We first consider the arguments with dominant premises and then the arguments with non-dominant ones. We define $K^\tau = \{B \in \mathcal{A} \mid \forall A \in \mathcal{A}(A \leq^\tau B)\}$ where $\mathcal{A}$ is the set of arguments on the basis of AT with a knowledge base K. So, by a given K^τ, we only collect all the arguments that have their premises as obligatory, permitted, or other language types. Given such an $\mathcal{A}$, an argument A is either in K^τ or in $K - K^\tau$, but not in both. Accordingly, we can have the following proposition with regard to the orderings on premises, which provides a more general method for searching for stable extensions. Briefly speaking, we first deal with the dominant arguments based on K^τ as in Proposition 18.1, and then we deal with the non-dominant ones based on $K - K^\tau$. During this process, we need to ensure that each new selected argument does not conflict with the old arguments.

PROPOSITION 23 *Consider the deontic language $\mathcal{L}$ and a pair of two monotonic logics $(\mathbf{S}^-; \mathbf{S}^+) \in \{(\mathbf{D}_{-2}; \mathbf{D}_{-1}), (\mathbf{D}_{-2}; \mathbf{D}), (\mathbf{D}_{-1}; \mathbf{D})\}$. Let AF, corresponding to $\langle AT, \leq^\tau \rangle$, be an abstract argumentation framework $(\mathcal{A}, \mathcal{D})$ such that AT is based on $(\mathbf{S}^-; \mathbf{S}^+)$, K is a knowledge base, and $\tau \in \{f, o^s, a^s, o, a, d\}$. We construct a τ-premise set generated by K as $\bigcup_{n \in \mathbb{N}} E_n$ such that :*

$$E_0 = \{D \in \mathcal{A} \mid F(D) \subseteq Cn_{\mathbf{S}^+}(\Gamma_1)\} \text{ for some } \Gamma_1 \in MC_{\mathbf{S}^+}(K^\tau)$$

$$E_{n+1} = \begin{cases} E_n \cup \{D \in \mathcal{A}\}, & \text{if } \exists \Gamma_2 \in MC_{\mathbf{S}^+}(K - K^\tau) \text{ such that} \\ & \quad (i)\, F(D) \subseteq Cn_{\mathbf{S}^+}(\Gamma_2) \text{ and} \\ & \quad (ii)\, F(D) \cup F(E_n) \text{ is } \mathbf{S}^+\text{-consistent;} \\ E_n, & \text{otherwise.} \end{cases}$$

Then:

- *E is a τ-premise set generated by K iff E is a stable extension regarding K.*

The following proposition shows two connections of stable extensions from the preferences they are based on. We say a preference $\leq^1$ is less informative than another $\leq^2$ if and only if $K^{\leq^1} \subseteq K^{\leq^2}$. First, roughly speaking, a stable extension based on the less informative preference contains all the information in one stable extension based on the more informative preference. Secondly, the more informative preference constructs more stable extensions than the less informative one. All this shows that a more informative preference leads to a larger stable extension.

PROPOSITION 24 *Consider the deontic language $\mathcal{L}$ and a combination of two monotonic logics $(\mathbf{S}^-; \mathbf{S}^+)$. Let AF_i, corresponding to $\langle AT, \leq^i \rangle$, be an abstract argumentation framework $(\mathcal{A}, \mathcal{D}_i)$ such that AT is based on $(\mathbf{S}^-; \mathbf{S}^+)$, K is a knowledge base, $i \in \{1, 2\}$, and $\leq^i$ is a preference on premises. Let $Stable(AF_i)$ be the set of all stable extensions w.r.t. AF_i.*

- *If $K^{\leq^1} \subseteq K^{\leq^2}$, then $E \in Stable(AF_1)$ implies $\exists E' \in Stable(AF_2)$ s.t. $E' \subseteq E$.*

- *If $K^{\leq^1} \subseteq K^{\leq^2}$, then $|Stable(AF_1)| \leq |Stable(AF_2)|$.*

This implies that $|Stable(\langle AT, \leq^{o^s} \rangle)| \leq |Stable(\langle AT, \leq^o \rangle)|$.

The following example illustrates the effects brought by the general undermining mechanism compared to those of rebuttal as proposed in Section 7.

EXAMPLE 25 (Air Pollution, continued) *Given the set $K = \{\Diamond(c \wedge a), O\neg a, Pc\}$ as the premises again, we have arguments A, A', B, B', C, C' defined as follows:*

- $A = O\neg a$

- $A' = A, C \Rrightarrow \neg Pc$

- $B = Pc$

- $B' = B, C \Rrightarrow \neg O\neg a$

- $C = \Diamond(c \wedge a)$

- $C' = A, B \Rrightarrow \neg\Diamond(c \wedge a)$

The preferences over arguments A, A', B, B', C, C' are presented as follows:

- $f \colon C \geq A, A', B, B', C'$

- $o^s \colon A \geq A', B, B', C, C'$

- $a^s \colon B \geq B', A, A', C, C'$

- $o \colon A, A', C \geq B, B', C'$

- $a \colon B, B', C \geq A, A', C'$

- $d \colon A, B, C' \geq A', B', C$

The dominant arguments can defeat the non-dominant ones. See Figure 3 for an example of $(\mathbf{D}_{-2}; \mathbf{D})$. This strategy leads to the different defeasible consequences in Table 3. All these consequences are consistent in specific defeasible deontic logics, and explain why the chosen language types for arguments are better than the others. However, they provide different intuitive results compared to those of the running example. In other words, the common-sense reasoning of knifed murder does not follow the argumentation machinery developed with reference to the language type.

Table 3 presents another way of showing how the methodology of formal argumentation has an effect on the logical consequences of defeasible deontic logic. In the Introduction, we mentioned that one assumption behind the defeasibilities is that obligations defeat permissions. This assumption is, for instance, illustrated by the defeasible inferences $\|\hspace{-0.3em}\sim_{\mathbf{D}_{-2}; \mathbf{D}_{-1}}^{o^s \forall}$ and $\|\hspace{-0.3em}\sim_{\mathbf{D}_{-2}; \mathbf{D}}^{o \forall}$. Some other examples in Table 3 illustrate the other assumptions regarding the deontic modalities, such as permission defeating obligation with the defeasible inferences $\|\hspace{-0.3em}\sim_{\mathbf{D}_{-2}; \mathbf{D}}^{a^s \forall}$ and $\|\hspace{-0.3em}\sim_{\mathbf{D}_{-1}; \mathbf{D}}^{a \forall}$. In other words, assumptions of how one type of language defeats another explain these defeasible consequences.

191

Huimin Dong   Beishui Liao   Réka Markovich   Leendert van der Torre

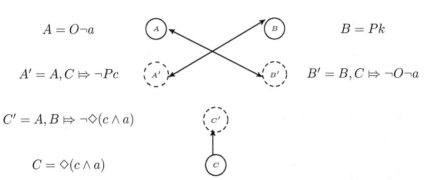

$$A = O\neg a \qquad\qquad\qquad\qquad B = Pk$$

$$A' = A, C \Rrightarrow \neg Pc \qquad\qquad\qquad B' = B, C \Rrightarrow \neg O\neg a$$

$$C' = A, B \Rrightarrow \neg\Diamond(c \wedge a)$$

$$C = \Diamond(c \wedge a)$$

Figure 3: Some of the defeats among arguments A, A', B, B', C, C' based on $(\mathbf{D}_{-2}; \mathbf{D})$ in the strictly factural ordering $\leq^f$. Straight arrows are defeats among these arguments.

	Order	Example of Consequences $\{\Diamond(c \wedge a), O\neg a, Pc\}$
$(\mathbf{D}_{-2}; \mathbf{D}_{-1})$	f	$\Diamond(c \wedge a)$
$(\mathbf{D}_{-2}; \mathbf{D}_{-1})$	o^s	$O\neg a, O\neg(c \wedge a)$
$(\mathbf{D}_{-2}; \mathbf{D})$	a^s	$Pc, P(c \wedge a), P(c \wedge m)$
$(\mathbf{D}_{-2}; \mathbf{D})$	o	$\Diamond(c \wedge a), O\neg a, O\neg(c \wedge a), \neg Pc, \neg P(c \wedge a)$
$(\mathbf{D}_{-1}; \mathbf{D})$	a	$\Diamond(c \wedge a), Pc, \neg O\neg a, P(c \wedge a), P(c \wedge m)$
$(\mathbf{D}_{-1}; \mathbf{D})$	d	$O\neg a, Pc, \neg\Diamond(c \wedge a), O\neg(c \wedge a), P(c \wedge a)$

Table 3: Various defeasible consequences of knowledge base $\{\Diamond(c \wedge a), O\neg a, Pc\}$, depending on various preferences on language types

8.2 Preference on knowledge bases

Section 6 mainly focuses on the influence of preference based on *rules*, while Section 8.1 discusses reasoning on arguments based on *premises* regarding language type. Notice that the premises of arguments are generated from the knowledge base. This section moves towards a further step—considering the effect of preference on the knowledge base. In general, ASPIC$^+$ takes two kinds of knowledge into consideration: defeasible and strict knowledge. The former takes the premises of arguments that are possible to defeat, while the latter takes the premises of arguments that cannot be defeated [Modgil and Prakken, 2018].

DEFINITION 26 (Argument Properties, continued) *Let $K = K_s \cup K_d$ be a knowledge base where K_s is called a set of strict knowledge and K_d is called*

192

a set of defeasible knowledge. Let A be an argument. Then A is firm iff $Prem(A) \subseteq K_s$, or plausible iff $Prem(A) \cap K_d \neq \emptyset$. The partial order $\leq^{fr}$ is firm iff ($A \leq B$ iff B is firm).

We then define $K^{fr} = \{B \in \mathcal{A} \mid \forall A \in \mathcal{A}(A \leq^{fr} B)\}$.

PROPOSITION 27 *Given the deontic language $\mathcal{L}$ and a pair of two monotonic logics $(\mathbf{S}^-; \mathbf{S}^+) \in \{(\mathbf{D}_{-2}; \mathbf{D}_{-1}), (\mathbf{D}_{-2}; \mathbf{D}), (\mathbf{D}_{-1}; \mathbf{D})\}$, let AF, corresponding to $\langle AT, \leq \rangle$, be an abstract argumentation framework $(\mathcal{A}, \mathcal{D})$ such that AT is based on $(\mathbf{S}^-; \mathbf{S}^+)$, $K = K_s \cup K_d$ is a knowledge base, and $\leq$ is firm. We construct a fr-premise set generated by K as $\bigcup_{n \in \mathbb{N}} E_n$ such that:*

$$E_0 = \{D \in \mathcal{A} \mid F(D) \subseteq Cn_{\mathbf{S}^+}(\Gamma_1)\} \text{ for some } \Gamma_1 \in MC_{\mathbf{S}^+}(K^{fr})$$

$$E_{n+1} = \begin{cases} E_n \cup \{D \in \mathcal{A}\}, & \text{if } \exists \Gamma_2 \in MC_{\mathbf{S}^+}(K - K^{fr}) \text{ such that} \\ & \quad (i) \, F(D) \subseteq Cn_{\mathbf{S}^+}(\Gamma_2), \text{ and} \\ & \quad (ii) \, F(D) \cup F(E_n) \text{ is } \mathbf{S}^+\text{-consistent}; \\ E_n, & \text{otherwise.} \end{cases}$$

Then:

- *E is a fr-premise set generated by K iff E is a stable extension regarding K.*

The defeasible inference defined below follows the sceptical account of defeasible reasoning [Horty, 1993]. In argumentation theory, these *sceptical* inferential consequences result from the arguments contained in the intersection of all stable extensions.

DEFINITION 28 (Defeasible Inferences) *Let $\Gamma \subseteq \mathcal{L}$ and let $\phi \in \mathcal{L}$. Let $(\mathbf{S}^-; \mathbf{S}^+) \in \{(\mathbf{D}_{-2}; \mathbf{D}_{-1}), (\mathbf{D}_{-2}; \mathbf{D}), (\mathbf{D}_{-1}; \mathbf{D})\}$ be a pair of two monotonic logics, and let $\leq^\tau$ be a τ-ordering such that $\tau \in \{f, o^s, a^s, o, a, d, fr\}$. Let AT be the Γ-argumentation theory based on $(\mathbf{S}^-; \mathbf{S}^+)$ iff the argumentation theory AT obtains with $K = \Gamma$, and let $AF^\tau = \langle AT, \leq^\tau \rangle$. The defeasible inference $\|\!\sim_{\mathbf{S}^-;\mathbf{S}^+}$ is defined as follows:*

- *$\Gamma \|\!\sim^{\tau\forall}_{\mathbf{S}^-;\mathbf{S}^+} \phi$ iff every stable extension of the Γ-AT based on $(\mathbf{S}^-; \mathbf{S}^+)$ corresponding to AF^τ contains an argument A with $Conc(A) = \phi$.*

We define the closure operator corresponding to this inference relation as usual: $C^{\tau\forall}_{\mathbf{S}^-;\mathbf{S}^+}(\Gamma) = \{\phi \mid \Gamma \|\!\sim^{\tau\forall}_{\mathbf{S}^-;\mathbf{S}^+} \phi\}$. Moreover, we write $\|\!\sim^{\tau\forall}_{\mathbf{S}^-;\mathbf{S}^+} \phi$ when $\emptyset \|\!\sim^{\tau\forall}_{\mathbf{S}^-;\mathbf{S}^+} \phi$.

The proposition below presents a uniform way to construct all defeasible inference relations for all these preferences on *premises* rather than *rules* based on the result of Proposition 27.

PROPOSITION 29 *Let* $\Gamma \subseteq \mathcal{L}$, $(\mathbf{S}^-; \mathbf{S}^+) \in \{(\mathbf{D}_{-2}; \mathbf{D}_{-1}), (\mathbf{D}_{-2}; \mathbf{D}),$ $(\mathbf{D}_{-1}; \mathbf{D})\}$ *be a pair of two monotonic logics, let $\leq^\tau$ be a τ-ordering with* $\tau \in \{p, f, o^s, a^s, o, a, d, fr\}$, *and let K be a knowledge base of AT. We define*

- *a P-set generated by K in $(\mathbf{S}^-; \mathbf{S}^+)$ as $\bigcup_{n \in \mathbb{N}} P_n$, such that*

$$P_0 = Cn_{\mathbf{S}^+}(\Gamma)$$

$$P_{n+1} = \begin{cases} P_n \cup \{\varphi\}, & \text{if } \exists \Gamma' \in MC_{\mathbf{S}^+}(K - K^\tau) \text{ such that} \\ & (i)\, \varphi \in Cn_{\mathbf{S}^+}(\Gamma') \text{ and} \\ & (ii)\, \{\varphi\} \cup P_n \text{ is } \mathbf{S}^+\text{-consistent;} \\ P_n, & \text{otherwise;} \end{cases}$$

where $\Gamma \in MC_{\mathbf{S}^+}(K^\tau)$.

The P-collection $P_{\mathbf{S}^-; \mathbf{S}^+}(K)$ generated by K in $(\mathbf{S}^-; \mathbf{S}^+)$ is the set of all P-sets generated by K in $(\mathbf{S}^-; \mathbf{S}^+)$. Then,

- $\mathcal{C}^{\tau\forall}_{\mathbf{S}^-; \mathbf{S}^+}(K) = \bigcap P_{\mathbf{S}^-; \mathbf{S}^+}(K)$.

COROLLARY 30 *Proposition 20.1 is a special case of Proposition 29.*

Now, we check the defeasible inferences based on the division of strict and defeasible knowledge in the mixed mechanism. We study how the argumentation machinery regarding the impact of this kind of category on a knowledge base helps to explain the results.

EXAMPLE 31 (Air Pollution, continued) *We consider the defeasible consequences $\mathcal{C}^{\tau\forall}_{\mathbf{S}^-; \mathbf{S}^+}(K_i)$ shown in Table 4, given the following divisions of knowledge bases K_i where $1 \leq i \leq 4$:*

- $K_1 = K_s \cup K_d$ *where* $K_s = \{\Diamond(c \wedge a)\}$ *and* $K_d = \{O\neg a, Pc\}$

- $K_2 = K_s \cup K_d$ *where* $K_s = \{\Diamond(c \wedge a), O\neg a\}$ *and* $K_d = \{Pc\}$

- $K_3 = K_s \cup K_d$ *where* $K_s = \{\Diamond(c \wedge a), Pc\}$ *and* $K_d = \{O\neg a\}$

- $K_4 = K_s \cup K_d$ *where* $K_s = \{\Diamond(c \wedge a), O\neg a, Pc\}$ *and* $K_d = \emptyset$

$(\mathbf{S}^-;\mathbf{S}^+)$	Order	K_i	$\mathcal{C}^\tau_{\mathbf{S}^-;\mathbf{S}^+}(K_i)$
$(\mathbf{D}_{-2};\mathbf{D}_{-1})$	fr	K_1	$\Diamond(c \wedge a)$
$(\mathbf{D}_{-2};\mathbf{D})$	fr	K_1	$\Diamond(c \wedge a)$
$(\mathbf{D}_{-1};\mathbf{D})$	fr	K_1	$\Diamond(c \wedge a)$
$(\mathbf{D}_{-2};\mathbf{D})$	fr	K_2	$\Diamond(c \wedge a), O\neg a, O\neg(c \wedge a), \neg Pc, \neg P(c \wedge a)$
$(\mathbf{D}_{-2};\mathbf{D})$	fr	K_3	$\Diamond(c \wedge a), \neg O\neg a, \neg O\neg(c \wedge a), Pc, P(c \wedge a), P(c \wedge m)$
$(\mathbf{D}_{-1};\mathbf{D})$	fr	K_3	$\Diamond(c \wedge a), \neg O\neg a, \neg O\neg(c \wedge a), Pc, P(c \wedge a), P(c \wedge m)$
$(\mathbf{D}_{-2};\mathbf{D}_{-1})$	fr	K_4	$\bigvee K_4$
$(\mathbf{D}_{-2};\mathbf{D})$	fr	K_4	$\bigvee K_4$

Table 4: Defeasible consequences based on a knowledge base K_i

Both the defeasible consequences based on the different language types and those based on the distinction between strict and defeasible knowledge only partially capture the intuition of knifed murder. See the latter case in Table 4.

The defeasible consequences in Table 4 reflect the idea in argumentation that an argument with strict knowledge defeats those with defeasible knowledge. In particular, the results of $\mathcal{C}^{fr}_{\mathbf{D}_{-2};\mathbf{D}}(K_2)$ illustrate how permissions are defeated by obligations generally, while the results of $\mathcal{C}^{fr}_{\mathbf{D}_{-2};\mathbf{D}}(K_3)$ show how permissions defeat obligations. See Figure 4 for an example of how K_2 generates the conclusions based on $(\mathbf{D}_{-2};\mathbf{D})$ in the firm ordering of $\leq^{fr}$.

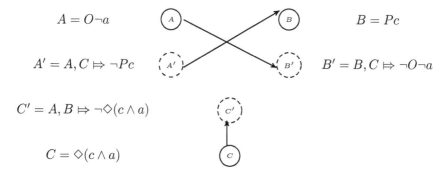

$A = O\neg a$

$B = Pc$

$A' = A, C \Mapsto \neg Pc$

$B' = B, C \Mapsto \neg O\neg a$

$C' = A, B \Mapsto \neg\Diamond(c \wedge a)$

$C = \Diamond(c \wedge a)$

Figure 4: Some of the defeats among arguments A, A', B, B', C, C' based on K_2 and $(\mathbf{D}_{-2};\mathbf{D})$ in the firm ordering $\leq^{fr}$. Straight arrows are defeats among these arguments.

9 Supra-classical inference

In the previous section, we presented various possible ways to define defeasible consequences. It can be defined according to preferences over *rules* (c.f. Section 6). It can also rely on preference orders over *premises*, like what we defined in Section 8. These variants define defeasible consequences depending on the ways in which different information in the knowledge base are considered to be more or less preferable: whether the formulas of the premises are obligated, permitted, or factual; or whether they are classed as strict or defeasible knowledge. We think they are good strategies for modelling defeasible consequences. They assume different assumptions behind defeasibilities regarding the structures of deontic modalities. In Section 7 and Section 8, we defined so-called sceptical inferences based on stable extensions. We could also consider the architectures of argumentation semantics, for instance credulous inference [Horty, 1994], which is another common inference in non-monotonic reasoning. We leave that discussion to future work. We call all the defeasible inferences defined previously *supra-classical* inferences [Makinson, 2005] because they provide more information than classical inferences.[2]

In this section, we check relations between supra-classical inferences and monotonic inferences. We define the subsystems in this way: $\mathbf{S}' \subseteq \mathbf{S}$, i.e. the theorems in subsystem $\mathbf{S}'$ are contained in its extension $\mathbf{S}$. And $\Gamma \vdash_\mathbf{S} \varphi$ is defined in Definition 8, representing derivations from premises Γ to conclusion φ. We first have the following proposition regarding atomic propositions:

PROPOSITION 32 *Let* $(\mathbf{S}^-; \mathbf{S}^+) \in \{(\mathbf{D}_{-2}; \mathbf{D}_{-1}), (\mathbf{D}_{-2}; \mathbf{D}), (\mathbf{D}_{-1}; \mathbf{D})\}$ *be a pair of two monotonic logics. Now we have* $p \mathrel{\|\!\sim}^{\tau\forall}_{\mathbf{S}^-;\mathbf{S}^+} p$ *but* $\{p, \neg p\} \mathrel{\|\!\not\sim}^{\tau\forall}_{\mathbf{S}^-;\mathbf{S}^+} p$, *with* $\tau \in \{p, r, f, o^s, a^s, o, a, d, fr\}$.

The supra-classical inferences we defined are non-monotonic. The following proposition offers a general result on their connections.

PROPOSITION 33 *Let* $(\mathbf{S}^-; \mathbf{S}^+) \in \{(\mathbf{D}_{-2}; \mathbf{D}_{-1}), (\mathbf{D}_{-2}; \mathbf{D}), (\mathbf{D}_{-1}; \mathbf{D})\}$ *be a pair of two monotonic logics. We have the following relation regarding supra-classicality:*

$$\vdash_{\mathbf{S}^-} \subseteq \; \mathrel{\|\!\sim}^{\tau\forall}_{\mathbf{S}^-;\mathbf{S}^+} \subseteq \; \vdash_{\mathbf{S}^+}$$

where $\tau \in \{p, r, f, o^s, a^s, o, a, d, fr\}$.

---

[2]It is also possible to define supra-classical inference in accordance with the 'classical' state of the art. For instance, recent work on substructural deontic logics [Dong *et al.*, 2019a; Governatori and Rotolo, 2019] studied several ways to exclude the undesired classical inferential patterns while still trying to maintain a certain amount of restricted monotonicity in control of different substructural rules for modal operators.

Now, we shall evaluate all the defeasible deontic logics defined in this chapter. First, we consider whether the extensions instantiated satisfy the rationality postulates. The main tool for studying formal argumentation in the setting of ASPIC$^+$ is based on using rationality postulates [Caminada, 2018]. It immediately follows from Propositions 18, 23 and 27, that all the rationality postulates are satisfied. This can also be proven as a corollary of the more general theorems of Caminada [2018] and those of Modgil and Prakken [2018].

Another evaluation we consider is that of a summary of the logical properties of all defeasible deontic logics. The following proposition shows whether these defeasible deontic logics satisfy some non-monotonic properties, which are the *rationality postulates* mentioned previously.

PROPOSITION 34 *Given $\tau \in \{p, r, f, o^s, a^s, o, a, d, fr\}$ as one of the preferences defined and $(\mathbf{S}^-; \mathbf{S}^+) \in \{(\mathbf{D}_{-2}; \mathbf{D}_{-1}), (\mathbf{D}_{-2}; \mathbf{D}), (\mathbf{D}_{-1}; \mathbf{D})\}$ as a pair of two monotonic logics, we will check whether the defeasible deontic logics defined in this chapter satisfy the following standard properties regarding non-monotonicity, where we simplify $\|\!\sim_{\mathbf{S}^-;\mathbf{S}^+}^{\tau\forall}$ to $\Vdash$:*

1. *Reflexivity: $\Gamma \Vdash \varphi$ where $\varphi \in \Gamma$*

2. *Cut: if $\Gamma \cup \{\psi\} \Vdash \chi$ and $\Gamma \Vdash \psi$, then $\Gamma \Vdash \chi$*

3. *Cautious Monotony: if $\Gamma \Vdash \psi$ and $\Gamma \Vdash \chi$, then $\Gamma \cup \{\psi\} \Vdash \chi$*

4. *Left Logical Equivalence: if $Cn_{\mathbf{S}^+}(\Gamma) = Cn_{\mathbf{S}^+}(\Gamma')$ and $\Gamma \Vdash \chi$, then $\Gamma' \Vdash \chi$*

5. *Right Weakening: if $\vdash_{\mathbf{S}^+} \varphi \to \psi$ and $\Gamma \Vdash \varphi$, then $\Gamma \Vdash \psi$*

6. *OR: if $\Gamma \Vdash \varphi$ and $\Gamma' \Vdash \varphi$, then $\Gamma \cup \Gamma' \Vdash \varphi$*

7. *AND: if $\Gamma \Vdash \psi$ and $\Gamma \Vdash \chi$, then $\Gamma \Vdash \psi \wedge \chi$*

8. *Rational Monotony: if $\Gamma \Vdash \chi$ and $\Gamma \not\Vdash \neg\psi$, then $\Gamma \cup \{\psi\} \Vdash \chi$*

The results are shown in Table 8.

Now, we provide some counterexamples to the non-monotonic properties.

EXAMPLE 35 (Invalidities of Reflexivity) *Let $\tau \in \{p, f, o^s, a^s, o, a, d\}$. By Examples 21, 25 and 31, we know that $\|\!\sim_{\mathbf{S}^-;\mathbf{S}^+}^{\tau\forall}$ is not reflexive.*

EXAMPLE 36 (Invalidities of Right Weakening) *Let $\Gamma = \{O\neg a, \Diamond(c \wedge a), Pc\}$ be a sentence illustrating the knifed murder scenario. Then,*

Properties	$\Vdash^{r\forall}_{\mathbf{S}^-;\mathbf{S}+}$	$\Vdash^{r\forall}_{\mathbf{S}^-;\mathbf{S}+}$
Reflexivity	✓*	No
Cut	✓	✓
Cautious Monotony	✓	✓
Left Logical Equivalence	✓	✓
Right Weakening	No	✓
OR	No	No
AND	✓	✓
Rational Monotony	✓	✓

Table 5: This is a summary regarding various principles of defeasibilities. Notice that $\tau \in \{p, f, o^s, a^s, o, a, d, fr\}$. The symbol ✓* indicates that this property is satisfied when the given knowledge base is consistent in $\mathbf{S}^-$.

- $\Gamma \Vdash^{r\forall}_{\mathbf{D}_{-2};\mathbf{D}} Pc$ but $\Gamma \not\Vdash^{r\forall}_{\mathbf{D}_{-2};\mathbf{D}} P(c \wedge a)$.

EXAMPLE 37 (Invalidities of OR) *Let* $\Gamma = \{\Diamond(c \wedge a), Pc\}$ *and* $\Gamma' = \{O\neg a, Pc\}$. *Then,*

- $\Gamma \Vdash^{r\forall}_{\mathbf{D}_{-2};\mathbf{D}} P(c \wedge a)$ *and* $\Gamma' \Vdash^{r\forall}_{\mathbf{D}_{-2};\mathbf{D}} P(c \wedge a)$ *but not* $\Gamma \cup \Gamma' \Vdash^{r\forall}_{\mathbf{D}_{-2};\mathbf{D}} P(c \wedge a)$.

10 Extending to various modal languages

In this section, we extend our discussion from monadic to conditional permission and obligation with different modal languages. We can extend the language into conditional obligation and permission, and then explore *deontic detachment* and *contrary-to-duty reasoning* [Horty, 1997; Makinson and van der Torre, 2001]. This deontic problem was originally phrased by Chisholm in 1963. We will discuss one variant of contrary-to-duty reasoning in Section 10.1. We will explore obligation and permission in legal reasoning in Section 10.2. Rights and duties are important concepts in Hohfeld's theory of legal rights [Hohfeld, 1923]. In particular, legal power and liability involve the notions of agency and actions, thereby capturing another dimension of legal rights. We need a modal language to express these concepts. The third approach we will explore focuses on permission to know [Aucher et al., 2011], in particular, the right to know as described in Section 10.3. Finally, we discuss permissive norms in Section 10.4.

10.1 Conditional permission

One important issue with conditional obligation, or prima facie obligation, is the problem of deontic detachment. It was first discussed by Chisholm [1963] and was later known as "Chisholm's paradox", or "contrary-do-duty paradox" [Prakken and Sergot, 1996]. As widely agreed, from an intuitive point of view, given a set of statements of conditional obligations like those in Example 38, the paradox is consistent and all its members are logically independent of one other. The challenge is that when formalising these statements, it turns out that they are neither logically consistent nor independent. This challenge can be addressed by the following variant.

EXAMPLE 38 (Deontic Detachment: Obligation) *Intuitively speaking, the following set of sentences are consistent, and their members are logically independent of one other.*

(A) *It ought to be the case that Jones does not eat fast food for dinner.*

(B) *It ought to be the case that if Jones does not eat fast food for dinner, then he does not go to McDonald's.*

(C) *If Jones eats fast food for dinner, then he ought to go to McDonald's.*

(D) *Jones eats fast food for dinner.*

A conditional obligation "It ought to be the case that if ψ then φ" can be represented by the formula $O(\varphi \mid \psi)$. Then, an unconditional obligation $O\varphi$ is stipulated as an abbreviation of $O(\varphi \mid \top)$. Then, the above-mentioned sentences are formulised as:

(A') $O\neg f$

(B') $O(\neg g \mid \neg f)$

(C') $f \to Og$

(D') f

where f is short for "Jones eats fast food for dinner" and g is short for "Jones goes to McDonald's". By the following CTO *pattern for cumulative transitivity*

$$\text{CTO:} \frac{O(\varphi \mid \psi \wedge \chi), O(\psi \mid \chi)}{O(\varphi \mid \chi)}$$

we then have conclusion $O\neg g$ from **(A')** *and* **(B')** *as well as conclusion Og from* **(C')** *and* **(D')**. *As the argument in Example 1 shows, the results turn out to be inconsistent.*

Many proposals have been suggested to solve this problem. One possible way is to interpret the conditionals as anankastic conditionals [Condoravdi and Lauer, 2016], also known as hypothetical imperatives. Another possible way is to adopt different kinds of non-monotonic tools for the representation and reasoning [Prakken and Sergot, 1996; Makinson and van der Torre, 2001; van der Torre and Tan, 1999a]. There is a consensus on deontic detachment that techniques from non-monotonic reasoning can be used to handle reasoning of prima facie obligation. However, there is less consensus about how these techniques can be used to deal with prima facie obligation. Please refer to the recent review by Pigozzi and van der Torre [2017] for details. We only present the key idea here in order to introduce a problem regarding prima facie permission.

The variant presented below illustrates a scenario of deontic detachment regarding prima facie permission.

EXAMPLE 39 (Deontic Detachment: Permission) *The following scenario is a variant of an example regarding permission by Prakken and Sergot [1996]. It contains statements that are consistent and intuitive in natural language:*

(A) *A dog is permitted if it is a guide dog for a blind man.*

(B) *It is permitted that if there is a dog, then there is a fence and it is painted white.*

(C) *It ought to be that there is no fence.*

(D) *It is possible that there is a fence and it is painted white.*

Now, a conditional permission "It is permitted that if ψ then φ" is formulated as $P(\varphi \mid \psi)$, and then the unconditional version $P\varphi$ is short for $P(\varphi \mid \top)$. These four statements can be represented as follows:

(A') $P(d \wedge g)$

(B') $P(w \wedge f \mid d)$

(C') $O\neg f$

(D') $\Diamond(w \wedge f)$

where d stands for "There is a dog", g for "It is a guide dog for a blind man", w for "It is painted white", and f for "There is a fence". We now consider two possible patterns of prima facie permission. The first one is the so-called strengthening antecedent, denoted as SA *and presented as follows:*

$$\text{SA:} \frac{P(\varphi \mid \psi), \Box(\chi \rightarrow \psi)}{P(\varphi \mid \chi)}$$

The second CTP pattern we consider is used as cumulative transitivity:

$$\text{CTP:} \frac{P(\varphi \mid \psi \wedge \chi), P(\psi \mid \chi)}{P(\varphi \mid \chi)}$$

There are two issues regarding the reasoning of prima facie permission. First, by using the SA pattern, we then infer (**B"**) $P(w \wedge f \mid d \wedge g)$ from (**B'**). And then by using CTP, we get (**C"**) $P(w \wedge f)$ from (**B"**) and (**A'**). Until now, we have not used the FCP pattern or the OWP pattern in the **D** system. Yet, we have already reached an uneasy situation according to our intuition. It is permitted to have a white fence no matter which precondition is given (i.e. $P(w \wedge f)$). Why is this situation uneasy? From (**C'**), we usually infer $O \neg (w \wedge f)$ by using K_O and NEC$_O$. Further, when taking this (**C"**) with the assumption (**C'**) by applying OWP, it implies something contrary to (**D'**). In other words, their results are inconsistent.

These two issues lead to two questions. The first question is which axioms or rules are appropriate for developing a defeasible logic of conditional permission? The second question is about preferences. What kind of preferences on arguments are more useful for distinguishing a reasonable prima facie permission from the others? Our ASPIC$^+$-based defeasible logic may help to handle the problems identified above. We leave the issue of how to apply our ASPIC$^+$-based defeasible logic to handling the problem of prima facie permission to future work.

10.2 Rights and duties

In legal reasoning, the terms rights and duties are more significantly used than permissions and obligations. It is necessary to consider agency when defining these legal notions. In this section, we review the discussion of rights and duties in legal and deontic literature [Hohfeld, 1923; Sergot, 2013]. We propose a basic representation of rights and duties by using additional modal operators for agency and actions. Various legal rights can be composed in our modal language, for instance, the right to privacy as well as active and passive rights.

Rights play a central role in deontic logic, since they point to a crucial social phenomenon: how agents' social or *normative positions* depend on others and and on others' positions. It is a well-known fact that talking about "rights" in itself is ambiguous. This ambiguity easily leads to conceptual obscurity, and so a hundred years ago, an American legal theorist differentiated between various possible meanings of legal rights [Hohfeld, 1923; Markovich, 2020]. In Hohfeld's system, which consists of four different right relations, there are four different rights, and each type of right matches a given type of duty on the other side: someone's right always means *someone*

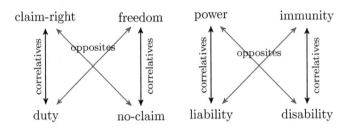

Figure 5: Hohfeldian right relations [Sergot, 2013]

else has a duty. Sergot [2013] calls these pairs of rights, or *normative positions*, correlative relations, as they always come together. From a logical point of view, the rights with the same correlative relation will be equivalent. The system Hohfeld designed can be graphically represented with rights in the upper row and duties in the lower row (see Figure 5). The opposite relations show the effect of a negation of someone's rights on another's duty and vice versa. More details will be shown in the next paragraphs.

These positions are most apparent in the case of a contract of sale. A seller's claim-right to the purchase price obviously means the buyer's duty to give her the money. But this phenomenon is far more general. Regarding epistemic positions, if an agent has a claim-right to know something, it means that another agent has a duty *directed towards* the previous agent to tell him: $R_a[b]K_a\varphi \Leftrightarrow O_{b,a}[b]K_a\varphi$, where $R_a\varphi$ is read as "Agent a has a right that φ", $[a]\varphi$ is read as "Agent a executes an action to make φ true", $K_a\varphi$ is read as "Agent a knows that φ", and directed obligation $O_{b,a}\varphi$ is read as "Agent b has a duty towards agent a that φ". However, if an agent has the freedom to know something, that only means that the other agent has no claim-right towards him that he doesn't get to know. We usually only consider this position as real freedom to know when no other agent has a claim-right that the previous agent shouldn't get to know that thing. We usually refer to such a position as *permission*, which we will analyse in Section 10.3.

The square on the right-hand side exhibits a very similar structure. However, those positions are dynamic [Kanger and Kanger, 1966; Lindahl, 1977] and are about the *potential* to change others' rights and duties [Markovich, 2020]. For example, if we consider the right to know something as a power, that means that the agent having this power can impose a duty directed towards another agent—whose position is called liability in this system—to let her know: $Power_{a,b}[a]O_{b,a}[b]K_a\varphi$. Meanwhile, if someone has an immunity regarding her knowledge, that would mean that the other agent has no

202

power to impose a duty on her to tell him. For details on formalising power and the related positions, please refer to recent discussions by Dong and Roy [2017; 2021] and Markovich [2020].

The agency of actions and the normative positions interact [Sergot, 2013] in the sense that we can have freedoms regarding actions, so-called active rights, while we can only have claim-rights regarding other agents' actions, i.e. passive rights. Power is active. It's about an agent's potential for action, commanding that the other agent does something in particular. In contrast, immunity is passive, because it is about the other agent's lack of potential to do or demand something. Formalising the rights expressed in natural language is already very decisive because it will expose whose action should concern us; though it is not always clear what that action is [Hohfeld, 1923]. As we see in the scope of a notion incorporating different things, there are different atomic rights pertaining to Hohfeldian types. The right to privacy covers many things, for example claim-rights towards everyone else to keep away from one's private zone, that is, not to get to know about one's private life. That means a long list of prohibitions: any action that might end up gathering and disclosing information pertaining to the private zone, as shown in Example 40.

These rights, like most rights apart from very few exceptions in modern constitutional democracies, are defeasible. This property means that their existence, the truth of the sentences expressing them, or the inferences we would draw from them, depend on the circumstances. It might happen that information subject to someone's right to know is considered to be a secret for some reason. In that case, there would be a stronger argument for keeping it private. Although it would go against the agent's right to know the information, there would be no obligation to let that agent know it. Or it can be the other way around. Someone's right to privacy, which would mean that others shouldn't know about her private life and information, can also be defeasible. It may be the case that what that individual does in her private life could be dangerous to others, and the public interest is often a strong argument against the interests of the individual.

Sometimes, it is far from easy to decide which argument is stronger, the right to know or the right to privacy, and then we face a dilemma. In this situation, both cases can be represented using formal argumentation, which may lead to a precise decision.

10.3 Permission to know

Defeasible deontic logic formalises the practical reasoning of intelligent autonomous agents in situations involving uncertainty, conflicts and exceptions. In this section, we explain how to extend defeasible deontic logic with modal operators for epistemic notions like knowledge and belief. In particular, we use techniques from formal argumentation to represent common-sense reasoning to handle permission to know.

Example 40 provides a case study on representing claims regarding the right to know and permission to know. To do this, our modal language will be extended with the modalities K_i for knowledge and $\langle i \rangle$ for agent i's ability to "see to it that", both indexed with agent i.

EXAMPLE 40 (Sensitive data scenario) *Anyone's health data counts as sensitive data and as such is subject to strong protection principles in most countries (in the European Union, there is the General Data Protection Regulation (the so-called GDPR) having the long title "Regulation (EU) 2016/679 of the European Parliament and of the Council of 27 April 2016 on the protection of natural persons with regard to the processing of personal data and on the free movement of such data, and repealing Directive 95/46/EC"). This means that others are not allowed to know the data. However, if someone is ill and in need of medical treatment, we would all agree that doctors have to provide this medical treatment. But fulfilling this obligation requires that they know the health data of the agent (in this case, the patient).*

Various claims arising from the example scenario above are visualised in Figure 6 below, together with a formalisation in ASPIC$^+$. Moreover, the claims in the figure are grouped into two camps of arguments by vertical arrows. The four claims on the left constitute the argument that the doctor is not permitted to know the sensitive information, and the three claims to the right constitute the argument that the doctor is permitted to know that information. The top claims are the conclusions of their arguments, and the other claims support those conclusions. The fact that the doctor's permission to know prevails is modelled by an arrow from the top right box to the left top box. In this section, we consider only the natural language statements and their formalisation as argumentation elements. Employing the previous techniques we have developed, we can put forward a defeasible epistemic deontic logic for permission to know. We only introduce the basic idea here and leave further development to future research.

10.4 Permissive norms

Given the defeasibility of legal reasoning, many people stop using standard deontic logic and develop new rule-based systems instead. A drawback of this approach is the resulting gap between standard deontic logic and defeasible deontic logics. In this chapter, we study an alternative solution that builds a bridge from standard deontic logic to defeasible deontic logic.

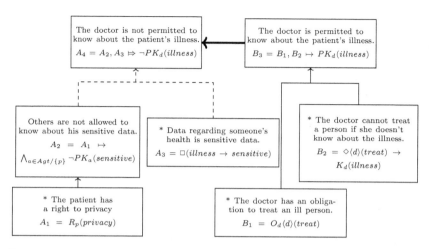

Figure 6: Two camps of arguments in the sensitive data scenario, each containing four claims. Each block is a claim containing the conclusion of an argument. The blocks marked with * are premises from the knowledge base.

Deontic logics range from the monadic modal logic of obligations and permissions, via the dyadic modal logic of conditionals, to rule-based systems for norms. Argumentation can be used at all three levels. A recent chapter in the Handbook of Normative Multiagent Systems (NorMAS) [da Costa Pereira *et al.*, 2018] focuses on the most complex level of rules or norms. In this chapter, we focus more on the basic level of obligations and permissions, but we also give pointers on using argumentation for norms.

The main contribution of this chapter is the development of a rule-based system for monadic modal logic, and we propose that one natural way to apply our method to rule-based systems for norms is to handle prima facie obligations and permissions. The discussion in Section 10.1 sets a good direction for future research. However, to distinguish norms from obligations and permissions and then study norm compliance and violation, we may need to differentiate between defeasibility among rules and defeasibility among premises. That would require us to build a new architecture for a more complex inferential relation than what we have now. In that case, a hypothetical style of inference [Makinson, 1994] would be worth considering. By doing so, we might not only provide a way to resolve conflicting norms and check compliance, but also study graded norms [da Costa Pereira *et al.*, 2018] in a quantitative setting. Then, it would be possible to interpret legal norms according to the presumptions assumed in particular contexts [Makinson, 1994].

11 Related work

There are many existing approaches to defeasible deontic logics, including input/output logic [Makinson and van der Torre, 2001; Parent, 2011], the logic of imperatives [Hansen, 2005; Hansen, 2006], paraconsistent deontic logic [Da Costa and Carnielli, 1986; Beirlaen et al., 2013], conditional deontic logic [Sergot, 2013; Dong et al., 2019a], non-normal deontic logic (including 'Seeing To It That' (STIT) logic [Horty, 2001; Broersen, 2011] and neighbourhood semantics [Anglberger et al., 2015]), default logic [Horty, 1994], deontic preference logic [Hansson, 1990], and dynamic deontic logic [van Benthem et al., 2014; Dong and Roy, 2017]. They emphasise different perspectives on handling inconsistency with obligations, permissions, and many other aspects of norms. We categorise this research into two groups: those that handle norms on a propositional level, and those that study norms based on the structures of their deontic modalities. The summary is shown in Table 6.

Many defeasible deontic logics investigate obligation, prohibition, and permission through their propositional components. Input/output logic [Makinson and van der Torre, 2001; Parent, 2011] is one main approach. It proposes studying the different structures of dependency between input and output in a normative propositional system, and then defining, for instance, different kinds of obligations in terms of their specific structured outputs. When constructing the normative code, it is possible to take preferences into consideration [Parent, 2011]. The resulting logical consequences of input/output logic satisfy the defeasibility requirement, and thus provide more results than classical logics. As such, their consequences are *supra-classical* relations. The logic of imperatives [Hansen, 2005; Hansen, 2006] and default logic [Horty, 1994] also have a similar spirit to handling norms: staying propositional, making it possible to have a preference, focusing on differently structured dependencies, and providing more consequences than classical logics. The logic of imperatives [Hansen, 2005; Hansen, 2006], however, has axiomatisations in modal language. On the other hand, conditional deontic logics [Sergot, 2013; Dong et al., 2019a] also treat norms on a propositional level, but usually their logical consequences are weaker or fewer than those of classical logics. These kinds of consequences are *infra-classical* relations.

Another key approach mainly considers norms on a modal level. Deontic preference logic [Hansson, 1990], dynamic deontic logic [van Benthem et al., 2014; Dong and Roy, 2017], and STIT logic [Horty, 2001; Broersen, 2011] are very famous modal frameworks in the literature. For instance, deontic preference logic [Hansson, 1990] and dynamic deontic logic [van Benthem et al., 2014; Dong and Roy, 2017] adopt Kripke models to capture preferential orders and then define modalities for obligation, prohibition, and permission. The preferences can be given [Dong and Roy, 2017] or derived [Hansson, 1990; van Benthem *et al.*, 2014]. To follow the character of non-monotonicity, these logics try to keep the derived consequences as much as possible while excluding inconsistency in normative reasoning. So they generate supra-classical relations. There is an exception. For instance, when adopting a non-normal Kripke framework like STIT logic [Horty, 2001; Broersen, 2011] or neighbourhood semantics [Anglberger *et al.*, 2015] to model norms, the logical consequences are fewer than usual. These infra-classical relations are the result of trade-offs in an attempt to balance the generality of their derivation results and their capacity to resolve a moral dilemma effectively [Broersen, 2011].

Paraconsistent logic [Da Costa and Carnielli, 1986; Beirlaen *et al.*, 2013] stands in between these two approaches. It usually handles norms at the propositional level, but still offers axiomatisation in the modal language [Beirlaen *et al.*, 2013]. Paraconsistent logic mostly concentrates on the dependent relations between the normative system and the results it leads to. Although the logical consequences in the early work of paraconsistent logic [Da Costa and Carnielli, 1986] are infra-classical, the most recent work [Beirlaen *et al.*, 2013] results in many more consequences, which we then call supra-classical.

Apart from these, adaptive logic [Batens, 2003; Batens *et al.*, 2003; Beirlaen and Straßer, 2013], a currently active approach to defeasible reasoning, provides a set-theoretical configuration, similar to our developments of logical systems based on ASPIC$^+$, to have a number of consistent sets derived from an inconsistent set if at all possible. In this logic, as with our approach, by having a lower-limit logic, each derivable formula is required to be consistent with those from the previous stage, given that abnormalities cannot be present. Two strategies, reliability and minimal abnormality, are used to develop sceptical or credulous inferences like our $\forall$- and $\exists$-types of inference. The key characteristic of adaptive logic is the way it interprets abnormality. In a "flat" adaptive logic, all the premises are equally preferred, while in a "prioritised" adaptive logic, premises are ordered in different layers [Batens *et al.*, 2003]. However, all priorities are premise-based [Batens *et al.*, 2003]. It is not clear how rule-based priorities can be captured in an adaptive framework.

Defeasible deontic logic [Nute, 1997] is a widely studied approach to normative reasoning and offers a lot of formal tools in non-monotonic reasoning. Its main idea is to define defeasibility either in terms of consistency, governed under a set of formulas combined with a set of inference rules [Goble, 2014; Straßer, 2014; Governatori and Rotolo, 2006], or by providing a priority mechanism for overtaking less normal conclusions [Horty, 1994; Governatori, 2018]. For instance, Goble [2014] provides an adaptive logic for handling different kinds of normative conflicts via the notion of abnormality. A formula is true from a set of formulas if and only if this formula is satisfied at every reliable and normal model. This inference relation highly depends on the sets of abnormalities and inferential rules on them. Straßer [2014] follows Goble's work and investigates dynamics in adaptive reasoning, while Governatori [2006] proposes that multi-layered consistency for conditional obligations is captured by sequential operators for computing norms and their violations. In contrast, Horty [1994] and Governatori [2018] define defeasible consequences in terms of priorities over default rules. They both define priorities among default rules rather than over the arguments. Riveret el al. [2019] propose a rule-based argumentation framework for representing conditional norms.

In a similar fashion, in order to be non-monotonic, facts in deontic update semantics [van der Torre and Tan, 1998; van der Torre and Tan, 1999a; van der Torre and Tan, 1999b] are updates that restrict the domain of the model. They make a fact 'settled' in the sense that it will never change again even after future updates of the same sort. Van Benthem et al. [2014] use dynamic logic to place such a dynamic approach within standard modal logic. Dynamic logic includes reduction axioms and standard model theory. They rehabilitate classical modal logic as a legitimate tool to do deontic logic, and position deontic logic within the growing dynamic logic literature [Dong and Roy, 2017; Dong and Roy, 2021]. In contrast to this dynamic approach, a recent work has been developed with weighted deontic modalities [Dong et al., 2021] in order to capture the ability of agents to make rational choices. Governatori et al. [2012] have developed a possible world semantics for defeasible normative reasoning.

Connecting formal argumentation to deontic logic has been an increasingly active area of research in recent years [Pigozzi and van der Torre, 2018]. An approach that is closely related to this chapter is called *logic-based instantiations of an argumentation framework* and can be traced back to the work of Benferhat et al. [1995] and Cayrol [1995]. Two key ideas highly related to this chapter were developed: Benferhat et al. [1995] suggested the methodology of handling preferences in Dung-style argumentation theory via the concept of "level of paraconsistency", while Cayrol [1995] provided a more concrete method: investigating the link between stable extension and Maximally consistent sets (MCS) based on classical logic. Recent studies focus on connections between logic and argumentation, including checking the application of Gentzen proof theory on formal argumentation, as proposed by Arieli et al. [2018], and instantiating ASPIC$^+$ based on deontic modal logics about obligation and permission but for complete and grounded extension, as proposed by Beirlaen et al. [2018]. A recent work that is close to our work, by Straßer and Arieli [2019], presents an argumentative approach to normative reasoning using standard deontic logic as base logic. Similarly related, Liao *et al.* [2019] represent three logics of prioritised norms by using argumentation. In addition, Glavaničová [2018] studies how to let the logical principle of free choice permission be defeasible in non-monotonic adaptive logic. In contrast, Governatori *et al.* [2013] provide a defeasible logic for computing strong and weak permissions, while Lam *et al.* [2016] have developed a connection between ASPIC$^+$ and defeasible logic. Dong *et al.* [2020] have identified a possible way to develop AI logic for social reasoning with this ASPIC$^+$-based method.

Table 6: This is a summary of various frameworks of handling norms. IOL is short for input/output logic, LI is short for logic of imperatives, PDL is short for paraconsistent deontic logic, CDL is short for conditional deontic logic, STIT is short for STIT-logic, NS is short for neighbourhood semantics, DL is short for default logic, DPL is short for deontic preference logic, and DYDL is short for dynamic deontic logic.

	based on a propositional level		
Properties	IOL	LI	PDL
Propositional Level	[Makinson and van der Torre, 2001; Parent, 2011]	[Hansen, 2005; Hansen, 2006]	[Da Costa and Carnielli, 1986]
Modal Axiomatization		[Hansen, 2005; Hansen, 2006]	[Beirlaen et al., 2013]
With Given Preference	[Parent, 2011]	[Hansen, 2006]	
With Derived Preference			
Dependency	[Makinson and van der Torre, 2001; Parent, 2011]	[Hansen, 2005; Hansen, 2006]	[Beirlaen et al., 2013]
Infra-Classicality			[Da Costa and Carnielli, 1986]
Supra-Classicality	[Makinson and van der Torre, 2001; Parent, 2011]	[Hansen, 2005; Hansen, 2006]	[Beirlaen et al., 2013]

Table 7: Summary of various frameworks of handling norms, part 2.

| | based on their deontic modalities | | | | |
CDL	STIT	NS	DL	DPL	DYDL
[Sergot, 2013; Dong et al., 2019a]			[Horty, 1994]		
	[Horty, 2001; Broersen, 2011]	[Anglberger et al., 2015]		[Hansson, 1990]	[van Benthem et al., 2014; Dong and Roy, 2017; Dong et al., 2021]
					[Dong and Roy, 2017]
	[Horty, 2001; Broersen, 2011]		[Horty, 1994]	[Hansson, 1990]	[van Benthem et al., 2014]
[Sergot, 2013; Dong et al., 2019a]	[Horty, 2001; Broersen, 2011]	[Anglberger et al., 2015]			
			[Horty, 1994]	[Hansson, 1990]	[van Benthem et al., 2014; Dong and Roy, 2017; Dong et al., 2021]

12 Conclusions and future work

In this chapter, ASPIC$^+$ connects formal argumentation to non-monotonic logic. We believe this approach benefits both areas. For formal argumentation, the resulting non-monotonic logics can be studied to provide new insights into the argumentation systems adopted, for example we can apply the logical results of our ASPIC$^+$-logic to learn more about the effect of the argumentation semantics adopted. For non-monotonic logics, the underlying argumentation theory can be used to explain deontic conclusions. Our case study on using the logic of obligations and permissions provides first evidence of this.

Within this general ambitious setting, the contributions of this chapter are as follows. First, with regard to the definitions, in Definitions 10 and 11 we show how to use two logics in ASPIC$^+$, and in Definitions 19 and 28 we show how to build a defeasible modal logic on top of ASPIC$^+$. With regard to formal results, Proposition 20 and 29 characterise the consequences of our defeasible deontic logics. As these representation theorems show, our defeasible deontic logics can be built without ASPIC$^+$. The role of ASPIC$^+$ is likely to be an interpreter. It provides an intuition as to why we accept certain conclusions and not others. Finally, the example illustrates how to apply this approach to formalising the analysis of strong permission by Glavaničová [2018].

We have also argued for many future research directions that may involve applying our method of building defeasible deontic logics. It is possible to handle various deontic challenges related to contrary-to-duty obligations, deontic detachment, and the formalism and legal interpretation of the right to privacy and the right to know if we extend the modal language properly in the ASPIC$^+$-based defeasible logics. The essential step is to have 'correct' preference among formulas in the logic, or arguments in ASPIC$^+$. What this 'correctness' is highly depends on what one wants to capture in the modelling. We are considering having a general approach to computing the construction of preference and then defeasible inference that may be based on, for instance, certain linguistic theories or legal theories.

Acknowledgments

We would like to thank the three referees for their valuable remarks and comments. Huimin Dong is supported by the Fundamental Research Funds for the Central Universities, Sun Yat-sen University (20221187). Beishui Liao is supported by the Key Program of the National Social Science Foundation of China (20&ZD047). Leendert van der Torre also acknowledges financial support from the Fonds National de la Recherche Luxembourg (INTER/-

Mobility/19/13995684/DLAl/van der Torre). This work was supported by the Fonds National de la Recherche Luxembourg through the project Deontic Logic for Epistemic Rights (OPEN O20/14776480).

BIBLIOGRAPHY

[Alchourrón and Bulygin, 1984] Carlos E Alchourrón and Eugenio Bulygin. Permission and permissive norms. *Theorie der Normen*, pages 349–371, 1984.

[Amgoud and Besnard, 2013] Leila Amgoud and Philippe Besnard. Logical limits of abstract argumentation frameworks. *Journal of Applied Non-Classical Logics*, 23(3):229–267, 2013.

[Anglberger et al., 2015] Albert J.J. Anglberger, Nobert Gratzl, and Olivier Roy. Obligation, free choice, and the logic of weakest permissions. *The Review of Symbolic Logic*, 8:807–827, December 2015.

[Arieli et al., 2018] Ofer Arieli, AnneMarie Borg, and Christian Straßer. Reasoning with maximal consistency by argumentative approaches. *Journal of Logic and Computation*, 28(7):1523–1563, 2018.

[Asher and Bonevac, 2005] Nicholas Asher and Daniel Bonevac. Free choice permission is strong permission. *Synthese*, 145(3):303–323, 2005.

[Aucher et al., 2011] Guillaume Aucher, Guido Boella, and Leendert van der Torre. A dynamic logic for privacy compliance. *Artificial Intelligence and Law*, 19(2-3):187, 2011.

[Barker, 2010] Chris Barker. Free choice permission as resource-sensitive reasoning. *Semantics and Pragmatics*, 3:10:1–38, 2010.

[Batens et al., 2003] Diderik Batens, Joke Meheus, Dagmar Provijn, and Liza Verhoeven. Some adaptive logics for diagnosis. *Logic and Logical Philosophy*, 11:39–65, 2003.

[Batens, 2003] Diderik Batens. A strengthening of the rescher–manor consequence relations. *Logique et Analyse*, pages 289–313, 2003.

[Beirlaen and Straßer, 2013] Mathieu Beirlaen and Christian Straßer. Two adaptive logics of norm-propositions. *Journal of Applied Logic*, 11(2):147–168, 2013.

[Beirlaen et al., 2013] Mathieu Beirlaen, Christian Straßer, and Joke Meheus. An inconsistency-adaptive deontic logic for normative conflicts. *Journal of Philosophical Logic*, 42(2):285–315, 2013.

[Beirlaen et al., 2018] Mathieu Beirlaen, Jesse Heyninck, and Christian Straßer. Structured argumentation with prioritized conditional obligations and permissions. *Journal of Logic and Computation*, 29(2):187–214, 2018.

[Benferhat et al., 1995] Salem Benferhat, Didier Dubois, and Henri Prade. A local approach to reasoning under inconsistency in stratified knowledge bases. In *European Conference on Symbolic and Quantitative Approaches to Reasoning and Uncertainty*, volume 946, pages 36–43. Springer, 1995.

[Blackburn et al., 2002] Patrick Blackburn, Maarten De Rijke, and Yde Venema. *Modal Logic*, volume 53. Cambridge University Press, 2002.

[Broersen, 2011] Jan Broersen. Deontic epistemic stit logic distinguishing modes of mens rea. *Journal of Applied Logic*, 9(2):137–152, 2011.

[Caminada, 2018] Martin Caminada. Rationality postulates: applying argumentation theory for non-monotonic reasoning. In Pietro Baroni, Dov Gabbay, Massimiliano Giacomin, and Leendert van der Torre, editors, *Handbook of formal argumentation*. College Publication, 2018.

[Cayrol, 1995] Claudette Cayrol. On the relation between argumentation and non-monotonic coherence-based entailment. In *International Joint Conference on Artificial Intelligence*, volume 95, pages 1443–1448, 1995.

[Chisholm, 1963] R.M. Chisholm. Contrary-to-duty imperatives and deontic logic. *Analysis*, 24:33–36, 1963.

[Chopra et al., 2018] Amit Chopra, Leendert van der Torre, Harko Verhagen, and Serena Villata, editors. *Handbook of normative multiagent systems*. College Publications, 2018.

[Condoravdi and Lauer, 2016] C. Condoravdi and S. Lauer. Anankastic conditionals are just conditionals. *Semantics and Pragmatics*, 9(8):1–69, November 2016.

[Da Costa and Carnielli, 1986] Newton CA Da Costa and Walter A Carnielli. On paraconsistent deontic logic. *Philosophia*, 16(3-4):293–305, 1986.

[da Costa Pereira et al., 2017] Célia da Costa Pereira, Beishui Liao, Alessandra Malerba, Antonino Rotolo, Andrea G. B. Tettamanzi, Leendert W. N. van der Torre, and Serena Villata. Handling norms in multi-agent systems by means of formal argumentation. *FLAP*, 4(9):3039–3073, 2017.

[da Costa Pereira et al., 2018] Célia da Costa Pereira, Beishui Liao, Alessandra Malerba, Antonino Rotolo, Andrea GB Tettamanzi, Leendert van der Torre, and Serena Villata. Handling norms in multiagent systems by means of formal argumentation. In Amit Chopra, Leendert van der Torre, Harko Verhagen, and Serena Villata, editors, *Handbook of normative multiagent systems*. College Publications, 2018.

[Dong and Roy, 2017] Huimin Dong and Olivier Roy. Dynamic logic of power and immunity. In *International Workshop on Logic, Rationality and Interaction*, pages 123–136. Springer, 2017.

[Dong and Roy, 2021] Huimin Dong and Olivier Roy. Dynamic logic of legal competences. *Journal of Logic, Language and Information*, 30(4):701–724, 2021.

[Dong et al., 2019a] Huimin Dong, Norbert Gratzl, and Olivier Roy. Open reading and free choice permission: A perspective in substructural logics. In *Dynamics, Uncertainty and Reasoning*, pages 81–115. Springer, 2019.

[Dong et al., 2019b] Huimin Dong, Beishui Liao, Réka Markovich, and Leendert W. N. van der Torre. From classical to non-monotonic deontic logic using aspic⁺. In *Logic, Rationality, and Interaction - 7th International Workshop, LORI 2019, Chongqing, China, October 18-21, 2019, Proceedings*, pages 71–85, 2019.

[Dong et al., 2020] Huimin Dong, Réka Markovich, and Leendert van der Torre. Developing ai logic for social reasoning. *Journal of Zhejiang University*, 5(50):31–50, 2020.

[Dong et al., 2021] Huimin Dong, Xu Li, and Yì N. Wáng. Weighted modal logic in epistemic and deontic contexts. In Sujata Ghosh and Thomas Icard, editors, *Logic, Rationality, and Interaction*, pages 73–87. Springer International Publishing, 2021.

[Gabbay et al., 2013] Dov Gabbay, John Horty, Xavier Parent, Ron van der Meyden, and Leendert van der Torre, editors. *Handbook of deontic logic and normative systems: Volume 1*. College Publications, 2013.

[Gabbay et al., 2021] Dov Gabbay, John Horty, Xavier Parent, Ron van der Meyden, and Leendert van der Torre, editors. *Handbook of deontic logic and normative systems: Volume 2*. College Publications, 2021.

[Gabbay, 1996] Dov M. Gabbay. Fibred semantics and the weaving of logics. part 1: Modal and intuitionistic logics. *The Journal of Symbolic Logic*, 61(4):1057–1120, 1996.

[Glavaničová, 2018] Daniela Glavaničová. The free choice principle as a default rule. *Organon F*, 25(4):495–516, 2018.

[Goble, 2014] Lou Goble. Deontic logic (adapted) for normative conflicts. *Logic Journal of the IGPL*, 22(2):206–235, 2014.

[Governatori and Rotolo, 2006] Guido Governatori and Antonino Rotolo. Logic of violations: A gentzen system for reasoningwith contrary-to-duty obligations. *The Australasian Journal of Logic*, 4, 2006.

[Governatori and Rotolo, 2019] Guido Governatori and Antonino Rotolo. Is free choice permission admissible in classical deontic logic? *arXiv preprint arXiv:1905.07696*, 2019.

[Governatori et al., 2012] Guido Governatori, Antonino Rotolo, and Erica Calardo. Possible world semantics for defeasible deontic logic. In *International Conference on Deontic Logic in Computer Science*, pages 46–60. Springer, 2012.

[Governatori et al., 2013] Guido Governatori, Francesco Olivieri, Antonino Rotolo, and Simone Scannapieco. Computing strong and weak permissions in defeasible logic. *Journal of Philosophical Logic*, 42(6):799–829, 2013.

[Governatori et al., 2020] Guido Governatori, Antonino Rotolo, and Giovanni Sartor. Deontics, logic, and the law. In Dov Gabbay, John Horty, Xavier Parent, Ron van der Meyden, and Leendert van der Torre, editors, *Handbook of Deontic Logic and Normative Systems*, volume 2. College Publication, 2020.

[Governatori, 2018] Guido Governatori. Practical normative reasoning with defeasible deontic logic. In *Reasoning Web International Summer School*, pages 1–25. Springer, 2018.

[Hansen, 2005] Jörg Hansen. Conflicting imperatives and dyadic deontic logic. *Journal of Applied Logic*, 3(3-4):484–511, 2005.

[Hansen, 2006] Jörg Hansen. Deontic logics for prioritized imperatives. *Artificial Intelligence and Law*, 14(1-2):1–34, 2006.

[Hansson, 1990] Sven Ove Hansson. Preference-based deontic logic (PDL). *Journal of Philosophical Logic*, 19(1):75–93, 1990.

[Hansson, 2013] Sven Ove Hansson. The varieties of permissions. In Dov Gabbay, John Horty, Xavier Parent, Ron van der Meyden, and Leendert van der Torre, editors, *Handbook of Deontic Logic and Normative Systems*. College Publication, 2013.

[Hilpinen, 1982] Risto Hilpinen. Disjunctive permissions and conditionals with disjunctive antecedents. *Acta Philosophica Fennica*, 35:175–194, 1982.

[Hohfeld, 1923] Wesley Newcomb Hohfeld. Fundamental legal conceptions applied in judicial reasoning. In Walter Wheeler Cook, editor, *Fundamental Legal Conceptions Applied in Judicial Reasoning and Other Legal Essays*, pages 23–64. New Haven : Yale University Press, 1923.

[Horty, 1993] John F. Horty. Deontic logic as founded on nonmonotonic logic. *Annals of Mathematics and Artificial Intelligence*, 9(1-2):69–91, 1993.

[Horty, 1994] John F Horty. Moral dilemmas and nonmonotonic logic. *Journal of philosophical logic*, 23(1):35–65, 1994.

[Horty, 1997] J. F. Horty. Nonmonotonic foundations for deontic logic. In D. Nute, editor, *Defeasible Deontic Logic*, pages 17–44. Kluwer, Dordrecht, 1997.

[Horty, 2001] John F Horty. *Agency and deontic logic*. Oxford University Press, 2001.

[Kamp, 1973] Hans Kamp. Free choice permission. In *Proceedings of the Aristotelian Society*, volume 74, pages 57–74. JSTOR, 1973.

[Kanger and Kanger, 1966] Stig Kanger and Helle Kanger. Rights and parliamentarism. *Theoria*, 32(2):85–115, 1966.

[Kanger, 1972] Stig Kanger. Law and logic. *Theoria*, 38(3):105–132, 1972.

[Kraus et al., 1990] Sarit Kraus, Daniel J. Lehmann, and Menachem Magidor. Nonmonotonic reasoning, preferential models and cumulative logics. *Artificial Intelligence*, 44(1-2):167–207, 1990.

[Lam et al., 2016] Ho-Pun Lam, Guido Governatori, and Régis Riveret. On aspic+ and defeasible logic. In *COMMA*, pages 359–370, 2016.

[Lewis, 1979] David Lewis. A problem about permission. In *Essays in honour of Jaakko Hintikka*, pages 163–175. Springer, 1979.

[Liao et al., 2019] Beishui Liao, Nir Oren, Leender van der Torre, and Serena Villata. Prioritized norms in formal argumentation. *J. Log. Comput.*, 29(2):215–240, 2019.

[Lindahl, 1977] Lars Lindahl. *Position and Change: A Study in Law and Logic*. Springer Science & Business Media, 1977.

[Makinson and van der Torre, 2001] D. Makinson and L. van der Torre. Constraints for input/output logics. *Journal of Philosophical Logic*, 30:155–185, 2001.

[Makinson and van der Torre, 2003] David Makinson and Leendert van der Torre. Permission from an input/output perspective. *Journal of philosophical logic*, 32(4):391–416, 2003.

[Makinson, 1984] David Makinson. Stenius' approach to disjunctive permission. *Theoria*, 50(2-3):138–147, 1984.

[Makinson, 1994] David Makinson. General patterns in nonmonotonic reasoning. In *Handbook of logic in artificial intelligence and logic programming (vol. 3)*, pages 35–110. Oxford University Press, 1994.

[Makinson, 2005] David Makinson. *Bridges from classical to nonmonotonic logic*. King's College, 2005.

[Markovich, 2020] Réka Markovich. Understanding Hohfeld and Formalizing Legal Rights: the Hohfeldian Conceptions and Their Conditional Consequences. *Studia Logica*, 108:129–158, 2020.

[Modgil and Prakken, 2018] Sanjay Modgil and Henry Prakken. Abstract rule-based argumentation. In Pietro Baroni, Dov Gabbay, Massimiliano Giacomin, and Leendert van der Torre, editors, *Handbook of formal argumentation*. College Publication, 2018.

[Nute, 1997] D. Nute, editor. *Defeasible deontic logic*. Springer Netherlands, 1997.

[Parent and van der Torre, 2017] Xavier Parent and Leendert W. N. van der Torre. Detachment in normative systems: Examples, inference patterns, properties. *FLAP*, 4(9):2995–3038, 2017.

[Parent and van der Torre, 2018] Xavier Parent and Leendert van der Torre. *Introduction to deontic logic and normative systems*. College Publications, 2018.

[Parent, 2011] Xavier Parent. Moral particularism in the light of deontic logic. *Artificial Intelligence and Law*, 19(2-3):75, 2011.

[Pigozzi and van der Torre, 2017] Gabriella Pigozzi and Leendert W. N. van der Torre. Multiagent deontic logic and its challenges from a normative systems perspective. *FLAP*, 4(9):2929–2993, 2017.

[Pigozzi and van der Torre, 2018] Gabriella Pigozzi and Leendert van der Torre. Arguing about constitutive and regulative norms. *Journal of Applied Non-Classical Logics*, 28(2-3):189–217, 2018.

[Prakken and Sartor, 2013] Henry Prakken and Giovanni Sartor. Formalising arguments about norms. In *Legal Knowledge and Information Systems (JURIX 2013)*, pages 121–130. IOS Press, 2013.

[Prakken and Sergot, 1996] Henry Prakken and Marek Sergot. Contrary-to-duty obligations. *Studia Logica*, 57(1):91–115, 1996.

[Prakken, 1996] Henry Prakken. Two approaches to the formalisation of defeasible deontic reasoning. *Studia Logica*, 57(1):73–90, 1996.

[Raz, 1975] Joseph Raz. Permissions and supererogation. *American Philosophical Quarterly*, 12(2):161–168, 1975.

[Riveret et al., 2019] Régis Riveret, Antonino Rotolo, and Giovanni Sartor. A deontic argumentation framework towards doctrine reification. *Journal of Applied Logics*, 6(5):903–940, 2019.

[Ross, 1930] David Ross. *The right and the good*. Oxford University Press, 1930.

[Searle, 1996] John R Searle. *The construction of social reality*. Penguin, London, 1996.

[Sergot, 2013] Marek Sergot. Normative positions. In Dov Gabbay, John Horty, Xavier Parent, Ron van der Meyden, and Leendert van der Torre, editors, *Handbook of Deontic Logic and Normative Systems*. College Publication, 2013.

[Straßer and Arieli, 2019] Christian Straßer and Ofer Arieli. Normative reasoning by sequent-based argumentation. *Journal of Logic and Computation*, 29(3):387–415, 2019.

[Straßer, 2014] Christian Straßer. A deontic logic framework allowing for factual detachment. In *Adaptive Logics for Defeasible Reasoning*, pages 297–333. Springer, 2014.

[van Benthem et al., 2014] J. van Benthem, D. Grossi, and F. Liu. Priority structures in deontic logic. *Theoria*, 80(2):116–152, 2014.

[van Benthem, 1979] Johan van Benthem. Minimal deontic logics. *Bulletin of the Section of Logic*, 8(1):36–42, 1979.

[van der Torre and Tan, 1998] L. van der Torre and Y. Tan. An update semantics for prima facie obligations. In *Proceedings of The 17th European Conference on Artificial Intelligence*, pages 38–42, 1998.

[van der Torre and Tan, 1999a] L. van der Torre and Y. Tan. Rights, duties and commitments between agents. In *Proceedings of the Sixteenth International Joint Conference on Artificial Intelligence, IJCAI 99, Stockholm, Sweden, July 31 - August 6, 1999. 2 Volumes, 1450 pages*, pages 1239–1246, 1999.

[van der Torre and Tan, 1999b] L. van der Torre and Y. Tan. An update semantics for defeasible obligations. In *UAI '99: Proceedings of the Fifteenth Conference on Uncertainty in Artificial Intelligence, Stockholm, Sweden, July 30 - August 1, 1999*, pages 631–638, 1999.

[van der Torre and Tan, 2000] L. van der Torre and Y.-H. Tan. Two-phase deontic logic. *Logique et analyse*, 43(171-172):411–456, 2000.

[van der Torre, 1997] L. van der Torre. *Reasoning about obligations: defeasibility in preference-based deontic logic*. PhD thesis, Erasmus University, 1997.

[van Fraassen, 1973] B.C. van Fraassen. Values and the heart command. *Journal of Philosophy*, 70:5–19, 1973.

[von Wright, 1951] Georg Henrik von Wright. Deontic logic. *Mind*, 1951.

[von Wright, 1963] Georg Henrik von Wright. *Norm and Action - A Logical Enquiry*. Routledge, 1963.

[Von Wright, 1968] Georg Henrik Von Wright. *An essay in deontic logic and the general theory of action*. North-Holland Publishing Company, 1968.

[Young et al., 2016] Anthony P. Young, Sanjay Modgil, and Odinaldo Rodrigues. Prioritised default logic as rational argumentation. In *Proceedings of AAMAS 2016*, pages 626–634, 2016.

Appendix: Proofs

PROPOSITION 41 *Consider the deontic language $\mathcal{L}$ and a pair of two monotonic logics $(\mathbf{S}^-;\mathbf{S}^+) \in \{(\mathbf{D}_{-2};\mathbf{D}_{-1}),(\mathbf{D}_{-2};\mathbf{D}),(\mathbf{D}_{-1};\mathbf{D})\}$. Let AF, corresponding to $\langle AT, \leq^\tau \rangle$, be an abstract argumentation framework $(\mathcal{A}, \mathcal{D})$ such that AT is based on $(\mathbf{S}^-;\mathbf{S}^+)$, K is a knowledge base, and $\tau \in \{p,r\}$. Given a set $\Gamma \subseteq \mathcal{L}$ of formulas, we define:*

- *a stable set generated by Γ as $\{D \in \mathcal{A} \mid F(D) \subseteq Cn_{\mathbf{S}^+}(\Gamma)\}$;*

- *a proper set generated by Γ as $\bigcup_{i\in\omega} E_i$, such that*

$$E_0 = \{D \in \mathcal{A} \mid F(D) \subseteq Cn_{\mathbf{S}^-}(\Gamma)\}$$

$$E_{n+1} = \begin{cases} E_n \cup \{D \in \mathcal{A}\}, & \text{if } F(D) \subseteq Cn_{\mathbf{S}^+}(\Gamma) \text{ and} \\ & \quad F(D) \cup F(E_n) \text{ is } \mathbf{S}^-\text{-consistent;} \\ E_n, & \text{otherwise.} \end{cases}$$

1. *When $\tau = p$, then E is a stable set generated by a $\Gamma \in MC_{\mathbf{S}^+}(K)$ iff E is a stable extension regarding K.*

2. *When $\tau = r$, E is a proper set generated by a $\Gamma \in MC_{\mathbf{S}^-}(K)$ iff E is a stable extension regarding K.*

Proof.

1. For the case of $\tau = p$.

   The left-to-right direction. Let E be the stable set generated by a $\Gamma \in MC_{\mathbf{S}+}(K)$.

   - E is conflict-free. Otherwise there are $A, B \in E$ such that A defeats B. Suppose A rebuts B by the conclusion $-\varphi$ of a top rule of a subargument of B, such that $Conc(A) = +\varphi$. Then, from $F(A), F(B) \subseteq Cn_{\mathbf{S}+}(\Gamma)$, we know that $-\varphi, +\varphi \in Cn_{\mathbf{S}+}(\Gamma)$. This implies that Γ is not $\mathbf{S}^+$-consistent, which contradicts $\Gamma \in MC_{\mathbf{S}+}(K)$. When A undermines B, the result is the same.

   - Given $B \notin E$, we need to find an $A \in E$ defeating B. We know that $F(B) \not\subseteq Cn_{\mathbf{S}+}(\Gamma)$. Then, there is a $\varphi \in F(B)$ which is not derived from Γ in the system $\mathbf{S}^+$. There are two cases to be considered.

     - φ is $\mathbf{S}^+$-consistent with $Cn_{\mathbf{S}+}(\Gamma)$. But then it contradicts the maximality of Γ.

     - φ is not $\mathbf{S}^+$-consistent with $Cn_{\mathbf{S}+}(\Gamma)$. Then, there are $\varphi_1, \cdots, \varphi_n \in \Gamma$ such that $\varphi_1, \cdots, \varphi_n \vdash_{\mathbf{S}+} \neg\varphi$. So, there is an argument $A \in E$ with the top rule $\varphi_1, \cdots, \varphi_n \Mapsto \neg\varphi$. Because $\tau = p$, the premise-based ordering $\leq^p$ ensures that $A \not< \varphi$, and then A undermines B.

   Then, E is a stable extension regarding K.

   The right-to-left direction. Let E be a stable extension regarding K. Let $\Gamma = E \cap K$.

   - We will show that $\Gamma \in MC_{\mathbf{S}+}(K)$.

     - Γ is $\mathbf{S}^+$-consistent. Otherwise, there are $\varphi_1, \cdots, \varphi_n, \varphi \in \Gamma$ such that $\varphi_1, \cdots, \varphi_n \vdash_{\mathbf{S}+} \neg\varphi$. There is an argument A with the top rule $\varphi_1, \cdots, \varphi_n \Mapsto \neg\varphi$. If $A \notin E$ and from that E there is a stable extension, assume that there is a $B \in E$ defeating A by the conclusion $\neg\varphi_n$. But both B and φ_n are in E, which contradicts that E is conflict-free.

     - Γ is maximal. Otherwise, there is a $\varphi \in K/\Gamma$ such that φ is $\mathbf{S}^+$-consistent with Γ. But then $\varphi \notin E$. There is an argument $A \in E$ undermining φ. Suppose the top rule of A is $\varphi_1, \cdots, \varphi_n \Mapsto \neg\varphi$, where $\varphi_1, \cdots, \varphi_n \in \Gamma$. It concludes that φ is not $\mathbf{S}^+$-consistent with Γ.

- Let $D \in E$. We will show $F(D) \subseteq Cn_{\mathbf{S}+}(\Gamma)$. If not, then there must be some $\varphi \in F(E)$ such that $\varphi \notin Cn_{\mathbf{S}+}(\Gamma)$. However, this leads to a contradiction when we bring together the maximality of $\Gamma \in MC_{\mathbf{S}+}(K)$ and the way it constructed $\Gamma = E \cap K$.

- Let $F(D) \subseteq Cn_{\mathbf{S}+}(\Gamma)$. We will show that $D \in E$. Otherwise, there is an argument $A \in E$ defeating D by A's top rule: $\varphi_1, \cdots, \varphi_n \mapsto \neg\varphi$, where $\varphi_1, \cdots, \varphi_n \in Cn_{\mathbf{S}+}(\Gamma)$ and $\varphi \in F(D)$. Then, $\varphi_1, \cdots, \varphi_n \vdash_{\mathbf{S}+} \neg\varphi$. However, by this assumption, we have $\neg\varphi, \varphi \in Cn_{\mathbf{S}+}(\Gamma)$. And that contradicts the consistency of Γ.

2. For the case of $\tau = r$.
   The left-to-right direction. Let E be a proper set generated by $\Gamma \in MC_{\mathbf{S}-}(K)$.

   - E is conflict-free. Otherwise, there are $A, B \in E$ such that A defeats B. There are four cases to be considered:
     - when both $A, B \in E_0$. Let $A = +\varphi$ and $B = -\varphi$. Then A undermines B. This implies $\Gamma \vdash_{\mathbf{S}-} \bot$, which contradicts the consistency of Γ.
     - when $A = \varphi \in E_0$ and $B \in E_n$ $(n > 0)$. We assume A rebuts B by the conclusion $\neg\varphi$ of the top rule of a subargument D of B. That then conflicts with the requirement that $F(B) \cup Cn_{\mathbf{S}-}(\Gamma)$ being $\mathbf{S}^-$-consistent.
     - when $A \in E_n$ and $B \in E_0$ $(n > 0)$. It is not possible for A to defeat B.
     - when $A \in E_n$ and $B \in E_m$ $(n, m > 0)$. Suppose $n < m$. We then know that $A \in E_n \subseteq E_{m-1}$. We assume that A rebuts B by the conclusion $\neg\varphi$ of the top rule of a subargument D of B. That contradicts the requirement that $F(B) \cup F(E_{m-1})$ should be $\mathbf{S}^-$-consistent.

   - For each $B \notin E$, we need to find a $A \in E$ defeating B. Consider:
     - when $B \in K/E$. Suppose $B = \varphi \in K$ and $B \notin \Gamma$. From $\Gamma \in MC_{\mathbf{S}-}(K)$, it implies that $\Gamma \cup \{\varphi\}$ is not $\mathbf{S}^-$-consistent. There are $\varphi_1, \cdots, \varphi_n \vdash_{\mathbf{S}-} \neg\varphi$ where $\varphi_1, \cdots, \varphi_n \in \Gamma$. Let $\varphi_1, \cdots, \varphi_n \mapsto \neg\varphi$ be the top rule of an argument A. Then A undermines B and $A \in E$.
     - when $B \notin K$ and $B \notin E$.
       * Suppose $\varphi \in F(B)/Cn_{\mathbf{S}-}(\Gamma)$ and φ is the conclusion of a top rule in R_s. If φ is $\mathbf{S}^-$-consistent with $Cn_{\mathbf{S}-}(\Gamma)$, that

conflicts with the maximality of $\Gamma \in MC_{\mathbf{S}^-}(K)$. Then, there are $\varphi_1, \cdots, \varphi_n \in \Gamma$ such that $\varphi_1, \cdots, \varphi_n \vdash_{\mathbf{S}^-} \neg\varphi$. Let $\varphi_1, \cdots, \varphi_n \mapsto \neg\varphi$ be the top rule of an argument $A \in E$. Then A undermines B.

* Suppose $\varphi \in F(B)/Cn_{\mathbf{S}^-}(\Gamma)$ such that φ is the conclusion of a top rule in R_d. Suppose φ is $\mathbf{S}^-$-consistent with $Cn_{\mathbf{S}^-}(\Gamma)$, which indicates that it is not possible to derive φ from Γ in system $\mathbf{S}^-$. Then we can assume that $\varphi \in Cn_{\mathbf{S}^+}(\Gamma)$, and that φ is the only element in B to make $B \notin E$, i.e. φ is not $\mathbf{S}^-$-consistent with $Cn_{\mathbf{S}^-}(\Gamma)$. Then, there are $\varphi_1, \cdots, \varphi_n \in Cn_{\mathbf{S}^-}(\Gamma)$ such that $\varphi_1, \cdots, \varphi_n \vdash_{\mathbf{S}^-} \neg\varphi$. According to the definition of E_0, there is an argument $A \in E_0$ with the top rule of $\varphi_1, \cdots, \varphi_n \mapsto \neg\varphi$ rebutting B.

Then E is a stable extension regarding K.

The right-to-left direction. Let E be a stable extension regarding K. Let $\Gamma = Cn_{\mathbf{S}^-}(E \cap K)$.

- First of all, $\Gamma \in MC_{\mathbf{S}^-}(K)$.

  - Γ is $\mathbf{S}^-$-consistent. Otherwise, there are $\varphi_1, \cdots, \varphi_n, \varphi \in \Gamma$ such that $\{\varphi_1, \cdots, \varphi_n\} \vdash_{\mathbf{S}^-} \neg\varphi$. We have an argument $A = \varphi_1, \cdots, \varphi_n \mapsto \neg\varphi$. If $A \in E$, then there is an argument $B = \varphi \in E$ such that A undermines B, which conflicts with E being conflict-free. If $A \notin E$, then because E is a stable extension, there is a $C = \psi_1, \cdots \psi_m \mapsto \neg\varphi_n \in E$ which undermines A for knowledge $\varphi_n \in Prem(A)$ where $\psi_1, \cdots \psi_m \in E$ (otherwise these premises would be defeated by some arguments contained in E, which contradicts that E is conflict-free). However, φ_n is already contained in E. This makes E not conflict-free. Given these two results, we know that Γ is $\mathbf{S}^-$-consistent.

  - Suppose Γ is not maximal. Let $\varphi \in K/\Gamma$. Then $\varphi \in K/E$. Because E is a stable extension, from $\varphi \notin E$ there is an $A \in E$ undermining φ. Assume that there is a top rule $\varphi_1, \cdots, \varphi_n \mapsto \neg\varphi$ of a subargument of A where $\varphi_1, \cdots, \varphi_n \in \Gamma$. Then $\varphi_1, \cdots, \varphi_n \vdash_{\mathbf{S}^-} \neg\varphi$. That implies that $\Gamma \cup \{\varphi\}$ is not $\mathbf{S}^-$-consistent.

- Given any $D \in E$, we show that either $D \in E_0$ or $D \in E_{n+1}$ ($n \geq 0$). Suppose $D \in E/E_0$. We show that $D \in E_{n+1}$ for some $n \geq 0$. Otherwise, given any E_n ($n \geq 0$), assume that

$F(D) \subseteq Cn_{\mathbf{S}^+}(\Gamma)$ but there is a $\varphi \in F(D)$ such that φ is not $\mathbf{S}^-$-consistent with $F(E_n)$. There are $\varphi_1, \cdots, \varphi_n \vdash_{\mathbf{S}^-} \neg\varphi$ where $\varphi_1, \cdots, \varphi_n \in F(E_n)$. So, there is an argument $A \in E_n$ with the top rule $\varphi_1, \cdots, \varphi_n \mapsto \neg\varphi$ in R_s, which defeats D. This conflicts with E being conflict-free.

- Given $D \in E_0$ or $D \in E_{n+1}$ ($n \geq 0$), we show $D \in E$. Consider:
  - when $D \in E_0$. Then by the way a stable set is defined, D is contained in E.
  - when $D \in E_{n+1}$ ($n \geq 0$) with $D \notin E_n$. Suppose $E_n \subseteq E$ and suppose $D \notin E$. Then, from that E is a stable extension, and there is an argument $A \in E$ defeating D. Let the top rule of A be $\varphi_1, \cdots, \varphi_n \mapsto \neg\varphi$ where $\varphi_1, \cdots, \varphi_n \in Cn_{\mathbf{S}^+}(\Gamma)$ and $\varphi \in F(D)$. Then $\varphi \notin Cn_{\mathbf{S}^+}(\Gamma)$. Then $D \notin E_{n+1}$.

Then E is a proper set generated by $\Gamma \in MC_{\mathbf{S}^-}(K)$.

■

PROPOSITION 42 *Let* $\Gamma \subseteq \mathcal{L}$, $(\mathbf{S}^-; \mathbf{S}^+) \in \{(\mathbf{D}_{-2}; \mathbf{D}_{-1}), (\mathbf{D}_{-2}; \mathbf{D}), (\mathbf{D}_{-1}; \mathbf{D})\}$ *be a pair of two monotonic logics and let* K *be a knowledge base of AT. We define*

- *an R-set generated by* K *in* $(\mathbf{S}^-; \mathbf{S}^+)$ *as* $\bigcup_{n \in \mathbb{N}} R_n$, *such that:*

$$R_0 = Cn_{\mathbf{S}^-}(\Gamma)$$

$$R_{n+1} = \begin{cases} R_n \cup \{\varphi\}, & \text{if } \varphi \in Cn_{\mathbf{S}^+}(\Gamma) \text{ and} \\ & \{\varphi\} \cup R_n \text{ is } \mathbf{S}^-\text{-consistent;} \\ R_n, & \text{otherwise;} \end{cases}$$

where $\Gamma \in MC_{\mathbf{S}^-}(K)$.

The R-collection $R_{\mathbf{S}^-;\mathbf{S}^+}(K)$ *generated by* K *in* $(\mathbf{S}^-; \mathbf{S}^+)$ *is the set of all R-sets generated by* K *in* $(\mathbf{S}^-; \mathbf{S}^+)$. *Then:*

1. $\mathcal{C}^{p\forall}_{\mathbf{S}^-;\mathbf{S}^+}(K) = \bigcap_{\Gamma \in MC_{\mathbf{S}^+}(K)} Cn_{\mathbf{S}^+}(\Gamma)$;

2. $\mathcal{C}^{r\forall}_{\mathbf{S}^-;\mathbf{S}^+}(K) = \bigcap R_{\mathbf{S}^-;\mathbf{S}^+}(K)$.

Proof. This proposition can be a direct result from Proposition 18.

1. When $\varphi \in \mathcal{C}^{p\forall}_{\mathbf{S}^-;\mathbf{S}^+}(K)$, then there is an argument A with $Conc(A) = \varphi$ such that A is contained in every stable extension regarding K. By Proposition 18.1, A is contained in every stable set generated by

221

$\Gamma \in MC_{\mathbf{S}+}(K)$, and then $\varphi \in Cn_{\mathbf{S}+}(\Gamma)$ for every $\Gamma \in MC_{\mathbf{S}+}(K)$. This result leads to $\varphi \in \bigcap_{\Gamma \in MC_{\mathbf{S}+}(K)} Cn_{\mathbf{S}+}(\Gamma)$. The other direction is similar.

2. When $\varphi \in \mathcal{C}^{r\forall}_{\mathbf{S}^-;\mathbf{S}+}(K)$, as in the previous case, by applying Proposition 18.2, we reach the same result. The other direction is similar by taking the definition into consideration.

■

PROPOSITION 43 *Consider the deontic language $\mathcal{L}$ and a pair of two monotonic logics $(\mathbf{S}^-;\mathbf{S}^+) \in \{(\mathbf{D}_{-2};\mathbf{D}_{-1}),(\mathbf{D}_{-2};\mathbf{D}),(\mathbf{D}_{-1};\mathbf{D})\}$. Let AF, corresponding to $\langle AT, \leq^\tau \rangle$, be an abstract argumentation framework $(\mathcal{A}, \mathcal{D})$ such that AT is based on $(\mathbf{S}^-;\mathbf{S}^+)$, $K = K_s \cup K_d$ is a knowledge base, and $\tau \in \{f, o^s, a^s, o, a, d, fr\}$. We construct a τ-premise set generated by K as $\bigcup_{n\in\mathbb{N}} E_n$ such that:*

$$E_0 = \{D \in \mathcal{A} \mid F(D) \subseteq Cn_{\mathbf{S}+}(\Gamma_1)\} \text{ for some } \Gamma_1 \in MC_{\mathbf{S}+}(K^\tau)$$

$$E_{n+1} = \begin{cases} E_n \cup \{D \in \mathcal{A}\}, & \text{if } \exists \Gamma_2 \in MC_{\mathbf{S}+}(K - K^\tau) \text{ such that} \\ & (i) F(D) \subseteq Cn_{\mathbf{S}+}(\Gamma_2) \text{ and} \\ & (ii) F(D) \cup F(E_n) \text{ is } \mathbf{S}^+\text{-consistent;} \\ E_n, & \text{otherwise.} \end{cases}$$

Then:

- *E is a τ-premise set generated by K iff E is a stable extension regarding K.*

Proof. The proof in this proposition is similar to the proof strategy in Proposition 18.
The left-to-right direction. Let $E = \bigcup_{n\in\mathbb{N}} E_n$ be a τ-premise set generated by K.

- E is conflict-free. Otherwise, there are $A, B \in E$ such that A defeats B. Consider:

  1. when $A, B \in E_0$. Then $+\varphi, -\varphi \in Cn_{\mathbf{S}+}(\Gamma_1)$ where $\Gamma_1 \in MC_{\mathbf{S}+}(K^\tau)$. But then that leads to a contradiction of Γ_1, which is $\mathbf{S}^+$-consistent.
  2. when $A, B \notin E_0$. We assume that $A \in E_m$ and $B \in E_n$ with $m < n$. By the construction of E, we can simply suppose that $B \in E_{m+1}$. Suppose A undermines B by having $+\varphi = Conc(A) \in F(E_m)$ and $-\varphi = Prem(B')$. Then, $F(B) \cup F(E_m)$ is not $\mathbf{S}^+$-consistent, which contradicts the construction of E.

- Given $B \notin E$, we need to find a $A \in E$ such that it defeats B. Consider:

  1. when $B \in K/E$. Suppose $B = \varphi \in K$ and $B \notin \Gamma$ where $\Gamma \in MC_{\mathbf{S}^+}(K^\tau)$. That simply implies that $\Gamma \cup \{\varphi\}$ is not $\mathbf{S}^+$-consistent. Then, there is $\varphi_1, \ldots, \varphi_n \vdash_{\mathbf{S}^+} \neg\varphi$ with $\varphi_1, \ldots, \varphi_n \in \Gamma$. Let $\varphi_1, \ldots, \varphi_n \mapsto \neg\varphi$ be the top rule of an argument A. Because all the premises of A and B come from K^τ, then A undermines B.

  2. when $B \notin K$ and $B \notin E$.

     (a) Suppose $\varphi \in F(B)/Cn_{\mathbf{S}^+}(\Gamma_1)$ where $\Gamma_1 \in MC_{\mathbf{S}^+}(K^\tau)$ such that φ is the conclusion of a top rule in R_s. Because of the maximality of Γ_1, there are $\varphi_1, \ldots, \varphi_n \in \Gamma_1$ such that $\varphi_1, \ldots, \varphi_n \vdash_{\mathbf{S}^+} \neg\varphi$. Let $\varphi_1, \ldots, \varphi_n \mapsto \neg\varphi$ be the top rule of an argument $A \in E_1$. Because all the premises of A come from K^τ, then A undermines B.

     (b) Suppose $\varphi \in F(B)/Cn_{\mathbf{S}^+}(\Gamma_1)$ where $\Gamma_1 \in MC_{\mathbf{S}^+}(K^\tau)$ such that φ is the conclusion of a top rule in R_d. We can still find such an $A \in E_1$, as above, that rebuts B.

     (c) Suppose $\varphi \in F(B)/Cn_{\mathbf{S}^+}(\Gamma_2)$ where $\Gamma_2 \in MC_{\mathbf{S}^+}(K - K^\tau)$ such that φ is the conclusion of a top rule (either in R_s or in R_d). The argument of proof is similar to that for the previous two cases.

Then E is a stable extension.

The right-to-left direction. Let E be a stable extension regarding K. Let $\Gamma = Cn_{\mathbf{S}^+}(E \cap K^\tau)$. Then:

- we will show that $\Gamma \in MC_{\mathbf{S}^+}(K^\tau)$.

  1. Γ is $\mathbf{S}^+$-consistent. Otherwise, there are $\varphi_1, \ldots, \varphi_n, \varphi \in \Gamma$ such that $\varphi_1, \ldots, \varphi_n \vdash_{\mathbf{S}^+} \neg\varphi$. Then, we have an argument $A = \varphi_1, \ldots, \varphi_n \mapsto \varphi$. If $A \in E$, then there is an argument $B = \varphi \in E$ such that A undermines B. This is because all the premises of A are in K^τ. But then, that conflicts with E being conflict-free. If $A \notin E$, then because E is a stable extension, there is a $C = \psi_1, \ldots, \psi_m \mapsto \neg\varphi_n \in E$ which undermines A for knowledge $\varphi_n \in Prem(A)$ where $\psi_1, \ldots, \psi_m \in E$. Then $Prem(C) \subseteq K^\tau$, otherwise C is not preferable enough to defeat A. However, φ_n is already contained in E. That leads to E not being conflict-free. In sum, Γ is $\mathbf{S}^+$-consistent.

2. Γ is maximal. Otherwise, let $\varphi \in K^\tau/\Gamma$ such that $\Gamma \cup \{\varphi\}$ is $\mathbf{S}^+$-consistent. Then $\varphi \notin E_0$. So, $\varphi \in Cn_{\mathbf{S}+}(\Gamma) = Cn_{\mathbf{S}+}(K^\tau) = \Gamma$, which leads to a contradiction.

- given any $D \in E$, we will show that there is an $n \in \mathbb{N}$ such that $D \in E_n$. We prove this by induction on the structure of D. Consider:

  - when $D \in K$. Since $D \in E$ and $\Gamma = Cn_{\mathbf{S}+}(E \cap K^\tau)$, from $D \in E \cap K$ it is implied that $D \in Cn_{\mathbf{S}+}(\Gamma)$. So $D \in E_0$.

  - when $D = \mapsto \in R_s^0$ or $D = \Mapsto \in R_d^0$. It is clear that $F(D) \subseteq Cn_{\mathbf{S}+}(\Gamma)$.

  - when we have an inductive hypothesis. All the subarguments of D are contained in some E_n where $n \in \mathbb{N}$.

  - when $D = D_1, \ldots, D_n \mapsto \varphi$. Then (@) $F(D_1), \ldots, F(D_n) \vdash_{\mathbf{S}-} \varphi$. Notice that $F(D_i)$ is $\mathbf{S}^+$-consistent for each $i \in [1, n]$ by inductive hyphothesis. If for all E_n it is the case that $D \notin E_n$, then $F(D_1) \cup \cdots \cup F(D_n) \cup \{\varphi\}$ is not $\mathbf{S}^+$-consistent. But then that conflicts with (@).

  - when $D = D_1, \ldots, D_n \Mapsto \varphi$. The proof is similar to that of the previous case.

- given a $D \notin E$, we will show that there is no E_n such that $D \in E_n$ is constructed from Γ. Since E is a stable extension, there is an argument $A \in E$ such that A defeats D. Then, there are $\varphi_1, \ldots, \varphi_n \vdash_{\mathbf{S}+} \varphi$ such that $\varphi_1, \ldots, \varphi_n, \varphi \in F(A)$ and $\neg\varphi \in F(D)$. Then, $A \in E_n$ for some $n \in \mathbb{N}$ by the case proven in the previous step. Now $\neg\varphi \notin E_n$ for any $n \in \mathbb{N}$, otherwise the result will be contrary to Γ being $\mathbf{S}^+$-consistent. It is then concluded that $D \notin E_n$ for any $n \in \mathbb{N}$.

∎

PROPOSITION 44 *Consider the deontic language $\mathcal{L}$ and a pair of two monotonic logics $(\mathbf{S}^-; \mathbf{S}^+)$. Let AF_i, corresponding to $\langle AT, \leq^i \rangle$, be an abstract argumentation framework $(\mathcal{A}, \mathcal{D}_i)$ such that AT is based on $(\mathbf{S}^-; \mathbf{S}^+)$, K is a knowledge base, and $i \in \{1, 2\}$. Let $Stable(AF_i)$ be the set of all stable extensions w.r.t. AF_i.*

1. *If $K^{\leq^1} \subseteq K^{\leq^2}$, then $E \in Stable(AF_1)$ implies $\exists E' \in Stbale(AF_2)$ s.t. $E' = E$.*

2. *If $K^{\leq^1} \subseteq K^{\leq^2}$, then $|Stable(AF_1)| \leq |Stable(AF_2)|$.*

Proof.

1. Consider the case when $K^{\leq^1} \subseteq K^{\leq^2}$. Suppose $E \in Stable(AF_1)$. Let $E = E_1 \cup E_2$ according to Proposition 23 and Proposition 27. We need to show that E is a stable extension w.r.t. AF_2.

   First, E is conflict-free in AF_2. Otherwise $\exists A, B \in E$ such that $(A, B) \in \mathcal{D}$ in AF_1. If A rebuts B, then $Conc(A) = \neg\varphi$ for some $B' \in Sub(B)$ and $TopRule(B') \in R_d$, $Con(B') = \varphi$, and $A \not\prec B'$. So B is generated from $K - K^{\leq^2}$ and then from $K - K^{\leq^1}$. This indicates that $(A, B) \in \mathcal{D}$ in AF_2. But then that contradicts E being conflict-free in AF_1. If A undermines B, then $Conc(A) = \neg\varphi$ for knowledge $\varphi \in Prem(B)$ of B and $A \not\prec \varphi$. No matter where A is generated from, whether from $K^{\leq^1}$ or from $K - K^{\leq^1}$, it keeps the preference in $K^{\leq^2}$. So A undermines B in AF_2. Again, this contradicts E being conflict-free in AF_1. Thus, we conclude that E is conflict-free in AF_2.

   Now, we prove that $\forall B \notin E \; \exists A \in E$ such that $(A, B) \in \mathcal{D}$ in AF_2. If that is not the case, then $\exists B \notin E$ such that $\forall A \in E$ and $(A, B) \notin \mathcal{D}$ in AF_2 (@). Notice that from E there is a stable extension in AF_1. We then have $\exists A' \in E$ such that $(A', B) \in \mathcal{D}$ in AF_1. Since $K^{\leq^1} \subseteq K^{\leq^2}$, this implies that $(A', B) \in \mathcal{D}$ in AF_2. That conflicts with (@). So the assumption is false.

   Now we conclude that E is a stable extension in AF_2.

2. From the first item, we can easily see that this statement holds. Notice that we have

$$\leq^{o^s} \subseteq \leq^o \text{ and } \leq^{a^s} \subseteq \leq^a \text{ and } \leq^f \subseteq \leq^o \text{ and } \leq^f \subseteq \leq^a .$$

   And thus it implies:

   - $|Stable(\langle AT, \leq^{o^s}\rangle)| \leq |Stable(\langle AT, \leq^o\rangle)|$;
   - $|Stable(\langle AT, \leq^{a^s}\rangle)| \leq |Stable(\langle AT, \leq^a\rangle)|$;
   - $|Stable(\langle AT, \leq^f\rangle)| \leq |Stable(\langle AT, \leq^o\rangle)|$;
   - $|Stable(\langle AT, \leq^f\rangle)| \leq |Stable(\langle AT, \leq^a\rangle)|$.

   ∎

PROPOSITION 45 *Let* $\Gamma \subseteq \mathcal{L}$, $(\mathbf{S}^-; \mathbf{S}^+) \in \{(\mathbf{D}_{-2}; \mathbf{D}_{-1}), (\mathbf{D}_{-2}; \mathbf{D}), (\mathbf{D}_{-1}; \mathbf{D})\}$ *be a pair of two monotonic logics, let* $\leq^\tau$ *be a* τ*-ordering (*$\tau \in \{p, r, f, o^s, a^s, o, a, d, fr\}$*), and let K be a knowledge base of AT. We define*

- a P-set generated by K in $(\mathbf{S}^-; \mathbf{S}^+)$ as $\bigcup_{n \in \mathbb{N}} P_n$, such that

$$P_0 = Cn_{\mathbf{S}^+}(\Gamma)$$

$$P_{n+1} = \begin{cases} P_n \cup \{\varphi\}, & \text{if } \exists \Gamma' \in MC_{\mathbf{S}^+}(K - K^\tau) \text{ such that} \\ & \quad (i)\, \varphi \in Cn_{\mathbf{S}^+}(\Gamma') \text{ and} \\ & \quad (ii)\, \{\varphi\} \cup P_n \text{ is } \mathbf{S}^+\text{-consistent;} \\ P_n, & \text{otherwise;} \end{cases}$$

where $\Gamma \in MC_{\mathbf{S}^+}(K^\tau)$.

The P-collection $P_{\mathbf{S}^-;\mathbf{S}^+}(K)$ generated by K in $(\mathbf{S}^-; \mathbf{S}^+)$ is the set of all P-sets generated by K in $(\mathbf{S}^-; \mathbf{S}^+)$. Then

- $\mathcal{C}_{\mathbf{S}^-;\mathbf{S}^+}^{\tau\forall}(K) = \bigcap P_{\mathbf{S}^-;\mathbf{S}^+}(K).$

Proof. Just like the proof in Proposition 20, by applying Proposition 23 and Proposition 27, the result can be reached. ∎

PROPOSITION 46 *Let* $(\mathbf{S}^-; \mathbf{S}^+) \in \{(\mathbf{D}_{-2}; \mathbf{D}_{-1}), (\mathbf{D}_{-2}; \mathbf{D}), (\mathbf{D}_{-1}; \mathbf{D})\}$ *be a pair of two monotonic logics. Now we have* $p \mid\hspace{-0.3em}\sim_{\mathbf{S}^-;\mathbf{S}^+}^{\tau\forall} p$ *but* $\{p, \neg p\} \mid\hspace{-0.3em}\not\sim_{\mathbf{S}^-;\mathbf{S}^+}^{\tau\forall} p$, *with* $\tau \in \{p, r, f, o^s, a^s, o, a, d, fr\}$.

Proof. This proposition can be argued by applying Proposition 20, Proposition 23 and Proposition 27. ∎

PROPOSITION 47 *Let* $(\mathbf{S}^-; \mathbf{S}^+) \in \{(\mathbf{D}_{-2}; \mathbf{D}_{-1}), (\mathbf{D}_{-2}; \mathbf{D}), (\mathbf{D}_{-1}; \mathbf{D})\}$ *be a pair of two monotonic logics. We have the following relations regarding supra-classicality:*

$$\vdash_{\mathbf{S}^-} \subseteq \mid\hspace{-0.3em}\sim_{\mathbf{S}^-;\mathbf{S}^+}^{\tau\forall} \subseteq \vdash_{\mathbf{S}^+}$$

where $\tau \in \{p, r, f, o^s, a^s, o, a, d, fr\}$.

Proof. Again, this proposition can be proved by applying Proposition 20, Proposition 23 and Proposition 27. ∎

PROPOSITION 48 *Given* $\tau \in \{p, r, f, o^s, a^s, o, a, d, fr\}$ *as one of the preferences defined and* $(\mathbf{S}^-; \mathbf{S}^+) \in \{(\mathbf{D}_{-2}; \mathbf{D}_{-1}), (\mathbf{D}_{-2}; \mathbf{D}), (\mathbf{D}_{-1}; \mathbf{D})\}$ *as a pair of two monotonic logics, we will now check whether the defeasible deontic logics defined in this chapter satisfy the following standard properties regarding non-monotonicity (where we simplify* $\mid\hspace{-0.3em}\sim_{\mathbf{S}^-;\mathbf{S}^+}^{\tau\forall}$ *to* $\Vdash$ *):*

1. *Reflexivity:* $\Gamma \Vdash \varphi$ *where* $\varphi \in \Gamma$

2. *Cut: If* $\Gamma \cup \{\psi\} \Vdash \chi$ *and* $\Gamma \Vdash \psi$, *then* $\Gamma \Vdash \chi$

3. *Cautious Monotony:* if $\Gamma \Vdash \psi$ and $\Gamma \Vdash \chi$, then $\Gamma \cup \{\psi\} \Vdash \chi$

4. *Left Logical Equivalence:* if $Cn_{\mathbf{S}+}(\Gamma) = Cn_{\mathbf{S}+}(\Gamma')$ and $\Gamma \Vdash \chi$, then $\Gamma' \Vdash \chi$

5. *Right Weakening:* if $\vdash_{\mathbf{S}+} \varphi \to \psi$ and $\Gamma \Vdash \varphi$, then $\Gamma \Vdash \psi$

6. *OR:* if $\Gamma \Vdash \varphi$ and $\Gamma' \Vdash \varphi$, then $\Gamma \cup \Gamma' \Vdash \varphi$

7. *AND:* if $\Gamma \Vdash \psi$ and $\Gamma \Vdash \chi$, then $\Gamma \Vdash \psi \wedge \chi$

8. *Rational Monotony:* If $\Gamma \Vdash \chi$ and $\Gamma \nVdash \neg\psi$, then $\Gamma \cup \{\psi\} \Vdash \chi$

The results are shown in Table 8.

Properties	$\Vdash^{\tau\forall}_{\mathbf{S}-;\mathbf{S}+}$	$\Vdash^{\tau\forall}_{\mathbf{S}-;\mathbf{S}+}$
Reflexivity	✓*	No
Cut	✓	✓
Cautious Monotony	✓	✓
Left Logical Equivalence	✓	✓
Right Weakening	No	✓
OR	No	No
AND	✓	✓
Rational Monotony	✓	✓

Table 8: This is a summary of various consequences we have based on different types of knowledge base. Notice that $\tau \in \{p, f, o^s, a^s, o, a, d, fr\}$. The symbol ✓* indicates that this property is satisfied when the given knowledge base is consistent in $\mathbf{S}^-$.

Proof. We first check whether the following properties hold for $\Vdash^{\tau\forall}_{\mathbf{S}-;\mathbf{S}+}$ by using Propositions 20 and 29. Consider:

1. Reflexivity (for the rule-based preference). First we know that for the rule-based preference, all the different knowledge are better than the other arguments. According to the construction shown in Proposition 20 and 29, we can see that all the different knowledge are contained in the consequences. Thus Reflexivity holds.

2. Cut. Suppose $\Gamma \cup \{\psi\} \Vdash^{\tau\forall}_{\mathbf{S}-;\mathbf{S}+} \chi$ and $\Gamma \Vdash^{\tau\forall}_{\mathbf{S}-;\mathbf{S}+} \psi$. From the latter, we have $\psi \in \mathcal{C}^{\tau\forall}_{\mathbf{S}-;\mathbf{S}+}(\Gamma)$. This implies that $\mathcal{C}^{\tau\forall}_{\mathbf{S}-;\mathbf{S}+}(\{\Gamma \cup \{\psi\}\}) \subseteq \mathcal{C}^{\tau\forall}_{\mathbf{S}-;\mathbf{S}+}(\Gamma)$. By applying the first assumption. we conclude that $\chi \in \mathcal{C}^{\tau\forall}_{\mathbf{S}-;\mathbf{S}+}(\Gamma)$.

3. Cautious Monotony. Assume that $\Gamma \cup \{\psi\} \vdash^{\tau\forall}_{\mathbf{S}^-;\mathbf{S}^+} \chi$ and $\Gamma \vdash^{\tau\forall}_{\mathbf{S}^-;\mathbf{S}^+} \psi$. From the second assumption, we get $\psi \in \mathcal{C}^{\tau\forall}_{\mathbf{S}^-;\mathbf{S}^+}(\Gamma)$. This indicates that $\mathcal{C}^{\tau\forall}_{\mathbf{S}^-;\mathbf{S}^+}(\Gamma \cup \{\psi\}) \subseteq \mathcal{C}^{\tau\forall}_{\mathbf{S}^-;\mathbf{S}^+}(\Gamma)$. Applying this result to the second assumption, we then conclude that $\chi \in \mathcal{C}^{\tau\forall}_{\mathbf{S}^-;\mathbf{S}^+}(\Gamma)$.

4. Left Logical Equivalence. Assume that $Cn(\Gamma) = Cn(\Gamma')$ and $\Gamma \vdash^{\tau\forall}_{\mathbf{S}^-;\mathbf{S}^+} \chi$. From the second assumption, we then have $\chi \in \mathcal{C}^{\tau\forall}_{\mathbf{S}^-;\mathbf{S}^+}(\Gamma)$. Because $Cn(\Gamma) = Cn(\Gamma')$, it is implied that $\mathcal{C}^{\tau\forall}_{\mathbf{S}^-;\mathbf{S}^+}(\Gamma) = \mathcal{C}^{\tau\forall}_{\mathbf{S}^-;\mathbf{S}^+}(\Gamma')$. This immediately indicates that $\chi \in \mathcal{C}^{\tau\forall}_{\mathbf{S}^-;\mathbf{S}^+}(\Gamma')$.

5. Right Weakening (for the preferences based on premises). Suppose $\vdash_{\mathbf{S}^+} \varphi \to \psi$ and $\Gamma \vdash^{\tau\forall}_{\mathbf{S}^-;\mathbf{S}^+} \varphi$. By $\Gamma \vdash^{\tau\forall}_{\mathbf{S}^-;\mathbf{S}^+} \varphi$ and Proposition 29, there are two cases of φ being contained in every stable extension. If φ is contained in the maximally consistent subset regarding K^τ, then ψ is also contained in K^τ because $\vdash_{\mathbf{S}^+} \varphi \to \psi$. By the construction of Proposition 29, we know that ψ is one of the best arguments, and thus cannot be defeated. It is also contained in $\mathcal{C}^{\tau\forall}_{\mathbf{S}^-;\mathbf{S}^+}(\Gamma)$. If φ is contained in the maximally consistent subset regarding $K - K^\tau$, then φ is always the conclusion of one of the second best arguments. Suppose such an argument is $A \in E' \in Stable(\Gamma)$ such that $Conc(A) = \varphi$ for any stable extension E' (@). Notice that $Prem(A) \subseteq K - K^\tau$. Let $E \in Stable(\Gamma)$ be a stable extension. Because $\vdash_{\mathbf{S}^+} \varphi \to \psi$, we then have an argument $A' = A \mapsto \psi$ where $TopRule(A') = \varphi \mapsto \psi$. Because A is contained in a stable extension E, the only way to defeat A' is to rebut it by the conclusion ψ. This indicates that there is an argument $B \in E$ such that $Conc(B) = \neg\psi$ and $B \not< A'$. On the other hand, we then have an argument $B' = B \mapsto \neg\varphi$. Notice that $Prem(A) = Prem(A')$ and $Prem(B) = Prem(B')$. Thus $B' \not< A$ because of the preference on premises. So A is defeated by B'. This indicates that there is a stable extension containing B' and thus excludes A. But then that conflicts with (@). So A' is not defeated in E. We then conclude that $\Gamma \vdash^{\tau\forall}_{\mathbf{S}^-;\mathbf{S}^+} \psi$.

6. AND. Assume that $\Gamma \vdash^{\tau\forall}_{\mathbf{S}^-;\mathbf{S}^+} \psi$ and $\Gamma \vdash^{\tau\forall}_{\mathbf{S}^-;\mathbf{S}^+} \chi$. So $\psi \in \mathcal{C}^{\tau\forall}_{\mathbf{S}^-;\mathbf{S}^+}(\Gamma)$ and $\chi \in \mathcal{C}^{\tau\forall}_{\mathbf{S}^-;\mathbf{S}^+}(\Gamma)$. We can have $\psi \wedge \chi \in \mathcal{C}^{\tau\forall}_{\mathbf{S}^-;\mathbf{S}^+}(\Gamma)$.

7. Rational Monotony. Assume that $\Gamma \vdash^{\tau\forall}_{\mathbf{S}^-;\mathbf{S}^+} \chi$ and $\Gamma \not\vdash^{\tau\forall}_{\mathbf{S}^-;\mathbf{S}^+} \neg\psi$. We want to show that $\Gamma \cup \{\psi\} \vdash^{\tau\forall}_{\mathbf{S}^-;\mathbf{S}^+} \chi$. By $\Gamma \not\vdash^{\tau\forall}_{\mathbf{S}^-;\mathbf{S}^+} \neg\psi$, there is a stable extension $E \in Stable(\Gamma)$ such that for any argument $A \in E$, then $Conc(A) \neq \neg\psi$ (@).

228

(a) If ψ is the conclusion of one argument in a stable extension of the Γ-AT, this indicates that ψ is $\mathbf{S}^+$-consistent with the conclusion χ of an argument in this stable extension. So adding ψ to the knowledge base Γ does not change its stable extensions. Then we have the desired result.

(b) If ψ is the conclusion of one argument that is excluded in every stable extension of the Γ-AT, then by the assumption (@), all the conclusions of all the arguments in E are $\mathbf{S}^+$-consistent with ψ. After adding ψ to the knowledge base, Γ does not change its stable extensions. Then we have the desired result again.

(c) If there is no argument from Γ has ψ as its conclusion, then adding ψ to the knowledge base Γ does not change its stable extensions. Then we have the desired result again.

According to the above cases, we conclude that $\Gamma \cup \{\psi\} \mathrel{|\!\!\sim}^{\tau\forall}_{\mathbf{S}^-;\mathbf{S}^+} \chi$.

∎

Huimin Dong
Sun Yat-sen University
Department of Philosophy (Zhuhai)
Zhuhai, China
Email: huimin.dong@xixilogic.org

Beishui Liao
Zhejiang University
School of Philosophy
Hangzhou, China
Email: baiseliao@zju.edu.cn

Réka Markovich
University of Luxembourg
Department of Computer Science
Eschr-sur-Alzette, Luxembourg
Email: reka.markovich@uni.lu

Leendert van der Torre
University of Luxembourg
Department of Computer Science
Eschr-sur-Alzette, Luxembourg
Email: leon.vandertorre@uni.lu

7
Normative Change: An AGM Approach

Juliano Maranhão
Giovanni Casini,
Gabriella Pigozzi
Leendert van der Torre

ABSTRACT.   Studying normative change is of practical and theoretical interest. Changing legal rules pose interpretation problems in
determining the content of legal rules. The question of interpretation
is tightly linked to questions about determining the validity of rules
and their ability to produce effects. Different formal models of normative change seem to be better suited to capturing these different
dimensions: the dimension of validity appears to be better captured
by the AGM approach, while syntactic methods are better suited to
modelling how the effects of rules are blocked or enabled. Historically, the AGM approach to belief revision (on which we focus in this
chapter) was the first formal model of normative change. We provide
a survey of the AGM approach along with the main criticisms of it.
We then turn to a formal analysis of normative change that combines
AGM theory and input/output logic, thereby allowing a clear distinction between norms and obligations. Our approach addresses some of
the difficulties of normative change, like combining constitutive and
regulative rules (and the normative conflicts that may arise from such
a combination), revision and contraction of normative systems, as well
as contraction of normative systems that combine sets of constitutive
and regulative rules. We end our chapter by highlighting and discussing some challenges and open problems with the AGM approach
regarding normative change.

1   Normative Change and Legal Reasoning

The study of normative change in identifying the law and understanding legal
reasoning and legal interpretation is of practical and theoretical interest.

Handbook of Legal AI
© *2022, Maranhão, et al.*

Juliano Maranhão   Giovanni Casini,   Gabriella Pigozzi   Leendert van der Torre

From a practical perspective, legal rules are the product of, or at least affected by, the continuous agency of authorities with the power to issue norms or make judicial decisions.[1] Such authoritative acts change the content of the normative order by including and excluding rules or by modifying their effects.

The problem lies in the fact that there are a variety of acts that perform such modifications in the lifetime of a normative system, which may have an effect on two dimensions:

(i) *validity*: the pertinence of rules to a normative system that may be changed by acts of abrogation, explicit derogation or implicit derogation;

(ii) *efficacy*: the capacity of rules to produce effects or apply in a certain time period, which may be changed by acts of annulment or invalidation, suspension, restriction, modulation etc.

Hence, there is a discrepancy between the period of the validity of a rule in a normative system (which also has its own time span of existence), and its period of efficacy, thus creating situations where a rule is invalid but applicable or where a rule is valid but inapplicable.

From a theoretical perspective, it is important to understand normative change in order to understand the status of entailed (derived) rules in a normative system and their relationship to explicitly promulgated rules. The debate about the status of entailed rules is connected to a central problem in the conception of modern law concerning the role of reason *versus* the role of authority in identifying the law [Maranhao, 2017b]. The question is whether the ultimate basis for identifying the legal status of an action are considerations of moral correction or goodness, or determination by a social source, i.e. whether the legal status of an action is determined by the content of an authoritative act, which is objectively identifiable independently of moral or political arguments [Raz, 1979].

1.1   Normative Change and Legal Validity

The inclusion of a new rule in a normative system is performed by an act of promulgation (or enactment). This new rule may represent new content, changing the content of the normative system by making new obligations, permissions or prohibitions derivable. Or the new rule may be redundant,

---

[1]Even scholars like Dworkin [1986] who refuse to reduce identifying the law to the content of authoritative social sources do acknowledge that those sources produce relevant legal material for legal interpretation, potentially affecting how the law is identified and causing modification to the law.

adding a new norm-formulation, new text, without actually introducing new content.

In turn, exclusion of a rule from the normative system or modification of its effects may be obtained by means of a variety of legislative or judicial acts. There are terminological variations and disputes concerning acts that either exclude content pertaining to normative systems or restrict its efficacy (applicability). There are also different practices depending on the jurisdiction, and particularly with respect to systems of common law vis-à-vis systems of statutory law. In order to avoid confusion, we shall use terms in accordance with their technical usage in legal practice, but will articulate their meanings where the terminology can be misleading. In general, we will use the terms *derogation* and *abrogation* to refer strictly to the *dimension of validity*, with the meaning that a statute is totally or partially excluded from (ceases to pertain to) the normative system. We prefer to restrict the term "annulment" to the dimension of efficacy, with the meaning that a rule or a set of rules has its effects cancelled (ceases to be applicable).

Derogation is a distinct normative act that excludes a rule or some rules from a set of valid rules. It may be explicit or implicit:

explicit derogation: a new rule that explicitly mentions the name of the rule or rules to be excluded.

implicit derogation: a new rule that adds normative content which is inconsistent with the content of previous rules in the normative system.

In the case of explicit derogation, the content of the new rule may consist of only excluding the named rule: for instance, "article 56 of Law 1234 is derogated". In such a case, the derogation rule exhausts its effects by performing that very derogation [Kelsen, 1973].

Abrogation means excluding the totality of the rules of a statute. Usually, abrogation is due to an act of promulgating a new statute that substitutes the content of a previous statute on the same subject. The exclusion is explicit because the set of excluded rules is indicated by either naming the statute or indicating the subject-matter. Abrogation also introduces new content whose effects hold after the previous statute has been derogated.

Derogation and abrogation (as well as promulgation) are usually nonretroactive normative acts, producing their effects immediately after publication or at a certain time in the future indicated by the same act. In the legal jargon, their effects are *ex nunc*, i.e. "from now on". That is, they are "established" by the legislative act.

We shall use the term "annulment"[2] to refer to acts that cancel the effects of a valid rule. If a rule is annulled, it becomes inapplicable, that is, one cannot derive obligations, permissions, powers or any legal consequences from it.

An annulment may be the consequence of a judicial declaration that a rule of the normative system is invalid, or it may be the product of legislative acts cancelling the effects of a rule. A judicial annulment recognises a "vice" or "defect" in the "pedigree" of the rule. Those "pedigree" defects are related to problems with the source of the rule, the *legitimate authority*, the procedure for creating the rule, or the incompatibility of the rule with the content of hierarchically superior rules. Depending on the gravity of the defect identified, the recognition may consider the rule to be invalid from the time of its promulgation (in the legal jargon, *ex tunc* effects) or from the moment the defect is declared (*ex nunc*).

To complicate matters, since the annulment may be a judicial act, the recognition of invalidity may be general, that is, applicable to all legal subjects, or it may have an effect on a particular legal relation or a particular individual. So there is a general dimension of effects, but there are also indirect effects where normative changes affect the legal positions of different individuals in different ways. The same also happens for derogation and abrogation, which cannot retroact, so that a derogated rule may still be applicable to facts that occurred before the derogation took place.

There are other ways to affect the efficacy of rules by authoritative acts. A statute or decree may suspend or restrict the applicability of a rule in a given period or to a given domain or context. For instance, the legal rules protecting moral rights for authors became inapplicable to software by the force of a new law (art. 2 §1 of the Brazilian Law 9609/1998 on Software Copyright). Or a rule may suspend the applicability of some rental of real estate or labour laws during a global pandemic.

Clearly, the temporal aspect is crucial to analysing normative change, and this temporal factor has two dimensions: the time span of the rule's validity, that is, the period of time in which the rule pertains to the normative system; and the time span of its applicability, that is, the period of time where the obligations/permissions derived by the rule are applicable.

---

[2]The term "revocation" is sometimes used in parallel with annulment and pertains to the dimension of validity. Revocation refers to the act of cancelling a previous declaration, contract or legislative act, but the term "annulment" is also used to refer to such a cancellation with the intent of producing legal effects, particularly when such a cancellation is performed by a different person or institution (e.g. a judicial court) to the one that issued the act (e.g. the parliament or the contracting parties). Annulment and invalidation may also refer to cancelling the *effects* or applicability of a particular act, and are therefore situated in the dimension of efficacy of rules.

These dynamics of normative change, which are performed by a variety of legal acts with different effects, bring a series of difficulties for determining the content and the effects of a normative system at a particular moment in time. Indeed, a promulgation and a derogation may involve choices between alternative and incompatible descriptions of the resulting normative system.

The practical import of the study of normative change is not only a matter of finding suitable formal and computable representations of an uncontroversial and standard practice. It is also relevant for clarifying that very practice by describing the impact of acts of promulgation and revocation on the content of a normative system, and especially how they affect the normative consequences or entailed rules of that system. We highlight three problems.

The first problem concerns the *network effects of normative change*, that is, the effects of a derogation or a promulgation on networks of regulative and constitutive rules [Searle, 1995]. Acts of promulgation or derogation may not only add or exclude *regulative rules*, which are authoritative rules demanding, prohibiting or permitting an action or the omission of an action. They may also add or exclude *constitutive rules*, whose role is to a) define under which factual conditions a certain object or action "counts as" an instance of a legal concept such as property right, or b) ascribe meaning to legal concepts via definitions (e.g. people under 18 years old count as minors).

Hence, stipulating a new definition or changing the definition of a legal concept may affect how the content of different regulatory rules are determined. In turn, the exclusion or addition of new rules that are related to a legal concept may affect the practical implications, and therefore the very understanding, of that very concept [Sartor, 2007]. Such an effect is neither immediately nor completely acknowledged by lawgivers, and leads to subsequent modifications and adaptations.

For instance, the legal definition of "software" as "literary work"[3] makes rules protecting the "expression" of a literary work applicable to the source code of software: the copyright owner may copy, share, or distribute the software, create "derivative work" etc. The equiparation also enhances new legal consequences by analogy, such as the additional copyright protection of the original "structure" of a code, considering that the "composition" of different non-original literary works are also protected. Thus, the addition of new rules or protections for "literary work" may also "expand" the protection of software. However, some undesirable legal consequences of that equiparation—for instance, the ascription of "moral rights" related to soft-

---

[3] Agreement on Trade-Related Aspects of Intellectual Property Rights (Trips Treaty, 1994)

ware, such as the right to regret and withdraw the work from distribution—have been derogated in several jurisdictions.[4] Such derogations in turn affect the understanding of the very concept of copyright—originally conceived as intrinsically bound to the author's personality—by linking the original notion of copyright to a network of personality rights. Thus, the ascription of new objects to a legal concept by definitional rules and the introduction or derogation of regulatory rules interferes with, and demands "reconfigurations" of, the links in the network of legal definitions and normative consequences.

The second problem concerns the *undecidability of implicit derogations*, which is a consequence of the potential conflict between different "collision criteria" in the law. New obligations, prohibitions, permissions or definitions added via lawgiving acts may create conflicts with the content of the previous version of the normative system. Such conflicts are solved by an *implicit derogation* operated by so-called *collision criteria*, which are legal principles of interpretation enunciating preference relations for solving conflicts between rules. There are three collision criteria:

lex superior: a *hierarchical* criterion according to which rules enacted by a source of a higher hierarchical degree prevail over rules from lower degree sources.

lex posterior: a *temporal* criterion according to which more recent rules take precedence over older ones.

lex specialis: a criterion of *specialisation* according to which a rule applicable to a specific circumstance or condition prevails over another rule applicable in a more general context.

Although it is clear that the hierarchical criterion prevails over the temporal and speciality criteria, the two last criteria may collide.

Example 1.1. Suppose that a new statute on public concessions is promulgated stating:

1. A private company operating a public concession of a federal road may explore its margins for commercial purposes.

This rule might conflict with a previous existing rule specific to electricity distribution companies stating:

---

[4]For instance, article 2º, §1, of the Brazilian Copyright Law considers all provisions of the law warranting moral rights to be inapplicable to software, except for the right to have authorship acknowledged and the right to oppose unauthorised modifications that may affect the reputation of the author.

2. Public energy distribution companies have the right to use road margins to the extent that such use is necessary to install its energy transmission network.

These rules conflict if one interprets the right to use, in which energy companies are invested, as the right to use free of charge, and if the right to explore the margins "for commercial purposes" is considered to include a right to charge a fee for the public energy distribution system. But the conflict cannot be solved by the existing collision criteria because there is a conflict in this case between *lex posterior*, which makes rule (1) prevail over rule (2), and *lex specialis*, which makes rule (2) prevail over rule (1). Actually, there is another possible source of dispute, which is the understanding of which rule is the more specific rule. One could argue that rule (2) is more specific because it relates to a public energy distribution company, while rule (1) relates to all kinds of potential users. However, one could also argue that rule (1) is more specific because it relates to roads, the object of public concessions to private companies, while rule (2) has a wider scope on this aspect.

Hence, given a conflict of rules created by a promulgation, there may be no fixed criteria for deciding which one should prevail.

The third problem concerns the *indeterminacy of implicit derogations*, that is, that the promulgation of a new rule may conflict with a rule derived from the combination of different explicit rules in the normative system.

Example 1.2. Suppose that a regulation contains the following rules:

3. Brasilia is the capital city of the Brazilian Federation.

4. The Brazilian Federal Administration must be located in the capital city of the Brazilian Federation.

Now suppose that the following rule is promulgated:

5. The Brazilian Federal Administration must be located in Rio de Janeiro.

Rule 3 does not conflict with either rule 1 or 2, but it does conflict with the entailed rule:

5'. The Brazilian Federal Administration must be located in Brasilia.

This would be a case of *implicit derogation* of an entailed rule resolved by the temporal criteria of collision. However, the entailed rule can only be suppressed if at least one of explicit rules (3) or (4) are derogated. Hence, the content of the normative system after the promulgation of (5) is undetermined, with three possible candidates for the outcome of this derogation: $S_1 = \{3,5\}$, $S_2 = \{4,5\}$ and $S_3 = \{5\}$.

From a domain-specific consideration, S_1 is plausible although it may have perplexing consequences (for instance, if there is a rule assigning a budget to the Brazilian capital that includes expenses for relocating and maintaining the offices of the Federal Administration). System S_2 would not properly imply that:

3'. Rio de Janeiro is the capital city of the Brazilian Federation.

But promulgating a norm specifying a city other than Rio de Janeiro as the capital city of Brazil would again lead to inconsistency.

Finally, system S_3 would leave the capital city of Brazil undefined, which could create uncertainty in the application of other rules employing that concept.

A similar problem of indeterminacy would appear when a rule entailed from a new and hierarchical superior rule is promulgated.

Example 1.3. Suppose that a normative system contains the following rule:

6. All industries are free economic activities except for the public services listed below: (...)

Suppose that the aviation industry is not listed in rule (6), implying that aviation is a free economic activity, and suppose also that there is a federal statute (the Aviation Code) stating the following:

7. Aviation companies must be controlled by national investors.

Now consider that a constitutional rule is enacted imposing the following:

8. There ought to be no discrimination between the national and foreign capital of companies dedicated to any free economic activity.

Considering that control by national investors counts as "discrimination" between foreign and national investors, rule (8) conflicts with rules (6) and (7), although originally the last two rules seemed to have no relevant connection to each other. The inconsistency is solved if either of these last two rules is derogated. The first option is to delete constitutive rule (6), which classifies the aviation industry as a free economic activity. The second option is to delete rule (7), thereby weakly permitting, that is not prohibiting, the control of aviation companies by foreign investors.

Hence, the interaction between constitutive and regulative rules, the problem of implicit derogation and the derogation of entailed rules all open up different possibilities for identifying the normative system resulting from normative revisions. Logical analysis of normative change should be faithful to such an indeterminacy, making the different possibilities for the resulting normative system transparent. Legal interpretation and argumentation may provide further constraints in order to select which, among all the possible candidates, would be the preferred outcome of a derogation, which may be domain-specific, or may have its rationality represented in formal models of normative change.

1.2 Normative Change and Legal Interpretation

Legal reasoning can be conceptually structured as three main tasks, as suggested by Wroblewski [1985; 1992]:

(i) **validity:** identifying the valid legal rules that are generally applicable to the subject-matter;

(ii) **interpretation:** determining the content of the rules identified as valid;

(iii) **application:** instantiating the content of the valid rules applied to concrete or hypothetical cases (this last task includes identifying the relevant facts of the case, identifying how they qualify according to the applicable rules, and determining the legal consequences based on those rules).

At first glance, normative change should only be concerned with questions of validity, since the dynamics of promulgation and derogation determines the timeframe for the applicability of rules in normative systems. However, the three problems highlighted above show an intrinsic connection between normative change and legal interpretation, given that one of the main triggers of normative dynamics is the need to handle inconsistencies between the *content* of different rules in the normative system.

The problem of *network effects* is connected to determining the content of regulative rules with conceptual definitions. The *undecidability* problem is also about choosing between rules with conflicting content. The *indeterminacy* problem of implicit derogation concerns a conflict between the content of the promulgated rule and the content entailed by the normative system.

Given that the core task of legal interpretation is to determine the content of legal rules, it is necessary to first identify inconsistencies between rules, and therefore to check whether an implicit derogation has undermined the validity of a rule. Hence, questions of validity and interpretation are not serial but circular. The object of interpretation is the content of valid rules, but interpretation is also necessary to the inquiry about validity. The same applies to interpretation and application. Since the conditions for applying the rule may not be isomorphic to the factors or circumstances of the case at hand [Peczenik, 1989, p. 77 ff.], the rule must be adapted to become "operational". Further qualifications to the facts must be introduced via definitions that match the factual properties of the case with the concepts employed in the rule in order to make them isomorphic [Aarnio, 1977]. Hence, although it is the content of the rule that is subsequently instantiated, that instantiation induces modifications to the content of the rule to be applied [Rotolo, 2001, p. 36 ff.].

Hence, interpretation is pervasive in legal reasoning, performing an important role from identifying the authoritative sources to determining the legal effects on a concrete or hypothetical case.

Broadly understood, legal interpretation encompasses both *linguistic* and *constructive* interpretation. Linguistic interpretation consists in identifying the semantic/pragmatic content that is conveyed by an authoritative legal text.[5] In turn, constructive interpretation, or "legal construction" [Solum, 2010], consists in determining the legal effect of that linguistic content, which means constructing the content of an "operational rule".

Some conceive of linguistic interpretation as an inquiry into the linguistic facts of a language community [Barak, 2005; Solum, 2010; Marmor, 2005], while others include an evaluative component in every linguistic inquiry [Fuller, 1958; Dworkin, 1986], and therefore consider the whole process of interpretation as constructing rules in the light of the purpose of legal practice. But even those who question the distinction accept that there would be a pre-interpretive stage where some preliminary meaning ascription takes place.

The linguistic interpretation or pre-interpretive stage may provide unsatisfactory solutions for a particular case. The linguistic meaning of the rule may not indicate a normative solution to a particular constellation of relevant facts [Alchourrón and Bulygin, 1971], leaving a so-called "gap" in the normative system that must be fulfilled. The linguistic inquiry may also provide conflicting commands deriving from the same rule or from different rules, in which case the contradiction must be corrected. It may provide an array of alternative meanings (ambiguity), from which only one must be chosen, or may provide an imprecise meaning (vagueness), demanding fur-

---

[5]Legal theorists disagree about what is the object of legal interpretation. While some contend that the object of interpretation is to formulate norms from authoritative sources [Raz, 2009], others, like Dworkin [1986] would also include the whole argumentative social practice of law [Dickson, 2016].

ther definitions to determine whether the case at hand fits the conditions for applying the rule. Finally, the rule's command as determined by the linguistic inquiry may violate the rule's underlying justification (the values promoted by the rule), which may necessitate the introduction of exceptions or the specification of new conditions for applying the rule so that its content aligns with its purpose.

These further processes of

- filling gaps by adding new content,

- eliminating ambiguities by choosing between different content,

- eliminating vagueness by adding definitions to make the rule precise,

- resolving inconsistencies between rules by excluding content, and

- resolving deviances to the rule's command with respect to its underlying justification by modifying its conditions of application,

all clearly involve changes not only to the rule to be applied but also to the very normative system. The process of constructing an operational rule to be applied presupposes that the interpreted rule coheres with the normative system, and therefore that what is instantiated is actually a reconstructed fragment of a normative order containing a set of rules that are relevant to defining the deontic status (obligatory, forbidden, permitted) of the action at stake [Alchourrón and Bulygin, 1971]. This reconstruction may be performed by a judge to solve a concrete case (judicial interpretation), or in legal doctrine when indicating solutions to hypothetical legal cases (doctrinal interpretation).

Note that in practice it is difficult to discriminate between these two different dimensions of legal interpretation—linguistic and constructive—considering that the very ascription of meaning to legal texts is constrained by a presumption of the lawgiver's rationality or "unity of will" [Bobbio, 1971], which requires that a text must be given a meaning that avoids inconsistencies or misalignments with the rule's purpose, and preferably avoids gaps and imprecision. Hence, construction may take place even when the identification of the meaning of a rule is uncontroversial.

For instance, consider the regulation on abortion in the Brazilian Criminal Code.

9. Causing an abortion; Punishment: imprisonment from 1 to 3 years.

10. Abortion performed by a physician is not punishable: (i) if there is no other way to save the pregnant woman's life; (ii) the pregnant woman

has consented to the abortion and the pregnancy is the result of sexual abuse.

A criminal lawyer would say that it is settled from the text above that it is forbidden to abort if the pregnant woman's life is not endangered and no sexual abuse took place. Some would even say that this conclusion is immediate and does not require interpretation. However, first of all, the interpretation of clauses (i) and (ii) as disjunctive and not conjunctive involves some evaluative considerations favouring women's freedom. Secondly, the plain language meaning actually reveals inconsistency between rules (9) and (10). Rule (10) is read as an exception, but this means that some interpretation cannons operate in order to first assume that inconsistent rules should be applicable to different hypothetical conditions, then to derogate (9) by specificity, and finally to reintroduce the prohibition of causing an abortion in scenarios that have not been exempted (*exceptio firmat regulam in casibus non exceptis*). The "operational rules" reconstructed from the original linguistic meaning are thus:

9*. Abortion is forbidden if not performed by a physician or if there are other ways to save the pregnant woman's life and the pregnancy is the result of sexual abuse or the pregnant woman has not consented to the abortion.

10*. Abortion is permitted if performed by a physician and there is no other way to save the pregnant woman's life or if the pregnancy is the result of sexual abuse and the pregnant woman has consented to the abortion.

The fact that what is assumed to be the "plain language meaning" of a norm already involves its construction leads some to consider the object of legal interpretation to be the legal community's set of settled instantiations of the valid rules [Marmor, 2005] rather than the ordinary meaning of legal texts. In this conception, legal interpretation would then be the process of construction from that restricted basis of settled law, in order to develop solutions for unclear cases with gaps, imprecision and/or conflicts, etc.

Legal construction allows flexibility in the law so that it can adapt to new circumstances and social demands while reinforcing the authority of the normative order. It can achieve this by keeping track of the original rules (taking as a starting point the legal text, the clear and settled instantiations, or the legal history) and making them align with community values. Assessment of this interpretative practice from the perspective of normative change reveals different strategies used in legal doctrine, or by the courts, to manipulate the legal material in the sources in order to justify choosing a particular legal solution. Particularly interesting is their stipulation of definitions affecting relevant concepts of the rule.

Consider, for instance, the controversy in many jurisdictions concerning police access to the content of mobile phones in search & seizure orders.

In 2014, a decision by the Brazilian Superior Court of Justice (STJ: HC 51.531-RO) held that a WhatsApp conversation on a mobile phone collected in a search procedure is analogous to ongoing correspondence and should count as "written communication". Therefore, an *order to intercept* was mandatory to access its content, otherwise the access would have violated freedom of communication. However, in a decision reached in 2016 (STJ: HC 75.800-PR), the same court affirmed that a message exchange on a mobile phone is just stored data and therefore a property item which, according to the statutes, may be accessed in a search & seizure procedure.

The German Constitutional Court (BVerfGE, 115,166, *Kommunikationsver-*

bindungsdaten) also concluded that access to data stored on a mobile phone collected during an investigation does not violate rules regarding search & seizure. Such data would be analogous to information in a physical document since both involve possession and the data or information could have been destroyed by the searched individual. Therefore, accessing the history of calls does not affect freedom of communication, and does not have a greater impact on informational autonomy or property rights deserving special protection.

Example 1.4. Consider a normative system with the following regulative rules:

11. Police officers have the power to access any property item if and only if authorised by a judicial search & seizure order.

12. Police officers have the power to intercept written or oral communication if and only if authorised by a judicial interception order.

The following conceptual rules are key to determining whether stored text messages may be accessed in a search & seizure order:

13. A message exchange stored on a mobile phone counts as ongoing communication;

14. A message exchange stored on a mobile phone counts as stored data;

15. Stored data counts as a property item.

Suppose that officers only hold a search & seizure order. Then there is an inconsistency between conceptual rule (13), on the one hand, and conceptual rules (14) and (15) on the other. The difficulty lies in the fact that the linguistic meaning of a message exchange supports its qualification as both communication and stored data. The link between stored data and property pertains to the legal language and derives from valid legal rules. The German court has just excluded rule (13), thus avoiding that the search procedure should become unconstitutional by affecting freedom of communication. One of the Brazilian courts chose to delete rule (14).

But those qualifications (data as property, stored messages as data, message exchanges as communication) are also relevant to the application of other rules. Another solution to keep rule (11) compatible with the constitutional value of freedom of communication, and with a lower impact on the network of conceptual and regulative rules, would be to refine rule (11) as follows:

11*. Police officers have the power to access any property item, except for the digital content of mobile phones, if and only if authorised by a judicial search & seizure order.

Indeed, this was the solution adopted by the U.S. Supreme Court in a similar case involving search powers in an arrest (*Riley v. California*, 2014).

Hence, legal construction involves manipulating conceptual definitions not only by legal doctrine, but also regulative rules. This possibility does not offend the authority of the rules provided that, first, conceptual definitions may also be stipulated by valid legal rules, and secondly, that valid regulative rules may be derogated or refined by introducing exceptions, in the name of consistency with constitutional values, as explicit and higher order rules [Alexy, 2000].

But it is clear that legal construction and legal interpretation in general have both a conservative and a creative component [Dickson, 2016]. On the one hand, construction must be faithful to the settled normative order. On the other hand, it must enhance new solutions by clarifying the content of that order. In other words, choices and changes to the content of the legal order are going to take place, but only to the extent that is minimal and necessary to clarify its content.

It is also characteristic of such constructions that their conclusion is presented as entailing a coherent interpretation of the normative system. Opposing conclusions in apparently similar cases are shown to align with the balance of the relevant values pursued by the normative system. Alignment is attained by using an array of different techniques in constructive interpretation: discarding possible conceptual qualifications e.g. excluding the rule that stored messages count as communication, introducing exceptions to rules e.g. excluding mobile phones from the general search powers of officials, and introducing or excluding values from consideration.

It is clear from this discussion and examples that legal construction as a fundamental dimension of legal interpretation consists in making changes to the content of the normative system, and that these changes are driven by both a demand for coherence and by a demand for conservatism or "minimal change" to the legal order. These drivers show how logics of theory change are suitable for modelling legal construction.

To conclude this practical perspective, we observe that the relationship between interpretation and normative change is twofold. On the one hand, legal interpretation is a precondition to the dynamics of normative systems, as the identification of inconsistencies between the content of rules depends on it. On the other hand, the very activity of legal interpretation may be seen as dynamics of change affecting constitutive and regulatory rules.

1.3 Normative Change and Implied Rules

From a theoretical perspective, normative change is an important factor in understanding the status of implied (derived) rules in a normative system and its relation to explicitly promulgated rules. The debate about the status of entailed rules is connected to a central problem in the conception of modern law concerning the role of reason *versus* the role of authority in identifying the law. The question is whether the ground for identifying the legal status of an action consists in reasoning about its correction or goodness or whether this status is determined by the will of an authority with respect to individual or collective behaviour or its outcome.

If one conceives that the binding force of the content of explicit rules is the outcome of the authority's will manifested in the norm-giving act, the question arises whether or to what extent obligations, prohibitions or permissions deductively derived from those original rules, albeit not explicitly endorsed by the authority, are also binding or should also be considered to be part of the normative system.

This problem may be explored from the perspective of normative dynamics. Instead of a synchronic epistemology considering the identification of a rule as a matter of examining the foundational or coherentist connection of its content to the content of the other rules of the system [Amaya, 2015], one may adopt a diachronic perspective of examining the vulnerability of the rule's content to changes in the normative system. If derived rules have the same "ontological status" as explicit rules, then, on the one hand, the promulgation (addition) of derived rules would be redundant and, on the other hand, their derogation would immediately mean a change in the normative system.

For instance, the Brazilian Criminal Code forbade sexual abuse with the following set of explicit rules:

16. It is forbidden to practice sexual intercourse without consent.

17. Sexual intercourse with a person under 14 years old shall be considered to be without consent.

Should we consider the derived rule (18) below a valid legal rule of the Brazilian criminal law system?

18. It is forbidden to practice sexual intercourse with a person under 14 years old.

A decade ago, a controversial decision by the Brazilian Supreme Court ruled that habeas corpus applied to an offender who maintained a sexual relationship with a 12 year old girl. The legal community has interpreted that ruling as *contra legem*, since it was widely assumed that the act violated the criminal code. It seems plain enough that although rule (18) was not explicitly promulgated, compliance with its content should be obligatory and any disregard would be a violation. And this follows from the fact that the content of (18) is deductively derived from rules (16) and (17).

Given that there is such a derived obligation, some would argue that rule (18) is also part of the normative system [Alchourrón and Bulygin, 1971; Navarro and Rodriguez, 2014]. Here, the binding force of the obligation is an outcome of reasoning (deduction), and if law is the system of binding rules, it should be part of the normative system as well.

Some, however, would accept the binding force of such derived rules, but would not acknowledge them as part of the normative system if their content is not explicitly willed [Marmor, 2005]. Accepting them as part of the normative system, Marmor argues, would imply a (most probably) false assumption that the set of legal rules is coherent. Others, like Joseph Raz [1985], would only accept them if such derivations were endorsed by the relevant authority (even though it is not quite clear what such endorsement means) as something distinct from explicitly willing its content but inferring such content from the explicit rules.

Curiously enough, that controversial decision by the Brazilian Supreme Court led to a legislative act (Law 12.015/2009) introducing rule (18) as an explicit rule of the Code. Did that law effectively change the Brazilian criminal law system? One could say that these are two different formulations of the Code representing the same criminal law system, provided that they contain the same set of derived obligations. If this is true, what led to the promulgation of the new legislative act?

One could say that it was fundamentally a political gesture with redundant or irrelevant legal consequences. Or one could say that the Supreme Court had actually changed the law, which was later modified by legislation again. But the interesting question is: if two different normative systems have identical normative consequences, is it the case that identical promulgations or derogations in each of these systems would lead to the same resulting normative system?

Example 1.5. Consider normative system $S1$ with the following formulations:

16. It is forbidden to practice sexual intercourse without consent.

19. Sexual intercourse with a legally incompetent person shall be considered to be without consent.

20. A person becomes legally competent by reaching 14 years of age.

Now consider normative system $S2$ containing rules (16), (19), (20) and, in addition, (18) as an explicit rule.

18. It is forbidden to practice sexual intercourse with a person under 14 years old.

Suppose now that the following rule is promulgated:

21. A person becomes legally competent by reaching 16 years of age.

Clearly, rule (18) is derived from $S1$. Hence, from the synchronic perspective, it is clear that $S1 = S2$, since the set of derived obligations is the same. But the effect of promulgating rule (21) in $S1$ is different from its promulgation in $S2$. In $S1$, promulgated rule (21) substitutes rule (20), and therefore the revised system ($S1*$) derives the following:

(18*) It is forbidden to practice sexual intercourse with a person under 16 years old.

However, in system $S2$, rule (18) would still be derived. And while rules (20) and (21) conflict, this is not necessarily a conflict between explicit rule (18) and derived rule (18*). Therefore rule (18) could still be derivable. It would be a matter of legal interpretation to determine whether the new definition of legal competence would be applicable only to civil law, that is, the ability to perform valid civil and contractual acts, or whether it would also be applicable to criminal law, specifically, the ability to consent to sexual intercourse or to be liable to criminal responsibility.

Hence, from a synchronic perspective, i.e. considering the normative system at a particular moment in time, one may assume that two normative systems are the same if they derive the same set of obligations/permissions, even if they have different formulations. That is, from that perspective, the formulation of the base of explicit rules is irrelevant. However, from a diachronic perspective, that is, considering the normative system's change from one moment to a second moment where a new rule is promulgated or derogated, the formulation of the base of explicit rules becomes relevant, given that the revision of different sets of explicit rules with the same derived obligations/permissions may lead to different outcomes. Therefore, changes in the base of explicit rules may not result in changes in the set of obligations/permissions, but every change in the set of obligations/permissions means a change in the base.

This observation makes it clear that even if one assumes that the content of derived rules is as equally binding as the content of explicit rules, which would make these rules share the same "normative status", it is not the case that they should share the same "pertinence status". That is, the fact that a derived obligation is binding does not imply that it is a rule pertaining to the normative system.

1.4   Modelling Normative Change

The distinction between the dimension of the validity of a rule (the time span of the pertinence of a rule to the normative system) and the binding force or efficacy of derived obligations or permissions (the time span where obligations and permissions are applicable) is also relevant for defining an appropriate methodology for the study of normative change. The different methods may focus on one or another aspect of normative change, namely, changes to the content of norms that are part of the normative order, or changes with respect to the effectiveness of obligations over time.

Suppose that there is a normative system $S3$ with the rule:

22. Abortion is forbidden.

Since this is an absolute prohibition, it applies to every possible circumstance. Therefore, the following prohibition is derived:

23. Abortion is forbidden if the pregnancy is the result of sexual abuse.

Suppose that a legislative or judicial authority wants to change rule (23) by permitting abortion in the case of sexual abuse (or a legal scholar argues that there is an "implicit exception" to the prohibition of abortion based on the constitutional value of a woman's dignity). This normative change may be described in at least three different ways corresponding to three different methods proposed in the literature on artificial intelligence & law for modelling normative change.

The first methodology, devised by Governatori and Rotolo [2010], may be called the *syntactic approach.* According to this approach, norm change is an operation performed on the rules contained in the code for determining whether a default rule is applicable or ceases to be applicable in defeasible deontic logic. So, the focus of the approach is not really the dimension of validity (the pertinence of the rule to the normative system) but the dimension of the efficacy (applicability) of derived obligations and permissions. They call "annulment" the operation where all the past and future effects of the rule are cancelled and "abrogation" the operation where only the effects to the future are cancelled while past effects still hold. They use a temporal extension of defeasible logic to keep track of changes in the normative system and to deal with retroactivity (the possibility of changing the applicability of obligations and permissions in the past). As we have seen, there are two temporal dimensions to be tackled: the time a norm is valid (when the norm enters the normative system) and the time it is effective (when the norm can produce legal effects). As a consequence, multiple versions of the normative system are needed [Governatori and Rotolo, 2010].

The logical machinery used to represent normative change in this approach is complex given that the default logic has to gather very different sorts of default rules providing information on: the content of rules, meta-rules regarding the applicability of other rules, preference between rules, and the timeframe of applicability. For instance, an "abrogation" of a default rule is represented by the addition of a defeater, which is a default rule of a higher order with void content, that is, from which no obligation or permission is derived.

For the example on the regulation of abortion above, the syntactic approach could be roughly illustrated by indicating that in the case of sexual abuse, rule (22) is *not applicable*, and therefore rule (23) is not derived. This could be achieved by introducing a sort of meta-rule to the normative set stating:

24. In the case of sexual abuse, rule (22) is not applicable.

Such a rule would be a *defeater* because it would block the derivation of consequences from rule (22) without excluding it from the normative system.

Notice that it adds no normative content by itself.

It is also possible to strengthen the contention that abortion is permitted in the case of sexual abuse by adding another rule to the normative system stating:

25. Abortion is permitted if the pregnancy is the result of sexual abuse.

In Governatori and Rotolo's approach, this addition is obtained by turning a defeater into a default rule that blocks the application of the original prohibition, but also derives the content of a permission in the case of sexual abuse.

This representation, however, does not capture the basic intuition that derogation is a sort of exclusion where the rule ceases to be a part of the normative system. Instead, since the model concerns the dimension of the efficacy of obligations, a derogation is captured only by blocking the effects of a default rule. Besides, what can be derived depends on which rules are valid at the time when we do the derivation. Thus, in order to keep track of norm changes, Governatori and Rotolo represent different versions of a legal system.

In order to reduce such complexity, Governatori *et al.* [2013] explored three AGM-like [Alchourrón and Makinson, 1981; Alchourrón and Makinson, 1982] contraction operators to remove rules, add exceptions and revise rule priorities. Governatori *et al.* [2019] also explored a model where, on particular occasions, normative change is reduced to a change of preference relations between default rules.

To illustrate this second method, which may be called the *preferential approach*, consider that from a moral order or a set of constitutional values one may derive inconsistent standards regarding abortion. One may derive permission of abortion from moral considerations, or from arguments about constitutional values, regarding the axiological contention that "women are free to dispose of their own bodies". But one may also derive prohibition of abortion (rule 22) from a moral contention, or from a constitutional value, stating that "all human beings are the subject of moral worth" and the determination that a "foetus is a human being".

Hence, this normative system would include rule (22) as well as the following rule:

26. Abortion is permitted.

The presence of rules (22) and (26) makes the normative system inconsistent, and thus the determination of the consequences of these conflicting rules for each relevant circumstance would depend on the addition and change of preference rules such as:

27. In the case of sexual abuse, rule (26) is preferred over rule (22).

In these two alternatives for representing change (syntactic and preferential), the corresponding logic cannot be classical (in particular, it cannot be monotonic). Otherwise rule (22) would conflict with rule (25) and rule (26), thereby making the normative system trivial. In these descriptions, rules (22), (25) and (26) are part of the normative system as "defaults", and there may be circumstances where each of these becomes inapplicable, or where one of them prevails over another. With the syntactic approach, normative change is a matter of adding new defaults or defeaters to block or enable the normative effects of the defaults over time and according to relevant factors or circumstances. With the preferential approach, normative change is reduced to changing the preference relations between default rules on particular occasions.

In both the syntactic and preferential approaches, a change in the normative system should include not only information about the content of the rules that are subject to change but also information about the applicability of these rules. It is this information about applicability and preference that determines the set of obligations and permissions derivable from the normative system. Actually, in both these approaches, the set of obligations and permissions may change without any modification to the content of the rules belonging to the normative system. It may be the result of modification to the time span of the applicability of the rules in that set, or the result of a change in the preference relations between defaults.

A third approach, which may be called the *AGM approach*, represents derogation and enactment, respectively, as effective exclusions and additions of content to the normative system. Historically, this was the first approach to modelling normative change, and was originally proposed by Alchourrón and Makinson [1981; 1982]. When Gärdenfors joined (at that time he was mainly working on counterfactuals), the trio became the founders of the well-known AGM theory, and started the fruitful research area of belief revision [Alchourrón *et al.*, 1985], which has found many applications in computer science and epistemology. Belief revision is the formal study of how a theory (a deductively closed set of propositional formulas) may change in view of new information that may cause inconsistency with existing beliefs. The basic operations of belief change are expansion (which corresponds to the promulgation of a rule to a code), revision (which corresponds to amendment of the code) and contraction (which corresponds to derogation of its normative application).

One of the first attempts to specify the AGM framework to tackling normative change was put forward by Maranhão [2001a; 2001b]. Maranhão introduced a *refinement* operator, which restricts the acceptance of new input to certain conditions in a revision, or keeps a more refined (weaker) version of a rule to be excluded in a contraction. Refinement thus represents the introduction of exceptions to rules in order to avoid conflicts in normative systems (see section 3.6).

More recently, Boella *et al.* [2016] also reconsidered the original inspiration for the AGM theory of belief revision as a framework for evaluating the dynamics of rule-based systems. They observed that if we wish to weaken a rule-based system from which we derive too much, we can use the theory of belief base dynamics [Hansson, 1993] to select a subset of the rules as a contraction of the rule-based system. Base contraction seems to be the most straightforward and safe way to perform a contraction; it always results in a subset of the original base. But it sometimes means removing too much. In turn, AGM theory contraction may retain some implications of the rule to be deleted. This was one of the motivations for the present contribution. Another advancement is to represent normative change in a formal framework that clearly distinguishes between the concepts of the pertinence of a rule in a normative system and the effectiveness of an obligation in a given context using the input/output logic framework developed by Makinson and van der Torre [2000]. A similar approach was proposed by Stolpe [2010]. In that work, AGM contractions and revision are used to define derogation and amendment of norms. In particular, the derogation operation is an AGM partial meet contraction obtained by defining a selection function for a set of norms in input/output logic. Norm revision defined via the Levi Identity characterises the amendment of norms. Stolpe can thus show that derogation and amendment operators are in one-to-one correspondence with the Harper and Levi Identities as inverse bijective maps (cf. section 2.1). Also, Tamargo *et al.* [2017; 2021] recently studied AGM-like revision operators that consider rules indexed by time intervals.

In the AGM approach, the operation of normative change is performed on the normative system (the set of rules that may be closed under logical consequence). The rules in the original system or in the system resulting from change does not carry meta-information about their applicability, time span or hierarchy (although these features may be added). Therefore, the set of applicable obligations or permissions at a given moment in time is the set of all logical consequences of the normative system valid at that specific time. Hence, information about hierarchy and the time span of validity and applicability is not part of the representation of its rules and does not interfere with the derivation rules of the underlying logic (although such information might be relevant to the revision functions).

To illustrate the AGM approach to the example of abortion discussed above, the normative change would consist in refining rule (22) with respect to the defeating factor "pregnancy resulting from sexual abuse", resulting in a normative system where rules (23) and consequently (22) are deleted and containing the following rules:

25. Abortion is permitted if the pregnancy is the result of sexual abuse.

28. Abortion is forbidden if it is not the case that the pregnancy is the result of sexual abuse.

With this last approach, every normative change, that is, every change in the set of obligations and permissions derived from the normative system, amounts to a change to the content of the rules that belong to the set of norms. This aspect makes the set of obligations and conditions for their application closer to the content of the revised normative system.

Research on formal models of normative change has also been concerned with representing legal interpretation.

In the field of artificial intelligence & law, legal interpretation has been mainly explored with models of case-based reasoning, where teleological reasoning is represented to derive solutions to new cases based on precedents. Following Berman and Hafner [1993], AI & Law research on teleological reasoning has provided multiple models of the relationship between cases, the factors that such cases include or express, and the values at stake. Bench-Capon and Sartor [2003] assign values to factors, and consequently to rules embedding such factors, to explain precedents according to the applicable rules and the importance of the values promoted by such rules. Prakken *et al.* [2015] formalise teleological reasoning using logics for defeasible argumentation, extended to allow the possibility of expressing arguments about values, supported by cases. Sartor [2013] explores the proportional balance of constitutional rights, where a legal outcome is compared to alternative outcomes based on their impact on the promotion and demotion of values. He examines the level of consistency between value-based decisions of cases given the factors present in those cases [Sartor, 2018].

In turn, AI & Law research on statutory interpretation has focused on the dynamic ascription of meanings to rules. These contributions are based on the distinction between *"constitutive"* (or *"conceptual"*) rules ascribing meanings to facts or objects and *"regulative"* rules demanding, prohibiting or permitting actions or states [Grossi *et al.*, 2008]. Interpretation is then modelled as introducing or changing conceptual rules. Governatori and Rotolo [2010] represent such changes, within the syntactic approach, as the introduction of exceptions, by blocking the application of default rules to a given condition or constellation of factors. Boella *et al.* [2010] developed that model by introducing values as coherence parameters guiding the change of conceptual rules, parameters whose meanings may be extended (weakening the antecedent of a conditional rule) or restricted (strengthening the antecedent of a conditional rule).

The incorporation of the AGM approach into input/output logics [Boella *et al.*, 2016] and, later, the representation of normative systems in an architecture of input/output logics combining constitutive and regulative rules, brought a new perspective to representing legal interpretation [Boella and van der Torre, 2006b]. Maranhão and de Souza [2018] introduced a contraction function for such combined normative sets in order to represent choices in legal doctrine between changing the definitions (or meaning ascriptions) of legal terms and changing the content of legal regulative rules, taking into consideration the network effects of those changes.

Maranhão [2017a] proposed an architecture of input/output logics for modelling doctrinal interpretation where values are represented as rules, and constitutive and regulative rules are the object of different contraction, revision and refinement functions. Differently from the work of Boella *et al.* [2010], where legal interpretation is conceived as a dynamic of syntactic modifications to constitutive rules (within the syntactic approach), in Maranhão's model it is not only constitutive rules, but also values and regulative rules, that are subject to change (with the AGM approach) in order to reach a coherent and stable description of the normative system. More recently, Maranhão and Sartor's [2019] research on statutory interpretation built on the case-based tradition of teleological reasoning and balancing with their representation of legal construction—where a model of balancing values is incorporated into an architecture of input/output logics—serving as a reference to the revision of constitutive (meaning ascriptions) and regulative rules.

Which is the best approach to representing normative change—syntactic, preferential or AGM?

This question was controversial in the 1990s in the context of Alchourrón's [1996] criticism that defeasible logics are philosophically inadequate. According to Alchourrón, defeasible logic unnecessarily weakens the inferential power of the underlying logic. It obscures the fact that the defeat of a conclusion is actually the result of the dynamic of revising the premises in a derivation, or the fact that the defeat of a consequence results from revising the antecedent of a conditional. According to Alchourrón, in an adequate account of the epistemology of law or of any domain, the revision processes of the premises of an argument or the antecedent of a conditional should be transparent [Maranhão, 2006].

Actually the reply to this question depends on what aspect of legal reasoning one would like to capture with the model of representation (without considering the technical issue of computational complexity).

As we have seen, there is a fundamental difference between the pertinence of a rule to a normative system and its effects in terms of the derivability of the corresponding obligations/permissions in the presence of given circumstances. There is the time span for when a rule pertains to the normative system, that is, the time the rule exists in the normative system. But, although pertinent to a system, a rule may still not produce its effects, for example because its conditions of application are dependent on an event or regulated by another rule, so there is another time span for when the norm is applicable. Furthermore, as mentioned above, there is the time span for when the conclusions of an instantiated rule apply to a particular individual, considering that the instantiated rule may be derogated or annulled (i.e. declared invalid) for that particular individual by a judicial authority.

The distinction between the validity and efficacy of a rule may be captured by all approaches. But the syntactic approach seems to be more congenial to the dimension of efficacy, that is, the applicability of rules, considering that the revision operations are represented as syntactical changes to the rules that affect their applicability. A contraction operator does not properly exclude a rule but interferes with the derivability of its consequence.

In turn, the AGM approach seems to be more congenial to modelling the dynamics of the pertinence of a rule in a normative system, since the suppression or addition of obligations of permissions, and obligations derived from the basic set of rules, are reflected in proper exclusion or expansion to the rules of the normative system.

In the end, the description of the obligations and permissions derived from the normative system may coincide in both approaches, the difference lying in the set of basic rules.

Lastly, the preferential approach seems to be more congenial to the dynamic of legal principles and values related to positively enacted rules. Such principles and values, both considered as external to the normative system or enshrined in the constitution, potentially conflict but coexist in the normative order or political morality underlying such an order of legal rules. Depending on the context, they are balanced in order to derive a solution. The preferential approach reflects the fact that the derivation of a normative solution from principles or values results from resolving potential conflicts by giving more weight to a preferred principle than another principle in a given context.

It seems that a closer correspondence between the content of the rules and the applicable obligations/permissions is also of interest for the representation of legal construction where a particular reconstruction of a fragment of

Juliano Maranhão   Giovanni Casini,   Gabriella Pigozzi   Leendert van der Torre

the normative system takes place before the instantiation of an operational rule.

Recent research on models of legal interpretation has shown that the three approaches must be combined since, as we have seen, the interpretive activity, particularly legal construction, involves all of the following three dimensions:

- manipulation and refinement of constitutive and regulative rules in a normative system (*validity*);

- consideration and weighing of underlying values (*balancing*);

- adaptation of definitions of legal terms to make the rules isomorphic and applicable to the facts of a particular case (*applicability*).

The first two approaches listed in this section are presented in the work of Tamargo *et al.* [2021]. This chapter focuses on the AGM option, presenting its reformulation for input/output logics—a family of logics dedicated to the analysis of normative reasoning in particular as well as rule-based reasoning in general. We consider the combination of these two formal approaches, AGM belief change and input/output logics, to be a promising framework for analysing normative change. On the one hand, the kind of analysis of information change that AGM-like approaches pursue is insightful and very clear at the same time, and often can be reformulated into specific solutions for other formal frameworks. On the other hand, input/output logics offer an analysis of rule-based reasoning that is along the same lines, since it combines the immediate clarity of characterising distinct rule-based systems via the structural properties they satisfy with an in-depth analysis of the different kinds of rule-based reasoning that can be modelled. In our view, applying an AGM-like approach on top of input/output systems allows an essential characterisation of change to be developed that focuses here on normative reasoning, but can actually be extended to other forms of rule-based reasoning.

2   Formal Framework

In this section, we briefly introduce the formal framework we will adopt in our analysis of normative change. In the last few decades, the area of knowledge representation and reasoning has proposed various formal approaches to modelling the dynamics of knowledge, and to modelling normative change in particular. As a result, one methodological issue that we need to address is what kind of analysis do we want to develop for normative change.

2.1 The AGM Approach

We will rely on the methodology of the *AGM approach* to belief change that we introduced in section 1.4. In the last 30 years, AGM has been the most popular formal approach to analysing the dynamics of beliefs, but it has been debated whether it is the best approach to analysing belief change in general, and normative change in particular. In this section, we briefly outline the main characteristics of this approach for the unfamiliar reader, and discuss why we still consider it to be a viable option for analysing normative change.

Let's start with a well-known example. Our knowledge base contains the following information:

a. Sweden is an European country.

b. All European swans are white.

c. The bird I just caught in the trap is a swan.

d. The bird I just caught in the trap is from Sweden.

e. No bird can be black and white at the same time.

This information entails that the bird I just caught in a trap is white. But then I look at it and I see that it is undoubtedly black. I add to my knowledge base the following proposition:

f. The bird I just caught in the trap is black.

From my knowledge base, I must conclude that the bird I just caught in the trap is both white and black. My knowledge base contains conflicting information, it is inconsistent. How should the situation be fixed? What constraints should we follow in changing our beliefs? And how should we give a formal characterisation to such constraints?

It is generally assumed that the constraints that a *rational* form of belief change should respect are based on considerations of two kinds:

1. *Logic.* Here the focus is on *consistency preservation*: the content of our knowledge base should always be devoid of contradictions.

   Looking at our example, we cannot accept that we can believe that a bird is black and that the bird is white at the same time. Once we rely on piece of information *f*, we need to change the content of our knowledge base, since propositions *a-f* together necessarily imply a contradiction.

2. *Pragmatic.* This point and Point 1 above are intertwined. If we are forced to modify the content of our knowledge base in order to satisfy logical constraints, e.g. in order to preserve consistency, we should do so taking into consideration also pragmatic issues, based on, for example, *economy of information.* According to that principle, information is valuable, some pieces of information are more relevant and reliable than others, and if we are forced to drop some pieces of information, we should "minimise the damage" by eliminating only the minimal amount of information that is necessary to preserve logical consistency.

What should we do in our example once we learn proposition f and we spot the conflict? We could simply erase the entire knowledge base, just eliminate all the propositions (a)-(e). But why should we do this given that, for example, it is sufficient to drop only one proposition among (a), (b), (c), (d), and (e)?

In order to describe belief change, the AGM approach gives a formal definition to the knowledge representation desiderata by defining formal constraints based on logical or pragmatic considerations.

To formally introduce the AGM approach, we need some formal preliminaries. We use a classical propositional language $\mathcal{L}$, built from atomic propositional letters and using the propositional connectives $\neg, \wedge, \vee, \rightarrow, \equiv, \perp$. Lower-case letters $a, b, c, \ldots, x, y, z$ will be used to represent propositions. A *knowledge base* is a set of propositional formulas, that will be indicated by capital letters as $\mathcal{K}$. In addition, $\vDash$ and Cn will represent the classical propositional entailment relation and entailment operator respectively.

The epistemic status of an agent is characterised by a knowledge base $\mathcal{K}$. Actually, the classical AGM approach embraces a perspective that has been dominant in epistemic logics: the epistemic status of the agent is characterised using a *belief set*, a logical theory closed under Cn. That is, the epistemic status of an agent is characterised by a knowledge base $\mathcal{K}$ such that $\mathcal{K} = Cn(\mathcal{K})$. Let $\mathcal{T}$ be the set of the belief sets (i.e. the closed theories) of language $\mathcal{L}$, that is, $\mathcal{T} := \{\mathcal{K} \subseteq 2^{\mathcal{L}} \mid \mathcal{K} = Cn(\mathcal{K})\}$.

The first question we need to address is what kind of changes we should consider. The AGM approach recognises three operations as the basic ones: *expansion, contraction,* and *revision.* Assume our agent A has a knowledge base $\mathcal{K}$:

- *Expansion* $+$: A is informed that proposition p holds, and simply adds it to $\mathcal{K}$ without caring whether this could generate some contradiction. The resulting knowledge base is indicated as $\mathcal{K} + p$.

- *Contraction* −: A believes that p holds ($p \in \mathcal{K}$), but then decides that it is better to abandon such a belief, for example because the source is not considered trustworthy anymore. The resulting knowledge base, indicated as $\mathcal{K} - p$, should be such that p is no longer implied by A's knowledge base.

- *Revision* ∗: A is informed that proposition p holds, and wants to add it to $\mathcal{K}$, but with the proviso that the resulting knowledge base should be logically sound. The resulting knowledge base is indicated as $\mathcal{K} * p$.

These three kinds of operations can be characterised using the function $\bullet : \mathcal{T} \times \mathcal{L} \mapsto \mathcal{T}$ with $\bullet \in \{+, -, *\}$.

Actually, the truly basic operations are generally considered to be the first two, *expansion* and *contraction*, since *revision* is usually built on top of those using the so-called *Levi Identity* [Levi, 1977]:

$$\mathcal{K} * p := (\mathcal{K} - \neg p) + p.$$

Revising knowledge base $\mathcal{K}$ by introducing a new proposition p requires that we guarantee that there are no pieces of information in our knowledge base that are in conflict with p. The reasonable way of obtaining this is to contract $\mathcal{K}$ to ensure that it does not imply $\neg p$, and only then introduce p. This is the revision procedure that is modelled by the Levi Identity.

In the swan example, in order to revise the belief set with the information that the swan is black, we should proceed as follows: the belief set corresponds to the set $\mathcal{K} := Cn(\{a, b, c, d, e\})$ and we want to introduce f ("The swan in the trap is black"). Using the Levi Identity, the revision

$$\mathcal{K} * f$$

will consist in first contracting the piece of information $\neg f$ ("It is not the case that the swan in the trap is black") from $\mathcal{K}$. The resulting belief set, $\mathcal{K} - \neg f$, should be a set of formulas that is smaller than $\mathcal{K}$ and does not imply $\neg f$ anymore. For example, let us opt for weakening proposition b ("All European swans are white") into a new proposition b' ("All European swans are white or black"), that is, $\mathcal{K} - \neg f = Cn(\{a, b', c, d, e\})$, and it is easy to check that $\mathcal{K} - \neg f$ does not imply $\neg f$ anymore. Only after the contraction do we add f, that is, we can set $\mathcal{K} * f = (\mathcal{K} - \neg f) + f = Cn(Cn(\{a, b', c, d, e\}) \cup \{f\})$, that is, $\mathcal{K} * f = Cn(\{a, b', c, d, e, f\})$.

We also have a complementary construction, the *Harper Identity*, in which revision is the primitive operator and contraction is defined on top of it:

$$\mathcal{K} - p := (\mathcal{K} * \neg p) \cap \mathcal{K}.$$

$\mathcal{K} - p$ should be a subset of $\mathcal{K}$ not implying p, while $\mathcal{K} * \neg p$ should be a theory as close as possible to $\mathcal{K}$ that implies $\neg p$ and does not imply p. The meaning of the Harper Identity is that since $\mathcal{K} * \neg p$ should not imply p, if we intersect it with $\mathcal{K}$, we obtain a contraction: a subset of $\mathcal{K}$ that does not imply p.

We can rephrase the above example to show that the Harper Identity and the Levi Identity can correspond to each other. Let $\mathcal{K}$ be our knowledge base containing propositions (a)-(e), and assume that we have a revision operator $*$, as described above and which is introduced here as a primary operator, such that $\mathcal{K} * f = Cn(\{a, b', c, d, e, f\}$. If we use the Harper Identity to define a contraction operator $-$ from $*$, we obtain $\mathcal{K} - f = Cn(\{a, b', c, d, e, f\} \cap Cn(\{a, b, c, d, e\}$ that, since $b \models b'$, corresponds to $\mathcal{K} - f = Cn(\{a, b', c, d, e\}$, that is, the contraction we have used above as a primitive operator to define $*$ via the Levi Identity. In what follows, we will use both Levi and Harper Identities, and we will soon give a more formal definition of the correspondence between the two.

Once we have identified the basic operations we are interested in, the second question we need to address is how we want to model and constrain such change operations. For each kind of operation, we want to determine a set of desired properties they should satisfy, and give a formal expression to such desiderata.

Expansion is considered to be a trivial operation, formalised by adding the formula we are interested in to the knowledge base and letting the agent commit to all the logical consequences of such an addition:

$$\mathcal{K} + a := Cn(\mathcal{K} \cup \{a\}).$$

In the *contraction* operation, an agent starts with a belief set $\mathcal{K}$ (e.g. the theory determined by sentences (a)-(e) above) and wants to eliminate some pieces of information in the belief set (e.g. that the swan is white). The AGM approach gives a formal representation to a basic set of desiderata using six *postulates*.

DEFINITION 1 (AGM contraction [Alchourrón *et al.*, 1985]).

Let $-$ be a function that, given a belief set $\mathcal{K}$ and a proposition a, returns a new belief set $\mathcal{K} - a$. Function $-$ is an *AGM basic contraction operator* iff it satisfies the following postulates:

$(- 1)$ $\mathcal{K} - a$ is closed under Cn \hfill (closure)

$(- 2)$ $\mathcal{K} - a \subseteq \mathcal{K}$ \hfill (inclusion)

$(- 3)$ If $a \notin \mathcal{K}$, then $\mathcal{K} - a = \mathcal{K}$ \hfill (vacuity)

$(-\ 4)$ If $\nvdash a$, then $a \notin \mathcal{K} - a$ (success)

$(-\ 5)$ If $a \in \mathcal{K}$, then $\mathcal{K} \subseteq (\mathcal{K} - a) + a$ (recovery)

$(-\ 6)$ If $\vDash a \equiv b$, then $\mathcal{K} - a = \mathcal{K} - b$ (extensionality)

Two extra postulates are introduced to relate the contraction of complex formulas to the contraction of their components:

$(-\ 7)$ $\mathcal{K} - a \cap \mathcal{K} - b \subseteq \mathcal{K} - (a \wedge b)$ (conjunctive overlap)

$(-\ 8)$ If $a \notin \mathcal{K} - (a \wedge b)$, then $\mathcal{K} - (a \wedge b) \subseteq \mathcal{K} - a$ (conjunctive inclusion)

Function $-$ is an *AGM contraction operator* iff it satisfies postulates $(-\ 1)$-$(-\ 8)$.

We will briefly go through the meaning of these postulates. Postulate $(-\ 1)$ enforces an idealisation we have already discussed: the epistemic status of the agent is described using logically closed theories (belief sets), hence every change operation must transform a closed theory into a new closed theory. Postulate $(-\ 2)$ imposes that the change operation must result in an actual *contraction* of the agent's belief set, that is, the set of formulas believed by the agent at the end is a subset of the initial beliefs. Postulate $(-\ 3)$ formalises a principle of an economical nature: if the contraction operation involves a formula that is already excluded from the agent's beliefs, the contraction operation is *vacuous*, that is, nothing changes, since the desired result is already satisfied. Postulate $(-\ 4)$ imposes that, whenever possible, that is, whenever the formula to be contracted is a *contingent* formula and not a tautology, the contraction operation must be successful, that is, the formula should no longer be in the resulting belief set. Let us jump to postulate $(-\ 6)$, leaving postulate $(-\ 5)$ aside for one moment. Postulate $(-\ 6)$ imposes independence from syntax, which is a classical logical principle: whenever two pieces of information are logically equivalent, they are indifferent from a logical point of view, and their impact on the agent's belief set is exactly the same. It is easy to see that this principle is strongly related to postulate $(-\ 1)$, the use of logically closed theories to model the epistemic states. While the use of closed theories imposes indifference with regard to the syntactic form of the knowledge base in the *static* model of the agent's epistemic state, the principle of *extensionality* extends such syntactic indifference also to operations modelling the *dynamics* of the agent's epistemic states. Postulates $(-\ 7)$ and $(-\ 8)$ are considered extra postulates, since they are the only ones that impose constraints on the way a contraction operator behaves with different formulas, in particular how the contraction of a formula should behave with the contraction of logically weaker formulas.

Juliano Maranhão   Giovanni Casini,   Gabriella Pigozzi   Leendert van der Torre

Postulate $(-\ 5)$, *recovery*, has a special status, since, probably together with postulate $(-\ 1)$, it is the most debated AGM principle, and in a certain sense it is also the one that mainly characterises the classical AGM approach. Its nature is purely economical, based on the idea that in order to contract, we "cut" as little as possible from the original knowledge base. So little that if the agent decides that contracting by formula a was not a good idea and that a should be added back, we should be able to return to the original knowledge base without any loss. In fact, together with postulate $(-\ 2)$, postulate $(-\ 5)$ implies that if $a \in \mathcal{K}$, then $\mathcal{K} = (\mathcal{K} - a) + a$, that is, if we put a back after a contraction, we go back to the initial state. It has been debated extensively whether *recovery* is a reasonable principle for contraction, and we will return to this issue later in this section.

Anyway, the reader can see that each of these eight postulates answers to either logical or pragmatic desiderata. For a more detailed explanation of their meaning, we refer the interested reader to the original AGM paper [Alchourrón et al., 1985] and many other publications in the field.

It is worth mentioning that Rott [2000] has disputed whether the AGM approach does actually satisfy any principle of informational economy. Despite the relevance of Rott's observations, postulates like $(-\ 3)$ and $(-\ 5)$ are generally seen as necessary conditions for defining contraction operators that satisfy the principle of informational economy. The principle of informational economy, which has been expressed in various forms and with different names, has always been addressed by researchers in the area as the main guideline for the definition of postulates.

In our presentation of AGM belief change, we first introduced a set of possible change operations (specifically, *expansion*, *contraction*, and *revision*), and then a set of *postulates* to give formal expression to the properties we think such operations should satisfy, specifically those for contraction. The next step is to present the formal tools that we can use to define such change operators. That is, given a set of postulates, the AGM approach is focused on providing a formal characterisation of the class of operations that satisfy such postulates. The classical results in the area define classes of change operations using maxiconsistent subsets and choice functions [Alchourrón et al., 1985], orderings over possible-world semantics representing which situations the agent considers to be more plausible [Grove, 1988; Katsuno and Mendelzon, 1991b], or orderings over the formulas (*epistemic entrenchment relations*) indicating which pieces of information the agent considers to be more or less reliable [Gärdenfors, 1988].

Regarding contraction, the initial characterisation of the class of operations satisfying the basic postulates is based on identifying the maximal subsets of the belief set that do not imply the contracted formula. The resulting belief set is defined by the intersection of some such maximal subsets. Which maximal subsets are used in the definition of the contraction is formalised via a dedicated choice function.

DEFINITION 2 (Partial meet contraction [Alchourrón *et al.*, 1985, p. 512]).

Let $\mathcal{K}\perp a$ be the *remainder set*, containing the maximal subsets $\mathcal{K}'$ of $\mathcal{K}$ such that $\mathcal{K}'$ is a closed theory and $a \notin \mathcal{K}'$. That is, $\mathcal{K}' \in \mathcal{K}\perp a$ iff

(i) $\mathcal{K}' \subseteq \mathcal{K}$,

(ii) $\mathcal{K}' \in \mathcal{T}$,

(iii) $a \notin \mathcal{K}'$, and

(iv) there is no set $\mathcal{K}'' \in \mathcal{T}$ such that $\mathcal{K}' \subset \mathcal{K}'' \subseteq \mathcal{K}$ and $a \notin \mathcal{K}''$.

Let pm be a choice function defined over the set of the remainder sets. Function pm is a *partial meet function* if for every KB $\mathcal{K}$ and every formula a:

- $pm(\mathcal{K}\perp a) \subseteq \mathcal{K}\perp a$, and
- if $\mathcal{K}\perp a \neq \emptyset$, then $pm(\mathcal{K}\perp a) \neq \emptyset$.

A *partial meet contraction operator* $-$ is defined as: $\mathcal{K}_A^- = \bigcap pm(\mathcal{K}\perp A)$.

The class of partial meet contractions is sufficient to give an operational characterisation of the class of AGM basic contraction operations.

OBSERVATION 3. [Alchourrón *et al.*, 1985, Observation 2.5] A contraction operator $- : \mathcal{T} \times \mathcal{L} \mapsto \mathcal{T}$ is an AGM basic contraction operator (satisfying (-1)-(-6)) iff it is a partial meet contraction operator.

An analogous analysis can be developed for *revision*. First of all, we can formalise our desiderata via appropriate postulates.

DEFINITION 4 (AGM revision $*$ [Alchourrón *et al.*, 1985]).

Let $*$ be a function that, given a belief set $\mathcal{K}$ and a proposition a, returns a new belief set $\mathcal{K} * a$. Function $*$ is an *AGM basic revision operator* iff it satisfies the following postulates:

$(* \, 1)$ $\mathcal{K} * a$ is closed under Cn (closure)

$(* \, 2)$ $a \in \mathcal{K} * a$ (success)

$(* \, 3)$ $\mathcal{K} * a \subseteq \mathcal{K} + a$ (inclusion)

$(* \, 4)$ If $\neg a \notin \mathcal{K}$, then $\mathcal{K} + a = \mathcal{K} * a$ (vacuity)

$(* \, 5)$ $\perp \in (\mathcal{K} * a)$ iff $\vDash \neg a$ (triviality)

(∗ 6) If $\vDash a \equiv b$, then $\mathcal{K} * a = \mathcal{K} * b$ (extensionality)

Two extra postulates are introduced also for revision. These postulates relate the revision of complex formulas to the revision of their components:

(∗ 7) $\mathcal{K} * (a \wedge b) \subseteq (\mathcal{K} * a) + b$ (Iterated (∗ 3))

(∗ 8) If $\neg b \notin \mathcal{K} * (a)$ then $(\mathcal{K} * a) + b \subseteq \mathcal{K} * (a \wedge b)$ (Iterated (∗ 4))

Function ∗ is an *AGM revision operator* iff it satisfies the postulates (∗ 1)-(∗ 8).

The meaning of the postulates for revision is very close to the meaning of the postulates for contraction. The parallel is clear for postulates (∗ 1), (∗ 2), (∗ 3), (∗ 4), (∗ 6) and the correspondent postulates for contraction. Postulate (∗ 5) imposes perhaps the key rational desideratum for modelling belief dynamics: preserving consistency. Whenever we add a new piece of information a, the only case where the resulting belief set can be inconsistent is when a itself is inconsistent.

We briefly summarise a series of well-known basic results in the area that show how the notions introduced up to this point are solidly connected to one other in AGM theory. First of all, the construction of AGM revision and contraction operators are intertwined via the Levi Identity.

OBSERVATION 5. [Alchourrón *et al.*, 1985] Let $* : \mathcal{T} \times \mathcal{L} \mapsto \mathcal{T}$ be a revision operator. Function ∗ is a basic AGM revision operator (it satisfies (∗ 1)-(∗ 6)) if and only if there is a contraction operator − such that:

- ∗ can be defined via the Levi Identity from −. That is, for every $\mathcal{K}$ and a,

$$\mathcal{K} * a = (\mathcal{K} - \neg a) + a$$

- − is a basic AGM contraction operator (it satisfies (− 1)-(− 6)).

Given Observation 3, Observation 5 connects the construction of basic AGM revision operators to the class of partial meet contractions via the Levi Identity.

An analogous result [Alchourrón *et al.*, 1985] holds for contraction and revision operators satisfying postulates (− 1)-(− 8) and (∗ 1)-(∗ 8) respectively.

Such a dependency of revision on contraction can also be reversed, moving from AGM revision operators to the definition of AGM contraction operators: the one-to-one correspondence between the Levi Identity and the

Harper Identity, that we have briefly exemplified above in revising and contracting our knowledge base about swans, can actually be formally proved. Let us translate the Levi and Harper Identities into transformation functions. Given a belief set $\mathcal{K}$, a formula a, a contraction operator $-$ and a revision operator $*$, let

- $\mathcal{K} \, \mathbb{R}(-) \, a := Cn((\mathcal{K} - \neg a) \cup \{a\})$

- $\mathcal{K} \, \mathbb{C}(*) \, a := (\mathcal{K} * \neg a) \cap \mathcal{K}$

where $\mathbb{R}(-)$ represents a revision operator obtained from contraction $-$ via the Levi Identity and $\mathbb{C}(*)$ represents a contraction operator obtained from revision $*$ via the Harper Identity. Using these operators, Makinson has proven that there is full correspondence between the Levi and Harper Identities.

OBSERVATION 6. [Makinson, 1987] Let $\mathcal{K}$ be a belief set, and let a be a formula, with $\mathbb{R}(-)$ and $\mathbb{C}(*)$ defined as above.

- Let $-$ satisfy the postulates of *closure, inclusion, vacuity, extensionality*, and *recovery*. Then $\mathbb{C}(\mathbb{R}(-)) = -$.

- Let $*$ satisfy the postulates of *closure, inclusion, success*, and *extensionality*. Then $\mathbb{R}(\mathbb{C}(*)) = *$.

As an immediate consequence, the Levi and Harper Identities have been shown to be interchangeable for AGM theory:

$$\mathcal{K} * a = (K \cap K * a) + a;$$

$$\mathcal{K} - a = K \cap ((\mathcal{K} - a) + \neg a).$$

What we have presented up to this point are some key results of the AGM approach that provide an essential introduction to the unfamiliar reader, and which are relevant to the sections that follow.

2.2 Criticisms of the AGM Approach

Simplifying, we could say that there are three main steps that characterise the AGM method:

- the identification of the typologies of change we want to model and of the properties we want them to satisfy;

- the translation of such desiderata into postulates, that is, into formal constraints;

- the characterisation of the classes of operators that satisfy the desired set of postulates. Such a characterisation is usually obtained by proving the correspondence of such operators to a class of constructions defined using a relevant formal tool (e.g. maxiconsistent sets, possible-world models...).

The AGM approach to belief change has quickly become standard in the field, and the last 30 years has seen many contributions [Fermé and Hansson, 2018]. Despite the fact that it has become a major research topic in knowledge representation, it is an approach that has been frequently and heavily criticised, and new lines of research have sprouted from some of these critiques. We briefly list some of the main critiques the AGM approach has received.

2.2.1 Too Many Constraints Imposed on the Underlying Logic

The AGM approach was originally developed for classical propositional logic (PL), and the classical results assume that the underlying logic, characterised by a language L and an entailment operator Cn, satisfies many of the formal properties that characterise PL:

1. The language L is closed under the propositional connectives.

2. The entailment operator Cn is *Tarskian*, that is, given two sets of formulas $\mathcal{K}, \mathcal{K}' \subseteq L$, it satisfies the following properties:

   - *monotonicity*: if $\mathcal{K} \subseteq \mathcal{K}'$, then $Cn(\mathcal{K}) \subseteq Cn(\mathcal{K}')$;
   - *idempotence*: $Cn(\mathcal{K}) = Cn(Cn(\mathcal{K}))$;
   - *iteration*: $\mathcal{K} \subseteq Cn(\mathcal{K})$.

3. The consequence operator satisfies some well-known properties of classical logic:

   - *deduction*: $b \in Cn(\mathcal{K} \cup \{a\})$ iff $(a \to b) \in Cn(\mathcal{K})$;
   - *disjunction in the premises*: if $a \in Cn(\mathcal{K} \cup \{b\})$ and $a \in Cn(\mathcal{K} \cup \{c\})$, then $a \in Cn(\mathcal{K} \cup \{b \vee c\})$.

4. *Compactness*: if $a \in Cn(\mathcal{K})$, then $a \in Cn(\mathcal{K}')$ for some finite $\mathcal{K}' \subseteq \mathcal{K}$.

266

Much recent research in belief revision has been dedicated to investigating whether the above constraints are essential to the definition of AGM operators and, when we are dealing with an underlying logic that does not allow the definition of classical AGM postulates, what other meaningful postulates can be defined and satisfied. For example, the AGM approach has been applied to logics that are not fully closed under propositional operators [Delgrande and Peppas, 2015; Zhuang *et al.*, 2016b], that are not monotonic [Zhuang *et al.*, 2016a; Casini and Meyer, 2017; Casini *et al.*, 2018], and that are not compact [Ribeiro *et al.*, 2018].

This chapter will also deal with a family of logics that do not satisfy all the properties listed above. Input/output logics are not closed under propositional operators and, because of that, cannot satisfy properties like *deduction* and *disjunction in the premises*. Some input/output logics also do not satisfy the property of *monotonicity* [Makinson and van der Torre, 2001]. Although we shall not discuss them in this chapter, application of the AGM methodology to normative change based on non-monotonic input/output logics is a promising field of inquiry.

2.2.2 Lack of Expressiveness

It has often been pointed out that the expansion/contraction/revision triad is not sufficient to account for the dynamics of information. It is also claimed that the AGM approach is not appropriate for handling multi-agent systems because it is suitable only for factual information.

With respect to the first line of criticism, it is worth mentioning that operations that are not reducible to the original ones have been introduced, such as *update* [Katsuno and Mendelzon, 1991a] and *merging* [Konieczny and Perez, 2002] among others. Besides, many refinements to the original operations have been proposed, based on alternative postulates and formal constructions, which introduce new dimensions to the original operations, such as the trustworthiness of the new information [Fermé and Hansson, 2018, Chapter 8]. Despite being a common place that the AGM operations of contraction and revision are not sufficient to cover all the relevant dynamics of information, it is generally accepted that analysing the operations of contraction and revision is a good starting point for modelling informational change in many contexts. Analysing contraction and revision in different formal contexts allows us to deal with the ideas of minimal change and consistency preservation in each of those contexts, and minimal change and consistency preservation are the two main stepping stones towards characterising rational informational change.

It is true that multi-agent contexts are not immediately compatible with the AGM approach, since some classical AGM postulates would be counter-intuitive in such a framework.

In the area of Dynamic Epistemic Logic (DEL), it has been pointed out that some sentences, for example those resembling the structure of that used in *Moore's paradox*, are not compatible with the *success* postulate [Van Ditmarsch and Kooi, 2006]. The DEL framework allows us to model the dynamics of epistemic states in which the agent also models higher-order sentences representing beliefs about its own beliefs and the beliefs of other agents. On the other hand, AGM is easier to understand, and allows a more in-depth analysis of specific kinds of operations. Working first at the AGM level, and later transporting the proposed solutions to other frameworks such as the DEL framework, can be seen as a good research strategy. Also, some domains, like formal ontologies or the domain under consideration in this chapter, normative bodies, do not usually need to deal with a multi-agent aspect in modelling change.

2.2.3   Logical Closure and the Recovery Postulate

Finally, let us consider two further lines of criticisms of the AGM approach that are particularly relevant for what follows. These are connected to the *recovery* $(- 5)$ and the *closure* $((- 1)/(* 1))$ postulates.

As mentioned above in this section, the recovery postulate has often been criticised. On the one hand, its desirability is intertwined with the use of logically closed belief sets. On the other hand, as many commentators have pointed out, the recovery postulate is not always desirable even if we are working with closed belief sets (see [Fermé and Hansson, 2018, Sect. 5.1] for an overview).

Moreover, if we define revision on top of contraction via the Levi Identity, it turns out that the recovery postulate is not necessary to characterise the class of the AGM basic revision operators. That is, the representation that results in Observation 5 remains valid if we drop postulate $(- 5)$.

OBSERVATION 7. [Gärdenfors and Rott, 1995] Let $* : \mathcal{T} \times \mathcal{L} \mapsto \mathcal{T}$ be a revision operator. Function $*$ is a basic AGM revision operator (it satisfies $(* 1)$-$(* 6)$) if and only if there is a contraction operator $-$ such that:

- $*$ can be defined via the Levi Identity from $-$. That is, for every $\mathcal{K}$ and a,

$$\mathcal{K} * a = (\mathcal{K} - \neg a) + a.$$

- $-$ satisfies $(- 1)$-$(- 4)$ and $(- 6)$.

The criticisms of the recovery postulate, together with the fact that it is not a necessary property in order to characterise well-behaved revision operators, has convinced many researchers to drop such a postulate in many contexts, looking for more significant alternatives [Fermé, 1998].

As mentioned above, the AGM approach models change over belief sets, that is, it does not consider arbitrary sets of formulas, but only logically closed theories.

This is a constraint that is in line with the classical modelling approach of epistemic logics, and it is prone to the same kind of criticisms. On the one hand, characterising epistemic states as closed logical theories is seen as the correct way to characterise rational agents, since it allows a description of knowledge that is syntax-independent and that models the commitment a rational agent should have towards all the consequences of what is explicitly stated in a knowledge base. On the other hand, depending on the modelling goals, exactly the same arguments can be considered as drawbacks. If we investigate the belief states and dynamics of agents with bounded rationality, committing to closed logical theories is too strong an idealisation, which in epistemic logics is labelled as *logical omniscience*. Moreover, the syntactic form of the knowledge base can actually play a role in modelling the way the agent manages the information at its own disposal, for example by making explicit how the agent clusters pieces of information together in a single formula. The belief change community has reacted by developing the theory of *base revision*, where the same approach as AGM to investigation is applied to finite knowledge bases rather than logically closed theories [Hansson, 1999].

2.3 Base Contraction and Revision

In base revision, the epistemic status of an agent is described using a set of formulas K that is not necessarily logically closed. The basic operation in base revision is Hansson's *kernel contraction* [Hansson, 1999], which is a re-interpretation at the level of finite base of the AGM notion of contraction based on remainder sets.

Hansson's base contraction is based on the notions of *kernels* and *incision functions* in a way that resembles the roles of the *remainder sets* and the *partial meet functions* in partial meet contraction. Given a knowledge base K and a formula a, the *a-kernels of K* are the minimal subsets of K that have a as a logical consequence. Eliminating some pieces of information from each kernel allows us to avoid deriving a, and such an elimination is made using an *incision function*.

DEFINITION 8 (Kernel set and incision function [Hansson, 1999]). Let $a \in \mathcal{L}$ and $K \subseteq \mathcal{L}$. The set $Kern_K(a) \subseteq 2^{2^{\mathcal{L}}}$ is the *kernel set of K with respect* *to a* if it is defined as follows. $X \in Kern_K(a)$ if and only if:

- $X \subseteq K$;
- $a \in Cn(X)$;
- if $X' \subset X$, then $a \notin Cn(X')$.

An incision function σ defined over the kernel sets is a choice function such that:

- $\sigma(Kern_K(a)) \subseteq \bigcup Kern_K(a)$;
- $\sigma(Kern_K(a)) \cap X \neq \emptyset$ for all $X \in Kern_K(a)$.

Once the incision function has specified the information that should be eliminated from K in order to avoid deriving a, we can use it to define a contraction operator on arbitrary sets of formulas.

DEFINITION 9 (Kernel contraction [Hansson, 1999]). Let $a \in \mathcal{L}$ and $K \subseteq \mathcal{L}$. Operator $-_\sigma : 2^{\mathcal{L}} \times \mathcal{L} \mapsto 2^{\mathcal{L}}$ is a *kernel contraction operator* if

$$K -_\sigma a = K \setminus \sigma(Kern_K(a)).$$

Hansson gives a postulate characterisation of kernel contractions.

OBSERVATION 10. [Hansson, 1999] A function $- : 2^{\mathcal{L}} \times \mathcal{L} \mapsto 2^{\mathcal{L}}$ is a kernel contraction if and only if it satisfies the following postulates:

$(-_\sigma \, 1)$ $K - a \subseteq K$ (inclusion)

$(-_\sigma \, 2)$ If $\nvdash a$, then $a \notin K - a$ (success)

$(-_\sigma \, 3)$ If $b \in K \setminus K - a$, then there is a $K' \subset K$ such that $a \notin Cn(K')$ but $a \in Cn(K' \cup \{b\})$ (core-retainment)

$(-_\sigma \, 4)$ If for all subsets K' of K, it holds that $a \in Cn(K')$ iff $b \in Cn(K')$, then $K - a = K - b$ (uniformity)

We can also define revision combining contraction and expansion using bases, but now we have two possible ways of combining the two operations [Hansson, 1993],

- $K *_\sigma a = (K -_\sigma \neg a) +_\sigma a$ (Levi Identity)

- $K *_\sigma a = (K +_\sigma a) -_\sigma \neg a$ (Reversed Levi Identity) where $\mathcal{K} +_\sigma a := \mathcal{K} \cup \{a\}$. The two options define revision operators with different properties [Hansson, 1993]. The Reversed Levi Identity is not a viable option when we are working with belief sets, since the first step, the expansion, could take us to an inconsistent theory, the contraction of which is not efficiently managed by the classical AGM approach.

3 Formal Analysis of Normative Change

The distinction between norms and obligations was articulated and formally developed in input/output logic [Makinson and van der Torre, 2000]. Input/output logic takes a very general view of the process used to obtain conclusions (outputs) from given sets of premises (inputs). To detach an obligation from a norm, there must be a context, and the norm must be conditional. Thus, norms are just particular kinds of rules, and one may view a normative system simply as a set of rules.

Makinson's iterative approach to normative reasoning distinguishes unconstrained from constrained output. Unconstrained is close to classical logic, whereas constrained output is much less similar, due to the existence of multiple output sets (or extensions), for example. Examples of constrained output are default reasoning, defeasible deontic reasoning etc.

Makinson and van der Torre introduced seven distinct input/output logics, including both a semantic definition and a proof theoretic characterisation [Makinson and van der Torre, 2001; Makinson and van der Torre, 2003a]. They showed that their seven unconstrained input/output logics cannot handle contrary-to-duty reasoning and thus cannot be used as logics representing normative reasoning. They therefore introduced constrained output in a companion paper, and they showed how that can be used as a logic of norms. However, the user has to make some seemingly arbitrary choices by, for example, choosing between a sceptical and a credulous approach. Moreover, the complex nature of constrained output makes it difficult to handle. This becomes apparent if we consider norm change, like contraction and revision of norms. The constrained input/output logic framework becomes relatively complex and cumbersome. Here, we follow the work of Boella *et al.* [2016] and call the generators of unconstrained output *rules*.

3.1 Input/Output Logic

In this section, we give a general introduction to input/output logic. For a deeper look into the input/output logic framework, the reader is referred to the work of Makinson and van der Torre [2003b] and Parent and van der Torre [2013].

A *rule* is a pair of propositional formulas,[6] called the antecedent and consequent of the rule.

DEFINITION 11 (Rules [Makinson and van der Torre, 2000]). Let L be a propositional logic built on a finite set of propositional atoms A. A rule-based system $R \subseteq L \times L$ is a set of pairs of L, written as $R = \{(a_1, x_1), (a_2, x_2), \ldots, (a_n, x_n)\}$.

Rules allow the derivation of formulas, like the derivation of obligations and prohibitions in a legal code. Which obligations and prohibitions can be derived depends on the factual situation (i.e. the *context* or *input*), which is a propositional formula.

DEFINITION 12 (Operational semantics [Makinson and van der Torre, 2000]). An input/output operation $out : \mathcal{P}(L \times L) \times L \to \mathcal{P}(L)$ is a function from the set of rule-based systems and contexts to a set of sentences of L.

Note that operator *out* satisfies the principle of irrelevance of syntax. The simplest input/output logic defined by Makinson and van der Torre is the so-called simple-minded output.

DEFINITION 13 (Simple-minded output [Makinson and van der Torre, 2000]). Proposition x is in the simple-minded output of the set of rules R in context a, written as $x \in out_1(R, a)$, if there is a set of rules $(a_1, x_1), \ldots, (a_n, x_n) \in R$ such that $a_i \in Cn(a)$ and $x \in Cn(x_1 \wedge \ldots \wedge x_n)$, where $Cn(a)$ is the consequence set of a in L.

A set of rules is said to 'imply' another rule (a, x) if and only if x is in the output in context a.

DEFINITION 14. Rule 'implication' by Makinson and van der Torre [2000]] Rule (a, x) is 'implied' by rule-based system R, written as $(a, x) \in out(R)$, if and only if $x \in out(R, a)$.

As Makinson and van der Torre observe, the relation between the 'implication' among rules $(a, x) \in out(R)$ and the 'operational semantics' $x \in out(R, a)$ has an analogy in classical logic, where the pair $a \models x$ is equivalent to the membership of x in the consequence set of a, written as $x \in Cn(a)$.

DEFINITION 15. [Boella *et al.*, 2016] Function *out* is a closure operation when the following three conditions hold:

reflexivity: $x \in out(R \cup \{(a, x)\}, a)$ (in other words, $R \subseteq out(R)$), and if the context is precisely the antecedent of one of the rules, then the

---

[6]One may also use a first-order, temporal or action logic. The choice of classical propositional logic is intended to stay closer to the AGM theory.

output contains the consequent of that rule.

monotony: $x \in out(R_1, a)$ implies $x \in out(R_1 \cup R_2, a)$ (in other words, $out(R_1) \subseteq out(R_1 \cup R_2)$), and if the set of rules increases, then no conclusions are lost.

idempotence: if $x \in out(R, a)$, then for all b, we have $out(R, b) = out(R \cup \{(a, x)\}, b)$ (in other words, $out(R) = out(out((R)))$), and if x is obligatory in context a, then (a, x) can be added to the rule-based system without changing the output.

Makinson and van der Torre show that their seven input/output logics satisfy the Tarskian properties, and their notion of 'implication' among rules is therefore a Tarskian consequence relation, a crucial characteristic to incorporating the AGM construction into the framework of input/output logics.

DEFINITION 16. [Makinson and van der Torre, 2000] Let $R(a) = \{x \mid (a, x) \in R\}$, and let v be a classical valuation (maxiconsistent set of propositions) or L. Simple-minded, basic, reusable and basic reusable output are defined as follows:

simple minded: $out_1(R, a) = Cn(R(Cn(a)))$

basic: $out_2(R, a) = \cap\{out_1(R, v) \mid a \in v\}$

reusable: $out_3(R, a) = \cap\{out_1(R, b) \mid a \in Cn(b), out_1(R, b) \subseteq Cn(b)\}$

basic reusable: $out_4(R, a) = \bigcap\{out_1(R, v) : a \in v \text{ and } out_1(R, v) \subseteq v\}$

Basic output handles reasoning by cases, and reusable output handles iterated detachment [Makinson and van der Torre, 2000]. Moreover, for each input/output logic, a corresponding throughput operator is defined by:

$$out_i^+(R, a) = out_i(R \cup \{(b, b) \mid b \in L\}, a).$$

As many of the examples discussed in section 1 have shown, normative change has to handle and solve inconsistencies and incoherencies (on the concept of incoherence, see section 3.2 below) between obligations and permissions as two distinctive kinds of regulative rules.

The implication (or derivation) of obligations from a set O of obligatory regulative rules is given by definition 14. With respect to permissions, it is important beforehand to distinguish, following Alchourrón [1969], between *weak* (or negative) permissions and *strong* (or positive) permissions. In its

273

weak sense, a permission to x in context b is just the absence of a prohibition to x in context b. That is, if we consider a set of obligation rules O, then a permission $\langle a, x \rangle$ is implied by O if and only if $\neg x \notin out(O, b)$ [Makinson and van der Torre, 2003a].

In its strong or positive sense, a permission is derived from explicit enactments of obligations as well as permissive rules. The output of a set of explicit permissions is defined below:

DEFINITION 17. *[Makinson and van der Torre, 2003a]* Let O be a set of obligations and let $P \subseteq (L \times L)$ be a set of explicit permissions. Then, $(a, x) \in perm_i(P, N)$ iff $(a, x) \in out_i(O \cup Q)$ for some singleton or empty $Q \subseteq P$.

As we have emphasised in section 1.1 when referring to the problem called *network effects*, some difficulties concerning normative change are related to the combination of constitutive and regulative rules in the normative system.

We may model this problem using input/output logics by making the output of a normative set (possibly joined with the input set) the input of the output operation on the other normative set. It is also possible to combine sets for deriving obligations and explicit permissions.

A typical combination of normative sets is given by the definition or qualification, by a constitutive rule, of a concept present in a regulative rule. For instance, a data protection legislation contains a regulative rule establishing that consent by the data subject (*consent*) is a condition for lawful processing of his/her personal data (*process*). Suppose that a platform processes the personal data of its users without explicit consent, considering that authorisation is implicit unless they explicitly object to that processing (*opt-out* model). If an user of that internet platform has not opted out, would the processing of her personal data be lawful? The answer may be found in a constitutive rule stipulating that only the data user's explicit and written authorisation for processing counts as consent (*opt-in* model). If the set of constitutive rules contain such a rule, then an opt-out model does not count as valid consent for personal data processing. This example of legal reasoning may be modelled by a combination of a set C of constitutive rules and sets O and P of regulative rules, where an output operator on the set of constitutive rules delivers the inputs for the output operator on the sets of regulative rules.

We shall use a general definition of the relation between a constitutive and a regulative rule in a derivation:

DEFINITION 18. Let $A \subseteq L$, $I \in \{A, \emptyset\}$, let out_i and out_j be output operators, and let C and R be constitutive and regulative sets of rules respectively. Then, the combined output of C and R is defined as:

$$out_{ij}(C, R, A) = out_i(R, out_j(C, A) \cup I).$$

The definition and the results regarding the contraction operator in section 3.7 covers, with straightforward adaptations, both cases of combinations, i.e. constitutive with permissive rules and constitutive with obligation rules, as follows:

$$out_{i,j}(O, C, A) = out_i(O, out_j(C, A) \cup I);$$
$$perm_{i,j}(P, C, A) = perm_i(P, out_j(C, A) \cup I).$$

In the examples used throughout this chapter, we shall consider combined *out* and *perm* operators in which $I = A$. To formalise the above example on consent for lawful data processing using a combination of sets of normative rules, let us consider the following normative sets:

$C = \{(opt\text{-}in, consent), (opt\text{-}out, \neg consent)\}$
$P = \{(consent, process)\}$
$O = \{(\neg consent, \neg process,\}$

The normative system implies that $(opt\text{-}in, process) \in perm_{1,1}(P, C)$ and that $(opt\text{-}out, \neg process) \in perm_{1,1}(O, C)$. That is, it is permitted to process personal data if authorisation was obtained by an opt-in model, while it is forbidden to process that data if the model used was opt-out.

3.2 Consistency and Coherence of Normative Systems

As example 1.4 in section 1.2 shows, constitutive rules may be responsible for genuine normative conflicts when combined with a regulative set. In order to model this feature, it should be possible to verify regulative sets that are consistent but whose combination with a constitutive set implies inconsistent conditional norms. To avoid confusion, let us qualify regulative sets as consistent or inconsistent and combinations of constitutive sets with regulative sets as coherent or incoherent.

Consistency is defined with respect to a given context. We say that a normative set N is *b-consistent* if and only if $(b, \perp) \notin out(N)$. Accordingly, a combination (C, R) is *b-coherent* if and only if $(b, \perp) \notin out(C, R)$. If we have a set of obligations O and a set of explicit permissions P, then such normative sets are *b-consistent* if and only if for any sentence x, it is not the case that $(b, x) \in perm(O, P)$ and $(b, \neg x) \in out(O)$. Accordingly, a combination of a set of constitutive rules and a set of obligations and the same set of constitutive rules and a set of permissions is *b-coherent* if and only if, for any sentence x, it is not the case that $(b, x) \in perm(O, P, C)$ and $(b, \neg x) \in out(O, C)$.

When should we then consider a normative system to be generally consistent or coherent? We may consider two extreme possibilities for such definitions.

The first extreme would be to consider a normative system *consistent* if it is consistent for all possible inputs, that is, to demand $\bot$-consistency. This conception would limit the possibility of giving opposite commands in logically independent conditions, since $N = \{(a, x), (b, \neg x)\}$ would be inconsistent.

The other extreme would be to consider a normative system *consistent* if it is consistent for a tautological input, i.e. to demand $\top$-consistency. This conception also seems inadequate because normative sets with genuine conflicts such as $N = \{(a, x), (a, \neg x)\}$ would be rendered consistent.

As a middle ground, we shall consider a normative set N consistent if it is b-consistent for every b such that $b \in Cl(a)$ and $a \in body(N)$ where $body(N) = \{b : (b, x) \in N\}$. That is, a normative set is consistent if there is no condition explicitly mentioned in its conditional rules that would, as input, deliver inconsistent outputs. Accordingly, a combination (C, R) is coherent if it is b-coherent for every b such that $b \in Cl(a)$ and $a \in body(C)$.

Therefore, we may have a consistent set R but an incoherent combination (C, R), which would demand a contraction to restore coherence.

Let us formalise example 1.4 in the model proposed here. Following Maranhão and de Souza [2018], we shall employ a basic reusable output operator (out_4) for the set of constitutive rules, and a basic output operator (out_2) for the sets of regulative (obligatory and permissive) rules. Recall that the example referred to a normative system where the police have the power to access (acc) property items ($prop$) in a search & seizure order ($sord$) but are forbidden from accessing ongoing communication (com) without an interception order ($iord$). The pertinent question is whether an exchange of messages stored on a mobile phone (sms) counts as data (dat) or as communication (or both). This normative system could be represented by the following normative sets of constitutive (C), regulative obligation (O) and regulative permission (P) rules:

$$C = \{(sms, com), (sms, dat), (dat, prop)\}$$
$$P = \{(prop \wedge sord, acc), (com \wedge iord, acc)\}$$
$$O = \{(com \wedge \neg iord, \neg acc), (prop \wedge \neg sord, \neg acc)\}$$

The corresponding normative theory is both consistent and coherent as there is no explicit condition in these normative sets that can, by itself, deliver a contradiction as output. However, given that a message exchange on a mobile phone collected during an authorised search is both stored data and a form of ongoing communication, a search & seizure order to check message exchanges would deliver a contradiction, that is, we have both $(sms \wedge sord \wedge \neg iord, acc) \in perm_{2,4}(O, P, C)$ and $(sms \wedge sord \wedge \neg iord, \neg acc) \in out_{2,4}(O, C)$. Hence, the normative system is $(sms \wedge sord \wedge \neg iord)$-incoherent, and a contraction should take place to restore coherence for that specific context.

There are different ways to reach this goal. And the task of legal interpretation, doctrinal or judicial, is to choose and justify such choices. It is possible to restore coherence by handling the definitions involved, that is, by contracting the set of constitutive rules, by contracting the set of regulative rules, or by deleting rules from both sets. We shall explore these alternatives in section 3.7 below.

3.3 Contraction of Normative Systems

Boella *et al.* [2016] defined a rule set as a set of rules closed under an input/output logic ($out(R)$), and generalised the AGM postulates as postulates for the revision of norms. In order to keep an abstract approach and obtain general results without specifying a particular logic, they used operator *out* to refer to any input/output logic. Operation $out(R) \oplus (a, x)$ indicates the expansion of a rule based-system R by a new rule, operation $out(R) \ominus (a, x)$ denotes the contraction of a rule (a, x) from $out(R)$, and operation $out(R) \circledast (a, x)$ indicates the revision of $out(R)$ by new rule (a, x).

Like AGM expansion, the definition of rule expansion is straightforward. The new rule that is enforced does not cause any conflict with the existing legal code. Hence, rule (a, x) is added to $out(R)$ together with all the rules that can be derived from the union of $deriv(R)$ and (a, x): $out(R) \oplus (a, x) = out(R \cup \{(a, x)\})$.

DEFINITION 19. [Boella *et al.*, 2016] Let *out* be an input/output logic. A rule contraction operator $\ominus$ satisfies the following postulates:

R-1: $out(R) \ominus (a, x)$ is closed under *out*   (closure or type)

R-2: $out(R) \ominus (a, x) \subseteq out(R)$ (inclusion or contraction)

R-3: If $(a, x) \notin out(R)$, then $out(R) = out(R) \ominus (a, x)$ (vacuity or min. action)

R-4: If $(a, x) \notin out(\emptyset)$, then $(a, x) \notin out(R) \ominus (a, x)$ (success)

R-5: If $(a, x) \in out(R)$, then $out(R) \subseteq (out(R) \ominus (a, x)) \oplus (a, x)$ (recovery)

R-6: If $out(\{(a,x)\}) = out(\{(b,y)\})$, then $out(R) \ominus (a,x) = out(R) \ominus (b,y)$ (extensionality)

As we have seen in definition 1, the last two AGM postulates $((-7)$-$(-8))$ are optional and refer to conjunctions. Since conjunctions are not defined for rules, we restrict ourselves to the basic postulates.

A few words are due about the success postulate. The *success* postulate for rule contraction says that if $x \notin out(\emptyset, a)$, then $x \notin out(R \ominus (a,x), a)$. There are several ways in which a set of rules can be contracted. The purpose of the postulates is to distinguish admissible solutions from inadmissible ones. However, unlike in AGM theory revision, the question here concerns not only what and how much to contract, but also *which inputs* to contract. Boella *et al.* [2016] show with the aid of an example that sometimes, in order to obtain a rule-based system that satisfies the success postulate, one needs to *add* some rules.

Another issue is the characterisation of the minimal rule contraction operators. We have seen that in AGM, one interpretation of the postulates is to impose the economical principle. That is, when performing a rule contraction operator, we want to keep as much as possible. However, a syntactic characterisation of minimal rule contraction encounters some problems. In AGM, thanks to the closure postulate (i.e. belief sets are closed under consequence), if $y \notin (K - x)$, then we also have that $x \wedge y \notin (K - x)$. Likewise, if $(a,x) \notin out(R) \ominus (a,x)$, then also $(a, x \wedge y) \notin out(R) \ominus (a,x)$. However, this is not the only consequence of the success postulate for rule contraction. For example, for all six input/output logics considered here, if $(a,x) \notin out(R) \ominus (a,x)$, then also $(a \vee b, x) \notin out(R) \ominus (a,x)$.

Other logical relations depend on the input/output logic used. For example, for basic output out_2, if $(a,x) \notin out(R) \ominus (a,x)$, then we have either $(a \wedge b, x) \notin out(R) \ominus (a,x)$ or $(a \wedge \neg b, x) \notin out(R) \ominus (a,x)$. In other words, if $(a,x) \notin out(R) \ominus (a,x)$ and $(a \wedge b, x) \in out(R) \ominus (a,x)$, then $(a \wedge \neg b, x) \notin out(R) \ominus (a,x)$. These relations do not hold for simple-minded output out_1. Likewise, a similar property based on the inverse of CTA holds for reusable output out_3.

The recovery postulate states that contracting a rule-based system by (a,x) and then expanding by the same (a,x) should leave $out(R)$ unchanged. We will see that such a postulate turns out to be problematic for rule contraction.

Boella *et al.* [2016] show that the five postulates considered so far are consistent only for some input/output logics, and not for others. In particular, if we adopt output out_1 or out_3, then there is no single rule contraction operator satisfying the postulates.

PROPOSITION 20. *[Boella et al., 2016]*
(R-1) to (R-5) cannot hold together for out$_1$ or out$_3$, but they can hold together for out$_2$.

We now turn to the postulates for rule revision.

3.4 Revision of Normative Systems

As in rule contraction, we consider only the first six AGM revision postulates and the rule revision postulates.

DEFINITION 21. [Boella *et al.*, 2016] Let *out* be an input/output logic, and *deriv*(R) a set of rules closed under out. A rule revision operator ⊛ satisfies the following postulates:

R ⊛ 1: $out(R) ⊛ (a, x)$ is closed under out   (closure or type)

R ⊛ 2: $(a, x) \in (out(R) ⊛ (a, x))$ (success)

R ⊛ 3: $out(R) ⊛ (a, x) \subseteq out(R) \oplus (a, x)$ (inclusion)

R ⊛ 4: If $(a, \neg x) \notin out(R \cup (a, x))$ then $out(R) \oplus (a, x) = out(R) ⊛ (a, x)$
(vacuity)

R ⊛ 5: $(a, \neg x) \in out(R) ⊛ (a, x)$ iff $(a, \neg x) \in out(\emptyset)$ (triviality)

R ⊛ 6: If $out(\{(a, x)\}) = out(\{(b, y)\})$, then $out(R) ⊛ (a, x) = out(R) ⊛ (b, y)$
(extensionality)

As seen in section 2, the Levi Identity defines revision $K * A$ as a sequence of a contraction and a expansion. We have seen the correctness of such a definition in observations 5 and 7.

It is worth noting that the controversial recovery postulate (-5) was not used in observation 7. Boella *et al.* [2016] show that the same result can be proven for rule change.

THEOREM 22. *[Boella et al., 2016] Given a rule contraction operator, we can define a rule revision operator via the Levi Identity:*

$$out(R) ⊛ (a, x) = (out(R) \ominus (a, \neg x)) \oplus (a, x).$$

When operator $\ominus$ satisfies rules (R-1) to (R-4) and (R-6), then operator ⊛ satisfies rules (R*1) -(R*6).

Not only can belief revision be defined in terms of belief contraction operators, belief contractions can also be defined in terms of belief revisions using the Harper and Levi Identities introduced in section 2 .

However, as recalled in proposition 20, for out_1 and out_3 the revision postulates are consistent and the contraction postulates are not. Thus, a result like observation 5 for normative change does not hold.

We recall from section 2 that the Levi and Harper Identities have been shown to be interchangeable in AGM theory. So, even though there is no theorem corresponding to observation 5 in the general case, one may want to check whether $out(R) \circledast (a, x) = (out(R) \cap out(R) \circledast (a, x)) \oplus (a, x)$ is a consequence of the basic postulates for rule revisions, and whether $out(R) \ominus (a, x) = out(R) \cap ((out(R) \ominus (a, x)) \oplus (a, \neg x))$ can be proven from the basic set of postulates for rule contractions (including the recovery postulate). Boella *et al.* [2016] show that the answer to the first question is positive:

PROPOSITION 23. *[Boella* et al., *2016]* $out(R) \circledast (a, x) = (out(R) \cap out(R) \circledast (a, x)) \oplus (a, x)$.

However, $out(R) \ominus (a, x) = out(R) \cap ((out(R) \ominus (a, x)) \oplus (a, \neg x))$ does not hold in general, i.e. it cannot hold for output out_1 or out_3.

3.5   Contraction of Normative Bases

Models of belief contraction and revision are built in order to satisfy the demand for minimal change to keep a theory consistent. As we have seen in section 2.1 above, there are two basic strategies for reaching this goal with the syntactic approach. The first consists in selecting the resulting contraction or revision among maximal consistent subsets of the original. The second consists in making an "incision" in the minimal subsets of the theory or base that derived the sentence to be deleted or revised. We shall now follow the second strategy, calling those minimal subsets "arguments", which are here the base of normative entailments from the set of rules. The construction proceeds basically by making minimal withdrawals from those arguments:

DEFINITION 24. *(Argument)* $X \subseteq L \times L$ is an *argument* for (a, x) based on a normative set N if and only if:
(i) $X \subseteq N$;
(ii) $(a, x) \in out(X)$;
(iii) if $X' \subset X$, then $(a, x) \notin out(X')$.

$Args_N(a, x)$ is the set of arguments for (a, x) based on N.

DEFINITION 25. An incision σ is a choice-like function on $Args_N(a, x)$ to $\wp(L \times L)$ such that:
(i) $\sigma(Args_N(a, x)) \subseteq \bigcup Args_N(a, x)$;
(ii) $\sigma(Args_N(a, x)) \cap X \neq \emptyset$, for all $X \in Args_N(a, x)$.

DEFINITION 26. Let N be a normative set and (a, x) a conditional norm. Then, the *contraction* of N by (a, x) is defined as:

$$N -_\sigma (a, x) = N \backslash \sigma(Args_N(a, x)).$$

The *contraction* of a normative set N by a conditional rule (a, x) may also be defined by postulates on a contraction function, as follows.

DEFINITION 27. The contraction of a normative set N by a conditional rule (a, x) is a function $N- : L \times L \longrightarrow \wp(L \times L)$ satisfying the following postulates:

N−1: if $(a, x) \notin out(\emptyset)$, then $(a, x) \notin out(N - (a, x))$ (success)

N−2: $N - (a, x) \subseteq N$ (inclusion)

N−3: if $(b, y) \in N \backslash N - (a, x)$, then there is $N' \subset N$ such that $(a, x) \notin out(N')$, but $(a, x) \in out(N' \cup \{(b, y)\})$ (core-retainment)

N−4: if for all $N' \subseteq N$, $(a, x) \in out(N')$, if and only if $(b, y) \in out(N')$, then $N - (a, x) = N - (b, y)$ (uniformity)

The representation theorem below is easily adapted from Hansson's representation theorem for base contraction (observation 10):

THEOREM 28. $N -_\sigma (a, x) = N - (a, x)$.

3.6 Refinement of Normative Bases

As we have noticed above for output operators stronger than basic output out_2, the following property holds: if $(a, x) \notin out(R) \ominus (a, x)$, then either $(a \wedge b, x) \in out(R) \ominus (a, x)$ or $(a \wedge \neg b, x) \in out(R) \ominus (a, x)$. Hence, in every contraction of a conditional obligation (a, x) from a closed normative set R, based on an underlying logic at least as strong as basic output, the resulting contracted set $out(R) \ominus (a, x)$ will include a "weakened" version of the conditional, that is, either $(a \wedge b, x)$ or $(a \wedge \neg b, x)$. It is possible to specify in the selection function which weakened version shall remain. This was the basic intuition underlying the operator called *refinement* proposed by Maranhão [2001b], which was aimed at modelling the introduction of exceptions to rules by legal interpretation. For instance, given a normative system that delivers absolute prohibition of abortion, $(\top, \neg abort) \in O$, a defence of abortion in the case of an anencephalic foetus would not be a proposal for permitting abortion in any context. Hence, the contraction of $(\top, \neg abort)$ from that system should make reference to that specific exception, which means that in the absence of anencephaly, abortion should remain forbidden in that normative system, in the name of minimal change. That is, $(\neg anenceph, \neg abort)$ should still be derivable from normative system O, while the prohibition should cease to hold in the exceptional case, that is $(anenceph, \neg abort) \notin out(O)$.

By specifying the exception in the selection function, this result follows from the principle of minimality if the normative set is closed and the logic is at least as strong as a basic output. However, for normative bases (not closed sets), deleting $(anenceph, \neg abort)$ from the set of consequences of O would be tantamount to excluding $(\top, \neg abort)$ from normative set O, and therefore $(\neg anenceph, \neg abort)$ would not be derived anymore.

But it is possible to define a refinement as a particular case of a *conservative contraction* [Maranhão, 2009]. That is, it expands the normative set with rules that are entailed by the rule to be contracted, and which include the exceptional factor and its negation in the antecedent.

DEFINITION 29. (*Refinement*) Let $f \in L$, N be a normative system and let $(a, x) \in out(N)$, where out is at least as strong as a basic output. Then, the refinement of N and (a, x) by factor f is $N \otimes^f (a, x) = N^* -_{\theta_{N^*}} (a, x)$ where $N^* = N \cup \{(f \wedge a, x), (\neg f \wedge a, x)\}$ and $(\neg f \wedge b, y) \notin \theta(Args_{N^*}(a, x))$. We call factor f an exception to (a, x) in the resulting refined normative system.

PROPOSITION 30. *The refinement operator satisfies the following success properties:*
$(a, x) \notin N \otimes^f (a, x)$;
$(a, x), (f \wedge a, x) \notin N \otimes^f (a, x)$;
$(\neg f \wedge a, x) \in N \otimes^f (a, x)$.

3.7   Contraction of Combined Normative Bases

As we have seen in section 3.2, the combination of a constitutive set of rules and regulative sets of permissions and obligations may give rise to genuine incoherencies, that is, the delivery of incompatible rulings, even though the sets of obligations and permissions are consistent. This happens when a given input activates definitions in the constitutive set that triggers logically independent rules with conflicting outputs. As we have suggested, restoring coherence would involve deciding between several alternatives that may change the set of constitutive rules, or the set of regulative rules, or both. In this section, we are going to introduce a formal framework for the operation of contracting normative systems that combine sets of constitutive rules (which we shall call a *constitutive set*) and regulative rules (which we shall call a *regulative set*).

For $A \subseteq L$, output operators out_i and out_j, constitutive set C and regulative set R, we shall use the following conventions:

(i) $out_i(C, R, A)$ if $i = j$;

(ii) $out_{ij}(C, R, a)$ denoting $out_{ij}(C, R, \{a\})$;

(iii) $(a, x) \in out_{ij}(C, R)$ if $x \in out_{ij}(C, R, a)$.

We call the pair of normative sets (C, R) the combination of C and R or the combination (C, R).

Below, we build and characterise operators to perform the three kinds of changes in normative systems that combine constitutive and regulative rules. The first operator, called *constitutive contraction*, contracts only the constitutive set. The second operator, called *regulative contraction*, contracts the regulative set. The *combined contraction* operator may contract both in order to delete a norm from the combination of the constitutive and regulative sets.

DEFINITION 31. (*Constitutive contraction*) The *constitutive contraction* of a combination (C, R) by a conditional norm (a, x) is a function $C-_R : L \times L \longrightarrow \wp(L \times L)$ satisfying the following postulates:

C−1: if $(a, x) \notin out_i(\emptyset, R)$, then $(a, x) \notin out_i(C -_R (a, x), R)$ (success)

C−2: $C -_R (a, x) \subseteq C$ (inclusion)

C−3: if $(b, y) \in C \backslash C -_R (a, x)$, then there is $C' \subset C$ such that $(a, x) \notin out_i(C', R), but (a, x) \in out_i(C' \cup \{(b, y)\}, R)$ (core-retainment)

C−4: if for all $C' \subseteq C$ it is the case that $(a, x) \in out_i(C', R)$ if and only if $(b, y) \in out_i(C', R)$, then $C -_R (b, y) = C -_R (a, x)$ (uniformity)

DEFINITION 32. (*Regulative contraction*) The regulative contraction of a combination C, R by a conditional norm (a, x) is a function $R-_C : L \times L \longrightarrow \wp(L \times L)$ satisfying the following postulates:

R−1: if $(a, x) \notin out_i(C, \emptyset)$, then $(a, x) \notin out_i(C, R -_C (a, x))$ (success)

R−2: $R -_C (a, x) \subseteq R$ (inclusion)

R−3: if $(b, y) \in R \backslash R -_C (a, x)$, then there is an $R' \subset R$ such that $(a, x) \notin out_i(C, R')$, but $(a, x) \in out_i(C, R' \cup \{(b, y)\})$ (core-retainment)

R−4: if for all $R' \subseteq R$, $(a, x) \in (C, R')$ if and only if $(b, y) \in out_i(C, R')$, then $R -_C (a, x) = R -_C (b, y)$ (uniformity)

We use the following conventions for the definition of the combined contraction of normative sets:

(i) if $(C, R)-(a, x) = (C^-, R^-)$, then $(C, R)\backslash (C, R)-(a, x) = (C\backslash C^-, R\backslash R^-)$;

(ii) $\bigcup(C, R) = \bigcup\{C, R\}$.

DEFINITION 33. (*Combined contraction*) The *combined contraction* of the combination (C, R) by a conditional norm (a, x) is a function $(C, R)-$: $L \times L \longrightarrow \wp(L \times L) \times \wp(L \times L)$ satisfying the following postulates:

C/R−1: if $(a, x) \notin out_i(\emptyset)$, then $(a, x) \notin out_i((C, R) - (a, x))$ (success)

C/R−2: if $(C, R) - (a, x) = (C^-, R^-)$, then $C^- \subseteq C$ and $R^- \subseteq R$ (inclusion)

C/R−3: if $(b, y) \in \bigcup(C, R)\backslash (C, R)-(a, x)$, then there is a $C' \subseteq C$ and $R' \subseteq R$ such that $(a, x) \notin out(C', R')$, but $(a, x) \in out_i(C' \cup \{(b, y)\}, R')$ or $(a, x) \in out_i(C', R' \cup \{(b, y)\})$ (core-retainment)

C/R−4: if for all $C' \subseteq C$ and $R' \subseteq R$, it is the case that $(a, x) \in out_i(C', R')$ if and only if $(b, y) \in out_i(C', R')$, then $(C, R) - (a, x) = (C, R) - (b, y)$ (uniformity)

Now we will define a general construction for kernel contraction of combined normative sets, from which we may specify constitutive, regulative and combined contraction operators.

DEFINITION 34. (*Combined argument*) A combination (X, Y) is a *combined argument* for (a, x) based on the combination (C, R) of a constitutive set C and a regulative set R if and only if:

(i) $X \subseteq C$;

(ii) $Y \subseteq R$;

(iii) $(a, x) \in out_i(X, Y)$;

(iv) if $X' \subset X$, then $(a, x) \notin out_i(X', Y)$;

(v) if $Y' \subset Y$, then $(a, x) \notin out_i(X, Y')$.

We denote by $Args_{(C,R)}(a, x)$ the set of combined arguments for (a, x) based on (C, R). Now we will define the incision function for choosing rules from the minimal arguments delivering the rule to be excluded.

DEFINITION 35. An *incision* is a choice-like function on $Args_{(C,R)}(a, x)$ to $\wp(L \times L)$ such that:

(i) if $Args_{(C,R)}(a,x) = \{(X_i, Y_i) : i \in I\}$,
   then $\sigma(Args_{(C,R)}(a,x)) \subseteq \bigcup_{i \in I}(X_i \cup Y_i)$;
(ii) $\sigma(Args_{(C,R)}(a,x)) \cap (X_i \cup Y_i) \neq \varnothing$ for every $(X_i, Y_i) \in Args_{(C,R)}(a,x)$.

The general definition encompasses incisions that choose rules from both normative sets at the same time, incisions that choose only regulative rules, and incisions that choose only constitutive rules. The definitions above restrict the incision functions to choosing only constitutive rules or only regulative rules.

DEFINITION 36.
   An incision on $Args_{(C,R)}(a,x)$ is *constitutive* if and only if $\sigma(Args_{(C,R)}(a,x)) \cap R = \emptyset$.

DEFINITION 37.
   An incision on $Args_{(C,R)}(a,x)$ is *regulative* if and only if $\sigma(Args_{(C,R)}(a,x)) \cap C = \emptyset$.

Now we will use a general definition for contraction based on the incision function. Of course, if we use a constitutive incision, the result will be a constitutive contraction. Similarly, if we use a regulative incision, the result will be a regulative contraction.

DEFINITION 38. (*Contraction*) Let (C, R) be a combination of normative sets and (a, x) a conditional norm. Then, the *contraction* of (C, R) by (a, x) based on incision σ is defined as $(C, R) -_\sigma (a, x) = (C^-, R^-)$ where $C^- = C \backslash \sigma(Args_{(C,R)}(a,x))$ and $R^- = R \backslash \sigma(Args_{(C,R)}(a,x))$.

The theorems below show that the postulates for constitutive, regulative and general contraction characterise the respective constructions.

THEOREM 39. *[Maranhão and de Souza, 2018] A contraction of (C, R) by (a, x) based on a constitutive incision σ is a constitutive contraction, that is, $(C, R) -_\sigma (a, x) = (C -_R (a, x), R)$. Moreover, given a constitutive contraction, there is a constitutive incision σ such that $(C, R) -_\sigma (a, x) = (C -_R (a, x), R)$.*

THEOREM 40. *[Maranhão and de Souza, 2018] A contraction of (C, R) by (a, x) based on a regulative incision σ is a regulative contraction, that is, $(C, R) -_\sigma (a, x) = (C, R -_C (a, x))$. Moreover, given a regulative contraction, there is a regulative incision σ such that $(C, R) -_\sigma (a, x) = (C, R -_C (a, x))$.*

THEOREM 41. *[Maranhão and de Souza, 2018]*
$(C, R) -_\sigma (a, x) = (C, R) - (a, x)$.

The contraction operators discussed here do not involve constraints on the choice of incision function that will determine the result of the contraction operation. Therefore, there is no preference for a regulative contraction over a constitutive or combined contraction.

This feature may be illustrated by example 1.4, which was formalised in section 3.2. In that case, a contraction to avoid $sms \land sord \land \neg iord$-incoherent would have the following alternatives for the incisions: $(C, O) -_\sigma (sms \land sord \land \neg iord, \neg acc)$ or $(C, P) -_\sigma (sms \land sord \land \neg iord, acc)$, each of which is determined by any of the following unitary incision functions: $\sigma_1 = \{(sms, dat)\}$, or $\sigma_2 = \{(sms, com)\}$, or $\sigma_3 = \{(data, prop)\}$, or $\sigma_4 = \{(prop \land sord, acc)\}$, or $\sigma_5 = \{(com \land \neg iord, \neg acc)\}$.

The controversy within the Brazilian Superior Court of Justice discussed in section 1.2 involved two of these alternative contractions. The first decision was a constitutive contraction based on σ_1, where the court contended that message exchanges are communications in flux, which demanded a specific order to intercept the conversation.

In turn, the second decision by the Brazilian court was a conservative contraction based on σ_2, contending that message exchanges should not be considered as ongoing communication. The same alternative contraction was chosen by the German court. The underlying reason for these choices was the weight given to the constitutional value of freedom of communication, which is demoted by such access to the content of an individual's mobile phone. The demotion of freedom of communication was considered stronger than the demotion of property rights. Hence, the association of "text messaging" with "stored data" and, therefore, with "property" (instead of its association with "personal communication") coheres with an underlying valuation where property rights are outweighed by public safety concerns. The German decision also involved a concern about the constitutional right of informational autonomy as the core of data protection. According to the court's argumentation, this right was not violated because the data subject could have destroyed the data in her possession.

Notice that both courts decided not to revise the regulative rules, only stipulate the conceptual qualification of text messaging. The contraction of the regulative set would be inadequate. The first alternative contraction, σ_4, would lead to the absence of an explicit authorisation to search property items, while the other alternative contraction, σ_5 would exclude the prohibition to intercept communications. Nevertheless, the court could have considered less intrusive interventions on the set of regulative rules by, for instance, treating the case of text messaging as an exception to search orders on data. That is, in order to reach a coherent normative system in that context (to avoid $sms \land sord \land \neg iord$-incoherence), the court could have refined the set of obligations, which in the model would be represented by a refinement operator ensuring that $(\neg sms \wedge prop \wedge sorder, acc) \in P \otimes^{sms} (prop \wedge sorder, acc)$.

The resulting contraction would then be either constitutive or regulative. However, there can be genuine combined contractions on sets of constitutive and regulative rules. Consider, for instance, a variation on example 1.4, where an order to investigate an individual ($order$) would encompass both a search & seizure procedure and the interception of any communication. We would have the following sets in the normative system:

$C = \{(sms, dat), (data, prop), (sms, com)\}$
$P = \{(com \wedge order, acc), (prop \wedge order, acc)\}$

According to that normative system, police officers are authorised to access the content of the message exchange stored on the cell phone with a general order authorising the investigation of an individual. Now suppose that the legislator derogates from the positive permission to access the content of text messages stored on a mobile phone, or that legal interpretation (judicial or doctrinal) considers such a permission to be unconstitutional for violating the fundamental right to privacy. In that case, a contraction $(C, P) - (sms \wedge order, acc)$ involves choosing from the following incisions:

$\sigma_1 = \{(sms, dat), (com, acc)\}$
$\sigma_2 = \{(dat, prop), (com, acc)\}$
$\sigma_3 = \{(sms, com), (prop, acc)\}$
$\sigma_4 = \{(sms, com), (sms, dat)\}$
$\sigma_5 = \{(sms, com), (dat, prop)\}$
$\sigma_6 = \{(prop, acc), (com, acc)\}$

The contractions based on σ_{1-3} are combined contractions, while those based on σ_{4-5} are constitutive contractions. The contraction based on σ_6 is the only alternative based on regulative contraction. The figure below illustrates incision σ_1, where each dash linking two nodes is a pair, and each node is proposition:

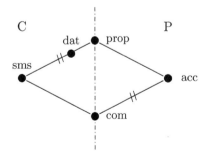

The contraction based on σ_1 is indeed the most reasonable choice. A regulative contraction is clearly undesirable, since it would make any search unauthorised, resulting in a normative system that completely disregards the value of public safety and containing useless definitions. On the other hand, a constitutive contraction based on σ_4 would not address the crucial question in this case, which is how to legally qualify text messaging. In turn, the constitutive contraction σ_5 would make it impossible to search for any document on the premises, in spite of defining that text messaging counts as data. The combined contraction σ_2 would be similar to σ_1, with the effect of favouring freedom of communication over public safety. However, it would also have the undesirable effect of hindering access to any data in a search procedure. For a similar reason, σ_3 would be inadequate with regard to the intuition that the protection of property rights has less weight than the protection of freedom of communication when balancing public safety concerns.

4   Challenges and Open Problems with the AGM Approach

In this final section, we will discuss some open problems and relevant questions that are the object of mainstream research on normative change with the AGM approach.

As we have seen in section 2.2, one of the main challenges and criticisms of the AGM approach is the potential indeterminacy of the result of a contraction, revision or refinement of the normative system, which depends on choices about the proper selection or incision functions to determine the result. This feature is sometimes seen as a disadvantage compared to the syntactic approach, where the syntax of a particular rule is the object of change.

Actually, as we have argued in section 1.1, what we have called the "indeterminacy problem" is not really a defect of the representational model, but is a real feature of legal reasoning about normative change that should be captured by the model itself. As a representation of the activity of legal interpretation, it is particularly interesting to show what are the alternative interpretations for different acts of the derogation, making it clear that a particular interpretation involves choices.

Although there may be some alternative interpretations that are clearly inadequate and would be immediately rejected by a jurist, it is important to investigate the criteria for rejection and represent them in the model. It is also a fact that there may be a doctrinal or judicial controversy concerning the defensible results of a normative change, as illustrated in example 1.4, and we believe that the model should be able to express these different available choices as an adequate representation of legal reasoning. So we see the indeterminacy reflected in the model as an advantage of the AGM approach.

However, there is also an *onus* on this model to provide criteria that would reflect the consensual choices (in the sense of consensus on action, not consensus on explicit convention) reached by legal practitioners and jurists on normative change. Hence, one of the main challenges to research on normative change is to find and model criteria for determining rational choices from alternative normative systems resulting from change operations.

When discussing the examples formalised in section 3.7, we provided some reasons for preferring certain incisions over others. The arguments used there to justify the choice of a particular incision were all domain-specific. Nevertheless, the discussion provided at least two important clues for developing more abstract constraints.

The first clue is related to Makinson and van der Torre's discussion on constraints for I/O-logics [Makinson and van der Torre, 2001] suggesting a distinction between rule maximisation (*maxrule*: maximising the preservation of rules in order to satisfy a constraint) and output maximisation (*maxout*: maximising the preservation of outputs in order to satisfy a constraint). The Mobius Strip example is a radical case and may be seen as a contraction. Consider $N = \{(\top, a), (a, b), (b, \neg a)\}$. The contraction $N - (\top, \bot)$ has two possible outcomes: $N_1 = \{(\top, a)\}$ or $N_2 = \{(a, b), (b, \neg a)\}$. While N_1 satisfies *maxout* and fails *maxrule*, N_2 satisfies *maxrule* and fails *maxout*.

Indeed, constitutive contractions tend to favour *maxrule* and sacrifice *maxout*, since intermediary concepts may be connected to different rules. As we have indicated in section 1.1, the network effects problem regarding normative change alerts us that suppressing relevant connections between normative concepts may render regulative rules inapplicable, while deleting regulative rules may change our understanding of some normative concepts. The construction of the contraction operators for combined normative sets in this chapter was based on rule maximisation, but future investigations should try to find reasonable constraints to temper the demand for *maxrule* with the demand for *maxout*.

The second clue is the role of values that drive the choices among possible outcomes of a change function. The positively enacted rules (constitutive and regulative) on which the legal order are built are the outcomes of (legislative or judicial) deliberations on relevant societal values (moral considerations, political goals, fundamental rights). Those societal values inform the interpretation of authoritative decisions in the application of the rules of the normative system when evaluating the legality of actions in particular contexts. Such values may be considered as external to the normative system or as internal to it in the form of constitutional rights and principles. Thus, if one conceives of legal interpretation as a dynamic of normative change, as suggested in section 1.2, then enriching the model with reasoning about balancing values would provide relevant criteria for choosing between the resulting contracted, revised or refined normative systems, a line of research recently pursued by Maranhão [2017a] and Maranhão and Sartor [2019].

If one takes seriously the representation of legal interpretation as normative change, and succeeds in modelling relevant criteria for choosing among possible systems resulting from contractions, revisions and refinements, then argumentation frameworks could be developed to model argumentation by legal doctrine to determine the best interpretation. That is, there could be a model of argumentation about the results of normative change. Such an argumentation process would put forward defeasible arguments about competing goals of legal interpretation (consistency, coherence with underlying political morality, completeness, precision, adherence to positively enacted rules and natural language, etc.).

The incorporation of tools to represent reasoning about values in the model of normative change will inevitably lead to the need to adapt the change functions to non-monotonic logic, including input/output logics where its rules are default (see [Parent, 2011]). There is a fairly dominant trend in legal theory [Alexy, 2003] and in the literature of artificial intelligence & law (see [Bench-Capon and Sartor, 2003], [Prakken et al., 2015] and [Sartor, 2013]) of considering reasoning about values as defeasible, where consideration of additional values in a particular context may defeat reasons for particular actions in a framework of an overall appreciation of those relevant values. Hence, as already mentioned in section 2.2, the AGM methodology should be adapted to systems with underlying logics that are not monotonic, as pursued recently by Zhuang et al. [2016a], Casini and Meyer [2017], and Casini et al. [2018]. Since the addition of new values or considerations related to values may defeat some implications or reasons for action, with the AGM approach such systems will reflect an aspect of the syntactic approach where a "contraction" is obtained by adding rules to the normative set [Maranhão, 2017a]. As argued in sections 1.2 and 1.4, the representation of legal interpretation should involve values, and that aspect may point to incorporating methods of revision provided by what we have called the preferential approach.

Another important observation concerning applications of the formal models of normative change, emphasised in sections 1.2 and 1.4, is how to adequately represent the two dimensions of normative change: the dimension of validity, which we believe is better reflected by the AGM approach, and the dimension of efficacy, which seems to be better captured by the syntactic approach. Integrating both perspectives would also demand formal comparisons between these approaches. Where the AGM approaches focus on changes in the normative system, it is pertinent to ask whether and how the resulting system can be captured by syntactic modifications of the rules and how alternative interpretations can be represented. Where the syntactic approaches focus on the syntactical representation of the time span of the efficacy of rules and how to block or enable their effects, it is pertinent to ask whether the enabled rules in a given time span can be represented by a temporal dynamic for subsystems of the whole system of valid rules (containing the rules that are enabled at a given period). Efforts to enrich the syntactic representation of rules within the AGM approach with, for instance, time labels [Tamargo et al., 2017], are also important for modelling reasoning that closely reflects real-life examples of the complex interaction between the period of a rule's efficacy and the time span of its validity in the legal system.

There are also conceptual and formal results to be pursued by researchers working on the AGM approach. For instance, there are still no formal characterisations of revision and refinement for changing combined normative sets. It is also relevant to explore constructions of revision from contraction and vice versa for some input/output logics where the Harper and Levi Identities would not hold (see section 3.4). A general theory of revision functions on different sorts of architectures of input/output logics (combinations of normative sets within the input/output logics framework) would also be a relevant theoretical achievement to ground future research of applications that explore particular architectures [Boella and van der Torre, 2006a; Maranhão and Sartor, 2019] for more complex architectures).

The constructions discussed in this chapter were based on original input/output logics (simple-minded, basic, reusable and basic reusable) introduced by Makinson and van der Torre [2000]. It would be interesting to apply the AGM approach to input/output logics with constraints [Makinson and van der Torre, 2001] and other variants [Parent and van der Torre, 2017; Parent and van der Torre, 2018].

Acknowledgments

Leendert van der Torre acknowledges financial support from the Fonds National de la Recherche Luxembourg (INTER/Mobility/19/13995684/DLAl/van der Torre). Giovanni Casini has been supported by TAILOR, a project funded by EU Horizon 2020 research and innovation programme under GA No 952215.

BIBLIOGRAPHY

[Aarnio, 1977] Aulis Aarnio. *On Legal Reasoning*. Turun Yliopisto, 1977.

[Alchourrón and Bulygin, 1971] Carlos E Alchourrón and Eugenio Bulygin. *Normative Systems*. Springer, 1971.

[Alchourrón and Makinson, 1981] Carlos E. Alchourrón and David Makinson. *Hierarchies of Regulations and their Logic*, pages 125–148. Springer Netherlands, 1981.

[Alchourrón and Makinson, 1982] Carlos E. Alchourrón and David Makinson. On the logic of theory change: Contraction functions and their associated revision functions. *Theoria*, 48:14–37, 1982.

[Alchourrón et al., 1985] Carlos E. Alchourrón, Peter Gärdenfors, and David Makinson. On the logic of theory change: Partial meet contraction and revision functions. *Journal of Symbolic Logic*, 50:510–530, 1985.

[Alchourrón, 1969] Carlos E Alchourrón. Logic of Norms and Logic of Normative Propositions. *Logique et analyse*, 12:242–268, 1969.

[Alchourrón, 1996] Carlos E. Alchourrón. Detachment and Defeasibility in Deontic Logic. *Studia Logica*, 57:5–18, 1996.

[Alexy, 2000] Robert Alexy. On the structure of legal principles. *Ratio Jurix*, 13:294–304, 2000.

[Alexy, 2003] Robert Alexy. Constitutional Rights, Balancing, and Rationality. *Ratio Juris*, 16:131–140, 2003.

[Amaya, 2015] Amalia Amaya. *The Tapestry of Reason: an inquiry into the nature of coherence and its role in legal argument*. Hart Publishing, 2015.

[Barak, 2005] Aharon Barak. *Purposive Interpretation in Law*. Princeton University Press, 2005.

[Bench-Capon and Sartor, 2003] Trevor J. M. Bench-Capon and Giovanni Sartor. A model of legal reasoning with cases incorporating theories and values. *Artificial Intelligence*, 150:97–142, 2003.

[Berman and Hafner, 1993] Donald H. Berman and Carole D. Hafner. Representing teleological structure in case-based reasoning: The missing link. In *Proceedings of the Fourth International Conference on Artificial Intelligence and Law (ICAIL)*, pages 50–9. ACM, 1993.

[Bobbio, 1971] Norberto Bobbio. Le bon législateur. *Logique & Analyse*, 14(53-54):243–249, 1971.

[Boella and van der Torre, 2006a] Guido Boella and Leendert van der Torre. A Logical Architecture of a Normative System. In *Deontic Logic and Artificial Normative Systems - DEON 2006*, pages 24–35. Springer, 2006.

[Boella and van der Torre, 2006b] Guido Boella and Leendert van der Torre. A logical architecture of a normative system. In *Deontic Logic and Artificial Normative Systems - DEON 2006*, pages 24–35. Springer, 2006.

[Boella et al., 2010] Guido Boella, Guido Governatori, Antonino Rotolo, and Leendert van der Torre. Lex minus dixit quam voluit, lex magis dixit quam voluit: A formal study on legal compliance and interpretation. In *AICOL-I/IVR-XXIV'09 Proceedings of the 2009 international conference on AI approaches to the complexity of legal systems: complex systems, the semantic web, ontologies, argumentation, and dialogue*, pages 162–183. Springer, 2010.

[Boella et al., 2016] Guido Boella, Gabriella Pigozzi, and Leendert van der Torre. AGM contraction and revision of rules. *Journal of Logic, Language and Information*, 25(3-4):273–297, 2016.

[Casini and Meyer, 2017] Giovanni Casini and Thomas A. Meyer. Belief change in a preferential non-monotonic framework. In *Proceedings of the Twenty-Sixth International Joint Conference on Artificial Intelligence, IJCAI 2017, Melbourne, Australia, August 19-25, 2017*, pages 929–935, 2017.

[Casini *et al.*, 2018] Giovanni Casini, Eduardo Fermé, Thomas Meyer, and Ivan Varzinczak. A semantic perspective on belief change in a preferential non-monotonic framework. In *Principles of Knowledge Representation and Reasoning: Proceedings of the Sixteenth International Conference, KR 2018, Tempe, Arizona, 30 October - 2 November 2018.*, pages 220–229, 2018.

[Delgrande and Peppas, 2015] James P. Delgrande and Pavlos Peppas. Belief revision in Horn theories. *Art. Int.*, 218:1 – 22, 2015.

[Dickson, 2016] Julie Dickson. Interpretation and Coherence in Legal Reasoning. In Edward N Zalta, editor, *The Stanford Encyclopedia of Philosophy*. Metaphysics Research Lab, Stanford University, 2016.

[Dworkin, 1986] Ronald M Dworkin. *Law's Empire*. Kermode, 1986.

[Fermé and Hansson, 2018] Eduardo L. Fermé and Sven O. Hansson. *Belief Change - Introduction and Overview*. Springer Briefs in Intelligent Systems. Springer, 2018.

[Fermé, 1998] Eduardo L. Fermé. On the logic of theory change: Contraction without recovery. *Journal of Logic, Language and Information*, 7(2):127–137, Apr 1998.

[Fuller, 1958] Lon L Fuller. Positivism and Fidelity to Law - A Reply to Professor Hart. *Harvard Law Review*, 71:630–672, 1958.

[Gärdenfors and Rott, 1995] Peter Gärdenfors and Hans Rott. Belief revision. In C.J. Hogger D.M. Gabbay and J.A. Robinson, editors, *Handbook of Logic in Artificial Intelligence and Logic Programming. Volume IV: Epistemic and Temporal Reaoning*, pages 35–132. Oxford University Press, 1995.

[Gärdenfors, 1988] Peter Gärdenfors. *Knowledge in Flux: Modeling the Dynamics of Epistemic States*. MIT Press, 1988.

[Governatori and Rotolo, 2010] Guido Governatori and Antonino Rotolo. Changing legal systems: legal abrogations and annulments in defeasible logic. *Logic Journal of IGPL*, 18(1):157–194, 2010.

[Governatori *et al.*, 2013] Guido Governatori, Antonino Rotolo, Francesco Olivieri, and Simone Scannapieco. Legal contractions: a logical analysis. In Enrico Francesconi and Bart Verheij, editors, *ICAIL*, pages 63–72. ACM, 2013.

[Governatori *et al.*, 2019] Guido Governatori, Francesco Olivieri, Matteo Cristani, and Simone Scannapieco. Revision of defeasible preferences. *Int. J. Approx. Reason.*, 104:205–230, 2019.

[Grossi *et al.*, 2008] Davide Grossi, John-Jules Ch. Meyer, and Frank Dignum. The many faces of counts-as: A formal analysis of constitutive rules. *Journal of Applied Logic*, 6:192–217, 2008.

[Grove, 1988] Adam Grove. Two modellings for theory change. *Journal of Philosophical Logic*, 17:157–170, 1988.

[Hansson, 1993] Sven O. Hansson. Reversing the Levi identity. *Journal of Philosophical Logic*, 22:637–669, 1993.

[Hansson, 1999] Sven O. Hansson. *A Textbook of Belief Dynamics: Theory Change and Database Updating*. Kluwer Academic Publishers, 1999.

[Katsuno and Mendelzon, 1991a] Hirofumi Katsuno and Alberto O. Mendelzon. On the difference between updating a knowledge base and revising it. In *Proceedings of the Second International Conference on Principles of Knowledge Representation and Reasoning, KR'91*, pages 387–394, San Francisco, CA, USA, 1991. Morgan Kaufmann Publishers Inc.

[Katsuno and Mendelzon, 1991b] Hirofumi Katsuno and Alberto O. Mendelzon. Propositional knowledge base revision and minimal change. *Artificial Intelligence*, 3(52):263–294, 1991.

[Kelsen, 1973] Hans Kelsen. Derogation. In *Essays in Legal and Moral Philosophy*, pages 261–275. Springer Netherlands, 1973.

[Konieczny and Perez, 2002] Sebastien Konieczny and Ramon Pino Perez. Merging information under constraints: A logical framework. *Journal of Logic and Computation*, 12(5):773–808, 10 2002.

[Levi, 1977] Isaac Levi. Subjunctives, dispositions and chances. *Synthese*, 34:423–455, 1977.

[Makinson and van der Torre, 2000] David Makinson and Leendert van der Torre. Input-output logics. *Journal of Philosophical Logic*, 29:383–408, 2000.

[Makinson and van der Torre, 2001] David Makinson and Leendert van der Torre. Constraints for input-output logics. *Journal of Philosophical Logic*, 30(2):155–185, 2001.

[Makinson and van der Torre, 2003a] David Makinson and Leendert van der Torre. Permissions from an input-output perspective. *Journal of Philosophical Logic*, 32(4):391–416, 2003.

[Makinson and van der Torre, 2003b] David Makinson and Leendert van der Torre. What is input/output logic? In L'owe Benedikt, Malzkom Wolfgang, and R'asch Thoralf, editors, *Foundations of the Formal Sciences II: Applications of Mathematical Logic in Philosophy and Linguistics*, pages 163–174. Kluwer, Dordrecht, 2003.

[Makinson, 1987] David Makinson. On the status of the postulate of recovery in the logic of theory change. *Journal of Philosophical Logic*, 16(4):383–394, Nov 1987.

[Maranhão and de Souza, 2018] Juliano Maranhão and Edelcio de Souza. Contraction of combined normative sets. In *Deontic Logic and Normative Systems: 14th International Conference, DEON 2018*, pages 247–261. Springer, 2018.

[Maranhão and Sartor, 2019] Juliano Maranhão and Giovanni Sartor. Value assessment and revision in legal interpretation. In *Proceedings of the 17th International Conference on Artificial Intelligence and Law, ICAIL 2019*, pages 219–223, New York, New York, USA, jun 2019. Association for Computing Machinery, Inc.

[Maranhão, 2001a] Juliano Maranhão. Refinement. A tool to deal with inconsistencies. In *Proc. of the 8th ICAIL*, pages 52–59, 2001.

[Maranhao, 2001b] Juliano Maranhao. Some Operators for Refinement of Normative Systems. In *Proceedings of Jurix 2001*, pages 103–115. IOS Press, 2001.

[Maranhão, 2006] Juliano Maranhão. Why was Alchourrón afraid of snakes? *Analisis Filosofico*, XXVI(1):62–92, 2006.

[Maranhão, 2009] Juliano Maranhão. Conservative Contraction. In *The many sides of logic*, pages 465–479. College Publications, 2009.

[Maranhão, 2017a] Juliano Maranhão. A logical architecture for dynamic legal interpretation. In *Proceedings of the Eight International Conference on AI and Law ICAIL '17,*, pages 129–38. ACM Press, 2017.

[Maranhao, 2017b] Juliano Maranhao. *Positivismo jurídico lógico-incluyente*. Marcial Pons, 2017.

[Marmor, 2005] Andrei Marmor. *Interpretation and Legal theory*. Hart, 2005.

[Navarro and Rodriguez, 2014] Pablo E Navarro and Jorge L Rodriguez. *Deontic Logic and Legal Systems*. Cambridge University Press, 2014.

[Parent and van der Torre, 2013] Xavier Parent and Leendert van der Torre. *Input/output logics*. College Publications, London, 2013.

[Parent and van der Torre, 2017] Xavier Parent and Leendert van der Torre. The pragmatic oddity in norm-based deontic logics. In *Proceedings of the International Conference on Artificial Intelligence and Law*, pages 169–178. Association for Computing Machinery, June 2017.

[Parent and van der Torre, 2018] Xavier Parent and Leendert van der Torre. - input/output logics with a consistency check. In *Proceedings of the 14th International Conference on Deontic Logic and Normative Systems (DEON2018)*, 2018.

[Parent, 2011] Xavier Parent. Moral particularism in the light of deontic logic. *Artificial Intelligence and Law*, 19:75–98, 2011.

[Peczenik, 1989] Aleksander Peczenik. *On Law and Reason*. Kluwer, 1989.

[Prakken et al., 2015] Henry Prakken, Adam Wyner, Trevor R. Bench-Capon, and Katie Atkinson. A formalisation of argumentation schemes for legal case-based reasoning in ASPIC+. *Journal of Logic and Computation*, 25:1141–1166, 2015.

[Raz, 1979] Joseph Raz. Legal Positivism and the Sources of Law. In *The Authority of Law*, pages 37–52. Oxford University Press, 1979.

[Raz, 1985] Joseph Raz. Authority, law and morality. *The Monist*, 68(3):295–324, jul 1985.

[Raz, 2009] Joseph Raz. *Authority and Interpretation*. Oxford University Press, 2009.

[Ribeiro *et al.*, 2018] Jandson S. Ribeiro, Abhaya Nayak, and Renata Wassermann. Towards belief contraction without compactness. In *Principles of Knowledge Representation and Reasoning: Proceedings of the Sixteenth International Conference, KR 2018, Tempe, Arizona, 30 October - 2 November 2018.*, pages 287–296, 2018.

[Rotolo, 2001] Antonino Rotolo. *Identità e somiglianza: saggio sul pensiero analogico nel diritto*. Clueb, 2001.

[Rott, 2000] Hans Rott. Two dogmas of belief revision. *Journal of Philosophy*, 97(9):503–522, 2000.

[Sartor, 2007] Giovanni Sartor. The Nature of Legal Concepts: Inferential Nodes or Ontological Categories. In Gianmaria Ajani, Ginevra Peruginelli, Giovanni Sartor, and Daniela Tiscornia, editors, *Proceeding of the Conference on "Approaching the Multilanguage Complexity of European Law: Methodologies in Comparison"*. European Press Academic Publishing, 2007.

[Sartor, 2013] Giovanni Sartor. The logic of proportionality: Reasoning with non-numerical magnitudes. *German Law Journal*, pages 1419–57, 2013.

[Sartor, 2018] Giovanni Sartor. Consistency in balancing: from value assessments to factor-based rules. In D. Duarte and S. Sampaio, editors, *Proportionality in Law: An Analytical Perspective*, pages 121–36. Springer, 2018.

[Searle, 1995] John R Searle. *The Construction of Social Reality*. Free Press, 1995.

[Solum, 2010] Lawrence B. Solum. The interpretation-construction distinction. *Constitutional Commentary*, 27:95–118, 2010.

[Stolpe, 2010] Audun Stolpe. Norm-system revision: theory and application. *Artificial Intelligence and Law*, 18:247–283, 2010.

[Tamargo *et al.*, 2017] Luciano H. Tamargo, Diego C. Martinez, Antonino Rotolo, and Guido Governatori. Temporalised belief revision in the law. In *Frontiers in Artificial Intelligence and Applications*, volume 302, pages 49–58. IOS Press, 2017.

[Tamargo *et al.*, 2021] Luciano H. Tamargo, Diego C. Martínez, Antonino Rotolo, and Guido Governatori. Time, defeasible logic and belief revision: Pathways to legal dynamics. *FLAP*, 8(4):993–1022, 2021.

[Van Ditmarsch and Kooi, 2006] Hans Van Ditmarsch and Barteld Kooi. The secret of my success. *Synthese*, 151(2):201–232, Jul 2006.

[Wróblewski, 1985] Jerzy Wróblewski. Legal Language and Legal Interpretation. *Law and Philosophy*, 4:239–255, 1985.

[Wróblewski, 1992] Jerzy Wróblewski. *The Judicial Application of Law*. Kluwer, 1992.

[Zhuang *et al.*, 2016a] Zhiqiang Zhuang, James P. Delgrande, Abhaya C. Nayak, and Abdul Sattar. Reconsidering AGM-style belief revision in the context of logic programs. In *ECAI 2016 - 22nd European Conference on Artificial Intelligence, 29 August-2 September 2016, The Hague, The Netherlands - Including Prestigious Applications of Artificial Intelligence (PAIS 2016)*, pages 671–679, 2016.

[Zhuang *et al.*, 2016b] Zhiqiang Zhuang, Zhe Wang, Kewen Wang, and Guilin Qi. DL-lite contraction and revision. *J. Artif. Intell. Res.*, 56:329–378, 2016.

Juliano S.A. Maranhão
University of São Paulo,
Law School,
São Paulo, Brazil.
Email: julianomaranhao@usp.br

Giovanni Casini
ISTI-CNR,
Pisa, Italy.
University of Cape Town,
Cape Town, South Africa.
Email: giovanni.casini@isti.cnr.it

Gabriella Pigozzi
LAMSADE,
Université Paris-Dauphine,
PSL Research University,
75016 Paris, France.
Email: gabriella.pigozzi@dauphine.fr

Leendert van der Torre
University of Luxembourg,
Computer Science and Communication Research Unit,
Luxembourg.
Email: leon.vandertorre@uni.lu

8

Time, Defeasible Logic and Belief Revision: Pathways to Legal Dynamics

LUCIANO H. TAMARGO
DIEGO C. MARTINEZ
ANTONINO ROTOLO
GUIDO GOVERNATORI

ABSTRACT. In order to properly model norm change in the law, temporal aspects of legal dynamics must be considered. Since there exist several time-based features of law that should be studied, we discuss two interesting approaches: one based on defeasible logic and the other based on belief revision. Each of these makes use of one of the two classic forms of reasoning about time: point-based and interval-based. Both formalisms provide the necessary logical infrastructure to address the characterization of complex behaviour of legal dynamics.

1 Introduction and Background

One peculiar feature of many normative systems, such as the law, is that it necessarily takes the form of a dynamic normative system [Kelsen, 1991; Hart, 1994]. Despite the importance of norm-change mechanisms, the logical investigation of legal dynamics is still relatively underdeveloped. However, recent contributions exist and this section is devoted to a brief sketch of this rapidly evolving literature.

Alchourrón and Makinson were the first to logically study the changes of a *legal code* [Alchourrón and Makinson, 1981; Alchourrón and Makinson, 1982; Alchourrón and Bulygin, 1981]. The addition of a new norm n causes an enlargement of the code, consisting of the new norm plus all the regulations that can be derived from n. Alchourrón and Makinson distinguish two other types of change. When the new norm is incoherent with the existing ones, we have an *amendment* of the code: in order to coherently add the new regulation, we need to reject those norms that conflict with n. Finally, *derogation* is the elimination of a norm n together with whatever part of the legal code that implies n.

Alchourrón, Gärdenfors and Makinson [1985] inspired by the works above proposed the so called general AGM framework for belief revision. This area has been proved to be a very fertile one and the phenomenon of revision of logical theories has been thoroughly investigated. As is well-known, the AGM framework distinguishes three types of change operation over theories. Contraction is an operation that removes a specified sentence ϕ from a given theory Γ (a logically closed set of sentences) in such a way as Γ is set aside in favour of another theory Γ_ϕ^- which is a subset of Γ not containing ϕ. Expansion operation adds a given sentence ϕ to Γ so that the resulting theory Γ_ϕ^+ is the smallest logically closed set that contains both Γ and ϕ. Revision operation adds ϕ to Γ but it is ensured that the resulting theory Γ_ϕ^* be consistent [Alchourrón et al., 1985]. Alchourrón, Gärdenfors and Makinson argued that, when Γ is a code of legal norms, contraction corresponds to norm derogation (norm removal) and revision to norm amendment.

It is then natural to ask if belief revision offers a satisfactory framework for the problem of norm revision in the law. Some of the AGM axioms seem to be rational requirements in a legal context, whereas they have been criticised when imposed on belief change operators. An example is the *success* postulate, requiring that a new input must always be accepted in the belief set. It is reasonable to impose such a requirement when we wish to enforce a new norm or obligation. However, it gives rise to irrational behaviours when imposed to a belief set, as observed in [Gabbay et al., 2003].

The AGM operation of contraction is perhaps the most controversial one, due to some postulates such as recovery [Governatori and Rotolo, 2010a; Wheeler and Alberti, 2011], and to elusive nature of legal changes such as derogations and repeals, which are all meant to contract legal effects but in remarkably different ways [Governatori and Rotolo, 2010a]. Standard AGM framework is of little help here: it has the advantage of being very abstract—it works with theories consisting of simple logical assertions—but precisely for this reason it is more suitable to capture the dynamics of obligations and permissions rather than the one of legal norms.

Difficulties behind AGM have been considered and some research has been carried out to reframe AGM ideas within reasonably richer rule-based logical systems able to capture the distinction between norms and legal effects [Stolpe, 2010; Rotolo, 2010]. However, these attempts suffer from some drawbacks: they fail to handle reasoning on deontic effects and are based on a very simple representation of legal systems.

In fact, it is hard in AGM to represent how the same set of legal effects can be contracted in many different ways, depending on how norms are changed. These difficulties have been addressed in logical frameworks combining AGM ideas with richer rule-based logical systems, such as standard or Defeasible Logic [Rotolo, 2010; Governatori et al., 2013] or Input/Output Logic [Boella et al., 2009; Boella et al., 2016; Stolpe, 2010]. [Wheeler and Alberti, 2011] suggested a different route, i.e., employing in the law existing techniques—such as iterated belief change, two-dimensional belief change, belief bases, and weakened contraction—that can obviate problems identified in [Governatori and Rotolo, 2010a] for standard AGM.

In general, any comprehensive logical model of norm change in the law has to take care of the following aspects:

1. the law usually regulates its own changes by setting specific norms whose peculiar objective is to change the system by stating what and how other existing norms should be modified; for instance, in most countries the Constitution states that only the Congress have powers to lay and regulate taxes. Even more, the Constitution states, by a norm, how to change or amend its own body of norms.

2. since legal modifications are derived from these peculiar norms, they can be in conflict and so are defeasible; for instance, some US states requires non-english foreign driver licenses to be accompanied by the International Drivers Permit. However, in 1989 US and Canada agreed to recognize each other's licenses, even french-written licenses. Hence, norms are contradictory regarding the documentation that a french-canadian driver must show to authorities.

3. legal norms are qualified by temporal properties, such as the time when the norm comes into existence and belongs to the legal system, the time when the norm is in force, the time when the norm produces legal effects, and the time when the normative effects hold. For instance, Belarus established that several laws passed before 1996 ceased to be enforced in the exact moment the President issues the new Constitution. In the United States, the 18th Amendment prohibiting the manufacture of liquor was passed in 1919 and repealed later in 1933. The end of this prohibition was established in turn by another Amendment (the 21st) that also establishes that this amendment *"shall be inoperative unless it shall have been ratified (...) within seven years from the date of the submission"*.

To sum up, AGM-like frameworks have the advantage of being very abstract but work with theories consisting of simple logical assertions. For this reason, it is perhaps suitable to capture the dynamics of obligations and permissions, not of norms: the former ones are just possible effects of the application of norms and their dynamics do not necessarily require to remove or revise norms, but correspond in most cases to instances of the notion of *norm defeasibility* [Governatori and Rotolo, 2010a].

Addressing the above aspects has triggered new research lines in recent years, which break down in the following two approaches:

- Normative dynamics can be modelled by combining logical systems for temporal and defeasible reasoning: previous works [Governatori *et al.*, 2005; Governatori *et al.*, 2007; Governatori and Rotolo, 2010a] have proposed to combine Defeasible Logic with some basic forms of temporal logics;

- Another route is rather to enrich belief revision techniques by adding several temporal dimensions: this has been done in works such as [Tamargo *et al.*, 2017; Tamargo *et al.*, 2019].

The layout of the chapter is as follows. Section 2 introduces the importance of time in legal norms and shows an example to motivate some ideas in the area of legal dynamics. Section 3 summarizes the first approach mentioned above, in which it is described how the Defeasible Logic was extended with temporal parameters to allow for reasoning about the times specified inside norms, and it is described how consider a legal system as a time-series of its versions, where each version is obtained from previous versions by some norm changes. Section 4 summarizes the second approach mentioned above, in which it is proposed a belief revision operator that considers time interval in the revision process. Finally, in Section 5 conclusions are offered and ideas for future work are given.

2   Preamble: Why Does Time Matter?

Legal norms are qualified by temporal properties, such as the time when the norm comes into existence and belongs to the legal system or the time when the norm is in force. Suppose that a municipality establishes that all taxis licensed since 2015 must be all-yellow, and a couple of years later the city adds a new rule establishing that all taxis with license starting in 2018 must be all-black. Hence, the yellow-taxi rule only applies for passenger cars with a valid license from 2015 to 2017. However, this is true only years later, after the introduction of the black-taxi rule.

Since all these properties can be relevant when legal systems change, [Governatori and Rotolo, 2010b] argued that failing to consider the temporal aspects of legal dynamics poses a serious limit to correctly model norm change in the law.

2.1   The Problem and a Motivating Example

As we have briefly mentioned above, belief revision, and specifically the AGM paradigm, has been advocated to be an elegant and abstract model for legal change. Its has been, however, argued that standard belief techniques do not capture the following aspects of the law [Governatori and Rotolo, 2010b]:

1. the law regulates its own changes by issuing norms stating what and how other norms should be modified;

2. legal modifications can be in conflict and so are defeasible;

3. legal norms are qualified by temporal properties, e.g., the time when the norm is in force.

The general temporal model, as proposed in [Governatori and Rotolo, 2010b] assumes that all legal norms are qualified by different temporal parameters:

- the time when the norm comes into existence and belongs to the legal system,

- the time when the norm is in force,

- the time when the norm produces legal effects (it is applicable), and

- the time when the normative effects (conclusions) hold.

Indeed, it is common legislative practice that, once a legal provision is enacted (for example, the Italian 2018 budget law was enacted on 23 December 2017), its force can for instance be postponed to a subsequent time (for example, the Italian 2018 budget law was in force since 1 January 2018). Similarly, a part of a certain provision, which is in force since a certain time t, can be effective (i.e., can be applied) since a different time t' (for example, the Italian 2018 budget law, which was in force since 1 January 2018, at art. 1, par. 253 states that par. 252 will be applicable since 1 January 2019), or any provision can produce effects that hold retroactively (for example, art. 1 of Italian 2018 budget law, par. 629, states that certain tax effects cover cases since December 2017).

In [Tamargo *et al.*, 2019], for example, the authors concentrate on issue 3 in the list above, i.e., how to integrate belief revision with time in the law. As regards issue 2, in that article, the authors do not work directly on rule-based defeasible reasoning, but they define a revision operator that may remove rules when needed or adapt intervals of time when contradictory norms are introduced in the system: for instance, if n is effective from 2001 to 2008 and a contradictory norm n' is added at 2006, we know that n is still effective from 2001 to 2005.

Let us now present a concrete example that serves to motivate the main ideas proposed in [Tamargo *et al.*, 2019], an approach that we will recall in Section 4. It involves information and rules referring to intervals of time in which some taxes applies.

EXAMPLE 1 *Consider the following pieces of information regarding a legislative attempt to ease tax pressure for people that have been unemployed.*

(a) A citizen was unemployed from 1980 to 1985.

(b) If unemployed from 1980 to 1983, then a tax exemption applies from 1984 to 1986, in order to increase individual savings.

(c) New authorities in government revoke tax exemption for years 1985 and 1986.

(d) Tax exemption reinstated for the year 1985 due to agreements with labor unions.

However, later on the legislator approved a new provision establishing that finally there is no tax-exemption for all citizens for the years 1985 and 1986.

Here some rules are produced and, as it happens in legislative bodies, norms change later according to the political and economical context. Rule (a) provides time-bounded information: only between 1980 and 1985 the status of being unemployed holds for a given citizen. Rule (b) states that if some property (unemployed) holds between 1980 and 1983, then other property (tax exemption) holds between 1984 and 1986. Rule (c) establishes that this is no longer valid for a certain interval of time. This means that, from now on, rule (b) of tax exemption should not be applied in its original text. In other words, the intervals of rule (b) are *revised* according to new political positions. Finally, rules are revised again as a consequence of labor unions, only to be revoked later. In this example the general rule of tax-exemption is revised several times. This revision is actually about the moments in which this benefit can be applied. In fact, rule (c) solely demands a revision of the interval for tax exemption. Hence, it cannot be the case that there is a rule in the normative system that entails a tax exemption for 1985 and 1986. From (c) and (b), it can be concluded that the benefit is only applied to 1984. Therefore, (b) should be not used anymore and a new rule for 1984 should be introduced.

3 Defeasible Logic with Time for Modelling Legal Dynamics

Before illustrating in Section 4 how belief revision can be integrated by temporal reasoning, we recall in this section the other approach that we mentioned in the introduction.

In [Governatori *et al.*, 2005; Governatori *et al.*, 2007; Governatori and Rotolo, 2010a] Defeasible Logic was extended with temporal parameters. In particular the authors *temporalised* propositional Defeasible Logic. This means that a temporal parameter is attached to the atomic elements of the logic, i.e., to the atomic propositions. For the logic it is assumed a discrete totally ordered set of instants of time $\mathcal{T} = \{t_0, t_1, t_2, \dots\}$. Based on this we can introduce the notion of *temporalised literals*. Thus if l is a plain literal, i.e., $l \in \mathrm{PlainLit}$, and $t \in \mathcal{T}$ then l^t is a temporalised literals. The intuitive interpretation of l^t is that l is true (or holds) at time t. Lit denotes the set of temporalised literals. Finally, given a time instant t and $y \in \{pers, tran\}$ we call the combination of (t, y) *duration specification*, and literals labelled with a duration specification are called *duration literals*. The labels *pers* and *tran* denotes the quality of being *transient* or *persistent*. A duration literal has the form $l^{(t,y)}$. We denote the set of duration literals DurLit. The reasoning mechanism occurs on a set of *rules*, which are supposed to represent legal rules. The signature of rules is

$$(1) \qquad\qquad \mathrm{Rule} \colon 2^{\mathrm{Lit}} \times \mathrm{DurLit}$$

this means that a rule has the following form

$$(2) \qquad\qquad r \colon a_1^{t_1}, \dots, a_n^{t_n} \hookrightarrow c^{(t,y)}$$

where $y \in \{tran, pers\}$ and hence the conclusion of the rule may be *transient* or *persistent*.

The idea behind the distinction between a transient and persistent conclusion is whether the conclusion is guaranteed to hold for a single instant or it continues to hold until it is terminated. This is particular relevant for legal rules, since their conclusions are for example obligations (or, in general deontic effects), and obligations, once triggered, remain in force until they are complied with, violated, or explicitly terminated. Accordingly we can use the duration specification $(t, tran)$ to indicate that an obligation is in force at a specific time t, and must be fulfilled at that time, while the duration specification $(t, pers)$ establishes that a legal effect enters in force at time t.

The inference mechanism extends that of Defeasible Logic taking into account the temporal and durations specification. As in article [Antoniou *et al.*, 2001], we equate arguments with rules, thus this is the same as saying that there is a (defeasible) rule such that all the elements in its antecedent are provable and the conclusion is $p^{(t',y)}$. To assert that p holds at time t we have the following steps:

1. Give an argument for p at time t';

2. Evaluate all counterarguments against it. Here, we have a few cases:

    (a) If the duration specification of p is $(t, tran)$ $(t' = t)$, then, the counterargument must be for the same time t given that p is ensured to hold only for t.

    (b) If the duration specification of p is $(t', pers)$, then t' can precede t and we can 'carry' over the conclusion from previous times. In this case, the counterarguments we have to consider are all rules whose conclusion has a duration specification (t'', z) such that $t' \leq t'' \leq t$.

3. Rebut the counterarguments. This is the same as the corresponding step of basic defeasible logic, the only thing to pay attention to is that when we rebut with a stronger argument, the stronger argument should have t'' in the duration specification of the conclusion.

The general idea of the conditions outline above is that it is possible to assert that something holds at time t, because it did hold at time t', $t' < t$, by persistence, but there must be no reasons to terminate it. Thus new information defeats previous one.

3.1   From Rules to Meta-Rules

The temporal Defeasible Logic just presented allows for reasoning about the times specified inside norms, but it is not able to capture the natural evolution of legal systems, where new norms are issued, and existing norms are revised or derogated. To obviate this problem [Governatori and Rotolo, 2010a] proposes to consider a legal system as a time-series of its versions, where each version is obtained from previous versions by some norm changes, e.g., norms entering in the legal system, modification of existing norms, repeals of existing norms, ... This means that we can represent a legal system LS as a sequence

$$(3) \qquad\qquad LS(t_1), LS(t_2), \ldots, LS(t_j)$$

where each $LS(t_i)$ is the snapshot of the rules (norms) in the legal system at time t_i. Graphically it can be represented by the picture in Figure 1.

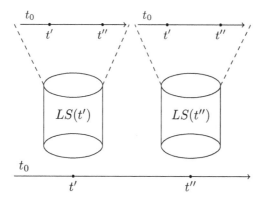

Figure 1. Legal System at t' and t''

A *rule* is a relation between a set of premises (conditions of applicability of the rule) and a conclusion. The admissible conclusions are either literals or rules themselves; in addition the conclusions and the premises will be qualified with the time when they hold. Two classes of rules can be considered: *meta-rules* and *proper rules*. Meta-rules describe the inference mechanism of the institution on which norms are formalised and can be used to establish conditions for the creation and modification of other rules or norms, while proper rules correspond to norms in a normative system. In what follows we will use Rule to denote the set of rules, and MetaRules for the set of meta-rules, i.e., rules whose consequent is a rule.

A *temporalised rule* is either an expression $(r: \bot)^{(t,x)}$ (the void rule) or $(r: \emptyset)^{(t,x)}$ (the empty rule) or $(r: A \hookrightarrow B)^{(t,x)}$, where r is a rule label, A is a (possibly empty) set of temporalised literals, B is a duration literal, $t \in \mathcal{T}$ and $x \in \{tran, pers\}$.

We have to consider two temporal dimensions for norms in a normative system. The first dimension is when the norm is in force in a normative system, and the second is when the norm exists in the normative system from a certain viewpoint. So far temporalised rules capture only one dimension, the time of force. To cover the other dimension we introduce the notion of temporalised rule with viewpoint. A *temporalised rule with viewpoint* is an expression

$$(4) \qquad (r: A \hookrightarrow B)^{(t,x)}@(t', y),$$

where $(r: A \hookrightarrow B)^{(t,x)}$ is a temporalised rule, $t' \in \mathcal{T}$ and $y \in \{tran, pers\}$.

Finally, meta-rules are introduced, that is, rules where the conclusion is not a simple duration literal but a temporalised rule. Thus a *meta-rule* is

305

an expression

$$(5) \qquad (s \colon A \hookrightarrow (r \colon B \hookrightarrow C)^{(t',x)})@(t,y),$$

where $(r \colon B \hookrightarrow C)^{(t',x)}$ is a temporalised rule, $r \neq s$, $t \in \mathcal{T}$ and $y \in \{tran, pers\}$. Notice that meta-rules carry only the viewpoint time (the validity time) but not the "in force" time. The intuition behind this is that meta-rules yield the conditions to modify a legal system. Thus they specify what rules (norms) are in a normative system, at what time the rules are valid, and the content of the rules. Accordingly, these rules must have an indication when they have been inserted in a normative system, but then they are universal (i.e., apply to all instants) within a particular instance of a normative system.

Every temporalised rule is identified by its rule label and its time. Formally we can express this relationship by establishing that every rule label r is a function

$$(6) \qquad r \colon \mathcal{T} \mapsto \text{Rule}.$$

Thus a temporalised rule r^t returns the value/content of the rule 'r' at time t. This construction allows us to uniquely identify rules by their labels[1], and to replace rules by their labels when rules occur inside other rules. In addition there is no risk that a rule includes its label in itself. In the same way a temporalised rule is a function from $\mathcal{T}$ to Rule, we will understand a temporalised rule with viewpoint as a function with the following signature:

$$(7) \qquad \mathcal{T} \mapsto (\mathcal{T} \mapsto \text{Rule}).$$

As we have seen above a legal system LS is a sequence of versions $LS(t_0)$, $LS(t_1), \ldots$. The temporal dimension of *viewpoint* corresponds to a version of the legal system, while the temporal dimension of a *temporalised rule* corresponds to the time-line inside a version. Thus the meaning of an expression $r^{t_v}@t_r$ is that we take the value of the temporalised rule r^{t_v} in $LS(t_r)$. Accordingly, a version of LS is just a repository (set) of norms (implemented as temporal functions).

Accordingly, given a rule r, the expression $r^t@t'$ gives the value of the rule (set of premises and conclusion of the rule) at time t in the repository t'. The content of a void rule, e.g., $(r \colon \bot)^t@t'$ is $\bot$, while for the empty rule the value is the empty set. This means that the void rule has a value

---

[1]We do not need to impose that the function is an injective: while each label should have only one content at any given time, we may have that different labels (rules) have the same content.

for the combination of the temporal parameters, while for the empty rule, the content of the rule does not exist for the given temporal parameters. Another way to look at the difference between the empty rule and the void rule is to consider that a rule is a relationship between a set of premises and a conclusion. For the void rule this relationship is between the empty set of premises and the empty conclusion; thus the rule exists but it does not produce any conclusion. For the empty rule, the relationship is empty, thus there is no rule. Alternatively, we can think of the function corresponding to temporalised rules as a partial function, and the empty rule identifies instants when the rule is not defined.

For a transient fully temporalised literal $l^{(t,x)}@(t', tran)$ the reading is that the validity of l at t is specific to the legal system corresponding to repository associated to t', while $l^{(t,x)}@(t', pers)$ indicates that the validity of l at t is preserved when we move to legal systems after the legal system identified by t'. An expression $r^{(t,tran)}$ sets the value of r at time t and just at that time, while $r^{(t,pers)}$ sets the values of r to a particular instance for all times after t (t included).

We will often identify rules with their labels, and, when unnecessary, we will drop the labels of rules inside meta-rules. Similarly, to simplify the presentation and when possible, we will only include the specification whether an element is persistent or transient only for the elements for which it is relevant for the discussion at hand.

Meta-rules describe the inference mechanism of the institution on which norms are formalised and can be used to establish conditions for the creation and modification of other rules or norms, while proper rules correspond to norms in a normative system. Thus a temporalised rule r^t gives the 'content' of the rule 'r' at time t; in legal terms it tells us that norm r is in force at time t. The expression

$$(8) \qquad (p^{t_p}, q^{t_q} \Rightarrow (p^{t_p} \Rightarrow s^{(t_s,pers)})^{(t_r,pers)})@(t, tran)$$

means that, for the repository at t, if p is true at time t_p and q at time t_q, then $p^{t_p} \Rightarrow s^{(t_s,pers)}$ is in force from time t_r onwards.

A legal system is represented by a temporalised defeasible theory, called *normative theory*, i.e., a structure

$$(9) \qquad (F, R, R^{\text{meta}}, \prec)$$

where F is a finite set of facts (i.e., fully temporalised literals), R is a finite set of rules, R^{meta} is a finite set of meta rules, and $\prec$, the superiority relation over rules is formally defined as $\mathcal{T} \mapsto (\mathcal{T} \mapsto \text{Rule} \times \text{Rule})$ accounting that we can have different instances of the superiority relation depending on the legal systems (external time) and the time when the rules involved in the superiority are evaluated[2].

The inference mechanism with meta-rules is essentially an extension of that of temporal defeasible logic, but it involves more steps. Rules are no longer just given, but they can be derived from meta-rules. Thus, to prove a conclusion x the first thing to do is to see if it is possible to derive a rule r supporting x. But we have to derive such rule at the appropriate time. Here, we want to remember that a rule is a function from time (validity time or version of a legal system) to time (when a rule is in force in a version of a legal system) to the content of the rule (relationship between a set of premises and a conclusion). The basic intuition is that a rule corresponds to a norm, and there could be several modifications of a norm, thus deriving a rule means to derive one of such modifications. As we shall see in the next section a meta-rule (or more generally a set of meta-rules) can be used to encode a modification of a norm. In general it is possible to have multiple (conflicting) modifications of a norm. Accordingly, to derive a rule, we have to check that there are no conflicting modifications[3] or the conflicting modifications are weaker than the current modification. The final consideration is that in this case we have two temporal dimensions, and the persistence applies to both.

3.2   An Example: Modifications on Norm Validity and Existence – Annulment vs. Abrogation

The expression *repeal* is sometimes used to generically denote the operation of norm withdrawal. However, at least two forms of withdrawal are possible: annulment and abrogation.

An *annulment* makes the target norm invalid and removes it from the legal system. Its peculiar effect applies *ex tunc*: annulled norms are prevented to produce all their legal effects, independently of when they are obtained. Annulments typically operate when the grounds (another norm) for annulling are hierarchically higher in the legal system than the target norm which is annulled: consider when a legislative provision is annulled (typically by the Constitutional Court) because it violates the constitution.

An *abrogation* works differently; the main point is usually that abrogations operate *ex nunc* and so do not cancel the effects that were obtained from the target norm before the modification. If so, it seems that abrogations cannot operate retroactively. In fact, if a norm n_1 is abrogated in 2012, its effects are no longer obtained after then. But, if a case should be decided

---

[2]For instance, if we have $s \prec^{2007}_{Monday} r$ and $r \prec^{2007}_{Tuesday} s$, it means that, according to the regulation in force in 2007, on Monday rule s is stronger than rule r, but on Tuesday r is stronger than s.

[3]Two meta-rules are conflicting, when the two meta-rules have the same rule as their head, but with a different content.

at time 2013 but the facts of the case are dated 2011, n_1, if applicable, will anyway produce its effects because the facts held in 2011, when n_1 was still in force (and abrogations are not retroactive). Accordingly, n_1 is still in the legal system, even though is no longer in force after 2012. Abrogations typically operate when the grounds (another norm) for abrogating is placed at the same level in the hierarchy of legal sources of the target norm which is abrogated: consider when a legislative provision is abrogated by a subsequent legislative act.

Consider this case:

EXAMPLE 2 (Abrogation vs Annulment)   *[Target of the mod-ification]* *Legislative Act n. 124, 23 July 2008*
Art. 1. With the exception of the cases mentioned under the Articles 90 and 96 of the Constitution, criminal proceedings against the President of the Republic, the President of the Senate, the President of the House of Representatives, and the Prime Minister, are suspended for the entire duration of tenure. [...]
In case of abrogation, we could have that the legislator enacts the following provision:

[Abrogation enacted and effective at 1 January 2011] *Legislative Act n. 124, 23 July 2008 is abrogated.*

In case of (judicial) annulment, we would rather have

[Annulment enacted and effective at 1 January 2011] *On account of Art. 3 of the Constitution [...] the Constitutional Court hereby declares the constitutional illegitimacy of Art. 1 of the Act n. 124, 23 July 2008.*

As we have recalled, the difference between the two cases is that the annulment has retroactive effects. In particular, let us focus on the following provisions from the Italian penal code:

Art. 157 Italian of Penal Code – Terms of statute-barred penal provisions.
When the terms for statute-barred penal effects expire, the corresponding crime is canceled [...]
Art. 158 Italian Penal Code – Effectiveness of the terms of statute-barred penal provisions
The effectiveness of terms of statute-barred penal provisions begins starting from the time when the crime was committed.
Art. 159 Italian of Penal Code – Suspension of time limits for

309

statute-barred penal effects.
The terms for statute-barred penal effects [...] are suspended
whenever the criminal proceedings are suspended under any legislative provisions [...]

Consider a hypothetical case where the Italian Prime Minister is accused
in 2007 of accepting bribes at the beginning of 2006. Clearly, if Legislative
Act n. 124 is abrogated in 2011, since abrogation has no retroactive effects,
art. 159 of Italian Penal Code applied from 2008 to 2011, and so the counting
of terms has been suspended between these two years. Hence, from the perspective of 2011 (immediately after the abrogation) the relevant time passed
is two years and six months (2006, 2007, and until July 2008). Instead, if
the act is annulled in 2011, more time has passed from the perspective of
2011, because it is as if the Legislative Act n. 124 were never enacted: from
2006 until 2011.

As we can see, modeling retroactive legal modifications is far from obvious.
The logical model proposed in [Governatori and Rotolo, 2010a] and recalled
in Section 3 offers a solution. In the next section we will illustrate the
intuition and apply to the above example of annulment and abrogation.

3.3   Intermezzo – Temporal Dynamics and Retroactivity

As we have previously argued, if $t_0, t_1, \ldots, t_j$ are points in time, the dynamics
of a legal system LS can be captured by a time-series $LS(t_0), LS(t_1), \ldots,$
$LS(t_j)$ of its versions. Each version of LS is like a norm repository: the
passage from one repository to another is effected by legal modifications or
simply by temporal persistence. This model is suitable for modeling complex
modifications such as retroactive changes, i.e., changes that affect the legal
system with respect to legal effects which were also obtained before the legal
change was done.

The dynamics of norm change and retroactivity need to fully make use of
the time-line within each version of LS (the time-line placed on top of each
repository in Figure 2). Clearly, retroactivity does not imply that we can
really change the past: this is "physically" impossible. Rather, we need to
set a mechanism through which we are able to reason on the legal system
from the viewpoint of its current version but *as if* it were revised in the
past: when we change some $LS(i)$ retroactively, this does not mean that we
modify some $LS(k)$, $k < i$, but that we move back from the perspective of
$LS(i)$. Hence, we can "travel" to the past along this inner time-line, i.e.,
from the viewpoint of the current version of LS where we modify norms.

Figure 2 shows a case where the legal system LS and its norm r persist
from time t' to time t'' and can have effects immediately from t'. Now,
the figure represents the situation where r is retroactively repealed at t'' by

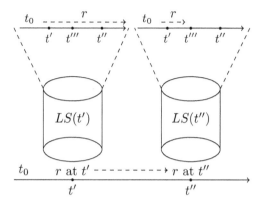

Figure 2. Legal System at t' and t''

stating that the modification applies from t''' (which is between t' and t'') onwards. The difference between abrogation and annulment is illustrated in Figures 1.3(a) and 1.3(b).

3.4 Modifications on Norm Validity and Existence: Annulment vs. Abrogation (Cont'd)

On account of our previous considerations, the cases in Example 2 can be reconstructed as follows.

EXAMPLE 3 (Abrogation vs Annulment (cont'd)) *First of all, for the sake of simplicity let us*

- *only consider the case of Prime Minister (Legislative Act n. 124 mentions other institutional roles),*

- *assume that the dates of enactment and effectiveness coincide and are generically 2008,*

- *the duration of tenure covers a time span from 2008 to 2012,*

and formalize the corresponding fragment of art. 1 of Legislative Act n. 124 (23 July 2008) as follows:

$L.\ 124 : (Crime^x, Tenure^{x+y} \Rightarrow_O Suspended^{(x+y,tran)})^{(2008,pers)})@(2008, pers)$

The duration of tenure spanning from 2008 to 2012 is represented as follows:

$$r1 : (Elected^{2008} \Rightarrow_O Tenure^{(2008,pers)})^{(2008,pers)})@(2008, pers)$$
$$r2 : (Elected^{2008} \leadsto_O \neg Tenure^{2012})^{(2008,pers)})@(2008, pers)$$

311

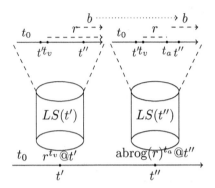
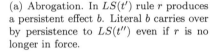
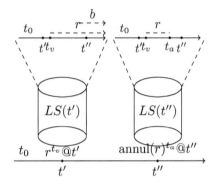

(a) Abrogation. In $LS(t')$ rule r produces a persistent effect b. Literal b carries over by persistence to $LS(t'')$ even if r is no longer in force.

(b) Annulment. In $LS(t')$ rule r is applied and produces a persistent effect b. Since r is annulled in $LS(t'')$, b must be undone as well.

Figure 3. Abrogation and Annulment

Arts. 157-159 of the Italian Penal Code state the following:

$$Art.\ 157\colon (Crime^x,\ Terms^{x+y} \Rightarrow_O CrimeCancelled^{(x+y,pers)})^{(z,pers)})@(z,pers)$$

$$Art.\ 158\colon (Crime^x \Rightarrow_O Terms^{(x,pers)})^{(z,pers)})@(z,pers)$$

$$Art.\ 159\colon (Crime^x,\ Suspended^{x+y} \Rightarrow_O \neg Terms^{(x+y,tran)})^{(z,pers)})@(z,pers)$$

As proposed by [Governatori and Rotolo, 2010a], the distinction between ab-rogation and annulment requires to distinguish between void *rules and* empty *rules. The content of a void rule, e.g., $(r\colon \bot)^t@t'$ is $\bot$, while for the empty rule the value is the empty set. This means that the void rule has value for the combination of the temporal parameters, while for the empty rule, the content of the rule does not exist for the given temporal parameters.*

Given a rule $(r\colon A \Rightarrow b^{tb})^{tr}@t$, the abrogation of r at t_a in repository t' is basically obtained by having in the theory the following meta-rule

$$(10) \qquad abr_r\colon\ \Rightarrow (r\colon \bot)^{(t_a,pers)})@(t',pers)$$

where $t' > t$. The abrogation simply terminates the applicability of the rule. More precisely this operation sets the rule to the void rule. The rule is not removed from the system, but it has now a form where no longer can produce effects. In the case of the Legislative Act n. 124 (23 July 2008) we would have

$$abr_{L.\ 124}\colon\ \Rightarrow (L.\ 124\colon \bot)^{(2011,pers)})@(2011,pers)$$

Hence, we can have the following, for example

- at time x, from the viewpoint x we derive $Suspended^x$, $2008 \leq x \leq 2010$;

- at time x, from the viewpoint x we show that we cannot derive $Terms^x$, $2008 \leq x \leq 2010$;

- at time 2011, from viewpoint 2011 we show that we cannot derive $Suspended^{2011}$;

- at time 2011, from viewpoint 2011 we can derive $Terms^{2011}$.

This is in contrast to what we do for annulment where the rule to be annulled is set to the empty rule. This essentially amounts to removing the rule from the repository. From the time of the annulment the rule has no longer any value. All past effects are thus blocked as well.

The definition of a modification function for annulment depends on the underlying variants of the logic, in particular whether conclusions persist across repositories. Minimally, the operation requires the introduction of a meta-rule setting the rule r to be annulled to $\emptyset$, with the time when the rule is annulled and the time when the meta-rule is inserted in the legal system:

$$(11) \qquad (annul_r\colon \; \Rightarrow (r\colon \emptyset)^{(t_a, pers)})@(t', pers)$$

Hence,

$$(annul_{L.\ 124}\colon \; \Rightarrow (L.\ 124\colon \emptyset)^{(2008, pers)})@(2011, pers)$$

If we assume that conclusions persist over repositories we need some additional technical machinery to block pasts effects from previous repositories. In this case, since L. 124 is modeled as a transient rule, we have basically to add a defeater like the following[4]:

$$((annul_{ef}\colon \; \leadsto_\circ \neg Suspended^{2008})^{(2008, pers)})@(2011, pers)$$

Hence, we now have, for example

- *we can show that we cannot derive at x, from viewpoint 2011, $Suspended^x$, $2008 \leq x$;*

- *we can prove at x, from viewpoint 2011 $Terms^x$, $2008 \leq x$.*

As stated before, another approach to address a logical model of norm change in the law is to enrich belief revision techniques by adding several temporal dimensions, as done in [Tamargo *et al.*, 2017; Tamargo *et*

---

[4]The general procedure to block conclusions when conclusions persist over repositories can be very complex: for all details, see [Governatori and Rotolo, 2010a].

al., 2019]. There, techniques from belief revision formalisms are integrated with interval-based logical rules for legal systems, formalizing a revision operator. This operator may remove rules when needed or adapt intervals of time when contradictory norms are added in the system. This is discussed in the following section.

4 Temporalising Belief Revision for the Law

Example 1 involves information and rules referring to intervals of time in which some taxes applies. Cases like this, need to go beyond AGM machinery. Some research has been carried out to reframe AGM ideas, some of these, within richer rule-based logical systems [Stolpe, 2010; Rotolo, 2010], and other, have aimed to study belief revision for situations in which non-monotonic reasoning is addressed [Zhuang *et al.*, 2016; Krümpelmann and Kern-Isberner, 2012]. However, also these attempts suffer from some drawbacks of standard AGM, among them the fact that the proposed frameworks fail to handle the temporal aspects of norm change.

Unlike rich but complex frameworks such as the one of [Governatori and Rotolo, 2010b]—which we have recalled in Section 3—we claim that belief revision techniques—which are based on an abstract and elegant machinery—can be reconciled with the need to consider several temporal patterns of legal reasoning. In [Tamargo *et al.*, 2019] the authors are thus interested in the formalization of a belief revision operator applied to an epistemic model that considers rules and time. They enrich a simple logic language with an interval-based model of time, to represent temporal dimensions such as the effectiveness of norms, i.e., when norms are applicable. There, the revision operator may remove rules when needed or adapt intervals of time when newer, contradictory norms are introduced in the system. In particular, the idea is the formalization of a belief revision operator that can address the evaluation of *timed rules* representing legal norms. Technical aspects of temporalised knowledge are considered in the following sections.

4.1 Legal System as Temporalised Belief Base

The problem of representing temporal knowledge and temporal reasoning arises in many disciplines, including Artificial Intelligence. A usual way to do this is to determine a *primitive* to represent time, and its corresponding *metric relations*. There are in the literature two traditional approaches to reasoning with and about time: a point based approach, as in [Governatori and Rotolo, 2010b], and an interval based approach as in [Allen, 1984; Budán *et al.*, 2017]. In the first case, the emphasis is put on *instants* of time (e.g., timestamps) and a relation of precedence among them. In the second case, time is represented as continuous sets of instants in which something relevant occurs. These intervals are identified by the starting and ending instants of time.

The approach introduced in [Tamargo *et al.*, 2019], time intervals (like in [Augusto and Simari, 2001; Budán *et al.*, 2017]) are considered. Following the semantics of the temporalised rules proposed in [Governatori and Rotolo, 2010b] and explained in Section 3 (in an adapted version), the revision operator, in essence, consists in the handling of intervals in order to maintain the consistency.

The above-mentioned temporal machinery is able to explicitly model two temporal dimensions among those mentioned above in Section 2.1, that is the time of norm effectiveness—i.e. when a norm can produce legal effects—and the time when the norm effects hold [Governatori and Rotolo, 2010b].

In [Tamargo *et al.*, 2019], a propositional language $\mathbb{L}$ with a complete set of boolean connectives: $\neg, \wedge, \vee, \rightarrow, \leftrightarrow$ is adopted and a consequence operator, denoted $Cn(\cdot)$, is used that takes sets of sentences in $\mathbb{L}$ and produces new sets of sentences. In general, in this chapter, we will write $\alpha \in Cn(A)$ as $A \vdash \alpha$.

Note that the AGM model [Alchourrón *et al.*, 1985] represents epistemic states by means of belief sets, that is, sets of sentences closed under logical consequence. Other models use belief bases; i.e., arbitrary sets of sentences [Fuhrmann, 1991; Hansson, 1992; Wassermman, 2000]. In [Tamargo *et al.*, 2019], epistemic model is based on an adapted version of belief bases which have additional information (time intervals).

4.2 Time Interval

In [Tamargo *et al.*, 2019] a universal finite *set of time labels* $\mathbb{T} = \{t_1, \ldots, t_n\}$ strictly ordered is considered; each time label represents a unique time instant. Simplifying the notation, $t_i - 1$ is the immediately previous instant to the instant t_i and $t_i + 1$ is the immediately posterior instant to the instant t_i. An interval is considered like a finite ordered sequence of time labels $t_i, \ldots, t_j$ where i, j are natural numbers ($i \leq j$) and $t_i, \ldots t_j \in \mathbb{T}$ denoting instances of time or *timepoints*. The discreteness of the flow of time is appropriate for modelling norms dynamics since norms usually refer to time in the spectrum of hours, days, months and years. Generally speaking, the law itself views time as determined by discrete steps. Thus, let $\alpha \in \mathbb{L}$, we have expressions of the type $\alpha^{interval}$, where *interval* can be as follow:

- $[t_i, t_i]$: meaning that α holds at time t_i. Following Governatori and Rotolo [2010b] α is transient (holding at precisely one instant of time). For simplicity $[t_i, t_i] = [t_i]$.

- $[t_i, \infty]$: meaning that α holds from t_i. Following Governatori and

Rotolo [2010b] α is (indefinitely) persistent from t_i.

- $[t_i, t_j]$: meaning that α holds from time t_i to t_j with $t_i < t_j$.

Then a set of time intervals $\mathbb{I}$ contains intervals as those described previously. Thus, for simplicity, we can have expressions like α^J where $J \in \mathbb{I}$. Intervals in $\mathbb{I}$ will be denoted by uppercase Latin characters: $A, B, C, \ldots, Z$. Then, throughout this work α^J is a *temporalised sentence* meaning the sentence α has an effectiveness time indicated by J. Then the semantics of classical propositional logic to a timed context is preserved. A temporalised sentence $\alpha^{[t_a, t_b]}$ is true when its non-temporalised expression α is true in every time point t between t_a and t_b. In other words, α holds at $[t_a, t_b]$.

Naturally, two intervals may not be disjoint, as defined next.

DEFINITION 4 (Contained interval) *Let $R, S \in \mathbb{I}$ be two intervals. R is contained in S, denoted $R \subseteq S$ if and only if for all $t_i \in R$ it holds that $t_i \in S$.*

DEFINITION 5 (Overlapped interval) *Let $R, S \in \mathbb{I}$ be two intervals. R and S are overlapped, denoted $R \top S$ if and only if there exists $t_i \in R$ such that $t_i \in S$.*

EXAMPLE 6 *Let $R, S, V \in \mathbb{I}$ where $R = [t_3, t_7]$, $S = [t_4, t_6]$ and $V = [t_5, t_9]$ with $t_3, t_4, t_5, t_6, t_7, t_9 \in \mathbb{T}$. Then $S \subseteq R$, $R \top V$ and $S \top V$.*

4.3 Temporalised Belief Base

As rules are part of the knowledge, they are subject of temporal effectiveness too. In this perspective, there may be expressions such as

$$\alpha^{[t_a, t_b]} \to \beta^{[t_c, t_d]}$$

meaning that the rule can derive that β holds from time t_c to t_d if it is proved that α holds from time t_a to t_b. The notion of persistence during a given interval could be also applied to rules, although we adopt here a general approach. Note that the above implication itself is not decorated with intervals, but α and β are. This means that the implication always holds at $[-\infty, \infty]$ and hence again the classical semantics of first order logic is preserved. Thus, if the implication holds (since it is not conditioned in time) and α holds at $[t_a, t_b]$ then β holds at $[t_c, t_d]$.

EXAMPLE 7 *The provision from Example 1 "If unemployed from 1980 to 1983, then a tax exemption applies from 1984 to 1986" can be formalised as follows:*

$$Unemployed^{[1980, 1983]} \to Tax\_Exemption^{[1984, 1986]}.$$

Thus, in [Tamargo *et al.*, 2017], *temporalised belief base* which will contain temporalised sentences (see Example 8) is defined. This base represents a legal system in which each temporalised sentence defines a norm whose time interval determines the effectiveness time.

EXAMPLE 8 *The set*

$$\mathbb{K} = \{\alpha^{[t_1,t_3]}, \alpha^{[t_4]}, \alpha^{[t_1,t_4]} \rightarrow \beta^{[t_4,t_6]},$$
$$\beta^{[t_5,t_6]}, \beta^{[t_6,t_8]}, \beta^{[t_{10}]}, \delta^{[t_{11}]},$$
$$\delta^{[t_{11}]} \rightarrow \beta^{[t_{15},t_{20}]}, \omega^{[t_2,t_8]},$$
$$\omega^{[t_4]} \rightarrow \beta^{[t_6,\infty]}, \epsilon^{[t_1,\infty]}\}$$

is a valid temporalised belief base for a legal system. Note that sentence ϵ is valid (or true) from t_1.

This type of belief base representation implies that a sentence can appear more than once in a temporalised belief base, but from the point of view of the temporalised sentences stored in the temporalised belief base there is no redundancy because each temporalised sentence has different time intervals. For instance, consider Example 8, where α and β appear twice, but with different intervals. Whenever a sentence appears more than once with different intervals, just like $\beta^{[t_5,t_6]}$ and $\beta^{[t_{10}]}$, this sentence is said to be **intermittent**. Also note that if the intervals of a sentence are overlapped or continuous through the knowledge base, like $\beta^{[t_5,t_6]}$, $\beta^{[t_6,t_8]}$ in Example 8, the different occurrences are not collapsed into one, producing $\beta^{[t_5,t_8]}$. This is for two main reasons. First, a knowledge base scanning procedure is needed for identifying overlapped or continuous temporalised sentences, adding extra, yet small, complexity which is not relevant for the belief revision operator discussed here. Second, in law this kind of reiteration of a sentence in different intervals is not uncommon. For instance, the government may decide that there is a tax exemption during quarantine in March, and some weeks later then decide that the same exemption also holds during April. Here there are two legal norms that conform a continuous benefit, but with separate identities that can be revised for different reasons. Even more, the continuity does not need to be so explicit: two different continuous sentences like $\alpha^{[t_1,t_n]}$, $\alpha^{[t_{n+1},t_m]}$ may be derived from different, separate portions of the knowledge base, and even when it is clear that α holds from t_1 to t_m, this wider interval will not be derived as it is. That is, as we will see below, a sentence can be implicitly represented on a belief base by several different derivations that maintain the validity of the sentence at overlapping intervals. In this case, it could not be explicitly represented with a single sentence the validity of it at all times.

4.4   Temporalised Derivation

Note that a norm can explicitly be in a temporalised belief base, as $\alpha^{[t_5]} \in \mathbb{K}$ in Example 8. However, a norm can implicitly be represented in a temporal belief base if some conditions hold. For instance, in Example 8, norm β is implicitly represented with $\omega^{[t_2,t_8]}$, $\omega^{[t_4]} \to \beta^{[t_6,\infty]}$ due to the antecedent of the rule is held in t_4 by the temporalised sentence $\omega^{[t_2,t_8]}$. Next, the notion of temporalised derivation for a sentence is introduced to capture this intuition. To do this, we first give a definition of temporalised derivation in a time instant and then we give a definition of temporalised derivation in time interval.

DEFINITION 9 (Temporalised derivation in a time instant) *Let* $\mathbb{K}$ *be a set of temporalised sentences and* $\alpha^{[t_i]}$ *be a temporalised sentence. We say that* $\alpha^{[t_i]}$ *is derived from* $\mathbb{K}$*, denoted* $\mathbb{K} \vdash^t \alpha^{[t_i]}$*, if and only if:*

- $\alpha^J \in \mathbb{K}$ *and* $t_i \in J$*, or*

- $\beta^H \to \alpha^P \in \mathbb{K}$ *and* $t_i \in P$ *and* $\mathbb{K} \vdash^t \beta^{[t_j]}$ *for all* $t_j \in H$.

DEFINITION 10 (Temporalised derivation in a time interval) *Let* $\mathbb{K}$ *be a set of temporalised sentences and* $\alpha^{[t_i,t_j]}$ *be a temporalised sentence. We say that* $\alpha^{[t_i,t_j]}$ *is derived from* $\mathbb{K}$ *(denoted* $\mathbb{K} \vdash^t \alpha^{[t_i,t_j]}$*) if and only if* $\mathbb{K} \vdash^t \alpha^{[t_p]}$ *for all* $t_p \in [t_i, t_j]$.

Computing the temporalised derivation of a sentence through checking each instant of the intervals is useful in special cases where implicit sentences need temporalised sentences with overlapped intervals as antecedents. To determine the time interval of the implicitly derived temporal sentence, the temporal consequence will be defined below.

DEFINITION 11 (Temporalised consequence) *Let* $\mathbb{K}$ *be a set of temporalised sentences and* $\alpha^{[t_i,t_j]}$ *be a temporalised sentence. We say that* $\alpha^{[t_i,t_j]}$ *is a temporalised consequence of* $\mathbb{K}$ *(*$\alpha^{[t_i,t_j]} \in Cn^t(\mathbb{K})$*) if and only if* $\mathbb{K} \vdash^t \alpha^{[t_i,t_j]}$.

EXAMPLE 12 *Consider again the temporalised belief base of Example 8. Then,* $\mathbb{K} \vdash^t \beta^{[t_4,\infty]}$*, that is,* $\beta^{[t_4,\infty]} \in Cn^t(\mathbb{K})$*; and* $\mathbb{K} \vdash^t \alpha^{[t_1,t_4]}$*, that is,* $\alpha^{[t_1,t_4]} \in Cn^t(\mathbb{K})$.

Following Definition 10, notice that the **interval of an implicitly derived sentence** will be the interval of the consequent of the rule that derives the conclusion of the proof. For instance, suppose that $\mathbb{K} = \{\gamma^{[t_2,t_5]}, \gamma^{[t_3,t_4]} \to \epsilon^{[t_6,t_9]}\}$ then the time interval of ϵ is $[t_6, t_9]$. Thus, a temporalised sentence $\alpha^{[t_i,t_j]}$ is **valid** (or true) in $\mathbb{K}$ if $\mathbb{K} \vdash^t \alpha^{[t_i,t_j]}$.

Thus, in [Tamargo *et al.*, 2019], a **contradiction** arises when two complementary sentences can be derived with time intervals overlapped. For instance, suppose $\mathbb{K} = \{\alpha^{[t_2,t_9]}, \neg\alpha^{[t_1,t_3]}\}$, in this case, there exists a contradiction. However, consider $\mathbb{K} = \{\alpha^{[t_5]}, \neg\alpha^{[t_1,t_3]}\}$, in this case, we will say that $\mathbb{K}$ does not have contradictions. Moreover, a temporalised belief base is **temporally consistent** if the base does not have contradictions. The temporalised belief base of Example 8 is temporally consistent.

REMARK 13 *If $\mathbb{K}$ represents a legal system then $\mathbb{K}$ should be temporally consistent.*

4.5 Legal Belief Revision

From a rational point of view, as was mentioned in Remark 13, a legal system should be temporally consistent, i.e., it cannot contain contradictory norms at any time. Hence, in [Tamargo *et al.*, 2019], the authors propose a **prioritised legal revision operator** that allows to consistently add a temporalised sentence $\alpha^{[t_i,t_j]}$ to a consistent legal system $\mathbb{K}$.

This special revision operator is inspired by the rule semantics explained above in Section 4.1 (an adapted version from the one proposed in [Governatori and Rotolo, 2010b]). Thus, following the concept of temporally consistency of Subsection 4.4, the revision operator may remove temporalised sentences or, in some cases, may only modify the intervals to maintain consistency.

To incorporate a norm $\neg\beta^J$ into a legal system, it is necessary to consider all possible contradictions that may arise if the norm is added without checking for consistency. For this reason, it is necessary to compute all proofs of β considering only those temporalised sentences β^P whose effectiveness time is overlapped with the time interval J, that is, $J\top P$. Note that it is optimal to compute all minimal proofs of a temporal sentence considering only those in which the time interval is overlapped with the time interval of the input sentence. Next, a set of minimal proofs for a sentence is defined.

DEFINITION 14 (Minimal proof) *Let $\mathbb{K}$ be a temporalised belief base and α^J a temporalised sentence. Then, $\mathbb{H}$ is a minimal proof of α^J if and only if*

1. $\mathbb{H} \subseteq \mathbb{K}$,

2. $\alpha^P \in Cn^t(\mathbb{H})$ with $J\top P$, and

3. if $\mathbb{H}' \subset \mathbb{H}$, then $\alpha^P \notin Cn^t(\mathbb{H}')$ with $J\top P$.

Given a temporalised sentence α^J, the function $\Pi(\alpha^J, \mathbb{K})$ returns the set of all the minimal proofs for α^J from $\mathbb{K}$.

REMARK 15 *Each set of $\Pi(\alpha^J, \mathbb{K})$ derives α in at least one time instant of J.*

EXAMPLE 16 *Consider the temporalised belief base of Example 8. Then $\Pi(\beta^{[t_5,t_6]}, \mathbb{K}) = \{\mathbb{H}_1, \mathbb{H}_2, \mathbb{H}_3, \mathbb{H}_4\}$ where:*

- $\mathbb{H}_1 = \{\alpha^{[t_1,t_3]}, \alpha^{[t_4]}, \alpha^{[t_1,t_4]} \to \beta^{[t_4,t_6]}\}$,

- $\mathbb{H}_2 = \{\beta^{[t_5,t_6]}\}$,

- $\mathbb{H}_3 = \{\beta^{[t_6,t_8]}\}$,

- $\mathbb{H}_4 = \{\omega^{[t_2,t_8]}, \omega^{[t_4]} \to \beta^{[t_6,\infty]}\}$

Note that $\mathbb{H}_1$ is minimal: α should be derived from t_1 to t_4 to use the rule $\alpha^{[t_1,t_4]} \to \beta^{[t_4,t_6]}$ hence, $\alpha^{[t_1,t_3]}$ and $\alpha^{[t_4]}$ should be in $\mathbb{H}_1$.

The construction of prioritised legal revision by a temporalised sentence is based on the concept of a minimal proof; to complete the construction, an incision function is used which selects in every minimal proof the sentence to be erased later and which can produce legal effects in favour of a possible contradiction with the new norm.

The operator is based on a selection of sentences in the knowledge base that are relevant to derive the sentence to be retracted or modified. In order to perform a revision, following kernel contractions [Hansson, 1994], this approach uses *incision functions*, which select from the minimal subsets entailing the piece of information to be revoked or modified. An incision function only selects sentences that can be relevant for α and at least one element from each $\Pi(\alpha^J, \mathbb{K})$:

DEFINITION 17 (Incision function) *Let $\mathbb{K}$ be a temporalised belief base. An incision function σ for $\mathbb{K}$ is a function such that for all $\alpha^J \in Cn^t(\mathbb{K})$:*

- $\sigma(\Pi(\alpha^J, \mathbb{K})) \subseteq \bigcup(\Pi(\alpha^J, \mathbb{K}))$.

- *For each $\mathbb{H} \in \Pi(\alpha^J, \mathbb{K})$, $\mathbb{H} \cap \sigma(\Pi(\alpha^J, \mathbb{K})) \neq \emptyset$.*

In Hansson's approach it is not specified how the incision function selects the sentences that will be discarded of each minimal proof. In this approach, this is solved by considering those sentences that can produce legal effects in favour of a possible contradiction with the new norm. Thus, if the new norm is $\neg\beta^J$ then the incision function selects the temporalised sentences β^P or $\alpha^Q \to \beta^F$ of each $\Pi(\beta^J, \mathbb{K})$.

DEFINITION 18 (Search consequence function) $Sc: \mathbb{L} \times \mathbb{K} \mapsto \mathbb{K}$, *is a function such that for a given sentence α and a given temporalised base $\mathbb{K}$ with $\mathbb{H} \subseteq \mathbb{K}$,*

$$Sc(\alpha, \mathbb{H}) = \{\alpha^J : \alpha^J \in \mathbb{H}\} \cup \{\beta^P \to \alpha^Q : \beta^P \to \alpha^Q \in \mathbb{H} \text{ and } \beta \in \mathbb{L}\}.$$

DEFINITION 19 (Consequence incision function) *Given a set of minimal proofs $\Pi(\alpha^J, \mathbb{K})$, σ^c is a consequence incision function if it is a incision function for $\mathbb{K}$ such that*

$$\sigma^c(\Pi(\alpha^J, \mathbb{K})) = \bigcup_{\mathbb{H} \in \Pi(\alpha^J, \mathbb{K})} Sc(\alpha, \mathbb{H}).$$

EXAMPLE 20 *Consider Examples 8 and 16. Then, $Sc(\beta, \mathbb{H}_1) = \{\alpha^{[t_1, t_4]} \to \beta^{[t_4, t_6]}\}$, $Sc(\beta, \mathbb{H}_2) = \{\beta^{[t_5, t_6]}\}$, $Sc(\beta, \mathbb{H}_3) = \{\beta^{[t_6, t_8]}\}$, and $Sc(\beta, \mathbb{H}_4) = \{\omega^{[t_4]} \to \beta^{[t_6, \infty]}\}$. Thus, $\sigma^c(\Pi(\beta^{[t_5, t_6]}, \mathbb{K})) = \bigcup_{\mathbb{H} \in \Pi(\beta^{[t_5, t_6]}, \mathbb{K})} Sc(\beta, \mathbb{H}) = \{\alpha^{[t_1, t_4]} \to \beta^{[t_4, t_6]}, \beta^{[t_5, t_6]}, \beta^{[t_6, t_8]}, \omega^{[t_4]} \to \beta^{[t_6, \infty]}\}$.*

As mentioned before, the revision operator may remove temporalised sentences or, in some cases, may modify the intervals to maintain consistency. Next, a temporal projection will be introduced based on a given time interval. The idea here is, given a temporalised belief base $\mathbb{K}$ and given a time interval $[t_i, t_j]$, to return a temporalised belief base $\mathbb{K}'$ containing those sentences from $\mathbb{K}$ whose time intervals be out of $[t_i, t_j]$.

DEFINITION 21 (Excluding temporal projection) *Let $\mathbb{K}$ be a temporalised belief base and let $[t_i, t_j]$ be a time interval where $t_i, t_j \in \mathbb{T}$. A excluding temporal projection of $\mathbb{K}$ from t_i to t_j, denoted $out(\mathbb{K}, [t_i, t_j])$, is a subset of $\mathbb{K}$ where for all $\alpha^{[t_p, t_q]} \in \mathbb{K}$, $out(\mathbb{K}, [t_i, t_j])$ will contain:*

- $\alpha^{[t_p, t_i - 1]}$ *if $t_p < t_i$, $t_q \geq t_i$ and $t_q \leq t_j$,*
- $\alpha^{[t_j + 1, t_q]}$ *if $t_p \geq t_i$, $t_q > t_j$ and $t_p \leq t_j$,*
- $\alpha^{[t_p, t_i - 1]}$ *and $\alpha^{[t_j + 1, t_q]}$ if $t_p < t_i$, $t_q > t_j$,*
- $\alpha^{[t_p, t_q]}$ *if $t_q < t_i$ or $t_p > t_j$.*

REMARK 22 *Note that when $t_p \geq t_i$ and $t_q \leq t_j$, the temporal sentence is not considered. In this case, this sentence is erased.*

REMARK 23 *Note that if $\delta^{[t_h, t_k]} \in out(\mathbb{K}, [t_i, t_j])$ and the interval $[t_h, t_k]$ is generated through excluding temporal projection of $\mathbb{K}$ from t_i to t_j then there exists a temporal sentence $\delta^{[t_p, t_q]}$ in $\mathbb{K}$ such that $[t_h, t_k] \subseteq [t_p, t_q]$.*

EXAMPLE 24 *Consider Example 20 and suppose that S is a temporalised belief base and $S = \sigma^c(\Pi(\beta^{[t_5,t_6]}, \mathbb{K}))$. Then, $out(S, [t_5, t_6]) = \{\alpha^{[t_1,t_4]} \to \beta^{[t_4]}, \beta^{[t_7,t_8]}, \omega^{[t_4]} \to \beta^{[t_7,\infty]}\}$.*

Following the notion of excluding temporal projection (Definition 21) a norm prioritised revision operator is defined. That is, an operator that allows to *consistently* add temporalised sentences in a temporalised belief base. If a contradiction arises, then the revision operator may remove temporalised sentences or modify the corresponding intervals in order to maintain consistency.

DEFINITION 25 *Let $\mathbb{K}$ be a temporalised belief base and α^J be a temporalised sentence. The operator "$\otimes$", called prioritised legal revision operator, is defined as follow:*

$$\mathbb{K} \otimes \alpha^J = (\mathbb{K} \setminus \sigma^c(\Pi(\neg\alpha^J, \mathbb{K}))) \cup out(\sigma^c(\Pi(\neg\alpha^J, \mathbb{K})), J) \cup \{\alpha^J\}.$$

Note that, to add α^J to $\mathbb{K}$, all temporized sentences that have $\neg\alpha$ as a consequence and contribute to derive some instant of $\neg\alpha^J$ are erased. Then, these same sentences are added but with their modified intervals (using the excluding temporal projection introduced in Definition 21). Finally, α^J is added.

EXAMPLE 26 *Consider Example 8 and suppose that a new norm $\neg\beta^{[t_5,t_6]}$ it is wished to add. To do this, it is necessary to do $\mathbb{K} \otimes \neg\beta^{[t_5,t_6]}$. Consider Examples 16 and 20. Then, $\mathbb{K} \otimes \neg\beta^{[t_5,t_6]} = \{\alpha^{[t_1,t_3]}, \alpha^{[t_4]}, \alpha^{[t_1,t_4]} \to \beta^{[t_4]}, \beta^{[t_7,t_8]}, \beta^{[t_{10}]}, \delta^{[t_{11}]}, \delta^{[t_{11}]} \to \beta^{[t_{15},t_{20}]}, \omega^{[t_2,t_8]}, \omega^{[t_4]} \to \beta^{[t_7,\infty]}, \epsilon^{[t_1,\infty]}, \neg\beta^{[t_5,t_6]}\}$. Note that, this new temporalised base is temporally consistent.*

The following example shows how our operator works in a particular situation when a legal system undergoes many changes and has rules that complement each other.

EXAMPLE 27 *Consider the following temporalised belief base $\mathbb{K} = \{\beta^{[t_1,t_{10}]}, \beta^{[t_1,t_5]} \to \alpha^{[t_1,t_5]}, \beta^{[t_6,t_{10}]} \to \alpha^{[t_6,t_{10}]}, \delta^{[t_4]}\}$. Note that, $\mathbb{K} \vdash^t \alpha^{[t_1,t_{10}]}$ because $\mathbb{K} \vdash^t \alpha^{[t_i]}$ for all $t_i \in [t_1, t_{10}]$. Suppose that it is necessary to adopt $\neg\alpha^{[t_1,t_{10}]}$. To do this, it is necessary to compute all the minimal proofs of $\alpha^{[t_1,t_{10}]}$ in $\mathbb{K}$. In this case, $\Pi(\alpha^{[t_1,t_{10}]}, \mathbb{K}) = \{\{\beta^{[t_1,t_{10}]}, \beta^{[t_1,t_5]} \to \alpha^{[t_1,t_5]}, \beta^{[t_6,t_{10}]} \to \alpha^{[t_6,t_{10}]}\}\}$. Then, $S = \sigma^c(\Pi(\alpha^{[t_1,t_{10}]}, \mathbb{K})) = \{\beta^{[t_1,t_5]} \to \alpha^{[t_1,t_5]}, \beta^{[t_6,t_{10}]} \to \alpha^{[t_6,t_{10}]}\}$. Thus, $out(S, [t_1, t_{10}]) = \emptyset$. Therefore, $\mathbb{K} \otimes \neg\alpha^{[t_1,t_{10}]} = \{\beta^{[t_1,t_{10}]}, \delta^{[t_4]}, \neg\alpha^{[t_1,t_{10}]}\}$.*

4.6 Others works that have discussed the relation between belief revision and temporal reasoning

There are some works in the literature that have discussed the relation between belief revision and temporal reasoning, though none of them addressed the issue in the normative domain. Two prominent lines of investigation are [Bonanno, 2007; Bonanno, 2009] and [Shapiro et al., 2011].

Bonanno [2007; 2009] address belief revision in a temporal logic setting. These articles consider sets of sentences closed under logical consequence. In contrast to this, the approach proposed in [Tamargo et al., 2019] is based on an adapted version of belief bases which have additional information (time intervals). The use of belief bases makes the representation of the legal system state more natural and computationally tractable. That is, following [Hansson, 1999, page 24] and [Wassermman, 2000], it is considered that legal systems sentences could be represented by a finite number of sentences that correspond to the explicit beliefs on the legal system. The main purpose of [Bonanno, 2007; Bonanno, 2009] is to represent the AGM postulates as axioms in a modal language. The assumption is that belief revision has to do with the interaction of belief and information over time, thus temporal logic seemed a natural starting point. The technical solution is to consider branching-time frames to represent different possible evolutions of beliefs. Hence, belief revision operators are interpreted over possible worlds. Unlike this, the authors in [Tamargo et al., 2019] work with legal system in which each temporalised sentence defines a norm whose time interval determines the effectiveness time. Then, the revision process defined in [Tamargo et al., 2019] may remove temporalised sentences or, in some cases, may only modify the intervals.

Shapiro [2011] is based on a well-developed theory of action in the situation calculus extended to deal with belief. The authors add to this framework a notion of plausibility over situations, and show how to handle nested belief, belief introspection, mistaken belief, belief revision and belief update together with iterated belief change.

An interesting line of investigation is to study possible correlations with these two last research lines in literature as compared to the system proposed in [Tamargo et al., 2019]. Such a comparison cannot be directly done from technical viewpoint for two reasons. First of all, [Tamargo et al., 2019] is specifically focused in a propositional language following kernel contraction construction proposed in [Hansson, 1994]. Second, the propositional language in [Tamargo et al., 2019] is equipped with explicit time-stamps and with temporal intervals, which allow them for expressing richer temporal specifications in the language.

5 Conclusions

In order to properly model norm change in the law, temporal aspects of legal dynamics must be considered. Several reasons support this idea. The law regulates its own changes by stating, within the system, what and how other existing norms should be modified. The introduced new norms can be in conflict and so norms are defeasible by nature. Even more, legal norms are qualified by diverse temporal properties, such as the time when the norm is added to the legal system, or when the norm is in force and it produces legal effects. Thus, all these aspects may be addressed by two different pathways, as reflected in the literature. First, normative dynamics can be modelled by combining logical systems for temporal and defeasible reasoning [Governatori *et al.*, 2005; Governatori *et al.*, 2007; Governatori and Rotolo, 2010a]. Second, belief revision techniques can be enriched with temporal dimensions: this has been done in works such as [Tamargo *et al.*, 2017; Tamargo *et al.*, 2019]. These are two different approaches to the consideration of time within a logical framework for legal dynamics.

Defeasible Logic was extended with temporal parameters to allow for reasoning about time specified inside norms. Two temporal dimensions are considered: the first one is when the norm is in force in a normative system, and the second is when the norm exists in the normative system from a certain viewpoint. Usually only the time of force is considered, but here the notion of *temporalised rule with viewpoint* is introduced, a mechanism through which it is possible to reason on the legal system from the viewpoint of its current version but as if it were revised in the past. This extension increases the expressive power of the logic and it allows us to represent meta-norms describing norm modifications by referring to a variety of possible time-lines through which conclusions, rules and derivations can persist over time. This formalism has been shown useful to model retroactive legal modifications, a complex timed behaviour of legal systems that requires special attention. Hence, this model is suitable for modeling changes that affect the legal system with respect to legal effects which were also obtained before the legal change was done. This is not a simple feature and the formalism addresses it properly.

On the other hand, a contrasting approach explores the importance of time in legal dynamics from the point of view of *revision of beliefs* in laws. This make sense since the law is a *dynamic* system of rules. Indeed, a very complex one: as times goes by, rules are introduced in the system, which may be either unexpectedly in conflict with existing rules or be intended to provide new, different norms for society. This demands a consistent revision of the rules of the system, so an extension of classic belief revision formalism seems to be appropriate. Then, we discussed here the second approach, which proposes a belief revision operator that considers time interval in the revision process. Intervals are used to model a period of time for a piece of knowledge to be effective or relevant, leading to the definition of a new kind of temporal rules. On these interval-decorated rules the corresponding temporalised derivation was defined. The consideration of time requires an adaptation of the notions of contradiction and inconsistency in the classical sense. Temporalised knowledge base is inconsistent only if contradictory information can be derived for the same moment of time. In that approach was defined a novel belief revision operator that allows the consistent addition of temporalised sentences in a temporalised belief base. If a contradiction arises, then the revision operator may either completely remove conflictive temporalised sentences or modify the intervals of some rules. This last action is made because a given consequence a at interval I may fall in contradiction during a sub-interval of I. Thus, a should be a consequence, after the revision, only for the rest of I. Then, intervals in rules should be taken into account for the revision process.

The central idea of this research topic is that formal models of norm change must address the fact that new norms may be elicited and old norms may need to be retracted, with complex consequences. Depending on the particular feature of legal dynamics intended to be modelled, any proposed framework requires an appropriate model of time. There are two mainstream approaches to reasoning with and about time: point based and interval based. Here we explored both flavours, by discussing two different, interesting approaches to the consideration of time within the study of legal dynamics. Both formalisms take time into account and provide the necessary logical infrastructure to address the characterization of complex behaviour of dynamics in normative systems, constituting solid foundations for further research.

Acknowledgments

This research was supported by the EUs Horizon 2020 research and innovation programme under the Marie Skodowska-Curie grant agreement No 690974 for the project MIREL: MIning and REasoning with Legal texts (http://www.mirelproject.eu).

BIBLIOGRAPHY

[Alchourrón and Bulygin, 1981] Carlos E. Alchourrón and Eugenio Bulygin. The expressive conception of norms. In Risto Hilpinen, editor, *New Studies in Deontic Logic*, pages 95–125. D. Reidel, Dordrecht, 1981.

[Alchourrón and Makinson, 1981] Carlos E. Alchourrón and David C. Makinson. Hierarchies of regulations and their logic. In Risto Hilpinen, editor, *New Studies in Deontic Logic*, pages 125–148. D. Reidel, Dordrecht, 1981.

[Alchourrón and Makinson, 1982] Carlos E. Alchourrón and David C. Makinson. The logic of theory change: Contraction functions and their associated revision functions. *Theoria*, 48:14–37, 1982.

[Alchourrón et al., 1985] C.E. Alchourrón, P. Gärdenfors, and D. Makinson. On the logic of theory change: Partial meet contraction and revision functions. *Journal of Symbolic Logic*, 50:510–530, 1985.

[Allen, 1984] James F. Allen. Towards a general theory of action and time. *Artif. Intell.*, 23(2):123–154, 1984.

[Antoniou et al., 2001] Grigoris Antoniou, David Billington, Guido Governatori, and Michael J. Maher. Representation results for defeasible logic. *ACM Trans. Comput. Log.*, 2(2):255–287, 2001.

[Augusto and Simari, 2001] Juan Carlos Augusto and Guillermo Ricardo Simari. Temporal defeasible reasoning. *Knowl. Inf. Syst.*, 3(3):287–318, 2001.

[Boella et al., 2009] G. Boella, G. Pigozzi, and L. van der Torre. A normative framework for norm change. In *Proc. AAMAS 2009*, pages 169–176. ACM, 2009.

[Boella et al., 2016] Guido Boella, Gabriella Pigozzi, and Leendert van der Torre. Contraction and revision of rules. *Journal of Logic, Language and Information*, 25(3):273–297, 2016.

[Bonanno, 2007] Giacomo Bonanno. Axiomatic characterization of the AGM theory of belief revision in a temporal logic. *Artif. Intell.*, 171(2-3):144–160, 2007.

[Bonanno, 2009] Giacomo Bonanno. Belief revision in a temporal framework. In *New Perspectives on Games and Interaction, volume 4 of Texts in Logic and Games*, pages 45–80. Amsterdam University Press, 2009.

[Budán et al., 2017] Maximiliano Celmo Budán, Maria Laura Cobo, Diego C. Marténez, and Guillermo Ricardo Simari. Bipolarity in temporal argumentation frameworks. *Int. J. Approx. Reasoning*, 84:1–22, 2017.

[Fuhrmann, 1991] André Fuhrmann. Theory contraction through base contraction. *Journal of Philosophical Logic*, 20(2):175–203, may 1991.

[Gabbay et al., 2003] Dov M. Gabbay, Gabriella Pigozzi, and John Woods. Controlled revision - an algorithmic approach for belief revision. *J. Log. Comput.*, 13(1):3–22, 2003.

[Governatori and Rotolo, 2010a] G. Governatori and A. Rotolo. Changing legal systems: Legal abrogations and annulments in defeasible logic. *Logic Journal of IGPL*, 18(1):157–194, 2010.

[Governatori and Rotolo, 2010b] Guido Governatori and Antonino Rotolo. Changing legal systems: legal abrogations and annulments in defeasible logic. *Logic Journal of the IGPL*, 18(1):157–194, 2010.

[Governatori et al., 2005] G. Governatori, M. Palmirani, R. Riveret, A. Rotolo, and G. Sartor. Norm modifications in defeasible logic. In *JURIX 2005*, pages 13–22. IOS Press, Amsterdam, 2005.

[Governatori et al., 2007] Guido Governatori, Antonino Rotolo, Régis Riveret, Monica Palmirani, and Giovanni Sartor. Variants of temporal defeasible logics for modelling norm modifications. In *The Eleventh International Conference on Artificial Intelligence and Law, Proceedings of the Conference, June 4-8, 2007, Stanford Law School, Stanford, California, USA*, pages 155–159, 2007.

[Governatori et al., 2013] Guido Governatori, Antonino Rotolo, Francesco Olivieri, and Simone Scannapieco. Legal contractions: a logical analysis. In *Proc. ICAIL 2013*, 2013.

[Hansson, 1992] Sven Ove Hansson. In defense of base contraction. *Syntheses*, 91(3):239–245, june 1992.

[Hansson, 1994] Sven Ove Hansson. Kernel Contraction. *The Journal of Symbolic Logic*, 59:845–859, 1994.

[Hansson, 1999] Sven Ove Hansson. *A Textbook of Belief Dynamics: Theory Change and Database Updating*. Kluwer Academic Publishers, 1999.

[Hart, 1994] H. L. A. Hart. *The Concept of Law*. Clarendon Press, Oxford, 1994.

[Kelsen, 1991] Hans Kelsen. *General theory of norms*. Clarendon, Oxford, 1991.

[Krümpelmann and Kern-Isberner, 2012] Patrick Krümpelmann and Gabriele Kern-Isberner. Belief base change operations for answer set programming. In *Logics in Artificial Intelligence - 13th European Conference, JELIA 2012, Toulouse, France, September 26-28, 2012. Proceedings*, pages 294–306, 2012.

[Rotolo, 2010] Antonino Rotolo. Retroactive legal changes and revision theory in defeasible logic. In G. Governatori and G. Sartor, editors, *DEON 2010*, volume 6181 of *LNAI*, pages 116–131. Springer, 2010.

[Shapiro *et al.*, 2011] Steven Shapiro, Maurice Pagnucco, Yves Lesprance, and Hector J. Levesque. Iterated belief change in the situation calculus. *Artificial Intelligence*, 175(1):165 – 192, 2011. John McCarthy's Legacy.

[Stolpe, 2010] Audun Stolpe. Norm-system revision: theory and application. *Artif. Intell. Law*, 18(3):247–283, 2010.

[Tamargo *et al.*, 2017] Luciano H. Tamargo, Diego C. Martinez, Antonino Rotolo, and Guido Governatori. Temporalised belief revision in the law. In Adam Z. Wyner and Giovanni Casini, editors, *Legal Knowledge and Information Systems - JURIX 2017: The Thirtieth Annual Conference, Luxembourg, 13-15 December 2017.*, volume 302 of *Frontiers in Artificial Intelligence and Applications*, pages 49–58. IOS Press, 2017.

[Tamargo *et al.*, 2019] Luciano H. Tamargo, Diego C. Martinez, Antonino Rotolo, and Guido Governatori. An axiomatic characterization oftemporalised belief revision inthelaw. *Artificial Intelligence and Law*, pages 1–21, 2019.

[Wassermman, 2000] Renata Wassermman. Resource bounded belief revision. *PhD Thesis, Institute for Logic, Language and Computation (ILLC), University of Amsterdam*, 2000.

[Wheeler and Alberti, 2011] Gregory R. Wheeler and Marco Alberti. No revision and no contraction. *Minds and Machines*, 21(3):411–430, 2011.

[Zhuang *et al.*, 2016] Zhiqiang Zhuang, James P. Delgrande, Abhaya C. Nayak, and Abdul Sattar. Reconsidering agm-style belief revision in the context of logic programs. In *ECAI 2016 - 22nd European Conference on Artificial Intelligence, 29 August-2 September 2016, The Hague, The Netherlands - Including Prestigious Applications of Artificial Intelligence (PAIS 2016)*, volume 285 of *Frontiers in Artificial Intelligence and Applications*, pages 671–679. IOS Press, 2016.

Luciano H. Tamargo
ICIC–UNS–CONICET, Universidad Nacional del Sur
San Andres 800, Baha Blanca, Argentina
Email: lt@cs.uns.edu.ar

Diego C. Martinez
ICIC–UNS–CONICET, Universidad Nacional del Sur
San Andres 800, Baha Blanca, Argentina
Email: dcm@cs.uns.edu.ar

Antonino Rotolo
CIRSFID, University of Bologna
Bologna, Italia
Email: antonino.rotolo@unibo.it

Guido Governatori
Data61, CSIRO
Melbourne, Australia
Email: guido.governatori@data61.csiro.au

9

Multi-agent Argumentation and Dialogue

Ruyta Arisaka
Jérémie Dauphin
Ken Satoh
Leendert van der Torre

ABSTRACT. This chapter provides an overview of multi-agent abstract argumentation and dialogue, and its application to formalising legal reasoning. The basis of multi-agent abstract argumentation is input/output argumentation, distinguishing between individual acceptance by agents and collective acceptance by the system. The former may also be seen as a kind of conditional reasoning, and the latter may be seen as the reasoning of an external observer. We extend input/output argumentation in two ways. First, we introduce epistemic trust and agent communication. The former is based on a social network representing epistemic trust, and the latter is based on so-called sub-framework semantics. Second, we introduce dialogue semantics for abstract argumentation by refining agent communication into dialogue steps. A dialogue is a sequence of steps from the framework to the extensions, where at each step an agent can commit to accepting some arguments, or commit to hiding or revealing one of his/her rejected arguments. The revealed arguments are then aggregated and an external observer, in our example a judge, can compute which arguments are finally accepted at a global level.

1 Introduction

In his historical overview of formal argumentation, Prakken [2018] distinguishes between two kinds of approaches, which he calls argumentation-as-dialogue and argumentation-as-inference. The former is based on protocols and game theory, and the latter is based on non-monotonic logic and graph theory. While in the former approach agents and time play a central role, in the latter approach they are often abstracted away.

In game theory, there is a related distinction between extensive games, which make agents and time explicit, and strategic games, which use the concept of a strategy or conditional plan to abstract time away. The relationship between extensive and strategic games is well understood, in

Handbook of Legal AI
© *2022, Ruyta Arisaka* et al.

the sense that they are two views of the same phenomenon at different levels of abstraction. This understanding is still missing in the relationship between argumentation-as-dialogue and argumentation-as-inference, despite some work relating these two traditions to the other. For example, Dung [1995] shows how his abstract theory can also be applied to reasoning in game theory, and various authors have developed dialogue-based decision procedures for abstract and structured argumentation [Caminada, 2018]. We believe that there is a common theory to be developed for argumentation-as-dialogue and argumentation-as-inference, bringing new insights to both. As a first step, we therefore raise the following research question:

Research question. How to introduce agent interaction and dialogue into Dung's abstract argumentation theory?

The starting point for abstract agent argumentation [Arisaka *et al.*, 2018], also called triple-A, is the concept of conditional acceptance. In particular, an argument that an agent does not accept can still be put forward as part of the discussion. For example, the agent can explain why (s)he does not accept an argument by presenting counter-arguments to the unaccepted argument, and (s)he may even be willing to accept the argument if convinced by the other agents that his/her counter-arguments are wrong. The following example illustrates how an agent's individual acceptance function is conditional on accepting the arguments of other agents attacking his/her argument, and how this allows us to model one kind of counter-factual argument.

EXAMPLE 1 (Conditional acceptance). Consider the agent argumentation framework visualised on the left-hand side of Figure 1, whose formal definitions are explained in Section 2. Agent A is an expert in healthcare management considering the argument that a new virus is contained (argument a) and the argument that an additional hospital needs to be built (argument b). Moreover, agent A assumes that if the first argument is accepted, the latter should not be accepted, which is represented by an attack visualised as an arrow from argument a to argument b. Now, consider the multi-agent argumentation framework visualised on the right-hand side of Figure 1. Agent B is an expert in virology who argues that the virus will not be contained (argument c), which attacks argument a of agent A. Since agent A is not an expert in virology, agent A cannot judge whether argument c should be accepted or not.

Whether agent A accepts his/her own argument b depends on whether agent B accepts argument c, and on whether agent A trusts agent B on argument c. In particular, if agent B accepts argument c and agent A trusts agent B, then agent A accepts argument b. Otherwise, agent A will accept argument a and reject argument b.

330

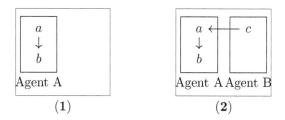

Figure 1. The agent and multi-agent framework of Example 1.

Finally, consider an external observer. Will (s)he accept argument b that an additional hospital must be built? That depends not only on the trust of agent A in agent B, but also whether agent A communicates argument b. In particular, when agent A does not accept argument b, (s)he may decide not to inform agent B or the external observer about the existence of the argument.

To formalise conditional and multi-agent argumentation, abstract agent argumentation uses the theory of input/output argumentation described by Baroni *et al.* [2014], also known as multi-sorted argumentation [Rienstra *et al.*, 2011]. This theory allows arguments to be assigned to agents, and individual acceptance functions to be associated with these agents. Following the above example, and building on various theories in the literature, abstract agent argumentation extends input/output argumentation in two ways.

First, whether an agent accepts an argument put forward by another agent depends on the trust the agents have in one other, which may be based on their respective reputations [Ramchurn *et al.*, 2004; Huynh *et al.*, 2006; Sabater and Sierra, 2005; Sabater and Sierra, 2001; Mui, 2002]. This is often represented by a social network [Degenne and Forsé, 1999; Heaney and Israel, 2008; Sabater and Sierra, 2002], and we follow that tradition in this chapter. For instance, in Example 1, agent A will only reject argument a and accept argument b if (s)he trusts agent B on argument c. Agents A and B may be part of the same coalition cooperating in building a common view of the situation.

Secondly, dialogue is strategic, in the sense that sometimes it is better not to reveal an argument. For example, agent A may not like argument b, and may thus decide not to reveal this argument to the other agents. This aspect is missing in Dung-style abstract argumentation in the sense that in the dialogue procedures [Caminada, 2018], the set of available dialogue actions does not change when arguments are put forward by other agents. Likewise, in most structured argumentation theories, the knowledge bases are assumed to be fixed. Therefore, there is no advantage for an agent in a dialogue game to not put forward an argument. We introduce a new concept: agents can decide whether to hide some of their arguments from the other agents. This concerns, in particular, arguments they do not accept themselves. For example, assume that a scientist knows how increased temperature leads to rising sea levels, but she does not accept this argument herself. She may decide to hide this argument from public debate, because she does not want to give ammunition to her opponents.

From the perspective of an external observer, the interaction is a game between agents. Since the arguments an agent reveals may depend on the arguments revealed by other agents, game-theoretic equilibrium among agents is necessary for the external observer. In a game-theoretic equilibrium, the behaviour of the agents depends on the behaviour of the other agents, in our case for both communicating and accepting arguments. Moreover, even if the agents do not accept an argument, an external observer may still accept it. A dialogue is a sequence of steps from the framework to the extensions, where at each step an agent can commit to accept or reject some arguments, or commit to hide or reveal one of his/her rejected arguments. The revealed arguments are then aggregated and an external observer can compute which arguments are finally acceptable at a global level.

Our use of input/output argumentation as a model for multi-agent argumentation contains some assumptions, which can be relaxed in further research. In particular, the conditional reasoning of the agents implies that they do not have a model of the arguments pertaining to the other agents, and therefore the only agent who considers the interaction between agents is the external observer. In more sophisticated models, agents can recursively model other agents, including the other agents' model of their own arguments.

This chapter also considers the application of our framework to legal reasoning, using an example from a court case. Here, the agents are the accused, the lawyers, the witnesses, the prosecutors and so on. The external observer is the jury or the judge, who has to take into account all the arguments put forward during the deliberation and decide which arguments to accept. For example, we can distinguish the collective argumentation of judges from the individual argumentation of the accused, prosecutors, witnesses, lawyers, and experts. In multi-agent argumentation, agents have partial knowledge of the arguments and attacks of other agents, and they decide autonomously whether to accept or reject their own arguments as well as whether to bring their arguments forward in court. The arguments accepted by the judge are based on a game-theoretic equilibrium of the argumentation of the other

	Name	Components
Sec. 2 (Def. 2)	Argumentation framework	$\langle \mathcal{A}, \mathcal{R} \rangle$
Sec. 2 (Def. 4)	Multi-agent argumentation framework	$\langle \mathcal{A}, \mathcal{R}, Ag, Src \rangle$
Sec. 3 (Def. 10)	Trust argumentation framework	$\langle \mathcal{A}, \mathcal{R}, Ag, Src, T \rangle$
Sec. 3 (Def. 10)	Trust argumentation framework of an agent A	$\langle \mathcal{A}_A, \mathcal{R}_A, I_A, R_{I_A} \rangle$

Table 1. The different frameworks defined throughout the chapter.

	Acceptance	Individual acceptance	Collective acceptance
Sec. 2	ac-arg(Def. 2)	iac-arg(Def. 6)	cac-arg(Def. 8)
Sec. 3	ac-trust(Def. 10)	iac-trust(Def. 10)	cac-trust(Def. 10)
Sec. 4	ac-sub(Def. 16)	iac-sub$_A$ (Def. 17)	cac-sub(Def.18)

Table 2. The different acceptance functions defined throughout the chapter.

agents. The multi-agent argumentation can be used to distinguish various direct and indirect ways in which an agent's arguments can be used against his/her other arguments. The novelty of the framework we introduce in this chapter is that not only do we have agents with local argumentation frameworks and individual acceptance functions, but we also consider a social network for the agents, and the semantics also specify whether the agents decide to hide or reveal the arguments they do not accept.

Tables 1 and 2 provide a list of the concepts introduced in Sections 2, 3 and 4 of this chapter. Table 1 provides a list of the different structures introduced throughout the chapter, specifying where they are introduced and which components they are made of. Table 2 provides a list of the different acceptance functions defined in this chapter, together with a note of where they first appear. The second column is comprised of general acceptance functions, while the third column focuses on the local acceptance functions of each agent. Finally, the last column recounts the global collective acceptance functions that aggregate the individual acceptance functions.

The layout of this chapter is as follows. In Section 2, we repeat the definitions and concepts of the input/output argumentation of Baroni *et al.* [2014], and we consider the limitations that arise when considering it as a kind of multi-agent argumentation. In Section 3 we extend input/output argumentation with a social trust network, and in Section 4 we introduce the possibility of communicating arguments to other agents via sub-frameworks. In Section 5 we introduce dialogue semantics by refining the sub-framework approach with dialogue steps. In Section 6 we discuss related work.

2   Conditional and multi-agent argumentation

In this section, we introduce the basic definitions that pertain to multi-agent argumentation, including individual agents' conditional acceptance of arguments based on other agents' acceptance of the arguments. The formal theory of multi-agent argumentation in this section is an interpretation of so-called input/output argumentation as described by Baroni *et al.* [2014]. Whereas input/output argumentation is a powerful theory for distinguishing the acceptance of arguments by individual agents from the acceptance of arguments by an external observer, we also explain why we need to extend input/output argumentation to make it applicable to multi-agent argumentation.

We first recall Dung's abstract argumentation semantics [Dung, 1995] which can be represented by a function associating sets of jointly acceptable arguments with argumentation frameworks. Though Dung introduced various ways of defining the semantics of argumentation frameworks, in this chapter we consider only so-called stable semantics in order to keep our formal exposition to a minimum.

DEFINITION 2 (Stable semantics for argument acceptance). Let $\langle \mathcal{A}, \mathcal{R} \rangle$ be a directed graph called an *argumentation framework*, where the elements of $\mathcal{A}$ are called *arguments* and the binary relation $\mathcal{R}$ over $\mathcal{A}$ is called an *attack* relation. A subset of the arguments is a *stable extension* of the argumentation framework if and only if it does not contain an argument attacking another argument in the extension, and for each argument that is not in the extension, there is an argument in the extension attacking it. We write $\texttt{ac-arg}(\langle \mathcal{A}, \mathcal{R} \rangle)$ for the set of all stable extensions of the argumentation framework $\langle \mathcal{A}, \mathcal{R} \rangle$.

The following example illustrates how Dung uses stable extensions of argumentation frameworks to define the concept of arguments that can be accepted together. It also explains how there can be multiple extensions of an argumentation framework.[1] To find all stable extensions, one can guess an extension and check whether it is stable.

EXAMPLE 3 (Four arguments). Consider the arguments $\mathcal{A} = \{a_1, a_2, a_3, a_4\}$ with attack relation $\mathcal{R} = \{(a_1, a_2), (a_2, a_1), (a_3, a_4), (a_4, a_3), (a_3, a_1), (a_2, a_4)\}$ visualised on the left-hand side of Figure 2. We have $\texttt{ac-arg}(\langle \mathcal{A}, \mathcal{R} \rangle) = \{\{a_1, a_4\}, \{a_2, a_3\}\}$ since for $\{a_1, a_4\}$, neither a_1 nor a_4 is attacked by a_1 or a_4, and the arguments attacking either of them, namely a_2 and a_3, are attacked by them; analogous reasoning goes for $\{a_2, a_3\}$.

---

[1]In fact, there can even be argumentation frameworks that do not have any stable extensions, for example argumentation frameworks consisting of a single argument attacking itself. This reflects the notion of incoherence in argumentation.

In Dung's semantics, acceptance firstly means no conflict. If we accept any argument, every argument attacked by it is thus certainly rejected. In a way, acceptance of an argument becomes the cause for rejecting other arguments. Each extension (member) of the stable semantics is stable in the sense that (1) no arguments in the extension are in conflict and (2) rejection of every other argument outside it is guaranteed.

Each extension in $\{\{a_1, a_4\}, \{a_2, a_3\}\}$ satisfies the two criteria. Moreover, no other sets of arguments are stable in this example. Any strict superset would involve a conflict. For instance, $\{a_1, a_3, a_4\}$ is in conflict since a_3 attacks a_1. Any strict subset does not ensure rejection of all the other arguments. Consider $\{a_2\}$, while it rejects a_1 and a_4, a_3 is not rejected by it.

Figure 2. An argumentation framework and a multi-agent argumentation framework.

A multi-agent argumentation framework is an argumentation framework with a set of agents and an assignment of the arguments to the agents. We also call the agents the *sources* of the arguments. Rienstra *et al.* [2011] call it a multi-sorted argumentation framework, and Baroni *et al.* [2014] call it an input/output argumentation framework.

DEFINITION 4 (Multi-agent argumentation). A multi-agent argumentation framework is a tuple $\langle \mathcal{A}, \mathcal{R}, Ag, Src \rangle$ where $\langle \mathcal{A}, \mathcal{R} \rangle$ is an argumentation framework, Ag is a set called agents and $Src : \mathcal{A} \to Ag$ is a function mapping each argument to the agent that put it forward (also known as its *source*).

EXAMPLE 5 (Two agents, continued from Example 3). Consider the multi-agent argumentation framework $\langle \mathcal{A}, \mathcal{R}, Ag, Src \rangle$ visualised on the right-hand side of Figure 2. We have $Ag = \{W_1, W_2\}$, $Src(a_1) = Src(a_2) = W_1$, and $Src(a_3) = Src(a_4) = W_2$.

For the semantics, we first define individual acceptance by an agent. We consider the part of the multi-agent framework that is relevant to the agent, which we call the *agent argumentation framework*. It contains its own arguments together with the attacks from and against those arguments, the relevant arguments of other agents, an extension of these other arguments, and an attack relation from these other arguments to its own arguments.

The agent semantics considers the agent argumentation framework as well as the arguments accepted by other agents. This conditional acceptance is called a local function by Baroni *et al.* [2014].

We slightly rewrite the definition of local function to make it explicit that agents' acceptance of arguments is conditional on the other agents' accepted arguments. Moreover, in contrast to Baroni *et al.* [2014], we do not consider attacks against input arguments. Since Baroni *et al.* [2014] define their local acceptance functions for all Dung semantics and not only for stable semantics, their definitions are more general than ours. Similar notions are defined also by Liao [2013]. We refer to these papers for further explanations and examples of local functions.

DEFINITION 6 (Individual conditional acceptance). For multi-agent argumentation framework $\langle \mathcal{A}, \mathcal{R}, Ag, Src \rangle$, the *argumentation framework of agent A* is a tuple $\langle \mathcal{A}_A, \mathcal{R}_A, I_A, R_{I_A} \rangle$, where $\mathcal{A}_A = \{a \in \mathcal{A} \mid Src(a) = A\}$ are the arguments of agent A, $\mathcal{R}_A = \mathcal{R} \cap (\mathcal{A}_A \times \mathcal{A}_A)$ are its attacks, $I_A = \{a \in \mathcal{A} \mid a \notin \mathcal{A}_A, (a,b) \in \mathcal{R}, b \in \mathcal{A}_A\}$ are the relevant arguments from other agents, and $R_{I_A} = \mathcal{R} \cap (I_A \times \mathcal{A}_A)$ is the corresponding attack relation. The stable semantics of agent A and context $E_{I_A} \subseteq I_A$, a set of arguments called the input extension, is defined by

$$
\begin{aligned}
\texttt{iac-arg}(\langle \mathcal{A}, \mathcal{R}, Ag, Src \rangle, A, E_{I_A}) = \\
\texttt{ac-arg}(\langle \mathcal{A}_A \cup E_{I_A}, \mathcal{R}_A \cup (\mathcal{R} \cap (E_{I_A} \times \mathcal{A}_A)) \rangle)_{\mathcal{A}_A}
\end{aligned}
$$

where for a set of extensions S, $S_{\mathcal{A}_A} = \{s \cap \mathcal{A}_A \mid s \in S\}$. We may denote a member of $\texttt{iac-arg}(\langle \mathcal{A}, \mathcal{R}, Ag, Src \rangle, A, E_{I_A})$ by E_A.

Conditional acceptance is illustrated in the example below.

EXAMPLE 7 (Two agents, continued from Example 5). Figure 3 visualises the agent argumentation frameworks from the running example. The left-hand side visualises the agent argumentation framework of agent W_1, and the right-hand side visualises the framework of agent W_2. The left framework represents a tuple $\langle \mathcal{A}_{W_1}, \mathcal{R}_{W_1}, I_{W_1}, R_{I_{W_1}} \rangle$ where $\mathcal{A}_{W_1} = \{a_1, a_2\}$ are the arguments of agent W_1, $\mathcal{R}_{W_1} = \{(a_1, a_2), (a_2, a_1)\}$ are its attacks, $I_A = \{a_3\}$ are the relevant arguments from other agents, and $R_{I_A} = \{(a_3, a_1)\}$ is the corresponding attack relation.

The stable semantics of agent W_1 depends not only on its agent framework, but also on its input extension. In other words, agent W_1's acceptance of arguments is conditional on its input extension, which is why we refer to the semantics of individual agents as conditional semantics. This input extension of agent W_1 is a subset of its input arguments $\{a_3\}$, so the input extension is either the empty set or $\{a_3\}$. The stable semantics for agent W_1 is now calculated to either reject or accept a_3.

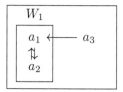
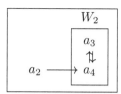

Figure 3. The two agent frameworks from the multi-agent framework in Figure 2.

In the former case, the agent accepts either a_1 or a_2, and in the latter case, the agent accepts a_2. We have $\texttt{iac-arg}(\langle \mathcal{A}_{W_1}, \mathcal{R}_{W_1}, I_{W_1}, R_{I_{W_1}} \rangle, W_1, \emptyset) = \{\{a_1\}, \{a_2\}\}$ and $\texttt{iac-arg}(\langle \mathcal{A}_{W_1}, \mathcal{R}_{W_1}, I_{W_1}, R_{I_{W_1}} \rangle, W_1, \{a_3\}) = \{\{a_2\}\}$.

Likewise, for agent W_2, the input contains only argument a_2 from agent W_1, and the input extension is either the empty set or $\{a_2\}$. In the former case, agent W_2 accepts either argument a_3 or a_4, and in the latter case, the agent accepts a_3. We have $\texttt{iac-arg}(\langle \mathcal{A}_{W_2}, \mathcal{R}_{W_2}, I_{W_2}, R_{I_{W_2}} \rangle, W_2, \emptyset) = \{\{a_3\}, \{a_4\}\}$ and also $\texttt{iac-arg}(\langle \mathcal{A}_{W_2}, \mathcal{R}_{W_2}, I_{W_2}, R_{I_{W_2}} \rangle, W_2, \{a_2\}) = \{\{a_3\}\}$.

We finally provide a definition for collective acceptance, which may be seen as the arguments accepted by an external observer.

DEFINITION 8 (Collective acceptance).

The collective stable semantics of multi-agent argumentation framework $\langle \mathcal{A}, \mathcal{R}, Ag, Src \rangle$, which we write as $\texttt{cac-arg}(\langle \mathcal{A}, \mathcal{R}, Ag, Src \rangle)$, is the set of extensions $S \subseteq \mathcal{A}$ such that for all agents $A \in Ag$ we have

$$S \cap \mathcal{A}_A \in \texttt{iac-arg}(\langle \mathcal{A}, \mathcal{R}, Ag, Src \rangle, A, S \cap I_A).$$

The following example illustrates how to check whether an extension is collectively accepted.

EXAMPLE 9 (Two agents, continued from Example 7). An external observer now has to combine the two semantic functions of agents W_1 and W_2 to find the collectively accepted arguments. Since each agent has only three possibilities, there are only nine cases to check. As it turns out, only two of them are compatible and thus lead to a collective extension. The stable extensions are $\texttt{cac-arg}(\langle \mathcal{A}, \mathcal{R}, Ag, Src \rangle) = \{\{a_1, a_4\}, \{a_2, a_3\}\}$.

	$E_{I_{W_1}} = \emptyset,$ $E_{W_1} = \{a_1\}$	$E_{I_{W_1}} = \emptyset,$ $E_{W_1} = \{a_2\}$	$E_{I_{W_1}} = \{a_3\},$ $E_{W_1} = \{a_2\}$
$E_{I_{W_2}} = \emptyset, E_{W_2} = \{a_3\}$	x	x	x
$E_{I_{W_2}} = \emptyset, E_{W_2} = \{a_4\}$	$\{a_1, a_4\}$	x	x
$E_{I_{W_2}} = \{a_2\}, E_{W_2} = \{a_3\}$	x	x	$\{a_2, a_3\}$

337

To compute the extensions, one can guess an extension and then check that it is in equilibrium in the sense that for every agent, if the input is part of the extension, then the agent accepts the arguments provided by the individual acceptance function.

The reader may observe that the two extensions of the collective semantics coincide with the two stable extensions of the argumentation framework in Example 3, and wonder whether this holds more generally. Perhaps surprisingly, Baroni *et al.* [2014] prove that this is no coincidence. For many semantics σ, including stable semantics, collective acceptance coincides with the σ of the underlying argumentation framework:

$$\texttt{cac-arg}(\langle \mathcal{A}, \mathcal{R}, Ag, Src \rangle) = \texttt{ac-arg}(\langle \mathcal{A}, \mathcal{R} \rangle)$$

In their approach, this represents a useful principle, because it allows for compositional computation of the semantics, and various applications such as summarisation. As for using input/output argumentation as a theory of multi-agent argumentation, it shows that the theory must be extended. For instance, Rienstra *et al.* [2011] study the case where the individual acceptance of the agents (sorts in their terminology) may use different semantics. As an example, one agent may use stable semantics as described in this chapter, while another agent may use grounded or preferred semantics. In this chapter, we extend the theory in other ways by introducing the notion of trust in Section 3, allowing agents to hide information in Section 4, and then considering communication between agents in Section 5.

3   Multi-agent argumentation with a social trust network

In this section, we extend multi-agent argumentation with a social network for agents reflecting epistemic trust. An agent trusts another agent if the first agent accepts the arguments the second agent accepts. If the social network is reflexive, symmetric and transitive, then the network consists of equivalence classes of agents, which may be called coalitions.

Individual and collective acceptance in trust argumentation frameworks are defined the same as before, using trust argumentation frameworks for individual agents.

DEFINITION 10 (Trust argumentation framework). A *trust argumentation framework* $\langle \mathcal{A}, \mathcal{R},\ Ag, Src, T \rangle$ extends a multi-agent argumentation framework $\langle \mathcal{A}, \mathcal{R}, Ag, Src \rangle$ with a binary relation of trust $T \subseteq Ag \times Ag$ such that each agent A trusts itself, i.e. $(A, A) \in T$, which we can write alternatively as $T(A, A)$. We write $T(A)$ for $\{B \mid T(A, B)\}$.

338

$$T(W_1) = T(W_2) = \{W_1, W_2\} \qquad\qquad T(W_1) = \{W_1, W_2\}, T(W_2) = \{W_2\}$$

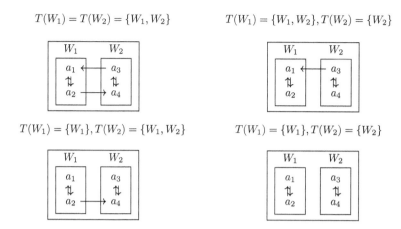

$$T(W_1) = \{W_1\}, T(W_2) = \{W_1, W_2\} \qquad\qquad T(W_1) = \{W_1\}, T(W_2) = \{W_2\}$$

Figure 4. MAF representations for a chosen trust relation.

For trust argumentation framework $\langle \mathcal{A}, \mathcal{R}, Ag, Src, T \rangle$, we say that $\langle \mathcal{A}, \mathcal{R}', Ag, Src \rangle$ with $\mathcal{R}' = \{(a, b) \in \mathcal{R} \mid T(Src(b), Src(a))\}$ is its Multi-agent Argumentation Framework (MAF) representation.

$$\texttt{iac-trust}(\langle \mathcal{A}, \mathcal{R}, Ag, Src, T \rangle, A, E_{I_A}) =$$
$$\texttt{iac-arg}(\langle \mathcal{A}, \mathcal{R}', Ag, Src \rangle, A, E_{I_A})$$
$$\texttt{cac-trust}(\langle \mathcal{A}, \mathcal{R}, Ag, Src, T \rangle) = \texttt{cac-arg}(\langle \mathcal{A}, \mathcal{R}', Ag, Src \rangle)$$

EXAMPLE 11 (Two agents, continued from Example 9). Let us consider the multi-agent argumentation framework $\langle \mathcal{A}, \mathcal{R}, Ag, Src \rangle$ on the right-hand side of Figure 2, and let us extend it with trust relation T to derive $\langle \mathcal{A}, \mathcal{R}, Ag, Src, T \rangle$. Figure 4 visualises its MAF representations for each choice of T.

- $T(W_1) = T(W_2) = \{W_1, W_2\}$ means that the agents trust each other. The top-left corner of Figure 4 shows the corresponding MAF representation.
  $\texttt{cac-arg}(\langle \mathcal{A}, \mathcal{R}, Ar, Src, T \rangle, W_1, \{a_3\}) = \{\{a_2\}\}$.
  $\texttt{cac-arg}(\langle \mathcal{A}, \mathcal{R}, Ar, Src, T \rangle, W_1, \emptyset) = \{\{a_1\}, \{a_2\}\}$.
  $\texttt{cac-arg}(\langle \mathcal{A}, \mathcal{R}, Ar, Src, T \rangle, W_2, \{a_2\}) = \{\{a_3\}\}$.
  $\texttt{cac-arg}(\langle \mathcal{A}, \mathcal{R}, Ar, Src, T \rangle, W_2, \emptyset) = \{\{a_3\}, \{a_4\}\}$.
  $\texttt{cac-trust}(\langle \mathcal{A}, \mathcal{R}, Ag, Src, T \rangle) = \{\{a_1, a_4\}, \{a_2, a_3\}\}$.

- $T(W_1) = \{W_1, W_2\}$, $T(W_2) = \{W_2\}$ means that only agent W_1 trusts agent W_2. The top-right corner of Figure 4 shows the corresponding MAF representation.

$\texttt{cac-arg}(\langle \mathcal{A}, \mathcal{R}, Ar, Src, T \rangle, W_1, \{a_3\}) = \{\{a_2\}\}.$
$\texttt{cac-arg}(\langle \mathcal{A}, \mathcal{R}, Ar, Src, T \rangle, W_1, \emptyset) = \{\{a_1\}, \{a_2\}\}.$
$\texttt{cac-arg}(\langle \mathcal{A}, \mathcal{R}, Ar, Src, T \rangle, W_2, \emptyset) = \{\{a_3\}, \{a_4\}\}.$
$\texttt{cac-trust}(\langle \mathcal{A}, \mathcal{R}, Ag, Src, T \rangle) = \{\{a_1, a_4\}, \{a_2, a_3\}, \{a_2, a_4\}\}.$

- $T(W_1) = \{W_1\}$, $T(W_2) = \{W_1, W_2\}$ means that only agent W_2 trusts agent W_1. The bottom-left corner of Figure 4 shows the corresponding MAF representation.
  $\texttt{cac-arg}(\langle \mathcal{A}, \mathcal{R}, Ar, Src, T \rangle, W_1, \emptyset) = \{\{a_1\}, \{a_2\}\}.$
  $\texttt{cac-arg}(\langle \mathcal{A}, \mathcal{R}, Ar, Src, T \rangle, W_2, \{a_2\}) = \{\{a_3\}\}.$
  $\texttt{cac-arg}(\langle \mathcal{A}, \mathcal{R}, Ar, Src, T \rangle, W_2, \emptyset) = \{\{a_3\}, \{a_4\}\}.$
  $\texttt{cac-trust}(\langle \mathcal{A}, \mathcal{R}, Ag, Src, T \rangle) = \{\{a_1, a_3\}, \{a_1, a_4\}, \{a_2, a_3\}\}.$

- $T(W_1) = \{W_1\}$, $T(W_2) = \{W_2\}$ means the agents do not trust one other. The bottom-right corner of Figure 4 shows the corresponding MAF representation.
  $\texttt{cac-arg}(\langle \mathcal{A}, \mathcal{R}, Ar, Src, T \rangle, W_1, \emptyset) = \{\{a_1\}, \{a_2\}\}.$
  $\texttt{cac-arg}(\langle \mathcal{A}, \mathcal{R}, Ar, Src, T \rangle, W_2, \emptyset) = \{\{a_3\}, \{a_4\}\}.$
  $\texttt{cac-trust}(\langle \mathcal{A}, \mathcal{R}, Ag, Src, T \rangle) = \{\{a_1, a_3\}\{a_1, a_4\}, \{a_2, a_3\}, \{a_2, a_4\}\}.$

In the above example, the lack of trust leads to an increase in the number of extensions in $\texttt{cac-trust}$. The following example illustrates that this is not always the case.

EXAMPLE 12 (Two agents, another example). Consider the trust argumentation framework in Figure 5. Let us extend it with a trust relation.

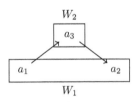

Figure 5. Multi-agent argumentation with 2 agents, W_1 and W_2.

Depending on which agents trust whom, we obtain four different MAF representations as shown in Figure 6.

- $T(W_1) = T(W_2) = \{W_1, W_2\}$ means that the agents trust each other. The top-left corner of Figure 6 shows the corresponding MAF representation.
  $\texttt{cac-trust}(\langle \mathcal{A}, \mathcal{R}, Ag, Src, T \rangle) = \{\{a_1, a_2\}\}.$

$T(W_1) = T(W_2) = \{W_1, W_2\}$ $T(W_1) = \{W_1, W_2\}, T(W_2) = \{W_2\}$

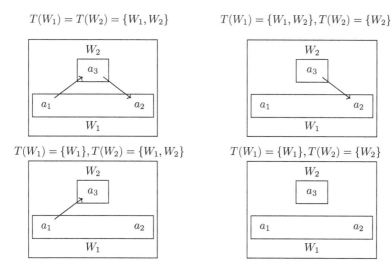

$T(W_1) = \{W_1\}, T(W_2) = \{W_1, W_2\}$ $T(W_1) = \{W_1\}, T(W_2) = \{W_2\}$

Figure 6. MAF representations for a chosen trust relation.

- $T(W_1) = \{W_1, W_2\}, T(W_2) = \{W_2\}$ means that only W_1 trusts the other. The top-right corner of Figure 6 shows the corresponding MAF representation.
  cac-trust$(\langle \mathcal{A}, \mathcal{R}, Ag, Src, T \rangle) = \{\{a_1, a_3\}\}$.

- $T(W_2) = \{W_1, W_2\}, T(W_1) = \{W_1\}$ means that only W_2 trusts the other. The bottom-left corner of Figure 6 shows the corresponding MAF representation.
  cac-trust$(\langle \mathcal{A}, \mathcal{R}, Ag, Src, T \rangle) = \{\{a_1, a_2\}\}$.

- $T(W_1) = \{W_1\}, T(W_2) = \{W_2\}$ means that each agent trusts only himself/herself. The bottom-right corner of Figure 6 shows the corresponding MAF representation.
  cac-trust$(\langle \mathcal{A}, \mathcal{R}, Ag, Src, T \rangle) = \{\{a_1, a_2, a_3\}\}$.

As is clear from these examples, it is not necessary that collective acceptance of a trust argumentation framework $\langle \mathcal{A}, \mathcal{R}, Ag, Src, T \rangle$ should consist solely of conflict-free extensions (*i.e.* those extensions in which no attacks occur), unlike in the multi-agent argumentation frameworks in the previous section. When we have an agent W in a trust argumentation framework $\langle \mathcal{A}, \mathcal{R}, Ag, Src, T \rangle$, and when, to ensure that W's arguments do not cause a conflict, collective acceptance of any of W's arguments necessarily implies non-acceptance of arguments put forward by other agents attacking it, it is in our interest to know what must be minimally added to this trust argumentation framework in order to break the no-conflict property of collective acceptance. By establishing the knowledge, we can consecutively learn what additions to the trust argumentation framework are safe to make without violating the no-conflict property.

It turns out that if an extension S'' in $\mathtt{cac\text{-}trust}(\langle \mathcal{A}, \mathcal{R}, Ag, Src, T\rangle)$ includes some agent W's argument a_1 and another agent W'''s argument a_2, then $\langle \mathcal{A}, \mathcal{R} \cup \{(a_2, a_1)\}, Ag, Src, T\rangle$ already breaks the no-conflict property provided that (1) W does not trust W', and provided also that (2) there is some extension S in $\mathtt{cac\text{-}trust}(\langle \mathcal{A}, \mathcal{R}, Ag, Src, T\rangle)$ and some extension S' in $\mathtt{cac\text{-}trust}(\langle \mathcal{A}, \mathcal{R} \cup \{(a_2, a_1)\}, Ag, Src, T\rangle)$ such that S includes a_1 and a_2, and that S' contains a_2 and any $a_x \in (S \backslash \mathcal{A}_W)$ attacking an argument in $\mathcal{A}_W$ but no other $a_y \in (\mathcal{A} \backslash \mathcal{A}_W)$ attacking an argument in $\mathcal{A}_W$. Furthermore, the opposite is also true. If either of the conditions (1) or (2) above is not satisfied, then no extension in $\mathtt{cac\text{-}trust}(\langle \mathcal{A}, \mathcal{R} \cup \{(a_2, a_1)\}, Ag, Src, T\rangle)$ contains both a_1 and a_2.

We make use of the following two lemmas to prove the result.

LEMMA 13. *For any* $\langle \mathcal{A}, \mathcal{R}, Ag, Src, T\rangle$, *any* $W_1, W_2 \in Ag$, *any* $a_1 \in \mathcal{A}_{W_1}$, *and any* $a_2 \in \mathcal{A}_{W_2}$, *if* $(a_2, a_1) \in \mathcal{R}$ *and if there is some* $S \in \boldsymbol{cac\text{-}trust}(\langle \mathcal{A}, \mathcal{R}, Ag, Src, T\rangle)$ *such that* $a_1, a_2 \in S$, *then* $W_2 \notin T(W_1)$.

Proof. We show the contrapositive. Let $\langle \mathcal{A}, \mathcal{R}', Ag, Src\rangle$ be its MAF representation. If $W_2 \in T(W_1)$, then for any $a \in \mathcal{A}_{W_1}$, $(a_2, a_1) \in \mathcal{R}'$ holds iff $(a_2, a_1) \in \mathcal{R}$ holds. By the definition of $\mathtt{iac\text{-}trust}$, for all $S_{W_1} \in \mathtt{iac\text{-}trust}(\langle \mathcal{A}_{W_1}, \mathcal{R}_{W_1}, I_{W_1}, R_{I_{W_1}}\rangle, W_1, \{a_2\})$, it holds that $a_1 \notin S_{W_1}$. Then, for any $S \in \mathtt{cac\text{-}trust}(\langle \mathcal{A}, \mathcal{R}, Ag, Src, T\rangle)$, if $a_2 \in S$, it must be the case that $a_1 \notin S$; and by the contrapositive, if $a_1 \in S$, it must also be the case that $a_2 \notin S$, as required. ∎

LEMMA 14. *For any* $\langle \mathcal{A}, \mathcal{R}, Ag, Src, T\rangle$, *any* $W \in Ag$, *and any* $a_1 \in \mathcal{A}_W$, *if there is some* $S \in \boldsymbol{cac\text{-}trust}(\langle \mathcal{A}, \mathcal{R}, Ag, Src, T\rangle)$ *such that* $a_1 \in S$, *then for any* $\langle \mathcal{A}, \mathcal{R}^*, Ag, Src, T\rangle$ *with* $\mathcal{R} \backslash (\bigcup_{W_x \in (Ag \backslash \{W\})} \mathcal{A}_{W_x} \times \{a_1\}) \subseteq \mathcal{R}^* \subseteq \mathcal{R}$, *there is some* $S' \in \boldsymbol{cac\text{-}trust}(\langle \mathcal{A}, \mathcal{R}^*, Ag, Src, T\rangle)$ *such that* $S_W = S'_W$.

Proof. Let $\langle \mathcal{A}, \mathcal{R}', Ag, Src\rangle$ be the MAF representation of $\langle \mathcal{A}, \mathcal{R}, Ag, Src, T\rangle$, let $\langle \mathcal{A}, \mathcal{R}'', Ag, Src\rangle$ be the MAF representation of $\langle \mathcal{A}, \mathcal{R}^*, Ag, Src, T\rangle$, let I'_W denote $\{a \in \mathcal{A} \backslash \mathcal{A}_W \mid \exists a_x \in \mathcal{A}_W.(a, a_x) \in \mathcal{R}'\}$, and let I''_W denote $\{a \in \mathcal{A} \backslash \mathcal{A}_W \mid \exists a_x \in \mathcal{A}_W.(a, a_x) \in \mathcal{R}''\}$. For any $E_{I'_W} \subseteq I'_W$, if $S_W \in \mathtt{iac\text{-}trust}(\langle \mathcal{A}, \mathcal{R}, Ag, Src, T\rangle, W, E_{I'_W})$, then for any $a_x \in (\mathcal{A} \backslash \mathcal{A}_W)$, if $(a_x, a_1) \in \mathcal{R}$, then $a_x \notin E_{I'_W}$, because no stable extension of $(\mathcal{A}_W \cup E_{I'_W}, \mathcal{R}_W \cup R_{E_{I'_W}})$ with $R_{E_{I'_W}} \equiv \{(a_2, a_1) \in \mathcal{R}' \mid a_2 \in E_{I'_W} \text{ and } a_1 \in \mathcal{A}_W\}$ contains two arguments with one (or both) attacking another. But this then implies that $S \cap I'_W = S \cap I''_W$. Meanwhile, for any $W_x \in (Ag \setminus \{W\})$, it trivially holds that $I'_{W_x} = I''_{W_x}$. Hence, for any $W_y \in Ag$, we have $S \cap I'_{W_y} = S \cap I''_{W_y}$, so $\texttt{iac-trust}(\langle A, R, Ag, Src, T \rangle, W_y, S \cap I'_{W_y}) = \texttt{iac-trust}(\langle A, R, Ag, Src, T \rangle, W_y, S \cap I''_{W_y})$. It then holds that $S \in \texttt{cac-trust}(\langle A, R^*, Ag, Src, T \rangle)$. Let S' thus denote S, to conclude. ∎

THEOREM 15 (Collective acceptance with trust). *For any $\langle A, R, Ag, Src, T \rangle$ and any $W \in Ag$, let I_a for $a \in A$ denote $\{a_3 \in A \mid Src(a_3) \neq Src(a)$ and $(a_3, a) \in R\}$. Given a $\langle A, R, Ag, Src, T \rangle$ and a $W \in Ag$, if $(\bigcup_{a \in S_W} I_a) \cap S = \emptyset$ for any $S \in \texttt{cac-trust}(\langle A, R, Ag, Src, T \rangle)$, then for any $a_1 \in A_W$, any $a_2 \notin A_W$ and any $\langle A, R \cup \{(a_2, a_1)\}, Ag, Src, T \rangle$, the first condition below holds just when the second condition holds.*

1. *(1) There is some $S \in \texttt{cac-trust}(\langle A, R, Ag, Src, T \rangle)$ and some $S' \in \texttt{cac-trust}(\langle A, R \cup \{(a_2, a_1)\}, Ag, Src, T \rangle)$ such that $a_1, a_2 \in S$, and that $S \cap (\{a_2\} \cup \bigcup_{a \in A_W} I_a) = S' \cap \bigcup_{a \in A_W} I_a$. (2) $Src(a_2) \notin T(W)$.*

2. *There is some $S'' \in \texttt{cac-trust}(\langle A, R \cup \{(a_2, a_1)\}, Ag, Src, T \rangle)$ such that $a_1, a_2 \in S''$.*

Proof. Let $\langle A, R', Ag, Src \rangle$ be the MAF representation of $\langle A, R, Ag, Src, T \rangle$, let $\langle A, R'', Ag, Src \rangle$ be the MAF representation of $\langle A, R \cup \{(a_2, a_1)\}, Ag, Src, T \rangle$, let I'_W denote $\{a \in A \setminus A_W \mid \exists a_x \in A_W.(a, a_x) \in R'\}$, and let I''_W denote $\{a \in A \setminus A_W \mid \exists a_x \in A_W.(a, a_x) \in R''\}$.

1 to 2: Due to (2), it holds that $\langle A, R' \rangle = \langle A, R'' \rangle$. Thus, for any $W_x \in Ag$, we have $I'_{W_x} = I''_{W_x}$. The reasoning for the rest is similar to that provided in the proof for Lemma 14.

2 to 1: (2) follows from Lemma 13. The first part of (1), i.e. that some such S includes a_1 and a_2, follows from the assumption on $\langle A, R, Ag, Src, T \rangle$. The second part of (1) is via Lemma 14. ∎

We can also refine the trust relation in terms of topics of expertise, such that an agent only accepts an argument put forward by another agent if it concerns a topic on which the first agent trusts the second agent to be informed.

4 Communication of arguments

In this section, we further extend multi-agent argumentation by allowing agents to communicate not only the arguments they accept, but also some of the arguments they reject, and we describe how they all interact.

The following definition generalises Dung's stable extensions as sub-frameworks. A stable sub-framework is a sub-framework having exactly one stable extension that also is a stable extension of the whole framework. A sub-framework semantics called AFRA (argumentation framework with recursive attacks) semantics was introduced by Baroni *et al.* [2011] and a sub-framework semantics called attack semantics was introduced by Villata *et al.* [2011].

DEFINITION 16 (Stable sub-frameworks). The framework $\langle \mathcal{A}', \mathcal{R}' \rangle$ is a *stable sub-framework* of $\langle \mathcal{A}, \mathcal{R} \rangle$ if and only if $\mathcal{A}' \subseteq \mathcal{A}$, $\mathcal{R}' \subseteq \mathcal{R} \cap (\mathcal{A}' \times \mathcal{A}')$ and $\langle \mathcal{A}', \mathcal{R}' \rangle$ has exactly one stable extension which is also a stable extension of $\langle \mathcal{A}, \mathcal{R} \rangle$. We write $\mathtt{ac\text{-}sub}(\langle \mathcal{A}, \mathcal{R} \rangle)$ for the set of all stable sub-frameworks of the argumentation framework $\langle \mathcal{A}, \mathcal{R} \rangle$.

Every Dung extension can be interpreted as a sub-framework containing only the accepted arguments and an empty attack relation. However, in general, there are several sub-frameworks corresponding to each Dung extension. We use this fact to define an agent's individual acceptance function $\mathtt{ac\text{-}sub}_A$. For example, $\mathtt{ac\text{-}sub}_A$ can be the minimal sub-framework corresponding to Dung's extension, but it can also be a maximal sub-framework communicating as much information as possible.

Given a $\mathtt{ac\text{-}sub}_A$, the definition of an agent's individual acceptance function stays exactly the same, except it replaces $\mathtt{ac\text{-}arg}$ with $\mathtt{ac\text{-}sub}_A$.

DEFINITION 17 (Individual acceptance). For a multi-agent argumentation framework $\langle \mathcal{A}, \mathcal{R}, Ag, Src \rangle$ with agent $A \in Ag$, an individual acceptance function $\mathtt{ac\text{-}sub}_A$ returns a set of stable sub-frameworks $\mathtt{ac\text{-}sub}_A(\langle \mathcal{A}, \mathcal{R} \rangle) \subseteq \mathtt{ac\text{-}sub}(\langle \mathcal{A}, \mathcal{R} \rangle)$ containing at least one sub-framework for each stable extension, so $\bigcup_{F \in \mathtt{ac\text{-}sub}_A(\langle \mathcal{A}, \mathcal{R} \rangle)} \mathtt{ac\text{-}arg}(F) \supseteq \mathtt{ac\text{-}arg}(\langle \mathcal{A}, \mathcal{R} \rangle)$.

For a multi-agent argumentation framework $\langle \mathcal{A}, \mathcal{R}, Ag, Src \rangle$ and an individual acceptance function $\mathtt{ac\text{-}sub}_A$, the stable semantics of agent A and context $E_{I_A} \subseteq I_A$ is defined by

$$\mathtt{iac\text{-}sub}_A(\langle \mathcal{A}_A, \mathcal{R}_A, I_A, R_{I_A} \rangle, E_{I_A}, \mathtt{ac\text{-}sub}_A) =$$

$$\mathtt{ac\text{-}sub}_A(\langle \mathcal{A}_A \cup E_{I_A}, \mathcal{R}_A \cup (R_{I_A} \cap (E_{I_A} \times \mathcal{A}_A)))\rangle)_{\mathcal{A}_A}.$$

Moreover, the definition of collective acceptance is adapted as follows.

DEFINITION 18 (Collective acceptance). A stable sub-framework of multi-agent argumentation framework $\langle \mathcal{A}, \mathcal{R}, Ag, Src \rangle$ with the set $\{\text{ac-sub}_A \mid A \in Ag\}$ of individual acceptance functions is a triple $\langle \mathcal{A}', \mathcal{R}', S \rangle$ such that S is a stable extension of $\langle \mathcal{A}', \mathcal{R}' \rangle$ and for all agents $A \in Ag$, we have

1. $\langle \mathcal{A}', \mathcal{R}' \rangle_A \in \text{ac-sub}_A(\langle \mathcal{A}_A, \mathcal{R}_A, I_A, R_{I_A} \rangle, S \cap E_{I_A})_A$, and

2. for all (a_1, a_2) such that $Src(a_1) \neq Src(a_2)$, we have $(a_1, a_2) \in \mathcal{R}'$ iff $(a_1, a_2) \in \mathcal{R} \cap (\mathcal{A}' \times \mathcal{A}')$.

We write $\text{cac-sub}(\langle \mathcal{A}, \mathcal{R}, Ag, Src \rangle, \{\text{ac-sub}_A \mid A \in Ag\})$ for the set of all such triples from multi-agent argumentation framework $\langle \mathcal{A}, \mathcal{R}, Ag, Src \rangle$ with individual acceptance functions $\{\text{ac-sub}_A \mid A \in Ag\}$.

The first item ensures that the collectively accepted framework locally corresponds to each agent's accepted sub-framework, while the second item states that attacks from one agent's individually accepted framework on another are as they are in the original framework. Trust networks and sub-framework semantics can be combined in the obvious way.

Example 19 below illustrates a multi-agent debate involving an accused, a witness, a prosecutor and finally a judge who is evaluating collective acceptance. We show how variations in individual conditional acceptance, i.e. variations in what to reveal for the judgment of collective acceptance, can lead to different outcomes, some good and some bad for the accused.

EXAMPLE 19. There was a murder at Laboratory C which Acc is accused of having committed. There is a witness Wit and a prosecutor Prc. Acc has two arguments:

a_1 : that he was at Laboratory A on the day of the murder (this is a fact known to Acc).

a_2 : that he is innocent (this is Acc's claim).

Prc entertains:

a_6 : that only Acc could have killed the victim (this is Prc's claim).

Meanwhile, Wit believes certain things. He has three arguments:

a_3 : Acc stayed at home on the day of the murder, having previously lost his ID card (Wit originally believes this to be a fact).

a_4 : Acc could enter any laboratory provided that he does so with his own ID card (this is a fact known to Wit).

a_5 : Acc could not have been at Laboratory C at the time of the murder (this is Wit's claim).

The multi-agent debate in Figure 7 (**A**) represents this example, showing the conflicts between the arguments. We denote this multi-agent argumentation framework by $\langle \mathcal{A}, \mathcal{R}, Ag, Src \rangle$.

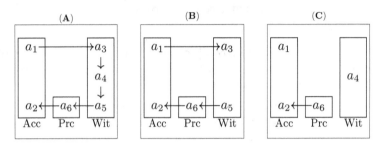

Figure 7. Accused (Acc), witness (Wit), and prosecutor (Prc).

In this example, Prc has no reason to drop her argument a_6. Neither does Acc, seeing no benefit in conceding to a_6, have any reason to drop a_2. Hence, we only consider contexts where $E_{I_{\mathrm{Acc}}} = E_{I_{\mathrm{Prc}}} = \emptyset$. How Wit responds to the fact known to Acc (a_1), however, can prove crucial for Acc to be judged innocent or guilty by the judge who computes collective acceptance.

Case A. Suppose that $E_{I_{\mathrm{Wit}}} = \emptyset$, which signifies that Wit is either not aware of a_1 or just ignores it. Then any individual acceptance function of Wit's will output a set of sub-frameworks of $\langle \mathcal{A}, \mathcal{R} \rangle_{\mathrm{Wit}}$ such that it has $\{a_3, a_5\}$ as its one and only stable extension. Thus, suppose that the acceptance function outputs only $\langle \mathcal{A}, \mathcal{R} \rangle_{\mathrm{Wit}}$, as shown in Figure 7 (**A**). Then, the stable sub-framework of $\langle \mathcal{A}, \mathcal{R}, Ag, Src \rangle$ is $\langle \mathcal{A}, \mathcal{R}, \{a_1, a_4, a_6\} \rangle$. Hence Acc is not judged innocent by the judge.

On the other hand, if Wit's acceptance function outputs only $\langle \{a_3, a_5\}, \emptyset \rangle$, as shown in Figure 7 (**B**), then the stable sub-framework is $\langle \mathcal{A} \backslash \{a_4\}, \mathcal{R} \backslash (\{a_4\} \times \mathcal{A} \cup \mathcal{A} \times \{a_4\}), \{a_1, a_2, a_5\} \rangle$. Acc is judged innocent by the judge.

Case B. Suppose that $E_{I_{\mathrm{Wit}}} = \{a_1\}$, which signifies that Wit takes a_1 into account. Then any individual acceptance function of Wit's will output a set of sub-frameworks of $\langle \mathcal{A}, \mathcal{R} \rangle_{\mathrm{Wit}}$ such that it has $\{a_4\}$ as its one and only stable extension. Thus, suppose that the acceptance function outputs only $\langle \{a_4\}, \emptyset \rangle$, as shown in Figure 7 (**C**). Then the stable sub-framework is $\langle \mathcal{A} \backslash \{a_3, a_5\}, \mathcal{R} \backslash (\{a_3, a_5\} \times \mathcal{A} \cup \mathcal{A} \times \{a_3, a_5\}), \{a_1, a_4, a_6\} \rangle$. Again, Acc is not judged innocent by the judge.

5 Dialogue semantics

In this section, we consider dialogical and dynamic aspects of multi-agent argumentation. Based on the work of Dauphin *et al.* [2018] that refines extensions into decision graphs, we observe the process of argument sharing between agents and how the individual attitude of each agent affects the global outcome of the argumentation process.

We apply the same commitment-graph structure to argumentation dialogue between agents. The agents first commit to a single extension to their internal framework when multiple frameworks exist, and then decide how to share it. They may opt to fully share their arguments, exposing counter-arguments that they know about but locally reject, or they may decide to share the arguments they accept without mentioning any of the counter-arguments they are aware of. We represent these strategic choices in a graph to have a clearer visualisation of the communication process between different agents. We later provide a way to reduce these graphs such that only the choices that impact the final outcome are displayed, thus providing a summary of the argumentation process.

In their original work, Dauphin *et al.* [2018] provided a framework for analysing the decisions made in the process of selecting one extension from a set of extensions. The decisions are represented in directed graphs where the nodes represent commitments made by the agent towards a progressively smaller subset of the set of extensions until only one extension remains.

We slightly adapt this framework when applying this approach to our multi-agent dialogue setting. When it is their turn, agents either simply decide which arguments to accept, or, once that is done, they also choose which arguments to share. While they will want to share every argument that they accept, that may not be the case for the arguments they reject. For each argument they are aware of but do not accept, agents have the opportunity to either leave them out or share them with their peers.

We first present a definition of commitments about arguments. We allow our agents to choose which arguments to accept or reject, and for the arguments they reject, to choose whether or not to communicate this. We therefore introduce pairs to represent these decisions.

DEFINITION 20. Given $c \in \{+, -, say, hide\}$ and an argument a, we say that a pair (c, a) is a *commitment on a*. Given a set C of commitments on arguments, we say that C is *coherent* if there is no argument a such that:

- $(say, a) \in C$ and $(hide, a) \in C$, or

- $(+, a) \in C$ and $(-, a) \in C$, or

- $(hide, a) \in C$ and $(+, a) \in C$.

For the sake of simplicity, we write $s(a)$ instead of (say, a), we write $h(a)$ instead of $(hide, a)$, we write $+(a)$ instead of $(+, a)$, we write $-(a)$ instead of $(-, a)$. And for a set of commitments C, we write C^s for $\{a \mid s(a) \in C\}$, we write C^h for $\{a \mid h(a) \in C\}$, we write C^+ for $\{a \mid +(a) \in C\}$ and we write C^- for $\{a \mid -(a) \in C\}$.

We then define a sub-framework acceptance semantics that takes these commitments into account.

DEFINITION 21. Let $\langle \mathcal{A}, \mathcal{R} \rangle$ be an argumentation framework and C a coherent set of commitments on arguments in $\mathcal{A}$. We define the C-committed stable sub-framework semantics to be

$$\texttt{ac-com}^C(\langle \mathcal{A}, \mathcal{R} \rangle) \;=\; \{\langle \mathcal{A} \setminus C^h, (\mathcal{R} \cap (\mathcal{A} \setminus C^h)^2) \setminus \mathcal{A} \times \mathcal{E} \rangle \mid \\ \mathcal{E} \in \texttt{ac-arg}(\langle \mathcal{A}, \mathcal{R}, \mathcal{E} \supseteq C^+ \rangle)\}$$

The C-committed stable semantics first removes all the arguments that an agent has committed to hide. It then looks at the remaining framework, and for each stable extension containing the arguments the agent has committed to accept, it proceeds to remove the attacks on any arguments in that stable extension. This then forces one stable extension to apply to each framework from the output.

We can now adapt the decision graph structure in [Dauphin $et\ al.$, 2018] to the triple-A frameworks. The individual agents still have to commit to which arguments they accept when their internal argumentation allows for multiple extensions, but then they also have to commit to which ones they communicate. We have defined the notion of C-committed stable semantics in order to let agents choose, for each argument they reject, whether or not to share it. We now examine the impact these commitments have on the final extensions determined by the overall observer, or in our running examples, the judge.

DEFINITION 22. Let $\langle \mathcal{A}, \mathcal{R}, Ag, Src, T \rangle$ be a trust argumentation framework. We say that a labelled directed acyclic graph $(\mathcal{C}, \mathcal{V}, l)$, where $\mathcal{C}$ is a set of sets of commitments about $\mathcal{A}$, $\mathcal{V}$ is a relation between elements of $\mathcal{C}$ and l is a function assigning labels to both $\mathcal{C}$ and $\mathcal{V}$ (as described below), is a $multi\text{-}agent\ commitment\ graph$ for $\langle \mathcal{A}, \mathcal{R}, Ag, Src, T \rangle$ iff all of the following hold:

1. $\emptyset \in \mathcal{C}$ and every other node can be reached from $\emptyset$ via $\mathcal{V}$;

2. for any non-leaf node C, it is the case that $l(C) \in Ag$;

3. for any edge $v \in \mathcal{V}$, it is the case that $l(v)$ is of the form $c(a)$ where $a \in \mathcal{A}$ and $c \in \{+, -, s, h\}$;

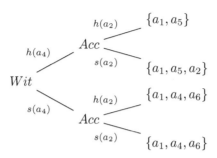

Figure 8. Commitment graph for the argumentation framework in Example 19.

4. for any edge $(C_1, C_2) \in \mathcal{V}$, if $l((C_1, C_2)) = c(a)$ for some $a \in \mathcal{A}$ and $c \in \{+, -, s, h\}$, then $Src(a) = l(C_1)$;

5. for all $e = (C_1, C_2) \in \mathcal{V}$, it is the case that $C_2 = C_1 \cup l(e)$;

6. for every leaf node C, it is the case that $l(C) = E$ where E is such that $\texttt{cac-sub}(\langle \mathcal{A}, \mathcal{R}, Ag, Src \rangle, \{\texttt{ac-com}^C\}) = \{(\mathcal{A}', \mathcal{R}', E)\}$.

The first constraint is that the starting point is where no decision has yet been made. All the cases considered can be reached from this starting point. The second constraint, together with the third constraint, forces the process to consider only the commitments made by one agent at a time. The fourth constraint represents the fact that a commitment on a certain argument can only be made by the agent who is its source. The fifth constraint represents carrying over commitments. The last constraint labels the nodes with the resulting collective extension. It computes the collective sub-framework semantics resulting from assigning the C-committed stable sub-framework semantics via individual acceptance functions for each agent.

EXAMPLE 23 (Three agents, continued from Example 19). Consider the scenario described in Example 19—the case where Acc trusts Prc, and Prc trusts Wit, but Wit does not trust Acc. Wit does not need to condition his local framework, and therefore accepts a_3 and a_5, and rejects a_4. Wit may now decide whether to share or hide a_4. If he hides a_4, he only communicates the framework $\langle \{a_3, a_5\}, \emptyset \rangle$. Now, Acc considers the possibility that a_6 is acceptable and thus a_2 is not. Acc can then decide whether to share or hide a_2, since he considers that the argument might not be accepted.

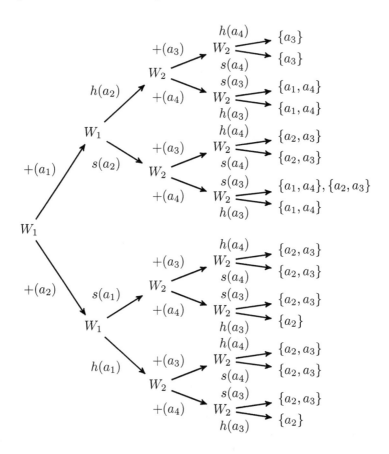

Figure 9. Multi-agent commitment graph for Example 24.

EXAMPLE 24 (Four arguments, continued from Example 11). Recall running example 11. Assume that neither agent trusts the other. In Figure 9, we can see that in this case, the decisions of the agents have a major impact on the reasoning of the judge. Note also that in this case, the agents also have to decide which extension to accept before making any decisions about how to communicate this extension. Following the notation of Dauphin *et al.* [2018], we represent this by using $+a$ when an agent commits to accepting an argument and $-a$ when the agent commits to rejecting it.

However, in Figure 9, we notice that there is a lot of redundancy between some nodes. By applying a similar method to [Dauphin *et al.*, 2018], we can reduce the graph to ensure that every node represents a meaningful commitment that isn't merely the logical consequence of a previous commitment.

We can define a reduction that collapses a node if for each child, the subgraphs that it can reach is isomorphic. We remove the node in question and replace it with one of its children, removing every other child from the original node. We first define what we mean by the subgraph that a given node generates.

DEFINITION 25. Let $(\mathcal{C}, \mathcal{V}, l)$ be a multi-agent commitment graph and $c \in \mathcal{C}$. We say that the *subgraph generated by* c is $(\mathcal{C}', \mathcal{V}', l')$ where $\mathcal{C}'$ is the set of all nodes accessible with $\mathcal{V}$ from c, where $\mathcal{V}' = \mathcal{V} \cap \mathcal{C}'^2$ and where l' is the restriction of l on $\mathcal{C}'$.

DEFINITION 26. Let $(\mathcal{C}, \mathcal{V}, l)$ be a multi-agent commitment graph and $c \in \mathcal{C}$. We say that a node is *reducible* iff for every node $c' \in \mathcal{C}$ such that $(c, c') \in \mathcal{V}$, the subgraphs generated by the c' have an isomorphic relationship[2] to one other. In this case, we say that the graph where the subgraph generated by such a c has been replaced by the graph generated by the graph of its child c' is a *reduction* of the graph. If no such reduction exists, we say that the graph is *minimal*.

EXAMPLE 27 (Four arguments, continued from Example 24). A minimal reduction of the decision graph from Figure 9 is depicted in Figure 10. Notice that every time a node used to be connected to two leaves labelled with the same extension, that node has now been replaced by a leaf labelled with that extension. Observe also that when W_1 committed to accepting a_2, it did not matter whether W_1 hid or revealed a_1. Therefore, the two subgraphs generated by those leaves could be merged, simplifying the resulting graph.

6 Related and future work

In this section, we provide an overview of existing related research and some ideas for future work.

6.1 Abstract argumentation

The *Handbook* series on formal argumentation provides an up-to-date overview of the area. The first volume [Baroni *et al.*, 2018] presents the foundations of abstract and structured argumentation, and connects it to the rest of the argumentation literature. The second volume (to appear) offers extensions to abstract argumentation, analyses its dynamic aspects, and investigates the field at a meta level.

Dung [1995] introduced the notion of admissibility-based semantics as a generalisation of stable sets. While the definitions in this chapter are based

---

[2]Two graphs are isomorphic iff there exists a one-to-one mapping from one graph to the other graph that preserves the relation and labels.

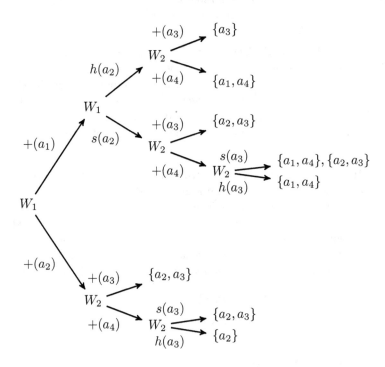

Figure 10. Reduction of the commitment graph in Figure 9.

on the idea of stable sets, they can easily be adapted to other notions of acceptability, such as admissibility. Since the work of Dung, many other notions have been introduced, such as naïve-based semantics [Bondarenko *et al.*, 1997], weak admissibility [Baumann *et al.*, 2020] and strong admissibility [Baroni and Giacomin, 2007]. It remains to be seen whether the approach described in this chapter generalises to all of these.

The idea of using sub-frameworks as an output of the semantics has been introduced previously in various contexts, most notably attack semantics [Villata *et al.*, 2011] and argumentation frameworks with recursive attacks [Baroni *et al.*, 2011]. The interpretation and application described in this chapter are, however, novel.

Baroni *et al.* [2005] had previously introduced the idea of local functions, and they have been used in subsequent work, most notably concerning principles [van der Torre and Vesic, 2018], multi-sorted argumentation [Rienstra *et al.*, 2011], and input/output argumentation [Baroni *et al.*, 2014]. In the work of Arisaka *et al.* [2018], the sorts were interpreted as different agents and combined with sub-framework semantics. The work of Giacomin [2017] and van der Torre *et al.* [2018] have a similar interpretation for the sorts.

Dialogue semantics has been widely studied, and a comprehensive overview of the work carried out in this direction is provided by Caminada [2018]. In these dialogues, two players exchange arguments from a given argumentation framework in order to prove or disprove the acceptability of a particular argument. These dialogues serve as a proof theory for the acceptability status (sceptical, credulous) of arguments with respect to various semantics, allowing one to prove the acceptability of an argument without requiring the computation of all the extensions. In this chapter, we considered a different kind of dialogue where all agents have their own sets of arguments and choose to hide or reveal them. We then observed how these choices affect the final verdict of an external observer. An interesting line of work would be to combine these two kinds of dialogues and provide a proof theory for acceptability statuses in the frameworks presented in this chapter.

Some researchers have followed a principle-based approach to the classification of argumentation semantics [Baroni and Giacomin, 2007; van der Torre and Vesic, 2018]. A natural related first step towards the further development of multi-agent argumentation would be a definition of principles.

The work of Amgoud and Ben-Naim [2013] aims to extract more information from argumentation frameworks by providing rankings pertaining to their degree of acceptability rather than sets of acceptable arguments. An interesting continuation of the work described in this chapter would be to investigate the effects of having agents share a ranking instead of a subframework. Then, the agents could also choose how much of their ranking to share, thereby hiding some of their arguments.

The dialogue semantics described in section 5 is based on the work of Dauphin *et al.* [2018], which examines the decisions made while choosing an extension from a set of extensions. Another work of theirs [Dauphin *et al.*, 2019] studies a similar structure for a different purpose. There, the focus is on detailing the process of getting from an argumentation framework to providing extensions to the semantics in order to allow different semantics to be combined in a meaningful way.

Many extensions of abstract argumentation frameworks have been proposed, together with more general notions of acceptance. Some example additions to the basic argumentation frameworks are preferences [Amgoud and Vesic, 2014], support relations [Cayrol and Lagasquie-Schiex, 2005], abstract dialectical frameworks [Brewka and Woltran, 2010], and higher-order relations [Baroni *et al.*, 2011]. Abstract dialectical frameworks are discussed in more detail in the first volume of the *Handbook of Formal Argumentation* [Brewka *et al.*, 2018], while other extensions are discussed in the second volume of the *Handbook* (to appear).

While the agent-to-agent relation of trust is natural, we could alternatively define a function that maps an agent to a set of arguments it trusts [Arisaka *et al.*, 2018], which adds to the expressiveness. Arisaka and Bistarelli [2018] have studied the usage of a version of the agent-to-agent relation with an extra parameter for determining the mode of interaction for characterising dynamic collaboration among agents through defence delegation.

6.2 Merging argumentation frameworks and social argumentation

Whereas our model of multi-agent argumentation takes its inspiration from game theory, and it can be further developed towards coalitional game theory by introducing the arguments of sets of agents, an alternative approach to multi-agent argumentation takes its inspiration from voting theory, and more generally from social choice. One way to generalise our model towards such approaches is to consider a *Src relation* (rather than a function) between arguments and agents, such that two agents share the same argument. Likewise we can consider the sharing of attacks.

Sharing arguments:

Sharing an argument may mean that two arguments were put forward independently (so that there are two independent sources), or that one agent learned the argument from the other agent and copied it (so that there is one source and one copycat), or that two agents working together have prepared an argument using their combined knowledge (so that there is one source consisting of two agents).

Sharing attacks:

Attacks among arguments either do or do not depend on the agent. For example, in the former case, if two agents A and B both have arguments a and b, it may be the case that for agent A we have that a attacks b, and vice versa for agent B i.e. argument b attacks argument a. This could be interpreted using agent-specific preferences where agent A prefers a to b, whereas agent B prefers argument b to argument a.

We can relate this sharing of arguments and attacks also to the trust social network we introduced in Section 3. In an extreme case, it could be that if an agent trusts another agent, then (s)he also incorporates his/her arguments and/or attacks into his/her own framework. Moreover, as we discuss in Section 3 of the chapter, if we assume the trust relation in Section 3 to be symmetric and transitive, then the equivalence classes of this trust relation may be called coalitions as well. If agents can share arguments, immediately the question arises: how is this related to coalitions? For example, do agents in a coalition share the same arguments? We believe this would be a natural assumption.

This can be related in different ways to existing theories of merging argumentation and social argumentation. For example, in social choice, the terms merging, fusion, voting and aggregation are often used interchangeably. Moreover, there are closely related approaches like negotiation with slightly different formal theories. There is a choice between combining the frameworks of the individual agents into a common framework by voting on the existence of arguments and attacks [Coste-Marquis *et al.*, 2007; Leite and Martins, 2011], or making it so that they can agree on the framework and vote on the extensions [Awad *et al.*, 2017; Caminada and Pigozzi, 2011; Bodanza and Auday, 2009; Tohmé *et al.*, 2008].

We believe that this raises the challenge of how to define a general research programme of multi-agent argumentation, of which all the above approaches are specific instances. Such a general theory would then explain precisely how a relatively simple procedure like voting can be compared to much more complex social phenomena like deliberation, negotiation, and argumentation.

6.3 Strategic dialogue games and 3+ multi-agent argumentation

In strategic dialogue games and agent persuasion (see [Thimm, 2014] for a somewhat dated survey on the former, and [Hunter, 2018] on the latter), multiple agents (most of the literature focuses on two parties) play a dialogue game, where the agents take turns in putting forward arguments with the aim of getting some arguments accepted (the goal of a proponent agent) or rejected (the goal of an opponent agent) in the end.

Ruyta Arisaka   Jérémie Dauphin   Ken Satoh   Leendert van der Torre

While there has been some discussion of argumentation games under perfect information [Rahwan and Larson, 2009; Riveret and Prakken, 2008; Procaccia and Rosenschein, 2005] that consider assigning payoffs to moves of putting forward a set of arguments and attacks, with the notion of equilibria then defined as in game theory, a dialogue game may not assume perfect knowledge of the environment on the part of the agents, thus opening up opportunities for opponent modelling, i.e. estimating their opponents' argumentation graphs, preferences, trusts, semantics and so on [Arisaka et al., 2019; Oren and Norman, 2009; Sakama, 2012; Hadjinikolis et al., 2013; Hadoux et al., 2015; Panisson et al., 2018] to gain strategic advantages.

Moreover, the arguments put forward may not always be truthful, since a greater strategic advantage may be gained by withholding information [Rahwan and Larson, 2008; Riveret and Prakken, 2008; Hadjinikolis et al., 2013] or even by bluffing (common in Poker, Mafia/Werewolf, Mah-jong, and other imperfect information games). Strategic deceptive argumentation was first modelled explicitly in [Sakama, 2012]. A variation is found in [Takahashi and Yokohama, 2016] which relaxes the assumption of attack-omniscience (every agent knows argument-to-argument relations between two arguments precisely as long as the arguments are known to the agents). Other assumptions and certain anomalies in both studies were examined in [Arisaka et al., 2019], which also linked detected deception/honesty to changes in trustworthiness. The work of Kuipers and Denzinger [Kuipers and Denzinger, 2010] studied exploitation in logic-based argumentation that may arise from agents' differing logical inference capabilities. There is also a study on measuring the accuracy of lying/hiding detection based on observations on an agent's traits [Kontarinis and Toni, 2015].

Multi-agent imperfect information argumentation among strictly more than two parties present other technicalities such as concurrency [Arisaka and Satoh, 2018; Arisaka and Ito, 2019] and collaboration [Arisaka et al., 2018; Arisaka and Bistarelli, 2018]. There has also been discussion of two-party perfect information dialogue games with an external observer, where the two agents aim to persuade the observer to accept some arguments by estimating the observer's belief about where argument-to-argument attacks are taking place [Grossi and van der Hoek, 2013].

In this chapter, we had a glimpse of opponent modelling, collaboration, information withholding, selective trust in other agents, and above all how these affect agent semantics, by letting the agent choose whether or not to take into account input argument(s) for computing its semantics, and what to share. As we observed in Example 11, Example 12 and Theorem 15, collective acceptance may not always match the stable semantics applied globally, depending on whom is trusted by which agents.

Some more recent work on persuasion also focuses on incorporating strategic aspects into natural language situations such as chatbots [Hunter *et al.*, 2019]. They combine domain modelling (predicting the arguments that could come up in the discussion), user modelling (representing the user's beliefs) and dialogue strategies (selecting the best argumentation moves for persuading the user). An interesting question is how to improve their system by incorporating the dialogue strategies outlined in this chapter.

7 Conclusion

Dung's abstract argumentation is the de facto standard for argumentation-as-inference. To bring it closer to the theories of argumentation-as-dialogue, we introduced agent interaction and dialogue into Dung's theory. This is a step towards a unified formal theory of argumentation covering both argumentation-as-inference and argumentation-as-dialogue, just like game theory is a unified theory for strategic and extensive games.

The starting point for multi-agent argumentation is the concept of conditional acceptance. In particular, an argument that an agent does not accept can be still be put forward as part of the discussion. For example, agents can explain why they do not accept particular arguments by presenting counter-arguments to the unaccepted arguments, and they may even be willing to accept the argument if convinced by the other agents that their counter-arguments are wrong.

Multi-agent argumentation assigns arguments to agents, and associates individual acceptance functions with these agents. Multi-agent argumentation extends input/output argumentation in two ways. First, whether an agent accepts an argument put forward by another agent depends on the trust the agents have in one another, which is represented by a social network. Secondly, agents can decide whether or not to hide some of their arguments from the other agents. This concerns, in particular, the arguments they do not accept themselves.

An example from a court case illustrates the application of the above to legal reasoning. The agent abstract argumentation model distinguishes the global reasoning of judges from the local reasoning of the accused, prosecutors, witnesses, lawyers, experts and so on. The agents decide autonomously whether to trust the other agents in the sense that they take some of their arguments into account. Moreover, they decide autonomously whether to accept or reject their own arguments, and whether to bring their arguments forward in court. The arguments that are globally accepted by the judge are defined using a game theoretic equilibrium definition. The example distinguishes between various direct and indirect ways in which agents' arguments can be used against their other arguments.

Ruyta Arisaka   Jérémie Dauphin   Ken Satoh   Leendert van der Torre

A dialogue is a sequence of steps from the framework to the extensions where at each step of the sequence, agents can commit to accepting some arguments, or commit to hiding or revealing one of their rejected arguments. The revealed arguments are then aggregated and an external observer, in our example the judge, can compute which arguments are finally accepted at a global level.

The theory of multi-agent argumentation discussed in this chapter can be generalised in the way that is described in the *Handbook of Formal Argumentation*, for example by studying other semantics, defining principles, and by using structured argumentation theory, algorithms, and extensions that involve other concepts like preference and support. These further developments can be guided by our desire to bring the theory of abstract argumentation closer to existing theories of argumentation-as-dialogue. Several concrete proposals are discussed in the related work section of this chapter.

Acknowledgements

We thank Massimiliano Giacomin and our two anonymous reviewers for insightful feedback on an earlier version of this chapter. Leendert van der Torre acknowledges financial support from the Fonds National de la Recherche Luxembourg (INTER/Mobility/19/13995684/DLAl/van der Torre)

BIBLIOGRAPHY

[Amgoud and Ben-Naim, 2013] Leila Amgoud and Jonathan Ben-Naim. Ranking-based semantics for argumentation frameworks. In *International Conference on Scalable Uncertainty Management*, pages 134–147. Springer, 2013.

[Amgoud and Vesic, 2014] Leila Amgoud and Srdjan Vesic. Rich preference-based argumentation frameworks. *International Journal of Approximate Reasoning*, 55(2):585–606, 2014.

[Arisaka and Bistarelli, 2018] Ryuta Arisaka and Stefano Bistarelli. Defence Outsourcing in Argumentation. In *Proceedings of the Seventh International Conference on Computational Models of Argument (COMMA)*, pages 353–360, 2018.

[Arisaka and Ito, 2019] Ryuta Arisaka and Takayuki Ito. Numerical Abstract Persuasion Argumentation for Expressing Concurrent Multi-Agent Negotiations. In *IJCAI Best of Workshops 2019*, 2019.

[Arisaka and Satoh, 2018] Ryuta Arisaka and Ken Satoh. Abstract Argumentation / Persuasion / Dynamics. In *Proceedings of the Twenty-First International Conference on Principles and Practice of Multi-Agent Systems (PRIMA)*, pages 331–343, 2018.

[Arisaka et al., 2018] Ryuta Arisaka, Ken Satoh, and Leendert van der Torre. Anything you say may be used against you in a court of law: Abstract Agent Argumentation (Triple-A). In *Proceedings of the Ninth Workshop on Artificial Intelligence and the Complexity of Legal Reasoning (AICOL)*, pages 427–442, 2018.

[Arisaka et al., 2019] Ryuta Arisaka, Makoto Hagiwara, and Takayuki Ito. Deception/Honesty Detection and (Mis)trust Building in Manipulable Multi-Agent Argumentation: An insight. In *Proceedings of the Twenty-second International Conference on Principles and Practice of Multi-Agent Systems (PRIMA)*, pages 443–451, 2019.

[Awad et al., 2017] Edmod Awad, Richard Booth, Fernando Tohmé, and Iyad Rahwan. Judgement Aggregation in Multi-Agent Argumentation. *Journal of Logic and Computation*, 27(1):227–259, 2017.

[Baroni and Giacomin, 2007] Pietro Baroni and Massimiliano Giacomin. On principle-based evaluation of extension-based argumentation semantics. *Artificial Intelligence*, 171(10-15):675–700, 2007.

[Baroni et al., 2005] Pietro Baroni, Massimiliano Giacomin, and Giovanni Guida. Scc-recursiveness: a general schema for argumentation semantics. *Artificial Intelligence*, 168(1-2):162–210, 2005.

[Baroni et al., 2011] Pietro Baroni, Federico Cerutti, Massimiliano Giacomin, and Giovanni Guida. AFRA: argumentation framework with recursive attacks. *International Journal of Approximate Reasoning*, 52(1):19–37, 2011.

[Baroni et al., 2014] Pietro Baroni, Guido Boella, Federico Cerutti, Massimiliano Giacomin, Leendert W. N. van der Torre, and Serena Villata. On the input/output behavior of argumentation frameworks. *Artificial Intelligence*, 217:144–197, 2014.

[Baroni et al., 2018] Pietro Baroni, Dov M Gabbay, Massimiliano Giacomin, and Leendert van der Torre. *Handbook of formal argumentation*. College Publications, 2018.

[Baumann et al., 2020] Ringo Baumann, Gerhard Brewka, and Markus Ulbricht. Revisiting the foundations of abstract argumentation–semantics based on weak admissibility and weak defense. In *Proceedings of the Thirty-Fourth International Conference on Artificial Intelligence (AAAI)*, 2020.

[Bodanza and Auday, 2009] G. Bodanza and M. Auday. Social argument justification: some mechanisms and conditions for their coincidence. In *Proceedings of the Tenth European Conference on Symbolic and Quantitative Approaches to Reasoning with Uncertainty (ECSQARU)*, pages 95–106, 2009.

[Bondarenko et al., 1997] Andrei Bondarenko, Phan Minh Dung, Robert A Kowalski, and Francesca Toni. An abstract, argumentation-theoretic approach to default reasoning. *Artificial intelligence*, 93(1-2):63–101, 1997.

[Brewka and Woltran, 2010] Gerhard Brewka and Stefan Woltran. Abstract dialectical frameworks. In *Twelfth International Conference on the Principles of Knowledge Representation and Reasoning*, 2010.

[Brewka et al., 2018] Gerhard Brewka, Stefan Ellmauthaler, Hannes Strass, Johannes P. Wallner, and Stefan Woltran. Abstract dialetical frameworks. In Pietro Baroni, Dov M Gabbay, Massimiliano Giacomin, and Leendert van der Torre, editors, *Handbook of formal argumentation*, volume 1, chapter 5, pages 237–285. College Publications, 2018.

[Caminada and Pigozzi, 2011] Martin Caminada and G. Pigozzi. On judgement aggregation in abstract argumentation. *Autonomous Agents and Multi-Agent Systems*, 22(1):64–102, 2011.

[Caminada, 2018] Martin Caminada. Argumentation semantics as formal discussion. In Pietro Baroni, Dov M Gabbay, Massimiliano Giacomin, and Leendert van der Torre, editors, *Handbook of formal argumentation*, volume 1, chapter 10, pages 487–518. College Publications, 2018.

[Cayrol and Lagasquie-Schiex, 2005] Claudette Cayrol and Marie-Christine Lagasquie-Schiex. On the acceptability of arguments in bipolar argumentation frameworks. In *European Conference on Symbolic and Quantitative Approaches to Reasoning and Uncertainty*, pages 378–389. Springer, 2005.

[Coste-Marquis et al., 2007] Sylvie Coste-Marquis, Caroline Devred, and Sébastien Konieczny. On the Merging of Dung's Argumentation Systems. *Artificial Intelligence*, 171(10-15):730–753, 2007.

[Dauphin et al., 2018] Jérémie Dauphin, Marcos Cramer, and Leendert van der Torre. Abstract and concrete decision graphs for choosing extensions of argumentation frameworks. *Computational Models of Argument*, 2018.

[Dauphin *et al.*, 2019] Jérémie Dauphin, Marcos Cramer, and Leendert van der Torre. A dynamic approach for combining abstract argumentation semantics. In *Dynamics, Uncertainty and Reasoning*, pages 21–43. Springer, 2019.

[Degenne and Forsé, 1999] Alain Degenne and Michel Forsé. *Introducing social networks.* Sage, 1999.

[Dung, 1995] Phan M. Dung. On the Acceptability of Arguments and Its Fundamental Role in Nonmonotonic Reasoning, Logic Programming, and n-Person Games. *Artificial Intelligence*, 77(2):321–357, 1995.

[Giacomin, 2017] Massimiliano Giacomin. Handling heterogeneous disagreements through abstract argumentation. In *International Conference on Principles and Practice of Multi-Agent Systems (PRIMA)*, pages 3–11. Springer, 2017.

[Grossi and van der Hoek, 2013] Davide Grossi and W. van der Hoek. Audience-based uncertainty in abstract argument games. In *Proceedings of the Twenty-third International Joint Conference on Artificial Intelligence (IJCAI)*, pages 143–149, 2013.

[Hadjinikolis *et al.*, 2013] Christos Hadjinikolis, Yiannis Siantos, Sanjay Modgil, Elizabeth Black, and Peter McBurney. Opponent modelling in persuasion dialogues. In *Proceedings of the Twenty-third International Joint Conference on Artificial Intelligence (IJCAI)*, pages 164–170, 2013.

[Hadoux *et al.*, 2015] Emmanuel Hadoux, Aurélie Beynier, Nicolas Maudet, Paul Weng, and Anthony Hunter. Optimization of Probabilistic Argumentation with Markov Decision Models. In *Proceedings of the Twenty-Fourth International Joint Conference on Artificial Intelligence (IJCAI)*, pages 2004–2010, 2015.

[Heaney and Israel, 2008] Catherine A Heaney and Barbara A Israel. Social networks and social support. *Health behavior and health education: Theory, research, and practice*, 4:189–210, 2008.

[Hunter *et al.*, 2019] Anthony Hunter, Lisa Chalaguine, Tomasz Czernuszenko, Emmanuel Hadoux, and Sylwia Polberg. Towards computational persuasion via natural language argumentation dialogues. In *Joint German/Austrian Conference on Artificial Intelligence (Künstliche Intelligenz)*, pages 18–33. Springer, 2019.

[Hunter, 2018] Anthony Hunter. Towards a framework for computational persuasion with applications in behaviour change. *Argument & Computation*, 9(1):15–40, 2018.

[Huynh *et al.*, 2006] Trung Dong Huynh, Nicholas R Jennings, and Nigel R Shadbolt. An integrated trust and reputation model for open multi-agent systems. *Autonomous Agents and Multi-Agent Systems (AAMAS)*, 13(2):119–154, 2006.

[Kontarinis and Toni, 2015] Dionysios Kontarinis and Francesca Toni. Identifying Malicious Behaviour in Multi-party Bipolar Argumentation Behaviour. In *Proceedings of the Thirteenth European Conference on Multi-Agent Systems and Third International Conference on Agreement Technologies (EUMMAS/AT)*, pages 267–278, 2015.

[Kuipers and Denzinger, 2010] Andrew Kuipers and Jörg Denzinger. Pitfalls in Practical Open Multi Agent Argumentation Systems: Malicious Argumentation. In *Proceedings of the Third International Conference on Computational Models of Argument (COMMA)*, pages 323–334, 2010.

[Leite and Martins, 2011] Joao Leite and Joao Martins. Social abstract argumentation. In *Twenty-Second International Joint Conference on Artificial Intelligence (IJCAI)*, 2011.

[Liao, 2013] Beishui Liao. Toward incremental computation of argumentation semantics: A decomposition-based approach. *Annals of Mathematics and Artificial Intelligence*, 67(3-4):319–358, 2013.

[Mui, 2002] Lik Mui. *Computational models of trust and reputation: Agents, evolutionary games, and social networks.* PhD thesis, Massachusetts Institute of Technology, 2002.

[Oren and Norman, 2009] Nir Oren and Timothy J. Norman. Arguing Using Opponent Models. In *Proceedings of the Sixth International Workshop on Argumentation in Multi-Agent Systems (ArgMAS*, pages 160–174, 2009.

[Panisson *et al.*, 2018] Alison R. Panisson, Simon Parsons, Peter McBurney, and Rafael H. Bordini. Choosing Appropriate Arguments from Trustworthy Sources. In *Proceedings of the Seventh International Conference on Computational Models of Argument (COMMA)*, pages 345–352, 2018.

[Prakken, 2018] Henry Prakken. Historical overview of formal argumentation. In Pietro Baroni, Dov M Gabbay, Massimiliano Giacomin, and Leendert van der Torre, editors, *Handbook of formal argumentation*, volume 1, chapter 2, pages 75–143. College Publications, 2018.

[Procaccia and Rosenschein, 2005] A. Procaccia and J. Rosenschein. Extensive-form argumentation games. In *Proceedings of the Third European Workshop on Multi-Agent Systems (EUMAS)*, pages 312–322, 2005.

[Rahwan and Larson, 2008] Iyad Rahwan and K. Larson. Mechanism design for abstract argumentation. In *Proceedings of the Seventh International Conference on Autonomous Agents and Multi-Agent Systems (AAMAS)*, pages 1031–1038, 2008.

[Rahwan and Larson, 2009] I. Rahwan and K. Larson. Argumentation and game theory. In *Argumentation in Artificial Intelligence*, pages 321–339. Springer, 2009.

[Ramchurn *et al.*, 2004] Sarvapali D Ramchurn, Dong Huynh, and Nicholas R Jennings. Trust in multi-agent systems. *The Knowledge Engineering Review*, 19(1):1–25, 2004.

[Rienstra *et al.*, 2011] Tjitze Rienstra, Alan Perotti, Serena Villata, Dov M. Gabbay, and Leendert W. N. van der Torre. Multi-sorted argumentation. In *Theory and Applications of Formal Argumentation - First International Workshop, TAFA 2011. Barcelona, Spain, July 16-17, 2011, Revised Selected Papers*, pages 215–231, 2011.

[Riveret and Prakken, 2008] R. Riveret and Henry Prakken. Heuristics in argumentation: A game theory investigation. In *Proceedings of the Second International Conference on Computational Models of Argument (COMMA)*, pages 324–335, 2008.

[Sabater and Sierra, 2001] Jordi Sabater and Carles Sierra. Regret: reputation in gregarious societies. In *Proceedings of the Fifth International Conference on Autonomous agents and Multi-Agent Systems (AAMAS)*, pages 194–195, 2001.

[Sabater and Sierra, 2002] Jordi Sabater and Carles Sierra. Reputation and social network analysis in multi-agent systems. In *Proceedings of the first international joint conference on Autonomous agents and multiagent systems: Part 1*, pages 475–482, 2002.

[Sabater and Sierra, 2005] Jordi Sabater and Carles Sierra. Review on computational trust and reputation models. *Artificial intelligence review*, 24(1):33–60, 2005.

[Sakama, 2012] Chiaki Sakama. Dishonest Arguments in Debate Games. In *Proceedings of the Fourth International Conference on Computational Models of Argument (COMMA)*, pages 177–184, 2012.

[Takahashi and Yokohama, 2016] Kazuko Takahashi and Shizuka Yokohama. On a Formal Treatment of Deception in Argumentative Dialogues. In *Proceedings of the Fourteenth European Conference on Multi-Agent Sytems and Fourth International Conference on Agreement Technologies (EUMMAS/AT)*, pages 390–404, 2016.

[Thimm, 2014] Matthias Thimm. Strategic Argumentation in Multi-Agent Systems. *Künstliche Intelligenz*, 28(3):159–168, 2014.

[Tohmé *et al.*, 2008] Fernando Tohmé, G. Bodanza, and Guillermo R. Simari. Aggregation of attack relations: a social-choice theoretical analysis of defeasibility criteria. In *Proceedings of the Fifth International Symposium on Foundations of Information and Knowledge Systems (FoIKS)*, pages 8–23, 2008.

[van der Torre and Vesic, 2018] Leendert van der Torre and Srdjan Vesic. The principle-based approach to abstract argumentation semantics. In Pietro Baroni, Dov M Gabbay, Massimiliano Giacomin, and Leendert van der Torre, editors, *Handbook of formal argumentation*, volume 1, chapter 16, pages 797–837. College Publications, 2018.

[van der Torre *et al.*, 2018] Leendert van der Torre, Tjitze Rienstra, and Dov Gabbay. Argumentation as exogenous coordination. In *It's All About Coordination*, pages 208–223. Springer, 2018.

Ruyta Arisaka   Jérémie Dauphin   Ken Satoh   Leendert van der Torre

[Villata *et al.*, 2011] Serena Villata, Guido Boella, and Leendert W. N. van der Torre. Attack semantics for abstract argumentation. In Toby Walsh, editor, *IJCAI 2011, Proceedings of the 22nd International Joint Conference on Artificial Intelligence, Barcelona, Catalonia, Spain, July 16-22, 2011*, pages 406–413. IJCAI/AAAI, 2011.

Ryuta Arisaka
Kyoto University
Graduate School of Informatics
Japan
Email: arisaka.ryuta.7e@kyoto-u.ac.jp

Jérémie Dauphin
University of Luxembourg
Luxembourg
Email: jeremie.dauphin@uni.lu

Ken Satoh
National Institue of Informatics
Principles of. Informatics Research Division
Tokyo 101-8430, Japan
Email: ksatoh@nii.ac.jp

Leendert van der Torre
University of Luxembourg
Luxembourg
Email: leon.vandertorre@uni.lu

10

The Law of Evidence and Labelled Deduction: Twenty Years Later[1]

Dov Gabbay
John Woods

ABSTRACT. The purpose of this chapter is to reveal, through examples, the potential for collaboration between the theory of legal reasoning on the one hand, and some recently developed instruments of formal logic. Three zones of contact are highlighted.

1. The law of evidence, in the light of labelled deductive systems (LDSs), discussed through the example of the admissibility of hearsay evidence.

2. The give and take of legal debate in general, and regarding the acceptability of evidence in particular, represented using the abstract systems of argumentation developed in logic, notably the coloured graphs of Bench-Capon. This is considered through an imaginary example.

3. The use of Bayesian networks as tools for analysing the effects of uncertainty on the legal status of actions, illustrated via the same example

These three kinds of technique do not exclude each other. On the contrary, many cases of legal argument will need the combined resources of all three.

1 Background: Logic and Law

In the first half of the past century, logic took a turn to the mathematical, and many were of the view that logic was the better for it. In the passage from Frege to Whitehead & Russell and on to the likes of Tarski and Church, first-order extensional logic would acquire the historically puzzling honorific "classical", notwithstanding that Frege's and W & R's logics did not fill that

---

[1] An earlier version was originally published in Φ News, Vol 4, October 2003, pp. 5–46. A revised book version was published in D. M. Gabbay, Canivez, P., Rahman, S., and Thiercelin, A. (Eds.) *Approaches to Legal Rationality, Logic, Epistemology and the Unity of Science 20*, 1st Edition, Springer 2010, pp. 295–331.

bill.[2] One of the main nonclassical forces in this period lay in propositional extensions of classical logic for the modalities necessity and possibility. These were adapted in turn to the-so-called modalities of knowledge, belief, time and tense, and obligation and permission. Also important was the development of propositional logics in which the classical theorem mislabelled "*ex falso quodlibet*" is blocked.[3] The theorem asserts that from a contradiction every sentence follows of necessity. It was often taken to mean that from a contradiction everything whatever can be *inferred*. It doesn't mean that in fact, and it is not true. Although many a "paraconsistentist" logician was guilty of this confusion, there was great value in the attention they called to inference from inconsistent information. There is reason to believe that humans routinely reason from inconsistent background information without ever going completely to the dogs see Woods [2015; 2018a]. Rational inconsistency-management remains an open problem in logic and computer science and yet an insufficiently recognized one [Gabbay and Hunter, 1991; Gabbay and Hunter, 1992; Mortensen, 1995; Mortensen, 2010; Hewitt and Woods, 2015]. It is a central problem in the logic of jury-trials and yet, there too, it wants for recognition and resolution [Woods, 2018a, appendix G, "Inconsistently based verdicts"].

At the turn of that century, the universal Turing machine made its début, and there was launched an unending quest to build a machine that's worth talking to. In time, it would be possible for computers to talk to computers of different kinds. What is sought now is a computer that can talk to us without having to be simulacra of us. Since the mere fact of human conversation is a standing invitation to voice differences of opinion, computer science has a large stake in analyzing human argument. This marks a return of the human individual to the focal exactions of formal methods [Gabbay, 1992a; Gabbay, 1992b]. Modal logics acquired their quantificational wings and certain logics of deduction would, in the company of information theory, take the turn to pragmatics [Gabbay, 1992a; Gabbay, 1992b; Hintikka, 1999; Gabbay and Woods, 2003a]. Meanwhile the philosophy of mathematics sorted itself into the standard *collegia* of logicism, intuitionism and formalism. In what remained of the final half of the 20th century, logic would lose much of its historically acknowledged claim to be the one and only authoritative canonical framework for deductive thought. It is not that the very idea of it lost all credence, but rather that no one theoretical claimant to the title managed to qualify itself for it. Not only had pluralism

---

[2]Frege's was a second-order functional calculus harnessed to a theory of what we now call sets. Whitehead and Russell's logic was a typed logic over propositional functions, hence not extensional.

[3]An accurate name is "*ex contradictione quodlibet*".

taken deep root in logic's deductive precincts [Carnielli *et al.*, 2009], computer scientists had turned their attention to what mathematical logicians had long ignored. It was an immensely profitable turning in which, again, the reasoning agent was restored to formal consideration in the modelling of inference, decision-making, and tactical and strategic thinking. Arising from these freshly restimulated contexts were solid theories of nonmonotonic reasoning, defeasible reasoning, default judgement, autoepistemic reasoning, abductive logic and the sundry operations of AI [Fisher *et al.*, 2005]. Fruitful crossovers were wrought between the modal logics of belief, time and obligation, various of which skillfully negotiated and softened the older boundaries that had somewhat lazily dispersed mathematical philosophy to the camps of the classical, intuitionist and the formalist [Kripke, 1959; Kripke, 1963].

Towards the end of the 1990s, logics of abductive inference started coming into flower [Aliseda, 1999; Kuipers, 1999; Flack and Kakas, 2000; Magnani, 2001; Magnani, 2009; Magnani, 2017; Walton, 2004; Gabbay and Woods, 2005a; Park, 2017; Niiniluoto, 2018], and efforts would soon be made to model aspects of legal reasoning abductively [Walton, 2007; Woods, 2010; Woods, 2018]. The emphasis of much of this work fell on reasoning as a practical matter, and since the agents who reason practically are beings like us ensuing logics would in time take a naturalistic turn to the analysis of human reasoning. It would be a turn for the better for the logic of law. Abductive logic, too, would take an expressly naturalistic turn [Magnani, 2019; Chifi and Pietarinen, 2019] against an enlarging background of naturalistic approaches to inference more generally [Woods, 2013; Magnani, 2015; Magnani, 2018; Ransom, 2019; Englebretsen, 2019].

Meanwhile, a full-scale rebellion against the mathematicised formal logics of the day was launched by informal logicians who had taken up the task of restoring the systematic studying of fallacies to the research programmes of logic. If we date this resistance from the year in which Charles Hamblin's book *Fallacies* appeared [Hamblin, 1970], we would see soon after an emerging and prosperous interweaving of logic and epistemology, some of it very high levels of mathematical abstraction, and others more closely tethered to what happens on the ground of everyday thought and action [Hendricks, 2006]. In virtually all these often rivalrous iterations, there are unmistakable commonalities. In the main, the target of these myriad approaches was the human actor, making his way through life in real time as best he can with the resources at his command. This common orientation called for consideration of goals, actions, time and resources. A fruit of this widely shared focus was the cross-disciplinary readiness, even among rival theorists, to adopt from one another aspects of their proceedings in hopes of using them to greater advantage in their own respective approaches [Gabbay and Woods, 2010]. Researchers would often approach problems in their own respective domains of enquiry by modelling them on the way theories in other domains treated the problems that cropped up there.[4] One day in London, Ray Reiter remarked to the present authors, "It is deliciously wild! Everyone is eating everyone else's lunch!" He did not say this complainingly.[5]

An earlier and also important influence on the development of informal logic was the appearance in 1958 of Stephen Toulmin's *The Uses of Argument* which, among other things, offered a more complex representation of argument structure than the more standard premiss + premiss + conclusion model such as would be found in such textbooks as Copi [1953]. Known as the Toulmin Model, it picked out features of legal reasoning which Toulmin believed to be generalizable to arguments of all subject matters [Toulmin, 1958]. Although the Toulmin Model has continued to play well in theories of argument, perhaps a more substantial jolt to received opinion was delivered in Toulmin's primer on the philosophy of science in the Hutchison Library series in 1953. In it Toulmin admonished theorists of inductive and probabilistic reasoning for their over-use of Bayesian methods, especially in contexts for which they are especially ill-suited. *The Uses of Argument* roiled mid-century thought about argument, to such an extent as to have brought it about that Stephen Toulmin was analytic philosophy's "most refuted author".[6]

Nineteen ninety-two marks a significant step in the logical investigation of legal reasoning, with the establishment of the journal *Artificial Intelligence and Law*, currently edited by Kevin Ashley, Trevor Bench-Capon and Giovanni Sartor. Soon after, T. F. Gordon's monograph on AI modelling of procedural justice would appear [Gordon, 1995]. In 2001, the present authors announced a research program in what came to be known as the practical logic of cognitive systems.[7] While not explicitly focused on ei-

---

[4]For example, the so-called Woods-Walton Approach to fallacy theory found profitable assistance in intuitionist logic, graph theory, relatedness logic, aggregate theory, plausibility logics, dialectics, dialogue logics, and decision theory.

[5]Also significant is the relaxation of logic's mathematical preclusion of the physical advocated in Putnam [Putnam, 1968]. The birth of quantum logic would have irritated Frege, but Putnam's suggestion that logic should be seen as a natural science would have infuriated him. But when it takes the practical turn to objects of nature, this is precisely what the logic of inference turns out to be. In due course, quantum logics would be a flourishing enterprise [Dalla Chiara *et al.*, 2007; Bruza, 2009; Engesser *et al.*, 2009].

[6]In the words of William Alston in 1962, when introducing Toulmin to a packed house at the University of Michigan. We find it surprising that Toulmin's probabilistic deviations didn't raise much dust in the philosophy of science.

[7]Gabbay DM and Woods J. 2001. The new logic, *Logic Journal of the IGPL*, 9, 157–186.

ther AI or the law, it was so structured as to be amenable to such uses. The turn was taken in 2003 in the first iteration of the present study in Φ News 4, 5–46. While it bore the same main title as does the present version, it carried a subtitle which no longer applies — "A Position Paper". That same year there appeared the first volume of our omnibus work, *A Practical Logic of Cognitive Systems* under the title, *Agenda Relevance: A Study in Formal Pragmatics* (2003b), in two sections of which we took up the question of legal relevance (5.3 and 9.7). Two years later legal relevance and legal presumption were taken up in volume 2. *The Reach of Abduction: Insight and Trial* (2005) in sections 8.4 and 8.5.[8] A significant step in the modelling of legal reasoning using AI techniques was Walton [2005]. Building on earlier work on the dialogical structure of legal reasoning [Walton, 1997; Walton, 2002] more AI-oriented work would follow [Walton, 2005; Walton, 2007; Walton, 2008; Walton, 2016], along with co-authored work [Gordon *et al.*, 2007; Reed and Walton, 2007; Walton and Gordon, 2005; Walton, 2008]. Further work in this area includes Gordon [1995], Verheij [2005], Keppens [2009] and Prakken and Sartor [2011]. A well-received reference work on this subject is Bongiovanni, Postema, Rotolo, Sartor and Walton, *Handbook of Legal Reasoning and Argumentation* [2016].

Once logic has evolved in this direction and has developed new logical tools for this purpose, these same kind of new logics and new tools can usefully be adapted to the consideration of similar issues in the law.

Here lies the connection between logic and law. We can say without serious exaggeration that the interface of logic and law is going to be central to the further advancement of logic in the next twenty years. If only we can bring the respective communities together and make them aware of their potential! This is the purpose of this chapter.

We envisage the following main benefits to the law community, in addition to the benefits from existing logical tools and aids available from Artificial Intelligence.

- The proper LDS logic tailored for law of evidence and other judicial arguments can help articulate and clarify (hidden) intuitive common sense principles behind existing practices.

- The LDS methodology includes a system of labelling and stylised hierarchical movements which have logical content. This kind of hierarchy

---

[8]Shortly after, our publisher adopted a new business model and changed course markedly, and among other things, shut down the venerable "Yellow Series", Studies in Logic and the Foundations of Mathematics. They denied us our continued use of the name "A Practical Logic of Cognitive Systems", so a third volume by Woods — *Errors of Reasoning: Naturalizing the Logic of Inference* — would appear in 2013 with College Publications under the new series title "Logic and Cognitive Systems".

can be added to legal specification formats thus giving a better specification language for law without sacrificing the use of ambiguities and variety of interpretations.

It is astonishing to realize that very few people are aware of the true potential of the interaction of the new logics and law. There are many reasons for that, most of them social. The new developments in logic are slow to spread around even among logicians, and certainly among researchers in legal reasoning and legal theory, many of whom still think of "logic" as "Aristotlian syllogism".[9]

Some bridging work between law and logic has been done by C.H. Perelman [Perelman, 1980], who kept in touch with both logicians and judges and lawyers, arguing that logic should play a different — more restricted — role. But when Perelman wrote, the new logical tools were not as available as they are now; and such as were available, Perelman made no use of.

The rise of Horn clause logic programming in the 1980s has helped turn some logicians in the direction of the law, but early attempts to apply logic to law, such as the formalisation of the British Nationality Act [Sergot and Kowalski, 1986], has rightly drawn a strong critical reaction from the legal community on the ground that Horn clause logic is not rich enough to allow for the wealth of nuances and interpretations/explanation/ revision so common in legal reasoning. See also [Aldisert, 1989] by Judge Ruggero J. Aldisert.

This criticism may have been valid in 1980, the objection is no longer valid now, especially in view of many advances made in logics of practical

---

[9]It is instructive to read the following passage on legal reasoning from the July 2003 edition of a basic textbook on legal philosophy, widely taught in the UK (J. W. Harris, *Legal Philosophies*, p 213):

"It is far from easy to get a comprehensive view of the subject [of legal reasoning]. Most writers who have discussed legal reasoning have either concentrated on the form as distinct from the substance of justificatory arguments, or else dealt with only part of the subject. Two forms of argument, the deductive and the inductive, have generally been considered inapposite characterizations of legal argument. Some take the view that deductive argument – from major and minor premises to a logically necessary conclusion – is inappropriate even in clear cases. This may be asserted on the general ground that deductive arguments only hold true of factual propositions not of norms; or on the more specific ground that even the clearest rule may be held not to apply to a case where that would frustrate the purpose of the law or produce absurd consequences, and the decision whether this so or not cannot be dictated by logic. On the other hand, reasoning in clear cases seems very close to deductive reasoning – here is a speed-limit rule applying to all car drivers, I am a car driver, so it applies to me. Even in unclear cases, it can be contended that the form of the argument is deductive, since what is at issue is which of competing rulings should be adopted, granted that the winner will be applied deductively in all cases of the present type – although here our major concern will be with the substantive arguments which dictate choice among the rulings.

reasoning and argumentation.

Logic programmers and deontic logicians have had a somewhat earlier interest in law, have their own conferences and journals [Deon,]. But we doubt if they are aware as a community of all relevant developments in logic. They appear not to realize (or believe) that law is an area of potentially evolutionary significance to logic.

Still valuable are survey works by two key researchers in the area, Trevor Bench-Capon's [2015] survey article for the *Encyclopaedia of Computer Science and Technology* and Henry Prakken's book [1997], *Logical Tools for Modelling Legal Argument*. Prakken's book, especially, takes note of many of the new developments in logic, and argues very strongly in favour of the theoretical connectedness of logic and law. He especially highlights the new developments in defeasible and non-monotonic logics and reasoning from inconsistent data. However, he is unaware of the methodology of labelled deductive systems which subsumes the logic of legal reasoning, among many others, as a special case. More importantly, Prakken believes that 'logic should be regarded as a tool rather than as a model of reasoning', [Prakken, 1997, Section 1.4]. Furthermore, the entire approach to date of the community to logic and law is further restricted by the view that:

> To understand the scope of the present investigations it is important to be aware of the fact that the information with which a knowledge-based system reasons, as well as the description of the problem, is the result of many activities which escape a formal treatment, but which are essential elements of what is called 'legal reasoning'. In sum, the only aspects of legal reasoning which can be formalised are those aspects which concern the following problem: *given* a particular interpretation of a body of information, and *given* a particular description of some legal problem, what are then the general rational patterns of reasoning with which a solution to the problem can be obtained? With respect to this question one remark should be made: I do not require that these general patterns are deductive; the only requirement is that they should be formally definable. [Prakken, 1997, p. 6]

Thus modelling the legal theory of evidence (which decides what 'body of information' we are 'given') still remains beyond the horizon of some current research in logic and law. In what follows, on the contrary, we shall develop a case study that will show just how important this area is.

A recent key collection of papers by Marylin MacCrimmon and Peter Tillers [2002] indicates very lively activity in law and logic. However, most of the papers take a fuzzy logic, uncertainty and probabilistic approach (in the sense of [Shafer, 1976; Guan and Bell, 1991]. See also [Prakken *et al.*, 2003] and the references there.

We must here add that the Bayesian reasoning community is actively involved in (Bayesian) logic and law. This is because of several high visibility court cases and evidence where probabilities are used. Part of the problem is that the probabilistic reasoning community is not so interactive with the ordinary logic communities (and so we also need to bring logic and probability together as part of our own ongoing work). However, for reservations about the reliability in their present formulations of the Bayesian norms for legal reasoning, see [Woods, 2018]. Suitably interpreted the theory of Labelled Deductive Systems is fully compatible with probabilistic reasoning and networks.

In the sections to come we examine some case studies to show how the new logics can play a role in the area of evidence and legal reasoning.

2 Legal Theory of Evidence and the New Logics

Our purpose here is to show how the new labelled logics, arising from research in computer science, can be applied to the legal theory of evidence. For a sample of Labelled Deductive Systems, see [Gabbay, 2002]. For the original monograph, see [Gabbay, 1996].

2.1 Some Labelled Logic

We start with logic. One of the most well known resource logics is linear logic [Girard *et al.*, 1989]. In this logic, the databases are multisets of formulas and each item of data must be used *exactly once*. So, for example, we have

$$A, A \rightarrow B \vdash B$$

But

$$A, A \rightarrow (A \rightarrow B) \nvdash B$$

This is because two copies of A are needed here, and we have only one. The proof would run as follows:

1. $A \rightarrow (A \rightarrow B)$, assumption

2. A, assumption

3. $A \rightarrow B$, from 1 and 2 using the rule of modus ponens.

4. B, from 1 and 3, using the rule of modus ponens.

In this proof, 2. is used twice.

To make this example more concrete, let

- $A =$ having a drunken driving conviction

- $B =$ driving licence suspended.

Then $A \to (A \to B)$ means that two convictions entail suspension (and of course you cannot count the same conviction twice!).

Linear logic allows for the connective $!A$, which means that A can be used as many times as needed.

Thus

$$!A, A \to (A \to B) \vdash B.$$

Let us modify the logic a bit[10] and add the connective ❤ A: ❤ A means that we can use A if we ask and get permission from some meta-level authority. So we can write

$$❤ A, A \to (A \to B), \text{ permission given } \vdash B.$$

There is a mixing here of object level and meta-level features. Such logics are best expressed as labeled deductive systems (LDS) [Gabbay, 1996; Gabbay, 2002]. A labelled system is comprised of formulas and labels. The labels contain additional information relating to the formulas. For example an item of data (called a *declarative unit*) may have the form

$$\Delta : \text{ John has cancer.}$$

Δ can be a medical file with data confirming the fact that John has cancer. This fact can be used in certain situations of legal argument; e.g. to attempt to release John from prison. The reasoning governing Δ is medical, while the reasoning governing the release from prison is legal. Labelled logic is the methodology of how to use such mixed reasoning.

We have in LDS the following form of modus ponens:

$$\frac{t : X, s : X \to Y, \varphi(s,t)}{f(s,t) : Y}$$

Here t, s are labels (their nature and mode of handling are defined in the system), which can be themselves entire databases; φ is meta-predicate indicating that there is the permission to apply modus ponens (φ is called the compatibility predicate); and f is a function giving the new label of the result Y.

Going back to our example, we write

---

[10]See footnote 30 for an anagram example.

1. $s : (A \to (A \to B))$, where s represents here a body of legal background data on how the substantive law of
   " two drunken driving convictions $\to$ licence suspended"
   has been established.

2. $t : A$, where t is a file indicating the data establishing the facts of the drunken driving incident.

3. $\varphi(s,t)$ is a meta-level argument looking into s and t and arguing that, although we have here only *one* incident of drunken driving, the intention of law (see file s) and the severe circumstances of the incident (see file t) call for suspension (that is, permission to count as two incidents is granted).

4. $f(s,t) : A \to B$, by modus ponens from (1), (2), (3).
   $f(s,t)$ is a file containing the arguments present in granting permission, i.e., $f(s,t) = t + s + \varphi$

5. $f(s,t) : B$, by modus ponens from (4) and (5).

   So formally, we have $f(f(s,t),t) = f(s,t)$.

We now show a further connection with the law of evidence.

One important feature of LDS is that it regulates the admissibility of data into the database together with the label it is permitted to have. In fact, using φ we can diplomatically admit a datum D into the database with a label "don't touch", with the effect that φ will never give permission to use it.

These kinds of logics were developed to accommodate the needs of artificial intelligence and the logic of language. It is surprising how well these logics fit the needs of theories of evidence.

Imagine a database (Barclays Bank) containing data about a customer. One kind of data includes home telephone number, mobile telephone number, etc. Assume that a security protocol will allow only certain individuals at the Bank to enter such data and it is up to them to decide whether to 'admit' an additional number. Suppose I call Barclays bank, identify myself and ask the represenative to add my mobile number to the database. The representative will ask me some questions (usually mother's maiden name). If correct answers are given, he will add (admit) the additional telephone number. If he is still uncomfortable with my identity (for whatever reasons) he can refuse to do so. We doubt, however, that he has the authority to decide to accept the phone number even if we fail to answer the questions correctly. In other words, security protocols allow the representative to refuse admissible data but do not allow him to overrule and accept non-admissible data!

2.2 What Some Books on Evidence Say

Let us go now to the website and to the book of Steve Uglow.

In his web course notes, and presumably also in his book, he says:

> "Evidence is about regulating the information produced at a trial.
>
> - What are the general principles regarding this?
> - What are exclusionary rules?
> - What logical processes are involved?"

In our labelled logic we can phrase these points as

- With what label do we insert the new data (evidence) in our database?

The challenge of this area to the research community is made clear at the very first paragraph of Uglow's 725-page book on evidence [Uglow, 1997] (*Textbook on Evidence*, 1997)

> "The law relating to evidence is a strange and unruly beast. It is unruly because, first, it refuses to fit into any easy structure for analysis and exposition and, second, it often adopts the characteristics of an uncharged minefield, by which is meant that any set of facts has the potential of throwing up evidential problems, not just of one but of several types, often unforeseen. It is strange because it fulfils different functions than the familiar areas of substantive law. It is in such areas that we see legal rules at their most visible, dealing with the *consequences* of facts – if a contract is broken, damages are paid; if a theft is committed, punishment is imposed. Damages, imprisonment and other civil and criminal remedies are the sanctions accompanying rules which require or prohibit certain types of conduct or which lay down conditions under which that conduct can take place. These rules are often referred to as the substantive law. Within most contested trials, such rules form the background to the case but play little part since there is no conflict over the substance of the rule. We know what the rule says and what the consequences of a breach will be: if there has been a road accident and a driver has been negligent, damages for personal injuries will be paid to any

plaintiff; if a sane defendant intentionally kills another person, he or she will be prosecuted and generally receive a life sentence.

But the real conflict in a court, before any substantive rule is brought to bear, is about establishing the facts: was the driver negligent? Did the defendant cause the victim's death? What happened? The law of evidence is not about determining the consequences of facts but about establishing those facts. In a contested trial, under the common law system of justice, the opposing parties will present differing, sometimes diametrically opposed, views of the same event. Having listened to these accounts, the trier of fact must decide what the facts are. It is this problem as to how 'facts' are established with which the law of evidence is concerned: what information can be presented to the court' through what means; how does a court decide whether that information proves whether an event happened in a particular way or not? Such rules, alongside the rules of civil and criminal procedure, can be described, not as *substantive*, but as *adjectival* law.[11]

---

[11]This is our footnote.

Note that a substantive law in labelled logic looks like $s : A \to (A \to B)$. Facts look like $t : A$. We can also have other testimony allowing for $t' : \neg A$. The rule that decides in *LDS*, whether to deduce A or $\neg A$ given say, $t_1 : A, t_2 : A, t_3 : \neg A$ is called a *flattening rule*. More precisely, a flattening rule tells us, given $t_i : A$ and $s_j : \neg A$, what is the resultant labels $t : A$ and $s : \neg A$. So, for example, if t_i, s_j are reliability measures of various sources supporting A and $\neg A$ respectively, t and s might be some averages.

What Professor Uglow calls here *Adjectival Law*, means in LDS the logic for reasoning *inside* the label t. For example, t may contain medical evidence and a lawyer may attack that!

If we take our example

Δ : John has cancer,

Δ may be a medical file about John. Δ may contain among other things an expert opinion of a certain Dr. Smith, giving a statement $\Gamma : X$, there X is the Doctor's statement and Γ is another file showing Dr.Smith is a world expert on this kind of cancer. A lawyer wishing to attack Δ might choose to attack Γ (i.e., Dr. Smith's credentials are false), thus weakening the value of X and overall weakening Δ. So we have a structure like

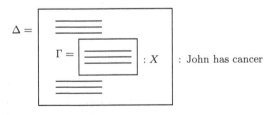

This means that these rules attach themselves to and qualify the operation of a substantive rule but never, by themselves, directly decide the rights and wrongs of any issue. The law of evidence qualifies the operation of a substantive rule because it controls the flow and nature of the information which can be presented to the court. Indirectly, of course, the law of evidence can be decisive since the outcome of a case can depend on whether a particular item of evidence is allowed to be presented to the court or not. For example, a guilty verdict or an acquittal can hang on whether the prosecution can meet the preconditions for the admissibility of a confession in a criminal trial; in a civil case where the weight of the evidence is evenly balanced, the decision may hinge on the question as to where the burden of proof rests.

Many of these evidential issues seem very technical to a layperson and, especially in criminal trials, to exclude relevant and important information from the proceedings. Examples might be given of the rule against the admission of hearsay evidence — a witness would be usually prevented from testifying that the victim, now dead, had identified the accused as the assailant; similarly the jury would rarely be allowed to hear about any previous convictions of the defendant. But these are not technicalities for their own sake and reflect the nature and characteristics of the common law trial."

Put in the language our own LDS, what Uglow is saying in this passage is that:
Given the situation

$$t : A, s : A \to B$$

he calls $A \to B$ "substantive law", (in logic it is called a "rule" or a "ticket"), and calls A the facts (called minor premises in logic), then the main part of the theory of evidence is whether to admit A into the database (i.e., establish A as a fact) and with what label t? t may be a label supporting A and what the book calls "adjectival law" is the theory (logic) of evidence.

Here now is another basic textbook on evidence [Dennis, 1992], I. H. Dennis, *Law of Evidence*, 1999.[12] He says (pages 4–6)

---

[12]Dennis also says in his introduction "Evidence is a notoriously difficult subject to organize in any logical basis".

B. Concepts and Terminology

The law of evidence uses a number of concepts which are fundamental to an understanding of the subject. This section attempts to introduce these concepts by stating a number of general propositions about them and about their relationships. The propositions are stated in summary form, with more detailed explanation given later.[13]

1. Evidence must be *relevant* in order for a court to receive it. This means that it must relate to some fact which is a proper object of proof in the proceedings.[14] The evidence must relate to the fact to be proved in the sense that it tends to make the existence (or non-existence) of the fact more probable, or less probable, than it would be without the evidence. A simple example is a case where a fact to be proved is the identity of the accused as the person who stole certain goods. Evidence that the goods were found in the accused's house is relevant because it makes the existence of the fact that he is the thief more probable.

2. Evidence must also be *admissible*, meaning that it can properly be received by a court as a matter of law. The most important rule of admissibiltiy is that the evidence must be relevant; irrelevant evidence is always inadmissible. Generally speaking evidence that is relevant is also admissible, but certain rules of law prohibit the reception of certain types of evidence, even though the evidence is relevant. An example is the rule against hearsay evidence, which, broadly speaking, forbids the reception of evidence of a statement made by a person on another occasion when the purpose of adducing[15] the evidence is to ask the court to accept that the statement was true. These rules are often called the *exclusionary rules*, to indicate their function of excluding certain evidence from the court's consideration. The rules are complex because they are often accompanied by excep-

---

[13] Also important from a dialogical perspective are works by Douglas Walton on evidence in law. See Walton [2002; 2007; 2016]. Woods emphasizes the artificialities of legal evidence in Woods [2018, chapters 8 and 10].

[14] The facts which are proper objects of proof are sometimes called material facts, but materiality is a slippery term which can be used with more than one meaning. See the discussion in the text below.

[15] "Adducing" evidence is a term often used to denote the process of presenting evidence to a court in one of the approved forms, most commonly in the form of the testimony of a witness.

tions, some of which may be narrow and precisely defined, others may be in broad and flexible terms.

3. In criminal cases, in addition to exclusionary rules, there is also *exclusionary discretion*. A trial judge may exclude prosecution evidence that is relevant and admissible (in the sense that it is not excluded by an exclusionary rule) in the exercise of a discretion conferred on him by the common law or by section 78 of the Police and Criminal Evidence Act 1984 (PACE). The statutory discretion is to prevent the admission of the evidence from adversely affecting the fairness of the proceedings. The main application of the common law discretion is to exclude evidence the prejudicial effect of which outweighs its probative value. Probative value refers to the potential weight of the evidence (see next paragraph), whereas prejudicial effect refers to the tendency of evidence to prejudice the court against the accused, so as to lead the court to make findings of fact against him for reasons not related to the true probative value of the evidence.[16]

4. At the end of a contested trial the court will have to evaluate the relevant and admissible evidence that it received. The *weight* of the evidence is the strength of the tendency of the evidence to prove the fact or facts that it was adduced to prove. This is a matter for the tribunal of fact to decide. In civil cases the judge who tries the case is generally the judge of issues of both law and fact. In criminal cases the tribunal of fact is different according to whether the case is tried on indictment or summarily. The jury is the tribunal of fact for cases tried on indictment. In summary trial the magistrates (justices) deal with issues of both law and fact; lay magistrates have the guidance of their clerk on questions of law. This book uses the term "factfinder" to refer generally to a tribunal of fact, unless the context requires a specific reference to a judge, jury or magistrate. When a factfinder has to determine the weight of evidence it will examine carefully, amongst other things, the *credibility* and *reliability* of the evidence. These terms are not always used with a consistent meaning. Credibility is most commonly used in connection with the testimony of a witness and refers to the extent to which the witness can be accepted as giving truthful evidence in the sense of honest or sincere

---

[16]In other situations a judge can find clearly probative evidence to be irrelevant in law if it would be too difficult for the jury to understand or would take too long for the jury to hear. ("Justice delayed is justice denied.") Woods [2018, pp. 182–283].

testimony. Reliability refers most commonly to the truthfulness of testimony in the sense of its accuracy. Honest witnesses may sometimes give evidence that is inaccurate; mistaken evidence of identification by eyewitnesses is a classic example.[17]

Note here the central role played by the notion of *relevance*. This is also an AI and natural language concept. It is no accident that the first book of our series of books on cognitive systems is a book on relevance [Gabbay and Woods, 2003].

3   Case Study: Hearsay Case, *Myers v DPP*

We begin by quoting from [Allen, 2001, p. 133].

A good statement of the hearsay rule was given originally in *Cross on Evidence*, [Cross, 1999].

> "An assertion other than one made by a person while giving oral evidence in the proceedings is inadmissible as evidence of any fact asserted".

Allen continued on page 135:

> "Hearsay law has been described as 'exceptionally complex and difficult to interpret' [RRCCJ, 1993]. What we need is a method of approach to the subject which will enable us to understand why some cases were decided as they were and why others are open to criticism. Above all, we need a technique [our comment: i.e., logic] for thinking about hearsay, ... '.

We now examine a key case, which seems to be quoted in every textbook on Evidence (and hearsay). This is a case of *written statements*, which may fall under hearsay law.

We quote two descriptions of this case, one from [Keane, 2000] and one from [Uglow, 1997], and then we model the arguments as quoted in [Uglow, 1997].

We begin with [Keane, 2000, pp. 250–252]

(b) Written statements

The leading case on written hearsay is *Myers v DPP* ([1965] AC 1001). The appellant was convicted of offences relating to the theft of motor cars. He would buy a wrecked car, steal a car resembling it, disguise the stolen car so that it corresponded with

---

[17]For some of the difficulties with eyewitness testimony, see Loftus [1975] and Loftus *et al.*, [2006].

the particulars of the wrecked car as noted in its log book, and then sell the stolen car with the log book of the wrecked one. The prosecution case involved proving that the disguised cars were stolen by reference to the cylinder-block numbers indelibly stamped on their engines. In the case of some cars, therefore, they sought to adduce evidence derived from records kept by a motor manufacturer. An officer in charge of these records was called to produce microfilms which were prepared from cards filled in by workmen on the assembly line and which contained the cylinder-block numbers of the cars manufactured. The Court of Criminal Appeal held that the trial judge had properly allowed the evidence to be admitted because of the circumstances in which the record was maintained and the inherent probability that it was correct rather than incorrect. The House of Lords held that the records constituted inadmissible hearsay evidence. The entries on the cards and contained in the microfilms were out-of-court assertions by unidentifiable workmen that certain cars bore certain cylinder-block numbers. The officer called could not prove that the records were correct and that the numbers they contained were in fact the numbers on the cars in question. Their Lordships, however, were divided as to whether the evidence should be admitted by the creation of a new exception to the hearsay rule.[18] Lords Pearce and Donovan were in favour of such a course, but the majority, comprising Lords Reid, Morris and Hodson, declined to do so, being of the opinion that it was for the legislature and not the judiciary to add to the classes of admissible hearsay.[19] It was argued before the House that the trial judge has a discretion to admit a record in a particular case if satisfied that it is trustworthy and that justice requires its admission. Lord Reid, while acknowledging that the hearsay rule was 'absurdly technical', held that 'no matter how cogent particular evidence may seem to be, unless it comes within a class which is admissible, it is excluded ... '

The actual decision in *Myers v DPP* was reversed by the Criminal Evidence Act 1965, which provided for the admissibility of cer-

---

[18]The Lords were unanimous in dismissing the appeal on the grounds that the other evidence of guilt being overwhelming, there had been no substantial miscarriage of justice.

[19]The minority view, that it was within the provenance of the judiciary to restate the exceptions to the hearsay rule, was adopted by the Supreme Court of Canada in *Ares v Venner* [1970] SCR 608. See also per Lord Griffiths in *R v Kearley* [1992] 2 All ER 345, HL at 348.

tain hearsay statements contained in trade or business records. Although the 1965 Act was repealed by the Police and Criminal Evidence Act 1984, ss 23 and 24 of the Criminal Justice Act 1988 are wider in scope than the provisions of the 1965 Act and provide for the admissibility of first-hand hearsay statements in documents generally as well as hearsay statements contained in documents created or received by a person in the course of, inter alia, a trade or business. The principles enunciated in *Myers v DPP*, however, remain of importance in relation to hearsay statements falling outside the statutory exceptions. Over 25 years later, another majority of the House of Lords, in *R v Kearley*,[20] although of the opinion that there may be a case for a general relaxation of the hearsay rule, affirmed the majority view in *Myers v DPP* that the only satisfactory solution is legislation following on a wide survey of the whole field.

Patel v Comptroller of Customs[21] also illustrates the application of the hearsay rule to written statements. The appellant was convicted of making a false declaration in an import entry form concerning certain bags of seed. Evidence was admitted that the bags of seed bore the words 'Produce of Morocco'. The Privy Council held that the evidence was inadmissible hearsay and advised that the conviction be quashed. The decision may be usefully compared with that in *R v Lydon*.[22] The appellant, Sean Lydon, was convicted of robbery. His defence was one of alibi. About one mile from the scene of the robbery, on the verge of the road which the getaway car had followed, were found a gun and, nearby, two pieces of rolled paper on which someone had written 'Sean rules' and 'Sean rules 85'. Ink of similar appearance and composition to that on the paper was found on the gun barrel. The Court of Appeal held that evidence relating to the pieces of paper had been properly admitted as circumstantial evidence: if the jury were satisfied that the gun was used in the robbery and that the pieces of paper were linked to the gun, the references to Sean could be a fact which would fit in with the appellant having committed the offence. The references were not hearsay because

---

[20] [1992] 2 All ER 345, HL, per Lords Bridge, Ackner and Oliver at 360–361, 366 and 382–383 respectively.

[21] [1966] AC 356, PC. See also *R v Sealby* [1965] 1 All ER 701 and *R v Brown* [1991] Crim LR835, CA (evidence of a name on an appliance inadmissible to establish its ownership); and cf *R v Rice* [1963] 1 QB 857, below.

[22] [1987] Crim LR 407, CA.

they involved no assertion as to the truth of the contents of the pieces of paper: they were not tendered to show that Sean ruled anything.[23]

In Steven Uglow's book [Uglow, 1997], we find his account of the same case.

> "*written statements*: the classic case here is *Myers v DPP* ([1964] 2 All E.R. 877) where the defendant bought wrecked cars for their registration certificates. He would then steal a similar car and alter it to fit the details in the document. He would sell the disguised stolen car along with the genuine log book of the wrecked car. The prosecution sought to show that the cars and registration documents did not match up by reference to the engine block numbers and introduced microfilm evidence kept by the manufacturer, showing that this block number did not belong in a car of this registration date. The microfilm was prepared from cards which were themselves prepared by workers on the assembly line. Lord Reid in the House of Lords held that the microfilm was inadmissible since it contained the out-of-court assertions by unidentified workers."

The labelled structure of the above is as follows.

Let

- $t : C$ The numbers assigned to the cars by the manufacturers are $x_1, x_2, \ldots$

- $t' : C'$ The numbers in the cars' logbook are $y_1, y_2, \ldots$.

If $x_i \neq y_i$, then we get:

---

[23]See also *R v McIntosh* [1992] Crim LR 651, CA (calculations as to the purchase and sale prices of 12 oz of an unnamed commodity, not in M's handwriting but found concealed in the chimney of a house where he had been living, admissible as circumstantial evidence tending to connect him with drug-related offences); and cf *R v Horne* [1992] Crim LR 304, CA (documents of unknown authorship, referring to H, containing calculations possibly relating to the cost of importing drugs, and found in the flat of a co-accused to which H was supposed to deliver the drugs, inadmissible against H). *R v McIntosh* was applied in *Roberts v DP* [1994] Crim LR 926, DC: documents found at R's offices and home, including repair and gas bills and other accounts relating to certain premises, were admissible as circumstantial evidence linking R with those premises, on charges of assisting in the management of a brothel and running a massage parlour without a licence.

- $t + t' : C'' = $ the numbers on the cars and numbers on the registration documents do not match

where

- $t = $ description of how the microfilm supporting C was obtained and compiled.

- $t' = $ the cars' logbooks.

The candidate item of data for admissibility is

- $t : C$.

The following passage is Lord Reid's argument that $t : C$ should be inadmissible, i.e., Lord Reid wants to argue that t should also contain the phrase "do not use me".

This is done in the logic of the labels. In other words, Lord Reid's argument has to do with the data inside t.

Here is Lord Reid's argument (technically it is part of t). It also quotes the arguments given in favour of admitting $t : C$.

Myers v DPP [1964] 2 All E.R. 877 at 886b–887h, per Lord Reid

It is not disputed before your Lordships that to admit these records is to admit hearsay. They only tend to prove that a particular car bore a particular number when it was assembled if the jury were entitled to infer that the entries were accurate, at least in the main; and the entries on the cards were assertions by the unidentifiable men who made them that they had entered numbers which they had seen on the cars. Counsel for the respondents were unable to adduce any reported case or any textbook as direct authority for their submission. Only four reasons for their submission were put forward. It was said that evidence of this kind is in practice admitted at least at the Central Criminal Court. Then it was argued that a judge has a discretion to admit such evidence. Then the reasons given in the Court of Criminal Appeal were relied on. And lastly it was said with truth that common sense rebels against the rejection of this evidence.

At the trial counsel for the prosecution sought to support the existing practice of admitting such records, if produced by the persons in charge of them, by arguing that they were not adduced to prove the truth of the recorded particulars but only to prove that they were records kept in the normal course of business. Counsel for the accused then asked the very pertinent question — if they were not intended to prove the truth of the entries, what were they intended to prove? I ask what the jury would infer from them: obviously that they were probably true records. If they were not capable of supporting an inference that they were probably true records, then I do not see what probative value they could have, and their admission was bound to mislead the jury.

The first reason given by the Court of Criminal Appeal for sustaining the admission of the records was that, although the records might not be evidence standing by themselves, they could be used to corroborate the evidence of other witnesses.[24] I regret to say that I have great difficulty in understanding that ... Unless the jury were entitled to regard them, I can see no reason why they should only become admissible evidence after some witnesses have identified the cars for different reasons ...[25]

At the end of their judgement, the Court of Criminal Appeal gave a different reason. 'In our view the admission of such evidence does not infringe the hearsay rule because its probative value does not depend upon the credit of an unidentified person but rather on the circumstances in which the record is maintained and the inherent probability that it will be correct rather than incorrect.' That, if I may say so, is undeniable as a matter of common sense. But can it be reconciled with the existing law? I need not discuss the question on general lines because I think that this ground is quite inconsistent with the established rule regarding public records. Public records are prima facie evidence of the fact which they contain but it is quite clear that a record is not a public record within the scope of that rule unless it is open to inspection by at least a section of the public. Unless we are to alter that rule how can we possibly say that a private record not open to public inspection can be prima facie evidence of the truth of its contents? I would agree that it is quite unreasonable to refuse to accept as prima facie evidence a record obviously

---

[24]This is our footnote. "corroborate evidence of other witnesses" means in our LDS language "help with the flattening process".

[25]Our footnote: i.e., $u_1 : X$ is admissible only if some other $u_2 : X$ is already admissible. See objection $s_{3,2}$ below. LDS allows formally for putting item $u_1 : X$ in the database in such a way that it can be used only in the flattening process to support other items but not in deduction.

well kept by public officers and proved never to have been discovered to contain a wrong entry though frequently consulted by officials, merely because it is not open to inspection. But that is settled law. This seems to me to be a good example of the wide repercussions which would follow if we accepted the judgement of the Court of Criminal Appeal. I must therefore regretfully decline to accept this reason as correct in law.

In argument, the Solicitor-General maintained that, although the general rule may be against the admission of private records to prove the truth of entries in them, the trial judge has a discretion to admit a record in a particular case if satisfied that it is trustworthy and that justice requires its admission. That appears to me to be contrary to the whole framework of the existing law. It is true that a judge has a discretion to exclude legally admissible evidence if justice so requires, but it is a very different thing to say that he has a discretion to admit legally inadmissible evidence. The whole development of the exceptions to the hearsay rule is based on the determination of certain classes of evidence as admissible or inadmissible and not on the apparent credibility of particular evidence tendered. No matter how cogent particular evidence may seem to be, unless it comes within a class which is admissible, it is excluded. Half a dozen witnesses may offer to prove that they heard two men of high character who cannot now be found discuss in detail the fact now in issue and agree on a credible account of it, but that evidence would not be admitted although it might be by far the best evidence available.

It was admitted in argument before your Lordships that not every private record would be admissible. If challenged it would be necessary to prove in some way that it had proved to be reliable, before the judge would allow it to be put before the jury. And I think that some such limitation must be implicit in the last reason given by the Court of Criminal Appeal. I see no objection to a judge having a discretion of this kind though it might be awkward in a civil case; but it appears to me to be an innovation on the existing law which decides inadmissibility by categories and not by apparent trustworthiness ...

Structure of Lord Reid's argument

$\Delta_1 : N =$ number on car A is a, (when assembled), and Δ_1 is the support of this claim.

$\Delta_1 =$ description of procedures of entering numbers during assembly.

We also have a common sense metalevel persistence principle: numbers on cars persist (don't fade away or change).

$$N \to \textbf{Always } N.$$

Thus, according to Lord Reid, t is equal to:

$$t = \{\Delta_1 : N, N \to \textbf{Always } N\}.$$

He wants to block the use of t by attacking the admissibility of Δ_1.

Four reasons were quoted for the admissibility of Δ_1 and three reasons for non-admissibility:

r_1:   Evidence of this kind is admitted in Central Criminal Court.

r_2:   Judge has discretion to admit such evidence.

r_3:   This is a list of reasons given in Court of Criminal Appeal, namely:

     $r_{3,1}$:   The records were produced to show that the records were kept in the normal course of business (but not to prove the truth of the recorded particulars).

     $r_{3,2}$:   Although the record may not be evidence by themselves, they may be used to corroborate other evidence.

     $r_{3,3}$:   We do not have dependency on the credit of an unidentified person but rather on a probably reliable process of record maintenance, and can therefore admit them.

r_4:   Common sense rebels against rejection of such evidence.

s_0:   No reported case or any textbook as direct authority for admission.

It seems at this point that r_1–r_4 are stronger than s_0.[26] So Lord Reid is trying to weaken the force of r_3 and r_2 by attacking them logically with s_3 and s_2:

s_2:   Judges do not have the discretion to admit legally inadmissible evidence.

---

[26] In other words, it seems that a reasonable flattening process, weighing $\{r_1, r_2, r_3, r_4\}$ against $\{s_0\}$ will decide in favour of the former and thus admit the records. Note that no rules are given at this stage of how the decision is made. In some logics, where labels are confidence numbers, we can give a rule; e.g. admit iff $r_1 + r_2 + r_3 + r_4 > s_0$, but not here.

s_3:   Counter argument to r_3 comprising of:

    $s_{3,1}$;   If the records are not intended to prove the truth of their entries, what are they intended to prove? (I.e., they are irrelevant!)

    $s_{3,2}$:   Either the records are admissible or not. There is no sense in which they can become admissible only after some other evidence to the same conclusion becomes admissible (see Footnote 25).

    $s_{3,3}$:   Such records are not public records which are admissible for reasons that they are open to the public for inspection and correction. The current law therefore does not support their admissibility.

Figure 1 shows the form of t, where E = admit evidence or 'use me'.

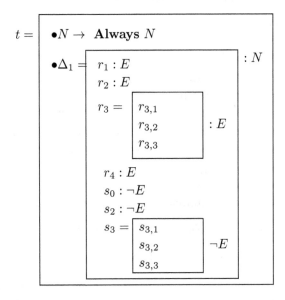

Figure 1.

To strengthen his case (i.e., strengthen the overall labels for $\neg E$, Lord Reid is attacking the label r_3 by putting forward $s_{3,1}, s_{3,2}$ and $s_{3,3}$. Note that the reasoning in the different boxes can be of different kinds!

Note that one of the points Lord Reid is making is s_2, namely that trial judges do not have discretion to 'admit legally inadmissible evidence'.

Compare this with the Barclays Bank example. So the force of the argument is to influence the flattening process: we have r_1–r_4 : E and s_0, s_2, s_3 : $\neg E$, which one wins?

In this case the evidence was not admitted.[27]

Uglow continues:

> The House of Lords recognized the absurdity of their position but felt strongly that it was for the legislature to reform the law and create new exceptions. Parliament dealt with the problem of documentary hearsay with the Criminal Evidence Act 1965 which created an exception for trade and business records This was later extended by section 68 of the Police and Criminal Evidence Act 1984 and now by sections 23 and 24 of the Criminal Justice Act 1988. Such records have all been admissible in civil proceedings since the Civil Evidence Act 1968.
>
> Myers has been regularly followed in such cases as *Patel v Comptroller of Customs* ([1965] 3 All E.R. 593) where the appellant was convicted of making a false declaration to customs, having stated that the bags of seed were originally from India. The prosecution sought to prove that the seed originated in Morocco and adduced evidence that the bags were stamped with 'Produce of Morocco'. The Privy Council, following *Myers* held that these words were hearsay and inadmissible. Unlike *Myers*, there was no evidence that the writing was at all reliable, there being no testimony as to how or by whom the bags were marked."

The reader should note that the main thrust of the argument and logic of the Lord Reid example is in weakening and strengthening labels. Put schematically we have a master argument, say E which can prove a conclusion on D. E is a labelled argument containing various labels within labels. Among this maze of labels there is a label t containing another argument, say Δ. To attack E we can attack Δ. Our argument attacking Δ can itself be attacked by attacking some label s in it and so on. This is reminiscent of systems of abstract argumentation theory. Bench-Capon [2003] has a paper on graphs of arguments and counterarguments, but his model is schematic. We can give actual proof rules and labelling disciplines so that questions like export from one label to another can also be considered. For example:

"If you weaken t then D will not follow from E, and that would be a bad

---

[27]This decision was made by vote as described in the quote from [Keane, 2000] on our page 17.

precedent."

One cannot argue in this way unless a specific labelled model is available. We shall examine the Bench-Capon paper in the next section. For the time being, we think that we have seen enough to be convinced that labelling logics can play a central role here, though we would understand if the cautious reader would prefer to reserve judgement until more case studies are presented.

4 Case Study. Sex Offender Case, Risk Assessment

Consider the argument structure of item Δ_1 of Figure 1. This can also be represented as a tree, as in

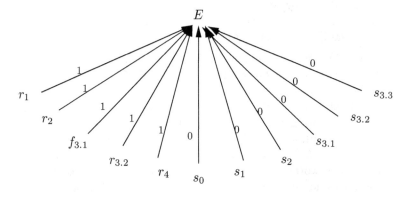

Figure 2.

where $x \overset{1}{\to} E$ means x supports E and $y \overset{0}{\to} E$ means y supports $\neg E$ (i.e., $y \overset{1}{\to} \neg E$).

Figure 2 is the same representation as Figure 2 presented as a different geometrical form.

Now imagine a legal reporter interviewing Lord Reid and asking him a question about each of his arguments x and Lord Reid gives an answer. We can add to the tree the respective question and the answer. We can write $a(x)$ for the question about x and write $b(x)$ for the answer to $a(x)$. The reporter can also ask Lord Reid to provide a strength number $m(x)$ for each argument x. If this is done we get a graph like Figure 3.

In fact the legal reporter (who is most likely a legal man himself) might prepare his interview and ask Lord Reid why he did not use certain other arguments which can maybe support E or support $\neg E$.

So we can assume, if we want, an additional set of arguments, say $t_1, ..., t_n$, which could be relevant and Lord Reid has not mentioned.

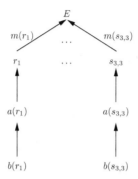

Figure 3.

The above discussion connects the structure of Δ_1 of Figure 3 with the formal structure of our present case study about sex offenders risk assessment.

When a sex offender is convicted he/she can join a therapy group in prison (a group of 12–15 other offenders and benefit from therapy for several years, see [Gabbay and Rozenberg, 2017]). He can also apply on the basis of his performance for a "good progress/behaviour" early release from prison. The decision is taken by a Judge, in consultation with a recognised expert in sex-offences, and it hinges on whether and how much risk there is to others in releasing the offender. The court deliberations are stylised and are structured as in Figure 3.

First the expert presents his qualifications and his report to the court and the sex offender's lawyer can ask questions and he expert answers. Then the expert's report is discussed. There are a fixed number of factors for and against:

E = this sex offender presents a risk to society.

The expert has to address each of them and give a risk number. The expert may have mentioned only some of the factors and then he may be asked why he did not mention other factors. This would be similar to the legal reporter asking Lord Reid why he did not mention some other relevant argument. The difference is in that in the sex offenders case there is an internationally recognized list of factors, while in the reporter case , he compiled a list himself. The lawyer can ask a question $a(x)$ about each factor x (i.e., what the expert assessed of x) and the expert answers $b(x)$.

The factors are fixed and there are international statistical packages giving a risk number $m(x)$ for each factor. These are updated all the time following international case studies data.

In this case study we give a sample of $x, m(x), a(x)$ and $b(x)$ written by Dr G. Rozenberg and based on 15 years' court experience of his court cases (see [Gabbay and Rozenberg, 2017]). For the purpose of this chapter the data can be considered almost as transcripts of a realistic court case.

Let us begin:

The following is almost an actual court case created by Dr G. Rozenberg based on the many court cases in which he participated. It lists the questions he was asked and his answers. The text presented is a translation of transcriptions taken by the official court clerk of the Military Court in Jaffa, Israel, in a court cases of a certain sex offenders. The expert witness is Dr Rozenberg. The text is the exact detail of the cross examination questions presented to Dr Rozenberg and his answers. The original is in Hebrew and it was faithfully and accurately translated by the authors of [Gabbay and Rozenberg, 2017]. Although their translation is not a legally accepted notarised "authorised translation", it is sufficient for the purpose of this chapter. Some slight modifications were made to avoid the possibility of identifying any offender.

It is a case study of an attack on the qualifications of the expert. It also has a stylised structure. It is comprised from questions about how the expert acquired/ studied for his qualifications, as well as how he went about (methodology used in) composing his report. There are also questions about specific items in his report, not with a view of attacking the item but with a view to see if the expert understands their significance. Other questions relate to whether the expert understands the limitation and margins of error of his report.

There are also traditional Fallacies, trick questions, tempting the expert to answer in such a way that he appears to be racist, over-confident and full of his own importance, unable to take criticism or timid, hesitant and unsure of himself. We must remember that these questions are asked on the witness stand in front of a Judge and are intended to discredit the expert.[28]

We shall not present the discussion of the qualification of the expert (see [Gabbay and Rozenberg, 2017], but reproduce here the discussion of his expert testimony.

---

[28]Doug Walton and John Woods jointly and separately have written many wonderful books on the Fallacies. The reader should consult the internet.

5   The Attack on the Expert Testimony

5.1   Background

There is consensus in the international community (ATSA — Association
for the Treatment of Sexual Abusers) on the factors which contribute to the
assessment of risk of sexual offenders. There are also several actuarial tools
to help the expert in assessing the risk of a given patient. The tool asks the
expert to evaluate/answer questions about the individual patient and then
gives a risk assessment a final grade which is a number x, $k < x < m$, where
x, m, n are integers (depending on the tool). The expert can use several tools,
as well as some additional clinical factors (determined by the experience of
the individual expert) and the expert integrates all these results (in his own
mind, as there is no Super Integrating Tool) into a final determination.

There is no super-tool which can integrate/reconcile the results of several
existing tools. The expert has to decide which tools to use and how to
integrate them. The ATSA list of factors are recognised by the Israeli courts,
and the expert witness is expected in court to address these factors and be
challenged by the defence attorney of the sex offender. The main tools are
listed in the Appendix and the typical questions and answers in court are
presented in this section. The list in this section does not represent any
particular court case but is based on 11 years practice and thousands of
expert opinions put forward by the second author. The courts follow Israeli
law. The defence lawyer may invite his own expert to present a possibly
different report and different conclusion. In this case the second expert
will also appear in court and be subjected to the same procedures as the
first expert with the prosecutor performing the attacks on the second expert
factors.

This section deals with the attacks on the expert testimony. The structure
of the testimony is as outlined in the previous section. Each numbered item
below represents an attack sequence on a factor s. Each item comprises of
three sub-items;

- what the expert says concerning factor i, denoted by s_i. (The expert
  can either introduce the factor in his considerations or not mention it
  at all. The factor may support the increasing of risk assessment of the
  offender or support the decreasing of the risk assess of the offender.
  There are international packages which assess the contribution of such
  factors s_i.)

- the attack on what the expert says, denoted by a_i. (This attack is
  mounted by the defence. So if the expert does not mention a factor
  which decreases the risk assessment the defence can ask why? If the

factor increases the assessment of risk the defence might add information which makes the increase smaller. If the expert gets his facts
wrong, then his entire testimony is at risk and the expert loses credibility. So this does not happen in practice. Note further that the node a_i
denotes all of what the defence says which can be comprised of several
attacks in the formal sense, or a joint attack or a higher level attack,
etc.)

- the experts answer to the attack denoted by b_i. (Many of the answers
  of the expert are explanations or more information, see [Gabbay and
  Gabbay, 2015].

The factors come with labelling of strengths: low, moderate and strong. We
shall see in the Appendix, which surveys Tools which assess the strength
of these factors, that numerical strength are assigned to them both positive
and negative numbers, the qualitative strengths can be derived from these
numbers. Note that the factors s_i can be factors which increase risk or
sometimes factors which decrease risk (such as participation in therapy).
We still view them as "supports" with negative input, which turns them as
"attacks". The examples below show that the "counter attacks" a_i on s_i can
either question the strength and the significance suggested by s_i or they can
question the validity of s_i in applying or not applying to the sex offender in
question or can be factual attacks on the factual part of the factor s. Some
attacks a_i are logical fallacies. The replies b_i to the items a_i are more in the
nature of explanations, rather than "counter-counter-attacks" on a_i.

We need to be more explicit here. Let us assume that the expert puts
forward factor s_i. Factor s_i has two parts, the factual part and the assessment part arguing its contribution to how dangerous the offender is. For
example The lawyer of the defence attacks s_i with counter argument a_i. If
the counter argument is successful against the factual part, then the credibility of the expert is shattered, and all his support arguments s_j for all j are
destroyed. Take s_{15} for example. The factual part is that the offence was in
a public place. The attack $a_{15}(b)$ simply says that the attack was at night
at an isolated part of the public place and so the factor should not be used.
This is not a factual attack. But if the defence proves $a_{15}(a)$, that the attack
was at home, then this is a factual attack and all the support arguments s_j
for all j are destroyed. On the other hand if the lawyer's attack $a_{15}(a)$ is
factually destroyed by b_{15}, then his other arguments can still be used. The
lawyer is not an expert, he is not committed to the same credibility criteria,
and he is expected to try all kinds of arguments. a_{15} may be destroyed but
his other arguments may survive. The defence lawyer may invite his own
expert to present a possibly different report and different conclusion. In this

case the second expert will also appear in court and be subjected to the same procedures as the first expert with the prosecutor performing the attacks on the second expert factors.

We finally would like to put the contents of this section (namely the attack on the expert testimony) into a general perspective from the point of view of argumentation: An influential classification of dialogue types is that of Walton and Krabbe [1995]. We recall their distinction between persuasion and deliberation dialogue. The goal of a deliberation dialogue is to solve a problem while the goal of a persuasion dialogue is to test whether a claim is acceptable The material of this section falls under the category of persuasion dialogues. In such dialogues, two or more participants try to resolve a difference of opinion by arguing about the tenability of a claim, (in our case the degree of risk of a given sex offender), each trying to persuade the other participants (in our case mainly the Judge) to adopt their point of view. General dialogue systems regulate such things as the preconditions and effects of speech acts, including their effects on the commitments of the participants, as well as criteria for terminating the dialogue and determining its outcome. Good dialogue systems regulate all this in such a way that conflicting viewpoints can be resolved in a way that is both fair and effective [Loui, 1998]. In our case the procedure as we described is a highly stylised tree of depth 4, and the final arbiter is the Judge.

Furthermore the particular arguments used are informational and numerical, as we shall see in later sections.

The reader would also benefit greatly from looking at the important paper of Gordon, Prakken and Walton, [2007] and the survey [Chesnevar et al., 2000].

Let us begin.

Full Matrix/List of Relevant parameters/ factors to assess sexual risk

Note that the attacks on these factors are taken from protocols of actual cases involving Dr Rozenberg and his actual replies. They are not from a single court case but a representative compilation. But each sequence was actually asked and answered in court. The wording describing the node s_i is the authors wording simply saying the factor was or was not introduced in the experts report. We could have written "+" and "−" . The entries for a_i and b_i are from transcripts of actual court cases.

5.2   This factor is the age

Sex offender's age taken into account when making the risk assessment. Below is the official table of the age groups and the risk strength assigned to them

Risk factor	Age group
1	18–34.9
0	35–39.9
-1	40–59.9
-2	60 or older

A significant factor with at least moderate importance

- s_1 The expert gives a contribution due to this age factor

- a_1 The attack says that the offender is older so according to the table the risk factor strength should be less.

- b_1 The expert reply: Recent literature shows the relationship between the age of the offender to a level of sexual risk is not so dichotomous, for example, we learn that the dangerousness decline in child molesters is milder and occurs in older ages than among rapists. Also, the person who committed the offence in an advanced age, his age should not be taken that seriously as a risk reducing factor.

5.3 Division/ classification of sex offenders by the official definition of the nature of their offence

child molester- victim under age 13
rapist- victim above 13 years old. A significant factor with at moderate importance

s_2 — The expert gives a contribution of risk due to this factor.

a_2 — The attack says that the expert should have taken into account that risk of rapists against the passage of time declines at a faster rate than that of in child molester.

b_2 — Expert reply: Recent literature shows the relationship between the age of the offender to a level of sexual risk is not so dichotomous, for example, we learn that a dangerousness decline in child molesters is milder and occurs in older ages than among rapists. Also, the person who committed the offence in an advanced age, his age as a factor that reduces dangerousness should be taken with a grain of salt.

5.4 Family status

The official classification is as follows:

Bachelor — a person who has not lived with an Intimate Partner nor had a joint household with a partner for a period of at least 2 Years. If bachelor then this factor raises the dangerousness.

This factor is of Low importance.

s_3 — The expert put forward this factor

a_3 — The attack: You can see that the accused person is acquainted with a woman, maybe even married her, and managed a relationship for almost 2 years. Technically he is considered a bachelor but arguably it teaches us about his capabilities and reduces risk.

b_3 — Expert reply: The literature indicates that the fact a person contacted and possibly married is insufficient. Only if he would be able to manage relationships with common household for two years it will show the ability to keep significant relationship.

5.5 Index Non-sexual Violence (NSV) - Any Convictions

If the offender's criminal record shows a separate conviction for a non-sexual violent offence at the same time they were convicted of their Index Offence, this factor raise the dangerousness.

A significant factor with at least moderate importance

s_4 — Expert mentions use of violence.

a_4 — The attack: If the offender's criminal record does not show a separate conviction for a non-sexual violent offence at the same time they were convicted of their Index Offence, this factor should be ignored.

b_4 — Expert Reply: Do not ignore the fact that almost all sex offences include aspects of coercion and violence and the choice to convict a person of a crime of violence is a legal issue rather than sex offence issue.

5.6 Prior Non-sexual Violence - Any Convictions

Having a history of violence is a predictive factor for future violence. A significant factor with moderate importance

s_5 — Expert did not address this factor, (meaning that in the court case this factor was not mentioned in the expert's report. Since this is a mitigating factor the defence asks why was it not mentioned).

a_5 – The attack: If not convicted, so arguably he usually keeps the law and it is one-time lapse and the current conviction probably discourages him.

b_5 — Expert reply: Sometimes the person tells us himself that once he used violence against family members or others and the absence of conviction of violence does not necessarily indicate that he never used violence.

5.7 Prior Sex Offences

The best predictor of future behaviour, is past behaviour. A meta-analytic review of the literature indicates that having prior sex offences is a predictive factor for sexual recidivism.

A significant factor with high importance

s_6 — expert mentioned that the person had previous offences which increase the risk.

a_6 — Attack : This was a long time ago. Since then for many years there were no conviction. So previous conviction probably discouraged him.

b_6 — Expert Reply. Criminal that have several conviction at any time in the past is still to be considered dangerous. The existence of a conviction for sex offence often indicates quality of functioning of law enforcement officials and victims readiness and motivation, (if such were indeed), to complain. Also, in law, sometimes for a similar offence the offender can be convicted on different offences, for example, reveals himself in public might be convicted of committing a public indecent assault, but charges may be ether wild behaviour in a public place.

5.8   Prior Sentencing Dates

This item relate to criminal history and the measurement of persistence of criminal activity. The Basic Rule: If the offender's criminal record indicates four or more separate sentencing dates prior to the Index Offence, the offender is more dangerous. Count the number of distinct occasions on which the offender was sentenced for criminal offences. The number of charges/convictions does not matter, only the number of sentencing dates.

A significant factor is law importance

s_7 — Expert used this factor, even though the past convictions were not sex related.

a_7— Attack: If not convicted before, so arguably he usually keeps the law and it is one-time lapse and the current conviction probably discourages him. We can claim that if the subject made prior offences that teach about his criminal lifestyle, the risk sex assessment should evaluate only sexually dangerous and nothing else and the index offence is one-time lapse. People with criminal life style mostly feel disgusted by sex offences and shy away of it and their self-esteem injured therefore current conviction probably discourages him

b_7 — Expert Reply: A person who has a background of criminal offences shows difficulty to maintain limits and respect the boundaries of correct behaviour and one of the main concerns is that reluctance not to respect the laws and other limits may result in repeated sex offences, too.

5.9   Any Convictions for Non-contact Sex Offences

Offenders with paraphilic interests are at increased risk for sexual recidivism. Offenders who engage in these types of behaviours are more likely to have problems conforming their sexual behaviour to conventional standards than offenders who have no interest in paraphilic activities. If the offender's criminal record indicates a separate conviction for a non-contact sexual offence, the offender is more dangerous.

A significant factor with high or very high importance

s_8 — Expert did use this factor

a_8 — Attack: You can argue that sex is contactless low threshold of severity of injury and despite the offence with high recidivism, even if a person carries the offence again, the damage it can cause to the potential victim not so strong a man performing very offensive offence with contact and entering offences. Typically, offenders who committed Non-contact Sex Offences contact offences are less likely to make contact sex offences.

b_8 — Reply: The person that makes risk sex assessment is not a judge, and it is not his job to determine severity of harm, but to indicate to which group the subject belongs and what are the chances that he will make again sex offences, regardless of the severity of the offence.

5.10 Unrelated Victims (victim known to the offender, but not family)

The items concerning victim characteristics. Sex offence on Unrelated Victims related to higher risk assessment. Research indicates that offenders who offend only against family members recidivate at a lower rate compared to those who have victims outside of their immediate family.

A significant factor with high importance

s_9 — Expert used this factor

a_9 — Attack: Offender who harm the victims in his family is less dangerous because he is often perceived as a "lazy" who probably will not look for victims outside the family.

b_9 — Reply: Despite the fact that the person who harm victims within the family hurts somebody outside the family is relatively low, but it still exists. In addition, the offence to be possible because of problematic family climate expressed within weak limits and if the family circumstances do not change, significant treatment, then the individual may return to the same environment that allowed the violation in the past and may again exploit his authority and hurt.

5.11 Any Stranger Victims?

The Basic Principle: Research shows that having a stranger victim is related to sexual recidivism. If the offender has victims of sexual offences who were strangers at the time of the offence (stranger is defined as a person known to offender for less than 24 hours prior to the offence), is related to higher sexual recidivism.

A significant factor with high importance

s_{10} — Expert says the victim was a stranger.

a_{10} — Attack: A strong connection formed between the offender and the victim, even though they met less than 24 hours (they had intimate conversation before the offence).

b_{10} — Reply: But he hurt the 'victim, who is not a relative and possibly in future is pushing a minimal introduction to compromise.

5.12 Any Male Victims?

The Basic Principle: Research shows that offenders who have offended against male children or male adult recidivate at a higher rate compared to those who do not have male victims.

A significant factor with high importance

s_{11} — The expert used this factor

a_{11} — attack- you say that a sex offender attacking male victims is more dangerous than offender who attacks female victims. This is clearly a prejudiced judgement between males and females. You see a man attacking another man as sick and therefore you make him more dangerous.

b_{11} — Reply There is no prejudice here, the observation is based on statistical data.

5.13 Alcohol consumption is clearly associated with violence

This is a strong factor in assessing risk. s_{12} — The expert increased the risk owing to the offender's high alcohol consumption

a_{12} — Attack 1: the offender has rehabilitated, he is no longer drinking.

$a_{12}(b)$ — Attack 2: the man has been alcoholic for a long time without offending, so there is no real connection.

b_{12} — Reply: The expert assertion about use of alcohol is based on the offender report of his use of alcohol, and it is well known that such reports can be unreliable. The offender report of alcoholism could be a cover for some more serious pathological causes.

$b_{12}(b)$ — Furthermore the use of alcohol can cause offence while drunk. This is a worrying factor because he might drink and be inhibited in the future and offend again.

5.14 The use of hard drugs

The connection between being a drug addict and sexual offence is not strong enough. Research identifies two types of drugs (excluding alcohol) contribute to hyper sexuality, namely Cocaine and Meta-amphetamines. To the extent that we get confirming scientific reports about the connection, we will consider drug abuse as a risk factor. At any rate this is a weak factor

s_{13} — The expert mentions this as a factor.

a_{13} - Attack 1 —The offender has rehabilitated, he is no longer drug addict.

$a_{13}(b)$ — Attack 2 The man has been addict for a long time without offending so there is no real connection.

b_{13} — Reply. The expert assertion about use of drugs is based on the offenders report of his use of drugs, and it is well known that such reports can be unreliable. The offender report of drug addiction could be a cover for some more serious pathological causes. Furthermore the use of drugs can cause inhibited behaviour and to lead to offence while under the influence. This is a worrying factor because he might use drugs in the future and offend again. Note that meta-amphetamines do increase /flood the sex drives and therefore might push the man to further offence.

5.15 Sexual offence while the offender was under court order

This could be, for example, a legal trial, conditional sentence, legal restrictions, etc. This is a strong factor

s_{14} — Expert used this factor.

a_{14} — Attack - the offender has been punished and will behave. Furthermore he did not understand at the time the full meaning of legal restrictions but now he does understand.

b_{14} — Reply: Maybe the offender just says he will now behave but this does not ensure that he will not offend again.

Furthermore the effects of the present trial and punishment will wear off as time goes by.

5.16 Sexual offence in a public place

This is a medium strength factor

s_{15} — The expert used this factor.

$a_{15}(b)$ — Attack- The offender made his offence at night at insulated place and the chance that somebody would see him is low.

b_{15} — It is still a public place and even at insulated places people can pass. It is known that offending in a public place indicates a deep difficulty to restrain oneself and control one's drives.[29]

---

[29] One of the referees made the following comment about this case (factor s_{15}), I quote:

"Why might someone not attack on the basis that it was raining, so there was a lower chance of being interrupted? Or in a place that was not visible to passers-by? Why is the attack a conjunction of night time and isolation — surely isolation could be enough to form an attack? What I would expect is that the typical attacks would be evidenced through reference to the court record — and then I would expect to see many different attacks that might be levelled arranged into groups, classes, or hierarchies perhaps. Similarly with defences against those attacks."

We note that s_{15} is a transcript of a case in court. The reader might ask whether we have

5.17   The use of force while offending

This includes using firearms or the threat of using firearms, or use of physical force, or threat of physical damage or kidnapping.

This is a medium strength factor.

s_{16} — Expert uses this factor.

a_{16} — Threat is not really use of force.

b_{16} — professional literature shows it is it. Threat is definitely count as a use of force. Many times it is enough to compel person to make things that he didn't. Conviction of violence in addition to conviction of sexual offence indicates the offender not only cannot control his sexual drives but also cannot control his aggression.

5.18   The offender subjected the victim to a variety of sexual violations

These include: Penis penetration to vagina, finger into vagina, foreign object into vagina, groping the victim, masturbating over the victim, forcing the victim to grope the offender, forcing victim to masturbate, Forcing victim to give offender oral sex, offender giving victim oral sex, offender exposes himself (excluding exposing for the purpose of executing the offence), forcing victim to make sex with a third party/object, penetration of penis to anus, penetration of finger to anus, penetration of object to anus, kiss, forcing the victim to masturbate the offender.

This is a weak factor

s_{17} — Expert lists the offences done by the offender

a_{17} — attack. These should be considered a single offence and not a list of multiple offences. Moreover, almost any rape or other sex offence including a variety of sexual violations. For example, it is almost impossible to rape without groping the victim.

---

collected an exhaustive list of transcripts and analysed them and examined them? Maybe the above suggested referee questions were asked in other cases? The answer is we did not assemble a larger set of transcript but a representative one. There is sufficient data and we learnt a lot from these examples already, namely the idea of the attack as information input, see [Gabbay and Gabbay, 2015].

Let us examine the transcript of s_{15} itself, to show the reader what we mean by representative. The attack a_{15} adds factual information, and tries to say, given this information, then the place was not really public. The response b_{15} is actually saying that the factor's contribution to the risk assessment of the sex offender was determined statistically based on the formal definition of public place (as opposed to the concept of not containing people) and the extra information is not relevant to the statistics. Again b_{15} is an attack by adding information.

In fact b_{15} is also a valid counter-attack to the referees suggestions above ("it was raining", or "it was in a place that was not visible to passers-by", etc...), again because such cases did not go into the statistics!. Compare with b_{20}.

b_{17} — Reply: yes legally it is a single offence, but statistics shows that multiple components increase risk of re-offending in the future. The offender needs multiple stimulations to satisfy his drive. The offender might even commit some unusual acts in the future, and if the indictment detail the violation, than probably is was a different offence and not a basis to perform another offence.

5.19 Sex offender with victims from different age groups

In such a case the offender is considered more dangerous because the offender has a larger group of potential victims.

The age groups are:

$$0\text{–}6.99; 7\text{–}12.99; 13\text{–}15.99; 16 \text{ and above}$$

s_{18} — Expert mentions this factor

a_{18} — Victims may not look their ages so it only an illusion that the offender is not focused on a single age group.

b_{18} — Reply. As an expert I have a choice and judgement on whether I work like a simple mathematical machine or try to decide on the correct evaluation and scenario. I try to understand the triggers motivating the offence and using that evaluate how dangerous the offender is and to what age groups. I especially examine the significance of cases where the victim's age is near the boundaries.

5.20 Age of victim is 13–15 years

An offender attacking this age group is more dangerous if the offender is 5 years older or more than the victim.

This is a medium factor

s_{19} — Expert mentions this factor

a_{19} — Attack. The age division into group is arbitrary and further teenagers.

Vary in how old they look, and many times 13–15 years old looks like elder.

b_{19} — Reply: the expert exercises judgement. The problem here is that the offender seeks an intermediate age group between children and grownups. There is the danger of a shift into the neighboring age groups. It is offenders responsibility to know the exact age of teenager. And mostly the confusion is a result of cognitive distortion of the offender.

5.21 Offender has not been able to maintain continuous employment up to the offence

This is a medium factor

s_{20} — Expert quotes this factor

a_{20} — There is an objective market difficulty in maintaining continuous employment. Many employers sack people in order not to give them tenure.

b_{20} — This is a statistical observation. The statistics show increase in risk. The statistics does not consider the reasons behind the lack of past continuous employment.

5.22 Offender violated some restrictions imposed by court orders, not necessarily sexually connected

This is a medium factor.

s_{21} — Expert mentions this factor

a_{21} — The past offences are not sexual, why are you mentioning them?

b_{21} — The offender cannot keep to proper boundaries, and his "internal policeman" is weak. If within the boundaries of court orders the offender could not police himself, he might reoffend if we release him now.

5.23 Empathy towards the victim

Weak factor

s_{22} — Expert mentions this factor

a_{22} — The literature shows there is no significant connection of this factor to risk.

b_{22} — If there is no empathy to the victim the offender will not appreciate the damage he is doing, and will not be interested or respond well to remedial treatment.

5.24 Disrespect to authority and institutions

s_{22} — expert mentions this aspect

a_{22} — The literature shows there is no significant connection of this factor to risk

b_{22} — If offender does not respect authority, then the offender if released with disrespect the officer supervising him/her and will try to out-manoeuver the officer and offend again

5.25 Medical treatment to lower the sexual drive

This is an important factor, medium strength, as long as the patient participates

s_{24} — expert mentions this.

a_{24} — The Offender agrees to a chemical castration without being forced to do it. He is risking his body and might have to face side effects. This is a proof of how much he appreciates his wrong doing in the past and shows commitment to be risk free in the future. This must be considered a significant factor.

b_{24} — This treatment affects the offender capabilities, not his personality and tendencies. Therefore without a genuine internal change there is still the risk of further offence, especially if the treatment is discontinued.

Furthermore the offender agreeing to the treatment may be just manipulative and not genuine, and we can be sure only if he continues with it for a considerable period of time. This is why this factor doesn't change the risk assessment in the long term..

5.26 No community or family support for the offender

Low factor.

s_{25} — Expert mentions this factor

a_{25} — Offender can take care of himself

$a_{25}(b)$ — It is bad enough that everyone abandoned the offender, you have also to punish him for it?!

b_{25} — This is not a punishment but the unfortunate fact that the offender will have no support to help him not offend again.

5.27 Offender is mentally retarded

This increases risk, medium factor.

s_{26} — Expert mentioned this factor

a_{26} — This is God's doing, what can the offender do?

b_{26} — Mental retardation leads to dis-inhibition. The offender cannot learn from experience or appreciate vague situations with unclear boundaries.

5.28 Mental illness

Medium factor for increase in risk

s_{27} — Expert mentions this factor

a_{27} — What can he do, it is not his fault.

b_{27} — Mental illness leads to dis-inhibition. The offender has difficulties to learn from experience or appreciate vague situations with unclear boundaries.

We are not supposed to be politically correct but we deal in science and it is proven that mental illness increases risk of re-offending.

5.29 Offender does not accept responsibility for his actions nor expresses regret

Factor of low importance

s_{28} — Expert mentions this factor.

a_{28} — The literature does not consider this significant

b_{28} — If the offender does not accept responsibility of regret he will not be interested in any change. Accordingly, his chance to integrate on treatment and to derive the usefulness from it is low.

5.30 Did the offender plead guilty?

This is low factor.

s_{29} — Expert mentioned this factor

a_{29} — A literature do not attach much importance to this factor with the possible exception of a small group of offenders.

b_{29} — For offences within the family unit this is an important factor.

Furthermore, it is less likely the offender will accept treatment nor benefit from it

5.31 The offender has a distorted way of thinking

Low importance.

s_{30} —- Expert mentions this factor

a_{30} — This factor is not identified in the literature. Besides, everyone has distorted ways of thinking one way or another.

b_{30} — Sex offenders have their own characteristic distortions, that form the basis to rationalise and justify his offences. We know there is a connection between thinking positions and behaviour.

5.32 Offender has low opinion of himself

Medium importance for increasing risk.

s_{31} — Expert presents this factor.

a_{31} — Person with low opinion of self the offender will not dare offend.

b_{31} — On the contrary offender will not dare approach normal relationship and will find someone weak to offend and attack.

5.33 Offender is physically or mentally impotent or is ashamed of his sexual organs

Factor of medium to high importance

s_{32} — Expert mentions this factor as increasing risk

a_{32} — On the contrary, there is no risk, he cannot do it he will not do it.

b_{32} — Not at all, we are dealing with frustration as a basis for action. To prove him-self the offender might prey on the weak such as children.

5.34 Impulsiveness, low tolerance to stimuli

Factor of medium importance.

s_{33} — Expert presents this factor

a_{33} — Usually his impulsiveness is not connected with sex

b_{33} — Impulsive people are unpredictable, you cannot be sure what the offender will do.

5.35 Strong sex drive

Factor of high importance for risk.

s_{34}- - Expert presents this factor

a_{34} – So what, the offender will just be busy masturbate more often and is less likely to offend.

b_{34} – Research shows that on the contrary, increase masturbation enhances existing sex drives and not diminishes them. The offender is more likely to seek real contact.

5.36 Sexual deviation

Such as pedophilia, exhibitionism, proterism, etc.

Factor with high risk.

s_{35} — Expert uses this factor.

a_{35} — The man is sick, he needs hospital, not punishment.

b_{35} — I am not a Judge, the fact is that people with sexual deviation are high risk offenders.

5.37 Offender completed medical treatment

This is medium factor in reducing risk.

s_{36} — Expert did not include this factor

a_{36} — The offender did conclude a treatment why did you not include it as a high risk reducing factor?

b_{36} — The treatment is not effective on some people. They emerge from it with some success but these fade in time. The real test is if the offender continues the program suggested by the treatment.

5.38 Sex offender treatment was interrupted and never completed

High risk factor.

s_{37} — expert uses this factor.

a_{37} — The interruption was due to objective factors such as the offender was sent to prison and was not allowed to complete the treatment.

b_{37} — Even if it is not the offender's fault the fact is that half a treatment is risky and makes the situation worse in confusing the patient.

5.39 Does the offender understand/ know the risk/ trigger situations? Can the offender use adaptive preventive measures?

Medium factor

407

s_{38} — The Expert said the offender did not know.

a_{38} — The offender did know but when you talked to him he was under stress and could not list them. Anyway there is not enough research about this factor

s_{38} — It is important to know the risk/ trigger situation for offence and learn to avoid them. It is important for the offender to know that even simple, seemingly unimportant decisions can put him at a risk of a trigger situation.

5.40   Personality disorder

Factor of low importance.

s_{39} — Expert mentions this factor.

a_{39} — There is not enough research on this factor.

b_{39} — Sometimes this can be the reason for the offence. For example a narcissist might think the victim actually wants sex and the offender is actually being helpful.

Personality disorders are very difficult to treat.

5.41   The offender has had a long prison sentence

Factor with low strength.

s_{40} — Expert mentions this factor.

a_{40} — Offender did not offend in prison and suffered long enough. Why don't you let go instead of continuing to support punishing him?

b_{40} — I don't deal with punishment. I deal only with risk assessment. Today there is literature that indicates that having served a long prison sentence does not reduce risk but might even increase risk.

6   Value-based Argument Framework

The purpose of this section is to compare our approach with that outlined in Bench-Capon [2003] and to show how labels can be used more effectively. We also give a Bayesian approach and a neural nets approach. In coming work we hope to offer an LDS mix of all approaches. We believe any realistic model needs to do that!

We can indicate at this stage how the abstract argumentation model can relate to LDS. Consider the Lord Reid argument as presented in Figure 1. It has arguments $r_1, \ldots, r_4$ in favour of E and counter arguments $s_0, \ldots, s_3$ in favour of $\neg E$, essentially attacking $r_1, \ldots, r_4$. LDS requires in this case a flattening function (or a process) to tell us which arguments win and at what strength we can use E or $\neg E$.

This flattening process can make use of abstract argumentation theory, either in its Bench-Capon form, or modified with probability or implemented

408

in neural nets. A taste of these options is given in this section.

6.1   The Framework

We begin by discussing and highlighting our method of modelling. The first principle is to work bottom up from the application area into the formal model, trying to reflect in the formal model more and more key properties of the application area. In the case of evidence this means we need to see and study many examples/case studies/debates about evidence and then try to construct a suitable logic for it. Chances are that existing logics, constructed for some other purpose, may not be the most suitable. Our starting formal system for this purpose is LDS. The theory of LDS was developed from the bottom up point of view, especially to model aspects of human behaviour, reasoning and action, and is very comprehensive, adaptable and incremental. It contains a large variety of existing logical systems as special cases. What is more important is that LDS is not a single system but a methodology for building *families* of systems, ready to be adapted to the needs of various application areas, in our case to the theory of evidence.

One very important side effect of this approach is that the logic can be worked up directly from the day-to-day activity of the practitioner of the laws of evidence, without necessarily forcing him to study logic. The 'logic' will be hidden in the stylised movements he will be asked to make, and the interplay between the labels and comments and arguments he will be using.[30]

---

[30]For recent work on the norms implicit and tacit in the cognitive behaviour of parties to a criminal trial, see Woods [2018, chapter 20, 'An epistemology for law'], and [2020]. Consider the widespread use of anagrams. Take as an example the pair of words 'read on'. We can rearrange the letters (including the space between the words) into 'no dear'. Let us write this as

$$\text{read on} \vdash \text{no dear}$$

We can also write equivalently

$$\text{space, a, d, e, n, o, r} \vdash \text{read on}$$
$$\text{space, a, d, e, n, o, r} \vdash \text{no dear}$$

where on the left we just listed the basic blocks we can use, including the space.
Now suppose we allow you some 'wildcard' of the form

$$\text{space} \mapsto \text{any other already listed letter}$$

Then we get

$$\text{space, a, d, e, n, o, r, (space} \mapsto \text{any other already listed letter)} \vdash \text{adorned}$$

We chose here space $\mapsto$ d.
What we have been doing here was linear logic!

409

In contrast to our approach, in a good deal of applicational work in logic, a logic is applied to various areas and tend to force the application area into a form suitable for its existing formalism. This tends to produce results intelligible mainly to the logician, ignoring that the ordinary human/lawyer/judge already knows intuitively how to handle his daily life, and that all he needs is some bottom up additional organisation of his activities which will enable him to understand it better and possibly solve some of his outstanding puzzles.[31]

The difference in this point of view is apparent when we look again at Prakken's book. The book does realise the potential in the interaction of logic and law. It also recognises some of the kinds of logics needed to model some aspects of the law. But having made and argued all of these points, the main part of the book gives an exposition of the relevant parts of the logic in a way that only a logician can understand. This is also true at the moment of this version of our chapter, but we hope in the full version to be able to do logic directly in the legal evidence application area. See Footnote 30.

Having said all that, we can now look at some specific model, namely that of abstract argumentation systems. These were put forward as a response to the realisation that no argument or proof is conclusive in real life, and that arguments have counterarguments. The argument framework has the form $AF = (AR, Attacks)$ where AR is a set of objects called arguments and $Attacks$ is a binary relation (usually irreflexive), saying which arguments x attacks which argument y. The following Figure 4 is an example

a attacks c, c attacks b and b attacks a.

There are no winning arguments here. This framework is too abstract to be of specific use. It equally applies to circuits and impending circuits, credits and debits, neural nets and counterweights or any system involving x and anti-x, whatever x is.

To apply such a system successfully we need to go into the structure of the arguments and analyse the mechanics of one argument attacking another.

So anagrams with wildcards is linear logic.

The idea that logic can be 'translated' into stylised proof movements was put forward in the Gabbay 1984 logic lectures at Imperial College, London. See the first chapter of [Gabbay, 1996] and see [Gabbay, 2001]. Peter Tillers says similar things in his paper in [MacCrimmon and Tillers, 2002, pp. 2–11]. We assume the word 'dynamics' in the title of [MacCrimmon and Tillers, 2002] is significant.

[31] The modelling practices of the social sciences generally are adaptations of the modelling paradigms of physics (rather than, say, biology), and are a reflection of the primacy of logical positivism as the social sciences were in process of articulating its philosophical presumptions. But it is almost never satisfactory to abstract from the data of human interactions in the same way that one abstracts from the interactions of physical particles.

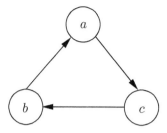

Figure 4.

Bench-Capon tried to improve upon such systems by introducing a clever idea; the value-based argumentation framework. In this framework we are given a set of colours (values) and a colouring of the arguments. The values are partially ordered and an argument of strictly lesser value cannot now attack an argument of stronger value.

So following Bench-Capon in the previous figure, if we make b red and a and c blue then

1. If blue is stronger than red, then b cannot attack and defeat a, a can attack c and the winning arguments are $\{a, b\}$, because c is out.

2. If red is stronger than blue then the winning arguments are $\{b, c\}$.

Certainly this colouring with values is an intuitively welcome improvement. However, this model is still too abstract. Real life has arguments within arguments in different levels and interconnections between the levels. We can extend the Bench-Capon model by using our technique of self-fibring of networks [Garcez and Gabbay, 2004]–[Gabbay, 1998]. This method allows for the recursive substitution of networks inside nodes of other networks [Barringer *et al.*, 2005a; Barringer *et al.*, 2008; Barringer *et al.*, 2012; Barringer *et al.*, 2012a; van Benthem, 2011; van Benthem, 2012]. We will work out the details in a later section. Still, we think using LDS is a much better option.

In LDS, this situation will arise if we have a labelled database which includes items such as $t : a, s : b$ and $r : c$ and some additional data, say $u_i : X_i$, such that the following can be proved, among others:[32]

- $\gamma(t) : \neg c$

---

[32]Note that we are assuming here that to defeat x we must put forward an argument for $\neg x$. This is only a simplifying assumption. In LDS, x comes with a label t and so to weaken $t : x$ we can attack t.

- $\beta(r) : \neg b$

- $\alpha(s) : \neg a.$

α, β, γ are the labels of $\neg a, \neg b$ and $\neg c$ respectively and t, r, s are mentioned in the respective labels to indicate that e.g. $t : a$ is used in the proof of $\gamma(t) : \neg c$ (a with label t attacks c, by proving $\neg c$ with label $\gamma(t)$). The label $\gamma(t)$ shows exactly what role a plays in this attack.

The flattening process acts here as value judgement of what can win, $r : c$ or $\gamma(t) : \neg c$, by comparing r and $\gamma(t)$.

Obviously the value based argumentation machinery can be utilised as part of our flattening mechanism.

The following LDS model will reflect the Bench-Capon coloured diagram:

$$\begin{aligned}
&\text{red: } b \\
&\text{blue: } a \\
&\text{blue: } c \\
&\text{red to blue: } b \to \neg a \\
&\text{blue to blue: } a \to \neg c \\
&\text{blue to red: } c \to \neg b
\end{aligned}$$

Using modus ponens in the form

$$\frac{\alpha : X, \beta : X \to Y, \varphi(\beta, \alpha)}{\alpha \cup \beta : Y}$$

We can prove:

red:$\neg a$	if red to blue is allowed
blue:$\neg c$	if blue to red is allowed
blue:$\neg b$	if blue to blue is allowed.

The flattening function has to flatten:

{red: b, blue: $\neg b$}
{blue: a, red: $\neg a$}
{blue: c, (blue: $\neg c$ is not allowed!)}

Case 1.
red stronger than blue i.e., *blue to red* not allowed.
    We get b and $\neg a$ and c.

Case 2.
Blue stronger than red (*red to blue* not allowed)
    We get
{blue: a, (red: $\neg a$ not allowed)}

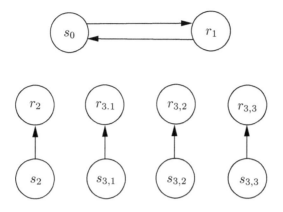

Figure 5.

{blue: c, blue: $\neg c$}
{red: b, blue: $\neg b$ if c is available}

We cannot decide between c and $\neg c$ since both are blue. If we leave them both out or take $\neg c$ then $\neg b$ will not be obtainable and hence we will have {a, b}.

We see that in the labelled formulation we have more options

1. We can have $X, \neg X$ or neither as choices

2. The label colour (value) can itself be a whole database and so arguments about the values and their strengths can also be part of the system.

The Bench-Capon system is only one level.

The following Figure 5 shows the abstract argumentation structure of Lord Reid's arguments.

Accordingly, Δ_1 in Figure 1 can be better rewritten as Figure 6 below

Assuming that the attack of Lord Reid is successful, then Figure 6 reduces to {$r_1 : E, r_4 : E$ and $s_0 : \neg E$}. The Lords indeed decided that s_0 was stronger, but they were uncomfortable about it and decided to recommend new legislation.

Note Lord Reid's argument $s_{3,2}$. This is a metalevel value argument like "you cannot colour something red".

Also note that s_0 and s_2 can be further counter-argued if possible by other Lords. The formal labelling of these additional arguments may require self-fibring. See section 6.5.

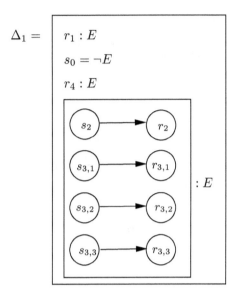

Figure 6.

6.2 Moral Debate Example

This section also follows Bench-Capon [2003, p. 442]. We consider an example cited by Bench-Capon, attributed to Coleman in [1992] and Christie [2000].

> "Hal, a diabetic, loses his insulin in an accident through no fault of his own. Before collapsing into a coma, he rushes to the house of Carla, another diabetic. She is not at home but Hal enters her house and uses some of her insulin. Was Hal justified, and does Carla have a right to compensation?"

The following are the arguments involved as presented in the Bench-Capon paper:

A = Hal is justified, since a person has a privilege to use the property of others to save their life - the case of necessity.

B = It is wrong to infringe the property rights of another.

C = Hal compensates Carla.

Bench-Capon [2003] quotes that Christie [2000] adds:

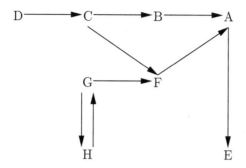

Figure 7.

D_1 = If Hal is too poor to compensate Carla, he should nonetheless be allowed to take the insulin, as no one should die because they are poor.

D_2 = Moreover, since Hal would not pay compensation if too poor, neither should he be obliged to do so even if he can.[33]

Bench-Capon further suggests:

E = Poverty is no defence for theft.

F = Hal is endangering Carla's life.

G = Fact: Carla has abundant insulin.

H = Fact: Carla does not have ample insulin.

Figure 7 now represents the situation. Note that $H = \neg G$.

Bench-Capon gives the following value properties to the arguments:

Life: A, D, F
Property: B, C, E
Fact: G, H

He says one might argue whether life is stronger than property or not but facts are always the strongest.

Since $H = \neg G$, and since we cannot have both facts, he regards that part of Figure 7 as a case of uncertainty.

---

[33]Christie puts $D_1 + D_2 = D$ together as D. The division into D_1 and D_2 is ours, for later discussion.

We cite this example because we want to analyse what is needed for a better representation of it.

We begin by listing the points:

1. The model needed for a proper analysis of this kind of problem in general (though maybe not necessarily the Hal problem) is a time/action model. There is a difference of values depending at what stage of the action sequence we are at. Has Hal entered Carla's house? Has he checked for insulin? Is it all over and Carla is dead? Each of these cases may have a different argument diagram, possibly with values depending on the previous one! We might add at this point that the need for time/action models has already been strongly emphasised in Gabbay [2001] in connection with puzzles involved in the logical analysis of conditionals. This is factors of connected to contrary-to-duty models[34] and also needed to incorporate uncertainty. We can get a quite complicated (but highly intuitive) model.[35]

2. We require a better metalevel hierarchy of values and rules, as are available in Labelled Deduction. Possibly such options can also be made adequately available to the abstract argumentation model via self-fibring.

3. The links $(X \to Y)$ should be given strength labels to help us model more realistic cases where an argument X is attacked by arguments $Y_1, \ldots, Y_k$ with strength measuring $m_1, \ldots, m_k$.

This is an essential generalisation. One of the quotes we cited from the car case study was (see footnote 18) had the Lords rejecting the written

---

[34] See the authoritative survey of A. Jones and J. Carmo [2002] in the *Handbook of Philosophical Logic*, 2nd edition.

[35] We take this opportunity to reinforce our methodological remark of footnote 31. In modelling human practical reasoning, actions and general behaviour it is often a disadvantage and a deficiency to try and use a stylised model and abstract too much from the actual reality (in contrast possibly with modelling physical nature). Often the details of the reality to be modelled suggests the solution to what otherwise is a puzzle. Let us look at the story and focus on the part which assumes Hal is too poor to replace Carla's insulin. We can ask how is he getting his insulin? Is he getting it on National Health Service? If yes, can't he call the NHS and try to get a replacement? So surely the question of replacement is not 'whether' but 'when', i.e., can he get a replacement in time before Carla runs out of insulin? If life is more important than property this is a good question. If property is more important, then we know he can replace it! Another question, if Hal steals the insulin from Carla and then calls for a replacement, would it not be more difficult to get a replacement (as opposed to calling the NHS first)? We need more details. We are *not* transforming the problem to one more suited to our framework. There are many other examples in other areas which need more details.

evidence because there was other ample evidence to the same effect (and they didn't want to create a precedent by admitting it).[36]

4. We can read the link $X \rightarrow Y$ as preventative action of X to stop Y and thus by giving probability of success turn any acyclic network into a Bayesian one. This will introduce uncertainty into the framework. Actually the probability of success is inversely proportional to the conditional probability of Y on X.

6.3 Bayesian aspects of the moral debate example

We begin this section with a closer look at Figure 7. We require a time/action model and contrary-to-duty considerations. We shall explain these features as we model the example.

We imagine an agent, such as Hal, who has available a stock of optional actions. These actions have the form $\mathbf{a} = (A, (B^+, B^-))$ where A is the precondition of the action and B^+, B^- are the post-conditions. A must hold in order for Hal to be allowed to perform the action, in which case the resulting state is guaranteed to satisfy B^+. However, the agent may take the action anyway, without permission (i.e., A does not hold), in which case the post-condition is B^-. Note that in most cases $B^- = B^+$.

We imagine we are at a state (or time) T_0, described by a logical theory Δ. The actions allowable to us to perform are $\mathbf{a}_1, \mathbf{a}_2, \ldots \mathbf{a}_i = (A_i, (B_i^+, B_i^-)), \ldots$. If $\Delta \vdash A_i$, then action $\mathbf{a}_i$ is allowable at time (state) T_0, otherwise not. If we perform the action $\mathbf{a}$, with post-condition B (B is either B^+ or B^-) then we move to time T_1, with state $\Delta_{\mathbf{a}} = \Delta \circ B$ where $\Delta \circ B$ is the revision of Δ by B. We have $\Delta \circ B \vdash B$.

So to have time action model we need

1. A language for the theories Δ to describe states

2. A language for pre-condition and a language for post-conditions for actions

3. A logic or algorithm for determining when $\Delta \vdash A$ holds, where A is a pre-condition.

4. A revision algorithm giving for each Δ and post-condition B a new theory $\Delta' = \Delta \circ B$. This algorithm can satisfy some reasonable axioms.

Note that the languages for Δ, the pre-conditions and the post-conditions need not be the same!

---

[36]This is a mixture of metalevel/strength/proof argument that only LDS can model. We shall address this kind of argument later.

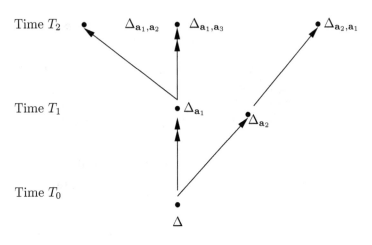

Figure 8.

The flow of time is future branching and is generated by the actions. So if for example our agent can perform actions $\mathbf{a}_1, \ldots, \mathbf{a}_k$ as options then after two steps in which he performs say $\mathbf{a}_1$ first and then say $\mathbf{a}_3$, we may get a situation as in Figure 8

The real history at time T_2 is $(\Delta, \Delta_{\mathbf{a}_1}, \Delta_{\mathbf{a}_1, \mathbf{a}_3})$. The states $\Delta_{\mathbf{a}_1, \mathbf{a}_2}$ and $(\Delta_{\mathbf{a}_2}, \Delta_{\mathbf{a}_2, \mathbf{a}_1})$ are hypotheticals.

At time T_0, our agent chose to take action $\mathbf{a}_1$ moving onto state $\Delta_{\mathbf{a}_1}$, but he could have chosen to take action $\mathbf{a}_2$ and done action $\mathbf{a}_1$ afterwards, ending up at state $\Delta_{\mathbf{a}_2, \mathbf{a}_1}$ at time T_2. In reality, however, he chose to perform $\mathbf{a}_1$ and then $\mathbf{a}_3$.

The pre-conditions of actions can talk about states and hypotheticals. They need not be in the same language as Δ or the same language as the post-conditions. What is important are the algorithms for '⊢' and '∘'.

We are now ready to analyse the moral debate example. First we tell the story in a more realistic way (see footnote 35!). Then we propose some probabilities as an example and we conclude by translating the Bench-Capon statements A–H (page 50) into our time/action set up.

Our story goes as follows. Hal needs insulin. So does Carla. Both are poor and get their insulin from the Health Service. They get it in batches, though not at the same time. So the question whether Carla has spare insulin (G) depends on the time, and is a matter of probability.

Hall loses all his insulin and would need to break into Carla's property to get hers. He has the option of calling the NHS and asking for replacement, which he can use either for himself if it arrives immediately or to replace

Carla's if necessary. He might get some money from friends. One thing is clear to him. If he steals Carla's insulin, it will complicate matters; it might be more difficult to find a replacement. So the question of compensation C is also a matter of probability. The following are the possible scenarios.

If property is valued more than life, then if Hal steals Carla's insulin, the probability of getting a replacement is lower in the case where Carla's life is not threatened.

If life is valued more than property, his chances of obtaining replacement is higher in case Carla's life is threatened.

We must clarify what 'getting a replacement' means. Hal will probably start a process for getting insulin for himself immediately at start time T_0. Since it might not arrive in time, he will break into Carla's home and use hers, and hope to use the insulin he 'ordered' to replace Carla's. If Carla has ample insulin, there is a higher chance or that the replacement will arrive in time before Carla's life is threatened. If Carla does not have ample insulin, Hal can use this as a further reason to rush the process of replacement. This further reason might be counterproductive if property is valued above life.

So the statement

$C = $ Hal gets a replacement

should be taken as (see footnote 35):

Hal gets a replacement before Carla is in need of it.

We may then have the following scenarios (P stands for Probability $P(x)$ and it should be indexed by case and time, i.e., $P_{1,a}, P_{1,b}, P_{2,a}$ and $P_{2,b}$:

Case 1. Property stronger than life

(a) Time = Before Hal breaks into Carla's house.
$P(G) = \frac{2}{3}$
$P(\neg G) = \frac{1}{3}$
$P(C/G) = 0.9$
$P(\neg C/G) = 0.1$
(Since Carla does have ample insulin, Hal has more time to replace what he might take.)

$P(C/\neg G) = 0.5$
$P(\neg C/\neg G) = 0.5$
(Admittedly, Carla's life is in danger but there may not be enough time to get a replacement. On the other hand, this very fact might help get the insulin more quickly. Note that the event C means 'getting replacement in time'.)

(b) Time = After Hal breaks into Carla's house.

At this stage the value of G is known: either $G = 1$ or $G = 0$. We get
$P(C/G = 1) = 0.7$
$P(\neg C/G = 1) = 0.3$
(less than before breaking into the house, because Hal committed a serious crime. He may not be favourable with the authority.)
$P(C/G = 0) = 0,4$
$P(\neg C/ G = 0) = 0.6$
Again, less than before. See also Gabbay and Woods [2008b].

Case 2. Property not stronger than life[37]

(a) Time = Before Hal breaks into Carla's house
$P(G) = \frac{2}{3}$
$P(\neg G) = \frac{1}{3}$
$P(C/G) = 0.9$
$P(\neg C/G) = 0.1$
$P(C/\neg G) = 0.9$
$P(\neg C/\neg G) = 0.1$

(b) Time = After Hal breaks into Carla's house
$P(G) = \frac{2}{3}$
$P(\neg G) = \frac{1}{3}$
$P(C/G = 1) = 0.9$
$P(\neg C/G = 1) = 0.1$
$P(C/G = 0) = 0.7$
$P(\neg C/G = 0) = 0.3$.

Let us now translate the arguments involved in the original moral debate example of Section 6.2.

When is Hal justified in breaking into Carla's home? The answer is yes only in the case that life is stronger than property and he can reasonably say he is not risking her life. That depends on finding a replacement. We therefore have to calculate the probability of C given all the data we have.

Thus our time/action axis has the form of Figure 9:

The actions available to Hal are:

1. **b** = breaking into Carla's house. The post-condition is breaking in and taking the insulin. The pre-condition of **b** is high probability

---

[37] Jon Williamson reminded us that it is reasonable to assume that the legal process does not make general value judgements like this, nor can a legal argument appeal to such judgements. Instead much more specific 'mitigating circumstances' can be used to reduce the length of a sentence on conviction ('I did it to save my life, guv').

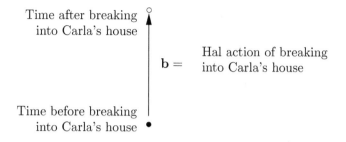

Figure 9.

of replacing Carla's insulin (in time before she needs it) in case *life is stronger than property* and ⊥ (falsity i.e., no permission to do the action) in case *life is not stronger than property*.

2. **r** = actions having to do with getting a replacement of insulin. We assume he can perform these actions at any time but the post-conditions are not clear.[38]

We need also agree the value of the threshold probability, e.g. only if there is at least 0.9 chance of replacement can Hal break into Carla's home to take the insulin. Consider now:

B = It is wrong to infringe the property of others.

B is an argument reflected in the pre-condition of the action **b**, it can be done when B satisfied otherwise not. I would write it as

$$\mathbf{b} = (\text{Justification, Break in and taking insulin}).$$

Let us now model the chain of events as a Bayesian network. The story is clear. Depending on the probability $P(G)$, Hal decides whether he wants to break into Carla's house **b** (no use breaking into her house if she does not have enough insulin). He is justified J in breaking **b** into Carla's house if there is high probability of compensation C. Thus C depends both on **b** and G, and **b** also depends on G. We have the following network, Figure 10. There are two problems with this representation.

1. The dependency of **b** on G is not on $G = 1$ or $G = 0$ but on $P(G)$. Say if $P(G) < 0.1$ then maybe **b** = 0.

   This is OK because the probabilities can be made to take account of that. This is allowed in the theory of Bayesian nets.

---

[38] We may need a temporal language for the post-conditions so that we can say something like 'insulin will be delivered in two days'.

2. The probabilities in Figure 10 depend on whether property is stronger than life or not. The best way to represent this is to have a Bayesian net with one variable only, *Case*.

Case =1 means property stronger than life and *case* =0 means property is not stronger than life.

For each case we get a different copy of Figure 10 with different probabilities.

So we get a substitution of the network of Figure 10 into a one point network:

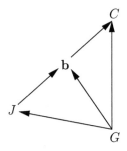

Figure 10.

- *Case*. This operation is in accordance with the ideas in [Williamson and Gabbay, 2004].

We can also allow for several justification variables to make it more realistic.

It is not difficult to work out the details of the rest of C–H, but the reader can already see that in the simple minded model there is lack of sensitivity to a variety of metalevels.

6.4   Neural Representation of Argumentation Frameworks

This subsection, based on [Garcez *et al.*, 2005] will outline how to represent (in neural nets) any value-based argumentation framework involving x and anti-x (i.e., arguments and counter-arguments). For instance, it can be implemented in neural networks with the use of Neural-Symbolic Learning Systems [Garcez *et al.*, 2002]. A neural network consists of interconnected neurons (or processing units) that compute a simple function according to the weights (real numbers) associated to the connections. Learning in this setting is the incremental adaptation of the weights [Haykin, 1999]. The

interesting characteristics of neural networks do not arise from the functionality of each neuron, but from their collective behaviour, thus being able
to efficiently represent (and learn) multi-part, cumulative argumentation, as
exemplified below.

Cumulative behaviour can be encoded in Neural-Symbolic Learning Systems with the use of a hidden layer of neurons in addition to an input and
an output layer in a feedforward network. Rules of the form $A \wedge B \rightarrow C$ can
be represented by connecting input neurons that represent concepts A and
B to a hidden neuron, say h_1, and then connecting h_1 to an output neuron
that represents C in such a way that output neuron C is activated (true)
if input neurons A and B are both activated (true). If, in addition, a rule
$B \rightarrow C$ is also to be represented, another hidden neuron h_2 can be added to
the network to connect input neuron B to output neuron C in such a way
that C is now activated also if B alone is activated.[39] This is illustrated in
Figure 11. The network can be used to perform the computation of the rules
in parallel such that C is true whenever B is true [Garcez *et al.*, 2002].

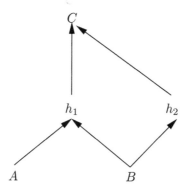

Figure 11. A simple example of the use of hidden neurons

In a neural network, positive weights can represent the support for an
argument, while negative weights can be seen as an attack on an argument.
Hence, a negative weight from a neuron A to a neuron B can be used to
implement the fact that A attacks B. Similarly, a positive weight from B to
itself can be used to indicate that B supports itself. Since we concentrate

---

[39]In the general case, hidden neurons are necessary to implement the following conditions: (**C1**) The input potential of a hidden neuron (N_l) can only exceed N_l's threshold
(θ_l), activating N_l, when all the positive antecedents of r_l are assigned the truth-value
true while all the negative antecedents of r_l are assigned *false*; and (**C2**) The input potential of an output neuron (A) can only exceed A's threshold (θ_A), activating A, when
at least one hidden neuron N_l that is connected to A is activated.

on feedforward networks, neuron B will appear on both the input and the output layers of this network as shown in Figure 12, in which dotted lines are used to indicate negative weights.

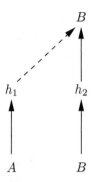

Figure 12. A simple example of the use of negative weights for counter-argumentation

In Figure 12, A attacks B via h_1, while B supports itself via h_2. Suppose now that, in addition, B attacks C. We need to connect input neuron B to output neuron C via a new hidden neuron h_3. Since B appears on both the network's input and output, we also need to add a feedback connection from output neuron B to input neuron B such that the activation of B can be computed by the network according to the chain 'A attacks B', 'B attacks C', etc. As a result, in Figure 13 (in which we do not represent B's feedback connection for the sake of clarity), if the attack from A on B is stronger (according to the network's weights) than B's support to itself, then A will block the activation of (output) B, and (input) B will not be able to block the activation of C. In this case, the network's final computation will include C and not B in a stable state. If, on the other hand, A is not strong enough to block B, then B will be activated and block C.

Let us take the example in which an argument A attacks an argument B, and B attacks an argument C, which in turn attacks A in a cycle. In order to implement this in a neural network, we need positive weights to explicitly represent the fact that A supports itself, B supports itself and so does C. In addition, we need negative weights from A to B, from B to C and from C to A (see Figure 14) to implement attacks. If all the weights are the same in absolute terms, no argument wins, as one would expect, and the network stabilises with none of $\{A, B, C\}$ activated. If, however, the value of A (i.e., the weight from h_1 to A) is stronger than the value of C (the weight from h_3 to C, which is expected to be the same in absolute terms as the weight from

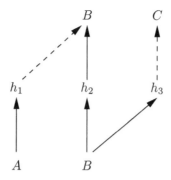

Figure 13. The computation of arguments and counter-arguments

h_3 to A), C cannot attack and defeat A. As a result, A is activated. Since A and B have the same value (as e.g., in the previous case of an unspecified priority), B is not activated, since the weights from h_1 and h_2 to B will both have the same absolute value. Finally, if B is not activated then C will be activated, and a stable state $\{A, C\}$ will be reached in the network. In Bench-Capon's model [Bench-Capon, 2003], this is exactly the case in which colour blue is assigned to A and B, and colour red is assigned to C with blue being stronger than red. Note that the order in which we reason does not affect the final result (the stable state reached). For example, if we started from B successfully attacking C, C would not be able to attack A, but then A would successfully attack B, which would this time round not be able to successfully attack C, which in turn would be activated in the final stable state $\{A, C\}$. This indicates that a neural (parallel) implementation of this reasoning process could be advantageous also from a purely computational point of view.

Note that (as in the general case of argumentation networks) in the case of neural networks, we can extend Bench-Capon's model with the use of self-fibring neural networks, which allow for the recursive substitution of neural networks inside nodes of other networks [Garcez and Gabbay, 2004].

The implementation of the network's behaviour (weights and biases) must be such that, when we start form a number of positive arguments (input vector $\{1, 1, \ldots 1\}$), weights with the same absolute values cancel each other producing zero as the output neuron's input potential. A neuron with zero or less input potential is then deactivated, while a neuron with positive input potential is activated. This allows for the implementation of the argumentation framework in neural-symbolic learning systems, in the style of the translation algorithms developed at [Garcez et al., 2002a].

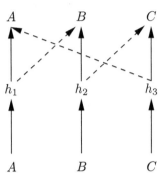

Figure 14. The moral-debate example as a neural network

6.5   Self-fibring of Argumentation Networks

We will conclude this section by indicating how to do self-fibring of argument networks. The mechanics of it is simple. We begin with one network, say the one in Figure 4. We pick a node in it, say node a, and substitute another network for that node, say we substitute the network of Figure 7. We thus get the 'network' of Figure 15.

The need of self-fibring may arise if additional arguments are available supporting the contents of the node.

The self-fibring problem has three aspects:

Aspect 1: Intuitive Meaning

What is the intended interpretation/meaning of this substitution? This can be decided by the needs of the application area. Here are some options:

(1.1) a is supposed to be an argument, so Figure 7 can be viewed as delivering some winning argument (A of Figure 7) which can combine/support a.

(1.2) Figure 7 is a network so b of Figure 4 can plug into it. We can connect b to all (or some) members of Figure 4 and similarly connect all (or some) members of Figure 7 into c of Figure 4.

For various options see [Williamson and Gabbay, 2004; Garcez and Gabbay, 2004; Gabbay, 1998].

Aspect 2: Formal aspect

(2.1) *Syntactical substitution*

Formally the node a is supposed to be an argument. So we need a

426

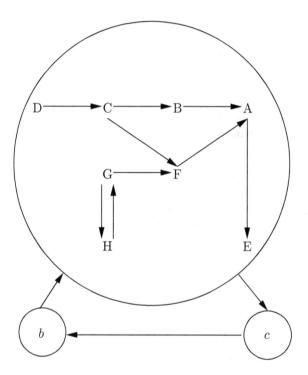

Figure 15.

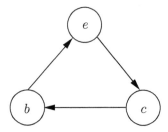

Figure 16.

fibring function **F**(node, network) $= e$ yielding a node e and so we end up with Figure 16

F might do, for example, the following: **F** can use the colour of node a to modify the colours of the nodes in Figure 7 (the substituted network), and maybe also modify some connections in Figure 7, and then somehow emerge with some winning argument e and a colour to be substituted/combined with a and its colour.

(2.2) *Semantic substitution*
If the original network has an interpretation, then the node a can get several possible semantic values. We can make the definition of the substitution context sensitive to those values. We may even go to the extent of substituting different networks for different options of values.

Aspect 3: Coherence
To enable successful repeated recursive substitution of networks within networks, we have to modify our definition of the original network. For example:

(3.1) Possibly extend the notion of network and allow arrows to either support or defeat arguments.

(3.2) Restrict the substitution of networks for nodes by compatibility/consistency conditions.

Example: Self-fibred argumentation network
We have a set of nodes and links of the form (a, b) meaning a attacks b. We also have valuation colours. A weaker colour cannot attack a stronger colour. So far this is the Bench-Capon definition.

Let a be a node. Define the notion of x is a supportive (resp. attacking) node for a as follows:

- a is supportive of a

- if x is supportive (resp. attacking) node of a and y attacks x then y is an attacking (resp. supportive) node of a.

Now let a be a node in a network A and suppose we have another network N which we want to substitute for a. We must assume a appears in N with the same colour value as it is in A. We substitute N for a and make new connection as follows:

- Any node x of A which attacks a in A is now connected to any node y in N which supports a in N.

- Any node y in N which supports a in N is now made connected to any node x of A which a of A is attacking.

This definition is reasonable. a is an argument in network A. N is another network which is supposed to support a (a in N). Thus anything which attacks a in A will attack of all a supporters in N and these in turn will attack whatever nodes a attacks in A. Note that he may be attacking facts in N by this wholesale connection of arrows. However, Bench-Capon has already remarked that facts should get the strongest colour and so the colours will take care of that!

See reference [Gabbay, 2009b].

Acknowledgements

We are grateful to A. Garcez, L. Lamb, D. Makinson, G. Pigozzi and J. Williamson for valuable comments.

BIBLIOGRAPHY

[Aldisert, 1989] Ruggero J. Aldisert. *Logic for Lawyers: A Guide to Clear Legal Thinking*, Clark Boardman, 1989.

[Aliseda, 1999] Aliseda A. 1999. *Seeking Explanation. Abduction in Logic, Philosophy of Science and Artificial Intelligence*, ILLC.

[Allen, 2001] Christopher Allen. *Practical Guide to Evidence*, 2nd ed. Cavdndish Pub, 2001.

[Barringer *et al.*, 2005] H. Barringer, D. M. Gabbay, and J. Woods. Temporal Dynamics of Argumentation Networks. In Volume Dedicated to Joerg Siekmann, D. Hutter and W. Stephan, editors. Mechanising Mathematical Reasoning, Springer Lecture Notes in Computer Science 2605, pp. 59-98, 2005.

[Barringer *et al.*, 2005a] Barringer H, Gabbay DM and Woods J. 2005. Temporal dynamics of support and attack networks: From argumentation to Zoology. In Hutler D and Stepham W (eds). *Mechanizing Mathematical Reasoning: Essays in Honor of Jörg Siekman on the Occasion of his 60th Birthday*, pages 59-98, Springer-Verlag.

[Barringer *et al.*, 2008] Barringer H, Gabbay DM and Woods J. 2008. Network modalities. In Gross G and Schulz U, eds. *Linguistics, Computer Science and Language Processing : Festschrift for Franz Guenthner on the Occasion of his 60th Birthday*, College Publications.

[Barringer et al., 2012] Barringer H, Gabbay DM and Woods J. 2012a. Temporal argumentation networks. *Argumentation and Computation*, 2-3, 143-202.

[Barringer et al., 2012a] Barringer H, Gabbay DM and Woods J. 2012b. Modal argumentation networks. *Argument and Computation*, 2-3, 203-227

[Bench-Capon, 2003] T. J. M. Bench-Capon. Persuasion in practical argument using value-based argumentation frameworks. *Journal of Logic and Computation*, **13**, 429–448, 2003.
See also: http://www.csc.liv. ac.uk/ tbc/FTP/kings2.ppt

[Bench-Capon, 2003a] T. Bench-Capon. Agreeing to differ: modelling persuasive dialogue between parties without a consensus about values. *Informal Logic*, forthcoming, 2003.

[Bench-Capon, 2015] T. Bench-Capon. Knowledge based systems in the legal domain. A survey article in *Encyclopaedia of Computer Science and Technology*, available on the web at http://www.csc.liv.ac.uk/~lial/lial/tut.html

[van Benthem, 2011] Benthem, JF van. 2011. *Logical Dynamics of Information and Interaction*, Cambridge University Press.

[van Benthem, 2012] Benthem, JF van. 2012 The nets of reason. *Argument and Computation*, 2-3, 83-86.

[Bongiovanni et al., 2016] Bongiovanni G, Postema G, Rotolo A, Sartor G, Walton D (eds). 2016 *Handbook of Legal Reasoning and Argumentation*, Cambridge Univ Press.

[Bruza, 2009] Bruza PD, Widdows D and Woods J. 2009. A quantum logic for down below. In Engesser K, Gabbay DM and Lehmann D (eds). *Handbook of Quantum Logic and Quantum Structures: Quantum Logic*, 625-660, North-Holland.

[Carmo and Jones, 2002] J. Carmo and A. Jones. Deontic logic and contrary-to-duties. *Handbook of Philosophical Logic*, Volume 8, 2nd edition, pp. 265–345, D. M. Gabbay and F. Guenthener, eds. Kluwer, 2002.

[Carnielli et al., 2007] W. Carnielli, M. Coniglio, D. M. Gabbay, P. Gouveia and C. Sernadas. *Analysis and Synthesis of Logics*. Springer, 2007, 500p.

[Carnielli et al., 2009] Carnielli WA, Coniglio ME and Loffredo D'Ottaviano IM (eds). 2009. *The Many Sides of Logic*, College Publications.

[Chesnevar et al., 2000] C. I. Chesnevar, A. G. Maguitman and R. P. Loui. Logical models of argument. *ACM Computing Surveys* (CSUR) Surveys Homepage archive Volume 32 Issue 4, Dec. 2000 Pages 337-383.

[Chifi and Pietarinen, 2019] Chiffi D and Pietarinen AV. 2019. The extended Gabbay-Woods schema and scientific practices. In Gabbay et al., 2019. 331-348.

[Christie, 2000] G. C. Christie. *The Notion of an Ideal Audience in Legal Argument*. Kluwer, 2000.

[Coleman, 1992] J. Coleman. *Risks and Wrongs*. Cambridge University Press, 1992.

[Copi, 1953] Copi I. 1953. *Introduction to Logic*, Macmillan.

[Cross, 1999] Sir Rupert Cross. *On Evidence*. Butterworth, 1999.

[Dalla Chiara et al., 2007] Dalla Chiara ML, Guintini R and Rédei M (eds). 2007. The history of quantum logics. In Gabbay DM and Woods J (eds). *The Many Valued and Nonmonotonic Turn in Logic*, volume 8 of Gabbay and Woods (eds.) *Handbook of the History of Logic*, 205-284, North-Holland.

[Dennis, 1992] H. Dennis. *Law of Evidence*, Sweet and Maxwell, 1992.

[Deon,] Deon Conferences. Journals.
Please see: http://www.doc.ic.ac.uk/deon02/, http://www.cert.fr/deon00/
ARTIFICIAL INTELLIGENCE AND LAW
http://www.denniskennedy.com/ailaw.htm, http://www.iaail.org/.
There are many useful Links to Evidence-Related Web Sites: at http://tillers.net

[Engesser et al., 2009] Engesser K, Gabbay DM and Lehmann D. 2009. Nonmonotonicity and holicity in quantum logic. In Engesser et al., 587-624, 2009

[Englebretsen, 2019] Englebretsen G. 2019. Is natural logic part of naturalized logic? In Gabbay et al., 2019, 593-620.

[Fisher et al., 2005] Fisher M, Gabbay DM, Vila L (eds). 2005. *Handbook of Temporal Reasoning in Artificial Intelligence: Foundations of Artificial Intelligence 1*, Elsevier.

[Flack and Kakas, 2000] Flack PA and Kakas A (eds) 2000. *Abduction and Induction: Essays on Their Relation and Integration*, Kluwer.

[Gabbay, 1992a] Gabbay DM. 1992. *Handbook of Logic and Computer Science, 1 Background: Mathematical Structures, and 2 Background: Computational Structures*, Clarendon Press.

[Gabbay, 1992b] Gabbay DM. 1992. Logic made reasonable. *Kunstliche Intelligenz*, 6, 39-41.

[Gabbay, 1996] D.M. Gabbay. *Labelled Deduction Systems*. Oxford University Press, 1996.

[Gabbay, 1998] D. Gabbay. *Fibring Logics*, Oxford University Press, 1998.

[Gabbay, 2001] D. M. Gabbay. Dynamics of practical reasoning, a position paper. In *Advances in Modal Logic 2, Proceedings of Conference October 1999*, K. Segerberg et al., eds, pp. 179–224. CSLI Publications, Cambridge University Press, 2001.

[Gabbay, 2002] D. M. Gabbay. Sampling LDS. In *A Companion to Philosophical Logic*, D. Jacquette, ed., pp. 742–769. Blackwell, 2002.

[Gabbay, 2002–12] D. M. Gabbay. Editorial to *Handbook of Philosophical Logic*, 2nd edition. Kluwer, 2002–2012.

[Gabbay, 2008] D. M. Gabbay. Reactive Kripke models and contrary-to-duty obligations. DEON-2008, *Deontic Logic in Computer Science*, Ron van der Meyden and Leendert van der Torre, eds. LNAI 5076, pp. 155–173, Springer, 2008.

[Gabbay, 2009] D. M. Gabbay. Semantics for higher level attacks in extended argumentation frames. Part 1: Overview. *Studia Logica*, 93:355–379, 2009.

[, Gabbay2009a] D. M. Gabbay. Modal foundations for argumentation networks. *Studia Logica*, 93(2-3): 181–198, 2009.

[Gabbay, 2009b] D. M. Gabbay. Fibring argumentation frames. *Studia Logica*, 93(2-3), 231-295, 2009.

[Gabbay, ??] D. M. Gabbay. Reactive Kripke models and contrary-to-duty obligations. Expanded version to appear in *Journal of Applied Logic*.

[Gabbay and Gabbay, 2015] D. Gabbay and M. Gabbay. Argumentation as information input, 2015. Short version published in *Proceedings COMMA 2016, Computational Models of Argument* , Pages 311 - 318 DOI10.3233/978-1-61499-686-6-311 A Volume in Series Frontiers in Artificial Intelligence and Applications IOS press Volume 287: Full version published by College Publication in the G. Simari Tribute *Argumentation-based Proofs of Endearment, Essays in Honor of Guillermo R. Simari on the Occasion of his 70th Birthday*, Carlos I Chesnevar, Marcelo A Falappa, Eduardo Ferme, eds. pp 145-197

[Gabbay and Garcez, 2009] D. M. Gabbay and A. d'Avila Garcez. Logical modes of attack in argumentation networks. *Studia Logica*, 93(2-3): 199–230, 2009.

[Gabbay and Hunter, 1991] Gabbay DM and Hunter A. 1991. Making inconsistency respectable. A logical framework for inconsistency in reasoning. In Jourand Ph and Kelemen T (eds). *Fundamentals of Artificial Intelligence Research*, 19-32, Springer.

[Gabbay and Hunter, 1992] Gabbay DM and Hunter A. 1992. Making inconsistency respectable part 2: Meta-level handling of inconsistency. In Clarke M, Kruse R and Seraffin S (eds). *Lecture Notes on Computer Science*, 129-136, Springer.

[Gabbay and Rozenberg, 2017] Dov Gabbay and Gadi Rozenberg. Reasoning Schemes, Expert Opinion and Critical Questions: Sex Offenders Case Study, *IFCoLog Journal of Logics and their Applications* Volume 4, Number 6 July 2017, PP 1687-1789.

[Gabbay and Woods, 1999] D. M. Gabbay and J. Woods. Cooperate with your logic ancestors. *Journal of Logic, Language and Information*, **8**, iii–v, 1999.

[Gabbay and Woods, 2003] D. M. Gabbay and J. Woods. *Agenda Relevance: A Study in Formal Pragmatics*, Elsevier, 2003, 521 pp.

[Gabbay and Woods, 2003a] Gabbay DM and Woods J. 2003. *Agenda Relevance: A Study in Formal Pragmatics*, North-Holland.

[Gabbay and Woods, 2005] D. M. Gabbay and J. Woods. *The Reach of Abduction: Insight and Trial*, Elsevier, 2005, 476 pp.

[Gabbay and Woods, 2005a] Gabbay DM and Woods J. 2005. *The Reach of Abduction: Insight and Trial*, North-Holland.

[Gabbay and Woods, 2008] D. M. Gabbay and J. Woods. Probability in the law. In *Dialogues, Logics and Other Strange Things: Essays in Honour of Shahid Rahman*, Cédric Dégremont, Laurent Keiff and Helge Rückert, eds. College Publications, 2008.

[Gabbay et al., 2008a] D. M. Gabbay, A. S. d'Avila Garcez and L. C. Lamb. *Connectionist Non-classical Logics: Distributed Reasoning and Learning in Neural Networks.* Monograph, Springer Verlag, 2008.

[Gabbay and Woods, 2008b] Gabbay DM and Woods, J. 2008. Probability in the law. In Dégremont C, Keiff L and Rukert H, eds. *Dialogues, Logics and Other Strange Things: Essays in Honour of Shahid Rahman*, College Publications.

[Gabbay and Woods, 2010] Gabbay DM and Woods J. 2010. Logic and the law: Crossing the lines of discipline. In Gabbay DM, Canivez P, Rahman S and Thiercelin (eds). 2010. *Approaches to Legal Rationality*, 165-202. Springer.

[Garcez et al., 2002] A. S. d'Avila Garcez, K. Broda and D. M. Gabbay, *Neural-Symbolic Learning Systems*, Springer-Verlag, 2002.

[Garcez et al., 2002a] A. S. d'Avila Garcez, L. C. Lamb, D. M. Gabbay and K. Broda, Connectionist Modal Logics for Distributed Knowledge Representation, submitted, 2002.

[Garcez and Gabbay, 2004] A. S. d'Avila Garcez and D. M. Gabbay, Fibring Neural Networks, In *Proceedings of 19th National Conference on Artificial Intelligence (AAA'04)*, pp. 342-347. San Jose, CA. AAAI Press, 2004.

[Garcez et al., 2005] A. S. D'Avila Garcez, D. M. Gabbay and L. Lamb. Value based argumentation frameworks as neural networks. *Journal of Logic and Computation*, 15(6):1041-1058, Dec. 2005.

[Girard et al., 1989] J. Y. Girard, Y. Lafont and P. Taylor. *Proofs and Types*. Cambridge University Press, 1989.

[Gordon, 1995] Gordon TF. 1995. *The Pleadings Game: An Artificial Intelligence Model of Procedural Justice*, Kluwer.

[Gordon et al., 2007] Gordon TF, Prakken H. and Walton D. 2007. The Carneades model of argument and burden of proof, *Artificial Intelligence*, 171, 875-896.

[Guan and Bell, 1991] J. W. Guan and D. A. Bell. *Evidence Theory*, 2 volumes. Elsevier, 1991.

[Hamblin, 1970] Hamblin CL. 1970. *Fallacies*, Methuen.

[Harris, 2003] J. W. Harris. *Legal Philosophies*, 2nd edition, 2003.

[Haykin, 1999] S. Haykin, *Neural Networks: A Comprehensive Foundation*, 2nd edition, Prentice Hall, 1999.

[Hendricks, 2006] Hendricks VE 2006. *Mainstream and Formal Epistemology*, Cambridge University Press.

[Hewitt and Woods, 2015] Hewitt C and Woods J. (eds). 2015 *Inconsistency Robustness*, College Publications.

[Hintikka, 1999] Hintikka J. 1999. *Inquiry as Inquiry: A Logic of Scientific Discovery*, Reidel.

[Keane, 2000] A. Keane. *The Modern Law of Evidence*, Butterworth, 2000.

[Keppens, 2009] Keppens J. 2009. Conceptions of vagueness in subjective probability for evidential reasoning. In Governatori (ed). *Proceedings of 22nd Annual Conference on Legal Knowledge and Information Systems*, 79-999 IOS Press.

[Kripke, 1959] Kripke S. 1959. A completeness theorem in modal logic, *Journal of Symbolic Logic*, 24, 1-14.

[Kripke, 1963] Kripke S. 1963. Semantical considerations on modal logic, *Acta Philosophica Fennica*, 16, 83-94.

[Kuipers, 1999] Kuipers, TAF. 1999. Abduction aiming at empirical progress of even truth approximation leading to a challenge for computational modelling. *Foundations of Science*, 4, 307-323.

[Loftus, 1975] Loftus EF, Leading questions and eyewitness reports *Cognitive Psychology*, 7 1975, 560-572.

[Loftus, 2006] Loftus EF, Wolchover D, and Page D, 2006. General review of the psychology of witness testimony, in Heath-Armstrong A. *et al.* (eds.) *Witness Testimony: Psychological, Investigative and Evidential Perspectives*, Oxford Univ Press.

[Loui, 1998] R.P. Loui. Process and policy: Resource-bounded non-demonstrative reasoning, *Computational Intelligence* 14 (1998) 138.

[MacCrimmon and Tillers, 2002] M. MacCrimmon and P. Tillers, eds. *The Dynamics of Judicial Proof*. Physica-Verlag, 2002.

[Magnani, 2001] Magnani L. 2001. *Abduction, Reason and Science: Processes of Discovery and Explanation*, Kluwer.

[Magnani, 2009] Magnani L. 2009. *Abductive Cognition. The Epistemological and Eco-Cognitive Dimensions of Hypothetical Reasoning*. Springer.

[Magnani, 2015] Magnani L. 2015. Naturalizing logic and errors of reasoning vindicated: Logic reapproaches cognitive science. *Journal of Applied Logic*, 13, 13-36.

[Magnani, 2017] Magnani L. 2017. *The Abductive Structure of Scientific Creativity. An Essay on the Ecology of Cognition*, Springer.

[Magnani, 2018] Magnani L. 2018. The urgent need of a naturalized logic. In Dodig-Crmkovic G and Schroeder MJ (eds). *Contemporary Natural Philosophy and Philosophies*, a special guest-edited number of Philosophies, 3, 44.

[Magnani, 2019] Magnani L. 2019. Errors of reasoning exculpated: Naturalizing the logic of abduction. In Gabbay *et al.* 2019, 269-308.

[Mortensen, 1995] Mortensen C. 1995. *Inconsistent Mathematics*, Kluwer.

[Mortensen, 2010] Mortensen C. 2010. *Inconsistent Geometry*, College Publications.

[Niiniluoto, 2018] Niiniluoto I. 2018. *Truth-Seeking by Abduction*, Springer.

[Park, 2017] Park, W. 2017. *Abduction in Context. The Conjectural Dynamics of Scientific Reasoning*, Springer.

[Perelman, 1980] Ch. Perelman. *Justice, Law and Argument*. Reider, 1980.

[Prakken, 1997] H. Prakken. *Logical Tools for Modelling Legal Argument*, Kluwer, 1997.

[Prakken and Sartor, 2011] Prakken H and Sartor G. 2011. On modelling burdens and standards of prof in structural argumentation. In Atkinson KD (ed).*Legal Knowledge and Information Systems*, 83-92, IOS Press.

[Prakken *et al.*, 2003] H. Prakken, C. Reed and D. Walton. Argumentation schemes and generalisation in reasoning about evidence. *ICAIL-03*, June 24–28, 2003.

[Putnam, 1968] Putnam H. 1968. Is logic empirical? In Cohen R and Warofsky M (eds). *Boston Studies in the Philosophy of Science*, 174-197, Reidel.

[Ransom, 2019] Ransom M. 2019. Naturalizing logic: A case study of the ad hominem and implicit bias. In Gabbay *et al.*, 573-589.

[Reed and Walton, 2007] Reed C and Walton D. 2007. Argument schemes in dialogue, dissensus and the search for common ground. In Hansen HV, Tindale, CW, Blair JA, Johnson RH and Godden DM (eds). *Proceedings of OSSA*, Windsor, ON (CD-ROM).

[RRCCJ, 1993] Report of the Royal Commission of Criminal Justice, M 2263, 1993. London: HMSO, Ch 8, para 26.

[Sergot and Kowalski, 1986] M. J. Sergot, R. A. Kowalski *et al.*. British Nationality Act. *Communications of the ACM*, **29**, 370–386, 1986.

[Shafer, 1976] G. Shafer. *A Mathematical Theory of Evidence*. Princeton University Press, 1976.

[Toulmin, 1958] Toulmin S. 1958. *The Uses of Argument*, Cambridge University Press.

[Uglow, 1997] S. Uglow. *Textbook on Evidence*, Sweet and Maxwell, 1997. (Second edition: Evidence Text and Materials Paperback — 29 Aug 2006).

[Verheij, 2005] Verheij B. 2005. *Virtual Arguments. On the Design for Lawyers and Other Arguers*, The Asser Press.

[Walton, 1997] Walton D. 1997. *Appeal to Expert Opinion*. Penn State University Press.

[Walton, 2002] Walton D. 2002. *Legal Argument and Evidence*, Penn State University Press.

[Walton, 2004] Walton D. 2004. *Abductive Reasoning*, University of Alabama Press.

[Walton, 2005] Walton D. 2005. *Argument Methods for Artificial Intelligence in Law*, Springer.

[Walton, 2007] Walton D 2007. *Character Evidence: An Abductive Theory*, Springer.

[Walton, 2008] Walton D. 2008. *Witness Testimony Evidence*, Cambridge University Press.

[Walton, 2016] Walton D 2016. *Argument Evaluation and Evidence*, Springer.

[Walton and Gordon, 2005] Walton D and Gordon TF. 2005. Critical question in computational models of legal argument. In Dunne PF and Bench-Capon T (eds). *Argumentation in Artificial Intelligence and Law*,103-111. Wolf Legal Publishers.

[Walton and Krabbe, 1995] D. Walton and E.C.W. Krabbe. *Commitment in Dialogue: Basic Concepts of Interpersonal Reasoning*, SUNY Series in Logic and Language, State University of New York Press, Albany, 1995.

[Williamson and Gabbay, 2004] J. Williamson and D. Gabbay. Recursive Bayesian Networks and self-fibring logics. In *Laws and models of Science*, D. Gillies, editor, College Publications, 2004, pp 173-247.

[Woods et al., 2002] J. Woods, R. H. Johnson, D. M. Gabbay and H. J. Ohlbach. Logic and the Practical turn. In *Handbook of the Logic of Argumentation and Inference: The Turn Towards the Practical*, D. M. Gabbay, R. H. Johnson and H. J. Ohlbach, eds. pp. 1–39. Volume 1 of *Studies in Logic and Practical Reasoning*, North-Holland, 2002.

[Woods, 2010] Woods, J (2010). Abduction and proof: A criminal paradox,. In Rahman et al. (eds), *Approaches to Legal Rationality*, 217-238, Springer.

[Woods, 2013] Woods, J (2013). *Errors of Reasoning: Naturalizing the Logic of Inference*, volume 45 of Studies in Logic, London: College Publications. Reprinted with corrections in 2014.

[Woods, 2015] Woods J. 2015. Inconsistency: Its present impacts and future prospects. In Hewitt and Woods 2015, 158-194.

[Woods, 2018] Woods J. 2018. *Is Legal Reasoning Irrational? An Introduction to the Epistemology of Law*, 2nd ed revised and extended. First edition in 2015. College Publications.

[Woods, 2018a] Woods J. 2018. *Truth in Fiction: Rethinking its Logic*, Springer.

[Woods, 2020] Woods J. (2020). Evidence probativity, and knowledge: A troubled trio. In Hansen HV (ed.) *Proceedings of the Twelfth Meeting of the Ontario Society for the Study of Argumentation*. To appear.

Dov Gabbay
King's College London
and University of Luxembourg
Email: dov.gabbay@kcl.ac.uk

John Woods
University of British Columbia
Vancouver, Canada
Email: john.woods@ubc.ca

11

Large-Scale Legal Reasoning with Rules and Databases

GRIGORIS ANTONIOU
GEORGE BARYANNIS
SOTIRIS BATSAKIS
GUIDO GOVERNATORI
MOHAMMAD BADIUL ISLAM
QING LIU
LIVIO ROBALDO
GIOVANNI SIRAGUSA
ILIAS TACHMAZIDIS

ABSTRACT. Traditionally, computational knowledge representation and reasoning focused its attention on rich domains such as the law. The main underlying assumption of traditional legal knowledge representation and reasoning is that knowledge and data are both available in main memory. However, in the era of big data, where large amounts of data are generated daily, an increasing range of scientific disciplines, as well as business and human activities, are becoming data-driven. This chapter summarises existing research on legal representation and reasoning in order to uncover technical challenges associated both with the integration of rules and databases and with the main concepts of the big data landscape. These challenges lead naturally to future research directions towards achieving large scale legal reasoning with rules and databases.

1 Introduction

Since the emergence of computational knowledge representation and reasoning (KR), the domain of law has been a prime focus of attention as it is a rich domain full of explicit and implicit representation phenomena. From early Prolog-based approaches [Satoh *et al.*, 2010; Sergot *et al.*, 1986] to elaborate logic-based mechanisms for dealing with, among others, notions of defeasibility, obligation and permission, the legal domain has been an inspiration for generations of KR researchers [Alberti *et al.*, 2008; Gavanelli *et al.*, 2015; Lam and Governatori, 2013; Snaith and Reed, 2012].

Handbook of Legal AI
© *2022, Grigoris Antoniou* et al.

Knowledge representation has been used to provide formal accounts of legal provisions and regulations, while reasoning has been used to facilitate legal decision support and compliance checking. Despite the variety of approaches used, they all share a common feature: the focus has always been on capturing elaborate knowledge phenomena while the data has always been small. As a consequence, one underlying assumption has been that all knowledge and data are available in main memory. This assumption has been reasonable until recently, but can be questioned with the emergence of *big data*. We now live in an era where unprecedented amounts of data become available through organisations, sensor networks and social media. An increasing range of scientific disciplines, as well as business and human activities, are becoming data-driven.

Since legislation is at the basis of and regulates our everyday life and societies, many examples of big data such as medical records in e-Health or financial data, must comply with, and are thus highly dependent on, specific norms. For instance, a sample database related to the US Food and Drug Administration (FDA) Adverse Event Reporting System (FAERS) contains over 3 million records to cover only the first quarter of 2014 [Islam and Governatori, 2018]. Any standard reasoning system would reach its limits if data over longer periods of time need to be audited.

Another source of huge amounts of data related to law is the financial domain, in which millions of transactions take place every single day and are subject to regulation on, among others, taxation, anti money laundering, consumer rights and data protection. While data mining is being used in the financial domain, it is arguably an area that would benefit from legal reasoning directly related to relevant legislation. This might indicatively entail checking for and ensuring compliance with reporting requirements, or traversing across financial transaction databases to check for potential violations of legislations.

Similarly, building applications and property/site development are covered by a variety of local and national laws and regulations. To develop and assess relevant applications, it may be necessary to consider the legal requirements in conjunction with geodata relating to morphology of the site and its surroundings, use of space and so on.

Industries in the aforementioned and other domains are feeling increasingly overwhelmed with the expanding set of legislation and case law available in recent years, as a consequence of the global financial crisis, among others. Consider, for example, the European Union active legislation, which was estimated to be 170,000 pages long in 2005 and is expected to reach 351,000 pages by 2020 assuming that legislation trends continue at the same rate [Miller, 2010]. As the law becomes more complex, conflicting and ever-changing, more advanced methodologies are required for analysing, representing and reasoning on legal knowledge.

While, the term "big data" is usually associated with machine learning, we argue that particularly in law there is also a need for symbolic approaches. Legal provisions and regulations are considered as being formal and legal decision making requires clear references to them. Stated another way, in the legal domain there is also a need for *explainable artificial intelligence*, as it has always been done in legal reasoning.

So what are the implications of this big data era on legal reasoning? On the one hand, as already explained above, a combination of legal reasoning with big data opens up new opportunities to provide legal decision support and compliance checking in an enhanced set of applications. On the other hand, there are new technical challenges that need to be addressed when faced with big data:

- Rules and data integration: while big data is stored in databases of various forms, reasoning is often performed using rule engines. Integrated solutions are necessary so that rule engines can seamlessly access and reason with big data in large scale databases.

- Volume: When the amount of data is huge, one cannot assume that all data is available in main memory. Hence, any approach that relies on this assumption needs to be adapted in order to work on larger scales.

- Velocity: In applications where one wishes to perform decision making close to the time data is generated, the dynamicity of data needs to be taken into account.

- Variety: In many applications, there is a need for a uniform manner of accessing and reasoning with data from disparate, heterogeneous sources, following different formats and structures.

The aim of this chapter is to present the state of the art in legal reasoning with rules and databases and explore the challenges faced by existing approaches when moving to larger scales and when integrating rule-based and database systems. In doing so, the chapter aims to stimulate the evolution of the area of legal reasoning so that it becomes more relevant in the new data-driven era.

The remainder of this chapter is organised as follows. Section 2 provides an overview of previous research in legal representation and reasoning. Section 3 discusses the application of legal reasoning in practice, first dealing with case studies of increasing scale, then discussing the integration of rules and databases and a possible solution through the RuleRS system. Then,

Section 4 provides a description of technical challenges arising both from the integration of rules and databases and large scale case studies. Finally, Section 5 summarises findings and briefly discusses their importance.

2 Legal Representation and Reasoning Approaches

2.1 Rule-based Approaches

A quite significant subset of legal representation and reasoning approaches relies on logic-based representation and rule-based reasoning. The benefits of rule-based approaches stem mainly from their naturalness, which facilitates comprehension of the represented knowledge [Ligeza, 2006]. Rules, representing domain knowledge, are normally in the "IF conditions THEN conclusion" form; in the legal domain, conditions are the norms and consequence is the legal effect. To apply rule-based reasoning in the legal domain, the meaning of legal texts needs to be interpreted and modelled, in order to transform the legal norms to logical rules for permitting reasoning [Cervone *et al.*, 2007].

According to [Negnevitsky, 2002], the main advantages of rule-based approaches are:

- compact representation of general knowledge,

- natural knowledge representation in the form of if-then rules that reflect the problem-solving procedure explained by the domain experts,

- modularity of structure where each rule is an independent piece of knowledge

- separation of knowledge from its process,

- justification of the determinations by explaining how the system arrived at a particular conclusion and by providing audit trails.

There are, however, a number of issues that pertain to the knowledge acquisition bottleneck, or inference efficiency, especially for large scale reasoning. Sections 2.2 to 2.4 summarise the most important rule-based legal reasoning approaches.

2.2 Early Logic-based Approaches

The earliest well-established approach to rule-based legal reasoning involved the use of subsets of first-order logic for knowledge representation and Prolog-based reasoning. The most prominent example is Sergot *et al.*'s seminal work on the British Nationality Act [Sergot *et al.*, 1986], where the authors expressed legal knowledge in the form of extended Horn logic programs that allow negation as failure. The authors present an excellent account of the intricacies of encoding actual legislation as rules, especially with regard to the treatment of negation and cases where double negation is introduced.

Subsequent work [Kowalski and Burton, 2011] focused, among others, on the encoding of exceptions within a particular legislation, representing them explicitly by negative conditions in the rules. While this is suitable for self-contained and stable legislation, it may require some level of rewriting whenever previously unknown exceptions (or chains of exceptions) are introduced or discovered. Moreover, in both of these works deontic concepts such as permission or obligation which are a common occurrence in legislation, have to be represented explicitly within predicate names. This is an expected characteristic when legal knowledge representation relies on standard predicate logic [Batsakis *et al.*, 2018].

2.3 Description Logic-based Approaches

Following the advent of the Semantic Web, several research efforts focused on examining whether description logics and ontologies are suitable candidates for representing and reasoning about legislation. An ontology is defined a formal, explicit specification of a shared conceptualization [Studer *et al.*, 1998]. The reusability and sharing features of ontologies are of critical importance to the legal reasoning domain, due to the complexity involved in legal documents. This complexity can be viewed from two different perspectives [Ghosh, 2018]:

- The language used in legal document is complex, especially the problem of open texture property, incomplete definition of many legal concepts of the law [Gardner, 1987].

- the amount of information that must be collected and processed in order for lawyers or judges to evaluate a case and litigation to proceed [White, 1992].

A prime example of legal reasoning approaches using description logics is HARNESS [Van de Ven *et al.*, 2008a] (also known as OWL Judge [Van de Ven *et al.*, 2008b]), which shows that well established sound and decidable description logic reasoners such as Pellet can be exploited for legal reasoning, if, however, a significant compromise in terms of expressiveness is made. The most important issue is that relationships can only be expressed between concepts and not between individuals: for instance, as exemplified in Van de Ven *et al.* [2008a], if we have statements expressing the facts that a donor owns a copyright donation and that a donor retains some rights, there is no way to express (in pure OWL) that the donor in both cases is the same individual. This can be expressed via rules (e.g., written in SWRL); however, to retain decidability these rules must be restricted to a so-called DL-safe subset [Parsia *et al.*, 2005].

Description logics provide an alternative formalisation to classical logic but still face similar issues with regard to the treatment of negation and the encoding of deontic notions. The issues related to negation are due to the fact that both classical and description logics are monotonic: logical consequences cannot be retracted, once entailed. However, the nature of law requires legal consequences to adapt in light of new evidence; any conflicts between different regulations must be accounted for and resolved [Batsakis *et al.*, 2018].

2.4 Defeasible and Deontic Logic-based Approaches

The aforementioned issues led researchers to employ non-monotonic logic for the purposes of legal reasoning. An example is the Defeasible Logic framework [Antoniou *et al.*, 2000], where rules can either behave in the classical sense (*strict*), they can be defeated by contrary evidence (*defeasible*), or they can be used only to prevent conclusions (*defeaters*). Defeasible Logic has been successfully used for legal reasoning applications [Antoniou *et al.*, 2001; Governatori, 2005; Governatori and Shek, 2013; Governatori, 2015] and it has been proven that other formalisms used successfully for legal reasoning correspond to variants of Defeasible Logic [Governatori, 2011].

As already mentioned, the notions of permission and obligation are inherent in legal reasoning but are not explicitly defined in any of the logic systems described so far; deontic logic was introduced to serve this purpose. As formalised in [Hilpinen, 2001], permission and obligation are represented by modal operators and are connected to each other through axioms and inference rules. While there has been some philosophical criticism on deontic logic due to its admission of several paradoxes (e.g., the gentle murderer), deontic modalities have been introduced to various logics to make them more suitable for reasoning with legal norms. [Sergot, 2001] uses a combination of deontic logic and the notions of action and agents to be able to derive all possible normative positions (e.g., right, duty, privilege) and assist in policy and contract negotiation. A similar proposal [Robaldo and Sun, 2017] uses reified I/O logic to formalise the EU General Data Protection Regulation (GDPR) in 966 if-then rules (https://github.com/dapreco/daprecokb/tree/master/gdpr).

Defeasible Deontic Logic [Governatori and Rotolo, 2008; Governatori *et al.*, 2013] is the result of integrating deontic notions (beliefs, intentions, obligations and permissions) to the aforementioned Defeasible Logic framework. Defeasible Deontic Logic has been successfully used for applications in legal reasoning and it is has been shown that it does not suffer from problems affecting other logics used for reasoning about norms and compliance [Governatori and Hashmi, 2015; Governatori, 2015; Islam and Governatori, 2018]. Thus, Defeasible Deontic Logic is a conceptually sound approach for the representation of regulations and at the same time, it offers a computationally feasible environment to reason about them [Governatori and Rotolo, 2008].

2.5 Case-based Approaches

Apart from rule-based approaches, a number of different solutions have been proposed for representation and reasoning in the legal domain. These are summarised next. This section discusses case-based approaches, followed by case-rule hybrids (Section 2.6) and argumentation-based approaches (Section 2.7).

Rule-based legal reasoning approaches are more suited to legal systems that are primarily based on civil law, due to their inherent rule-based nature and the fact they focus on conflicts arising from conflicting norms and not from interpretation [Bench-Capon and Prakken, 2008]. On the other hand, common law places precedents at the center of normative reasoning, which makes case-based approaches more applicable. Case-based representations store a large set of previous cases with their solutions in the case base (or case library) and use them whenever a similar new case has to be dealt with. The case-based system performs inference in four phases known as the CBR cycle [Aamodt and Plaza, 1994]: retrieve, reuse, revise and retain. Quite often, the solution contained in the retrieved case(s) is adapted to meet the requirements of the new case.

An important advantage of case-based representation is its ability to express specialized knowledge. This allows them to circumvent interpretation problems suffered by rules (due to their generality). Also, knowledge acquisition may be slightly easier than rule-based approaches, due to the availability of cases in most application domains. However, case-based approaches face a number of issues such as the inability to express general knowledge, poor explanations and inference inefficiency, especially for larger case bases [Prentzas and Hatzilygeroudis, 2007].

The most prominent examples of case-based legal reasoning are HYPO [Ashley, 1990], CATO [Aleven, 2003] and GREBE [Branting, 2000]. HYPO represents cases in the form of dimensions which determine the degree of commonality between two precedent cases: a precedent is more "on-point", if it shares more dimensions with the case at hand than another. CATO replaces dimensions with boolean factors organised in a hierarchy. GREBE is actually a rule/case hybrid, since reasoning relies on any combination of rules modeling legislation and cases represented using semantic networks (a precursor to ontologies in the Semantic Web). As noted in [Bench-Capon,

2012], using dimensions or factors to determine legal consequences is relatively tractable, but the initial step of extracting these dimensions or factors from case facts is deeply problematic.

2.6 Hybrid Approaches

A number of attempts have been made to integrate rule-based and case-based representations [Prentzas and Hatzilygeroudis, 2007]. Since rules represent general knowledge of the domain, whereas cases encompass specific knowledge gained from experience, the combination of both approaches turns out to be natural and useful.

In legal reasoning, such hybrid solutions are capable of addressing issues arising due to the existence of "open-textured" (i.e., not well defined and imprecise) rule terms or unstated prerequisite conditions and exceptions or circularities in rule definitions [Rissland and Skalak, 1991]. Examples of hybrid legal representation and reasoning systems are CABARET [Rissland and Skalak, 1991], DANIEL [Brüninghaus, 1994], GREBE [Branting, 1991; Branting, 2003], and SHYSTER-MYCIN [A O'Callaghan *et al.*, 2003].

2.7 Argumentation-based Approaches

Regardless of the legal system applied, legal reasoning at its core is a process of argumentation, with opposing sides attempting to justify their own interpretation. As succinctly stated in [Prakken and Sartor, 2015], legal reasoning goes beyond the literal meaning of rules and involves appeals to precedent, principle, policy and purpose, as well as the construction of and attack on arguments. This became especially apparent when Dung's influential work on argumentation frameworks [Dung, 1995] started being applied in AI and law research AI and law research has addressed this with models that are based on Dung's influential work on argumentation frameworks. A notable example is Carneades [Gordon *et al.*, 2007], a model and a system for constructing and evaluating arguments that has been applied in a legal context. Using Carneades, one can apply pre-specified argument schemes that rely on established proof standards such as "clear and convincing evidence" or "beyond reasonable doubt".

ASPIC+ [Prakken, 2009] takes a more generic approach, providing a means of producing argumentation frameworks tailored to different needs in terms of the structure of arguments, the nature of attacks and the use of preferences. However, neither Carneades nor any ASPIC+ framework can be used as-is for legal reasoning: they need to be instantiated using a logic language. For instance, versions of Carneades have used Constraint

Handling Rules to represent argumentation schemes, while any ASPIC+ framework can be instantiated using a language that can model strict and defeasible rules, such as those in the previously mentioned Defeasible Logic framework.

3 Legal Reasoning with Rules and Databases in Practice

As detailed in the previous section, researchers have proposed a multitude of different approaches to legal representation and reasoning, each with their own advantages and disadvantages. Focusing on rule-based approaches specifically, regardless of their individual characteristics, two major issues have not yet been adequately addressed, to the best of our knowledge. These involve handling significantly large datasets and achieving efficient integration between legal rules and databases. In this section, we explore how current rule-based legal reasoning approaches fare in relation to these issues.

3.1 Exploring Case Studies of Different Scale

As part of the MIREL project, practical legal reasoning applications were explored to complement theoretical analysis. For instance, in [Batsakis *et al.*, 2018], several legal reasoning approaches were applied on real-world use cases. The approaches examined included answer set programming (ASP), defeasible logic and ASPIC+-based argumentation. The use cases involved the presumption of innocence axioms, blockchain-based contracts use case and the FDA Adverse Event Reporting System.

The first use case (presumption of innocence) involves only a few rules but demonstrates the importance of semantics and how different formalisms deal with conflicting facts and rules, especially in the case of missing preferences between rules. The second use case is an example of rules within a contract, and is interesting due to including notions of permission, obligation and reparation. The third use case involves part of the rules applied in the FDA reporting system mentioned in the introduction. Since the number of rules and cases is big, the third use case is very relevant to the challenges of large scale reasoning.

The three formalisms were selected because of their support for complex rules involving conflicts and priorities, as is typically the case of legal reasoning, and the availability of stable tools for reasoning. All three formalisms were expressive enough for representing rules involved in the three use cases, but the user must be familiar with the underlying semantics, since in some cases the rules must be modified accordingly in order to achieve the desired behaviour. But besides their differences, the three approaches can form the basis of a large scale reasoning implementation.

The advantage of ASP is its expressiveness since it offers support for disjunction, strong negation and negation as failure and additional constructs such as aggregation functions; however, ASP reasoning has high computational complexity. Argumentation and defeasible logic offer reasoning with lower complexity, but argumentation has significantly restricted expressiveness. Overall, defeasible logic seems to provide the best trade-off between expressiveness and complexity.

The most complex use case in [Batsakis *et al.*, 2018], a subset of FDA Adverse Event Reporting System, when implemented contains approximately 100 rules for all three formalisms. Reasoning times for three formalisms did not exceed a few seconds. This means that reasoning is efficient for hundreds of rules, but challenges may arise for even larger rule sets or in case reasoning results in one rule set depend on completing reasoning on another set. The main bottleneck identified, however, is representation, since manual encoding of rules and case related facts is time consuming and requires expertise in knowledge representation, and specifically in the formalism used for reasoning.

3.2 Integration Between Legal Rules and Databases

For many applications, necessary data is stored in (relational) databases. Various organizations may use the data from existing databases to comply with various regulations and guidelines, take decisions and create reports based on regulations (and other normative and legislative documents). For example, Australian financial institutions are subject to Financial Sector (Collection of Data) Act 2001, with regard to what (financial) information to report to the relevant regulators (e.g., Australian Prudential Regulator Authority); government departments and agencies are required to comply with the Public Governance Performance and Accountability Act 2013 and Public Governance Performance and Accountability Rule 2014 for their annual financial reporting. The requirements about what, when and in what forms to comply (and related exceptions) are given in the (relevant) regulations while the (financial and other) data is stored in the databases of the institutions that have to generate reports about the data using legal reasoning.

Accordingly, in these scenarios, one has to perform some legal reasoning (for example to understand what are the actual requirements that apply in a given case) based on the information stored in enterprise databases. In fact, legal reasoning consists of five elements which lead to a decision that can be decided as either accepted or rejected [1]. The components are: issues or cases (legal), rules, facts, analysis and conclusion. The argument for a particular

---

[1]https://groups.csail.mit.edu/dig/TAMI/inprogress/LegalReasoning.html

issue has to align with the legal rule and relevant facts corresponding to the rule. Overall, the process is analysed and apply the facts from database to the rules for generating a conclusion. Consequently, the facts stored in the enterprise database are required to apply the rules and perform legal reasoning.

Typically, database management systems involve a relatively small number of relations or files holding a large number of records, whereas rule-based systems consist of a large number of relationships with a small number of records [Risch *et al.*, 1988]. Additionally, relational databases essentially represent knowledge in a first-order logic formalism and query languages mostly exploit first-order logic features. However, as detailed in Section 2, first-order logic is not fully suitable to represent legal knowledge. This means that in general, we cannot use solely database queries, but we have to integrate the information stored in a database with rule systems specialised in legal reasoning.

A possible solution to integrating rules with databases would be to encode and store rules in a separate application program and then align with databases. However, in this manner, it would often be difficult to adapt the program if regulations change. Additionally, it could not be guaranteed that databases and rule-based systems are consistently amended. Another solution would be to couple databases with an expert system, but this would not solve the consistency problem since data is in one system, and the rules are in another one [Stonebraker, 1992]. Stonebraker suggests that rule systems integrated into the (relational) database system could be the possible solution. In this circumstance, it is required to integrate a database to serve legal obligations since traditional database architecture is not capable of reporting regulatory requirements.

3.3   RuleRS: A Solution to the Integration Problem

This section demonstrates RuleRS [Islam and Governatori, 2018], a possible solution where rules and databases are integrated. Initially, we are focusing on the mapping between the two vocabularies representing rules and databases. The fundamental idea behind the mapping is that data stored in the database corresponds to facts in a legal norms and these facts can be retrieved from the database using queries (SQL, JSON). Thus, each fact corresponds to a query and a mapping is a statement that can be true or false depending on the value of its arguments/variables.

The *RuleRS* design architecture, shown in Figure 1, consists of five main system components. In particular, the key system components of RuleRS are: 1) I/O Interface, 2) Database facts 3) Formal Rules, 4) Predicates, and 5) Rule engine (SPINdle Reasoner). The following subsections provide a short outline of the RuleRS internal components and their functions.

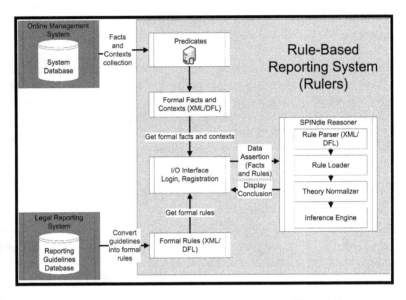

Figure 1. Rule-based Reporting System (RuleRS)

3.4 I/O Interface

The I/O Interface is implemented in Java to bridge RuleRS components and interacting with each other. The I/O interface is used to query data predicates (SQL or JSON files) and to generate facts and contexts in formal notation in Defeasible Logic syntax, and the rule engine (SPINdle reasoner) receives this as a parameter. The I/O interface also displays the final remarks or comments for each of the incidents and predicates.

3.5 Database facts

This section describes how to obtain facts from databases. In RuleRS, facts can be true or false for specific information from the database which is mapped with the literals rules. We have used either SQL or JSON (JavaScript Object Notation) syntax[2] syntax (or a combination of them) to represent database facts. Each of the facts are generated by queried database and send it to reasoner for further processing.

---

[2]http://json.org

3.6 Formal Rules base

One of the prominent features of the RuleRS system is its ability to perform reasoning based on legal requirements. As we alluded to in the introduction, such regulatory requirements are represented as formal rules in Defeasible Deontic Logic [Governatori and Rotolo, 2008; Governatori *et al.*, 2013]. To enable their use with the rule engine used by RuleRS (SPINdle, see the next section) the rules are stored in the DFL format [Lam and Governatori, 2009]. At this stage, the rules are created manually and (semi-)automatically by legal knowledge engineers and stored in a knowledge base.

3.7 Predicates

As specified earlier, since there is no direct correspondence between the literals encoding rules and the table/attributes of the database schema, we have to establish a mapping among them to enable the integration of rules and instances in the database. We named this mapping "predicates". The fundamental idea behind predicates is that data stored in the database correspond to facts in a defeasible theory and these facts can be retrieved from the database using queries. Thus, each fact corresponds to n SQL/JSON query and a predicate is a statement that can be true or false depending on the value of its arguments/variables. A predicate with n arguments is an $n - ary$ relation mapping literals and a set of attributes. A predicate in RuleRS corresponds to a database view, i.e.; a named query, where the name is literal to be used by the defeasible rules. The details are the query to be run to determine if the predicate is true or false for a given set of parameters. In case the output of the query is not empty, the predicate is true and is passed to the defeasible theory as fact.

In RuleRS, predicate consists of two components: (1) predicate name and (2) predicate details. *Predicate name* represents the action(s), condition(s) or indisputable statement(s), and passed on to the rule engine, SPINdle as defeasible fact (literal and modal literal) [Governatori and Rotolo, 2004; Governatori and Rotolo, 2008; Governatori and Rotolo, 2010] or actions that have been performed. For example, the fact "There is a risk for an incident" is represented by "*riskForIncident*" and passed as "$>> riskForIncident$" to SPINdle if it is returned as true from the relational database. "Predicate details" includes the "incident details" and may be stored as an SQL statement or converted to JSON to create a bridge between the data stored in the database and the terms passed as predicates (input case) to the rule engine. The SQL or JSON statements can be created in the initialisation of RuleRS with all of the incidents along with all of the predicates for each of the incidents or dynamically add it later.

Incident ID and relevant details of the incidents are also included for each of the predicates and named the predicates with relevant incident information such as "riskForIncident.sql" (for SQL statement) or "riskForIncident.json" (for JSON Statement). The following snippet illustrates the SQL syntax adopted by RuleRS for the example of the "riskForIncident" predicate:

```
SELECT incidentID, IncidentDetails, IncidentDetails1,
IncidentDetails2  FROM tblIncident
WHERE incidentID='XXXXXX'
```

In this example, $\boxed{\text{IncidentDetails}}$, $\boxed{\text{IncidentDetails1}}$, $\boxed{\text{IncidentDetails2}}$ are substituted for the place- holders in the "riskForIncident" predicate from relational databases for the $\boxed{\text{incidentID}}$ $\boxed{\text{'XXXXXX}}$. Using JSON, the syntax for the "riskForIncident" predicate is:

```
{"riskForIncident":
{ "incidentID":"XXXXXX",
"IncidentDetails":"ABC",
"IncidentDetails1":null,
"IncidentDetails2":"XYZ"}}
```

In the next step, the records and incidents for which there is a match in the relational database are transformed into predicates to be used by the SPINdle rule engine [Lam and Governatori, 2009], and forwarded to SPINdle for further processing using the I/O interface to make the process dynamic.

3.8 The rule reasoner

RuleRS uses SPINdle Reasoner [3] [Lam and Governatori, 2009], a Java-based implementation of Defeasible Logic that computes the extension of a defeasible theory. SPINdle supports Modal Defeasible Logic and all types of Defeasible Logic rule, such as facts, strict rules, defeasible rules, defeaters, and superiority. In summary, SPINdle is a powerful tool which accepts rules, facts, monotonic and non-monotonic (modal) rules for reasoning with inconsistent and incomplete information. In RuleRS, SPINdle Reasoner receives the formal facts, contexts as predicates from predicate file generated for data stored in the associated relational databases and computes definite or defeasible inferences which are then displayed by the I/O interface.

---

[3]SPINDle Reasoner is available to download freely from http://spin.nicta.org.au/spindle/tools.html under LGPL license agreement (https://opensource.org/licenses/lgpl-license)

4 Challenges and Future Research Directions

A number of different challenges arise when attempting to move towards large scale legal reasoning with rules and databases. Some of these challenges are directly related to the integration between rules and data and are discussed in Section 4.1. Others are linked to issues raised by large scale data and are discussed in Section 4.2.

4.1 Integration between Rules and Databases

In [Stonebraker, 1992], three possible forms that bring rules with database systems are discussed:

- rule policy can be written down in a booklet and distributed to people,

- the rules can reside in an application program which accesses the databases,

- a knowledge base can reside inside the DBMS by which we can guarantee that the data is consistent with the rules

The author expected that the last form will be the one to be adopted as a major approach. However, we argue that the last form may work well for a single database with small amount of rules but poses some significant challenges for large scale legal reasoning. A number of challenges are raised when attempting to integrate rules and databases, especially at larger scales and these are detailed next.

4.1.1 Common languages

The values encoding regulation and guidelines (legal documents) and the databases (schemas) used in conjunction with the rules are in general developed independently and are likely to have a different vocabulary in general. This may lead to "Tower of Babel" issues, due to the absence of "common languages" between regulations and databases. There is no direct correspondence between the literals used by the rules and the table/attributes of the database schema. Accordingly, we have to establish a mapping between them to enable the integration of rules and instances in the database.

4.1.2 Integrating varieties of data sources with rule engines

Another challenge involves the integration of data coming from disparate sources with rule engines. Each source could publish data in their own format and all of these formats would need to be brought together to construct schema-based conditions for rules. This is quite a big asking for knowledge engineering. Furthermore, when database schemas or rules change, schema-based indices will also be affected due to the strong coupling.

4.1.3 Inference efficiency

In the case of defeasible deontic logic in legal domain, each condition in a rule could be represented by a complex query that involves multiple selections, projections and joins across multiple tables and databases. Existing schema-based index approaches cannot address this complexity well. Furthermore, rules in the legal domain have not only dependent relationship but also defeater relationship. Together with issues such as reparation chain handling, they bring more dynamics during reasoning process which places even heavier burden to inference engines.

4.1.4 Reactive inference

The existing reasoning process in systems such as RuleRS is that the inference engine looks for rules which match facts stored in the working memory or provided by users. One rule is selected from the "conflict set" and executed to generate a new fact. Then the inference engine will continue the reasoning based on the new fact together with the previous given facts. We call this as reactive inference because the inference engine only reasons based on what is given but does not interact with databases to seek "unknown" facts proactively. Proactive inference is critically important when it is highly unlikely for users to know all facts beforehand. Furthermore, the assumption of storing facts "in memory" does not hold for large scale reasoning, as detailed in Section 4.2.2.

4.1.5 Rules as data

Rules could be treated as data and stored in database systems, to make it easier for the rules to be triggered and executed as and when required [Paul and Polamraju, 1991]. The main issue with storing rules in the database is that the database is not capable of handling deontic concepts. To correctly model the provision corresponding to prescriptive norms, we have to supplement the language with deontic operators, and the databases are not capable of handling these specific features.

Rules treated as data could create further challenges. Legal reasoning integrating rules and databases are not limited to any particular regulations. Hence, the database could be aligned to one-to-many regulations, establishing n-ary relations among these. If such rules are treated as data and stored in databases, then the task of amending them if necessary becomes even harder, since each of the rules could connect with another rule leading to nested and correlated queries. Such queries are usually avoided due to their complexity.[4] Query maintainability and filtering also create further challenges.

---

[4]http://www.sqlservice.se/sql-server-performance-death-by-correlated-subqueries/

4.2 Large-Scale Legal Reasoning

4.2.1 Representation

As discussed in Sections 2 and 3.1, there are several formalisms that can be used for representing legal norms and facts about cases, such as answer set programming, argumentation and defeasible logic. Although such formalisms are expressive enough for representing legal rules and efficient reasoning mechanisms and tools exist for them, encoding the rules is a complex process. For example in [Batsakis *et al.*, 2018] some implementations required approximately 100 rules, and creating these rules was a time consuming process requiring expertise in logic programming. In case of large scale reasoning the encoding process will face severe scalability issues and it is a potential bottleneck for efficient large scale reasoning. Automating this process with the help of efficient natural language processing tools is an open research problem.

4.2.2 Volume

Traditional legal reasoning has been focused on storing and processing data in main memory over a single processor. This approach is indeed applicable to small legal documents. However, there is a limit on how many records an in-memory system can hold. In addition, utilising a single processor can lead to excessive processing time.

RuleRS [Islam and Governatori, 2018] indicates that data can be processed record by record, namely querying the database and performing reasoning for each record separately. Experimental evaluation shows that this approach can evaluate each record within seconds. However, for 3 millions of records this approach requires an estimated time of 8 hours. A record by record processing approach cannot be guaranteed for any given application. Thus, in other applications where all records need to be loaded and processed together, main memory would be a hard constraint considering applicability.

Recent advances in mass parallelisation could potentially the limitations related to memory and processing time. It has been shown in literature [Antoniou *et al.*, 2018] that mass parallelisation can be applied to various types of reasoning. Both supercomputers (e.g., a single large machine with hundreds of processors and a large shared main memory) and distributed settings (e.g., a large number of combined commodity machines that collectively provide multiple processors and a large main memory) can be used in order to speed up data processing. The advantages are twofold, since mass parallelisation: (a) could significantly reduce processing time as multiple cores can be used simultaneously, and (b) virtually alleviates the restriction on main memory as more memory can be easily added to the system.

4.2.3 Velocity

Financial transactions could potentially require real-time monitoring of day-to-day activity. Such functionality would depend on processing large amounts of transactions within seconds. For cases where reasoning needs to take place during a short window of time, close to the time that events take place, batch reasoning is no longer a viable solution. A prominent challenge in this situation is the efficient combination of streaming data with existing legal knowledge (e.g., applicable laws and past cases), essentially updating the latter. Stream reasoning has been studied in literature [Hoeksema and Kotoulas, 2011; Urbani *et al.*, 2013], showing that only relatively simple rules could allow high throughput. In general, stream processing is intended for use cases where data is processed towards a single direction. However, in stream reasoning, recursive rules (i.e., rules that lead to inference loops) may lead to performance bottlenecks. In addition, within such a dynamic environment, incoming data could potentially invalidate previously asserted knowledge leading to a new set of knowledge, which would in turn change the set of conclusions.

4.2.4 Variety

One of the main challenges in large-scale legal reasoning could be the integration of data coming from disparate sources. Each source could publish data in any possible format, ranging from images of scanned pages to machine processable files. Thus, the first challenge is to translate all available data into machine processable data that can be readily stored and retrieved. Once this data transformation is achieved managing data that are stored in different formats (e.g., plain text, JSON, XML, RDF) would complicate legal reasoning as all data would need to be translated into a single format in order to have a uniform set of facts. Thus, in order to tackle data variety, all available data would need to be stored in a uniform format that would allow automated translation into facts of the chosen legal reasoning framework.

Existing work on semantic technologies can be used to address these challenges. Through the use of upper ontologies that provide definitions for a wide range of concepts, specialised legal ontologies such as LKIF [Hoekstra *et al.*, 2007] or bespoke ontologies, it can be ensured that all available data sources related to a large scale legal reasoning effort are eventually mapped into a unified body of knowledge.

5 Conclusion

This chapter argued that there is scope for research in AI and law with regard to performing effective legal reasoning when the associated knowledge and data is on a large scale and there is also a need for integration between rules and databases. A number of potential scenarios were discussed where this kind of reasoning would be useful, with use cases ranging from the pharmaceutical and financial to property development sectors.

Through a summary of state of the art and an analysis of applying rule-based legal reasoning and integrating rules and databases in practice, it becomes evident that current approaches are not fully equipped to handle large scale legal reasoning with rules and databases and face several challenges.

With regard to the problem of integration between rules and databases, the identified challenges relate to: (a) common languages; (b) integrating rule engines with various data sources; (c) inference efficiency; (d) reactive inference; and (e) rules as data. Additional challenges are encountered when moving towards larger scales, dealing with: (a) representation; (b) volume; (c) velocity; and (d) variety.

It is envisioned that these challenges, among others, will drive research on legal representation and reasoning in the near future, providing researchers at the confluence of AI and law with a multitude of potential avenues of investigation. By addressing some of these challenges, efficient, effective and successful large scale legal reasoning with rules and databases will be achievable in the era of big data.

BIBLIOGRAPHY

[A O'Callaghan et al., 2003] Thomas A O'Callaghan, James Popple, and Eric McCreath. Shyster-mycin: A hybrid legal expert system. In *Proceedings of the Ninth International Conference on Artificial Intelligence and Law (ICAIL-03)*, pages 103–4, 06 2003.

[Aamodt and Plaza, 1994] Agnar Aamodt and Enric Plaza. Case-based reasoning: Foundational issues, methodological variations, and system approaches. *AI Communications. IOS Press*, 7:1:39–59, 1994.

[Alberti et al., 2008] Marco Alberti, Federico Chesani, Marco Gavanelli, Evelina Lamma, Paola Mello, and Paolo Torroni. Verifiable Agent Interaction in Abductive Logic Programming: The SCIFF Framework. *ACM Trans. Comput. Logic*, 9(4):29:1–29:43, 2008.

[Aleven, 2003] Vincent Aleven. Using background knowledge in case-based legal reasoning: A computational model and an intelligent learning environment. *Artif. Intell.*, 150(1-2):183–237, 2003.

[Antoniou et al., 2000] Grigoris Antoniou, David Billington, Guido Governatori, and Michael J. Maher. A Flexible Framework for Defeasible Logics. In Henry A. Kautz and Bruce W. Porter, editors, *AAAI/IAAI*, pages 405–410. AAAI Press / The MIT Press, 2000.

[Antoniou et al., 2001] Grigoris Antoniou, David Billington, Guido Governatori, and Michael J Maher. Representation results for defeasible logic. *ACM Transactions on Computational Logic*, 2(2):255–287, 2001.

[Antoniou et al., 2018] Grigoris Antoniou, Sotiris Batsakis, Raghava Mutharaju, Jeff Z. Pan, Guilin Qi, Ilias Tachmazidis, Jacopo Urbani, and Zhangquan Zhou. A survey of large-scale reasoning on the web of data. *Knowledge Eng. Review*, 33:e21, 2018.

[Ashley, 1990] Kevin D. Ashley. *Modeling Legal Argument: Reasoning With Cases and Hypotheticals*. The Bradford Books, MIT Press, 1990.

[Batsakis *et al.*, 2018] Sotiris Batsakis, George Baryannis, Guido Governatori, Ilias Tachmazidis, and Grigoris Antoniou. Legal Representation and Reasoning in Practice: A Critical Comparison. In *Legal Knowledge and Information Systems - JURIX 2018: The Thirty-first Annual Conference, Groningen, The Netherlands, 12-14 December 2018.*, pages 31–40, 2018.

[Bench-Capon and Prakken, 2008] Trevor J. M. Bench-Capon and Henry Prakken. Introducing the Logic and Law Corner. *J. Log. Comput.*, 18(1):1–12, 2008.

[Bench-Capon, 2012] Trevor J. M. Bench-Capon. What Makes a System a Legal Expert? In Burkhard Schfer, editor, *JURIX*, volume 250 of *Frontiers in Artificial Intelligence and Applications*, pages 11–20. IOS Press, 2012.

[Branting, 1991] L.Karl Branting. Building explanations from rules and structured cases. *International Journal of Man-Machine Studies*, 34(6):797 – 837, 1991. AI and Legal Reasoning. Part 1.

[Branting, 2000] L. Karl Branting. *Reasoning with Rules and Precedents: A Computational Model of Legal Analysis*. Springer Netherlands, 2000.

[Branting, 2003] Karl Branting. A reduction-graph model of precedent in legal analysis. *Artif. Intell.*, 150:59–95, 2003.

[Brüninghaus, 1994] Stefanie Brüninghaus. Daniel: Integrating case-based and rule-based reasoning in law. In *AAAI*, 1994.

[Cervone *et al.*, 2007] Luca Cervone, Monica Palmirani, and Tommaso Ognibene. Legal rules, text and ontologies over time. In *Proceedings of the RuleML2012@ECAI Challenge, at the 6th International Symposium on Rules*, volume 874, 01 2007.

[Dung, 1995] P. M. Dung. On the Acceptability of Arguments and Its Fundamental Role in Nonmonotonic Reasoning, Logic Programming, and n-Person Games. *Artificial Intelligence*, 77(2):321–357, 1995.

[Gardner, 1987] Anne von der Lieth Gardner. *An Artificial Intelligence Approach to Legal Reasoning*. MIT Press, Cambridge, MA, USA, 1987.

[Gavanelli *et al.*, 2015] Marco Gavanelli, Evelina Lamma, Fabrizio Riguzzi, Elena Bellodi, Riccardo Zese, and Giuseppe Cota. Abductive logic programming for normative reasoning and ontologies. In *JSAI-isAI Workshops*, volume 10091 of *Lecture Notes in Computer Science*, pages 187–203, 2015.

[Ghosh, 2018] El Ghosh. *Automation of legal reasoning and decision based on ontologies.* PhD thesis, INSA de Rouen, 2018.

[Gordon *et al.*, 2007] T. F. Gordon, H. Prakken, and D. N. Walton. The Carneades model of argument and burden of proof. *Artificial Intelligence*, 171(10-15):875–896, 2007.

[Governatori and Hashmi, 2015] Guido Governatori and Mustafa Hashmi. No time for compliance. In *Enterprise Distributed Object Computing Conference (EDOC), 2015 IEEE 19th International*, pages 9–18. IEEE, 2015.

[Governatori and Rotolo, 2004] Guido Governatori and Antonino Rotolo. Defeasible logic: Agency, intention and obligation. In *Proceedings of the DEON 2004*, number 3065 in LNCS, pages 114–128. Springer, 2004.

[Governatori and Rotolo, 2008] Guido Governatori and Antonino Rotolo. Bio logical agents: Norms, beliefs, intentions in defeasible logic. *Autonomous Agents and Multi-Agent Systems*, 17(1):36–69, 2008.

[Governatori and Rotolo, 2010] Guido Governatori and Antonino Rotolo. A conceptually rich model of business process compliance. In *Proceedings of the APCCM 2010*, number 110 in CRPIT, pages 3–12. ACS, 2010.

[Governatori and Shek, 2013] Guido Governatori and Sidney Shek. Regorous: A business process compliance checker. In *Proceedings of the Fourteenth International Conference on Artificial Intelligence and Law*, pages 245–246, 2013.

[Governatori *et al.*, 2013] Guido Governatori, Francesco Olivieri, Antonino Rotolo, and Simone Scannapieco. Computing Strong and Weak Permissions in Defeasible Logic. *J. Philosophical Logic*, 42(6):799–829, 2013.

[Governatori, 2005] Guido Governatori. Representing business contracts in RuleML. *International Journal of Cooperative Information Systems*, 14(2-3):181–216, June-September 2005.

[Governatori, 2011] Guido Governatori. On the relationship between Carneades and defeasible logic. In *Proceedings of the ICAIL 2011*, pages 31–40. ACM, 2011.

[Governatori, 2015] Guido Governatori. The Regorous approach to process compliance. In *2015 IEEE 19th International Enterprise Distributed Object Computing Workshop*, pages 33–40. IEEE Press, 2015.

[Hilpinen, 2001] Risto Hilpinen. Deontic logic. In Lou Goble, editor, *The Blackwell Guide to Philosophical Logic*. Wiley-Blackwell, 2001.

[Hoeksema and Kotoulas, 2011] Jesper Hoeksema and Spyros Kotoulas. High-performance Distributed Stream Reasoning using S4. In *Proccedings of the 1st International Workshop on Ordering and Reasoning*, 2011.

[Hoekstra et al., 2007] Rinke Hoekstra, Joost Breuker, Marcello Di Bello, Alexander Boer, et al. The LKIF Core Ontology of Basic Legal Concepts. *LOAIT*, 321:43–63, 2007.

[Islam and Governatori, 2018] Mohammad Badiul Islam and Guido Governatori. RuleRS: a rule-based architecture for decision support systems. *Artificial Intelligence and Law*, 2018.

[Kowalski and Burton, 2011] Robert Kowalski and Anthony Burton. WUENIC - A Case Study in Rule-Based Knowledge Representation and Reasoning. In Manabu Okumura, Daisuke Bekki, and Ken Satoh, editors, *JSAI-isAI Workshops*, volume 7258 of *Lecture Notes in Computer Science*, pages 112–125. Springer, 2011.

[Lam and Governatori, 2009] Ho-Pun Lam and Guido Governatori. The Making of SPINdle. In Guido Governatori, John Hall, and Adrian Paschke, editors, *RuleML*, volume 5858 of *Lecture Notes in Computer Science*, pages 315–322. Springer, 2009.

[Lam and Governatori, 2013] Brian Lam and Guido Governatori. Towards a model of UAVs navigation in urban canyon through defeasible logic. *Journal of Logic and Computation (JLC)*, 23(2):373–395, 2013.

[Ligeza, 2006] Antoni Ligeza. *Logical Foundations for Rule-Based Systems, 2nd Ed.* Springer, 01 2006.

[Miller, 2010] Vaughne Miller. How much legislation comes from Europe? House of Commons Library Research Paper, 10-62, 13 October 2010.

[Negnevitsky, 2002] M. Negnevitsky. *Artificial Intelligence: A Guide to Intelligent Systems*. Addison-Wesley, 2002.

[Parsia et al., 2005] Bijan Parsia, Evren Sirin, Bernardo Cuenca Grau, Edna Ruckhaus, and Daniel Hewlett. Cautiously Approaching SWRL. Preprint submitted to Elsevier Science, 2005.

[Paul and Polamraju, 1991] V. Paul and R. V. Polamraju. Rule management and inferencing in relational databases. In *IEEE Proceedings of the SOUTHEASTCON '91*, pages 695–697 vol.2, April 1991.

[Prakken and Sartor, 2015] Henry Prakken and Giovanni Sartor. Law and logic: A review from an argumentation perspective. *Artif. Intell.*, 227:214–245, 2015.

[Prakken, 2009] Henry Prakken. An Abstract Framework for Argumentation with Structured Arguments. *Argument and Computation*, 1(2):93–124, 2009.

[Prentzas and Hatzilygeroudis, 2007] Jim Prentzas and Ioannis Hatzilygeroudis. Categorizing approaches combining rule-based and case-based reasoning. *Expert Systems*, 24:97–122, 2007.

[Risch et al., 1988] Tore Risch, René Reboh, Peter E. Hart, and Richard O. Duda. A functional approach to integrating database and expert systems. *Commun. ACM*, 31(12):1424–1437, 1988.

[Rissland and Skalak, 1991] Edwina L. Rissland and David B. Skalak. Cabaret: Rule interpretation in a hybrid architecture. *International Journal of Man-Machine Studies*, 34:839–887, 1991.

[Robaldo and Sun, 2017] Livio Robaldo and Xin Sun. Reified Input/Output logic: Combining Input/Output logic and Reification to represent norms coming from existing legislation. *Journal of Logic and Computation*, 27(8):2471–2503, 04 2017.

[Satoh *et al.*, 2010] Ken Satoh, Kento Asai, Takamune Kogawa, Masahiro Kubota, Megumi Nakamura, Yoshiaki Nishigai, Kei Shirakawa, and Chiaki Takano. PROLEG: An Implementation of the Presupposed Ultimate Fact Theory of Japanese Civil Code by PROLOG Technology. In *JSAI-isAI Workshops*, volume 6797 of *Lecture Notes in Computer Science*, pages 153–164. Springer, 2010.

[Sergot *et al.*, 1986] Marek J. Sergot, Fariba Sadri, Robert A. Kowalski, F. Kriwaczek, Peter Hammond, and H. T. Cory. The British Nationality Act as a Logic Program. *Commun. ACM*, 29(5):370–386, 1986.

[Sergot, 2001] Marek J. Sergot. A computational theory of normative positions. *ACM Trans. Comput. Log.*, 2(4):581–622, 2001.

[Snaith and Reed, 2012] Mark Snaith and Chris Reed. TOAST: Online ASPIC+ implementation. In Bart Verheij, Stefan Szeider, and Stefan Woltran, editors, *Proc. of the 4th International Conference on Computational Models of Argument (COMMA 2012)*, volume 245 of *Frontiers in Artificial Intelligence and Applications*. IOS Press, 2012.

[Stonebraker, 1992] Michael Stonebraker. The integration of rule systems and database systems. *IEEE Trans. Knowl. Data Eng.*, 4:415–423, 1992. This paper provides a survey on rule and database integration for a decade. The author discuss possible issue with separating two systems as consistancy of the data and knowledge base is not guranteed. Instead of coupling two system it is better to intergrate two systems. The paper also discuss the classfication and implementation of DBMS rules system.

[Studer *et al.*, 1998] Rudi Studer, V.Richard Benjamins, and Dieter Fensel. Knowledge engineering: Principles and methods. *Data and Knowledge Engineering*, 25(1):161 – 197, 1998.

[Urbani *et al.*, 2013] Jacopo Urbani, Alessandro Margara, Ceriel J. H. Jacobs, Frank van Harmelen, and Henri E. Bal. DynamiTE: Parallel Materialization of Dynamic RDF Data. In Harith Alani, Lalana Kagal, Achille Fokoue, Paul T. Groth, Chris Biemann, Josiane Xavier Parreira, Lora Aroyo, Natasha F. Noy, Chris Welty, and Krzysztof Janowicz, editors, *The Semantic Web – ISWC 2013*, volume 8218 of *Lecture Notes in Computer Science*, pages 657–672. Springer, 2013.

[Van de Ven *et al.*, 2008a] Saskia Van de Ven, Joost Breuker, Rinke Hoekstra, and Lars Wortel. Automated Legal Assessment in OWL 2. In Enrico Francesconi, Giovanni Sartor, and Daniela Tiscornia, editors, *JURIX*, volume 189 of *Frontiers in Artificial Intelligence and Applications*, pages 170–175. IOS Press, 2008.

[Van de Ven *et al.*, 2008b] Saskia Van de Ven, Rinke Hoekstra, Joost Breuker, Lars Wortel, and Abdallah El-Ali. Judging Amy: Automated Legal Assessment using OWL 2. In Catherine Dolbear, Alan Ruttenberg, and Ulrike Sattler, editors, *OWLED*, volume 432 of *CEUR Workshop Proceedings*. CEUR-WS.org, 2008.

[White, 1992] Michelle J. White. Legal complexity and lawyers' benefit from litigation. *International Review of Law and Economics*, 12(3):381 – 395, 1992.

Grigoris Antoniou
University of Huddersfield
Queensgate, Huddersfield, HD1 3DH, UK
Email: g.antoniou@hud.ac.uk

George Baryannis
University of Huddersfield
Queensgate, Huddersfield, HD1 3DH, UK
Email: g.bargiannis@hud.ac.uk

Sotiris Batsakis
University of Huddersfield
Queensgate, Huddersfield, HD1 3DH, UK
Email: s.batsakis@hud.ac.uk

Guido Governatori
Independent Researcher
Email: guido@governatori.net

Mohammad Badiul Islam
Data61, CSIRO
Dutton Park, QLD 4102, Brisbane, Australia
Email: Badiul.Islam@data61.csiro.au

Qing Liu
Data61, CSIRO
Sandy Bay, Tas 7005, Tasmania, Australia
Email: Q.Liu@data61.csiro.au

Livio Robaldo
Legal Innovation Lab Wales, Hillary Rodham Clinton School of Law,
Swansea University, Singleton Park, Swansea, SA2 8PP, UK
livio.robaldo@swansea.ac.uk

Giovanni Siragusa
University of Turin
Via Pessinetto 12, 10149 Torino, Italy
Email: siragusa@di.unito.it

Ilias Tachmazidis
University of Huddersfield
Queensgate, Huddersfield, HD1 3DH, UK
Email: i.tachmazidis@hud.ac.uk

12

Computational Complexity of Compliance and Conformance: Drawing a Line Between Theory and Practice

Silvano Colombo Tosatto
Guido Governatori

ABSTRACT. In the present chapter we focus our attention on the computational complexity of proving regulatory compliance of business process models. While the topic has never received the deserved attention, we argue that the theoretical results, both existing and yet to find, are far reaching for many areas related to the problem of proving compliance of process models. Therefore, we provide here and discuss the existing results concerning the theoretical computational complexity of the problem, as well as discussing some further areas that can potentially advance the knowledge about the issue, and other closely related disciplines that can either bring or take insights to this area.

1 Introduction

In this chapter we investigate the computational complexity of the problem of proving regulatory compliance of process models. This problem consists of verifying whether a process model, representing a set of executions of an organisation's procedures, complies with some given regulations. We consider an execution to be compliant with some regulations when no violations occurs in such execution with respect of the regulations. Different degrees of compliance are determined depending on whether every execution in a model comply with the regulations, when some comply, and when none comply.

Proving regulatory compliance has been receiving more attention during the past years, as shown by approaches of varying complexity being proposed in the literature (Some of the recently proposed approaches: [Indiono et al., 2018; Groefsema et al., 2018; Haarmann et al., 2018].) Analysis of the current expenses [PWC, 2017] from real businesses and companies towards showing their compliance with the relevant regulations, have brought an interests in

Handbook of Legal AI
© *2022, Silvano Colombo Tosatto, Guido Governatori*

finding automated solutions in order to bring down such costs. For a recent survey of the approaches to business process compliance and open research question in the field see Hashmi *et al.* [2018].

Despite the various approaches proposed to address the problem of proving the regulatory compliance of business process models, meaning "ensuring that, executing such a business process model to achieve a business objective, is compliant with the regulations", or dealing with conformance: "verifying whether existing executions, usually logs, have been performed in accordance to the regulatory requirements", in general, the computational complexity of the problem it has been for the most part ignored. Despite knowing that in general the problem is NP-complete [Colombo Tosatto *et al.*, 2015a], many approaches have shown to be able to solve current real problem without being hindered by the theoretical complexity of it. While this allows currently to use this kind of solutions without any sort of big issue, due to the current race towards automation, it is only bound that the business process models and the regulatory frameworks required to be verified in the future are increasing in size and complexity. This, in turn could potentially put a hard stop to the approaches currently used, due to them ignoring such theoretical complexity concerns.

In this chapter we first provide a computational complexity analysis of the general problem of proving regulatory compliance of business process models, and its variants obtainable by manipulating the properties of the regulatory framework being used. We consider three different properties that a regulatory framework can have: the number of regulations contained in the framework, whether the regulations affect the entirety of the executions of a business process model, or whether some parts of them given some additional conditions. The third property concerns whether the regulations are expressed using atomic boolean propositions, or full formulae. Given these binary properties we identify 8 variants of the problems, for which we study and provide their computational complexity classes.

Additionally, the computational complexity of the problem can change depending on the features of the business process models being verified. Taking as the basic variant in this scenario structured business process models, namely process models whose structure can be defined as a properly nested structure, which has technical advantages over processes not following such constraints, which in turn ends up being more expressive. We consider some additional features that can be desirable to represent real life processes, such as unstructured process models and the inclusion of loops, and we discuss how these additions influence the computational complexity of the problem's variants.

After having discussed the theoretical computational complexity of the problem, we consider some of the existing approaches aimed at solving the problem of proving regulatory compliance of business process models, and we assign them to the problem variants identified in this chapter, hence associating them to a computational complexity class. Starting form this classification, we provide a preliminary study of the behaviour of these approaches in a future where the components of the problem increase in size and complexity, namely the business process models and / or the regulatory frameworks. We aim with this preliminary analysis to provide some insights concerning which approaches may be hindered by the theoretical complexity limitations of the problem as bigger and more complex problems will be required to be solved, and which may be potentially be still used to tackle these larger problems.

Furthermore, we discuss a problem related to the problem of proving regulatory compliance: conformance, discussing a few of the techniques used to solve this tangential problem.

Finally, we conclude this chapter by discussing some of the open problem concerning the computational complexity analysis of the problem of proving regulatory compliance of business process models.

2 The Problem: Proving Regulatory Compliance

In this section, we introduce the problem of proving regulatory compliance of business process models analysed in this chapter. The problem consists of two components:

i) the business process model compactly describing a set of possible executions, and

ii) a regulatory framework, describing the compliance requirements.

2.1 Structured Business Processes

Generally, process models can be seen as a compact way to represent the set of possible ways that a company have to achieve some given business objectives. These models contain the tasks, which correspond to the atomic activities that can be executed to bring forward the achievement of the business objective pursued by the executions included in the model. These tasks are organised within the process model and describe a set of possible orders in which they can be executed. Example 2.1 illustrates an instance of a process that can be possibly used to describe the sale procedures in a shop.

Example 2.1 (Shop Sale Process) *Considering the scenario of a shop selling goods to costumers, the sale procedure can be summarised as a process by considering the sequence of steps listed below:*

1. *The customer chooses the goods he/she wants to purchase.*

2. *The total cost of the goods is tallied up.*

3. *The customer pays the calculated amount.*

4. *The sale is concluded.*

Using such formal models to represent their business procedures, companies allow to ensure that such procedures follow the required regulations by checking these models.

In this chapter we focus our analysis on structured process models, such type of processes is similar to structured workflows defined by Kiepuszewski *et al.* [2000]. The advantage of focusing our initial analysis on these kind of processes is that their soundness[1] can be verified in polynomial time with respect to their size, and that the amount of possible executions belonging to the process model is finite, as it does not contain *loops* that can be potentially iterated any number of times, leading to business process models containing an infinite amount of possible executions.

Despite their simplicity, such kind of business process models can be used to represent 406 out of 604 processes in the SAP reference model [Keller and Teufel, 1998], as shown by Polyvyanyy *et al.* [2012], illustrating also that unstructured processes, under certain conditions, can be translated into structured process models.

Definition 2.2 (Process Block) *A process block B is a directed graph: the nodes are called* elements *and the directed edges are called* arcs. *The set of elements of a process block are identified by the function $V(B)$ and the set of arcs by the function $E(B)$. The set of elements is composed of tasks and coordinators. There are 4 types of coordinators:* and_split, and_join, xor_split *and* xor_join. *Each process block B has two distinguished nodes called the* initial *and* final *element. The initial element has no incoming arc from other elements in B and is denoted by $b(B)$. Similarly the final element has no outgoing arcs to other elements in B and is denoted by $f(B)$.*

A directed graph composing a process block is defined inductively as follows:

- *A single task constitutes a process block. The task is both initial and final element of the block.*

- *Let $B_1, \ldots, B_n$ be distinct process blocks with $n > 1$:*

---

[1]A process is sound, as defined by van der Aalst [1997; 1998], if it avoids livelocks and deadlocks.

- SEQ$(B_1, \ldots, B_n)$ *denotes the process block with node set* $\bigcup_{i=0}^{n}$ $V(B_i)$ *and edge set* $\bigcup_{i=0}^{n}(E(B_i) \cup \{(f(B_i), b(B_{i+1})) : 1 \leq i < n\})$. *The initial element of* SEQ$(B_1, \ldots, B_n)$ *is* $b(B_1)$ *and its final element is* $f(B_n)$.

- XOR$(B_1, \ldots, B_n)$ *denotes the block with vertex set* $\bigcup_{i=0}^{n} V(B_i) \cup$ $\{$xsplit, xjoin$\}$ *and edge set* $\bigcup_{i=0}^{n}(E(B_i) \cup \{($xsplit$, b(B_i)), (f(B_i),$ xjoin$) : 1 \leq i \leq n\})$ *where* xsplit *and* xjoin *respectively denote an* xor_split *coordinator and an* xor_join *coordinator, respectively. The initial element of* XOR$(B_1, \ldots, B_n)$ *is* xsplit *and its final element is* xjoin.

- AND$(B_1, \ldots, B_n)$ *denotes the block with vertex set* $\bigcup_{i=0}^{n} V(B_i) \cup$ $\{$asplit, ajoin$\}$ *and edge set* $\bigcup_{i=0}^{n}(E(B_i) \cup \{($asplit$, b(B_i)), (f(B_i),$ ajoin$) : 1 \leq i \leq n\})$ *where* asplit *and* ajoin *denote an* and_split *and an* and_join *coordinator, respectively. The initial element of* AND$(B_1, \ldots, B_n)$ *is* asplit *and its final element is* ajoin.

By enclosing a process block as defined in Definition 2.2 along with a start and end task in a sequence block, we obtain a *structured process model*. Therefore, a structured process model can be understood as a structure recursively composed by process blocks, where at the lowest recursion level are the process blocks representing the tasks of the process model.

The effects of executing the tasks contained in a business process model are described using annotations as shown in Definition 2.3.

Definition 2.3 (Annotated process) *Let P be a structured process and T be the set of tasks contained in P. An annotated process is a pair: (P, ann), where* ann *is a function associating a consistent set of literals to each task in T:* ann $: T \mapsto 2^{\mathcal{L}}$.

The status of the process execution is represented by a process' state. Such state contains a set of literals representing what is considered to be the case at that step of the execution. The literals contained in the process' state is determined by the sequence of the task being executed, and it is updated after each task execution.

The update between the states of a process during its execution is inspired by the AGM[2] belief revision operator [Alchourrón *et al.*, 1985] and is used in the context of business processes to define the transitions between states [Ghose and Koliadis, 2007; Hoffmann *et al.*, 2012], which in turn are used to define the *traces*.

---

[2]The approach is named after the initials of the authors introducing it: Alchourrón, Gärdenfors, and Makinson.

Definition 2.4 (State update) *Given two consistent sets of literals L_1 and L_2, representing the process state and the annotation of a task being executed, the update of L_1 with L_2, denoted by $L_1 \oplus L_2$ is a set of literals defined as follows:*

$$L_1 \oplus L_2 = L_1 \setminus \{\neg l \mid l \in L_2\} \cup L_2$$

Definition 2.5 (Executions and Traces) *Given a structured process model identified by a process block B, the set of its executions, written $\Sigma(B) = \{\epsilon \mid \epsilon$ is a sequence and is an execution of $B\}$. The executions contained in $\Sigma(B)$ are recursively constructed as follows:*

1. *If B is a task t, then $\Sigma(B) = \{(t)\}$*

2. *if B is a composite block with sub-blocks $B_1, \ldots, B_n$:*

   (a) *If $B = \mathsf{SEQ}(B_1, \ldots, B_n)$, then $\Sigma(B) = \{\epsilon_1 +_\varepsilon \cdots +_\varepsilon \epsilon_n \mid \epsilon_i \in \Sigma(B_i)\}$ and $+_\varepsilon$ the operator concatenating two executions.*

   (b) *If $B = \mathsf{XOR}(B_1, \ldots, B_n)$, then $\Sigma(B) = \Sigma(B_1) \cup \cdots \cup \Sigma(B_n)$*

   (c) *If $B = \mathsf{AND}(B_1, \ldots, B_n)$, then $\Sigma(B) = \{$the union of the interleavings of: $\epsilon_1, \ldots, \epsilon_n \mid \epsilon_i \in \Sigma(B_i)\}$*

Given an annotated process (B, ann) and an execution $\epsilon = (t_1, \ldots, t_n)$ such that $\epsilon \in \Sigma(B)$, a trace θ is a finite sequence of states: $(\sigma_1, \ldots, \sigma_n)$. Each state $\sigma_i \in \theta$ is a pair: (t_i, L_i) capturing what holds after the execution of a task t_i, expressed by a set of literals L_i. A set L_i is constructed as follows:

1. $L_0 = \emptyset$

2. $L_{i+1} = L_i \oplus \mathsf{ann}(t_{i+1})$, *for $1 \leq i < n$.*

To denote the set of possible traces resulting from a process model (B, ann), we use $\Theta(B, \mathsf{ann})$.

Example 2.6 *Annotated Process Model. Fig. 1 shows a structured process containing four tasks labelled t_1, t_2, t_3 and t_4 and their annotations. The process contains an AND block followed by a task and an XOR block nested within the AND block. The annotations indicate what has to hold after a task is executed. If t_1 is executed, then the literal a has to hold in that state of the process.*

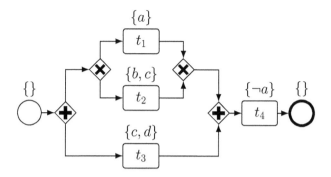

Figure 1. An annotated process

$\Sigma(B)$	$\Theta(B, \text{ann})$
$(\text{start}, t_1, t_3, t_4, \text{end})$	$((\text{start}, \emptyset), (t_1, \{a\}), (t_3, \{a, c, d\}), (t_4, \{\neg a, c, d\}), (\text{end}, \{\neg a, c, d\}))$
$(\text{start}, t_2, t_3, t_4 \text{end})$	$((\text{start}, \emptyset), (t_2, \{b, c\}), (t_3, \{b, c, d\}), (t_4, \{\neg a, b, c, d\}), (\text{end}, \{\neg a, b, c, d\}))$
$(\text{start}, t_3, t_1, t_4 \text{end})$	$((\text{start}, \emptyset), (t_3, \{c, d\}), (t_1, \{a, c, d\}), (t_4, \{\neg a, c, d\}), (\text{end}, \{\neg a, c, d\}))$
$(\text{start}, t_3, t_2, t_4 \text{end})$	$((\text{start}, \emptyset), (t_3, \{c, d\}), (t_2, \{b, c, d\}), (t_4.\{\neg a, b, c, d\}), (\text{end}, \{\neg a, b, c, d\}))$

Table 1. Executions and Traces of the annotated process in Fig. 1.

2.2 Regulatory Framework

When considering a compliance problem, one of its components is the set of regulations that the model is required to follow. We refer to such component as the regulatory framework, and we consider it as a set obligations, representing the set of regulations governing the process model within the scope of the problem.

As such, we use a subset of Process Compliance Logic (PCL), introduced by Governatori and Rotolo [2010a; 2010b], to specify the semantics for different types of obligations proposed by [Hashmi *et al.*, 2016].

The first distinction in the semantics of obligations, is that obligations can be either *global* or *local*. A global obligation is in force for the entire duration of an execution, while the in force interval of a local obligation is determined by its trigger and deadline conditions. Additionally, an obligation can be either an achievement or a maintenance obligation and it determines how such an obligation is fulfilled by an execution when in force.

Definition 2.7 (Global and Local Obligations) *The in force interval of an obligation depends on whether it is a global or a local obligation, described as follows:*

Global *A global obligation* $\mathcal{O}^o\langle c \rangle$, *where* $o \in \{a, m\}$ *represents whether the* *obligation is achievement or maintenance. The element c represents the fulfilment condition of the obligation.*

Local *A local obligation $\mathcal{O}^o\langle c, t, d \rangle$, where $o \in \{a, m\}$ represents whether the obligation is achievement or maintenance. The element c represents the fulfilment condition of the obligation, the element t the trigger, and the element d the deadline.*

While the in force interval of a global obligation spans the entire duration of a trace, the in force interval of a local obligation is determined as a sub-trace where the first state of such a sub-trace satisfies the trigger, and the last state satisfies the deadline.

Generally the trigger, deadline and condition of an obligation are defined as propositional formulae. Assuming the literals from $\mathcal{L}$ contained in a state to be true, then a propositional formula is true when that state implies it.

Finally, in the semantic we study for each obligation we allow a single in force interval at any given time. Meaning that when an in force interval is already active for an obligation, further triggers would not produce additional in force intervals. This has the consequence that it simplifies the analysis as it is not required to keep track of multiple in force instances, and which in force instance is satisfied by which event when executing a task.

2.2.1 Evaluating the Obligations.

Whether an in force obligation is fulfilled or violated is determined by the states of the trace included in the in force interval of the obligation. Moreover, whether an in force obligation is fulfilled depends on the type of an obligation, as described in Definition 2.8.

Definition 2.8 (Achievement and Maintenance Obligations) *How an in force obligation is fulfilled depends on its type as follows:*

Achievement *If this type of obligation is in force in an interval, then the fulfilment condition specified by the obligation must be satisfied by the execution in at least one point in the interval before the deadline is satisfied. If this is the case, then the obligation in force is considered to be satisfied. Otherwise it is violated.*

Maintenance *If this type of obligation is in force in an interval, then the fulfilment condition must be satisfied continuously in all points of the interval until the deadline is satisfied. Again, if this is the case, then the obligation in force is then satisfied, otherwise it is violated.*

2.2.2 Process Compliance.

The procedure of proving whether a process is compliant with a regulatory framework can return different answers. A process is said to be *fully compliant* if every trace of the process is compliant with the regulatory framework[3]. A process is *partially compliant* if there exists at least one trace that is compliant with the regulatory framework, and *not compliant* if there is no trace complying with the framework.

Definition 2.9 (Process Compliance) *Given a process (P, ann) and a regulatory framework composed by a set of obligations $\mathbb{O}$, the compliance of (P, ann) with respect to $\mathbb{O}$ is determined as follows:*

- ***Full compliance*** $(P, \text{ann}) \vdash^F \mathbb{O}$ *if and only if* $\forall \theta \in \Theta(P, \text{ann}),\ \theta$ *satisfies each obligation in $\mathbb{O}$.*

- ***Partial compliance*** $(P, \text{ann}) \vdash^P \mathbb{O}$ *if and only if* $\exists \theta \in \Theta(P, \text{ann}),\ \theta$ *satisfies each obligation in $\mathbb{O}$.*

- ***Not compliant*** $(P, \text{ann}) \not\vdash \mathbb{O}$ *if and only if* $\neg\exists \theta \in \Theta(P, \text{ann}),\ \theta$ *satisfies each obligation in $\mathbb{O}$.*

Note that we consider a trace to be compliant with a regulatory framework if it satisfies every obligation belonging to the set composing the framework.

3 Theoretical Computational Complexity in Structured Process Models

In this section we discuss the existing results concerning verifying regulatory compliance of structured business process models. We first introduce the acronyms used through the section to identify the different variants of the problem, and then we separately analyse and discuss the computational complexity results related to full, and partial compliance separately.

3.1 Problem Acronyms

Before discussing the existing computational complexity results, we first introduce a compact system to refer to different variants of the problem dealing with verifying compliance of structured process models. Notice that the acronyms refer to the properties of the regulatory framework being evaluated against the structured process model.

---

[3]Notice that by "compliant with the regulatory framework", we refer to a trace fulfilling each in force interval along the trace itself for each obligation belonging to the regulatory framework.

Definition 3.1 (Compact Acronyms) *The variants of the problem we refer to in this Chapter constantly aim to check regulatory compliance of a structured process model. The acronym system refers to the properties of the obligations being checked against the process model.*

1/n *Whether the structured process is checked against a single (**1**) or a set of (**n**) obligations.*

G/L *Whether the in force interval of the obligations is **G**lobal, meaning that it spans the entirety of an execution of the model, or it is **L**ocal, meaning that the in force interval is determined by the trigger and deadline elements of an obligation.*

-/+ *Whether the elements of the obligation being checked on the structured process model are composed by literals (-), or by propositional formulae (+).*

For instance, the variant **1G-** consists of verifying whether a structured process model is compliant with a single obligation, whose condition is expressed as a propositional literal and its in force interval spans the entire execution of the process model.

Note that in the binary properties of the problems considered in this Chapter, the leftmost, i.e., **1** in **1/n** represents a subset of the right side. Intuitively, the case on the right side is at least as complex as the left case. For instance, a solution for a problem including a set of regulations requires also to solve the case where the set of regulations is composed of exactly one regulation.

3.2 Partial Compliance

We focus now on discussing the computational complexity of proving partial compliance of structured business process models. As we see in the remainder of this section, many of the variants belong to the **NP**-complete computational complexity class. Thus we provide quick reminder before proceeding by discussing the existing results.

Definition 3.2 (NP-complete) *A decision problem is **NP**-complete if it is in the set of **NP** problems and if every problem in **NP** is reducible to it in polynomial-time.*

To prove membership in **NP** of a variant of the problem of proving partial compliance, we show that a process is partially compliant with a set of obligations if and only if there is a certificate whose size is at most polynomial in terms of the length of the input (comprising the business process model and the set of obligations) with which we can check whether it fulfils the regulatory framework in polynomial time. As a certificate we use a trace of the model and we check whether it satisfies the regulatory framework.

We illustrate in the following Algorithm 3.3 how **1G-** is solvable in time polynomial. Notice that, while the algorithm reported applies only to achievement obligations, in the original paper by Colombo Tosatto *et al.* [2015b], from which we took this approach, an algorithm dealing with a regulatory framework composed of a maintenance obligation is also provided. Moreover, notice that the algorithm reported is capable to prove either partial, full, and non-compliance in polynomial time.

Algorithm 3.3 (1G- is in P) *Given an annotated process* (P, ann) *and a regulatory framework* $\mathbb{O}$ *containing a single global achievement obligation* $\mathcal{O}^a \langle c \rangle$, *this algorithm returns whether* (P, ann) *is compliant with* $\mathbb{O}$.

1: **if** $\forall$ *task* t *in* $P, c \notin \mathsf{ann}(t)$ **then**
2:     **return** $(P, \mathsf{ann}) \not\vdash \mathbb{O}$
3: **else**
4:     **if** $\mathsf{Remove}(P, \{t \mid t$ *is a task in* P *and* $c \in \mathsf{ann}(t)\}) = \perp$ **then**
5:         **return** $(P, \mathsf{ann}) \vdash^F \mathbb{O}$
6:     **else**
7:         **return** $(P, \mathsf{ann}) \vdash^P \mathbb{O}$
8:     **end if**
9: **end if**

Where the Remove *functions removes the tasks from* P *having* c *annotated, and later checks whether there is a path, in other words an execution, from the start to the end of the process. If no such path exists then the function returns* $\perp$, *which means that there is no execution that does not execute a task having* c *annotated. Meaning that the process is fully compliant.*

In Reduction 3.5 we show the reduction provided by Colombo Tosatto *et al.* [2015a], and showing that the problem of finding whether a graph contains an Hamiltonian path can be reduced to the problem of proving partial compliance in **nL-**. Meaning that the computational complexity of **nL-** is at least the same as proving whether a graph contains an Hamiltonian path, which is in **NP**-complete.

Definition 3.4 (Hamiltonian Path) *Let* $G = (N, D)$ *be a directed graph where the size of* N *is* n. *A hamiltonian path* $ham = (v_1; \ldots; v_n)$ *satisfies the following properties:*

1. $N = \{v_1, \ldots, v_n\}$

2. $\forall i, j((v_i, v_j \in ham \wedge j = i + 1), ((v_i, v_j) \in D)$

Reduction 3.5 (Hamiltonian Path to Proving Partial Compliance in nL-) *Considering the problem of finding an Hamiltonian Path in a graph as described in Definition 3.4.*

Given a hamiltonian path problem containing a directed graph $G = (N, D)$, it can be translated into a regulatory compliance problem involving a process (P, ann) and a set of obligations $\mathbb{O}$ as follows:

1 *Consider a process model P that contains a task labeled $Node_i$ for each vertex v_i contained in N (Figure 2).*

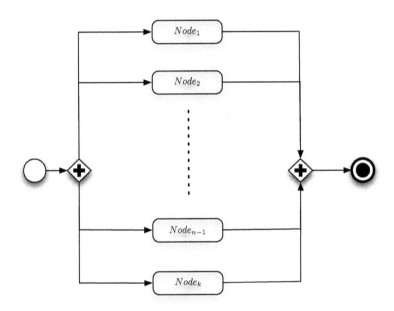

Figure 2. Hamiltonian path problem as verifying partial compliance.

The process block of P is structured as an AND block. The AND block contains in each branch a single task $Node_i$ for each node in the given directed graph: AND($Node_1, \ldots, Node_n$).

Intuitively a serialisation of the AND block represents a tentative hamiltonian path. Annotations and obligations are used to verify that two adjacent nodes in the serialisation can be indeed also adjacent in an hamiltonian path (explained in detail in 2).

Problem Variant	Source			Complexity Class
1G-	Colombo Tosatto *et al.*	[2015b]		**P**
nG-	Colombo Tosatto *et al.*	[2019]		**NP**-complete
1G+	Colombo Tosatto *et al.*	[2019]		**NP**-complete
nG+	Colombo Tosatto *et al.*	[2019]		**NP**-complete
nL-	Colombo Tosatto *et al.*	[2015a]		**NP**-complete
1L+	Colombo Tosatto *et al.*	[2019]		**NP**-complete
nL+	Colombo Tosatto *et al.*	[2015a]		**NP**-complete

Table 2. Partial Compliance Complexity

2 *In this reduction we use the annotations to identify which node is being
selected in the sequence constituting the tentative hamiltonian path.
Thus we use for the annotations a language containing a literal for each
node in G. The annotation of each task in* (P, ann) *is the following:*

- $\forall i | 1 \leq i \leq k, \mathsf{ann}(Node_i) = \{\neg l_1, \ldots, \neg l_n\} \oplus \{l_i\}$

*The obligations are used to represent the directed edges departing from
a vertex, in other words which vertices are the suitable successors in the
hamiltonian path. The set* $\mathbb{O}$ *contains the following local maintenance
obligations:*

- $\forall v_i, v_j | (v_i, v_j) \notin D, \mathcal{O} = \mathcal{O}^m \langle \neg l_j, l_i, \neg l_i \rangle$

*Using the proposed reduction, verifying whether the constructed process
model is partially compliant corresponds to identifying whether the original
graph contains a hamiltonian path. Concluding that the problem of verifying
partial compliance is at least as hard as finding whether a graph contains a
hamiltonian path.*

We collect in Table 2 the existing computational complexity results concerning solving the variants of the problem of proving partial compliance of
structured process models.

Notice that given the three binary properties associated to the regulatory framework being checked against the structured process model, of the
8 possible problem variants, only 7 computational complexity results are
provided in Table 2. This is more apparent by illustrating the results in
Figure 3, where the problem's variants have their computational complexities
associated and the relations between the variants are highlighted by the
connections in the picture. Notice that the directed arrows connecting one
variant of the problem to another refer, according to their direction, that

the computational complexity of a variant of the problem at the origin of an arrow, is at most as difficult as the variant of the problem which is pointed at by the same arrow.

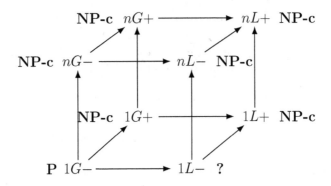

Figure 3. Partial Compliance Complexity Lattice.

It can be noticed in Figure 3, that the variant **1L-** does not have a computational complexity classification yet. While the computational complexity analysis for the considered problem is currently incomplete, Colombo Tosatto *et al.* [2019] conjectured that this variant of the problem to in **P**. However, while we have not yet managed to provide a conclusive computational complexity classification, we conjecture that **1L-** is instead in **NP-c** as explained in Conjecture 3.6

Conjecture 3.6 (1L- is in NP) *We currently have no information about the computational complexity of **1L-**. That is, we cannot infer its belonging to a computational complexity class in a similar way as for **nG+**, as in this case the simpler variant (**1G-**) is in **P**.*

*While it seems like that moving from **G** to **L** seems to not increase the complexity of the problem as much as when moving from - to +, or from **1** to **n**, we believe that such movement should be still be capable of bringing the computational complexity of the problem's variant into **NP-c**.*

*We back our conjecture using the intuition that by moving towards conditional obligations, allows multiple instances of the same obligation to be in force over a single trace. Which means that even for the variant **1L-**, multiple instances would be required to be verified for every trace. Which resembles the variant **nG-**, where multiple obligations are required to be verified over a trace, and it is in **NP-c**.*

Mind that the conjecture does not represent a computational complexity result in itself, hence identifying the computational complexity of the variant **1L-** remains an open problem.

3.3 Full Compliance

We focus now on discussing the computational complexity of the variants of the problem of proving full compliance of a structured process model. As many of the variants of the problem belong to the co**NP**-complete computational complexity class, we provide its definition before proceeding with the discussion.

Definition 3.7 (coNP-complete) *A decision problem is co**NP**-complete if it is in co**NP** and if every problem in co**NP** is polynomial-time many-one reducible to it. A decision problem is in co**NP** if and only if its complement is in the complexity class **NP**.*

We show in Reduction 3.9 how Colombo Tosatto *et al.* [Colombo Tosatto *et al.*, 2015a] have shown that checking for full compliance in a variant of the problem **1L+** is in co**NP**-complete.

Definition 3.8 (Tautology) *A formula of propositional logic is a tautology if the formula itself is always true regardless of which evaluation is used for the propositional variables.*

Reduction 3.9 (Tautology to Proving Full Compliance in 1L+)
Considering the problem to decide whether a given formula is a Tautology as described in Definition 3.8.

Let φ be a propositional formula for which we want to verify whether it is a tautology or not, and let L be the set of literals contained in φ. We include in L only the positive version of a literal, for instance if l or $\neg l$ are contained in φ, then only l is included in L.

For each literal l belonging to L we construct an XOR *block containing two tasks, one labeled and containing in its annotation the positive literal (i.e., l) and the other the negative literal (i.e., $\neg l$). All the* XOR *blocks constructed from L are then included within a single* AND *block. This* AND *block is in turn followed by a task labeled "test" and containing a single literal in its annotation: l_{test}. The sequence containing the* AND *block and the task* test *is then enclosed within a* start *and an* end, *composing the process (P, ann), graphically represented in Figure 4.*

The set of obligations, to which the constructed process has to be verified to be fully compliant with, is composed of a single obligation constructed as follows from the propositional formula φ:

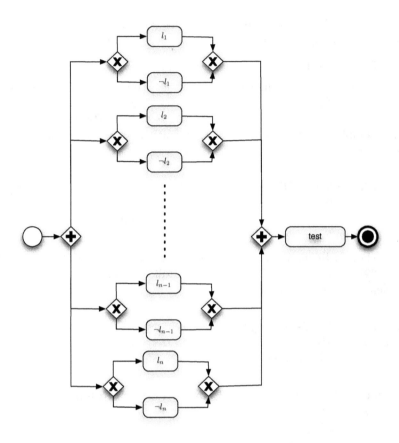

Figure 4. Tautology problem as verifying full compliance.

$$\mathcal{O}^a \langle \varphi, l_{test}, \bot \rangle$$

Notice that Algorithm 3.3 can also be used to prove full compliance of the variant **1G-**. For full compliance, we informally describe in Algorithm 3.11 the procedure introduced by Colombo Tosatto *et al.* [Colombo Tosatto *et al.*, 2020], capable of proving full compliance of the variant **nL-** of the problem in time polynomial with respect to the problem size.

Definition 3.10 (Process Tree Model) *Let P be a structured process model. A Process Tree PT is an abstract hierarchical representation of P, where:*

- *Each process block B in P corresponds to a node N in PT.*

- *Given a process block $B(B_1, \ldots, B_n)$, where $B_1, \ldots, B_n$ are the process blocks directly nested in B, the nodes $N_1, \ldots, N_n$ in PT, corresponding to $B_1, \ldots, B_n$ in P, are children of N, corresponding to B in P. Mind that the order between the sub-blocks of a process block is preserved between the children of the same node.*

Algorithm 3.11 *The approach is based on identifying whether a structured business process model, in its tree representation form as described in Definition 3.10, contain a trace violating one of the obligations belonging to the regulatory framework.*

The advantage of looking for a violating condition, is that finding a single instance within a process model where such condition is positively evaluated, it is a sufficient condition to return the answer that the structured process being evaluated is not fully compliant with the regulatory framework.

The tree representation of a process model has as its leaves the tasks composing the process. Considering a generic obligation $\mathcal{O}^o \langle c, t, d \rangle$, each of the leaves in a process tree associated to a task having t annotated are considered trigger leaves. A bottom up aggregation of the properties of the leaves of the tree, in accordance to their associated annotated tasks, and to the violation condition being looked for, leads to allow whether a process tree contains a violation for a given trigger leaf in a number of steps equal to the number of nodes in the process tree.

Repeating this procedure for each trigger leaf, for each violation condition of each obligation in a regulatory framework, allows to decide, when no violation condition is satisfied, that the business process model being evaluated is fully compliant, and this is decidable in time polynomial with respect to the size of the problem.

Table 3 outlines the existing complexity results concerning some of the variants of the problem of proving full compliance of structured process models.

Similarly as for partial compliance, we illustrate the result concerning the computational complexity of proving full compliance of a process model graphically in Figure 5.

Notice that Figure 5 contains a result for the problem variant **nG-**, which is not included in Table 3. This result is derived from other existing ones. As the relations in the lattice in Figure 5 represent the relation $\leq$ between the computational complexities of the variants of the problem, if we consider the three variants **1G-**, **nL-**, and **nG-**, the follow relationship holds regarding

Problem Variant	Source		Complexity Class
1G-	Colombo Tosatto *et al.*	[2015b]	**P**
1L-	Colombo Tosatto *et al.*	[2020]	**P**
nL-	Colombo Tosatto *et al.*	[2020]	**P**
1G+	Colombo Tosatto *et al.*	[2021]	co**NP**-complete
nG+	Colombo Tosatto *et al.*	[2021]	co**NP**-complete
1L+	Colombo Tosatto *et al.*	[2015a]	co**NP**-complete
nL+	Colombo Tosatto [2015]		co**NP**-complete

Table 3. Full Compliance Complexity

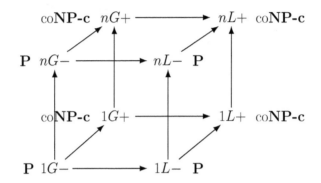

Figure 5. Full Compliance Complexity Lattice.

their computational complexity: **1G-** ≤ **nG-** ≤ **nL-**. Therefore, by knowing that both **1G-** and **nL-** are in **P**, it follows that also **nG-** is in **P**.

3.4   Climbing the Polynomial Hierarchy

The computational complexity results reported so far concerning the problems of proving both partial and full compliance of structured process model, rely on an assumption regarding how formulae composing the obligations are evaluated over the states composing the traces.

Assumption 3.12 (States Satisfying Formula) *Given a state σ, composed by a set of positive and/or negative literals, and a propositional formula φ, φ is satisfied by σ if and only if considering every literal in σ true, is a sufficient interpretation to make φ true. This is equivalent to evaluate a formula over a partial set of possible interpretations, the ones that explicitly appear in the state.*

While the assumption does not appear to be too surprising, it can lead to some interesting behaviours, such as the following: consider the formula $\alpha \vee \neg\alpha$, which is a tautology. Now, if we consider whether an empty state of a trace would satisfy, the formula, then the answer is counter-intuitively *no* in accordance to Assumption 3.12.

The effect of Assumption 3.12 on how formulae composing the obligations are verified over the states of the traces, is to simplify the verification, as the only interpretation required to be verified is the one where every proposition in the state is considered as true. If such interpretation is sufficient to evaluate the formula as true, then its associated effects, according to its place in the obligation, are applied. Differently, if the interpretation provided by the state is not sufficient to fully evaluate the formula, then it is assumed to be false in that state. Normally, without Assumption 3.12, when a state does not contain a sufficient interpretation, then the various cases are considered for the propositions which have not an assigned truth value. This can potentially increase the computational complexity of solving the problem, as evaluating a formula over a state can be reduced to a *Satisfiability* problem, which is known to be **NP**-complete. In order to properly classify the variants of the problem when Assumption 3.12 is dropped, we need first to introduce the *Polynomial Hierarchy*.

The Polynomial Hierarchy is a hierarchy of computational complexity classes describing both the classes already discussed in the present chapter (**P, NP** and co**NP**), as well as more complex classes. In the Polynomial Hierarchy **P** is also represented as either Σ_0^P or Π_0^P, while **NP** and co**NP** are respectively represented as Σ_1^P and Π_1^P.

Definition 3.13 (Σ_1^P) *A problem P is in Σ_1^P if there exists a polynomial time Turing machine T and a polynomial p such that:*
for each instance x of P: there exists a solution s, $|s| \leq p(|x|), T(x, s) =$ true

Definition 3.14 (Π_1^P) *A problem P is in Π_1^P if there exists a polynomial time Turing machine T and a polynomial p such that:*
for each instance x of P: for each solution s, $|s| \leq p(|x|), T(x, s) =$ true

Considering now the problem of proving partial compliance of a structured process model, when Assumption 3.12 is dropped. We have that for the variants of the problem allowing formulae to describe the elements of the obligations, the problem becomes the following: there exists a trace of the model such that, for each state state in the trace, and for each possible interpretations of the state the formulae composing the obligations are satisfied in such a way that no obligation is violated. It can be noticed, that this problem involves an existential quantifier followed by two universal quantifiers: $\exists \forall \forall$. While not delving too much into the technical details, when multiple quantifier of the same type directly follow each other, they

477

can be collapsed as a single quantifier of the same type. Given that, and Definition 3.15, we can see that the variants of the problem of proving partial compliance, and allow formulae in their obligations, can be classified as Σ_2^P. Furthermore, notice that the variants restricting the expressivity of their obligations to simple propositions are not affected and remain in Σ_1^P.

Definition 3.15 (Σ_2^P) *A problem P is in Σ_2^P if there exists a polynomial time Turing machine T and a polynomial p such that:*
for each instance x of P: there exists a solution s, $|s| \leq p(|x|)$ such that each s', $|s'| \leq p(|x|)$, $T(x, s, s') = true$

The lattice with the computational complexity classifications according to the Polynomial Hierarchy, after dropping Assumption 3.12, is shown in Figure 6.

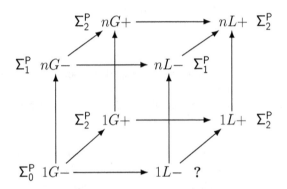

Figure 6. Partial Compliance Complexity Lattice with Polynomial Hierarchies.

Similarly, we can consider the problem of proving full compliance of structured process models, when Assumption 3.12 is dropped. Again, we have that for the variants allowing formulae in their obligations the problem becomes: for each trace of the model such that, for each state state in the trace, and for each possible interpretations of the state the formulae composing the obligations are satisfied in such a way that no obligation is violated. It can be noticed, that this problem involves three universal quantifiers: $\forall\forall\forall$. Again, we can collapse the quantifiers of the same type with the neighbouring ones, which leads to a single universal quantifier in this case. It can be noticed that these problems do not have the sufficient properties to be classified as Π_2^P, as described in Definition 3.16, but they can be classified as Π_1^P, as described in Definition 3.14.

Definition 3.16 (Π_2^P) *A problem P is in Π_2^P if there exists a polynomial time Turing machine T and a polynomial p such that:*

for each instance x of P: for each solution s, $|s| \leq p(|x|)$ such that there exists a s', $|s'| \leq p(|x|)$, $T(x, s, s') = true$

Therefore we can conclude that for the problem of proving full compliance, releasing Assumption 3.12 does not increase the complexity, as the variants allowing propositional formulae are still in co**NP**. For completeness we show the lattice with the Polynomial Hierarchy classifications for the variants of the problem of proving full compliance if Figure 7.

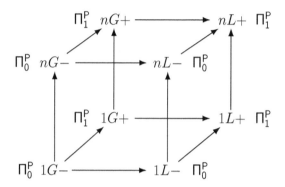

Figure 7. Full Compliance Complexity Lattice with Polynomial Hierarchies.

3.5 Summary

The computational complexity results illustrated in this section show that, when considering variants of the problem only allowing literals to represent the components of the obligations, proving full compliance of structured process model is generally easier than proving partial compliance. Intuitively, the former is easier since it is sufficient to find a violation for an obligation in one of the traces of the model, while for the former, it is required to identify a trace, and ensure that no obligation is violated in such a trace.

Moreover, it can be noticed from the computational complexity lattice in Figure 7, that for full compliance the computational complexity is be governed by the complexity of the language, namely by how expressively we can represent the elements representing the obligations.

Differently, partial compliance seems to be more complex to verify, as it does not seem to allow an easy way to identify its complement, and identifying a compliant trace in a process model is shown to be intractable apart from the the easiest, or maybe two easiest, variant(s) of the problem as illustrated in Figure 6.

Finally, we have also shown that by dropping Assumption 3.12, the computational complexity of the problem of proving partial compliance starts to climb the Polynomial Hierarchy.

4 Computational Complexity of Additional Business Process Features

The variants of the problem discussed earlier in this chapter have their computational complexity depending solely on the varying properties of the regulatory framework while keeping the properties of the process model static. Additional computational complexity analysis can be done when considering more complex variants of the process models used.

In this section we discuss about the computational complexity of proving compliance of process models by including additional features in the process models. In particular we discuss about the computational complexity of verifying compliance of unstructured process model, and the computational complexity impact of including loops in business process models.

4.1 Unstructured Process Models

The computational complexity analysis included in Section 3 focused on problems where the the process models were structured. As mentioned earlier, one of the advantages of such models is that their soundness can be verified in time polynomial with respect to the size of the model. Verifying soundness means to check whether every execution in the model is a proper execution, and capable of reaching the *end* of the model. In other words checking that the process model do not contain livelocks and or deadlocks preventing any of the contained execution to successfully complete.

Unstructured business process models, which are not composed by properly nested process blocks, as the instance shown in Figure 8, do not guarantee that their soundness can be verified in polynomial time. As it has been shown by van der Aalst [1995], and Lohmann *et al.* [2009], the semantics of business process models can be captured by Petri Nets [Murata, 1989]. While this does not provide any direct result concerning the computational complexity about verifying compliance of unstructured process model, it still provides an upper complexity bound, as coloured petri nets, one of the more complex variants of this formalism, is known to be undecidable [Esparza, 1994; Makungu *et al.*, 1999].

4.1.1 Open Problem

Studying the computational complexity of the problem of proving regulatory compliance of unstructured process models is still an open problem. Knowing

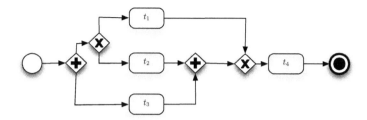

Figure 8. Unstructured Process Model

already that if a unstructured process model is complex enough to require a coloured petri net to represent its semantics, then also the corresponding problem of verifying compliance becomes undecidable. Therefore, one option is to study which classes of unstructured processes do not require coloured petri nets to represent their semantics, and how they affect the computational complexity of solving the problem of proving regulatory compliance.

When studying how unstructured process models affect the computational complexity of the compliance problem, it is also crucial to consider that such models can be potentially translated into structured models, as discussed by Polyvyanyy *et al.* [2014]. However the computational complexity cost of such translations should be still factored in the computational complexity of the problem, which still requires to be studied.

4.2 Loops

Loops are structures that allow to repeat the execution of parts of a process model. Figure 9 shows a process model containing a loop structure, in this model, the execution of the pair of tasks t_4 and t_5 can be executed any number of times between one and infinite. By allowing repeated executions of some of its elements, some issues can arise affecting the computational complexity of the problem of verifying regulatory compliance. In this section we discuss some of out intuitions behind these possible issues affecting the computational complexity of the problem.

4.2.1 Infinite Possible Executions

By allowing repeated executions of some components of a process model, the maximal length of their executions is not constrained anymore by the number of tasks contained in the process model, but can become potentially infinite as a task within a loop can be executed an infinite number of times. Therefore, approaches based on verifying directly whether the traces[4] of

---

[4]As a reminder, a trace is the sequence of the tasks in an execution with associated process' states at every step of the execution.

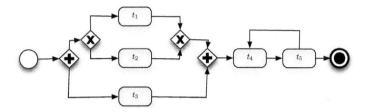

Figure 9. Process Model containing Loop

a model comply with the regulatory framework, are not applicable to this variant of the problem as some of these traces can in theory be infinite, and such approaches could never terminate and return a result.

Therefore, introducing loops into the model would make pure brute force approaches, the ones analysing the generated traces of a model, completely obsolete. We argue that similar issues would apply to every approach analysing the traces instead of the structure of the model, however techniques to recognise repeating patterns in the process' states could be potentially used to recognise loops and study their compliance effects. However whether this techniques would work, and the actual computational complexity of the problem including loops are both unanswered research questions.

4.2.2 Structural Analysis

Differently, approaches that analyse the process's structure without the need to analyse each trace explicitly, would still be able to terminate in a finite amount of steps. Thus, we argue that such kind of approaches, which do not need to explicitly analyse the traces, are the only viable approaches when dealing with process models containing loops.

However, the theoretical computational complexity of the variants of the problem identified in Section 3, with the inclusion of loops, is at least as difficult as the ones not including loops. This is due to the additional complexity brought by including the loops in the process model. While the added complexity may not necessarily be enough to increase the computational complexity class of the variants to harder ones, a through analysis of the computational complexity of the new variants including loops is still required in order to properly classify them.

4.2.3 Relating to Complete Turing Machines

We discuss now the intuition concerning why introducing loops in business process model, in addition to including conditions in the decision points[5], would allow potentially to simulate universal Turing machines using these extended business process models.

Definition 4.1 (Turing Completeness) *In computability theory, a system of data-manipulation rules (such as a computer's instruction set, a programming language, or a cellular automaton) is said to be Turing complete or computationally universal if it can be used to simulate any Turing machine.*

Considering now adding into the business process models conditions for its loops, like starting and exit conditions, and decision condition for the mutual exclusive paths in the process model, it becomes more and more evident how the elements of a business process model can simulate different structures common to programming languages, such as various type of cycles and decision blocks. As these programming languages are generally known to be Turing complete languages, such as for instance *Java* and *C++*, considering the process state as the computational state of Turing machine, and the possible executions of a model as the possible computations of the Turing machine, then we can conclude that with these additions, such models become Turing complete.

As a consequence, considering the *halting problem*[6] [Turing, 1937] affecting Turing machines, it would then also affect the problem of proving regulatory compliance of business process models including loops. Which, in turn, would make the problem of proving compliance in general *undecidable*.

4.2.4 Relation to Fairness

Given the relation between the problem of proving regulatory compliance of business process models and computer programs, which becomes particularly clear when loops and conditions are introduced within the process model. It is only fair to discuss some of the related work dealing with the termination of computer programs, in particular as the computational complexity of dealing with such more advanced variants of the problem is related to the undecidability of halting problem.

The relation we are going to discuss is the one with the concept of *fairness for model checking verification* as discussed earlier by Francez [1986], which

---

[5]We consider as decision points XOR blocks and loops, where a decision is required to be made concerning which branch to execute, or whether to exit the loop.

[6]The halting problem is the problem of determining, from a description of an arbitrary computer program and an input, whether the program will finish running or continue to run forever.

can be intuitively understood as the following: given two properties of comparable importance for a problem, if a certain effort is put into the verification of one of the property, then it is only *fair* that the same amount of effort is put towards the verification of the other property. Such concept led to Cook *et al.* [2007] to investigate the verification of liveness properties of programs in addition to their safety properties. Others, such as Dobrikov *et al.* [2016] proposed implementations under *fairness* assumptions, capable of verifying how fairly model checking approaches perform, with limited overhead. Moreover, Kesten *et al.* [2006] propose a fairness based approach based on LTL for model checking verification, showing that the introduction of fairness allows to close the gap with other approaches using CTL, as by using strong fairness, LTL properties can be verified on the model being checked without having to completely unfold the model to generate the possible states.

Adopting fairness to verify properties of models allows to do so without having to unfold these models and explicitly verify the possible states, in particular by adopting *strong fairness*, which is also referred as *compassion*. This requirement, compassion, stipulates that, given two types of states, then in every computation which verifies infinitely many of one of the types, is also required to verify infinitely many of the other type.

Considering now the problem of verifying regulatory compliance of business process models including loops, and assuming the existence of conditions governing choices such as mutually exclusive paths in the model, and whether a loop should be repeated or exited. It can be noticed that fairness based approached for model checking can be adapted to deal with such kind of problems. In particular, if we consider loops in a process model and its entering and exiting conditions as conditions leading to two different types of states for which we require *strong fairness*, then approaches verifying compliance, even by analysing the traces of the model explicitly, would be required to analyse an equivalent amount of states within and outside loops, guaranteeing to consider in such a way traces that represent full executions of the model. While this technique can prove useful to verify partial compliance of process models, as it requires to find a compliant trace, further analysis may be necessary when dealing with full compliance, as in order to be classified as such, every possible trace must be considered and verified.

4.3 Summary

Despite the added expressivity introduced by using unstructured business process models and loops can be useful to represent real world problems more faithfully, how such additions would affect the computational complexity of the variants of the problem discussed in Section 3 remain for the major part an unanswered research question.

5 Classification of Existing Approaches

In this section we consider and classify according to the variants identified in the present chapter some of the existing approaches proposed in the literature, and aiming to prove regulatory compliance of business process models. We organise the approaches according to the main technique used to solve the problem of proving regulatory compliance.

5.1 Control-Flow Based

These approaches focus on checking the execution order of the tasks in the business process models. To do so, temporal logic is generally used to verify properties over the execution orders of the tasks, some instances of this type of solution have been provided by Awad *et al.* [2008], and by Lu *et al.* [2007]. As the properties expressed through temporal logic formulae apply through the whole extents of the executions of the model, and refer directly to the tasks[7], then we can assign these approaches to the variant **nG-** of the problem.

Other approaches based on the control-flow can use different formalisms to represent the constraints between the execution order of the tasks. One of such approaches proposed by Groefsema *et al.* [2018], uses *CTL**[8] to describe the constraints between the execution order of the tasks. As this approach allows to express conditional constraint, it can then be classified as belonging to the variant **nL-**. Mind that the approach proposed by Groefsema *et al.* adopts also some practical optimisation, as it does reduce the space-state while preserving the information contained in the concurrent components of the model. This provides only a practical optimisation for the problem, while the theoretical computational complexity still holds for its worst case scenarios.

5.2 Temporal Logic Related

The approach proposed by Elgammal *et al.* [2016] introduces a new language to represent the execution constraints between the tasks of a business process model. This language, named *Compliance Request Language*, is used by Elgammal *et al.* to define patterns that must be followed by the executions of the model. While the language proposed allows to compactly express

---

[7]Having constraints referring directly to the tasks, in this case where temporal logic is used, it means that some constraint over the execution order is expressed between two particular tasks. When this is the case, the constraints refer to the labels of the tasks, which can be considered as propositional literal.

[8]CTL* is a combination of computational tree logic and linear temporal logic, which allows to combine path quantifiers and temporal operators.

these patterns, the authors shows that *Linear Temporal Logic* can be used to represent the patterns. As the constraints over the executions of the business process model are conditional, we can assign this approach to the variant **nL-**.

5.3 Classical Logic Related

Considering now approaches [Knuplesch *et al.*, 2010; Ghose and Koliadis, 2007; Indiono *et al.*, 2018; Haarmann *et al.*, 2018] adopting classical logic formalisms to represent the constraints over the execution of the process model, the introduction of logical formulae allows to represent more complex conditions and constraints. For instance the constraint over the order execution of a task can be conditional with respect to the execution of a set of tasks, or the combined effects of a set of tasks must be achieved before a given deadline. Given the expressivity that can be achieved by such approaches, then we classify as belonging to the variant **nL+**.

5.4 Modal Logic Related

Other approaches, such as the ones proposed by Sadiq *et al.* [2007], and Governatori [2015], adopt modal logic to represent the constraints over the allowed execution orders of the tasks of a business process model. While the inclusion of modalities over classical logic based approaches allows to improve the expressivity of the constraints, the more expressive constraints are still compatible with the variant **nL+** of the problem.

5.5 Practical Optimisations

Given the inherent computational complexity of the problem, several approaches have adopted techniques allowing to reduce the search state-space of the problem to limit the state explosion in concurrent processes. However, these approaches either generate large amounts of overhead, such as for instance the one introduced by Nakajima [2002], or lose information on concurrency and the orders of local tasks due to the linearisation of the concurrent components of the process model, as shown in the following approaches [Choi and Zhao, 2005; Sadiq *et al.*, 2005; Feja *et al.*, 2009; Hoffmann *et al.*, 2012]. We classify the approaches based on practical optimisations as belonging to the variant **nL-**.

5.6 Summary

We conclude this section by summarising the classification of some of the existing approaches in Table 4.

The first thing that can be noticed is that every single approach falls into the **NP**-complete computational complexity class when the goal is to prove partial compliance of a business process model. Differently, if the aim is to

Problem Variant	Approach
nG-	Control-Flow Based [Awad *et al.*, 2008]
	Control-Flow Based [Lu *et al.*, 2007]
nL-	Control-Flow Based using CTL* [Groefsema *et al.*, 2018]
	Temporal Logic [Elgammal *et al.*, 2016]
	Practical Optimisation [Nakajima, 2002]
	Practical Optimisation [Choi and Zhao, 2005]
	Practical Optimisation [Sadiq *et al.*, 2005]
	Practical Optimisation [Feja *et al.*, 2009]
	Practical Optimisation [Hoffmann *et al.*, 2012]
nL+	Classical Logic [Knuplesch *et al.*, 2010]
	Classical Logic [Ghose and Koliadis, 2007]
	Classical Logic [Indiono *et al.*, 2018]
	Classical Logic [Haarmann *et al.*, 2018]
	Modal Logic [Sadiq *et al.*, 2007]
	Modal Logic [Governatori, 2015]

Table 4. Classifying Existing Approaches

verify whether a model is fully compliant with the given regulations, then the logic based approaches are in coNP-complete, while the others can be theoretically solved in polynomial time.

The second and final observation over Table 4, concerns the distribution of the approaches over the various variants of the problem. We would like to point out that when global ordering constraints, as given in *control-flow* based approaches, then the problem lies in the nG- variant. Introducing conditional constraints, usually through the adoption of *temporal logics* or derivates, moves the problems into the nL- variant. Finally, when full fledged *logical formalisms* are used to represent the constraints, then the problem reaches the most difficult variant discussed in this chapter: nL+.

6 Conformance and Normative Reasoning

In this section we discuss some disciplines related to the problem of proving regulatory compliance of business process models. In particular we discuss *conformance*, verifying whether a trace from a log is a proper execution of a given process model, and normative reasoning, the discipline tasked with reasoning and deal with normative concepts, such as obligations and violations.

In addition to discuss the relations of these disciplines with the problem discussed in this chapter, we also discuss their computational complexity and how it relates to the results presented in this chapter for the problem of proving regulatory compliance.

6.1   Conformance Checking

Conformance checking, as defined by van der Aalst [2012], refers to the discipline of verifying whether the executions contained in a given event log are the proper executions of a given process model. To put it differently, using van der Aalst words: "The goal is to find commonalities and discrepancies between the modeled behaviour and the observed behaviour."

While conformance checking and compliance checking are orthogonal disciplines, mainly related as both deal with business process models, both prove useful in verifying the properties of models and their actual behaviour, and used together allows to ensure the compliance of the actual behaviours of business process models in real life scenarios. Considering a business process model used by an organisation, its compliance can be verified by using one of the many available techniques. In particular, if we focus on the case where *full compliance* is being proven for such a model, what is verified is that every proper execution of the model is compliant with the regulatory framework in place. However, while this is indeed a desirable property of a business process model, as van der Aalst mentions, its not always the case that the modelled behaviour of a business process model in an organisation, perfectly reflects the actual observed behaviour of how such organisation performs its business. Therefore, *conformance* becomes extremely important to verify whether the actual behaviour follows the modelled one, ensuring in this way that the organisation is compliant with the regulations. Moreover, when discrepancies are detected, it is desirable to realign the modelled behaviour of the organisation with the observed one, using available techniques such as for instance *process mining* [van der Aalst, 2016][9], in such a way the compliance of the realigned model can be rechecked and if the actual behaviour of the organisation keeps following the realigned model, then regulatory compliance is assured.

6.1.1   Token Replay

A technique to verify conformance of traces in a given event log with respect to a business process model is by using token replay [Rozinat and Van der Aalst, 2008]. This technique, as the name suggests, consists of trying to replay the traces over the model. One thing to notice, is that this technique is originally designed to verify the conformance of event logs with workflow models based on petri nets, such as the approach proposed by Adriansyah

---

[9]With the term process mining, we refer to techniques capable of distilling a business process model fitting a given event log of traces. Such techniques can be used to construct a process model from scratch, or to adapt existing process models to properly fit the actual observed behaviour. While this is another relevant discipline related to business process models, we do not delve in its details in this chapter as it is only marginally related to the problem of proving regulatory compliance.

et al. [2010], as described in Chapter 4, Part 2, Section 2.2. Despite this difference, the technique can be adapted to deal with business process models as well, especially given their similarities as pointed out by Kiepuszewski *et al.* [2000].

The original technique, replaying traces over workflow models constructed using petri nets, is based on going through the list of tasks representing the trace being checked whether it conforms with the workflow model. The workflow is setup having a token in its starting *place*, and each task in the trace is then checked to verify whether the current state of the model allows its execution, in accordance to the state of the tokens[10]. After, tokens in the precondition set are consumed and recreated in the postcondition set of the task in the model. This is repeated for every task composing the trace, and at the end of the analysis, every discrepancy detected, like missing required tokens to execute a task in the order defined by the trace, as well as remaining tokens in the model's places, with the exception of the final place[11], is considered to determine how much deviation there is between the observed behaviour and the expected behaviour of a model. Naturally, when the trace is a proper trace of the model, then no discrepancies are detected.

6.1.2 Data Driven Conformance

Understanding whether an execution, composed by simple sequence of tasks, belongs to a process model is important. Considering only the execution sequence may be in fact not enough to properly measure conformance. The execution of business process models involves additional factors, such as the state of the execution, in other words the data corresponding to the execution. This is represented in the present chapter as the process' states and associated to the execution of the tasks of the process in their corresponding traces.

Efforts towards this taking into account data while measuring conformance has already been made, as for instance by De Leoni *et al.* [2012], which adopt an approach using A^* to calculate the alignment[12] between the trace being evaluated and the process model, which allows to evaluate data and resources in addition to the execution order of the tasks in a trace.

While De Leoni *et al.* [2012] claim their approach to be sub-linear in time with respect to the size of the log and model being evaluated, it must be considered that being A^* heuristic based, hence trying to optimise the search space being investigated by smartly reducing it, there is always the

---

[10]As a reminder, in a Petri Net a task, also referred to as a transition, can be executed if every place in its precondition set contains a token.

[11]A workflow model based on Petri Nets, is considered to be sound if it is executable without leaving tokens within its internal places after the execution is concluded.

[12]Alignment is a measure related to conformance, and it measure how close, aligned, is a given execution with the possible executions of a given process model.

possibility that part of the search space containing the optimal solution (or a solution) for the problem to be discarded. In general, conformance verification procedures are solvable in time polynomial with respect to the size of the problem, as for instance the approach proposed by Sun and Su [2014], based on solving syntactic characterisations of some subclasses of *DecSerFlow* constraints[13].

6.1.3   Conformance and Legal Requirements

In addition to data, sometimes it is necessary to verify whether the actual behaviour of an organisation (its logs) conforms with the legal requirements in place. While business process regulatory compliance represents a way to indirectly verify this through its pairwise use with conformance checking, sometimes a more direct approach is desirable in particular to determine if the actual execution of instances of the process do not violate legal requirements. In this case, we can speak of run-time compliance (if checked while a process instance is executed) or auditing (if it is a post-mortem analysis of the instances). Generally, run-time compliance with the legal requirements can be handled with the same techniques adopted for design-time compliance. However, there are a few differences: the first is about the data to be used for the annotations. At design time, we do not know the actual value for the data (and most approaches assume annotations expressed as propositional/boolean variables) and those values must be instantiated by the actual value occurring in the instances of the processes. After the data has been instantiated, the theoretical complexity of auditing is reduced to the complexity of the underlying logic/framework given that the number of states is linear and it is determined by the number of entries in the process log (and every instance corresponds to a single trace of the process model). For run-time compliance, the issue is whether one is interested to check if the current instance at the then current task is compliant, in which case the complexity is the same as the complexity of auditing (given that the problem is reduced to the case of a single trace); alternatively, one can check if it is possible to terminate the current instance with no violations or all possible terminations are compliant. Clearly, both cases reduce to the situation where we have to determine if a sub-process model is compliant; in particular the (sub-)process model obtained by the original process model where we delete all paths not passing from the current task, and identifying the start of the (sub-)process model with the current task. Hence, the problem of determining if there is a compliant termination is reduced to the case of partial compliance, and all

---

[13]DecSerFlow is an extensible language, which stands for: *declarative service flow* language. It can be used to specify and monitor service flows, in addition to verify their conformance.

possible termination are compliant to full compliance.

6.2 Normative Reasoning

Finally, after having discussed the relation between business process compliance and conformance, we discuss the further relations with the area of *Normative Reasoning*, tasked about reasoning about norms and normative concepts, and how they affect various type of environment. While many different formalisms/logics/frameworks have been proposed for normative reasoning, ranging from various deontic logics [Gabbay *et al.*, 2013], different systems of non-monotonic reasoning [Prakken and Sartor, 2015; Horty, 1993; Governatori *et al.*, 2013], event calculus [Sergot *et al.*, 1986], Input/Output logic [Makinson and van der Torre, 2003] and various forms of expert systems and AI and Law systems [Bench-Capon *et al.*, 2012], the study of the complexity of legal and normative reasoning has been largely neglected. Despite this, the complexity classes for the different approach is well understood: modal logic [Ladner, 1977; Halpern and Moses, 1992] for deontic logics, though, with almost no results for conditional and dyadic deontic logic[14]; complexity of default logic, argumentation [Cadoli and Schaerf, 1993] for non-monotonic reasoning, and ad hoc results for event calculus [Chittaro and Montanari, 1996]. Practically, all approaches are **NP**-complete or with higher computational complexity. In what follows we briefly discuss some notable exceptions.

Some of the work dedicated to the complexity of normative reasoning concerns the investigation of the complexity of Input/Output logic [Sun and Ambrossio, 2015; Sun and Robaldo, 2017] where the complexity of some I/O variants is investigated also in connection to the representation of norms (including I/O with permissive norms; however, the work is dedicated to the study the complexity of logics, and not to normative reasoning problems. Most the problems (e.g., consistency, fulfilment) discussed by Sun and co-workers are not tractable. For example, consistency is some of the basic I/O logic (simple-minded I/O logic) is **NP**-complete, and fulfillment is **coNP**-complete, with higher complexity for constrained I/O logics.

The second area of research related to computational complexity and normative reasoning is the work on Defeasible Deontic Logic. Contrary to the work reported above the Defeasible Deontic Logic (also known as PCL[15] [Governatori and Rotolo, 2010b]), is computationally feasible. Governatori and Rotolo [2008b] and Governatori and Pham [2009] extended the result by Maher [2001] proving that the extensions of Defeasible Logic with deontic

---

[14]In general conditional logics received much less attention than their modal counterparts, for some complexity results see [Alenda *et al.*, 2016].

[15]Process Compliance Logic.

operators and violation operator of Governatori and Rotolo [2006] is still computationally feasible, and the extension of a defeasible theory can be computed in **P**, more specifically, the problem is linear in the size of the theory, where the size of a theory is given by the number of rules and instances of literals in the theory. The result was further extended to included permission and weak permissions [Governatori *et al.*, 2013]. Similarly, [Governatori and Rotolo, 2019] prove that temporalising PCL, allowing for explicit deadlines, and compensation does not increase the complexity of the logic, and the temporal extension can still be computed in time linear to the size of the theory, where, in this case, the size depends also on the distinct instants of time explicitly appearing in the given theory; this extends the result in [Governatori and Rotolo, 2013].

Governatori and Pham [2009] applied the work to the execution of business contracts, thus the performance of a contract can be executed in linear time. Furthermore, they discussed the issue of comparing contracts and proposed a normalisation procedure to this end. However, they did not investigate the complexity of the normalisation problem. Governatori and Rotolo [2019] address this issue in the context of a temporal extension of the logic, and while they do not give a complexity result they provide an (exponential) upper-bound. Accordingly, they conjecture the problem to be computationally hard but argue that it might not be a problem for real life applications since the problematic cases are typically not very frequent and limited in the number of parameters.

In [Governatori and Rotolo, 2008a] the logic was used for modelling agents, in particular to the modelling of the so called social agents, i.e., agents where there is a conflict between one of their intention and a norm, they give an higher preference to the norm, dropping thus the conflicting intention. However, Governatori and Rotolo shown that there are situations where, even for social agents, adhering to the agent plan ends up in a non-compliant situation. Accordingly, the restoring sociality problem is to identify a set of agent's intentions to drop to prevent the agent's plan to be non-compliant. Governatori and Rotolo proved that when norms and agents are represented using Defeasible Deontic Logic the restoring sociality problem is **NP**-complete. The logic employed in [Governatori and Rotolo, 2008a] can be used to model business processes, after all, one can consider a business process as the set of traces, where each trace is a sequence of task, where the annotations corresponds to the effects of the tasks, and the states include the preconditions of the tasks. Hence, the plan library of an agent can be understood as business process (or a set of business processes), where the intentions and the facts of a theory determine what are the traces/processes/sub-processes to be executed.

Accordingly, the restoring sociality problem can be seen as a special case to recovery from non-compliance for business processes (in the **nL-** space).

7 Summary and Open Problems

In this chapter we focused our attention on the computational complexity of proving regulatory compliance of business process models. We first describe the variants of the problem by reusing the same classification used by Colombo Tosatto *et al.* [2019]. After discussing the existing computational complexity results, we moved to discussing neighbouring areas which still require much investigation, in order to understand the computational complexity of a broader spectrum of the variants of the problem.

Finally, we conclude this chapter by listing the open problems identified.

7.1 Proving Partial Compliance for the Variant 1L-

This particular variant of the problem of proving regulatory compliance, identified by Colombo Tosatto *et al.* [2019], involves verifying whether a structured business process model is compliant with a single conditional obligation whose parameters are represented by using propositional literals.

While Colombo Tosatto *et al.* proposed a conjecture, reported in Conjecture 7.1, stating that the variant **1L-** should be able to be solved in time polynomial with respect to the size of the problem, we proposed in the present Chapter the opposite conjecture in Conjecture 3.6. However, no formal proof have been provided to show that the conjecture is correct. Therefore, proving that either **1L-** belongs to the computational complexity class **NP-c**, or to the class **P**, remains a problem to be solved.

Conjecture 7.1 (1L- is in P) *We currently have no information about the computational complexity of **1L-**. That is, we cannot infer its belonging to a computational complexity class in a similar way as for **nG+**, as in this case the simpler variant (**1G-**) is in **P**.*

*Our conjecture is that the computational complexity of **1L-** is in **P**. We have proven that moving from - to +, or from **1** to **n**, definitely brings the complexity into **NP-c**. In general, solutions tackling such variants have to explore the entire set of possible executions in the worst case scenarios, which precludes efficient solutions. Despite moving from **G** to **L** seems to definitely increase the complexity, we strongly believe that it does not influence the computational complexity of the problem enough to move it into **NP-c**, and polynomial solutions are still possible.*

7.2 Proving Regulatory Compliance of Unstructured Process Models

While the computational complexity of proving regulatory compliance of structured business process models has been extensively studied, the same cannot be said for unstructured process models. Therefore, a thorough analysis of the computational complexity for these unstructured variants of the problem is still an open problem. Considering that unstructured process models become structurally very similar to petri nets, investigating this similarity can be the initial step towards this analysis.

Moreover, as currently for structured process models, the variants of the problem are identified solely on adopting different properties of the regulatory framework being used to check regulatory compliance, identifying a set of structural properties of the models would allow to identify additional variants of the problem on the top of the ones already identified. The advantage in this case could be to allow a *divide and conquer* approach for studying the computational complexity of the problem, and possibly identifying simpler and harder versions of the problem.

Finally, given the relations with petri nets, correlating the structural properties of the variants of the compliance problems involving unstructured processes with known issues of petri nets (i.e., the undecidability of coloured Petri Nets) may be able to provide interesting results, which can potentially benefits both problems.

7.3 The Impact of Loops

Loops can be included in the business process models to improve the expressivity of the problem, allowing the repeated execution of tasks. Despite the obvious usefulness of including these type of constructs in process models, how much their inclusion increases the computational complexity of the problem in either structured and unstructured variants has not yet been studied.

As discussed in this chapter, introducing loops in business process models brings them closer to *complete Turing machines*, which also leads to the inheritance of the problems affecting them (i.e., undecidability due to the *halting problem*). Therefore, as mentioned while discussing the open problems related to proving compliance of unstructured processes, identifying a set of properties allowing to identify a relevant number of variants can help in the computational complexity analysis, as well as allowing to identify, if it exists, the line between these problem's variants separating the ones which can be considered complete Turing machines from the ones which cannot.

7.4 Conformance

While only tangentially related to the problem of proving regulatory compliance of business process models, the solutions for these problem can be used in combination to ensure stronger properties. While the computational complexity of verifying conformance has been shown to not be a big obstacle for the problems considered, their scope can be definitely broadened to cover more interesting variants, such as for instance considering the regulatory requirements provided by a regulatory framework while conformance is being verified, where the additional challenges are related to the data (how to ensure that the "concrete" data at run-time/auditing correspond to the "abstract" data specified in the annotations of the tasks. In addition, normative requirements can span across multiple instances of the process (and multiple processes) and, in general, the instances are not synchronised.

BIBLIOGRAPHY

[Adriansyah et al., 2010] Arya Adriansyah, Boudewijn F. van Dongen, and Wil M.P. van der Aalst. Towards robust conformance checking. In *International Conference on Business Process Management*, LNBIP 66, pages 122–133, Berlin, Heidelberg, 2010. Springer.

[Alchourrón et al., 1985] Carlos E. Alchourrón, Peter Gärdenfors, and David Makinson. On the logic of theory change: Partial meet contraction and revision functions. *Journal of Symbolic Logic*, 50(2):510–530, 1985.

[Alenda et al., 2016] Régis Alenda, Nicola Olivetti, and Gian Luca Pozzato. Nested sequent calculi for normal conditional logics. *Journal of Logic and Computation*, 26(1):7–50, 2016.

[Awad et al., 2008] Ahmed Awad, Gero Decker, and Mathias Weske. Efficient compliance checking using BPMN-Q and temporal logic. In *Business Process Management*, LNCS 5240, pages 326–341. Springer, Berlin, Heidelberg, 2008.

[Bench-Capon et al., 2012] Trevor Bench-Capon, Michał Araszkiewicz, Kevin Ashley, Katie Atkinson, Floris Bex, Filipe Borges, Daniele Bourcier, Paul Bourgine, Jack G. Conrad, Enrico Francesconi, et al. A history of AI and Law in 50 papers: 25 years of the international conference on AI and Law. *Artificial Intelligence and Law*, 20(3):215–319, 2012.

[Cadoli and Schaerf, 1993] Marco Cadoli and Marco Schaerf. A survey of complexity results for non-monotonic logics. *The Journal of Logic Programming*, 17(2-4):127–160, 1993.

[Chittaro and Montanari, 1996] Luca Chittaro and Alberto Montanari. Efficient temporal reasoning in the cached event calculus. *Computational Intelligence*, 12(3):359–382, 1996.

[Choi and Zhao, 2005] Yongsun Choi and J. Leon Zhao. Decomposition-based verification of cyclic workflows. In *Automated Technology for Verification and Analysis*, LNCS 3707, pages 84–98. Springer, Berlin, Heidelberg, 2005.

[Colombo Tosatto et al., 2015a] Silvano Colombo Tosatto, Guido Governatori, and Pierre Kelsen. Business process regulatory compliance is hard. *IEEE Transactions on Services Computing*, 8(6):958–970, 2015.

[Colombo Tosatto et al., 2015b] Silvano Colombo Tosatto, Pierre Kelsen, Qin Ma, Marwane El Kharbili, Guido Governatori, and Leendert W.N. van der Torre. Algorithms for tractable compliance problems. *Frontiers of Computer Science*, 9(1):55–74, 2015.

[Colombo Tosatto *et al.*, 2019] Silvano Colombo Tosatto, Guido Governatori, and Nick van Beest. Checking regulatory compliance: Will we live to see it? In *Business Process Management*, LNCS 11675, pages 119–138. Springer, Cham, 2019.

[Colombo Tosatto *et al.*, 2020] Silvano Colombo Tosatto, Guido Governatori, and Nick R.T.P. van Beest. Business process full compliance with respect to a set of conditional obligation in polynomial time. https://arxiv.org/abs/2001.10148, 1 2020.

[Colombo Tosatto *et al.*, 2021] Silvano Colombo Tosatto, Guido Governatori, and Nick R.T.P. van Beest. Proving regulatory compliance: A comprehensive computational complexity analysis. https://arxiv.org/abs/2105.05431v1, 2021.

[Colombo Tosatto, 2015] Silvano Colombo Tosatto. *Proving Regulatory Compliance: Business Processes, Logic, Complexity*. PhD thesis, University of Luxembourg and Università di Torino, 2015.

[Cook *et al.*, 2007] Byron Cook, Alexey Gotsman, Andreas Podelski, Andrey Rybalchenko, and Moshe Y. Vardi. Proving that programs eventually do something good. In *Proceedings of the 34th Annual ACM SIGPLAN-SIGACT Symposium on Principles of Programming Languages*, POPL '07, pages 265–276, New York, NY, USA, 2007. ACM.

[de Leoni *et al.*, 2012] Massimiliano de Leoni, Wil M.P. van der Aalst, and Boudewijn F. van Dongen. Data- and resource-aware conformance checking of business processes. In *Business Information Systems*, LNBIP 117, pages 48–59. Springer, Berlin, Heidelberg, 2012.

[Dobrikov *et al.*, 2016] Ivaylo Dobrikov, Michael Leuschel, and Daniel Plagge. LTL model checking under fairness in PROBB. In *Software Engineering and Formal Methods*, LNCS 9763, pages 204–211. Springer, Cham, 2016.

[Elgammal *et al.*, 2016] Amal Elgammal, Oktay Turetken, Willem-Jan van den Heuvel, and Mike Papazoglou. Formalizing and appling compliance patterns for business process compliance. *Software & Systems Modeling*, 15(1):119–146, 2016.

[Esparza, 1994] Javier Esparza. On the decidability of model checking for several μ-calculi and petri nets. In Sophie Tison, editor, *Trees in Algebra and Programming — CAAP'94*, LNCS 787, pages 115–129. Springer, Berlin, Heidelberg, 1994.

[Feja *et al.*, 2009] Sven Feja, Andreas Speck, and Elke Pulvermüller. Business process verification. In *GI Jahrestagung*, pages 4037–4051, 2009.

[Francez, 1986] Nissim Francez. *Fairness*. Springer-Verlag, Berlin, Heidelberg, 1986.

[Gabbay *et al.*, 2013] Dov Gabbay, Jeff Horty, Xavier Parent, Ron van der Meyden, and Leendert W.N. van der Torre, editors. *Handbook of deontic logic and normative systems*. College Publication, 2013.

[Ghose and Koliadis, 2007] Aditya Ghose and George Koliadis. Auditing business process compliance. In *Service Oriented Computing*, LNCS 4749, pages 169–180. Springer, Berlin, Heidelberg, 2007.

[Governatori and Pham, 2009] Guido Governatori and Duy Hoang Pham. DR-CONTRACT: an architecture for e-contracts in defeasible logic. *International Journal of Business Process Integration and Management*, 4(3):187–199, 2009.

[Governatori and Rotolo, 2006] Guido Governatori and Antonino Rotolo. Logic of violations: A Gentzen system for reasoning with contrary-to-duty obligations. *Australasian Journal of Logic*, 4:193–215, 2006.

[Governatori and Rotolo, 2008a] Guido Governatori and Antonino Rotolo. BIO logical agents: Norms, beliefs, intentions in defeasible logic. *Journal of Autonomous Agents and Multi Agent Systems*, 17(1):36–69, 2008.

[Governatori and Rotolo, 2008b] Guido Governatori and Antonino Rotolo. A computational framework for institutional agency. *Artificial Intelligence and Law*, 16(1):25–52, 2008.

[Governatori and Rotolo, 2010a] Guido Governatori and Antonino Rotolo. A conceptually rich model of business process compliance. In *7th Asia-Pacific Conference on Conceptual Modelling*, CRPIT 110, pages 3–12. ACS, 2010.

[Governatori and Rotolo, 2010b] Guido Governatori and Antonino Rotolo. Norm compliance in business process modeling. In *RuleML 2010*, LNCS 6403, pages 194–209. Springer, Berlin, Heidelberg, 2010.

[Governatori and Rotolo, 2013] Guido Governatori and Antonino Rotolo. Computing temporal defeasible logic. In *RuleML 2013*, LNCS 8035, pages 114–128. Springer, Berlin, Heidelberg, 2013.

[Governatori and Rotolo, 2019] Guido Governatori and Antonino Rotolo. Time and compensation mechanisms in checking legal compliance. *Journal of Applied Logics – IFCoLog Journal of Logics and their Applications*, 6(5):817–847, 2019.

[Governatori et al., 2013] Guido Governatori, Francesco Olivieri, Antonino Rotolo, and Simone Scannapieco. Computing strong and weak permissions in defeasible logic. *Journal of Philosophical Logic*, 42(6):799–829, 2013.

[Governatori, 2015] Guido Governatori. The Regorous approach to process compliance. In *2015 IEEE 19th International Enterprise Distributed Object Computing Workshop*, pages 33–40. IEEE, 2015.

[Groefsema et al., 2018] Heerko Groefsema, Nick R.T.P van Beest, and Marco Aiello. A formal model for compliance verification of service compositions. *IEEE Transactions on Services Computing*, 11(3):466–479, 2018.

[Haarmann et al., 2018] Stephan Haarmann, Kimon Batoulis, and Mathias Weske. Compliance checking for decision-aware process models. In *Business Process Management Workshops. BPM 2018*, LNBIP 342, pages 494–506. Springer, Cham, 2018.

[Halpern and Moses, 1992] Joseph Y. Halpern and Yoram Moses. A guide to completeness and complexity for modal logics of knowledge and belief. *Artificial intelligence*, 54(3):319–379, 1992.

[Hashmi et al., 2016] Mustafa Hashmi, Guido Governatori, and Moe Thandar Wynn. Normative requirements for regulatory compliance: An abstract formal framework. *Information Systems Frontiers*, 18(3):429–455, 2016.

[Hashmi et al., 2018] Mustafa Hashmi, Guido Governatori, Ho-Pun Lam, and Moe Wynn. Are we done with business process compliance: State-of-the-art and challenges ahead. *Knowledge and Information Systems*, 01 2018.

[Hoffmann et al., 2012] Jörg Hoffmann, Ingo Weber, and Guido Governatori. On compliance checking for clausal constraints in annotated process models. *Information Systems Frontiers*, 14(2):155–177, 2012.

[Horty, 1993] John F. Horty. Deontic logic as founded on nonmonotonic logic. *Annals of Mathematics and Artificial Intelligence*, 9(1-2):69–91, 1993.

[Indiono et al., 2018] Conrad Indiono, Walid Fdhila, and Stefanie Rinderle-Ma. Evolution of instance-spanning constraints in process aware information systems. In *OTM Confederated International Conference "On the Move to Meaningful Internet Systems"*, LNCS 11229, pages 298–317. Springer, Cham, 2018.

[Keller and Teufel, 1998] Gerhard Keller and Thomas Teufel. *SAP R/3 Process Oriented Implementation*. Addison-Wesley Longman Publishing Co., Inc., Boston, MA, USA, 1st edition, 1998.

[Kesten et al., 2006] Yonit Kesten, Amir Pnueli, Li-On Raviv, and Elad Shahar. Model checking with strong fairness. *Formal Methods in System Design*, 28(1):57–84, Jan 2006.

[Kiepuszewski et al., 2000] Bartek Kiepuszewski, Arthur H.M. ter Hofstede, and Christoph Bussler. On structured workflow modelling. In *CAISE 2000*, LNCS 1789, pages 431–445. Springer-Verlag, Berlin, Heidelberg, 2000.

[Knuplesch et al., 2010] David Knuplesch, Linh Thao Ly, Stefanie Rinderle-Ma, Holger Pfeifer, and Peter Dadam. On enabling data-aware compliance checking of business process models. In *Conceptual Modelling, ER 2010*, LNCS 6412, pages 332–346. Springer, Berlin, Heidelberg, 2010.

[Ladner, 1977] Richard E. Ladner. The computational complexity of provability in systems of modal propositional logic. *SIAM journal on computing*, 6(3):467–480, 1977.

[Lohmann et al., 2009] Niels Lohmann, Eric Verbeek, and Remco Dijkman. Petri net transformations for business processes – a survey. In Kurt Jensen and Wil M.P. van der Aalst, editors, *Transactions on Petri Nets and Other Models of Concurrency II: Special Issue on Concurrency in Process-Aware Information Systems*, LNCS 5460, pages 46–63. Springer, Berlin, Heidelberg, 2009.

[Lu et al., 2007] Ruopeng Lu, Shazia Sadiq, and Guido Governatori. Compliance aware business process design. In *Business Process Management WOrkshop*, LNCS 4928, pages 120–131. Springer, Berlin, Heidelberg, 2007.

[Maher, 2001] Michael J. Maher. Propositional defeasible logic has linear complexity. *Theory and Practice of Logic Programming*, 1(6):691–711, 2001.

[Makinson and van der Torre, 2003] David Makinson and Leendert W.N. van der Torre. Permission from an input/output perspective. *Journal of philosophical logic*, 32(4):391–416, 2003.

[Makungu et al., 1999] Mediatrix Makungu, Michel Barbeau, and Richard St-Denis. Synthesis of controllers of processes modeled as colored petri nets. *Discrete Event Dynamic Systems*, 9:147–169, 05 1999.

[Murata, 1989] T. Murata. Petri nets: Properties, analysis and applications. *Proceedings of the IEEE*, 77(4):541–580, 1989.

[Nakajima, 2002] Shin Nakajima. Verification of Web service flows with model-checking techniques. In *Proceedings of First International Symposium on Cyber Worlds*, pages 378–385. IEEE, 2002.

[Polyvyanyy et al., 2012] Artem Polyvyanyy, Luciano García-Ba nuelos, and Marlon Dumas. Structuring acyclic process models. *Information Systems*, 37(6):518 – 538, 2012.

[Polyvyanyy et al., 2014] Artem Polyvyanyy, Luciano García-Bañuelos, Dirk Fahland, and Mathias Weske. Maximal structuring of acyclic process models. *The Computer Journal*, 57, 01 2014.

[Prakken and Sartor, 2015] Henry Prakken and Giovanni Sartor. Law and logic: A review from an argumentation perspective. *Artificial Intelligence*, 227:214–245, 2015.

[PWC, 2017] PWC. *2017 Risk and Compliance Benchmarking Survey*, 2017.

[Rozinat and Van der Aalst, 2008] Anne Rozinat and Wil M.P. Van der Aalst. Conformance checking of processes based on monitoring real behavior. *Information Systems*, 33(1):64–95, 2008.

[Sadiq et al., 2005] Shazia Sadiq, Maria E. Orlowska, and Wasim Sadiq. Specification and validation of process constraints for flexible workflows. *Information System*, 30(5):349–378, 2005.

[Sadiq et al., 2007] Shazia Sadiq, Guido Governatori, and Kioumars Namiri. Modeling control objectives for business process compliance. In *Business Process Management*, LNCS 4714, pages 149–164. Springer, Berlin, Heidelberg, 2007.

[Sergot et al., 1986] Marek J. Sergot, Fariba Sadri, Robert A. Kowalski, Frank Kriwaczek, Peter Hammond, and H. Terese Cory. The british nationality act as a logic program. *Communications of the ACM*, 29(5):370–386, 1986.

[Sun and Ambrossio, 2015] Xin Sun and Diego Agustín Ambrossio. Computational complexity of input/output logic. In *Multi-disciplinary Trends in Artificial Intelligence, MIWAI 2015*, LNCS 9426, pages 72–79. Springer, Berlin, Heidelberg, 2015.

[Sun and Robaldo, 2017] Xin Sun and Livio Robaldo. On the complexity of input/output logic. *Journal of Applied Logic*, 25:69–88, 2017.

[Sun and Su, 2014] Yutian Sun and Jianwen Su. Conformance for decserflow constraints. In *Service-Oriented Computing*, LNCS 8831, pages 139–153. Springer, Berlin, Heidelberg, 2014.

[Turing, 1937] A. M. Turing. On Computable Numbers, with an Application to the Entscheidungsproblem. *Proceedings of the London Mathematical Society*, s2-42(1):230–265, 01 1937.

498

[van der Aalst, 1995] Wil M.P. van der Aalst. *A class of Petri nets for modeling and analyzing business processes.* Computing science reports. Technische Universiteit Eindhoven, 1995.

[van der Aalst, 1997] Wil M.P. van der Aalst. Verification of workflow nets. In *Application and Theory of Petri Nets 1997*, LNCS 1248, pages 407–426. Springer-Verlag, Berlin, Heidelberg, 1997.

[van der Aalst, 1998] Wil M.P. van der Aalst. The application of petri nets to workflow management. *Journal of Circuits, Systems, and Computers*, 8(1):21–66, 1998.

[van der Aalst, 2012] Wil M.P. van der Aalst. Distributed process discovery and conformance checking. In Juan de Lara and Andrea Zisman, editors, *Fundamental Approaches to Software Engineering*, LNCS 7212, pages 1–25. Springer, Berlin, Heidelberg, 2012.

[van der Aalst, 2016] Wil M.P. van der Aalst. *Process Mining: Data Science in Action.* Springer, Heidelberg, 2 edition, 2016.

Silvano Colombo Tosatto
Data61 CSIRO
41 Boggo Road, Dutton Park
QLD 4102, Australia
Email: silvano.colombotosatto@data61.csiro.au

Guido Governatori
Brisbane, Queensland 4121, Australia
Email: guido@governatori.net

13

An Exploratory Study on the Use of Artificial Intelligence to Initiate Legal Understanding for Business Development

ALESSIA GRASSI
MAURO VALLATI

ABSTRACT. Given the dynamic environment and the ever-changing international context, it is pivotal for companies to be able to quickly and effectively identify potential threats and opportunities. This can be done via environmental scanning, that allows to develop and analyse potential scenarios which help in proactively plan responses to potential risks. Yet, the process of scanning, and the design and analysis of scenarios, is extremely expensive, as it has to be done manually. Therefore, they cannot be exploited as often as they should to deliver the maximal benefit to a company.

In this Chapter, we propose the use of Artificial Intelligence (AI) techniques to support the PESTLE analysis, a managerial tool used to identify those external factors which might affect a company. In particular, we focus on one of the environments scanned through PESTLE, the legal environment, and how AI can support this time and labour consuming process.

1 Introduction

Companies operate in an ever-changing and dynamic environment. It is not sufficient being able to react to these changes, in order to be competitive and capable to provide consumers with the right product or service. By the time a business has reacted on the information collected, and has implemented the right strategy to react to a change, it would be probably too late. The most effective way to maintain a company competitive is to dynamically anticipate these changes. By undertaking environmental scanning, from which it is possible to develop scenarios, this might be successfully achieved [Brassington and Pettitt, 2005]. There are evident limitations in scanning the environment, and one of this is the approach utilised which might vary from significantly organised and principled to totally random. This not only influences the kind of information which is possible to collect and exploit, but also the level of costs which the business has to tackle. To avoid waste of resources, being aware of what is needed is key to make the most of environmental scanning and scenarios strategies. This Chapter is focusing on one specific approach widely utilised in business management to help articulate the macro-factors which can influence a business, the PESTLE analysis. This framework considers Political, Economical, Social, Technological, Legal, and Environmental factors as the main external macro-factors influencing a business strategy.

The recent advancement in technology, and especially the growing abilities of Artificial Intelligence (AI) techniques, might facilitate businesses in collating information and ease the scanning and strategising process. There has been, in particular, a significant amount of work in AI for dealing with laws and regulations. Dedicated conferences and workshops, such as JURIX[1] and ICAIL[2], and journals such as *Artificial Intelligence and Law* (Springer) focus on the design and development of AI approaches fit for the purpose of analysing and processing legal documents. Recent related works in the area focused, for instance, on the recently introduced EU General Data Protection Regulation (GDPR)[3], and include the use of machine learning systems to automatically check the compliance and adequacy of privacy policies [Contissa *et al.*, 2018], and the introduction of a dedicated GDPR ontology [Palmirani *et al.*, 2018]. More general works include the possibility to query a knowledge base of laws, in order to be provided with relevant paragraphs as answer [Collarana *et al.*, 2018]; the automated analysis of the interaction between legal systems in terms of possible arising conflicts for agents that have to operate in accordance to them [Li *et al.*, 2013]; and the use of a compliance management framework to expressively represent the specifications of normative requirements that impose constraints on various activities of a business process [Hashmi and Governatori, 2018]. On related topics, there has also been a significant amount of work in investigating the use of AI approaches in courts [Arisaka *et al.*, 2017; Bench-Capon *et al.*, 2009].

Here the authors discuss the possible benefits deriving from the exploitation of AI techniques to one of the macro-factors considered in the PESTLE analysis, the legal environment. This specific environment was chosen because it presents clear opportunities for classifications, due to its structured nature. Thus, it might foster the design of a modular approach, where each

---

[1] http://jurix.nl
[2] https://icail2019-cyberjustice.com
[3] https://eugdpr.org

module is capable of addressing the needs of a specific class, while maintaining flexibility and extensibility. Each module can therefore be designed and developed in isolation, and the most appropriate approaches can be exploited according to needs and requirements. The main contribution of this work, beside the classification of main aspects that businesses have to deal with in regards to the legal environment, is the analysis of potentially-suitable AI methods, and the description of an overall framework that can be used as a basis for the design of the aforementioned modules.

The remainder of this Chapter is organised as follows. The next section further explores the PESTLE framework and its importance in businesses' decision-making process. Section 3 gives details of the legal environment, and Section 4 introduces the proposed classification of legal aspects to be dealt with in the context of the PESTLE analysis. The modular AI framework is described in Section 5. Finally, Section 6 gives the conclusions and highlights future works in the area.

2 The PESTLE Analysis

Despite being called PESTLE analysis, PESTLE is not an analysis instrument but more a framework used to remember all the important factors which might influence the operations of a company. In particular, it is one of the most exploited models used to analyse the main variables which might influence the company's decision-making processes at a macro level. [Marmol and Feys, 2015]. The name of the model is an acronym for the six external variables –the first version included only four– which are fundamental considering when developing or expanding a business: Political, Economical, Social, Technological, Legal, and Environmental (Figure 1). Companies utilise this model to investigate macroeconomics changes which are uncontrollable and unavoidable [Baines *et al.*, 2017b]. By being able to identify, investigate, and classify the impact of all these variables, managers are facilitated in spotting potential threats which is not possible to directly control, evaluate potential high risks, and anticipate and limit these risks by developing possible future scenarios [Baines *et al.*, 2017a]. By doing so companies can conceptualise different scenarios, and develop alternative cases. The model is particularly utilised when business are developing new products, or are expanding in new countries or new markets. However, it is also used on a regular base for understanding markets dynamics and cycles, and as such to eventually evaluate the position, potential and direction for a business [Baker, 2014].

Currently, PESTLE analysis is still performed manually: human experts have to collect relevant information and analyse them to be in the position to suggest the most promising strategy to adopt in order to achieve the company's goals, or to avoid potential threats. Political and Legal factors are particularly demanding to investigate in terms of human labour and costs. Different countries and industries have specific bodies of law and principles which regulate any aspects of their market, contracts, business and stakeholders relationship. Moreover, these bodies of regulations tend to be updated and revised often, and even keep control of the changes requires some effort. Big companies inclusive of internal legal teams might face an easier process when collecting and analysing information aimed at developing new business opportunities. Yet, the time-cost and labour-cost for the collection and analysis of information are still high. For what concerns small companies, to time-cost needs to be added the cost of relaying on external legal experts which might facilitate gathering and analysing the information needed. On top of these costs, when entering new countries other barriers might complicate the process for both big and small companies, such as the language. There are organisations (private and governmental) which help small medium enterprises when exports are concerned: such as the JETRO to enter Japan, or Austrade to exit Australia [Albaum *et al.*, 2008]. In any case, even lawyers cannot always be knowledgeable of all the details concerning domestic, international and foreign legal aspects [Terpstra *et al.*, 2012]. As a consequence, by being able to initiate an understanding of a legal environment without the need for employing a significant amount of resources, companies could drastically reduce the initial costs of these processes and positively effect their performances.

The use of AI techniques to scan the legal environment for information and potential threats might help scanning even the smallest creases of laws and regulations and help firms avoiding the risk of missing some critical aspects which a human being even if well trained might miss. The implementation of AI techniques in this scenario has to be considered as an aid for firms' initial explorations regarding new opportunities for business, to assist people and not to substitute them. AI could facilitate the planning for the launch of a new product, the opening of a new retail store, or even to prepare in view of important legislation changes as recently the mandatory implementation of the EU General Data Protection Regulation. Finally, AI techniques could also facilitate the comparison between different potential strategies and help decide which one might be more effective under specific circumstances.

3   The Legal Environment

The number of legislation and regulations affecting businesses has significantly increased in the past decades, mainly due to global markets, and the expansion of e-commerce. Three are the main purposes that these legislation are attempting to achieve: protecting markets and society from irresponsi-

Figure 1. The PESTLE model, which emphasises the Political, Economical, Social, Technological, Legal, and Environmental aspects to take into account. For each aspect, examples of relevant elements to take into account are listed.

ble behaviours; protecting consumers' rights; and protecting companies from unfair competition [Wilson and Gilligan, 2012]. It is important for companies and managers to be aware not only of current legislation and practices, but also of possible future development of public interest groups and legislation directions [Wilson and Gilligan, 2012]. The possibility to utilise AI techniques to investigate the legal environment is an important perspective to avoid excessive costs at the beginning of a new process. This does not mean that firms will not need legal teams and consultants anymore; in fact, the modular approach we propose is based on interactions with humans. However, an initial automated scanning of the legislation might ease companies' processes, despite the fact that law bodies are still largely depending on human interpretation. It might be worth considering also that different cultures have different way of approaching potential legal issues. For example in Japan although an increase in the number of lawyers per capita, the demand for legal services is not as high as in other countries.[4]

As it will be properly analysed in section 4, one of the most difficult things to grasp in the legal environment is the different institutions and interest groups involved in a market and the hierarchical level they are operating at. There are national, international, and global legislation to consider, together with extra-jurisdictional bodies and institutions. Thus, it is pivotal to know who is jurisdictionally responsible at a specific level. There might be a national regulation in place regarding contracts, which might be overridden by an extra-national body. An example of international institution is UNCITRAL, a commission established by the United Nations to help in filling a communication gap between different countries and they created a Convention regarding contracts which is quite similar to an article of the United States Commercial Code, so to facilitate tradings between the US and other countries [Terpstra et al., 2012]. It is because of this diversification of bodies involved that this Chapter is providing an initial framework which collates the most significant levels to consider in a legal scanning.

3.1 Why AI might help the Legal Scanning

There are several reasons which brought the Authors to focus on the opportunities of applying AI techniques to a business tool such as PESTLE. One of these is that the number of news regarding law infringements committed by big corporations is exponentially increasing, especially due to the perfection of regulations concerning global markets and grey areas. In the UK there has been an increase of corporate fines up to 18 percent from 2016 to 2017 and only referring to health and safety regulations breach.[5] There are several other examples of law infringement: from trademark, to tax evasion; from unfair competition, to violation of labours' and humans' rights. Not to mention law suites between corporations due to suspect copyright infringements and copycats. Apple vs Microsoft, Google vs Apple, Gucci vs Guess.[6] Of course many examples might lead back to unfair business behaviour, where corporations are well aware of their acting borderlines. Yet, there are many cases where law violations are due mainly to lack of knowledge and information. It is for these cases that the use of AI techniques might be of aid and help to avoid not only the waste of resources before starting the process, but also the waste of money after due to having broken the law. It is important to consider that law violations have a significant financial repercussion on the business. However, another crucial aspect which derives from breaking

---

[4]https://blogs.wsj.com/briefly/2016/04/03/the-legal-industry-in-japan-the-numbers/

[5]https://www.hsmsearch.com/Corporate-fines-up-in-one-year

[6]https://realbusiness.co.uk/6-famous-copyright-cases

the law is the business' image damage. The bad publicity and PR which might derive from these episodes is sometimes even more dangerous than a fine and might permanently damage the ability of a firm to compete and generate profits.

The implementation of AI techniques in analysing the legal environment might prevent significant damage for companies. One of the most significant and recent example where AI might have helped in preventing significant losses is the breach of data protection. Many times these breaches happened because of the inability of companies to adhere to the GDPR regulations: among others, Yahoo and Ebay were asked to pay billions for having breached GDPR requirements. Although it is one of the most nasty issue for businesses at the moment, data breach is only one of numerous legal problems which a firm might need to face during its lifetime, and this is mainly due to the fast changing legal environment they are operating within. For example, Google was accused of tax evasion which derived from an uncertainty of the international tax system which is changing[7]; the Royal mail faced accusations of abuse of dominant position –breaking competition laws[8]; and Hugo Boss was caught in health and safety breach[9]. In all the examples, the existence of an AI system would have greatly benefit these companies and would have allowed them to avoid paying fines and, as previously said, image damages.

4   A Legislative Classification Framework

As mentioned in the previous section, the legal environment is very complex and investigating it requires a significant effort of time and resources. Although there are numerous shades in any country legal system, it is possible to create an initial classification framework which describes the main layers a business needs to consider when approaching a new market (Figure 2). Far from being a mere academic exercise, this classification plays a major role in fostering the use of AI for the legislative environment in the context of the PESTLE analysis. As better detailed in Section 5, the notion of classes can be helpful in selecting the most relevant body of laws to be analysed and considered for the reasoning, and can also characterise the sort of interaction that human experts may require to investigate corresponding aspects.

The idea behind the framework is to be a checklist or a road map for

---

[7]https://www.theguardian.com/technology/2016/jan/22/
google-agrees-to-pay-hmrc-130m-in-back-taxes

[8]https://www.theguardian.com/business/2018/aug/14/
royal-mail-fined-competition-law-ofcom-whistl

[9]https://www.shponline.co.uk/news/breaking-hugo-boss-fined-1-2m-for-health-
and-safety-breaches/

businesses through their initial legal scanning. Businesses are subject to numerous regulations, and all these regulations affect the businesses at different levels. There are global agreements such as those implemented by the World Trade Organisation (WTO), but also extra-jurisdictional regulations such as those overseen by the European Union, and finally national and local legislation issued by the hosting country. Furthermore, in some cases, companies are free to negotiate special agreements which might set them in a position of control over prices and competitors, allowing them to create entry barriers for other industries. These kinds of negotiations (and contracts) have to be considered as bodies of regulations which is not often easy to identify, especially if the company is new in the specific market. To facilitate the understanding of the different layers involved in a legal scanning a hierarchical framework was created as represented in Figure 2.

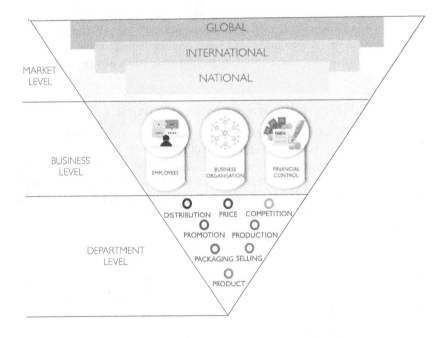

Figure 2. The classification of the legal environment into a hierarchical structure.

4.1 Market Level

4.1.1 Global Jurisdiction

The first issue a company might face when starting a legal scanning is to understand the hierarchical jurisdiction which is operating at a market level. This is particularly difficult if the company is considering to operate in an unfamiliar market. For example, consumer protection and fraud prevention regulations are generally shifting the burden of responsibility between countries and international bodies. Hence, be aware of the boundaries and limitations of regulations is a first fundamental step to avoid nasty issues and possible law suits. By being able to understand the rules which apply in a specific market and their jurisdictional hierarchies, a company might save significant resources. Yet, quick reactions and adaptations to the complexity and the continuous changes of the legal landscape could be an extreme burden for some companies. On this matter, a straightforward exploitation of AI may automatically analyse the changes in the legal landscape, and assess whether the current policies used by the company are complying or not.

As represented in Figure 2, a general classification of this first level divides the market jurisdiction into global, international, and national. An example of how a regulation could become global is the application of the GSM standard when the mobile communication revolution started. In 1987 the EU circulated a technical mandatory standard to regulate hardware and services related to mobile communication technological transformation. The transformation quickly became global and the regulation generated large economies of scales affecting the entire world. Furthermore, as mentioned in Section 3, in an effort of creating a globalised market, in 1966 the United Nation established the Commission on International Trade Law (UNCITRAL). In 1983, UNCITRAL developed the Convention on Contracts for the International Sales of Goods. This convention was an attempt of creating a single language among nations and harmonising different legal systems when regarding selling goods. Sometimes, as for the GSM example, not being able to quickly respond to changes in standards and regulations might turn into losses of market shares or of competitive advantages. Hence, it is fundamental to have a clear picture of what are the main forces operating on the market the business is attempting to approach.

4.1.2 International Jurisdiction

The same principle applies to international regulations, the second hierarchical layer at market level (Fig. 2). There are agreements and laws which can affect businesses which are operating in the European Union but, for example, not those which are operating in China or in the US. One of the most significant, and recent, examples is the modernisation of the European

Union (EU) gave to the data protection regulations by revoking the Directive (95/46/EC) in 2016 through the introduction of what is widely known as the GDPR (General Data Protection Regulation - regulation 2016/679). This is a regulation which affects all businesses operating in the European Union boundaries, and requires businesses to have appropriate mechanism in place to guarantee consumers with the opportunity to decide on how and if businesses can use their personal data. However, US businesses operating on the US soil are not obliged to respect this regulation, unless they decide to start operating on EU markets. Since the introduction of this strict regulations, there has been numerous cases of businesses fined because in breach of the regulation, as mentioned in section 3. This is one of the clearer case in which the ability of quickly identifying loopholes in the business procedures might have spared business from monetary losses and image damages, where these kinds of breaches can also influence the kind of image a firm is projecting towards consumers by not respecting their privacy. Another fundamental aspect which often is regulated internationally to avoid anti-competitive practices is price. An example is the legal battle which Microsoft have fought against the EU with regard to specific components integrated in the operating system which the EU wanted the business to make available separately. This dispute went on for several years and cost the business precious resources in terms of time and especially of money. These kinds of regulations are fundamental in the attempt of maintaining a fair competitive environment, but yet, not being able to react quickly might cost businesses a fortune.

4.1.3   National Jurisdiction

The third and final hierarchical layer at market level is the national jurisdiction. There are numerous business aspects which are not regulated globally nor internationally; sometimes international bodies provide suggestions to the single countries, but then depend on the country the decision to implement or not the provided suggestion - as often happens in the EU. Examples of these kinds of legislations, to mention some, are: the opening hours of retail stores; the imposition of specific products' taxation such as VAT in UK or IVA in Italy; safety regulation of products and work environments; and patent and copyright.

4.2   Business Level

As previously discussed, there are numerous aspects to consider when initiating a legal scanning, and the jurisdiction is the first important layer to investigate. Once the firm knows which bodies are regulating that aspect of the market, it is possible to go further in depth to a more specific level: the business level. As represented in Figure 2, this level can be divided in three macro-categories which encompass all major regulations which might impact the most significant business practices: Employees, Business Organisation, and Financial Control.

The Employees category regards all those laws and agreements which concern a business workforce. Part of this category are employees contract legislations which involve salaries, pension schemes, employees' benefits; but also working hours, annual leave regulations, work safety and environmental conditions and so on. The second category is the business organisation category. Here are considered all those regulations which might influence the organisation structure of the business: from the business hierarchical organisation, to consumers' data management. The third and final category at business level is the financial control category. Part of this group are all those regulations regarding the financial aspect of a business: from tariffs, quotas and taxes to pay; to the way profits are managed and divided among shareholders.

4.3 Department Level

Finally, the department level represented in Figure 2 is the most specific of the three levels and exemplifies all the divisions which might be involved in the business. These regulations vary from specific legislations regarding advertisement content, to product safety, packaging and labels; from competitive behaviours, to price regulations; from trade marks and patents regulations, to selling techniques legislations.

To conclude this section, there are numerous aspects which need to be considered according to the market and the country the business is operating in. The framework provided in this Chapter is an attempt of hierarchically categorise these aspects so to make it easier to design AI modules that can deal with them. Some regulations, as previously mentioned, might be established by an international organisation, some others might depend on the specific legislation of a single country, or might be a global agreement. Some agreements might affect the financial control of a business, or the human resources management; or might be even more specific and dictate specific opening hours for the retail store. By considering these three levels and all their specifications, it is safe to say that a business would be able to scan the legal environment and cover all the critical aspects involved.

5 A Modular Framework for Fostering the use of AI in Support of Legal Investigation for Businesses

The AI discipline has been increasingly turning its attention to the automated processing of complex information encoded in a non-formal structure, as it is the case of laws and regulations. In fact, two main issues arise when dealing with such type of documents and knowledge: a large body of rules and regulations are not electronically stored; and these rules strongly rely on (potentially very different) interpretations, that can depend on the context or on other involved aspects. The first issue presents mostly barriers related to limiting the human effort which is necessary to encode and classify the knowledge stored in paper-based documents. However, there is a growing interest in encoding laws and regulations in some digital form, to ease the search and analysis (also for human experts). The latter issue is extremely challenging from an AI perspective, and is now object of significant research. On the one hand, it is envisaged that the use of machine learning –that can learn from past decisions and interpretations– may help on this matter. However, on the other hand, such techniques tend to lack of explainability, and can therefore lead to hard-to-understand and non-trustworthy results.

The large amount of work done in the area, particularly in the areas of Argumentation and Knowledge Representation, suggest that a large part of the process of the PESTLE analysis can be supported by AI-based agents. This is mainly the case of the process of capturing knowledge and reasoning on top of it, for supporting the subsequent human decision process. Leveraging on recent advancements, and on the classification introduced in Section 4, we are now in the position to introduce a framework for supporting legal investigation for businesses in the context of the PESTLE analysis. The proposed framework depicted in Figure 3 includes the following four elements.

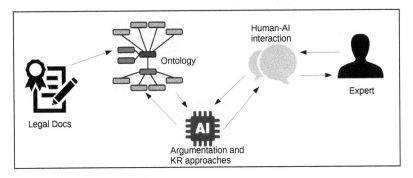

Figure 3. The proposed framework for fostering the use of AI in legal reasoning for businesses in the PESTLE context.

- **Legal documents**. There is of course the need of an appropriate corpus of legal documents, that can be encoded into suitable knowledge representation structures. On this matter, in order to reduce the burden on human experts, a number of automatic or semi-automatic approaches have been introduced. Examples include [Boella *et al.*, 2019; Nazarenko *et al.*, 2016]. Notably, it is not necessary to incorporate all the possible legal documents, but the classification provided in Section 4 has to be used to identify relevant articles. This approach can help in reducing the size of the data to analyse, and foster the use of more complex and more demanding AI techniques in the other modules.

- **Ontology**. Ontologies represent the standard way to model the knowledge regarding specific domains. In a nutshell, an ontology provides a structured way to store, process, and search knowledge [Staab and Studer, 2010]. In a typical ontology, *entities* can be defined, and relations between entities can be described and established. Furthermore, characteristics and attributes of each entity can be specified, so that an overall structure can be designed and exploited for processing purposes. An ontology has to be structured according to the specific kind of legal reasoning and knowledge that it has to support: it is not possible to design a single general ontology to be used for supporting any kind of reasoning. Thus, the classification provided in Section 4 has to guide the design of appropriate ontologies, according to the desired type of reasoning. In literature, several ontologies have been put forward to model specific kind of legal knowledge, and different methods have been introduced to compare this knowledge [Leone *et al.*, 2019]. Examples of ontologies for the legal domain include [Nguyen *et al.*, 2017; Palmirani *et al.*, 2018; Alexander, 2009; Casellas, 2011].

- **Query and Reasoning**. This component focuses on dealing with the requests made by users by querying the available ontology and performing appropriate reasoning. The knowledge stored in the ontology can then be analysed using argumentation approaches [Bongiovanni *et al.*, 2018], so to provide an overview of the specific legal matter to the user, through paragraphs pointers and a first argumentative feedback. The field of argumentation provide means that can support automated reasoning. They propose arguments and counter-arguments to support or defeat a given statement, similarly to the way in which human experts would argue and debate. In that, conclusions reached by the approach can be easily investigated and explained, and the strength and validity of raised arguments can be assessed. It should be noted that other approaches, for instance techniques based on ASP [Aravanis *et al.*, 2018] or machine learning [Collarana *et al.*, 2018; Do *et al.*, 2017] have also been investigated for querying purposes. The former class, similarly to argumentation, can provide answers to specific questions –potentially with explanations for the answer given.

The latter is more focused on identifying paragraphs or articles where elements of potential interest for the user can be found. Here the reasoning is left to the human experts, but there is the advantage that the person can work directly on unstructured text.

- **Human-Computer Interaction**. The proposed framework involves and relies on human experts. It is not supposed to be fully autonomous, but to support the decision-making process of businesses. This architecture is designed to maintain humans in the loop, and to make sure that provided results are properly evaluated and assessed, in order to minimise risks for businesses. Given this perspective, it is pivotal to design appropriate means for supporting the interaction between humans and the system, and to support the explainability of answers provided by the system. This is in line with recent trends of research in the area [Kirsch, 2017; Abdul *et al.*, 2018].

It is worth noting that the depicted AI framework has to be used as a blueprint to deal with different classes of the legislative framework identified in Section 4. This structure includes the main modules that have to be taken into account when dealing with any of the legislative classes. Yet, the actual techniques and approaches to exploit in each component can significantly vary according to the kind of questions the expert can pose, and the type of answers that are expected. There is a spectrum of potential interactions which might occur while implementing this framework, and the following two questions exemplify the two extremes:

- *What is the actual taxation in country X with regards to the class of products Y?* which requires a number (and possibly the corresponding legal article) as an answer;

- *Are our current internal regulations complying with the recently modified employment laws?* which requires a more complex answer, in terms of identified issues and corresponding laws and articles.

Intuitively, different classes of the legal framework may require only one type of interaction, with regards to the examples described above. In that case, the corresponding module could be tuned to the specific needs. In other cases, different types of interactions may be required, thus increasing the complexity of the AI modules. For instances, classes like price and promotion can be better suit for the first kind of interaction, while elements of financial control and employees rights may need the second type of interaction.

The human expert is still an important part of the process, and this is for two main reasons. First, the human expert can make sure that the analysis performed by the framework, as well as the provided reasons and arguments, is sound. It may of course be the case that some notions have been misinterpreted by the framework, or that some conclusions are based on, for instance, debatable or controversial articles and bodies of text. It is of pivotal importance that results obtained from the framework are reviewed by experts, and not blindly followed [Cerutti *et al.*, 2018]. Second, the human should be able to interact with the framework in order to explore different scenarios and possibilities, either by changing the posed query or by objecting on some steps of the argumentative process.

6 Discussion and Conclusions

Companies are operating an extremely dynamic environment, where frequent and substantial changes to rules and regulations can have a disruptive impact on businesses if not timely and effectively dealt with. Companies can no longer just react to changes, but they are forced to constantly scan the environment to proactively identify threats and opportunities.

In this work, we investigated how AI can be used to support PESTLE analysis, which is a managerial tool widely utilised to articulate all those macro-factors which might influence a business. In particular, we focused on the legal environment, one of the most challenging due to large bodies of laws and regulations which have to be taken into account, and to its frequent changes. We introduced a classification of the aspects that companies have to deal with regards to legislation, and we positioned the different classes in terms of market, business, and department levels. The classification poses the pillars of the AI modular framework we introduced in Section 5. The framework incorporates all the relevant aspects that need to be taken into account in order to support companies when dealing with the legislation environment. Moreover, the classification helps in understanding the kind of interaction which is likely needed.

The proposed framework could not be extensively empirically tested, due to the required amount of information and strong involvement of companies and marketing experts. However, we had some qualitative discussions with PESTLE and marketing experts. Such discussions clearly indicate that an AI-based support for dealing with legal aspects would be favourably received by companies. As said, companies are struggling to quickly react to changes, and they are increasingly forced to take complex decisions based on limited knowledge.

Noteworthy, while it is clear that businesses can benefit from the exploitation of AI, some scholars suggest that AI might also help consumers to protect themselves [Lippi *et al.*, 2019]. It may be the case that an AI-empowered PESTLE analysis can provide an additional tool to support consumers to identify potentially dangerous circumstances.

We see several avenues for future work. We plan to engage with experts who generally support companies in accessing new and international markets, such as the UK Department for International Trade[10]; or other similar departments and institutions. Such collaboration may lead to real-world case studies where the introduced frameworks can be validated. We are also interested in running some experiments with potential users, to better understand their requirements and needs. Finally, we are of course interested in extending the proposed framework to deal with all the other macro-factors considered by the PESTLE analysis tool, so to provide a comprehensive support system to perform environmental scanning.

Acknowledgements

This work has been partially supported by EU H2020 research and innovation programme under the Marie Sklodowska-Curie grant agreement No. 690974 for the project "MIREL: MIning and REasoning with Legal texts". The authors would also like to express their gratitude to Prof. Ken Satoh, National Institute of Informatics, Tokyo, Japan, for the useful discussions and support.

BIBLIOGRAPHY

[Abdul et al., 2018] Ashraf Abdul, Jo Vermeulen, Danding Wang, Brian Y. Lim, and Mohan Kankanhalli. Trends and trajectories for explainable, accountable and intelligible systems: An hci research agenda. In *Proceedings of the 2018 CHI Conference on Human Factors in Computing Systems*, pages 582:1–582:18, 2018.

[Albaum et al., 2008] Gerald S Albaum, Gerald Albaum, and Edwin Duerr. *International marketing and export management*. Pearson Education, 2008.

[Alexander, 2009] BOER Alexander. Lkif core: Principled ontology development for the legal domain. *Law, ontologies and the semantic web: channelling the legal information flood*, 188:21, 2009.

[Aravanis et al., 2018] Theofanis Aravanis, Konstantinos Demiris, and Pavlos Peppas. Legal reasoning in answer set programming. In *2018 IEEE 30th International Conference on Tools with Artificial Intelligence (ICTAI)*, pages 302–306, 2018.

[Arisaka et al., 2017] Ryuta Arisaka, Ken Satoh, and Leendert W. N. van der Torre. Anything you say may be used against you in a court of law - abstract agent argumentation (triple-a). In *AI Approaches to the Complexity of Legal Systems - AICOL International Workshops 2015-2017: Revised Selected Papers*, pages 427–442, 2017.

[Baines et al., 2017a] P. Baines, C. Fill, and S. Rosengren. *Marketing*. Oxford University Press, 2017.

[Baines et al., 2017b] P. Baines, C. Fill, S. Rosengren, and P. Antonetti. *Fundamentals of marketing*. Oxford University Press, 2017.

[Baker, 2014] M. J. Baker. *Marketing strategy and management*. Palgrave Macmillan, 2014.

---

[10]https://www.gov.uk/government/organisations/department-for-international-trade

[Bench-Capon et al., 2009] Trevor Bench-Capon, Henry Prakken, and Giovanni Sartor. *Argumentation in Legal Reasoning*, pages 363–382. Springer US, 2009.

[Boella et al., 2019] Guido Boella, Luigi Di Caro, and Valentina Leone. Semi-automatic knowledge population in a legal document management system. *Artificial Intelligence and Law*, 27(2):227–251, 2019.

[Bongiovanni et al., 2018] Giorgio Bongiovanni, Gerald Postema, Antonino Rotolo, Giovanni Sartor, Chiara Valentini, and Douglas Walton. *Handbook of legal reasoning and argumentation*. Springer, 2018.

[Brassington and Pettitt, 2005] Frances Brassington and Stephen Pettitt. *Principles of marketing*. FT Prentice Hall London, NY, 2005.

[Casellas, 2011] Núria Casellas. *Legal ontology engineering: Methodologies, modelling trends, and the ontology of professional judicial knowledge*, volume 3. Springer Science & Business Media, 2011.

[Cerutti et al., 2018] Federico Cerutti, Alessia Grassi, and Mauro Vallati. Unveiling the oracle: Artificial intelligence for the 21st century. *Intelligent Decision Technologies*, 12(3):371–379, 2018.

[Collarana et al., 2018] Diego Collarana, Timm Heuss, Jens Lehmann, Ioanna Lytra, Gaurav Maheshwari, Rostislav Nedelchev, Thorsten Schmidt, and Priyansh Trivedi. A question answering system on regulatory documents. In *Legal Knowledge and Information Systems - JURIX 2018: The Thirty-first Annual Conference*, pages 41–50, 2018.

[Contissa et al., 2018] Giuseppe Contissa, Koen Docter, Francesca Lagioia, Marco Lippi, Hans-Wolfgang Micklitz, Przemyslaw Palka, Giovanni Sartor, and Paolo Torroni. Automated processing of privacy policies under the EU general data protection regulation. In *Legal Knowledge and Information Systems - JURIX 2018: The Thirty-first Annual Conference*, pages 51–60, 2018.

[Do et al., 2017] Phong-Khac Do, Huy-Tien Nguyen, Chien-Xuan Tran, Minh-Tien Nguyen, and Minh-Le Nguyen. Legal question answering using ranking svm and deep convolutional neural network. *arXiv preprint arXiv:1703.05320*, 2017.

[Hashmi and Governatori, 2018] Mustafa Hashmi and Guido Governatori. Norms modeling constructs of business process compliance management frameworks: a conceptual evaluation. *Artificial Intelligence and Law*, 26(3):251–305, 2018.

[Kirsch, 2017] Alexandra Kirsch. Explain to whom? Putting the User in the Center of Explainable AI. In *Proceedings of the First International Workshop on Comprehensibility and Explanation in AI and ML 2017 co-located with 16th International Conference of the Italian Association for Artificial Intelligence (AI*IA 2017)*, 2017.

[Leone et al., 2019] Valentina Leone, Luigi Di Caro, and Serena Villata. Taking stock of legal ontologies: a feature-based comparative analysis. *Artificial Intelligence and Law*, 2019.

[Li et al., 2013] Tingting Li, Tina Balke, Marina De Vos, Julian Padget, and Ken Satoh. Legal conflict detection in interacting legal systems. In *Legal Knowledge and Information Systems - JURIX 2013: The Twenty-Sixth Annual Conference*, pages 107–116, 2013.

[Lippi et al., 2019] Marco Lippi, Giuseppe Contissa, Francesca Lagioia, Hans-Wolfgang Micklitz, Przemysław Pałka, Giovanni Sartor, and Paolo Torroni. Consumer protection requires artificial intelligence. *Nature Machine Intelligence*, 1(4):168, 2019.

[Marmol and Feys, 2015] del Thomas Marmol and Brigitte Feys. *PESTLE Analysis: Understand and Plan for Your Business Environment*. Namur: Lemaitre Publishing., 2015.

[Nazarenko et al., 2016] Adeline Nazarenko, Francois Levy, and Adam Wyner. Towards a methodology for formalizing legal texts in legalruleml. In *Legal Knowledge and Information Systems - JURIX 2016*, volume 294, pages 149–154, 2016.

[Nguyen *et al.*, 2017] Ha-Thanh Nguyen, Viet-Ha Nguyen, and Viet-Anh Vu. A knowledge representation for vietnamese legal document system. In *2017 9th International Conference on Knowledge and Systems Engineering (KSE)*, pages 30–35. IEEE, 2017.

[Palmirani *et al.*, 2018] Monica Palmirani, Michele Martoni, Arianna Rossi, Cesare Bartolini, and Livio Robaldo. Legal ontology for modelling gdpr concepts and norms. In *Legal Knowledge and Information Systems: JURIX 2018: The Thirty-first Annual Conference*, volume 313, page 91, 2018.

[Staab and Studer, 2010] Steffen Staab and Rudi Studer. *Handbook on ontologies.* Springer Science & Business Media, 2010.

[Terpstra *et al.*, 2012] Vern Terpstra, James Foley, and Ravi Sarathy. *International marketing.* Naper Press, 2012.

[Wilson and Gilligan, 2012] Richard MS Wilson and Colin Gilligan. *Strategic marketing management.* Routledge, 2012.

Alessia Grassi
University of Leeds
Woodhouse, LS2 9JT
Leeds, UK
Email: a.grassi@leeds.ac.uk

Mauro Vallati
University of Huddersfield
Queensgate, HD1 3DH
Huddersfield, UK
Email: m.vallati@hud.ac.uk

14

Artificial Intelligence and Space Law

GEORGE ANTHONY LONG
CRISTIANA SANTOS
LUCIEN RAPP
RÉKA MARKOVICH
LEENDERT VAN DER TORRE

ABSTRACT. In the next few years, space activities are expected to undergo a radical transformation with the emergence of new satellite systems and new services incorporating artificial intelligence and machine learning. This transformation covers a wide range of innovations from autonomous objects with their own decision-making power to increasingly sophisticated services exploiting very large volumes of information from space. This chapter identifies some of the legal and ethical challenges linked to their use. These legal and ethical challenges call for solutions that the international treaties currently in force are not able to determine and implement sufficiently. For this reason, a methodology must be developed that makes it possible to link intelligent systems and services to a system of applicable rules. Our proposed methodology refers to existing legal AI-based tools amenable to making space law actionable, interoperable and machine readable for future compliance tools.

1 Introduction

Governance of space activities is faced with progressive transformation associated with the emergence of satellite systems and space-based services employing artificial intelligence (AI), including machine learning (ML). This chapter identifies and examines some fundamental legal challenges related to the use of AI in the space domain. Ascertaining such legal challenges requires ascertaining that space systems and services that use AI are linked to a system of governing rules and guiding legal principles.

The nature of the space and satellite industry presents a quintessential use case for AI. Virtually all space activities and ventures constitute fertile ground for employing AI. In fact, AI is ready for use in Earth orbit activities like active debris removal (ADR), near Earth ventures like abiotic resource extraction, and deep space exploration. Generally, AI applications take place in two principal ways:

- *autonomous robots* (or space objects). Whether in the form of autonomous spacecraft or satellite constellations, autonomous or intelligent space objects have the ability to not only collect, analyse, and use data for information and operational purposes but also to go where no human has ever gone or could go to collect probes and data. This application also includes autonomous spacecraft and swarm intelligence that assist in space activities such as: mining and using abiotic resources, exploring, in-orbit servicing (IoS), active debris removal, and protecting space assets — which includes protecting themselves from rogue and unknown natural space objects;

- analysing and, if necessary, acting upon *big data from space* related to: (1) debris monitoring, (2) self-preservation against potential threats from rogue and unknown natural objects in the space domain and perceived threats from other human-manufactured objects, (3) predictive analytics using very high resolution (VHR) satellite imagery, (4) real-time geospatial data analysis, and (5) analysis of data products derived from the convergence of a wide spectrum of sources (e.g. satellites, drones, the Internet of Things (IoT), unmanned aerial vehicles (UAV) imagery and UAV location data). Big data from space also enables the provision of space cloud computing services where data is stored on space-based assets.[1] Indeed, the development of AI-based technologies combined with space data can enhance the production, storage, access and dissemination of data in outer space and on Earth.

Space is undergoing seismic shifts driven by: New Space (promoting a Smart, Fast and Now Space) [Gattle, 2019]; the Google, Amazon, Facebook and Apple (GAFA) web giants; venture capital firms; and start-ups. There has been significant growth in the number of space activities, space objects, and space actors. However, **new challenges** are emerging in the course of such active exploration and use while deploying AI in space. Harnessing (using and misusing) AI (and specifically ML) technologies to access and explore outer space, and engaging in space-enabled downstream commercial applications and services will, in all likelihood, **lead to a wide range of intended and unintended consequences** that cannot be downplayed or disregarded. The following risks merit attention:

(i) privacy issues associated with the use of these technologies, e.g. citizen tracking and surveillance; potential re-identification of individuals; function creep; fake imagery; biased automatic decision-making and unjust discrim-

---

[1]This is done to increase data capacity, reduce the cost of services and allow real-time access to data storage.

ination based on nationality, gender, race and geographic localisation; lack of transparency etc.; and

(ii) liability issues emerging from the potential for damage caused by, for example, collisions with autonomous spacecraft or hacking/malware aimed at weaponising AI, and the consequences of such damage for space data (security problems for sensitive data stored in outer space, and malicious data capture).

These risks are more acute when **important facets of the space field are acknowledged.** First, space is a service- and needs-oriented market, dominated mostly by demand and competitive **industry logics,** and **without a centralised regulatory body** to govern it. Second, **space activities on Earth will have increasingly pervasive repercussions** as the benefits and solutions that space provides for the problems and needs of mankind (transport, smart city management, security, agriculture, climate change monitoring etc.) become ubiquitous.[2]. The European Space Agency (ESA) estimates that for every euro spent on the sector, six euros benefit society. This correlation reflects the **Earth's more marked dependence on space-based services.**

The range of these space-based services – many of them AI-enabled – requires consideration of a wide range of legal and regulatory issues that cannot be answered by the space industry alone. However, **UN space treaties** leave much uncertainty as to which AI uses and activities are permitted in space. Clearly, there is a need to develop or reinterpret the 'rules of the road' to enable commercial and civilian actors to have continued and legally compliant access to space. The principal objectives of this chapter are as follows:

1. to identify and discuss potential risks and challenges associated with implementing AI and ML in space;

2. to analyse the extent to which the current *corpus iuris spatialis* (from the 1970s) can still provide answers to these risks and challenges, and choose which methodology to follow going forward; and

3. to discuss how AI-based legal tools can support space law.

In accordance with these objectives, **Section 2** examines the specifics of AI in space, describes the distinct features of AI on Earth, and demonstrates the usefulness and benefits of AI in space. **Section 3** analyses some legal, ethical and governance risks associated with AI in space. **Section 4** discusses limitations in the current space law legal framework relating to AI in

---

[2]According to Hon. Philip E. Coyle, Senior Advisor, Center for Defense Information [Space Security Index, 2014]

space. **Section 5** offers a methodological approach to determining the legal regime applicable to AI in space. **Section 6** discusses AI-based tools that enable knowledge representation and reasoning about space law. **Section 7** summarises our analysis of AI in space.

2 Contextual Dynamics of Space and the Specifics of AI in Space

Space technology, data and services have become indispensable to the daily lives of Europeans and most people on Earth. Space-based services and activities also play an essential role in preserving the strategic and national security interests of many States. The European Union (EU) is seeking to cement its position as one of the major spacefaring powers by allowing extensive freedom of action in the space domain to encourage scientific and technical progress and support the competitiveness and innovation capacity of its space sector industries.

To boost the EU's space leadership beyond 2020, the European Parliament and Council proposed a regulation to establish the EU's space programme and the European Union Agency for the Space Programme.[3] The proposed budget allocation of **EUR 16 billion for the post-2020 EU space programme**[4] was received by the European space industry as a clear and strong signal of the EU's political willingness to reinforce the EU's leadership, competitiveness, sustainability and autonomy in space.[5] AI is one area where the EU is exerting its leadership in space.

The use of AI in space capitalises on the emergence of **'New Space'** which is creating a more complex and challenging environment physically, technologically and operationally. The current contextual dynamics of space and the **specifics of space activities amenable to AI are discussed below.**

2.1 Contextual dynamics of space

Current space activities are defined as belonging to the *Space 4.0 era*, characterised by proactiveness and open-mindedness to both technology disruption and opportunity [ESA, 2016], and whose trends include big data

---

[3]In a vote on 17 April 2019, the European Parliament endorsed a provisional agreement reached by co-legislators on the EU Space Programme for 2021-2027, bringing all existing and new space activities under the umbrella of a single programme to foster a strong and innovative space industry in Europe. See [Council of the European Union, 2019]

[4]These benefits represent a return on investment for the European Union of between 10 and 20 times the cost of the programme.

[5]This budget will be used first to maintain and upgrade the existing infrastructures of Galileo and Copernicus, so that EU systems remain on top. Second, the EU will adapt to new needs, such as fighting climate change, security, and the Internet of Things.

from space (e.g. data imagery) and applied predictive and geospatial analytics. In particular, this era is supported by AI-based technology, machine learning, and the Internet of Things (IoT). IoT is expected to be pervasive by 2025. Data explosion will be driven by connected "things" with sensors deployed by mega constellations of small satellites (smallsats), such as those produced by Hiber and Astrocast.

The use of these technologies is bringing about a *digital revolution*, unlocking access to space-based benefits [Space News, 2019]. The space industry is now moving towards leveraging full digitalisation of its *products* (high-performance spacecraft infrastructure, onboard computers, antennas and microwave products), *new processes* (increasing production speed and decreasing failure rates), and *data uptake* (the ability to access data right away) for the purpose of data distribution, as well as data analytics, processing, visualisation and value adding. All this is enabling Earth observation (EO) to become part of the larger data and digital economy.

These space-based benefits (products/processes/data uptake) increase the *repercussions of space activities on Earth*. A growing number of key economic sectors (in particular land and infrastructure monitoring, security, the digital economy, transport, telecommunications, the environment, agriculture, and energy) use satellite navigation and EO systems.

Space democratisation and privatisation reflect access to and participation in space by spacefaring nations and non-governmental entities such as privately owned juridical entities. Among space actors, the **private sector** currently accounts for 70% of space activity.[6] This percentage will only increase with the emergence of new private actors who, thanks to frontier technologies such as AI and the data revolution [de Concini and Toth, 2019], are seeking commercial opportunities from the exploration and exploitation of space and its resources.

Apart from emerging new technologies such as AI, new actors are developing *new global business models* driven by demand for satellite constellations, tourism, asteroid and lunar mining, in-situ resource utilization (ISRU) [Lucas-Rhimbassen *et al.*, 2019], fifth-generation technology (5G), in-orbit servicing (IoS), three-dimensional (3D) printing of satellite parts (e.g. solar panels etc.), and commercial space stations, among others. These new business segments[7] are leveraging the space economy. The space economy is expanding enormously, with predictions that it will generate revenues of

---

[6] "Nowadays, private sector augments all segments of the space domain, from ground equipment and commercial space transportation to satellite manufacturing and Earth observation services" [UNOOSA, 2018].'.

[7] And others, like scalability and agility, media/advertising, business-to-consumer (B2C), vertical integration, and position in value chains.

US\$ 1.1—2.7 trillion or more by 2040 [UNOOSA, 2019].

New high-end technologies and small-satellite design characterise the current landscape of the space industry. Smaller, lightweight satellites based on affordable off-the-shelf hardware, less expensive spacecraft (small-, nano- and pico-satellites) can be replaced more easily, thereby stimulating rapid improvements in technology [Sharma, 2018]. This, as well as the fact that thousands of these satellites can be launched into mega constellations, opens up the possibility for more missions and applications using space infrastructure.

2.2 Specifics of space amenable to AI

It is still important to consider the specifics of how AI is used in outer space and why that usage is distinct from terrestrial usage:

i. Space conditions are difficult and are only amenable to AI machines. Space is a remote, hostile and hazardous environment for human life[8], and certain activities are impossible for humans to carry out and survive the ordeal. This renders space technologies dependent on AI-based technologies and processes [Soroka and Kurkova, 2019]. AI-based technologies are a good fit for operational decision-making because they are robust, resilient, adaptable and responsive to changing threats.

ii. Upstream and downstream impact of AI in space. AI in a fast-approaching future will impact all sectors of the space industry: launch, constellation control, satellite performance analysis [Harebottle, 2019], AI logic in onboard payload used in deep space applications, the downstream sector of telecommunications, and Earth observation in commercial applications such as image classification and predictive analysis of phenomena.

iii. Autonomy of intelligent space objects. Using AI, a spacecraft may be able [Werner,] to recognise a threat, capture relevant data, understand the nature of the threat, and counteract it or take evasive action. The spacecraft can even share its newly acquired knowledge with other satellites. For example, a rover exploring Mars that needs to contact Earth takes up to 24 minutes to pass a signal. That leaves rather a long time for making crucial decisions that can affect the mission, which is why engineers are increasingly providing space robots with the ability to make decisions themselves [Soroka and Kurkova, 2019]. With AI, space objects can, without any human involvement, collect and analyse data and decide what information to send back to Earth and when. An AI system can predict and self-diagnose problems so that it can fix itself while continuing to perform [Harebottle,

---

[8]Due to e.g. difficult accessibility, the complexity of extra-atmospheric missions, the extreme physical and climatic conditions, new gravitational forces, different temperature ranges and unknown collisions with dust or asteroids.

2019]. When collisions occur between intelligent space objects and debris, this brings issues relating to liability to the fore, some of which are discussed in Sections 3.1 and 4.

iv. Asset protection. Space assets could be protected with the development of an AI-based automatic collision avoidance system that can assess the risk and likelihood of in-space collisions, improve the process of deciding whether an orbital manoeuvre is needed, and transmit warnings to other space objects that are potentially at risk [ESA, 2019].

v. Big Data from space. Big data from space [Soille *et al.*, 2019] refers to massive spatio-temporal Earth and space observation data collected by a variety of sensors (ranging from ground-based to space-borne) and their synergy with data from other sources and communities. Big data from space combined with "big data analytics" delivers "value" in terms of volume, velocity, variety and veracity. Traditional tools cannot capture, store, manage and analyse huge volumes of data to the same extent. Geospatial intelligence is one of many ways artificial intelligence is used in outer space. The term refers to employing AI to extract and analyse images and other geospatial information relating to terrestrial, aerial, and/or spatial objects and events. It allows events like disasters, the migration and safety of refugees, and agricultural production to be interpreted in real time. These aspects are analysed in Section 3.2 of this chapter.

3   Risks of AI in Space

AI in space is leading to a gradual shift from "computer-assisted human choice and human-ratified computer choice" [Cuellar, 2017] towards non-human analysis, decision-making and actions. The emerging deployment and use of intelligent space objects[9] brings novel challenges to the current space law regime, especially when (and not if) the use of such objects for the purposes of AI systems or services causes terrestrial and/or extraterrestrial injury such as violation of privacy rights, violation of data protection requirements, or injury resulting from collision with a space object [Stewart, 2019].

The space law treaty regime consists of the foundational Treaty on Principles Governing the Activities of States in the Exploration and Use of Outer Space, including the Moon and Other Celestial Bodies (the "Outer Space Treaty" or OST)[10] and its progeny treaties. The OST embeds the corner-

---

[9]A space object is limited to the object, including its component parts, that was "launched" into space. The issue can become a bit murkier if intelligent space objects can be manufactured and deployed in situ in outer space.

[10]Entered into force Oct. 10, 1967, 18 UST 2410; TIAS 6347; 610 UNTS 205; 6 ILM 386 (1967).

stone principles of current international space law jurisprudence [von der Dunk, 2001]. Its principles have been elaborated on in the following progeny treaties: the Agreement on the Rescue of Astronauts, the Return of Astronauts and the Return of Objects Launched into Outer Space (the "Rescue Agreement")[11], the Convention on International Liability for Damage Caused by Space Objects (the "Liability Convention")[12], the Convention on Registration of Objects Launched into Outer Space (the "Registration Convention")[13], and the Agreement Governing the Activities of States on the Moon and Other Celestial Bodies (the "Moon Treaty")[14]. Liability issues associated with AI risks require analysis of the Outer Space Treaty and the Liability Convention.

3.1 Liability of intelligent space objects

Liability under the space law treaty regime is based on Article VII of the Outer Space Treaty, which is the genesis of the Liability Convention. Article VII imposes international liability only on the launching State.[15] The Liability Convention establishes a restricted framework for assessing international liability which also applies only to launching States [Long, 2018]. Determination of liability and allocation of fault is based on where the damage occurred. Article II of the Liability Convention imposes absolute or strict liability for damage caused by a space object on Earth or to an aircraft in flight. On the other hand, if a space object causes damage in outer space or to a celestial body, then liability is based on the degree of fault, as stipulated in Article III. This section applies these liability rules to intelligent space objects.

---

[11]Entered into force Dec. 3, 1968, 19 UST 7570; TIAS 6599; 672 UNTS 119; 7 ILM 151 (1968).

[12]Entered into force Sept. 1, 1972, 24 UST 2389; TIAS 7762; (961 UNTS 187; 10 ILM 965 (1971).

[13]Entered into force Sept. 15, 1976, 28 UST 695; TIAS 8480; 1023 UNTS 15; 14 ILM 43 (1975).

[14]Entered into force July 1, 1984, 1363 UNTS 3; 18 ILM 1434 (1979). The Moon Treaty is viewed differently to the other space treaties because it has not received the international ratification of the other space law treaties. Major spacefaring nations such as the United States, Russia and China have neither signed nor ratified the treaty.

[15]Article 1(c) of the Liability Convention defines the term "launching State" as the State that launches or procures the launch of the space object and the State from whose territory or facility the space object is launched. A non-governmental space actor does not have international liability under the Liability Convention for damage caused by the space object regardless of its culpability. This means that a State space actor can only have international liability if it comes within the definition of a "launching State".

3.1.1 Some notes on liability and intelligent space objects

The concept of "damage" in the Liability Convention is neither comprehensive nor unambiguous. Article 1(a) defines "damage" as **"loss of life, personal injury or other impairment of health; or loss of or damage to property of States or of persons, natural or juridical, or property of international intergovernmental organizations."** This definition creates uncertainty about the parameters or scope of damage covered by the convention. It is unclear whether the damage is limited to physical damage caused by the space object [Waldrop, 2004] or whether it extends to non-kinetic harm, indirect damage and purely economic injury [Long, 2014]. Similarly, the scope of the phrase "other impairment of health" is not yet settled. For instance, is the phrase limited to physical injury or does it extend to emotional and/or mental injury? Like all legal issues associated with the Liability Convention, the scope of a damage claim is resolved according to whether the definition of damage is given a restrictive or extended interpretation. Intelligent space objects, i.e. autonomous space objects utilising AI, present challenges for the strict and fault liability scheme imposed on launching States.

Article III of the Liability Convention reads as follows:

> In the event of damage being caused elsewhere than on the surface of the Earth to a space object of one launching State or to persons or property on board such a space object by a space object of another launching State, **the latter shall be liable only if the damage is due to its fault or the fault of persons** for whom it is responsible. (Emphasis added)

Intelligent space objects disrupt Article III's fault-based liability scheme because the decisions, acts and omissions of an intelligent space object may be construed as not being the conduct of a person and may not always be attributable to a launching State.

3.1.2 Fault liability is predicated on human fault

Generally, we think of a person as a human being, but in the legal arena, the term "person" generally refers to an entity that is subject to legal rights and duties [Solum, 1992]. The law considers artificial entities like corporations, partnerships, joint ventures and trusts to be "persons" as they are subject to legal rights and duties, and the law sometimes recognises and imposes legal rights and duties on certain inanimate objects like ships, lands and goods, with the result that those inanimate objects are subject to judicial jurisdiction and therefore liable to judgments made against them [Solum, 1992]. However, the legal rights and duties imposed on artificial entities and inanimate objects flow from the actions or conduct of human beings.

This is not necessarily the case with intelligent **machines**. A machine can learn independently from human input and can make decisions based on what it has learnt and other available information, but those abilities do not necessarily equate to natural or legal personhood. As noted, the decisions and conduct of legal persons are ultimately decisions made by human beings. This means that the decisions are not based solely on intellect or data but are also the product of human factors such as consciousness, emotions and discretion [Solum, 1992]. Thus, the concept of legal personhood is ultimately premised on humanity, and AI-based decisions and conduct divorced from human oversight or control arguably lack such human factors [Solum, 1992]. Moreover, no law currently grants "personhood" to an intelligent space object. The lack of direct or indirect human considerations in the decision-making of an intelligent machine, together with the fact that such an object has no legal rights or duties under existing law, strongly suggest that decisions made by an intelligent space object are not made by a natural or legal person.[16]

Since fault liability under Article III of the Liability Convention is premised on a State or persons being at fault, a decision by an intelligent space object will, in all likelihood, not be the "fault of persons". Accordingly, assessing fault liability under Article III for a decision made by an intelligent space object may very well depend on whether such a decision can be attributable to the launching State.

3.1.3 Fault liability in the absence of human oversight in the decision-making process

In general, a State's liability for damage or injury is traceable to human acts or omissions. This basis for imposing liability appears to be inapplicable when damage or injury in outer space is caused by a machine's own analysis, decision and course of action all carried out without human approval [Karnow, 1996].

Liability premised on human acts or omission does not work when no particular human had the ability to prevent the damage, short of making the decision whether to utilise AI in a space object [Karnow, 1996]. Certainly, it is substantively difficult to draw the line between relying on AI to supplant the judgement of a human decision-maker and allowing a machine, or a non-human, to decide on a course of action and go through with it [Karnow, 1996]. To that extent, it seems that the fault-based liability of a launching State should not be premised solely on a decision to launch an intelligent space object, because such a sweeping basis for liability would effectively retard the development and deployment of intelligent space objects.[17] Thus, the appropriate question would seem to be: what conduct

---

[16] [[Long, 2014] Note 39, at page 7.

[17] See [Long, 2014] Note 39, at page 7. See also [Kowert, 2017].

is necessary to attribute fault liability to a State for damage caused by an intelligent space object when human oversight is not involved in the event causing the damage?

Resolving this dilemma presents novel and complex issues associated with standard of care, foreseeability and proximate cause, which are crucial elements in establishing fault (under Article III of the Liability Convention).[18] This matter is further complicated by the distinct possibility that it may not be possible to ascertain how an intelligent space object has made a particular decision [Long, 2014].

Nevertheless, untangling these nuanced legal obstacles may not be necessary to assess fault liability. Article VI of the Outer Space Treaty requires a State to assure that the space activities of its governmental and non-governmental entities comply with the Outer Space Treaty. It not only makes a State internationally responsible for its national activities in outer space, but also imposes a dual mandate of "authorization and continuing supervision" that is not limited to the launching State or the space actor's home State [Long, 2014].

Article VI of the Outer Space Treaty does not expressly burden the launching State with the obligation to authorise and supervise. Instead, it bestows powers of authorisation and continuous supervision on the **"appropriate State"**. Since neither Article VI of the Outer Space Treaty nor any other provision of the space law treaty regime defines the term "appropriate State", or sets out any criteria for establishing the appropriate State(s), there are no agreed legal standards for determining what constitutes an "appropriate State". Nevertheless, some scholars have stated that a launching State is generally always an appropriate party for the purposes of Article VI of the Outer Space Treaty [Cheng, 1998]. This is a reasonable and accurate extrapolation since the liability scheme is predicated on launching State status.

Since fault liability is generally predicated on a breach of a standard of care[19], the dual responsibility of "authorization and continuing supervision by the appropriate State party" arguably establishes a standard of care that a launching State must comply with[20], especially in connection with an intelligent space object. This essentially means that **a launching State bears the responsibility for ensuring that appropriate authorisation and supervision is exercised in connection with an intelligent space object that it launches for a non-governmental entity, regardless of**

---

[18][Long, 2014] Note 39, at page 8. While the decision to launch an intelligent space object may not be the basis for fault liability, as discussed infra, how the decision was made may serve as a vehicle for assessing fault liability.

[19]See [Dennerley, 2018], Note 3.

[20]See generally [Cheng, 1998], Note 67.

whether the object is owned or operated by the national entity.
The standard of care analysis, therefore, shifts from the specific event that
caused the damage to examining whether the launching State exercised sufficient authorisation and supervision over the activities of the intelligent space
object.

In analogy with the **"due diligence"** standard under international law
[Dennerley, 2018], a **flexible** and fluid standard is used when determining
whether a launching State exercised sufficient authorisation and supervision.
"Due diligence" is not an obligation to achieve a particular result; rather it
is an obligation of conduct that requires a State to engage in sufficient effort
to prevent harm or injury to another State, its nationals[21] or the global commons (see [Gray, 1996]; [Rosenstock and Kaplan, 2002]). Breach of this duty
is not limited to State action, but also extends to the conduct of a State's
nationals.[22] While there is "an overall minimal level of vigilance" associated
with due diligence, "a higher degree of care may be more realistically expected" from States that have the ability and resources to provide it [Gray,
1996]. In any event, it would appear that a launching State's standard of
care entails assuring that there is some State authorisation and supervision
over the space activities engaged in by the intelligent space object. However,
with the **flexible** standard of care, it seems that the appropriate degree of
human oversight required, if any, depends on the function of the intelligent
space object.

This flexibility is consistent with the approach of the **European Commission** (EC) to artificial intelligence in general. In its White Paper on AI
[European Commission, 2020], the EC adopted the policy that **human oversight is a necessary component in the use of AI**, based on the reasoning
that human oversight ensures that an "AI system does not undermine human autonomy or cause other adverse effects" [European Commission, 2020,
p. 21]. The White Paper further stipulates that human oversight requires
"appropriate involvement by human beings", which may vary depending on
the "intended use of the AI system" and the "effect", if any, it can have on
people and legal entities. It then enumerates certain non-exhaustive kinds of
human oversight including 1) human review and validation of an AI decision
either before or immediately after the decision is made, 2) monitoring of the
AI system while in operation and the ability to intervene in real time and
deactivate it, and 3) imposing operational restraints to ensure that certain
decisions are not made by the AI system. This EC policy presents a flexible

---

[21]See Seabed Mining Advisory Opinion at ¶117 (Seabed Dispute Chamber of the International Tribunal of the Law of the Sea, Case No 17, 1 February 2011) and United States
Diplomatic and Consular Staff in Tehran (U.S. v. Iran), 1980 I.C.J. 3, 61 - 67 (May 24).
[22]See [Gray, 1996] Note 73 at page 243.

framework for determining whether a launching State has met its standard of care in relation to a non-governmental intelligent space object that causes damage in outer space.

The flexible standard of due diligence can also be used by the launching State to negate or mitigate its liability for damage caused by an intelligent space object. The flexible standard will allow a launching State to argue that the home State of the non-governmental space actor has a greater degree of oversight responsibility than the launching State. Accordingly, it should be reasonable and sufficient for a launching State to rely on assurances that the non-national's home State exercises adequate authorisation and oversight procedures for its nationals' use of intelligent space objects. This shifts the supervisory obligation from the launching State to the home State of the non-governmental space actor. The home State's failure to properly exercise its standard of care may, depending upon the circumstances, mitigate or absorb the launching State's fault liability under Article III of the Liability Convention. This shift, however, is not automatic as the due diligence standard makes it dependent on the home State's technological prowess in the area of AI or its financial ability to contract out such expertise.

3.1.4 Intelligent space objects and absolute liability

Article II of the Liability Convention imposes strict liability on a launching State if a space object causes damage on the Earth's surface or to aircraft in flight. Article VI(1), however, allows **exoneration** from absolute liability if the damage results "either wholly or partially from gross negligence or from an act or omission done with intent to cause damage on the part of a claimant State or of natural or juridical persons it represents." This defence, however, may not be available if the damage resulted "wholly or partially" from the act or omission of an intelligent space object deployed or controlled by the claimant State or a natural or juridical person the claimant State represents.

"Gross negligence", the mental element of an act or omission, is the product of human thought, which is absent in the machine's decision-making process. Even more so, Article VI of the Liability Convention may also defeat exoneration from absolute liability if the claimant State is able to show that the launching State's deployment of the intelligent space object breached its State responsibility under international law, including the United Nations Charter or the Outer Space Treaty. This counter-argument to the negation of absolute liability thrusts Article VI of the Outer Space Treaty into consideration.

3.1.5 Intelligent space objects and liability under Article VII of the Outer Space Treaty

Article VII of the Outer Space Treaty imposes international liability on the launching State, without qualification or exception. Moreover, Article VII does not predicate fault liability on human involvement in the damage-causing event or fault being otherwise attributable to the launching State. Bestowing unqualified liability on the launching State may present an alternative way to obtain compensation for damage in space caused by an intelligent space object. Monetary compensation under Article VII of the Outer Space Treaty may well be pursued when fault cannot be assessed under Article III of the Liability Convention because the decision that caused the damage was not made by a person and the decision is not otherwise attributable to a launching State. The issue can also surface if a claimant State seeks financial compensation for an injury or harm caused by an intelligent space object that does not come within the meaning of "damage" under Article 1(a) of the Liability Convention. For instance, if an intelligent space object is used to interfere with, jam or hijack a commercial satellite transmission, then the financial injury suffered as a consequence of such conduct may not be compensable under the Liability Convention given its definition of "damage." However, Article VII of the Outer Space Treaty may provide the basis for recovery in such circumstances.

Of course, a party seeking to pursue such a remedy under Article VII of the Outer Space Treaty may, in all likelihood, encounter the objection that since the Liability Convention is the progeny of Article VII of the Outer Space Treaty, the State is precluded from pursuing a remedy directly under Article VII of the Outer Space Treaty. Such an objection may be premised on the public international law principle that "when a general and a more specific provision both apply at the same time, preference must be given to the specific provision" [Perrazzelli and Vergano, 1999]. It is unclear if this principle applies to the relationship between Article VII of the Outer Space Treaty and the Liability Convention.

Although the Liability Convention expressly proclaims that one of its principal purposes is to establish rules and procedures "concerning liability for damage caused by space objects",[23] the treaty does not assert that its rules and procedures are exclusive when assessing liability through means other than the Liability Convention. Most importantly, neither the Outer Space Treaty nor the Liability Convention precludes recovery of damage under Article VII of the Outer Space Treaty. This point is significant given

---

[23]Liability Convention Preamble, 4th Paragraph. The other purpose is to ensure prompt payment "of a full and equitable measure of compensation to victims" in accordance with the Convention.

that one of the general principles of international law is that what is not prohibited is permitted.[24] In other words, "in relation to a specific act, it is not necessary to demonstrate a permissive rule so long as there is no prohibition".[25]

Determining whether Article III of the Liability Convention precludes a State from having recourse to Article VII of the Outer Space Treaty for an injury caused by a space activity is, like most current space law issues, purely an academic exercise inasmuch as there is not much guidance from national or international courts, tribunals, or agencies on how to interpret the provisions of the space law treaty regime. Nevertheless, resolving the issue involves a binary choice as to whether the Liability Convention does or does not preclude resorting to Article VII of the Outer Space Treaty. Resolution of the issue will have a significant impact on whether the Liability Convention needs to be amended or supplemented to accommodate the deployment and use of intelligent space objects. Certainly, if relief can be obtained under Article VII of the Outer Space Treaty when a remedy is not available under the Liability Convention, then Article VII of the Outer Space Treaty should provide sufficient flexibility to address liability issues associated with intelligent space objects during this period of AI infancy.

3.2 Data protection and ethical challenges related to AI in space

Every year, commercially available satellite images are becoming **sharper** and are being taken more frequently. Commercially available cutting-edge imagery resolution software limit each pixel in a captured image to approximately 31 cm.[26] There is increasing demand from private commercial entities to lower the resolution restriction threshold to 10 cm [Wang, 2019; Hollingham, 2014]. The significance of using AI with satellite imaging is best illustrated by the immediate interim export controls imposed by the United States in January 2020 to regulate the dissemination of AI software. AI software subject to these controls include those that can automatically scan aerial images to recognise anomalies or identify objects of interest such as vehicles, houses, and other structures.[27]

Speculation abounds regarding satellite imagery that can discern car plates, individuals, and "manholes and mailboxes" [BBC, 2014]. In fact, in 2013, police in Oregon used a Google Earth satellite image that showed marijuana growing illegally on a man's property [CBS, 2013]. In 2018, Brazilian

---

[24]S.S. Lotus, P.C.I.J. Ser. A, No. 10 at 18 (1927).

[25][Tricot and Sander, 2011] quoting Accordance with International Law of the Unilateral Declaration of Independence in Respect of Kosovo (Kosovo Advisory Opinion), Advisory Opinion, 2010 I.C.J. 403 (July 22) (declaration of Judge Simma at 2).

[26]http://worldview3.digitalglobe.com/

[27]85 Fed. Reg. 459 (January 6, 2020)

police used real-time satellite imagery to detect the spot where trees had been ripped out of the ground to illegally produce charcoal, and they arrested eight people in connection with the scheme [Global Forest Watch, 2018]. In China, human rights activists used satellite imagery to show that many of the Uigur re-education camps in the Xinjiang province are surrounded by watchtowers and razor wire [Wen and Auyezov, 2018]. In one recent case, ML was used to create a system that could autonomously review video footage and detect patterns of activity at a particular location. This system was used to monitor a video of a parking lot and identify moving vehicles and pedestrians. The system established a baseline of normal activity from which anomalous and suspicious actions could be detected [Aerospace, 2018].

Even if such image and video resolution systems are not able to identify individuals or their features [Santos *et al.*, 2019], they are **no longer in a sweet spot**. The broad **definition of personal data** in the General Data Protection Regulation (GDPR)[28] allows *all* information from EO data related to an *identified* or *identifiable* natural person (like location data) to be considered as personal data. The attribute "identified" refers to a known person, and "identifiable" refers to a person who has not yet been identified but whose identification is still possible. An individual is directly identified or identifiable with reference to *"direct or unique identifiers"*. These "direct and unique identifiers" cover data types that can be easily referenced and associated with an individual, including descriptors such as name, identification number, username, location data, the Subscriber Identity Module (SIM) cards of mobile phones, online identifiers etc., as described in Article 4(1) of the GDPR. An individual is *"indirectly identifiable"* by a combination of indirect (and therefore non-unique identifiers) that allow an individual to be singled out; these are less obvious information types which can be related to, or "linked" to an individual — for instance video footage, public keys, signatures, internet protocol (IP) addresses, device identifiers, metadata and so forth.

A picture may show a whole person, and very high resolution (VHR) arguably allows the identification of that person when considering, for example, that person's height, body type and clothing. Likewise, very high resolution images could enable a person to be identified via the objects (home, cars, boats etc.) and places (location data) associated with that person [Aloisio, 2017]. The lawfulness of processing such images needs to be assured.

---

[28] Regulation (EU) 2016/679 (General Data Protection Regulation) on the protection of natural persons with regard to the processing of personal data and on the free movement of such data, OJ L 119, 04.05.2016.

As **massive constellations of small satellites**[29] are becoming a staple in low Earth orbits (LEOs), larger influx of data, observation capabilities and high-quality imagery from EO satellites [Popkin, 2018] is expected to become more widely available on a regular basis. EO massive constellations may provide more frequent image capture and updates (capturing a single point several times a day) at a much lower cost. Users can plan both the target and frequency, allowing more specific analysis on a particular track. Ordinarily, these collected terabytes of data must be downlinked to a ground station before being processed and reviewed. But now, enabled satellites can carry out **mission applications on board, and this includes using AI that would carry out such processing in the satellite** [Harebottle, 2019]. This means that only the most relevant data would be transmitted, not only saving on downlink costs but also allowing ground analysts to focus on the data that matters the most. For example, one company has **developed algorithms that rely on AI to analyse stacks of images and automatically detect changes, allowing users to track changes** at individual properties in any country: "This machine learning tool, it's constantly looking at the imagery and classifying things it finds within them: that's a road, that's a building, that's a flood, that's an area that's been burned" [Yeo, 2018]. Other analytics companies feed visual data into algorithms designed to derive added value from mass images.

AI may be used, in **breach** of EU data protection and other rules, by public authorities or other private entities for mass surveillance. **VHR optical data** may have the same quality as aerial photography, and could therefore **raise privacy** [Beam, 2019], **data protection and ethical issues** [ITU, nd; von der Dunk, 2012; Aranzamendi et al., 2010; Santos and Rapp, 2019; Santos et al., 2019].

In addition, **EO data** could be explored by smart video or **face recognition technologies** [CNIL, 2019; FRA, 2019] and **combined with other data streams such as the Global Positioning System (GPS), security cameras**, etc., thus raising privacy concerns, even if the raw or pre-processed data itself does not. **We can anticipate several scenarios where the identifiability of individuals is at stake.** Applying very high resolution satellites to scan and inspect the landscape, images can be captured of buildings, cars or real estate for the purpose of showcasing, stock images, footage for publicity purposes, and such like. Those familiar with the areas captured and/or individuals in the vicinity may be able to identify those individuals and their movements and their social patterns. These are

---

[29]The EO constellation will be centred at 600 km, which spans a large range of altitudes. It comprises 300 non-manoeuvrable 3U cubesats so is much smaller in both total areal cross-section and aggregate mass.

the actual risks posed by making this data available open source to be used for **any unforeseen purpose**.

The aim of the **European strategy for data** [European Commission, nd] is to give the EU a secure and dynamic **data-agile economy** in the world – empowering the EU with data to improve decision-making and improve the lives of all its citizens. **The EU's future regulatory framework for AI** aims to create an **'ecosystem of trust'**. To do so, it must ensure compliance with EU rules, including rules protecting fundamental rights and consumer rights, particularly for AI systems that pose high risks, as explained in this chapter [European Commission, 2020]. If a clear EU regulatory framework is required to build trust among consumers and businesses using AI in space, and therefore hasten uptake of the technology, it is necessary to **be aware of the risks of AI in space**.

While AI can do much good, it can also do **harm**. This harm might be both **material** (affecting the safety and health of individuals, including loss of life and damage to property) and **immaterial** (loss of privacy, limitations to rights including freedom of expression and human dignity, or discrimination in e.g. access to employment), and can relate to a wide variety of risks. Harnessing AI technologies to access and explore outer space and engaging in space-based commercial activities will, in all likelihood, **lead to a broad array of intended and unintended consequences** flowing from the use and misuse of such technologies, and these consequences cannot be downplayed or disregarded. However, the two most prominent and complex legal issues are considered to be privacy and data protection, and liability for erroneous positioning [von der Dunk, 2015].

3.2.1   Privacy and data protection issues

The use of AI in connection with satellite imaging raises concerns relating to personal privacy and data protection. Some of the potential risks forecasted by the [European Commission, 2019] include the following:

- *ubiquity of "facial recognition data"* [CNIL, 2019]. Facial recognition data can potentially be obtained from a plethora of sources. Facial images collected and stored in a multitude of widely available databases can be used to track the movements of people through time and space. They therefore constitute a potential source for identifying individuals. Individuals may be identified via analysis of images captured by various facial recognition systems. More generally, any photograph can potentially become a piece of biometric data with more or less straightforward technical processing. Dissemination of data collected by facial recognition devices is taking place in a context of continuous self-exposure on social media, which increases people's vulnerability to facial recognition data. A massive amount of data is technically accessible for which AI can potentially be mobilised for the purpose of facial recognition-based identification.

- *lack of transparency.* Transparency requires that the data controller informs the data subject of the personal information collected, the purpose of the collection, and use of the data. Transparency also entails that imagery operators inform data subjects of their right to access, correct and erase their personal data, and the procedure for exercising such rights. The transparency obligation is difficult to document, monitor and enforce given the number of different companies involved in the collection and intelligent processing of personal data.

- *data maximisation and disproportionality of data processing.* Space technology has a tendency towards extensive collection, aggregation and algorithmic analysis of all the available data for various reasons, which hampers the data minimisation principle. In addition, irrelevant data are also being collected and archived, undermining the storage limitation principle.

- *lack of purpose limitation and repurposing of data.* Since data analytics can mine stored data for new insights and find correlations between apparently disparate datasets, big data from space is susceptible to reuse for secondary unauthorised purposes, profiling, and surveillance [Wiewiórowski, 2020]. This undermines the purpose specification principle, which stipulates that the purpose for which the data is collected must be specified and lawful. As for repurposing, personal data should not be further processed in a way that the data subject might regard as unexpected, inappropriate or otherwise objectionable and, therefore, unconnected to the delivery of the service. Moreover, once the infrastructure is in place, facial recognition technology can easily be used for **"function creep"** [Wiewiórowski, 2020]: for instance, the purpose of VHR usage may expand to include either additional operations or additional activities compared to that originally envisaged. Function creep also describes situations when such imagery is disseminated over the Internet, which naturally increases the risk of the data being reused widely. Given these circumstances, it is difficult to ensure that the data subject can effectively control the use of the facial recognition data by giving or withholding consent.

- *retracing.* By analysing large amounts of data and identifying links among them, AI can be used to retrace and deanonymise data about persons [European Commission, 2020], thereby creating new personal data protection risks even with datasets that do not include personal data per se.

- *lack of rights of access, correction and erasure*. Results obtained from data analysis may not be representative or accurate if the sources of the data are not subject to proper validation. For instance, AI analysis combining online social media resources are not necessarily representative of the whole population. Moreover, machine learning may contain hidden biases in its programming or software, which can lead to inaccurate predictions and inappropriate profiling of persons. Hence, AI interpretation of data collected by high-resolution images need human validation to ensure the trustworthiness of a given interpretation and avoid an incorrect image interpretation. 'At best, satellite images are interpretations of conditions on Earth – a "snapshot" derived from algorithms that calculate how the raw data are defined and visualized' [Laituri, 2018]. This can create a black box, making it difficult to know when or why the algorithm gets it wrong. For example, one recently developed algorithm was designed to identify artillery craters on satellite images – but the algorithm also identified locations that looked similar to craters but were not craters. This demonstrates the need for metrics to assist in formulating an accurate interpretation of big space data.

- *potential identification of individuals*. If footage taken via VHR imaging only shows the top of a person's head and one cannot identify that person without using sophisticated means, it is not personal data. However, if the same image was taken with the backyard of a house in view using additional imaging analytical algorithms that may enable the house and/or the owner to be identified, then that footage would be considered to be personal data. Thus, personal data is very much context-dependent. The situation escalates with the advance of "ultra-high" definition images being published online by commercial satellite companies, and the subsequent application of big data analytics tools. It might be possible to identify an individual indirectly (and show the individual's house etc.), when high-resolution images are combined with other spatial and non-spatial datasets. Thus, while footage of people may be restricted to "the tops of people's heads", once these images are contextualised by particular landmarks or other information, individuals may become identifiable. *"Combination of publicly available data pools with high resolution image data coupled with the integration and analysis capabilities of modern GIS [Geographic Information Systems] providing geographic keys[,] such as longitude and lat-*

itude, can result in a technological invasion of personal privacy" [Chun and Atluri, 2002].

- **erosion of anonymity in the public space** [CNIL, 2019]. Erosion of anonymity by public authorities or private organisations is likely to jeopardise some of the fundamental privacy principles established by the GDPR. Facial recognition in public areas can end up making harmless behaviour look suspicious. Wearing a hood, sunglasses or a cap, or looking at one's telephone or the ground can have an impact on the effectiveness of facial recognition devices, and such behaviour can be the basis for suspicion [CNIL, 2019]. Additionally, the interface between facial recognition systems and satellite imaging creates an opportunity for an unprecedented level of surveillance, whether by a governmental or private entity. It is not inconceivable that coupling satellite imagery with facial recognition software and other types of technology, such as sound capturing devices, may further increase the level of surveillance of people and places.

- **fallible technologies producing unfair biases** [Buolamwini and Gebru, 2018] **and outcomes** [CNIL, 2019; Louradour and Madzou, 2020]. Like any biometric processing, facial recognition is based on statistical estimates of a match between the elements being compared. It is therefore inherently fallible because it is a match based on probability. Furthermore, as the French data protection law explains, the biometric templates are always different depending on the conditions under which they are calculated (lighting, angle, image quality, resolution of the face image etc.). Every device therefore exhibits variable performance according, on the one hand, to its aims, and, on the other hand, to the conditions involved in collecting images of the faces to be compared. Space AI devices embedded with facial recognition technology can thus lead to "false positives" (a person is wrongly identified) and "false negatives" (the system does not recognise a person who ought to be recognised). Depending on the quality and configuration of the device, the rate of false positives and false negatives may vary. The model's result may be incorrect or discriminatory if the training data renders a biased picture of reality, or if it has no relevance to the area in question. Such use of personal data would be in contravention of the fairness principle.

- **lack of transparency and (in)visibility.** This risk applies when individuals on the ground may not know that VHR satellites are in operation, or if they do, may be unsure about who is operating them and the purpose for which they are being used, which somehow causes discomfort.

- *seamless and ubiquitous processing.* VHR combined with facial recognition technologies allows remote, contactless data processing [CNIL, 2019]. Such a "contactless" system means that processing devices are excluded from the user's field of vision. It allows remote processing of data without people's knowledge, and without any interaction or relationship with those persons. In this scenario, data controllers need to declare the data subject's rights and the procedures for exercising these rights (Articles 13(2)(b) of the GDPR).

- *loss of privacy and non-public areas.* Using AI with satellite imaging presents issues about loss of control over one´s personal information and activities [Nissenbaum, 2010, p. 70-72.][Solove, 2008, p. 24-29], which encompasses the right of individuals to move in their own home (including yards and gardens) and/or other non-public places without being identified, tracked or monitored [R. L. Finn and Friedewald, 2013, p. 16.].

- *loss of privacy of association.* This refers to people's freedom to associate with others [R. L. Finn and Friedewald, 2013, p. 16]. It is related also to the fact that footage might indicate, for example, the number of adults living in a house (based on the number of vehicles) or provide clues as to their relationships. Satellite imaging and AI provide an opportunity to ascertain and/or monitor personal associations.

- *lack of means to verify compliance.* The specific characteristics of many AI technologies, including opacity (the 'black-box effect'), complexity, unpredictability and partially autonomous behaviour, may make it hard to verify compliance with rules of existing EU law intended to protect fundamental rights, and may hamper the effective enforcement of those rules. Enforcement authorities and affected persons may lack the means to verify how a decision was made if it involved AI in space and, therefore, whether the relevant rules were respected. Individuals and legal entities may face difficulties obtaining effective access to justice in situations where such decisions can affect them negatively.

3.2.2 Ethical issues

The use of AI in connection with satellite imaging raises the following ethical issues:

- *discrimination.* Profiling consists of "pattern recognition, comparable to categorization, generalization and stereotyping" [Hildebrandt and Gutwirth, 2008]. VHR satellite imaging combined with analytic technologies can lead to discriminatory profiling [E. Denham. Big Data and Protection, 2017]. Also, satellite-based VHR may be used more on certain populations or areas where people are less likely to be able to effectively voice or act upon such concerns (i.e. marginalised populations or areas). With the use of ML and data mining, individuals may be clustered according to generic behaviours, preferences and other characteristics without necessarily being identified [der Sloot, 2014]. Profiling ultimately involves creating derived or inferred data and occasionally leads to incorrect and biased decisions (based on discriminatory, erroneous and unjustified judgements about, for instance, their behaviour, health, creditworthiness, recruitment potential, insurance risks etc.) [Edwards, 2016].

- *public dissatisfaction.* People could become disillusioned with surveillance and use of imagery based on the possibility that these activities can compromise privacy and data protection rights or due to a feeling that they are being "overrun" by such technologies.

- *chilling effect.* There are situations where individuals may be unsure if they are being observed (even if there are no VHR satellites processing data about them), and they attempt to adjust their behaviour accordingly [R. L. Finn and Friedewald, 2013, p. 16].

- *imbalance.* In one prospective scenario, space technologies might produce situations of imbalance where data subjects are not aware of the fundamental elements of data processing and related consequences and are unable to negotiate what information may be kept about them and for what purpose, which has the side effect of enhanced information asymmetry. Even exercising the right to be forgotten seems difficult. Images captured for use in Google Street View may contain sensitive information about people who are not aware that they are being observed and photographed [Holdren and Lander, 2014].

If these risks materialise, the lack of clear requirements and the characteristics of space-based AI technologies make it difficult to trace potentially problematic decisions made with the involvement of AI systems. This in turn may make it difficult for persons who have suffered harm to obtain compensation under current EU and national liability legislation [European Commission, 2019].

4 Limitations of space treaties in determining the law applicable to intelligent systems and services

Limitations naturally exist in the space law treaty regime because it employs broad legal principles accompanied by ambiguous terms and provisions. Moreover, the regime does not sufficiently reflect how access to and use of outer space has metamorphosed due to the escalation and diversification of space activities engaged in by private actors and other non-governmental entities, and due to technological advancements such as AI. The lack of international standardisation in the space law treaty regime comes to light generally when some sort of unforseen event occurs, such as i) damage to a space asset[30] or ii) an act that increases the hazards of access to and use of outer space.[31] This section will analyse and discuss limitations associated with the State-centric space legal regime, and will discuss jurisdiction and choice of substantive law issues related to the restrictive State-centric space law treaty regime.

4.1 State-centric space legal regime

The **space law treaty regime does not impose any direct obligation on non-governmental entities.** Instead, it puts all the responsibilities and obligations on only one class of space actor, the State. For instance, Article VI of the Outer Space Treaty establishes that the outer space activities of non-governmental entities are subject to restraint and control by States and not the treaty regime directly (provided that the non-governmental actor's space activity does not involve piracy, genocide or any other recognised international crimes).

The most fundamental limitation is apparent in Article XIII of the Outer Space Treaty, which recognises that the treaty provisions apply only to the activities of States, albeit including international governmental organisations and related entities. Limiting the obligations and remedies associated with space activities to States essentially **relegates the space law treaty regime to the rule of politics rather than the rule of law.** As the space economy matures, it will become necessary to have a space law legal regime directly applicable to all space actors and rooted in the rule of law rather than politics. Until international space law goes beyond the State-centric space legal regime, it will suffer from the limitation of restricted direct application and other limitations in areas such as jurisdiction and choice of

---

[30]Injury or harm is not limited to physical collision with a space object but also includes conduct such as jamming a satellite transmission, hijacking a satellite signal, or seizing command and control of a space object.

[31]The creation of space debris by testing an anti-satellite weapon is an example of an act that increases the hazards of access and use of space.

applicable substantive law.

4.2 Jurisdictional limitation

There is no international body that has the jurisdiction to adjudicate space-based disputes between States and bind the States to its judgments. International jurisdiction over space-based disputes depends on the consent of all the States that are parties to the dispute [Firestone, 1985]. Moreover, since the space law treaties do not impose direct obligations and duties on non-governmental entities, there is no basis for international jurisdiction over a non-governmental space actor, provided that the non-governmental actor's space activity does not involve piracy, genocide or any other recognised international crime.

The jurisdictional limitations of the space law treaty regime is also apparent whenever a private individual or non-governmental entity wants to pursue a remedy directly for harm caused by some space activity. In such circumstances, jurisdiction is determined by State law unless the parties to the dispute consent to private arbitration. Although space law precludes a State from exercising sovereignty in outer space, space law incorporates international law that recognises a State's power to exercise jurisdiction over extraterritorial acts under certain circumstances.[32] Accordingly, State law governing jurisdiction can arguably extend to AI-related disputes arising in space. Moreover, a State can enact specific legislation granting its courts or agencies jurisdiction over AI-based disputes arising from space activities. Either way, jurisdiction is properly determined only if such legislation satisfies one of the five grounds for extraterritorial jurisdiction.[33]

An example of a State extending its jurisdiction to the space context is when the United States enacted a statute criminalising interference with the operation of a satellite i.e. any activity that "intentionally or maliciously interferes with the authorized operation of a communications or weather satellite or obstructs or hinders any satellite transmission."[34] Noticeably, the statute did not: 1) limit its application to a satellite launched by or registered in the United States, or 2) limit its application to situations affecting the national security of the United States, citizens of the United States, the economic interests of the United States or any other interest pertaining to

---

[32]United States v. Ali, 885 F.Supp.2d 17, 25-26 rev. in part on other grounds 885 F.Supp.2d 55 (D.D.C. 2012). Customary international law generally recognises five tenets for a State exercising jurisdiction over the extraterritorial conduct of a non-governmental entity. As the United States judiciary has recognised in the context of the United States v. Ali piracy case, the five tenets are: territorial jurisdiction, protective jurisdiction, national jurisdiction, passive personality jurisdiction, and universal jurisdiction.

[33]See Id.

[34]18 U.S.C. § 1367.

or connected with the United States [Long, 2019]. In the absence of universal jurisdiction over interference with satellites, the statute's jurisdictional scope appears to be overbroad and extends beyond jurisdictional reach consistent with international law.

In any event, there is no international harmonisation or standardisation on matters of jurisdiction over AI-related disputes arising from space activities that do not cause damage as defined by the Liability Convention, or covering situations when a remedy is being directly pursued by a private person or non-governmental entity.

4.3 Limitations of space law

The space treaties do not address the use of AI, and there is no international treaty regulating AI in space. This means that domestic legislation must be the principal source of substantive law on the use of AI in space. The lack of international regulation of AI **potentially poses complex problems relating to the applicable substantive law in disputes involving the use of AI in space.** For instance, if the use of AI or an intelligent space object causes damage to another space object which is cognisable under the Liability Convention, it is unclear what substantive law applies when it comes to important issues for resolving the merits of the claim, issues such as the appropriate standard of care and what constitutes fault. Article XVIII of the Liability Convention stipulates that the "Claims Commission shall decide the merits of the claim for compensation and determine the amount of compensation payable, if any." However, neither Article XVIII nor any other provision of the Liability Convention indicates which substantive law should be used to decide the merits of the claim and determine the compensation issue. Is the appropriate substantive law the domestic law of: 1) the launching State of the space object causing the damage, 2) the State where the space object causing the damage was registered, 3) the State that owned the damaged space object or whose national owned the object, 4) the State where the damaged space object was registered, 5) the home State of the software developer who created the AI used by the space object that caused the damage? Or is it the substantive law formulated by the Claims Commission?[35]

There is a similar choice of substantive law problem when the dispute involves a space-based injury that is not subject to the Liability Convention or when an injured non-governmental entity decides to pursue a claim directly for injury caused by space activity. If such a claim is brought to the State's judiciary, then that State's conflict of law provisions may help determine

---

[35]Liability Convention Article XVI(3) allows the Claims Commission to determine its own procedure, which should include how it chooses the applicable substantive law.

which substantive law applies. It is an open question whether the Liability Convention's liability scheme for allocating fault can apply to private persons or non-governmental entities. The judiciary in Belgium and the United States have both adopted customary international law principles embodied in an international treaty as the substantive law for resolving disputes between two private parties arising in the international arena of the high seas.[36] Thus, the Liability Convention's fault allocation scheme may conceivably be used in proceedings for space-based damage or harm arising from the use of AI. However, that does not eliminate the choice of law dilemma when it comes to determining causation, fault, and other merit-related issues.

As we have seen, the lack of substantive law at the international level limits the ability of the space law treaty regime to establish a harmonious or uniform legal standard for deciding claims involving AI-related space-based damage or harm.

Given that the Liability Convention employs fault-based liability for extraterrestrial damage caused by a space object, it is sensible and practical that the same liability scheme should be applicable to a legal action involving extraterrestrial harm attributable to AI outside the scope of the Liability Convention, or where a non-governmental entity is a party. Otherwise, there will not be any international standard for, among other things, allocating fault and determining liability for extraterrestrial harm arising from space activities. The lack of international standardisation means that the plethora of potential substantive law choices becomes a critical issue. State laws can vary based on whether the State is a common law jurisdiction like the United States and Great Britain, a civil law jurisdiction as in most European States, a jurisdiction based on Islamic law, a State that practises some form of Marxism, or a State that has some other political or legal system.

Selecting from the buffet of substantive law choices in matters involving AI is complicated by the fundamental conceit that the space law treaty regime, like all State legal systems, is based on controlling and regulating the decisions, acts, errors, and omissions of a person or people even if made in the guise of a juridical person. AI is machine conduct. The fundamental distinction between AI conduct and human conduct is an issue that is currently facing the legal systems of technologically advanced States.

The United States is a technologically advanced State that is struggling to find the right "fit" for legal actions arising from an event involving AI. Generally, in the United States, legal actions seeking compensation for harm

---

[36] *Castle John v. NV Mabeco*, 77 ILR 537 (Belgium Court of Cassation 1986); *Institute of Cetacean Research v. Sea Shepherd Conversation Society*, 708 F.3d 1099 (9th Cir. 2013). The two cases involved plaintiffs seeking injunctive and declaratory relief against a non-State actor for conduct alleged to constitute piracy under international law.

caused by a device or machine either claim negligence on the part of the owner/operator or are based on a theory of product liability [Giuffrida, 2019]. However, both theories require that fault should be determined based on human conduct. Negligence requires human involvement. Product liability concerns a defect in software design or manufacturing, and failure to provide a warning of reasonable foreseeable injury [Chung and Zink, 2018; Sword, 2019]. According to these studies, a design defect occurs when a foreseeable risk of harm exists and the designer could have avoided or reduced the risk by using a reasonable alternative design; a manufacturing design fault occurs when a product is not produced according to specifications; and failure to warn occurs when the responsible party fails to "provide instructions regarding how to safely use the software" [Sword, 2019].

Liability for an AI design defect can incur either strict liability or fault liability depending on which particular industry is involved or what kind of application is using the AI [Sword, 2019]. However, the EC's White Paper on AI [European Commission, 2020], seems to adopt the fault-based approach to injury caused by an AI system. In suggesting that product liability law may not be a "good fit" for AI-related injury, the White Paper recognises that "it may be difficult to prove that there is a defect in the product, the damage that has occurred and the causal link between the two". It further notes that "there is some uncertainty about how and to what extent the Product Liability Directive applies in the case of certain types of defects, for example if these result from weaknesses in the cybersecurity of the product".

Nevertheless, since strict and fault liability are predicated on human conduct, a new perspective is emerging that perhaps a new liability scheme is needed for AI. Two new liability concepts proposed for AI are some form of legal personhood specifically for AI and "robot common sense" as a substitute for the "reasonable man" standard used in current jurisprudence [Giuffrida, 2019]. There is also a suggestion that agency law should be used in connection with AI systems since the autonomous machine is actually an agent of the owner or operator. Regardless of how necessary it is to have a new liability standard for AI, especially in the context of outer space, any such development will, in all likelihood, have to emerge from the domestic law of States. This is a substantial limitation in the space law treaty regime for the development of uniform substantive law governing fault liability for space-based damage caused by a space object using AI.

5 Elements of legal methodology for determining the law applicable to intelligent systems and services

Legal methodology is a way of reaching a legal result in a coherent and deductive way [Schadbach, 1998]. The most common legal methodology involves a three-pronged approach consisting of 1) a method of description, 2) a method of conceptual analysis and 3) a method of evaluation [Jovanović, 2019]. This section will examine AI in space in the light of these three prongs.

5.1 Method of description

The "method of description" describes the state of affairs as it exists at present [Jovanović, 2019, p. 2.]. The previous section articulated the current status on matters of jurisdiction and choice of law relating to disputes involving the use of AI in space.

5.2 Method of conceptual analysis

The "method of conceptual analysis" concerns an abstract idea or theory and usually involves: "(1) analysis of the existing conceptual framework of and about law; (2) construction of new conceptual frameworks with accompanying terminologies".[37] Since the previous section focused on the existing conceptual framework and its limitations, this section will examine a new conceptual framework for determining the applicable jurisdictional and substantive law in space-based disputes caused by an AI system, at least when one party to the dispute is an EU Member State or entity. The approach would be consistent with the EC's White Paper on AI [European Commission, 2020], which recognises the need to avoid fragmented and divergent national rules by juridical entities of its Member States on the use of AI within its markets.

The ruling delivered by the Court of Justice of the European Union (CJEU) on December 19, 2019, regarding the online accommodation-sharing platform Airbnb[38] could serve as an important benchmark for establishing jurisdictional boundaries. It may provide important tangential clues as to how to extend the existing frames of reference used to determine the applicable legal regimes governing **AI systems and services in space. Although the CJEU ruling pertains exclusively to terrestrial online platforms providing consumer-related intermediation services**, the extent of which falls considerably below the scope of in-orbit servicing, the extrapolation of this judgment to extraterrestrial matters potentially provides an alternative route to determining the legal regime for service providers and the larger issue of territoriality and State jurisdiction in space.[39]

---

[37][Jovanović, 2019] quoting [Summers, 1966].

[38]Aff. C-390/18, YA and Airbnb Ireland UC versus Hotelière Turenne SAS et Association pour un hébergement et un tourisme professionnel (AHTOP) et Valhotel, Concl. Maciej Szpunar, Press Release n°162/19.

[39]In the legal context of the European Union, this judgment is particularly significant in that it achieves this result without attempting to redefine the distribution of powers (as was done by the Lisbon Treaty) where space activities are concerned. Indeed, space

547

5.2.1 Overview of the solution adopted by the Court of Justice of the European Union

The CJEU provides a legal characterisation of Airbnb's activities which is in accordance with the recommendations set out in the Directive on Electronic Commerce (the e-Commerce Directive), concluding that the Airbnb *platform* fits the definition of *"information society services"* provided in Article 2(a) of the e-Commerce Directive.

In attempting to characterise Airbnb's service offering, the Court carried out a comprehensive examination of Airbnb's online marketplace as well as its wider business model. It ultimately found that the defendant's digital platform provides a direct intermediation service supplied remotely via electronic means, linking potential tenants and landlords, and offering to facilitate their entering into contractual agreements about future transactions.

Although the Airbnb ruling seems prima facie far removed from the realms of space and **AI systems and services**, it offers, nonetheless, a potentially new framework from which to examine broader issues of jurisdiction and extraterritoriality, and determine appropriate legal regimes for novel phenomena spawned by emerging technologies that elude regulatory oversight.

In this context, the CJEU's ruling of December 19, 2019, on Airbnb is a landmark decision that could prompt new insights into how **jurisdictional conflicts may be litigated in the future**. In particular, the decision raises two distinct avenues for inquiry, namely: i) its characterisation of the platform as a neutral vehicle (a delivery system) devoid of inherent liability and unconnected to jurisdiction; and ii) the territorialisation of the service delivered. In other words, the legal regime that is applicable to a platform — whether that platform is deployed on Earth or in outer space — is pegged on the content (the purveyor and/or beneficiary of the services) rather than the container (the physical platform and its operator).

(a) Emphasis on the nature of the service provided

What appears to be important to the Court is not so much the features or functionality of the platform used but the nature of the service provided. What it regards as constituting an information society service is really the purpose of that service: putting potential tenants in contact, in return for payment, with professional or non-professional landlords offering short-term accommodation services, so that tenants can book accommodation.

---

as well as the attendant technological research & development activities remain fully entrenched within the realm and jurisdiction of shared competence between the Union and its Members States, in complete agreement with Article 4 of the Treaty on the Functioning of the European Union, which specifies that space is an area over which "the Union shall have competence to carry out activities, in particular to define and implement programmes; however, the exercise of that competence shall not result in Member States being prevented from exercising theirs".

The fact that this service is provided by means of an electronic platform seems to be less important than the fact that it is provided at a distance, albeit by electronic means, or that it is provided at an individual's request on the basis of an advertisement disseminated by the landlord and an individual request from the tenant interested in the advertisement.

The fact that this service is provided by means of an electronic platform seems to be less important than the fact that it is provided at a distance, albeit by electronic means, or that it is provided at an individual's request on the basis of an advertisement disseminated by the landlord and an individual request from the tenant interested in the advertisement.

The platform only appears in the Court's reasoning as technical support for the service, and the main characteristic of that technical support, as far as the Court is concerned, is that it is provided remotely. The Court of Justice of the European Union notes that the service is provided *"by means of an electronic platform"* (§47), although it acknowledges that the technical support plays an essential role in the provision of the service, noting that the parties come into contact only through the electronic platform of the same name (§47).

(b) Unbundling of intermediation and hosting services

This approach is all the more interesting in that the reasoning of the Court of Justice of the European Union concerning the Airbnb electronic platform articulates a second argument: the intermediation service provided by Airbnb by means of the eponymous electronic platform must be disassociated from the real estate transaction *"in so far as it does not consist solely in the immediate provision of accommodation"* (§54). In the Court's view, it consists more in making available on an electronic platform *"a structured list of short-term accommodation (...) corresponding to the criteria adopted by persons seeking short-term accommodation"*, so that that the service (and hence the platform itself) is regarded only as *"an instrument facilitating the conclusion of contracts relating to future transactions"* (§53).

As the Court points out, *"it is the creation of such a list for the benefit of both guests with accommodation for rent and those seeking such accommodation which is the key feature of the electronic platform managed by Airbnb Ireland"* (§53).

Put differently by the same Court, the service provided by Airbnb Ireland by means of its electronic platform *"cannot be regarded as merely ancillary to an overall service falling within a different legal classification, namely the provision of accommodation"* (§54). Nor is it indispensable to the provision of accommodation, since this is provided directly by the landlords, whether professional or non-professional. It only provides one more channel, in addition to other ways and means, for the parties to the accommodation contract to meet and conclude the contract.

By recognising its independence, the Court renders Airbnb a service providing additional support, which serves the objectives of competition and, consequently, the market, especially since the electronic platform does not intervene in determining the price of accommodation. It is merely a means of facilitation, which includes all associated services (photographs of the asset rented, an optional instrument for estimating the rental price in relation to market averages calculated by the platform, a rating system for landlords and tenants), considered as part of *"the collaborative logic inherent in intermediation platforms, which allows, on the one hand, housing applicants to make a fully informed choice from among the housing offers proposed by landlords on the platform and, on the other hand, allows landlords to be fully informed about the seriousness of the tenants with whom they are likely to engage"* (§60).

(c) Consecration of the law of the country of establishment of the service provider

By classifying the intermediation service provided by the Airbnb platform as an information society service, the Court of Justice of the European Union makes it subject to the aforementioned Directive 2000/31. This means that, *"in order to ensure effectively the freedom to provide services and legal certainty for service providers and their recipients, such information society services must in principle be subject to the legal regime of the Member State in which the service provider is established"* (Recital 22).

The attachment of an activity, whether terrestrial or space-based, to the jurisdiction of a State implies submission of that activity to the legal system of that State. According to the logic of the internal market of the European Union, the activity may be linked to a particular State that is *"the State in which the service provider is established"*. Indeed, since the legal orders of each Member State are supposed to integrate the provisions of the regulations or directives of the European Parliament and the Council, these legal orders are made up of harmonised legislative or regulatory texts.

This is all the more true since the principle of the primacy of Community law gives precedence to European rules over national law and since this particular European rule is itself directly applicable. An European citizen can therefore ensure that it will be applied by the national court whether or not the national law is in conformity with European law.

This is why, in the logic of European integration, the principle adopted to determine which law is applicable to a service activity is that it must be the law of the country in which the service provider is established or, in the case of broadcasting by means of satellite systems, the law of the country in which the signal is transmitted.

Comparable reasoning can be articulated with regard to a platform deployed in space. Application of the law of the country of the origin of the service provided by means of an intelligent space platform is preferable, in our view, to applying the law of the country of consumption of the service.

(d) Obligation of prior notification of national provisions

The Airbnb decision is also interesting in that it obliges Member States to notify the European Commission when their national legislation is more restrictive than the EU legislation. This is an interesting idea that can be transposed to international relations. Moreover, a comparable practice exists in the air transport sector, which leaves States sovereign over their respective airspaces and, in the name of this sovereignty, allows them to have differences between their national legislation and international rules known to the International Civil Aviation Organization (ICAO). These differences are accepted and respected on the condition that they have been notified to the ICAO. The same mechanism could be transposed to space law.

In the Airbnb judgment, the European Court of Justice did not proceed differently. It set aside the national law of the country of consumption of service, in this case French law, on two separate grounds. The first arises from the principle of the free movement of information society services between Member States, which the Court of Justice considers to be one of the objectives of Directive 2000/31, going so far as to point out that "this objective is pursued by means of a mechanism for monitoring measures liable to undermine it" (§91). The second is a corollary of the first, since it follows from the obligation imposed on Member States, by Directive 2000/31, to notify the Commission of measures restricting or liable to restrict the free movement of information society services prior to their entry into force.

The Court pointed out that the obligation to notify is not "*a mere information requirement*", but corresponds in fact to "*a procedural requirement of a substantive nature justifying the non-applicability to individuals of non-notified measures restricting the free movement of information society services*" (§94). As the Court also pointed out, this is indeed "*a standstill obligation on the part of the State intending to adopt a measure restricting the freedom to provide an information society service*" (§93).

In its judgment of 19 December 2019, the Court of Justice of the European Union did not reject this eventuality. On the contrary, it recognised that, in extending the provisions of Article 3(4) of Directive 2000/31, Member States have the option of taking measures that derogate from the principle of the free movement of information society services with regard to a given information society service falling within a relevant field. However, in addition to the procedural obligation to notify referred to above, it laid down three substantive conditions which must be satisfied (§84):

- the restrictive measure concerned must be necessary in order to guarantee public policy, protect public health, ensure public security or protect the consumer AND,
- it must be taken against an information society service that effectively undermines or constitutes a serious and grave risk of undermining these objectives, AND,
- it must be proportionate to these objectives.

(e) Key takeaways from the Airbnb case

From a space law perspective, this ruling is especially significant as its rationale may be extended to space platforms that are assembled in outer space and that are used to provide AI systems and services in space and whose connections to terrestrial jurisdictions are inconclusive.

Such stations and platforms, regardless of their complexity, purpose and functionality, remain in essence supporting tools and instruments designed to facilitate the provision of a service. In other words, they are a means to an end. As such, the ruling of the CJEU would retain its role as a deciding factor to help courts determine the true nature and scope of an information communication technology related service, whether on Earth or in outer space. In other words, when examining the concept of platform, the Court excluded all metonymic reasoning and retained that it is the nature of the service that is being provided via that platform that is the primary consideration in making a legal characterisation, not the characteristics of the platform as a vehicle for delivering that service. Further, the ruling argues that even in circumstances where the provision of a service must in fine be conflated with the medium that is used to deliver it[40], the provision of the service must be considered over the medium that is used to deliver it, which must be considered a secondary aspect.

5.3   Method of evaluation

The "method of evaluation" involves examining "whether rules work in practice, or whether they are in accordance with desirable moral, political, economic aims, or, in comparative law, whether a certain harmonisation proposal could work, taking into account other important divergences in the legal systems concerned".[41] As discussed below, the Airbnb case may be applicable to disputes involving AI systems and services in space.

A similar rationale can be equally replicated in the context of AI systems and services in space **supplied** via outer space platforms powered by AI technologies. Drawing on a concept that has been common to both telecommu-

---

[40]Likely because the contracting parties could only establish contact through the intermediation of this service/tool.

[41][Jovanović, 2019] quoting [Hoecke, 2011, p. v.]

nications law and electronic communications law ever since those industries opened up to market competition, the support service delivered by a given platform is in and of itself a bearer service (or data service) that makes an infrastructure available to users. Such a service must be distinguished from the global service provision supplied through the platform-as-a-medium. As the service becomes increasingly dematerialised, it too becomes progressively disassociated from its medium.

In the case of in-orbit servicing, if the bulk of that service is actually delivered in orbit[42], the foreseeable legal challenge lies in accurately identifying the substance and nature of this service provision and defining its governing legal regime. This must apply even where the service provision merges with its delivery platform to such an extent that a platform governed by artificial intelligence becomes materially indivisible from the services that it is designed to deliver. From a legal perspective, the delivery of such a service calls for a distinct characterisation that falls under the authority of the principles governing the activities of States in the exploration and use of outer space, including the moon and other celestial bodies (i.e. the principles of the Outer Space Treaty).

This particular requirement raises the larger question of how to define the boundaries of the legal forum and the jurisdictional competence of the State i.e. the range of the applicability of national laws over matters beyond the traditional purview of national legislation. The CJEU's judgment of December 19, 2019, on the matter of Airbnb's digital platform offers an important contribution to this question as well. In characterising the intermediation service delivered by the Airbnb digital platform as an information society service, the CJEU places the defendant's business under the scope of Directive 2000/31. The directive lays down that *"in order to improve mutual trust between Member States [and] to effectively guarantee freedom to provide services and legal certainty for suppliers and recipients of services, such information society services should in principle be subject to the law of the Member State in which the service provider is established"*.[43]

Beyond the basic principles of the freedom to provide services and legal certainty[44], binding in-orbit service delivery provided via a smart space platform to the legal jurisdictional authority and to the legal regime of a particular State provides a fresh outlook on the leading doctrine established by Article VIII of the OST.[45] Where weighing the various connecting fac-

---

[42]Be it remote computation, temperature-controlled storage, maintenance operations, rescue missions, remote sensing and Earth observation or big data storage, etc.

[43]Directive 2000/31/CE, Recital n°22.

[44]Which are not unique to the internal European Union market, and which apply in equal measure to terrestrial commerce as to outer space commerce.

[45]With its twofold implication of jurisdictional boundary and government control.

tors enables an Earth or space-bound activity to be ascribed a given national jurisdiction, the activity is bound by the legal regime of that State. Therefore, in keeping with the internal market rationale of the EU, jurisdiction can be established on the basis of *the State in which the service provider is domiciled* (see [de Poulpiquet, 2018]).

Within the particular context of EU law, considering that the legal regime of each Member State is required to integrate the statutory and regulatory provisions issued by the European Parliament and the Council, all the national legislative and regulatory frameworks are supposed to be harmonised across EU jurisdictions, in compliance with the overarching principle of the primacy of Community law.[46] This principle requires that the EU rule of law must always prevail over national law where there is a conflict of laws, and that EU regulations have direct application within national jurisdictions. As a result, all EU citizens have the prerogative to avail themselves of the right to petition a national court to enforce the application of an EU statutory or regulatory provision over national law, regardless of whether the national law is compliant with EU legislation.

As is consistent with the guiding principles of European integration, the basic legal principle used when determining the appropriate legal regime applicable to the provision of a commercial service tethers the legal forum to the service provider's place of establishment, or, in the case of satellite frequency broadcasting, to the law of the country from which the signal is emitted. For our purposes, the latter criterion can be a particularly helpful connecting factor where, in the case of sophisticated information and communications technology (ICT) semi-autonomous applications developed by international teams cutting across traditional jurisdictions, the original place of establishment cannot be conclusively determined.

In the light of the preceding discussion, one proposed way out of the jurisdictional quandary raised by emerging intelligent technologies in outer space would be to bind the provision of the service to the legislation and to the jurisdictional forum of the beneficiary of that service i.e. the customer or the consumer of that service. Such an approach would have the advantage of bringing an added level of clarity to determine the appropriate legal forum and address the lingering difficulty of establishing clear connecting factors that bind orbital operators to terrestrial jurisdictions.

The latter situation arises when the country of registration is designated as the sole applicable jurisdiction where the "customer" is an actual space

---

[46]Declaration 17 concerning primacy in Declarations annexed to the Final Act of the Intergovernmental Conference which adopted the Treaty of Lisbon (December, 13, 2007). See also the consolidated protocols, annexes and declarations attached to the treaties of the European Union.

object that is subject to mandatory registration. This particular situation brings many challenges in the context of the intersection of the digital economy and the space industry. Rethinking liability around service users and service purveyors might be a way forward that is more in line with the direction that the industry seems to be taking as a whole.

The proposed solution might also put a stop to the growing practice of many States, due to the difficulties of tracking and controlling the activities of private operators in space, of starting to *"[relax] the registration and supervision of corporations [incurring the risk] of possible liability"* and failing to respect the duty of care imposed by the treaties [Zhao, 2004].

Going forward, the applicable legislation could be the national jurisdiction of the natural or legal entity that benefits either directly or indirectly from the service that is being supplied in orbit.

Such a solution would usher in an unprecedented level of transparency and legal certainty to all the stakeholders involved, and would further benefit from existing legal scholarship and regulatory frameworks that are already in place in other areas of international law as well as regulations to streamline oversight mechanisms while also stimulating industrial development. For instance, with particular regard to State subsidies and EU community State aid rules, there is ample legal expertise and established jurisprudence to help lawmakers trace international finance networks to determine State accountability and expose hollow intermediaries [Rapp and Terneyre, 2020].

Finally, such a solution would provide the flexibility required to enable any concerned State to introduce appropriate oversight and control mechanisms with its own legislation. This aligns with the observable trend of States relying ever more on national legislation rather than international consensus to regulate competitive markets.

6   AI techniques to support space law

The triad of "law, space, and AI" is an instance of the "law, science, and technology" triad. The intersection between the elements of the latter triad is quite extensive and goes beyond the scope of this whole handbook. The relationship between the first triad and this chapter is fairly similar. There are several open questions and developments in AI that concern the law and legal compliance. Those that concern the legal questions raised in this chapter so far are, of course, relevant. For instance, the developments of machine learning (federated learning, transfer learning, generative adversarial networks) or real-time analysis with big data in general are approaches that might facilitate compliance with the General Data Protection Regulation and are relevant for space applications too. The big question of liability related to automated decision-making or machine learning algorithms, or the possible accountability of autonomous agents, are also open questions for law. For now, answering these questions means relying on State law and general principles of international law where space law is inapplicable or uncertain. Space is an area where legal and technical solutions to the unresolved issues are of great significance because of our increasing reliance on AI for space activities. Autonomous space agents will need to reason about legal obligations under applicable law when making decisions. Accordingly, the processes discussed in the Handbook of Legal AI should be applied to general questions of legal reasoning, relevant formal systems and other AI applications related to space technologies and space law. In the next section, we highlight only one approach introduced in this book that is applicable to the current and foreseeable state of space law.

6.1 Legal knowledge representation in the space AI domain

Machine-readable modelling of a consensually shared domain of space law would increase the chance that such legal knowledge will be connected across the Web and used in different applications. As discussed, the normative sources in this domain are multiple and heterogeneous, thus ontologies would appear to be the most suitable way of mapping this body of knowledge [Humphreys *et al.*, 2015]. The interconnections within the space law framework makes it a natural domain for knowledge representation, sharing and reuse.

Legal fragmentation suitable for ontologies

The space law treaty regime is complemented and supplemented **by national legislation** from each country providing thorough provisions and sufficient clarify regarding activities that are not directly addressed in the vague, imprecise, overly broadly formulated and ambiguous provisions of the Outer Space Treaty [Rapp, 2018]. Analysis of some of the most significant space legislation immediately confirms that space law is not **a unified single text** but is a combination of **separate legal texts** (that do not all have the same legal value), **i.e. what we have is legal fragmentation.** And while we can observe an intention to keep some questions subject to international treaties and others subject entirely to national jurisdictions, these questions are highly interconnected in legal practice, as we saw above, and thoroughfares are required between supposedly separate areas.

Convergence of legal mechanisms as classes of a space law ontology

Alongside the heterogeneity of the form and contents of national legal texts — simultaneously reflecting the legal traditions of each State, their degree of involvement in the space economy and, more and more often, their willingness to differentiate themselves from other nations by offering more favourable conditions for space traders (forum shopping) — their **conver-**

gence is reflected in the fact that the most relevant legal mechanisms are used in each different jurisdiction. The following eight provision types represent the basic schema (domain-specific classes) for any space law ontology that describes the know¬ledge embedded in the different legal documents:

1. authorisation and licensing

2. continuous supervision of non-governmental activity

3. liability

4. insurance

5. space debris removal

6. State strategic interest

7. registration process or registry

8. transfer of ownership in space

6.2   Relevant knowledge resources

To develop a domain-specific legal ontology, it is necessary to use the most authoritative relevant knowledge resources [Opijnen and Santos, 2017] from that specific legal domain. We have therefore obtained both non-ontological and ontology-based resources to be further engineered.

Non-ontological resources. Non-ontological resources (NOR) in the legal domain are knowledge resources whose semantics have not been formalised yet in an ontology but which have related semantics that allows ontological interpretation of the legal knowledge they hold [Santos *et al.*, 2015]. In fact, using non-ontological resources about the space domain that conveys consensus in the field brings certain benefits e.g. interoperability in terms of the vocabulary used, information browse/search capabilities, decrease in the knowledge acquisition bottleneck, reuse etc. The following non-exhaustive resources are recommended because they comprise highly reliable domain-related content from the websites of organisations that have knowledge of the domain. They serve as domain knowledge resources for the development of a space ontology. They are structured and semantically rich taxonomies that serve to annotate the data elements in an ontology. Reuse of these resources can enable the development of a common terminology, i.e. a harmonised high-level taxonomy of space legal concepts and terms, to characterise space law. More concretely, we suggest that the following resources can be used for automatic ontology population:

- Space Legal Tech [SIRIUS, ndb], a tool representing the regulations and national space agencies of 100 countries (depicted in 1);

- the USA National Aeronautics and Space Administration (NASA) Thesaurus (accessible in machine-readable form) [NASA, 2012], and Taxonomy [NASA, 2009], documenting a high-level set of terms that can be used to map various data structures;

- the Union of Concerned Scientists (UCS) Satellite Database [UCS, 2005];

- glossaries, such as the European Space Agency Science's Glossary [ESA, nd] and others [NASA, nda; UNOOSA and PSIPW, nd; Fact Monster, 2017; NASA, ndb];

- the ESA Earth Observation Knowledge Navigational System [Zingler and di Marcantonio, 1998], a knowledge management system for EO imagery;

- A Guide to Space Law Terms [Hertzfeld, 2012]; and

- "Spationary" [SIRIUS, nda], a work-in-progress database with structured business and space law concepts and terms (illustrated in 2).

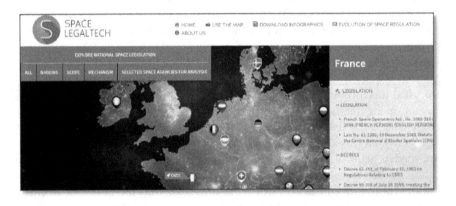

Figure 1. National space legislation from France [SIRIUS, ndb]

Ontological Resources. We leverage existing space-related ontological resources (semantically structured information about this domain) which can be reused or extended to any ontology modelling space law, which means that classes and/or instantiations from these existing ontologies can be imported.

Concept	Common definition	Laws and Treaties	Governmental, institutional or official sources	Legal Scholarship	Related terms	Examples
International Liability	A State Party's obligation to compensate another Third State for any injury that it caused to the people or property of the latter	"Each State Party to the Treaty that launches or procures the launching of an object into outer space, including the moon and other celestial bodies, and each State Party from whose territory or facility an object is launched, is internationally liable for damage to another State Party to the Treaty or to its natural or juridicalpersons by such object or its component parts on the Earth, in air or in outer space[.]", Outer Space Treaty Art. VII	"It is important to note that international responsibility under Article VI [of the] Outer Space Treaty is born for 'national activities in outer space' while the matter of international liability is tied to 'space objects.' Arguably, only the latter may raise the definitional issue of whether space debris is or is not a 'space object.'", Comm. on the Peaceful Uses of Outer Space, Scientific & Tech. Subcomm. Rep. on its 48th Sess., Feb. 7-18, 2011, U.N. Doc. A/AC.105/C.1 (Feb. 3, 2011)	States are, under Article VII of the Outer Space Treaty, "liable for damage caused to another state through its own space activities or of those subject to its jurisdiction, licensing and supervision. Such an extension of responsibility and liability of a state to damage caused by its non-state entities is unusual in international law.", Francis Lyall & Paul B. Larsen, Space Law: A Treatise 66 (2009)	International Responsibility and Liability	**Soviet Kosmos 954:** Soviet Union launched a radioactive satellite in 1978 which failed and crashed in Northern Canada, and deposited debris over a wide area. The Canadian government spent over $14M cleaning up the debris. OST – Liability Convention: Soviet Union held responsible, as the launcher state. However it only paid half of the damages. **Soviet Satellite Out Of Control**

Figure 2. Excerpt of the concept of liability from Spationary [SIRIUS, nda]

Ontological resources	Description
Ontology for space object [Rovetto, 2016b]	Analysis of the category of space object and its subcategories. Space objects include artificial objects such as spacecraft, space stations, and natural space objects.
Ontology-based knowledge management for space data [Rovetto, 2017a]	Discusses aspects of ontological engineering in knowledge management architectures for space data.
Ontology for Satellite Databases [Rovetto, 2017b]	Offers a domain-specific terminology and knowledge model for space data systems. Where data is drawn from multiple sensors or databases, ontologies can foster information fusion via this backbone terminology.
Space Surveillance Ontology in XML Schema [Pulvermacher et al., 2000]	Captures data structures, content and semantics from a targeted military domain of space surveillance.
Orbital Debris Ontology [Rovetto, 2016a]	Seeks to support orbital debris remediation by modelling orbital debris in an ontology and developing accurate and reusable debris classification.
Space Situational Awareness Ontology [Rovetto and	Domain coverage of all space objects in the orbital space environment and relevant space situational awareness (SSA) entities

In furtherance of the development of any ontological artefact, members of the space community should provide domain expertise, including verifying the accuracy of the knowledge expressed in the logical formalisations of the ontologies.

Ontology-based resources in the legal domain. Building on the risks for privacy and data protection described and assessed in Section 3.2, we aim to reuse ontologies that model concepts relating to the protection of personal data such as the Data Protection Ontology [Bartolini *et al.*, 2015], PrivOnto [Oltramari *et al.*, 2018], PrOnto [Palmirani *et al.*, 2018] and GDPRtEXT (GDPR text extensions) [Pandit *et al.*, 2018]. Core legal domain ontologies, such as Eurovoc, Legal RuleML [Palmirani *et al.*, 2011], and the European Legal Identifier (ELI) ontology, are also useful.

7 Conclusion

In this chapter, we discussed how "intelligent" systems and services raise legal problems, starting with the applicable law relating to privacy, data protection and liability. These legal challenges call for solutions that the international treaties in force cannot determine and implement sufficiently. For this reason, we suggested a legal methodology that makes it possible to link intelligent systems and services to a system of applicable rules. We also proposed legal informatics tools that could be used for the domain of space law.

BIBLIOGRAPHY

[Aerospace, 2018] Aerospace. Artificial intelligence gets ahead of the threats. https://aerospace.org/Annual-Report-2018/artificial-intelligence-gets-ahead-threats, 2018. 13 December, 2018.

[Aloisio, 2017] G. Aloisio. Privacy and data protection issues of the european union copernicus border surveillance service, 2017. Master's thesis, University of Luxembourg.

[Aranzamendi *et al.*, 2010] M. S. Aranzamendi, R. Sandau, and K. Schrogl. *Current Legal Issues for Satellite Earth Observation*. European Space Policy Institute, 2010.

[Bartolini *et al.*, 2015] C. Bartolini, R. Muthuri, and C. Santos. Using ontologies to model data protection requirements in workflows. In M. Otake, S. Kurahashi, Y. Ota, K. Satoh, and D. Bekki, editors, *Proceedings of the 9th International Workshop on Juris-informatics (JURISIN, 2015)*, volume 10091 of *New Frontiers in Artificial Intelligence. JSAI-isAI 2015, Lecture Notes in Computer Science*, pages 27–40. Springer, 2015.

[BBC, 2014] British Broadcasting Corporation BBC. Us lifts restrictions on more detailed satellite images. https://www.bbc.com/news/technology-27868703, 2014. 16 June, 2014.

[Beam, 2019] C. Beam. Soon, satellites will be able to watch you everywhere all the time—Can privacy survive?, 2019. MIT Technology Review.

[Buolamwini and Gebru, 2018] J. Buolamwini and T. Gebru. Gender shades: Intersectional accuracy disparities in commercial gender classification. In *Proceedings of the*

First Conference on Fairness, Accountability and Transparency, PMLR, pages 81:77–91, 2018.

[CBS, 2013] CBS. Google earth used to bust oregon medicinal marijuana garden, police say, 2013. CBS News. 22 October, 2013.

[Cheng, 1998] B. Cheng. Article vi of the 1967 space treaty revisited: 'international responsibility', 'national activities', and 'the appropriate state'. *Journal of Space Law*, 26(1):7-32, 1998.

[Chun and Atluri, 2002] S. Chun and V. Atluri. Protecting privacy from continuous high-resolution satellite surveillance. In B. Thuraisingham et al., editor, *Data and Application Security*, volume 73 of *International Federation for Information Processing*. 2002.

[Chung and Zink, 2018] J. Chung and A. Zink. Hey watson - can i sue you for malpractice? examining the liability of artificial intelligence in medicine. *Asia Pacific Journal of Health Law and Ethics*, 11:51-68, 2018.

[CNIL, 2019] Commission nationale de l'informatique et des libertés CNIL. Facial recognition. for a debate living up to the challenges. https://www.cnil.fr/sites/default/files/atoms/files/facial-recognition.pdf, 2019. 15 November, 2019.

[Council of the European Union, 2019] Council of the European Union. Outcome of proceedings: Proposal for a Regulation of the European Parliament and of the Council establishing the space programme of the Union and the European Union Agency for the Space Programme and repealing Regulations (eu) no 912/2010, (EU) no 1285/2013, (EU) no 377/2014 and Decision 541/2014/EU. https://data.consilium.europa.eu/doc/document/ST-7481-2019-INIT/en/pdf, 2019.

[Cuellar, 2017] M. F. Cuellar. A simpler world? on pruning risks and harvesting fruits in an orchard of whispering algorithms. *University of California Davis Law Review*, November; 51:27, 2017.

[de Concini and Toth, 2019] A. de Concini and J. Toth. The future of the european space sector—How to leverage Europe's technological leadership and boost investments for space ventures. https://www.eib.org/attachments/thematic/future_of_european_space_sector_en.pdf, 2019. European Investment Bank.

[de Poulpiquet, 2018] J. de Poulpiquet. *L'immatriculation des satellites. Recherches sur le lien de rattachement à l'Etat d'un objet lancé dans l'espace*. PhD thesis, 2018.

[Dennerley, 2018] J. A. Dennerley. State liability for space object collisions: The proper interpretation of 'fault' for the purposes of international space law. *European Journal of International Law*, 29(1):281-301, 2018.

[der Sloot, 2014] B. Van der Sloot. Privacy in the post-nsa era: Time for a fundamental revision? *Journal of Intellectual Property, Information Technology and E-Commerce Law*, 5:2, 2014.

[E. Denham. Big Data and Protection, 2017] Machine Learning E. Denham. Big Data, Artificial Intelligence and Data Protection. Information Commissioner's Office, UK, 2017.

[ESA, 2016] The European Space Agenc ESA. What is space 4.0? https://www.esa.int/About_Us/Ministerial_Council_2016/What_is_space_4.0, 2016. [accessed 4 May 2019)].

[ESA, 2019] The European Space Agency ESA. Automating collision avoidance. https://www.esa.int/Safety_Security/Space_Debris/Automating_collision_avoidance, 2019.

[ESA, nd] The European Space Agency ESA. Glossary. https://www.esa.int/Our_Activities/Space_Transportation/Glossary, n.d.

[European Commission, 2019] European Commission. Ethics guidelines for trustworthy ai. https://data.europa.eu/doi/10.2759/346720, 2019. Directorate-General for Communications Networks, Content and Technology, Publications Office.

[European Commission, 2020] European Commission. White Paper on Artificial Intelligence—A European approach to excellence and trust. https://ec.europa.eu/info/sites/info/files/commission-white-paper-artificial-intelligence-feb2020_en.pdf, 2020. COM 65 Final. European Union. 10 June, 2020.

[European Commission, nd] European Commission. A European Strategy for data. Sharing Europe's digital future. https://digital-strategy.ec.europa.eu/en/policies/strategy-data, n.d.

[Fact Monster, 2017] Fact Monster. Space glossary. https://www.factmonster.com/math-science/space/universe/space-glossary, 2017.

[Firestone, 1985] M. S. Firestone. Problems in the resolution of disputes concerning damage caused in outer space. *Tulane Law Review*, 59:747-763, 1985.

[FRA, 2019] European Agency for Fundamental Rights FRA. Facial recognition technology: fundamental rights considerations in the context of law enforcement. https://fra.europa.eu/en/publication/2019/facial-recognition, 2019.

[Gattle, 2019] B. Gattle. Moving from Newspace to "Nowspace". https://www.satellitetoday.com/innovation/2019/07/03/moving-from-newspace-to-nowspace/, 2019.

[Giuffrida, 2019] I. Giuffrida. Liability for ai decision-making: some legal and ethical considerations. *Fordham Law Review*, 88:439, 2019.

[Global Forest Watch, 2018] Global Forest Watch. Amapá police use forest watcher to defend the brazilian amazon. https://www.globalforestwatch.org/blog/people/amapa-police-use-forest-watcher-to-defend-the-brazilian-amazon/, 2018.

[Gray, 1996] M. A. Gray. The international crime of ecocide. *California Western International Law Journal*, 26:215, 1996.

[Harebottle, 2019] A. Harebottle. Space 2.0: Taking ai far out. https://interactive.satellitetoday.com/via/december-2019/space-2-0-taking-ai-far-out/, 2019.

[Hertzfeld, 2012] H. R. Hertzfeld, editor. *A Guide to Space Law Terms*. Space Policy Institute. George Washington University and Secure World Foundation, 2012.

[Hildebrandt and Gutwirth, 2008] M. Hildebrandt and S. Gutwirth. *Profiling the European Citizen*. Springer, Dordrecht, 2008.

[Van Hoecke, 2011] M. Van Hoecke, editor. *Methodologies of Legal Research — Which Kind of Method for What Kind of Discipline?* Hart Publishing, Oxford and Portland, Oregon, 2011.

[Hollingham, 2014] R. Hollingham. Google earth has given us a new way of looking at our cities and neighbourhoods—from space. richard hollingham visits the satellite factory building to see what's coming next. https://www.bbc.com/future/article/20140211-inside-the-google-earth-sat-lab, 2014. BBC. 11 February, 2014.

[Humphreys *et al.*, 2015] L. Humphreys, C. Santos, L. Di Caro, G. Boella, L. van der Torre, and L. Robaldo. Mapping recitals to normative provisions in eu legislation to assist legal interpretation. In A. Rotolo, editor, *Legal Knowledge and Information System*, volume 279 of *Frontiers in Artificial Intelligence and Applications*, pages 41–49. IOS Press, 2015.

[ITU, nd] International Telecommunication Union ITU. Study group 17 at a glance. https://www.itu.int/en/ITU-T/about/groups/Pages/sg17.aspx, n.d.

[Jovanović, 2019] M. Jovanović. Legal methodology and legal research and writing - a very short introduction. http://147.91.244.8/prof/materijali/jovmio/mei/Legal%20methodology%20and%20legal%20research%20and%20writing.pdf, 2019.

[Karnow, 1996] C. E. A. Karnow. Liability for distributed artificial intelligences. *Berkeley Technology Law Journal*, 11:147:189–190, 1996.

[Kowert, 2017] W. Kowert. The foreseeability of human-artificial intelligence interactions. *Texas Law Review*, 96:181-183, 2017.

[Laituri, 2018] M. Laituri. Satellite imagery is revolutionizing the world. but should we always trust what we see? `https://theconversation.com/satellite-imagery-is-revolutionizing-the-world-but-should-we-always-trust-what-we-see-95201`, 2018. The Conversation, 4 June, 2018.

[Long, 2014] G. A. Long. Small satellites and state responsibility associated with space traffic situational awareness. `https://commons.erau.edu/stm/2014/thursday/17/`, 2014. First Annual Space Traffic Management Conference "Roadmap to the Stars" at Embry-Riddle Aeronautical University, Daytona Beach, Florida, November 6, 2014.

[Long, 2018] G. A. Long. Artificial intelligence and state responsibility under the outer space treaty. In *Proceedings Of The International Institute Of Space Law*. Eleven International Publishing, 2018.

[Long, 2019] G. A. Long. Legal basis for a state's use of police power against non-nationals to enforce its national space legislation, 2019. 70th International Astronautical Congress, Washington, D.C., 23 October, 2019.

[Louradour and Madzou, 2020] S. Louradour and L. Madzou. White paper. a framework for responsible limits on facial recognition. use case: Flow management paper, 2020. World Economic Forum, 2020.

[Lucas-Rhimbassen et al., 2019] M. Lucas-Rhimbassen, C. Santos, G. Long, and L. Rapp. Conceptual model for a profitable return on investment from space debris as abiotic space resource, 2019. At 8TH European Conference for Aeronautics and Space Sciences (EUCASS). Held in Madrid, Spain, 1-4 July, 2019.

[NASA, 2009] NASA. Nasa taxonomy 2.0. `https://www.loc.gov/item/lcwaN0014329/`, 2009. Web Archive—Retrieved from the Library of Congress.

[NASA, 2012] STI Program NASA. Nasa thesaurus. `https://sti.nasa.gov/nasa-thesaurus/`, 2012. Data file.

[NASA, nda] NASA. Basics of space flight glossary. nasa science solar system exploration. `https://solarsystem.nasa.gov/basics/glossary/`, n.d.

[NASA, ndb] NASA. Glossary. `https://hubblesite.org/glossary`, n.d.

[Nissenbaum, 2010] H. Nissenbaum. *Privacy in Context: Technology, Policy, and the Integrity of Social Life*. Stanford Law Books. Stanford, California, 2010.

[Oltramari et al., 2018] A. Oltramari, D. Piraviperumal, F. Schaub, S. Wilson, S. Cherivirala, T. B. Norton, N. C. Russell, P. Story, J. Reidenberg, and N. Sadeh. Privonto: A semantic framework for the analysis of privacy policies. *Semantic Web*, Jan 1;9(2:185–203, 2018.

[Opijnen and Santos, 2017] M. Van Opijnen and C. Santos. On the concept of relevance in legal information retrieval. *In Artificial Intelligence and Law Journal*, 25:65—87, 2017.

[Palmirani et al., 2011] M. Palmirani, G. Governatori, A. Rotolo, S. Tabet, H. Boley, and A. Paschke. Legalruleml: Xml-based rules and norms. In F. Olken, M. Palmirani, and D. Sottara, editors, *Rule-Based Modeling and Computing on the Semantic Web, RuleML 2011*, volume 7018 of *Lecture Notes in Computer Science*, 2011.

[Palmirani et al., 2018] M. Palmirani, M. Martoni, A. Rossi, C. Bartolini, and L. Robaldo. Pronto: Privacy ontology for legal reasoning. In *International Conference on Electronic Government and the Information Systems Perspective*, pages 139–152. Springer, 2018.

[Pandit et al., 2018] H. J. Pandit, K. Fatema, D. O'Sullivan, and D. Lewis. Gdprtext-gdpr as a linked data resource. In *European Semantic Web Conference 2018, Jun 3*, pages 481–495. Springer, 2018.

[Perrazzelli and Vergano, 1999] A. Perrazzelli and P. R. Vergano. Terminal dues under the upu convention and the gats: An overview of the rules and of of their compatibility. *Fordham International Law Journal*, 23:736-747, 1999.

[Popkin, 2018] G. Popkin. Technology and satellite companies open up a world of data. `https://www.nature.com/articles/d41586-018-05268-w`, 2018. 29 May, 2018.

[Pulvermacher *et al.*, 2000] M.K. Pulvermacher, D. L. Brandsma, and J. R. Wilson. A space surveillance ontology captured in an xml schema, 2000. MITRE, Center for Air Force C2 Systems, Bedford, Massachusetts.

[R. L. Finn and Friedewald, 2013] D. Wright R. L. Finn and M. Friedewald. *Seven types of Privacy.* Springer, Dordrecht, 2013.

[Rapp and Terneyre, 2020] L. Rapp and P. Terneyre. Lamy droit public des affaires, 2020. Lamy Kluwer n°774 et seq.

[Rapp, 2018] L. Rapp. Space lawmaking. https://www.thespacereview.com/article/3523/1, 2018. The Space Review, 2 July, 2018.

[Raskin and Pan, 2005] R. G. Raskin and M. J. Pan. Knowledge representation in the semantic web for earth and environmental terminology (sweet). *Computers and Geosciences*, November 1;31(9):1119–25, 2005.

[Rosenstock and Kaplan, 2002] R. Rosenstock and M. Kaplan. The fifty-third session of the international law commission, 2002. 96(2):412-9.

[Rovetto and Kelso, 2016] R. J. Rovetto and T. S. Kelso. Preliminaries of a space situational awareness ontology, 2016. At 26th AIAA/AAS Space Flight Mechanics meeting, Napa, California, 17 Feb 17, 2016.

[Rovetto, 2016a] R. J. Rovetto. An ontological architecture for orbital debris data. *Earth Science Informatics*, Mar;9(1):67–82, 2016.

[Rovetto, 2016b] R. J. Rovetto. Space object ontology. https://philarchive.org/archive/ROVSOO, 2016.

[Rovetto, 2017a] R. J. Rovetto. Ontology-based knowledge management for space data, 2017. In 68th International Astronautical Congress, Adelaide, Australia.

[Rovetto, 2017b] R. J. Rovetto. An ontology for satellite databases. *Earth Science Informatics*, Dec;10(4):417–27, 2017.

[Santos and Rapp, 2019] C. Santos and L. Rapp. Satellite imagery, very high-resolution and processing-intensive image analysis: Potential risks under the GDPR. *Air and Space Law*, 1;44(3):275—295, 2019.

[Santos *et al.*, 2015] C. Santos, P. Casanovas, V. Rodríguez-Doncel, and L. van der Torre. Reuse and reengineering of non-ontological resources in the legal domain. In *AI Approaches to the Complexity of Legal Systems AICOL*, pages 350–364. Springer, 2015.

[Santos *et al.*, 2019] C. Santos, D. Miramont, and L. Rapp. High resolution satellite imagery and potential identification of individuals. In P. Soille, S. Loekken, and S. Albani, editors, *Proceedings of the 2019 conference on Big Data from Space (BiDS'2019)*, pages 237–240. Publications Office of the European Union, Luxembourg, 2019.

[Schadbach, 1998] K. Schadbach. The benefits of comparative law: A continental european view. *Boston University International Law Journal*, 16:331, 1998.

[Sharma, 2018] V. Sharma. Mini satellites, maximum possibilities. https://www.livemint.com/Leisure/yEXAKO6kOUWRLtV6rzdQaP/Mini-satellites-maximum-possibilities.html, 2018. published 10 November 2018; accessed 4 May 2019.

[SIP, nd] SIP. Official repository for Semantic Web for Earth and Environmental Terminology (SWEET) Ontologies. https://github.com/ESIPFed/sweet, n.d.

[SIRIUS, nda] Space Institute for Research on Innotative Use of Satellites SIRIUS. Spationary. https://chaire-sirius.eu/en/research/spationary, n.d.

[SIRIUS, ndb] Space Institute for Research on Innovative Use of Satellites SIRIUS. Space Legal Tech. https://spacelegaltech.com/, n.d.

[Soille *et al.*, 2019] P. Soille, S. Loekken, and S. Albani. Proceedings of the 2019 conference on big data from space (BiDS'2019), 2019. Publications Office of the European Union, Luxembourg.

[Solove, 2008] D. Solove. *Understanding Privacy.* Cambridge, Massachusetts, 2008.

[Solum, 1992] L. B. Solum. Legal personhood for artificial intelligences. *North Carolina Law Review*, 70:1231-1287, 1992.

[Soroka and Kurkova, 2019] L. Soroka and K. Kurkova. Artificial intelligence and space technologies: legal, ethical and technological issues. *Advanced Space Law*, April;3(1):131–139, 2019.

[Space Security Index, 2014] Space Security Index. https://spacesecurityindex.org/wp-content/uploads/2014/10/spacesecurityindexfactsheet.pdf, 2014.

[Space News, 2019] Space News. Digital endeavours in space. https://spacenews.com/digital-endeavors-in-space/, 2019.

[Stewart, 2019] E. Stewart. Self-driving cars have to be safer than regular cars. the question is how much. https://www.vox.com/recode/2019/5/17/18564501/self-driving-car-morals-safety-tesla-waymo, 2019.

[Summers, 1966] R. S. Summers. The new analytical jurists. *New York University Law Review*, 41:861, 1966.

[Sword, 2019] M. Sword. To err is both human and non-human. In *University of Missouri-Kansas City Law Review*, 88:211, 2019.

[Tricot and Sander, 2011] R. Tricot and B. Sander. Recent developments: The broader consequences of the international court of justice's advisory opinion on the unilateral declaration of independence in respect of kosovo. *Columbia Journal of Transnational Law*, 49:321-327, 2011.

[UCS, 2005] Union of Concerned Scientists UCS. UCS Satellite Database. https://www.ucsusa.org/resources/satellite-database, 2005.

[UNOOSA and PSIPW, nd] United Nations Officer for Outer Space Affairs UNOOSA and Prince Sultan Bin Abdulaziz International Prize for Water PSIPW. Space4water glossary. https://www.space4water.org/glossary, n.d.

[UNOOSA, 2018] The United Nations Office for Outer Space Affairs UNOOSA. Inter-agency meeting on outer space activities: Thirty-eighth session. https://www.unoosa.org/oosa/en/ourwork/un-space/iam/38th-session.html, 2018.

[UNOOSA, 2019] The United Nations Office for Outer Space Affairs UNOOSA. Annual report 2018, 2019.

[von der Dunk, 2001] F. G. von der Dunk. Sovereignty versus space—public law and private launch in the asian context. *Singapore Journal of International and Comparative Law*, 5:22, 2001.

[von der Dunk, 2012] F. G. von der Dunk. Outer space law principles and privacy. In D. Leung and R. Purdy, editors, *Evidence from Earth Observation Satellites: Emerging Legal Issues*, page 243—258. Martinus Nijhoff Publishers, 2012.

[von der Dunk, 2015] F. G. von der Dunk. Legal aspects of navigation. the cases for privacy and liability: An introduction for non-lawyers. http://mycoordinates.org/legal-aspects-of-navigation/, 2015. Coodinates magazine, May 2015.

[Waldrop, 2004] E. S. Waldrop. Integration of military and civilian space assets: legal and national security implications. *AFL Review*, 55, 157, 2004.

[Wang, 2019] B. Wang. Us spy satellites at diffraction limit for resolution since 1971, 2019.

[Wen and Auyezov, 2018] P. Wen and O. Auyezov. Tracking china's muslim gulag, 2018. 29 November, 2018. Reuters Investigates.

[Werner,] D. Werner. Self-driving spacecraft? the challenge of verifying ai will work as intended. https://spacenews.com/self-driving-spacecraft-the-challenge-of-verifying-ai-will-work-as-intended/. Space News, 2019.

[Wiewiórowski, 2020] W. Wiewiórowski. Ai and facial recognition: Challenges and opportunities, 2020. European Data Protection Supervisor, 21 February, 2020.

[Yeo, 2018] S. Yeo. How satellites can help catch disaster insurance fraudsters. https://psmag.com/environment/new-satellites-can-help-foil-fraud-in-disaster-insurance, 2018. 3 April.

[Zhao, 2004] Y. Zhao. Revisiting the 1975 registration convention: Time for revision? *Australian Journal of International Law*, 11:106-127, 2004.

[Zingler and di Marcantonio, 1998] M. Zingler and R. di Marcantonio. Navigating through earth observation knowledge. *The European Space Agency Bulletin*, 96, 1998.

George Anthony Long
Legal Parallax, LLC, USA
Email: gal@spacejurist.com

Cristiana Santos
Utrecht University, The Netherlands (The work conducted by Cristiana Santos was carried out under a service contract with the University of Luxembourg prior to her joining Utrecht University.)
Email: c.teixeirasantos@uu.nl

Lucien Rapp
Université Toulouse Capitole 1, SIRIUS Chair, France
Email: lucien.rapp@ut-capitole.fr

Réka Markovich
University of Luxembourg, Luxembourg
Email: reka.markovich@uni.lu

Leendert van der Torre
University of Luxembourg, Luxembourg
Email: leon.vandertorre@uni.lu